D1196837

GENDER
Blending

EDITED BY
BONNIE BULLOUGH, Ph.D., R.N.
VERN L. BULLOUGH, Ph.D., R.N.
& JAMES ELIAS, Ph.D.

GENDER
Blending

TRANSVESTISM
(CROSS-DRESSING)

GENDER HERESY

ANDROGYNY

RELIGION &
THE CROSS-DRESSER

TRANSGENDER
HEALTHCARE

FREE EXPRESSION

SEX CHANGE SURGERY

WHO LOVES
TRANSVESTITES?

THE LAW AND
TRANSSEXUALS

AND MUCH MORE...

Prometheus Books

59 John Glenn Drive
Amherst, New York 14228-2197

The photographs included in section 6 are © Mariette Pathy Allen.

Published 1997 by Prometheus Books

01 00 99 98 97   5 4 3 2

Library of Congress Cataloging-in-Publication Data

Gender blending / edited by Bonnie Bullough, Vern Bullough & James Elias.
     p.   cm.
    Includes bibliographical references.
    ISBN 1–57392–124–6 (cloth : alk. paper)
     1. Transsexualism. 2. Transvestism. 3. Gender identity. I. Bullough, Bonnie.
II. Bullough, Vern L. III. Elias, James.
HQ77.G46   1997
305.3—dc21   96–51743
                                                       CIP

Printed in the United States of America on acid-free paper

To Bonnie Bullough,
a compassionate and dedicated researcher
and an outstanding woman.

Contents

1. The Emergence of the Transgender Phenomenon

2. Transsexual Research and Comment

3. Men Who Cross-Dress

9. Law and Legal Issues

10. Personal Observations

Acknowledgments

We the editors would like to thank the officials at California State University for their cooperation and support of the Center for Sex Research, the faculty of which planned and put on the conference that resulted in this book. We also want to thank the members of various organizations serving the transgender community who participated and cooperated with the Center in bringing together those living in the transgender life with researchers and therapists. Cosponsoring the conference with the Center were the Society for the Scientific Study of Sex, the Society for the Second Self (SSS), American Educational Gender Information Service (AEGIS), International Foundation for Gender Education (IFGE), Outreach Institute of Gender Studies, Renaissance Education Association, and FTM International. The result has been a unique collaborative effort which we believe will mark a major advance in understanding transgenderism. Much of the compilation and initial editing of the book was done by Bonnie Bullough, who died while the book was in press. The book is dedicated to her.

Special thanks are due to all the editors and staff at Prometheus who worked on the book, particularly Steven Mitchell, Eugene O'Connor, Barbara Bergstrom, and Kathy Deyell. Without them this book would not have been possible.

Introduction

Current concepts of cross-dressing and cross-gender behavior had their origins in the nineteenth century. Probably the first description in the medical literature was by Carl Westphal (1833–1890) who confused the behavior of his two cross-dressers (one male and one female) with what later came to be called homosexuality (Westphal 1869). Richard von Krafft-Ebing, who pathologized much of sexual behavior, included case studies of three individuals whom he classified as dress fetishists and one whom he included in his section on homosexuality. All four today would be classed as exhibiting nonconforming gender behavior (Krafft-Ebing 1933).

Taking a radically different tack in the study of sexuality was Magnus Hirschfeld (1868–1935) who in 1910 published what was the pathbreaking book on what he called "transvestism" (Hirschfeld 1991). Hirschfeld presented the cases of sixteen male and one female cross-dresser. He reported that the dominant view in psychiatry during this period was that female impersonators were all homosexual, a view that he disputed. He argued that transvestites differed from fetishists because fetishists tend to attach the object of the fetish to a beloved person while transvestites focused on themselves and their clothing. He found that masochism was often linked to the transvestite phenomenon but felt that this linkage by itself could not explain transvestism (Hirschfeld 1991).

Hirschfeld's study was followed by one by Havelock Ellis, the English sexologist. For the most part Ellis agreed with Hirschfeld about the components of transvestism, but he did not adopt the term itself. In his first paper on the topic Ellis used the term *sexo-aesthetic inversion* (1913). Later, he decided the use of

15

the term *inversion* was misleading and implied homosexuality and he dropped it. He was also opposed to *transvestism*, Hirschfeld's term, because he felt much more was implied than simply wearing the clothing of the opposite sex. Eventually he settled on the term *Eonism*, based on the case of the Chevalier d'Éon, an eighteenth-century cross-dresser. Ellis believed that the term avoided the problems inherent in the other terms, and it also followed the precedent used for sadism and masochism in invoking names of well-known models of the behavior.

Ellis, like Hirschfeld, did not consider cross-dressing to be a particularly troublesome problem since most of the people he (and Hirschfeld) studied were able to lead lives they found satisfactory and did not harm others. Both Ellis and Hirschfeld were trying to understand the phenomenon, and neither made any proposal to change the individuals he studied.

Neither Hirschfeld nor Ellis, however, seemed to be particularly influential in the medical community, which essentially preferred to follow a pathological model. Particularly influential was Wilhelm Stekel and his colleague Emil Gutheil. They classed transvestism as a *paraphilia*, a term invented by Stekel, and defined by him as a perversion (1930). A description of transvestism was given in Stekel's book by Emil Gutheil (Gutheil 1930). Ellis and Hirschfeld were generally ignored by the psychiatric community, and Hirschfeld's work on the topic was not translated into English until 1991. In fact, Gutheil and Stekel were highly critical of Hirschfeld for his failure to realize the obvious (to psychoanalysis) tendencies present in most cross-dressers. Those psychiatrists who did write on the topic had a variety of explanations. Karl Abraham (1910) explained transvestism as a homosexual impulse component, while Lukianowicz (1959) saw it as an attempt to overcome the fear of castration by creating an imaginary phallic woman and then identifying with her. Otto Fenichel held that the fantasy of the phallic woman reassured the cross-dresser that he could not lose his penis because both men and women would thus have phalluses (1930, 1945). Often this fear of castration and its denial through the creation of a phallic woman were precipitated by an incident wherein a boy accidentally saw his mother or sister undressed and noted the absence of a penis (Peabody et al. 1953; Lukianowicz 1959). Some observers tried to search out hereditary factors, while others looked for childhood traumas (Lukianowicz, 1959). Even those in the cross-dressing community who wrote about their own lives tended to turn to psychoanalysis for explanation (Thompson 1956).

Additionally complicating the issue was a further refinement of diagnoses to include transsexualism. Hirschfeld had described such a case in his original studies (1991) but it was the Christine Jorgensen case in 1952 that brought the issue to the attention of the professional community. The person most involved with setting new diagnostic criteria for transsexualism and distinguishing it from transvestism was Harry Benjamin, who conceived of transsexualism and transvestism on a continuum with the transvestite showing the milder symptoms and the transsexual being the more troubled (Benjamin 1964).

Except for the Thompson study, which was autobiographical, most studies were based upon clients of the therapists. Few had more than one or two clients, but this was not true of John Randell (1959), a British physician-psychologist, who reported on fifty of his patients, thirty-seven males and thirteen females who had cross dressed more or less since childhood. He broke his sample down into two groups, a homosexual group (where he placed most transsexuals), and an obsessive-compulsive group (transvestites). This last category continued to appear in later literature even though his categorization of transsexuals as homosexual soon disappeared.

Less willing to diagnose a client was Vernon W. Grant (1960), who believed there had been too much theorizing based on too little data. He chose to describe and to classify. Few followed his example, and Winfield Scott Pugh (1964) devised five categories to describe cross-dressers of various kinds: heterosexual, bisexual, homosexual, narcissistic, and asexual. One of the more influential psychiatrists was Robert Stoller (1971). He held that while most transvestite men were primarily heterosexual, most of their phallic-centered erotic activity focused on women's clothing. Stoller had strong views about the etiology of transvestism in men, arguing that it was caused by mothers or other females who wanted revenge on their boys for being masculine. Stoller recognized that questionnaire studies or interviews usually did not identify a cross-dressing mother figure such as he posited, but held that it could be found with deeper probing. He was determined that such a figure must exist.

Not all psychoanalytic observers agreed with him. Ethel Person and Lionel Ovesey tried to get away from labeling cross-dressing as a perversion, but rather a neurosis developed as a compromise solution to unconscious conflict (Person and Ovesey 1978). Stoller seemingly marked the height of the psychoanalytic influence in examining transgender individuals. In part this was because the client base for data, the basis of psychoanalytic insights, was essentially replaced by wide-ranging surveys of cross-dressing individuals, most of whom had never seen a psychiatrist. The pathbreaking study in this respect was conducted by Virginia Prince and P. M. Bentler (1972) who, utilizing existing organized groups of cross-dressers, reported on 504 cases of transvestism, most of whom had not sought medical or psychiatric treatment. Other studies quickly followed by Neil Buhrich and Neil McConaghy (1978), Bullough, Bullough, and Smith (1983a, 1983b, 1985), and many others (Bullough and Bullough 1993).

One of the major studies in this new era was by Richard Docter (1988), who combined a therapy goal with his large-scale sampling and held that there were stages that many cross-dressers go through. Two major studies, however, approached the topic in order to describe it, rather than to prescribe or to advocate cures. Marjory Garber (1992), for example, felt it important to escape the bipolar notions of male and female in order to advocate a third category, a new mode of articulation, a way of describing a space of possibilities. Bipolar approaches, male-female or man-woman, create what she calls a "category crisis" because they lead to a failure of definitional distinction and result in a border that becomes permeable and permits crossing. Border crossing itself threatens established class, race, and gender norms, and cross-dressing, she holds, is a disruptive element in our society that involves not just a category crisis of male and female, but also the crisis of the category itself. Also challenging the duo-category model were Bonnie and Vern Bullough (1993), although they relied less on the literary tradition than Garber and more on the social and behavioral sciences.

Aiding these challenges has been a new element in the study of cross-dressing and transgenderism, namely, the growing ability of people in the gendered community to speak for themselves. In a sense this new development parallels what appeared in the homosexual and lesbian community. With this new direction in research in the gay community, it was found that there was not just one homosexuality or lesbianism, but as Alan Bell and Martin Weinberg (1978) pointed out, there was a tremendous variation in what could be called homosexual or lesbian or in the gay and lesbian community. No one description fit all, and in fact they emphasized this by the title of their book, *Homosexualities.*

Homosexuals themselves had realized this earlier than the scholarly and scientific community, and one of the results was to challenge the traditional psychiatric definitions of homosexuality. The eventual outcome was a history-making decision by the American Psychiatric Association in 1974 to remove homosexuality from its category of "mental illnesses" and to declare it instead a "sexual orientation disturbance" (Bayer 1981). Even this designation was later dropped.

It is in this setting that this book should be read. It grew out of a Congress on Cross-Dressing, Sex, and Gender, sponsored by the Center for Sex Research at the California State University in Northridge, California. It is not a record of the proceedings but a selection of papers from the meeting demonstrating the change taking place in the cross-gendered community. The organizers of the congress, the editors of this book, were conscious of the rapid changes taking place—so rapid that the old nomenclature was no longer valid. Though some people still identify themselves as transsexuals or transvestites, others prefer to call themselves transgenderists because they live their lives in the role of the opposite gender without benefit of surgery. Some call themselves or are called by others *she males* or *male woman*, while the term *gender blender* is also increasingly used by both sexes and genders, as is the term transgenderist. Those people who cross the gender barriers include both males and females, homosexuals, heterosexuals, bisexuals, and asexuals.

Increasingly also the number of membership groups not only in the gender community has escalated until there are membership groups not only in every state and province in the United States and Canada, but also in almost every major country of the world. The pioneer group, the Society for the Second Self, which emerged in the early 1960s is still on the scene but it is no longer dominant and its viewpoint is not always accepted by other groups. In examining the magazine *Tapestry*, which is aimed at the community and which strives to be a magazine of record, it is apparent that events occur somewhere in the United States and Canada every week, if not every day, in the year. There is a vast mail-order business in clothing by merchants oriented to the community, and many large cities have special shops where cross-dressers can go to purchase everything from wigs to body forms to beards (for female-to-males). Many of the groups as well as some individuals run their own publishing programs and books on everything from the latest information on hormone supplements to a variety of fantasy fiction are available.

This book is unique since it represents a dialogue between those in the gender community and those who do research on or offer therapy to the members of that community. It represents a scholarly version of Stonewall, the riot in New York City that focused media attention on the gay and lesbian communities. Increasingly many members of the community have come out publicly about their cross-gender identity. The gender blender who goes public is still regarded as a kind of oddity, but there is also a sort of halfhearted admiration for those who do, as illustrated by the 1995 profile in the *New Yorker* on a Tennessee Republican from Nashville who enjoys dressing up as a woman and going out in public to his country club and elsewhere (Berendt 1995). It is just something he does, just as he flies his own plane or plays golf.

We believe there are large numbers of people out there who engage in some aspect of gender blending, trying their best to keep it secret and fearful of exposure. Probably only a small minority belong to the club movement. This is our (Bonnie and Vern Bullough's) second book on cross-dressing (Bullough and Bullough 1993), and it builds upon the earlier one in an effort to make the public aware of the changes taking place in our society, the nature of the research being done, and what the members of this community think.

References

Abraham, Karl. 1910. Über hysterische Traumzustande. *Jahrbuch für Psychoanal. Forsch.*, 2. Cited by Havelock Ellis, in "Eonism," in *Studies in the Psychology of Sex,* 2 vols. New York: Random House, 16.

Bayer, Ronald. 1981. *Homosexuality and American psychiatry: The politics of diagnosis.* New York: Basic.

Bell, Allan, and Martin Weinberg. 1978. *Homosexualities.* New York: Simon and Schuster.

Benjamin, Harry. 1964. Trans-sexualism and transvestism. In *Transvestism: Men in female dress,* edited by David Cauldwell. New York: Sexology Corporation.

———. 1966. *The transsexual phenomenon.* New York: Julian Press.

Berendt, John. 1995. High heel Neil. *New Yorker* (January 16): 38–45.

Buhrich, Neil, and Neil McConaghy. 1978. Parental relationships during childhood in homosexuality, transvestism, and transsexualism. *Australian and New Zealand Journal of Psychiatry* 12: 103–108.

Bullough, Bonnie, Vern Bullough, and Richard Smith. 1985. Masculinity and femininity in transvestite, transsexual and gay males. *Western Journal of Nursing Research* 7: 317–32.

Bullough, Vern L., and Bonnie Bullough, 1993. *Cross dressing, sex, and gender.* Philadelphia: University of Pennsylvania Press.

Bullough, Vern L., Bonnie Bullough, and Richard Smith. 1983a. Childhood and family of male sexual minority groups. *Health Values* 7 (July-August): 19–26.

———. 1983b. A comparative study of male transvestites, male to female transsexuals and male homosexuals. *Journal of Sex Research* 19 (August): 238–57.

Cauldwell, David, ed. 1956. *Transvestism: Men in female dress.* New York: Sexology Corporation.

Docter, Richard F. 1988. *Transvestites and transsexuals: Toward a theory of gender behavior.* New York: Plenum Press.

Ellis, Havelock. 1913. Sexo-aesthetic inversion. Parts 1 and 2. *Alienist and Neurologist* 34 (May): 3–14; (August): 1–31.

———. 1936. Eonism. In *Studies in the Psychology of Sex*, vol. 2, pt. 2. New York: Random House, 10–120.

Fenichel, Otto. 1930. The psychology of transvestism. *International Journal of Psychoanalysis* 11: 212–37.

———. 1945. *The psychoanalytic theory of neuroses.* New York: Norton.

Garber, Marjorie. 1992. *Vested interests: Cross-dressing and cultural anxiety.* New York: Routledge.

Grant, V. 1960. The cross-dresser: A case study. *Journal of Nervous and Mental Disease,* 149–59.

Gutheil, Emil. 1930. An analysis of a case of transvestism. In *Sexual aberrations*, by W. Stekel, 281–318. New York: Liveright Publishing Co.

Hirschfeld, Magnus. 1991. *Transvestites: An investigation of the erotic drive to cross-dress.* Amherst, N.Y.: Prometheus Books.

Krafft-Ebing, Richard von. [1906] 1933. *Psychopathia sexualis.* Translated and adapted by F. J. Rebman from the 12th German ed. New York: Physicians and Surgeons Book Company.

Lukianowicz, N. 1959. Survey of various aspects of transvestism in light of our present knowledge. *Journal of Nervous and Mental Disease* 128: 36–64.

Peabody, G. A., A. T. Rowe, and J. M. Wall. 1953. Fetishism and transvestism. *Journal of Nervous and Mental Disease* 119: 339–50.

Person, Ethel, and Lionel Ovesey. 1978. Transvestism: New perspectives. *Journal of the American Academy of Psychoanalysis* 6: 304–22.

Prince, Virginia, and P. M. Bentler 1972. Survey of 504 cases of transvestism. *Psychological Reports* 31: 903–17.

Pugh, Winfield Scott. 1964. Transvestism and homosexuality. In *Transvestism: Men in female dress,* edited by David Cauldwell, 23–32. New York: Sexology Corporation.

Randell, John B. 1959. Transvestism and trans-sexualism: A study of 50 cases. *British Medical Journal* 2 (25 December): 1448–52.

Stekel, Wilhelm. 1930 *Sexual aberrations: The phenomenon of fetishism in relation to sex*. Translated by S. Parker. New York: Liveright Publishing Co.

Stoller, Robert J. 1971. The term "transvestism." *Archives of General Psychiatry* 24 (March): 230–37.

Thompson, Janet. 1956. Transvestism: An empirical study. *The Mattachine Review* 2: 6, 8–9, 44–46.

Westphal, Carl. 1869. Die konträre sexualempfindung. *Archiv für Psychiatrie und Nervenkranheiten* 2: 73–108.

1

THE EMERGENCE OF THE TRANSGENDER PHENOMENON

Introduction

Although in the last half of the twentieth century most of those who have sought to change their gender identity have been men, historically it was women who were unhappy and dissatisfied with their gender role (Bullough and Bullough 1993). We know of thousands of women over the centuries who changed roles, and only a handful of men. Some of the women who passed as men did so because they felt they belonged in the masculine gender, while others sought to escape the strictures and deprivations of the women's role.

This situation started to change in the nineteenth century and has become more marked as the twentieth century has progressed. The change in ratios might well have resulted from the improvement in women's roles and in women's opportunities, while at the same time the strictures on self-expression for men seemed to grow. Some men, such as the homosexuals, never did conform to the traditional male role, but many others turned to cross-dressing as a way to escape some of the strictures. With the development of transsexual surgery and electrolysis for removal of facial hair (and the availability of hormones) after 1952, many turned to surgical solutions, although here also the males outnumbered the females seeking to change their anatomical sex and continue to do so. The psychiatrists who screened the potential patients and the surgeons who did sex reassignment surgery became the high priests who granted permission for gender transformation.

One of the most severe critics of the SRS (sex reassignment surgery) was Janice Raymond, who labeled it an invention of the "medical psychiatric complex" (1979). Although her hostility to the process was too great to appeal to many of those who were looking for a surgical answer to their gender dysphoria, her ideas were adopted by a small group of militant feminists who continue to express hostility to both sexes who go through SRS. There are less strident critics, however, including Virginia Prince, the earth mother of the cross-dressing movement. She moved from part-time cross-dressing to full-time life as a woman in the 1960s, and in seeking to explain herself she eventually hit upon the term *transgenderist*. Both aspects of the crusade she founded, the cross-dressing clubs and the transgender movement, have been growing.

Another kind of sympathetic critic was Anne Bolin, a researcher (1988) who saw a "rite of passage" in SRS, a step that physically authenticated the gender change. Her writing and that of several of her contemporaries helped encourage the idea that there were different alternatives to be explored and that increasing numbers of men and women have opted to live in the opposite gender without going through surgery or have adopted a variety of lifestyles that depart from the dimorphic norms (Docter 1993; Bullough and Bullough, sect. 2, ch. 2, this book).

The four selections in this section analyze this transgender phenomenon from a variety of vantage points, emphasizing that this major shift in the gender world has upset old definitions and classification systems. Some have even called the 1990s the decade of the emergence of the role of the transgenderist.

References

Bolin, Anne. 1988. *In search of Eve: Transsexual rites of passage.* South Hadley, Mass.: Bergin & Garvey.

Bullough, Vern L. and Bonnie Bullough. 1993. *Cross dressing, sex and gender.* Philadelphia: University of Pennsylvania Press.

Docter, Richard. 1993. Dimensions of transvestism and transsexualism. *Journal of Psychology and Human Sexuality* 5: 15–37.

Raymond, Janice. 1979. *The transsexual empire: The making of the she-male.* Boston: Beacon Press.

Transforming Transvestism and Transsexualism: Polarity, Politics, and Gender

Anne Bolin

The purpose of this paper is to focus on culture change in gender variant social identities over a fifteen-year span. Ethnographic data from my research a decade ago on male-to-female transsexual and male transvestite identities are provided as historical background (Bolin 1982, 1987a, 1987b, 1988). Current information was collected over the past three years through methods including ethnographic forays at paracultural ritual events, informal interviewing, and an open-ended questionnaire, among other qualitative methods (Bolin 1994).[1]

Euro-American gender variance among those who self-identify as pre-operative, post-operative, non-surgical transsexuals and cross-dressers/transvestites is testimony to the complexity of gender, offering serious challenges to scientific paradigms that conflate sex and gender (cf. Foucault 1988; Gallagher and Laqueur 1987, Bordo 1989, 1990). Such individuals are part of a newly emerging transgender community that embraces the possibility of numerous genders and multiple social identities.

Ten years ago male-to-female transsexualism supported the binary gender schema by dividing dysphoric individuals into men and women where transvestites (argot TV) were variant or ersatz men, and transsexuals (argot TS) were women upon whom nature had erred and whose condition, in the words of one transsexual consultant, "can be corrected through surgery." Male-to-female transsexuals defined themselves by a bottom-line criterion of a desire for hormonal reassignment and surgery, privileging their status within the Berdache Society, a local grassroots TV/TS organization, as only a temporarily marginal status. Male-to-female transsexual ethnotheory stated that if one was not

25

absolutely committed to having the surgery, then one was de facto a transvestite, therefore, a man with a desire to cross-dress.

The transsexual dichotomization in the Berdache Society of "TS and TV" reflects social currents and technologies of the late 1960s. Surgical conversion and hormonal reassignment have come to dominate the medical designation and psychological diagnosis of transsexuals (Bolin 1987a). During the 1970s and early 1980s more than forty North American clinics, many affiliated with medical schools and universities, were offering programs leading to the performance of surgical reassignments (Denny 1992, 9–20).

From its inception, the transsexual identity sustained the Western paradigm that the sexes are oppositional and therefore differences in behavior, temperament, emotions, and sexual orientation are constituted in biological polarity. This opposition is represented in the genitals, symbols of reproductive differences and the basis for assigning biological sex. "Gender attribution, for the most part, is genitals attribution," according to Kessler and McKenna (1978, 153). But paradoxically the transsexual phenomenon also disobeyed this Western biocentricity. As a social identity, transsexualism necessarily posits the analytic independence of four gender markers—physiological sex, gender identity, social identity, and sexual orientation as witnessed by lesbian male-to-female transsexuals who subvert the conflation of femininity and heterosexual eroticism (Bolin 1988, 72).

As a result of this defiance to biology as gender, peoples of various gender-transposed identities have come to recognize themselves as part of a greater community, facing similar concerns of stigmatization, acceptance, treatment, and so on. This recognition of commonality, fostered by a growing political agenda offered by cross-gender organizations, has facilitated the burgeoning of a new gender option, transgenderism. The formation of a transgender community denotes a newfound kinship that supplants the dichotomy of transsexual and transvestite with a concept of continuity, indicative of a growing acceptance of non-surgical options for men wishing to live as women. An emerging sense of collectivity has propelled the recognition of the multiplicity of gender variant identities (Lynn 1988, n.d.; Denny 1991, 6; Boswell 1991, 29–31).

Diversity in the personal identity of male-to-female transsexual and male transvestite populations has been an important source of change in the social construction of identities over the past fifteen years. Although diversity of personal identity occurred among transsexuals and transvestites around 1989, this was suppressed by paracultural and clinical segregation into either TV or TS (Bolin 1988, 15). Underlying this dichotomy was a continuum of gender identities that included a pantheon of personal motives. This continuum of identities was artificially severed along the dimension of the extreme desire for surgical alteration. Through the course of time, the expression of heterogeneity in the subjective experience of individuals has been given voice.

Pluralism in gender variation is both cause and consequence of at least three sociocultural influences intersecting with diversity in personal gender identity. These are (1) the closing of university-affiliated gender clinics (Denny 1992); (2) the grassroots organizational adoption of a political agenda; and (3) the increasing availability in wider society of alternatives to embodiments of femininity as somatic frailty.

The university clinics subscribed to "a-man-trapped-in-a-woman's-body" notions of transsexualism. According to Denny,

> Transsexual people were considered to be homogenous. Those men who had not played with dolls in childhood, who did not report feeling like a girl from the earliest age, or who had any history of enthusiasm or success at masculine activities were in trouble. The directors and staff of the clinics tended to view SRS [sex reassignment surgery] as essential for satisfactory adjustment in the new gender. They did not seem to realize that it is possible to live as a woman or a man without the expected genitalia. . . . Those who were not accepted for SRS were not offered hormonal therapy. Those who were not offered services were often told that they were "not transsexual." (Denny 1992, 13, 17)

Denny warns this is not an indictment of all gender clinics or of the surgery itself, but that it does reflect the experience of thousands of transsexual persons.

Just as clinics contributed to the bipolarization of gender-variant identities through promoting sex-reassignment surgery, their widespread closing in the 1980s expedited the merging and blending of gendered identities. The termination of the Johns Hopkins Gender Clinic was followed by a closing down of university-affiliated clinics throughout the United States. Only about a dozen gender clinics remain. Because these are unaffiliated with the research interests of universities, client-centered approaches are dominant (Denny 1992, 19). Such client-centered gender clinics may contribute to greater flexibility in the expression of gender identities. The research agenda of university-sponsored treatment programs possibly biased the selection of the male-to-female transsexual clinic population through the use of stereotypical entrance criteria, thereby denying treatment to more divergent individuals.

Sharon, a fifty-year-old post-operative transsexual, provides a classic profile of a likely candidate for surgery in a traditional gender clinic:

> When I was a child my favorite pastime was playing dress-up. When I told people I wanted to be a girl, no one listened. . . . In 1953, the Christine Jorgensen story became headlines. It confirmed my belief that I could be a female. In 1962 I admitted to myself that I was not a man, and never would be. I was a "God

knows what," with a male anatomy. By 1979 my life-long dream was to be a legal and functional female. (Bolin 1994, 463)

In contrast, client-centered programs may cater to the diverse interests and personal goals inherent in gender-variant peoples, allowing for a pluralism in the expression of gender.

Karen, who waited until forty-five years of age to pursue full female attire, self-identifies in this way:

> To use the more common terminology, I would say I am transgendered. I cross-dress but not for sexual display or attraction. There is a feeling that is feminine, pretty, and desirable. Yet, I don't change as a "person." My gestures and walk are compatible with a feminine appearance, but not exaggerated, my voice unchanged. I don't consider myself a different person, just another visage or aspect of the same person. My friends that observe me in both modes would substantiate this. In addition, passing is of no concern to me. I don't really "do outreach" or "in your face" but only subject myself to situations in which people are aware of my maleness. At times I prefer feminine gestures and expressions, but more often masculine responses. When societal binarism insists I choose one pole or the other—I choose masculine. I have been raised as a male, my sexual anatomy is male, etc. Nonetheless, I insist that I am ambigenderal. I claim all gender space, if you will, and exist within this spectrum at different points at different times. (Bolin 1994, 464)

Pat considers her/himself an androgyne. "I currently maintain a full-time androgynous person, eliciting as many 'ma'ams' as I do 'sir' responses. My goal is to be free to present myself full female all the time, while still expressing a healthy degree of androgyny. Living as a woman gives me a much fuller range of expression than as a man. In time, I may feel more comfortable confronting the world with the unabashed ambiguity of total androgyny." (Bolin 1994, 465).

The transgender community grew out of expanding political concerns of individuals who wanted a voice in treatment, in defining themselves, and in offering support and services for a growing cohort. The American Education Gender Information Service (AEGIS) and the International Foundation for Gender Education (IFGE) are two prominent national organizations with political concerns.

Although there is not universal agreement on the term transgendered, there is an emerging generic semanticity that is inclusive of all people who cross-dress. It incorporates those who self-identify as male-to-female transsexuals, female-to-males, male transvestites, cross-dressers, and those who lie between the traditional identity of transsexual and male transvestite, as well as those persons ". . . who steer a middle course, living with the physical traits of both genders. Transgenderists may alter their anatomy with hormones or surgery, but they may purposefully retain many of the characteristics of the gender to which they were originally assigned. Many lead part-time lives in both genders, most cultivate an androgynous appearance" (Denny 1991, 6).

Transgenderism is a very inclusive category, incorporating the self-proclaimed androgyne. Ariadne Kane, director of the Human Achievement and Outreach Institute, has promoted androgyny as a flexible approach to living one's gender variation. Kane has a variety of personal expressions of "felt" gender that vary from day to day or even within the day and uses cultural symbols of masculinity/femininity to express inner-felt dimensions of gender.

The agenda of valuing and respect has advanced the possibility of a permanent and nonsurgical transsexual social identity rather than a temporary one, an "out" transvestism, and a pride in one's past social history as gender-variant people. Lydia, a middle-aged post-operative transsexual, argues that "transsexualism has two closets. . . . That's where people go after their transitions to deny their pasts and their transsexualism. In the past, there was little choice but to go into the closet at the end of the rainbow, for public identity as a transsexual person meant media attention, ridicule, loss of employment and employability, and even physical danger. As times have changed, it has become possible to have a public identity as transsexual and still have a reasonably normal life" (Bolin 1994, 473).

Fifteen years ago, organizations kept a low profile and focused on service. The focus was inward and it lacked a political emphasis. For example, in the Berdache Society, both the transsexual and transvestite constituency felt that education of the public at large could result in making it more difficult to pass. Impacting media stereotypes was regarded as an impossible task without "outing" themselves. In other words, the less the mainstream America knew about male-to-female transsexuals the better.

In contrast, today the Congress of Representatives (a fictive name), a national umbrella organization that encompasses all the gender organizations and groups in the United States, provides a community-based approach that emphasizes serving the needs of the various organizations and extant gender constituencies. This national network is a vehicle for the further blending and expansion of identity borders.

The growing transgender community has also been influenced by changes and challenges to traditional embodiments of femininity. Femininity in the late-twentieth century is in a process of redefinition socially, economically, and somatically. Feminine fragility is contested by an empowered athletic soma. Women's bodies have undergone radical revision since the hour-glass and corseted ideal of the 1800s prevailed and the very thin silhouette of the 1960s offered its new kind of tyranny. A worldwide movement toward health and fitness dovetailing with feminism has opened new embodiments that include toned and muscular physiques (Bolin 1992a and 1992b). Since bodies in the Western gender paradigm are regarded as "naturally" constituted contours, this has implications for the social mapping of transgenderism. The process of somatic revisioning may include backlashes, but it nevertheless continues to march forward in betraying biological sex as the singular determinant of bodily form.

Women bodybuilders in particular with their stout muscles, and other women athletes more generally, have contested the male equation of muscularity, strength, and masculinity embedded in biologistic readings of the body. The new muscular soma of women reinscribes other changes in women's status. Women athletes' physiques may even appear androgynous. Sports like track, long-distance running, and heptathlon and tri-athlete events create new embodiments of femininity that defy the traditional soma of women as soft and curvaceous.

Have such widespread changes in the feminine body and its implicit query to biology inspired changes in the transgender community? Will the changes in women's body shapes and roles contribute to a lessening of male cross-gender identification? Although these questions cannot be answered at this time, it may be tentatively assumed that the relaxing of bodily gender rules generally and the undermining of the biological paradigm ongoing since the 1960s have contributed to the trend toward a transgendered community and the option of a non-surgical transsexual identity. This corrodes constructs of behaviors and bodies by suggesting the unimaginable, and by extension the possibility of a social woman with a penis and of social man with a clitoris.

The androgynous-appearing soma of some women athletes combines symbols of masculinity and femininity that have indeed not gone unnoticed by the transgender community. Kathy, a middle-aged cross-dresser, testifies to a neo-femininity of an empowered body and psyche:

> The women I have always found attractive and try to emulate are assertive, self-sufficient, and emotionally and physically strong. This body-type and personality type have become increasingly accepted. The image I portray is essentially that of an alert, athletic, highly-trained female bodybuilder. Acceptance by society of this type of woman has benefitted me greatly. Ten years ago, there were no female body-types such as mine thought to be attractive. Cory Everson, Florence Griffith Joyner, and others have broken new ground. (Bolin 1994, 479)

In conclusion, the recently emerging transgendered identity offers an account of gender as a social product. The transgenderist may or may not feminize: some appear androgynous and others pass. The possible permutations within transgenderism are innumerable and lay bare the point that gender is not biology but is socially produced. The transgenderist harbors great potential either to deactivate gender or to create in the future the possibility of "supernumerary" genders as social categories no longer based on biology (cf. Martin and Voorhies 1975).

Note

1. An extended and earlier version of this paper appeared as "Transcending and Transgendering. Male to Female Transsexuals, Dichotomy and Diversity," in *Third Sex, Third Gender: Beyond Sexual Dimorphism in Culture and History,* edited by Gilbert Herdt (New York: Zone Publishing), pp. 447–85. Notes, pp. 589–96.

References

Bolin, Anne. 1982. Advocacy with a stigmatized minority. *Practicing Anthropology* 4, no. 2: 12–13.

———. 1987a. Transsexualism and the limits of traditional analysis. *American Behavioral Scientist* 31, no. 1: 41–65.

———. 1987b. Transsexuals and caretakers: A study of power and deceit in intergroup relations. *City and Society* 1, no. 2: 64–79.

———. 1988. *In search of Eve: Transsexual rites of passage.* South Hadley, Mass.: Bergin & Garvey.

———. 1992a. Flex appeal, food, and fat: Competitive body building, gender and diet. *Play and Culture* 5, no. 4: 378–99.

———. 1992b. Vandalized vanity: Feminine physiques betrayed and portrayed. In *Tattoo, torture, mutilation, and adornment: The denaturalization of the body in culture and text,* edited by Frances E. Mascia-Lees and Patricia Sharpe, 79–99. Albany: State University of New York Press.

———. 1994. Transcending and transgendering: Male-to-female transsexuals, dichotomy and diversity. In *Third sex, third gender: Beyond sexual dimorphism in culture and history,* edited by Gilbert Herdt, 448–85; Notes, 589–96. New York: Zone Books.

Bordo, Susan R. 1989. The body and the reproduction of femininity: A feminist appropriation of Foucault. In *Gender body/knowledge/feminist reconstructions of being and knowing,* edited by Alison M. Jaggar and Susan R. Bordo, 13–33. New Brunswick, N.J.: Rutgers University Press.

———. 1990. Reading the slender body. In *Body/politics: Women and the discourses of science,* 83–112. New York: Routledge Press.

Boswell, Holly. 1991. The transgender alternative. *Chrysalis Quarterly* 1, no. 2: 29–31.

———. N.d. Getting it together in the gender community (unpublished paper). 1–2.

Denny, Dallas. 1991. Dealing with your feelings. *The AEGIS Transition Series.* Decatur, Ga.: Aegis.

———. 1992. The politics of diagnosis and a diagnosis of politics. *Chrysalis Quarterly* 1, no. 3: 9–20.

Foucault, Michel. 1988. Technologies of the self. In *Technologies of the self: A seminar with Michel Foucault,* edited by Luther B. Martin et al., 16–49. Amherst: University of Massachusetts Press.

Gallagher, Catherine, and Thomas Laqueur. 1987. *The making of the modern body.* Berkeley: University of California Press.

Kessler, Suzanne J., and Wendy McKenna. 1978. *Gender: An ethnomethodological approach.* New York: John Wiley.

Lynn, Merissa Sherrill. 1988. Definitions of terms used in the transvestite-transsexual community. *Tapestry* 51: 19–31.

———. N.d. *Definitions of terms commonly used in the transvestite/transsexual community.* Wayland, Mass.: IFGE Educational Resources Committee.

Martin, M. Kay, and Barbara Voorhies. 1975. *Female of the species.* Irvington, N.Y.: Columbia University Press.

Transgender: Some Historical, Cross-Cultural, and Contemporary Models and Methods of Coping and Treatment

Dallas Denny

The ways in which transgendered and transsexual persons are treated are highly dependent upon the ways in which they are viewed by society. Expectations about sex and gender that channel the individual into pre-programmed channels of self-expression can result in unhappiness, depression, and various forms of self-destructive behavior, including suicide. Ideally, we should be working to examine a variety of current and historical models and to develop a variety of ways, or models, by which transgendered and transsexual persons can identify themselves and be viewed by society. These models should maximize individual self-expression and self-determination, while simultaneously minimizing the chance of harm coming to the individual from his or her interactions with medical and psychological professionals.

I have provided some initial criteria by which such models can be evaluated. Table 1 represents but a "first pass" at such criteria. As they begin to actually be applied to the various models of transgender and transsexual behavior, they can and should be modified and expanded.

Some Non-Western Roles

I have been able to identify more than thirty ways of looking at the transgender and transsexual experience. Table 2 lists them, giving the cultures in which they have been found and citing one or more authorities for each.

Hijra (Nanda 1989, 1994), Khushra (Gooren 1992), and Acault (Coleman et

Table 1

Some Criteria by Which to Evaluate Various Models of Transgender and Transexual Behavior

- How has the model impacted the way transgendered and transexual persons see themselves and the way they are viewed by others?
- Does the model treat the transgendered and transexual individual with self-respect and dignity?
- Does the model maximize the amount of choice of the transgendered and transexual individual (allow the individual to set his or her own pace, to participate in decisions to change/not change the body, and to decide upon particular life goals)?
- Does the model require the individual to surrender autonomy?
- Does the model build a sense of transgendered and transexual persons as healthy and productive, or does it pre-suppose abnormality and pathology?
- Does the model allow a healthy range of personal styles, as opposed to promoting gender stereotypes?
- Does the model provide a variety of outcome choices, including sex reassignment, genital surgery, hormonal therapy, androgyny, transgenderism, and remaining in the original gender role?
- Does the model provide procedural safeguards for medical procedures and treatment?
- Does the model provide continuity from early "coming-out" stages through coping with circumstances of the new life?
- Does the model provide the individual with opportunities to explore alternative gender roles before taking irrevocable steps? Does it allow "fall-back" positions when a step proves undesirable?
- Does the model provide for a hierarchy of treatment, with less aversive and intrusive methods considered before more aversive and intrusive methods are tried?
- Does the model provide for peer support?
- What are the relative costs associated with the model?
- What have been the outcomes of past applications of the model?

al. 1992) are institutionalized roles that are found in traditional Indian, Pakistani, and Myanmar (Burmese) societies, respectively. Like the Polynesian Mahu role (Besnier 1994) and Native North American Two-Spirit roles (Roscoe 1988, 1990; Williams 1986), these roles provide a "fit" for transgendered persons in society. Often, these roles are intermediate between those of males and females, comprising a "third sex" role.

The Xanith of Oman (Wikan 1977, 1982) comprise a fluid "third sex" role into which a male can enter or exit. Xaniths have an intermediate role in Omani society, wearing clothing which is much like that of women, but distinctly different from both men and women. Like the Hijras of India, Xaniths are often prostitutes, however, emasculation lies at the core of Hijra (and, presumably, Khushra and Acault) roles, while Omani men can opt to move in and out of the Xanith role.

Transgender behavior is often associated with shamanism. It has been commonly believed in many "primitive" societies that the liminal role of the transgendered person allowed him/her special insights into the human condition and the spirit world. Dr. William Dragoin, at the conference that inspired this book, distributed a tracing of a cave painting over 15,000 years old, showing a transgendered priest(ess). Hijras, who inspire both fear and awe in the larger society, are thought to have a variety of powers, and for this purpose are sought out to bestow blessings at births and weddings (Nanda 1994).

Historical Western Roles

Although factions within the Christian church, both in the Middle Ages and at the present time, have worked hard to eradicate any mention of transgendered behavior from the Bible and from history (and, indeed, sometimes to eradicate transgendered persons themselves), there is considerable evidence of transgender roles throughout Western history (Bullough and Bullough 1993; Feinberg n.d.). For a time, the worship of the Magna Mater, or Great Mother, co-existed with other religions in ancient Rome (O'Hartigan 1993)—but for the most part, transgender roles were underground or legitimated only when nontransgendered persons considered it fashionable or expedient to have transgendered persons around. For instance, when it was deemed unsuitable for women to take stage roles in Elizabethan England, men (or rather, for the most part, young boys) were sanctioned to take female roles. Non-Western cultures—for instance, the Japanese—have similar stage roles (Ackroyd 1979; Bullough and Bullough 1993; Garber 1991). Similarly, castration was considered acceptable (if controversial) in Europe because it produced persons with voices desirable for certain opera roles

Table 2

Some Historical, Cross-Cultural, and Contemporary Models of Transgenderism

Non-Western

Role	Culture	Authority(ies)
Hijra	India	Nanda 1989, 1994
Khushra	Pakistan	Gooren 1992
Acault	Burma	Coleman et al. 1992
Xanith	Oman	Wikan 1977, 1982
Mahu	Polynesia	Besnier 1994
Two-Spirit (Winkte, Berdache)	North American Indian	Williams 1986
		Roscoe 1988, 1990
Female Husbands	Bantu	Bolin 1993
Shamanism	Various	Dragoin 1995
Eunuchs		Ackroyd 1979
Stage and Ceremonial Roles		Ackroyd 1979

Western, Historical

Transgendered Priest(esses)	Roscoe 1994
	O'Hartigan 1993
Castrati	Bullough and Bullough 1993
	Judd 1988
Passing Women/Passing Men	Dekker and Van de Pol 1989
	Wheelright 1989
Stage Roles	Garber 1991
Circus Freaks	Fiedler 1978
Uranians	Ulrichs 1994
Mannish Lesbians	Devor 1995

Western, Contemporary

Stage Roles	Garber 1991
Androgyny	Singer 1977, 1989
	Bell-Metereau 1994
Gender Blending	Devor 1989
Butch/Femme	Burana et al. 1994
	Nestle 1992
Female Impersonator	Baker 1968
Queens	Alpert 1975
Drag Queen	Woodlawn 1992
Drag King	Feinberg 1993

Table 2 (continued)

He/She	Feinberg 1993
Sex Workers	Newton 1979
She-Males	Blanchard 1993
Transvestic Fetishism	Docter 1988
Guy-in-a-Dress	Berendt 1995
Heterosexual Cross-Dresser	Prince 1962
	Prince and Bentler 1972
Cross-Dresser-in-Denial	Denny 1994b
Gay Cross-Dresser	Kirk and Heath 1984
Bisexual Cross-Dresser	Denny 1994b
Third Sex/Third Gender	Heidt 1994
Transgenderism	Boswell 1991
Transexualism	
FTM (female-to-male)	Green 1994
	Sullivan 1990
Pre-/Post-/Non-op	Bolin 1988
Pathologizing	Barr et al. 1974
	Lothstein 1983
	Milliken 1982
Assimilationism	Benjamin 1966
	Hollis 1993
	Montgomery and
	Montgomery 1994
Empowerment	Bockting 1995
	Bockting and Coleman 1992
	Bolin 1994
Activism	Wilchins 1994
Pen Names, Pseudonyms	Alaya 1970
Virtual Gender	Denny 1995
Transcendent	Bornstein 1994
	Butler 1990, 1993
	Feinberg 1994
	Rothblatt 1995

(Judd 1988). As a blue-collar equivalent to the castrati, intersexed and transgendered persons were openly exhibited as freaks by circuses in both North America and Europe (Fiedler 1978).

Because openly transgendered persons were historically persecuted and sometimes executed for their manner of dress (as was Jean d'Arc [Bullough and Bullough 1993]), most transgendered persons in Western society have lived in secrecy. By examining historical records, Dekker and Van de Pol (1989) were able to discover several hundred instances of "passing women" (women who live as men) in the Netherlands during the Middle Ages. Females have been especially adept at passing for men in the military services (Wheelright 1989). Several hundred "male" soldiers in the American Civil War were female (Meyer 1994). There are also accounts of passing men, but they are less frequent, perhaps because without hormonal therapy (which was not available before the 1950s), it is more difficult for males to pass as females than vice-versa.

When homosexual identity began to be consolidated in the late nineteenth century (cf. Duberman et al. 1989), gay men were considered to have feminine spirits, and gay women to have masculine spirits. This was the result of the writings of Karl Ulrichs, whose works have been only recently translated into English (1994). This view of the effeminate gay male and the masculine lesbian was the dominant one until the 1950s (Devor 1995). Recently, in the wake of the publication of Leslie Feinberg's *Stone Butch Blues* (1994), there has been a re-emergence of butch identity among some members of the lesbian community. Certainly, there are ever-increasing numbers of female-to-male cross-dressers and transexual people visible in the support groups of the transgender community.

Contemporary Western Roles

Due to the writings of Virginia Prince (cf. Prince, 1962; Prince and Bentler 1972), it has been frequently proclaimed that most cross-dressers are heterosexual, and a large community of predominantly heterosexual cross-dressing males has formed. However, if there are large numbers of heterosexual cross-dressers, there are also large numbers of gay and bisexual cross-dressers. Their relative absence from the "transgender community" is not necessarily evidence of a low incidence (Denny 1994a). Gay cross-dressers congregate in large numbers in bars and at pageants, and bisexual cross-dressers communicate by way of sexual contact ads in newspapers and magazines, which outsell the magazines and newsletters of the "transgender community" by orders of magnitude. Fetishistic transvestites engage in solitary dressing for their own sexual pleasure; their sexual orientation may be toward males, females, or other transgendered persons (Docter 1988).

Following the media feeding frenzy about Christine Jorgensen that began in late 1952, the category called transexualism arose (Bullough and Bullough 1993).[1] This was a condition in which individuals insisted that they required medical intervention, and it gave rise to a pathology-based system that was very damaging to the individual's view of him- or herself as a whole and actualized person (cf. Barr et al. 1974; Lothstein 1983; Milliken 1982). For several decades, those who were transgendered could escape from the traditional male and female categories only at the price of being fit by the medical community into the categories ("boxes") of heterosexual transvestism or transexualism (Denny 1992). This resulted in a large number of "heterosexual" cross-dressers who were actually gay or bisexual or who had transexual issues that they hid to escape peer pressure from other "heterosexual" cross-dressers who often had similar issues (Denny 1994b).[2] Only the gay and lesbian community had nonpathology-based roles. These included drag queens, who used cross-dressing as a form of empowerment, both political and personal (Serian 1988); drag kings (Feinberg 1993); female impersonators, who made their living as performers (Baker et al. 1994), trans-gendered sex workers (Newton 1979); butch lesbians; "nellie" males; she-males (also called "chicks with dicks") (Blanchard 1993); or as "queens," a catchall term that included all of the above (in the male-to-female direction), as well as transexual persons who had found a home in the gay community (Alpert 1975).

For many years, transexualism was considered a "condition" that was "cured" by sex reassignment (Benjamin 1966). An emerging sensibility—or rather, a paradigm shift, in the classic Kuhnian (Kuhn 1962) sense—has made it clear that this is not the inevitable outcome of being transexual, or even a desirable one. I have called assimilation "the closet at the end of the rainbow." Other transexual people call those who wish to assimilate "woodworkers" or "stealth" transexuals. More and more transexual people are accepting their transgendered condition as a permanent state of being; this has opened the door for political and scientific activism and, moreover, to the realization that being pre-operative is not inevitably a way-station on the road to surgery, but perhaps a permanent state of non-operativeness. The clinical community is learning this lesson as well, with this new sensibility being discussed by Anne Bolin (1994), Walter Bockting (1995), Bockting and Coleman (1992), and others.

The changing of the paradigm has led to the emergence of a class of people known as transgenderists (Boswell 1991). Transgenderists define themselves, rather than asking or allowing themselves to be defined by helping professionals, doing as little or as much as they wish to their bodies, but stopping short of genital surgery. Transgenderism encompasses an older term, androgyny, as well as the "gender blending" observed by Devor (1989), who studied women who were socially perceived to be males in some contexts, and females in others. Cross-dressers are increasingly coming to realize that they need not "pass" (Goffman 1963) or even strive to emulate women or men—they can just dress as they damn well please (Berendt 1995).

Recently, the proliferation of computer networks like the Internet has opened the door to what I call "virtual gender." In cyberspace, one's gender is limited to a "handle," and sex reassignment can be as easy as changing one's log-on name. I find this similar to the adoption of feminine personae via correspondence, as happened with the writer William Sharp, whose "Fiona MacCleod" personality became very real to him (Alaya 1970). Sharp's experience as a "social female" is the cybernetic equivalent of social males in Bantu (Bolin 1993), and sworn virgins in Slavic tribes (Gremaux 1994), in which women take on the dress and social status of males.

If all of the ways of looking at transgender behavior seem arbitrary, dependent upon the sensibilities of the observer, so too do the terms male and female, man and woman. Many writers, including Kate Bornstein (1994), Judith Butler (1990, 1993), Leslie Feinberg (1994), and Martine Rothblatt (1994), take the view that these categories are no less constructed than any other, and exist not in reality, but only in the ways in which we are enculturated to believe in them. Any number of other societies believe there are more than two sexes (for some examples, see Bolin 1993), and even within the framework of Western science, there are those who believe there are more than two (Fausto-Sterling 1993).

Notions of a highly pathological condition called "gender dysphoria" are giving way to an empowerment model in which it is not the unwillingness or inability of some persons to fit into the rigidly bipolar gender roles of Western society, but the inability of society to look beyond binary roles that is viewed as pathological.

There are doubtless many ways of looking at gender other than those I have written about in this article. It would be of interest to identify them and examine them empirically in light of the evaluation criteria in table 1.

Based upon my personal experience and after a great deal of thought about the various ways of looking at transgender and transexual experience I have presented, I have some suggestions for future research.

1. Develop models that allow the greatest range of personal choice without forcing individuals into fixed outcomes. Models with fixed outcomes will inevitably force people into outcomes that may not be best for them. Individuals must not only be made aware that they have a range of choices, but also must be allowed to choose among them.

2. Develop models that provide procedural safeguards while at the same time maximizing individual autonomy. There is a delicate balance between the right of the individual to the freedom of his or her own body, and the duty of a medical or psychological professional to do what is in the best interest of the client. This balance will be reached only by ongoing, respectful dialogue between those who are transexual or transgendered, and those who provide the services they need. The recent rise of a class of transgendered and transexual physicians, psychologists, anthropologists, sociologists, and researchers is already providing valuable input in this area.

3. Avoid use of stigmatizing language in research reports (use of quotations around pronouns; use of terms like "male transexual," "female transexualism"; use of terms like "deviancy"). Instead, use more identity-affirming terms, such as "transexual woman" and "transexual man," and the words transgender and transexual instead of pathology-based terms like "gender dysphoria." Much of the supposedly objective literature of transexual and transgender issues is needlessly pejorative. Authors have tended to let their personal biases prevail, and editors have been very lax in catching and removing offending statements and usages. This shows a fundamental lack of respect for transgendered and transexual persons that must be resolved if respectful communication is to take place.

4. Look closely at the research question that is being asked. Does it reinforce obsolete models? Is it needlessly pathologizing? Do we really need one more research paper about the ways in which the MMPI scores of transgendered and transexual people differ from a control group? The assumptions that have driven much of the research have been faulty, based on the assimilationist model of transexualism, and upon the presupposition that transgender feelings are a sign of weakness or sickness. For future research to have any meaning or usefulness, underlying assumptions must be closely examined.

5. Avoid the ivory-tower syndrome. Base research questions on the realities of transgendered and transexual people, rather than the highly pathologizing existing literature. Take advantage of sociological and anthropological studies of transgendered and transexual people. The attacks on transexualism have been made by those who know the least about the phenomenon. Janice Raymond (1979, 1994) interviewed only fifteen transexual people before writing her antitransexual polemic, *The Transexual Empire: The Making of the She-Male.* Raymond made a career of talking against transexualism, going so far as to testify against SRS (sexual reassignment surgery) to the U.S. government. Paul McHugh, a psychiatrist who reported having gone to Johns Hopkins University specifically to shut down their gender clinic (McHugh 1992), in a letter to another physician in 1994, expressed disbelief at the idea that a postoperative transexual woman could be attracted to other women. Such "contributions" to the literature are political, and not scientific, and must be considered as such, while valuable work by anthropologists, sociologists, and transgendered scholars must not be ignored.

6. Don't needlessly empower genital surgery. Avoid use of words like "preoperative," "post-operative," and "non-operative," which define the entire transgender and transexual experience as secondary to one three-hour event.

Structure research so that it focuses on landmarks other than surgery (e.g., beginning of a real-life test). There is a great tendency in our society to define maleness and femaleness by the absence or presence of a penis, and neither transexual persons nor helping professionals are immune to this type of thinking. Bullough (1994) has noted that it was the synthesis of artificial sex hormones in the third decade of this century, and not modern surgical techniques, that made modern-day sex reassignment possible. This should constantly be kept in mind by those doing research with transexual persons.

7. Understand that the logical goal of sex reassignment is not necessarily assimilation, but rather integration of one's transgendered or transexual status into one's self-identity. The idea that sex reassignment and subsequent assimilation into the dominant culture were a "cure" for transexualism led to a great deal of shame and guilt. With this model, transexual people were once again in the closet and could never live with dignity or pride; instead, they had to hide, out of communication with one another. Those whose physical characteristics did not lend themselves to "passing" were especially likely to be disempowered.

It was only when transexual people began to realize that assimilation was not the inevitable consequence of sex reassignment that it became possible to develop a sense of transgender pride and begin to build community. Many people having sex reassignment will wish to assimilate, and if they so desire, they should not be discouraged, but it is important that they be given the information that there are other options.

My purpose in this article has been to describe a number of ways in which transgendered persons have been viewed throughout history, in our society and in others, and to provide tools by which to evaluate these and future models and to guide future research.

Notes

1. In keeping with the emerging transexual sentiment that those who are transexual have the ultimate right of self-definition, throughout this paper I have used the word *transexualism* rather than the more commonly used *transsexualism*.

2. This condition is unfortunately still common today. Organizations for heterosexual cross-dressers often act as if it were a defection when someone acknowledges his or her bisexual or transexual issues.

References

Cross-Cultural

Ackroyd, P. 1979. *Dressing up. Transvestism and drag: The history of an obsession.* New York: Simon & Schuster.

Besnier, N. 1994. Polynesian gender liminality through time and space. In *Third sex, third gender: Beyond sexual dimorphism in culture and history,* edited by G. Herdt, 285–328. New York: Zone Books.

Bolin, A. 1993. An interview with Anne Bolin, Ph.D. *Chrysalis Quarterly* 1, no. 6: 15–20.

Coleman, E., P. Colgan, and L. Gooren. 1992. Male cross-gender behavior in Myanmar (Burma): A description of the acault. *Archives of Sexual Behavior* 21, no. 3: 313–21.

Dragoin, W. 1995. The gynemimetic shaman: Evolutionary origins of male sexual inversion and associated talent? Paper presented at the International Congress on Cross-Dressing, Gender, and Sex Issues, Van Nuys, California, 24–26 February 1995.

Gooren, L. J. G. 1992. Gender dysphoria in Pakistan: The Khusra. A traveller's report. *Gender Dysphoria* 1, no. 2: 35–36.

Gremaux, R. 1994. Woman becomes man in the Balkans. In *Third sex, third gender: Beyond sexual dimorphism in culture and history,* edited by G. Herdt, 241–81. New York: Zone Books.

Herdt, G. ed. 1994. *Third sex, third gender: Beyond sexual dimorphism in culture and history.* New York: Zone Books.

Nanda, S. 1989. *Neither man nor woman: The Hijras of India.* Belmont, Calif.: Wadsworth Publishing.

———. 1994. Hijras: An alternative sex and gender role in India. In *Third sex, third gender: Beyond sexual dimorphism in culture and history,* edited by G. Herdt, 373–418. New York: Zone Books.

Roscoe, W. 1990. *The Zuni man-woman.* Albuquerque: University of New Mexico Press.

———, ed. 1988. *Living the spirit: A gay American Indian anthology.* New York: St. Martin's Press.

Wikan, U. 1977. Man becomes woman: Transsexualism in Oman as a key to gender roles. *Man* 12, no. 2: 304–319.

———. 1982. Xanith: A third gender role? In *Behind the veil in Arabia: Women in Oman,* edited by U. Wikan, 168–86. Baltimore: The Johns Hopkins University Press.

Williams, W. L. 1986. *The spirit and the flesh: Sexual diversity in American Indian culture.* Boston: Beacon Press.

Western, Historical

Alaya, F. 1970. *William Sharp—"Fiona Macleod," 1855–1905.* Cambridge, Mass.: Harvard University Press.

Bullough, V. L., and B. Bullough. 1993. *Cross dressing, sex, and gender.* Philadelphia: University of Pennsylvania Press.

Dekker, R. J., and L. C. van de Pol. 1989. *The tradition of female transvestism in early modern Europe.* New York: St. Martin's Press.

Duberman, M. B., M. Vicinus, and G. Chauncey, Jr., eds. 1989. *Hidden from history: Reclaiming the gay and lesbian past.* New York: Penguin.

Feinberg, L. N.d. *Transgender liberation: A movement whose time has come.* World View Forum, 55 W 17th St., 5th Floor, New York, NY 10011.

Fiedler, A. 1978. *Freaks: Myths and images of the secret self.* New York: Simon & Schuster.

Judd, R. 1988. *Origins of cross-dressing: A history of performance en travesti.* Ph.D. diss., Clayton University.
Meyer, E. L. 1994. The soldier left a portrait and her eyewitness account. *Smithsonian* 24, no. 10: 96–104.
O'Hartigan, M. 1993. The gallae of the Magna Mater. *Chrysalis* 1, no. 6: 11–13.
Roscoe, W. 1994. Priests of the goddess: Gender transgression in the Ancient World. Paper presented at the 109th Annual Meeting of the American Historical Association, San Francisco, California.
Ulrichs, K. H. 1994. *The riddle of "man-manly" love: The pioneering work on male homosexuality.* Translated by Michael A. Lombardi-Nash. Vols. 1 and 2. Amherst, N.Y.: Prometheus Books.
Wheelright, J. 1989. *Amazons and military maids: Women who dressed as men in pursuit of life, liberty, and happiness.* London: Pandora Press.

Western, Contemporary

GENERAL

Denny, D. 1994b. Heteropocracy: The myth of the heterosexual crossdresser. Unpublished paper.
Garber, M. 1991. *Vested interests: Cross-dressing and cultural anxiety.* New York: Routledge.

ANDROGYNY

Bell-Metereau, R. 1994. *Hollywood androgyny.* 1985. Reprint, New York: Columbia University Press.
Singer, J. 1977. *Androgyny: Toward a new theory of sexuality.* Garden City, N.J.: Anchor.
———. 1989. *Androgyny: The opposites within.* Boston: Sigo Press.

BUTCH/FEMME

Burana, L., and L. D. Roxxie, eds. 1994. *Dagger: On butch women.* New York: Cleis Press.
Findlay, H. 1995. What is stone butch—now? *Girlfriends* (March/April): 20–22, 44–45.
Nestle, J. 1992. *A femme/butch reader.* Boston: Alyson Publications, Inc.

DRAG, FEMALE IMPERSONATION

Baker, R. 1994. *Drag: A history of female impersonation on the stage.* London: Triton Books.
Serian, R. 1987. Big hair and new makeup. *Whole Earth Review* 56: 2–7.

GAY CROSS-DRESSING

Alpert, G. 1975. *The Queens.* New York: Da Capo.
Blanchard, R. 1993. The she-male phenomenon and the concept of partial autogynephilia. *Journal of Sex and Marital Therapy* 19, no. 1: 69–76.
Kirk, K., and E. Heath. 1984. *Men in frocks.* London: GMP Publishers, Ltd.
Newton, E. 1979. *Mother camp: Female impersonators in America.* Chicago: University of Chicago Press.

HETEROSEXUAL CROSS-DRESSING

Berendt, J. 1995. High-heel Neil. *The New Yorker* (January 16): 38–45.
Prince, C. V., and P. M. Bentler 1972. Survey of 504 cases of transvestism. *Psychological Reports* 31, no. 3: 903–17.
Prince, V. 1962. *The transvestite and his wife.* Los Angeles: Chevalier Publications.

TRANSVESTIC FETISHISM

Docter, R. F. 1988. *Transvestites and transsexuals: Toward a theory of cross-gender behavior.* London: Plenum Press.

TRANSEXUAL (ASSIMILATIONIST)

Benjamin, H. 1966. *The transsexual phenomenon: A scientific report on transsexualism and sex conversion in the human male and female.* New York: Julian Press. Currently available in reprinted form from The Human Outreach and Achievement Institute, 405 Western Avenue, Ste. 345, South Portland, ME 04106.
Blanchard, R., and B. Steiner, eds. 1990. *Clinical management of gender identity disorders in children and adults.* Washington, D.C.: American Psychiatric Press.
Green, R. 1974. *Sexual identity conflict in children and adults.* New York: Basic Books, Inc. Reprint, Penguin Books, 1975.
Hollis, C. M. 1993. *Beyond belief: "The discovery of my existence."* Galena, Ill.: Genesis Publications.
Montgomery, L., and J. Montgomery. 1994. *Transition to completion.* Decatur, Ga.: Montgomery Institute.

TRANSEXUALISM (FEMALE-TO-MALE)

Devor, H. 1995. How female-to-male transsexuals reject lesbian identities. Paper presented at the International Congress on Cross-Dressing, Gender, and Sex Issues, Van Nuys, California, 24–26 February 1995.
Green, J. 1994. The story of a transsexual man. San Francisco: FTM International (Audiotape)
Sullivan, L. 1990. *Information for the female-to-male cross-dresser and transsexual.* Seattle: Ingersoll Gender Center.

ANTI-TRANSEXUAL

McHugh, P. R. 1992. Psychiatric misadventures. *American Scholar* 61, no. 4: 497–510.
Raymond, J. 1979. *The transsexual empire: The making of a she-male.* Boston: Beacon Press. Reprinted 1994, New York: Teachers College Press.

TRANSEXUAL (PATHOLOGIZING)

Barr, R. F., B. Raphael, and N. Hennessey. 1974. Apparent heterosexuality in two male patients requesting change of sex operation. *Archives of Sexual Behavior* 3, no. 4: 325–30.

Lothstein, L. 1983. *Female-to-male transsexualism: Historical, clinical and theoretical issues.* Boston: Routledge & Kegan Paul.
Milliken, A. D. 1982. Homicidal transsexuals: Three cases. *Canadian Journal of Psychiatry* 27, no. 1: 43–46.

Transexual (Empowerment)

Bockting, W. 1995. Transgender coming out: Implications for the clinical management of gender dysphoria. Paper presented at the International Congress on Cross-Dressing, Gender, and Sex Issues, Van Nuys, California, 24–26 February 1995.
Bockting, W., and E. Coleman, eds. 1992. *Gender dysphoria: Interdisciplinary approaches in clinical management.* New York: Haworth Press.
Bolin, A. 1988. *In search of Eve: Transsexual rites of passage.* South Hadley, Mass.: Bergin & Garvey.
Denny, D. 1992. The politics of diagnosis and a diagnosis of politics: The university-affiliated gender clinics, and how they failed to meet the needs of transsexual people. *Chrysalis Quarterly* 1, no. 3: 9–20.
Wilchins, R. 1994. Clothes are for closets, not transpersons. *Tapestry* 70.

Transcendent

Bornstein, K. 1994. *Gender outlaw: On men, women, and the rest of us.* New York: Routledge.
Bolin, A. 1994. Transcending and transgendering: Male-to-female transsexuals, dichotomy, and diversity. In *Third sex, third gender: Beyond sexual dimorphism in culture and history,* edited by G. Herdt, 447–85. New York: Zone Books.
Boswell, H. 1991. The transgender alternative. *Chrysalis Quarterly* 1, no. 2: 29–31.
Butler, J. 1990. *Gender trouble: Feminism and the subversion of identity.* New York: Routledge.
———. 1993. *Bodies that matter: On the discursive limits of "sex."* New York: Routledge.
Devor, H. 1989. *Gender blending: Confronting the limits of duality.* Bloomington: Indiana University Press.
Fausto-Sterling, A. 1985. *Myths of gender: Biological theories about women and men.* New York: Basic Books.
———. 1993. The five sexes: Why male and female are not enough. *The Sciences* (March/April): 20–25.
Feinberg, L. 1993. *Stone butch blues.* New York: Firebrand Books.
Rothblatt, M. 1994. *The apartheid of sex: A manifesto on the freedom of gender.* New York: Crown Publishers.
Woodlawn, H., with J. Copeland. 1992. *A low life in high heels: The Holly Woodlawn Story.* New York: St. Martin's Press.

Miscellaneous

Bullough, V. L. 1994. Preface to *Gender dysphoria: A guide to research,* by D. Denny, xv–xix. New York: Garland Publishers.
Denny, D. 1994a. *Gender dysphoria: A guide to research.* New York: Garland Publishers.
———. 1995. Transgender: Some historical, cross-cultural, and modern-day models and methods of coping and treatment. Workshop presented at the International Congress on Cross-Dressing, Gender, and Sex Issues, Van Nuys, California, 24–26 February, 1995.

Goffman, E. 1963. *Stigma: Notes on the management of spoiled identity.* Englewood Cliffs, N.J.: Prentice-Hall.

Kuhn, T. S. 1962. *The structure of scientific revolutions.* Chicago: The University of Chicago.

Transgender Coming Out:
Implications for the Clinical Management
of Gender Dysphoria

Walter O. Bockting

Recent developments in conceptualization and expression of transgender identities in North America suggest a paradigm shift in this field signified by an emerging transgender consciousness that includes changes on a sociocultural, interpersonal, and intrapsychic level. Socioculturally, the prevailing gender schema of Western culture is challenged by transgender identities that transcend the gender dichotomy. Interpersonally, transgendered individuals are coming out to their families, friends, and workplaces, and no longer hide their unique identity. Intrapsychically, affirmation of one's identity as transgender alleviates shame and is experienced as liberating. A growing transgender community provides the necessary support.

This paradigm shift has implications for the clinical management of gender dysphoria. Treatment is no longer limited to assisting gender dysphoric individuals to adjust in one and/or the other gender role, but includes the possibility of affirming a unique transgender identity. Transgender identities are diverse and may or may not include partial or complete changes in primary or secondary sex characteristics. The merits of physical changes should be evaluated in the context of the individual's identity development with an emphasis on personal comfort and well-being.

What we today call cross- or transgender behavior has existed throughout history and across cultures. Examples are Chevalier D'Eon, Joan of Arc, the Native American two-spirited people (Williams 1986; Roscoe 1988, 1991), and the Acault in Myanmar (Coleman, Colgan, and Gooren, 1992).

In the beginning of this century, in 1910, Magnus Hirschfeld wrote "Die

Transvestiten" and coined the terms transvestite and transsexual. Magnus Hirschfeld is considered one of the founders of sexology, and has been given the status of "gender studies pioneer, feminist, and gay liberation hero." As with homosexuality, he medicalized transgender behavior, at that time as a way to counter the strong societal rejection and condemnation of sexual variance. He conceptualized transvestism as "woundedness" due to an inborn anomaly, and called for compassion and acceptance. By doing so, he was able to assist in defending in court those who were arrested for homosexuality or for cross dressing (Hirschfeld 1991).

When psychotherapy wasn't successful in alleviating transsexuals' discomfort with their birth sex and gender, pioneers such as Harry Benjamin took the risk of supporting sex reassignment to alleviate intense gender dysphoria. For those individuals falling on Benjamin's scale toward the extreme of "true transsexualism" sex reassignment was indicated.

The focus of sex reassignment was to help "true transsexual" males adjust as women and "true transsexual" females adjust as men. In other words: Sex reassignment conformed to a binary conceptualization of gender. A "true transsexual" was characterized by feeling like a member of the opposite sex trapped in the wrong body, "asexual," or desiring "relations with normal male as 'female,' if young" (Benjamin 1966). Sex reassignment became the option of choice to treat such transsexuality.

In the Netherlands, the term "de-transsexualization" (Verschoor 1986) was used to refer to hormonal and surgical sex reassignment, which reflects that the aim of treatment was to assist male and female transsexuals in changing toward "no longer transsexual" women and men.

In North America in the past five years, a paradigm shift has occurred signified by an emerging transgender consciousness that challenges this binary conceptualization of gender.

The need for this paradigm shift was well articulated by Sandy Stone in her 1991 article: "The Empire Strikes Back: A Posttranssexual Manifesto." Based on transsexuals' accounts (Lili Elbe's *Man into Woman,* Hedy Jo Star's *I Changed My Sex,* and Jan Morris's *Conundrum*) Stone concludes: "the authors reinforce a binary, oppositional mode of gender identification. They go from being unambiguous men, albeit unhappy men, to unambiguous women. There is no territory in between."

This type of gender identification is illustrated by the following 1974 quote from Jan Morris on the evening of her surgery: "I went to say good-bye to myself in the mirror. We would never meet again, and I wanted to give that other self a long last . . . wink for luck . . ."; and Sandy Stone's own experience: "I was reminded of this account on the eve of my own surgery. Gee, I thought on that occasion, it would be interesting to magically become another person in that binary and final way. So I tried it myself—going into the mirror and saying good-bye to the person I saw there—and unfortunately it didn't work. A few days later, when I could next get to the mirror, the person looking back at me was still me. I still don't understand what I did wrong."

This points to the shame that many transsexuals struggle with as a result of the expectation to "pass" as a nontranssexual woman or man and start a new life as such.

Subsequently, Stone goes on to call for transsexuals to come out and affirm their unique identity and experience, from outside the boundaries of gender and beyond its binary conceptualization.

In 1989 (*Pleasures of a Tangled Life*) Jan Morris's writings indicate a change in her thinking: "There was a time, when new to life as a woman, I tried to forget that I had ever lived as a man. But it had grown on me over the years that this was not only intellectually dishonest, but actually rather dull of me. Now I realized I enjoyed the present largely in reflection to the past; the tangle was part of me."

This represents a change away from the view of having started a new life as a member of the "opposite" sex, toward an integrated transsexual identity. As one of my clients stated: "I always knew I wasn't a man. I thought for a long time I was a woman, and tried very hard to be a woman. Now, many years after sex reassignment surgery, I recognize: I am neither a man nor a woman. I am a trans-sexual, period."

The paradigm shift regarding the transgender and transsexual experience includes changes on a sociocultural, interpersonal, and intrapsychic level.

Socioculturally, the prevailing gender schema of Western culture is chal-lenged by transgender identities that transcend the gender dichotomy. For exam-ple, there is a growing number of transsexual men with vaginas and women with penises and breasts. And individuals who cross or transcend culturally defined gender lines come out as transgendered and are members of transgender organi-zations, some of which have entered coalitions with gay, lesbian, and bisexual communities. People who are differently gendered are becoming a more visible part of society.

Interpersonally, transgendered individuals are coming out to their families, friends, and workplaces. Rather than attempting to "pass" as a nontransgender or nontranssexual man or woman, many affirm their unique transgender or trans-sexual identity (Warren 1993). This can contribute to comfort in interpersonal sit-uations. In intimate relationships, sex and gender roles do not always conform to a conventional heterosexual *or* homosexual pattern, but include exploration and discovery of unique gender creative roles and sexual scripts.

Intrapsychically, self-affirmation of one's identity as transgender or transsexual alleviates shame and is experienced as liberating. The never-ending pressure of trying to conform to how a man or woman is supposed to look and behave, the fear of being "read," the secrecy and isolation associated with hiding one's transsexual status, can form an incredible burden that can be released through coming out.

Applied to sexuality, one transgendered individual stated to me: "My sexuality is a transgender sexuality, different from both male and female sexuality." Having started out with Hirschfeld's biological determinism, this illustrates the contribution of social construction to one's identity and sexuality.

This paradigm shift has implications for the clinical management of gender dysphoria. As one of my clients stated: "Previous treatment let me believe that I was going to be a woman, not a transsexual. I wasn't prepared for that."

The treatment we now offer at the Program in Human Sexuality is no longer aimed at identifying the "true transsexual." Options for identity management are no longer limited to adjustment in one and/or the other gender role, but include the possibility of affirming a unique transgender identity and role.

Transgender identities are diverse and may or may not include partial or complete changes in primary or secondary sex characteristics. The merits of physical changes are evaluated in the context of the individual's identity development with an emphasis on personal comfort and well being.

Our treatment program is client-centered; acknowledges a spectrum of gender identities; does not require conformity to conventional social sex roles; does not consider sexual orientation relevant in the indication for sex reassignment; and assesses the appropriateness of hormone therapy and sex reassignment surgery separately (i.e., hormone therapy does not necessarily have to be followed by sex reassignment surgery and is a valid option in and of itself) (Bockting and Coleman 1992). To foster identity development and integration through psychotherapy, we have found a "coming out" model helpful.

This (trans)gender paradigm shift that includes community empowerment is accompanied by distrust and conflict between health care providers and transgender community activists. Therefore, in order to enhance treatment effectiveness and satisfaction, I support forums between providers and community representatives in which dialogue can take place.

As a university-based program serving the transgender population, our research has paralleled this paradigm shift. Our studies on homosexual and bisexual identity of sex reassigned female-to-male transsexuals indicated that gender identity, social sex role, and sexual orientation are separate dimensions of one's sexual identity and that a homogenderal sexual orientation is not a contraindication for sex reassignment (Coleman and Bockting 1988; Coleman,

Bockting, and Gooren 1993). Our cross-cultural research in Myanmar and Thailand explored the unique place cross-gender behavior assumes in non-Western cultures (Coleman, Colgan, and Gooren 1992). And our transgender HIV prevention project, developed and implemented in collaboration with transgender community organizations, targets health concerns for transgender-identified individuals and their families (Bockting, Rosser, and Coleman 1993).

In a time of renewed conservatism and health care reform in the United States, I believe providers, researchers, and community representatives need to work together to advance knowledge and educate the health care and service community as well as policymakers on transgender and transsexual health and on effective treatment of gender dysphoria.

References

Benjamin, H. 1966. *The transsexual phenomenon.* New York: Julian Press.

Bockting, W. O., and E. Coleman. 1992. A comprehensive approach to the treatment of gender dysphoria. In *Gender dysphoria: Interdisciplinary approaches in clinical management,* edited by W. O. Bockting and E. Coleman. Binghamton, N.Y.: The Haworth Press.

Bockting, W., B. R. Rosser, and E. Coleman. 1993. *Transgender HIV—prevention manual.* Minneapolis: Program in Human Sexuality.

Coleman, E., and W. Bockting. 1988. "Heterosexual" prior to sex reassignment—"homosexual" afterwards: A case study of a female-to-male transsexual. *Journal of Psychology and Human Sexuality* 1, no. 2: 69–82.

Coleman, E., W. Bockting, and L. Gooren. 1993. Homosexual and bisexual identity in sex-reassigned female-to-male transsexuals. *Archives of Sexual Behavior* 22, no. 1: 37–50.

Coleman, E., Colgan, P., and Gooren, L. 1992. Male cross-gender behavior in Myanmar (Burma): A description of the Acault. *Archives of Sexual Behavior* 21, no. 3: 313–21.

Elbe, L. 1993. *Man into woman: An authentic record of a change of sex: The true story of the miraculous transformation of the Danish painter, Einar Wegener.* New York: E. P. Dutton & Company, Inc.

Hirschfeld, M. 1991. *Transvestites: An investigation of the erotic drive to cross-dress.* Amherst, N.Y.: Prometheus Books.

Morris, J. 1974. *Conundrum.* New York: Harcourt Brace Jovanovich.

———. 1989. *Pleasures of a tangled life.* London: Arrow Books Limited.

Roscoe, W. 1991. *The Zuni man-woman.* Albuquerque: University of New Mexico Press.

———, ed. 1988. *Living the spirit: A gay American Indian anthology.* New York: St. Martin's Press.

Star, Hedy Jo. 1955. *I changed my sex.* Publisher Unknown.

Stone, S. 1991. The empire strikes back: A posttranssexual manifesto. In *Body guards,* edited by J. Epstein and K. Straub. New York: Routledge.

Verschoor, A. 1986. *De Transseksuele Mens.* Amsterdam: Een uitgave van de Stichting Nederlands Gender Centrum.

Warren, B. 1993. Transsexuality, identity, and empowerment: A view from the front lines. *SIECUS Report* (February/March): 14–16.

Williams, W. 1986. *The spirit and the flesh.* Boston: Beacon Press.

The Transgender Paradigm Shift toward Free Expression

Holly Boswell

What is transgender? What is it like to be transgendered? How many forms might this actually take? Is this paradigm shift new, and if so, how? What will it mean, not only for transgendered people, but for everyone?

Up until this decade, the emerging transgender community consisted of three recognizable components: transsexuals, cross-dressers (usually heterosexual), and our seldom-acknowledged cousins of gay drag. While the need to challenge culturally imposed stereotypes remains just as strong today, these three models have proven to be far too restrictive of the true range of transgender expression, ironically reinforcing the very myth that there are only two genders, as defined by most contemporary assimilationist cultures. This is changing (Boswell 1991).

In the primary cases of transsexualism and cross-dressing, notions of femininity and masculinity are thoroughly emulated—even to the point of undergoing radical surgery, or at least by challenging conformance to societal expectations of gender expression. The transgenderist, as defined by Virginia Prince, is usually no different from the non-operative transsexual who expresses only one of two genders. Still, this is risky business, often involving the loss of marriages, children, parents, family, friends, and livelihood. Such is the depth of the quest for selfhood, struggling to survive against social stigmatization and rejection.

What we are now beginning to experience is a new—yet anciently rooted—way of being that defies and transcends the absurd linkage between biological sex and gender expression. While biological sex manifests between our legs, the complexity of sexual and gender expression occurs between our ears. Even so, the concept of sex itself must be challenged as an artificial construct (Rothblatt

1995), especially in view of recurrent hermaphroditism and a host of other persistent psycho/social deviations from so-called male or female characteristics. Sex, in spite of how we have been conditioned to perceive it, is far from black or white, and is as much a state of mind—distinct from anatomy—as the outward expression we call gender. It is time to move beyond the bipolar masculine/feminine model of sex and gender based solely on anatomy. Manifesting our true humanity has much more to do with the rainbow of possibilities emanating from within our hearts, minds, and spirits.

It is important to recognize that this new paradigm of gender is coming from, and is finally being articulated by, the very people who are living it. For us, the experience comes first, then our conceptual explanation of it—unlike the academic approach of postulating a hypothesis that must then be proven. Many of us have become living proof of transgender reality. Some of us have been the willing subjects of research, but we are also recognizing the need to assert our own voices—some voices dialogue within our transgender community, and other voices remind us evermore of our rich diversity.

We are discovering how difficult it is to describe to others what it is like to be transgendered. I used to be amazed that, despite my elaborate explanations, no one could ever quite understand my experience of transgender, until I finally realized that neither have I ever understood what it is to be a man or a woman (Bornstein 1994). I seem to be neither, or maybe both, yet ultimately only myself. So, is transgender simply a result of being more honest with oneself and resistant to socialization, or is it chromosomally or hormonally induced, or better described as spirit taking precedence over form? All I know is that I could no longer live any other way, and have since found many others who share this experience.

So the word "transgender" describes much more than crossing between the poles of masculinity and femininity. It more aptly refers to the transgressing of gender norms, or being freely gendered, or transcending gender altogether in order to become more fully human. Transgender has to do with reinventing and realizing oneself more fully outside of the current systems of gender (Williams 1995). There are probably as many genders as there are people. Gender may be nothing more than a personal matrix of personality traits.

In fact, once the concept of gender is freed from various cultural and biological expectations of sex, the terms "masculine" and "feminine" become so relative that they are virtually meaningless. The Bem Sex Role Inventory lists two hundred personality characteristics such as analytical, gentle, independent, sympathetic, idealistic, and worldly. It is understood that each culture assigns different groupings of traits to each anatomical sex and leaves some in a neutral category. No trait is intrinsically masculine or feminine, though a few are more commonly attributable. As a culture evolves, it defines and re-defines which traits are appropriate for each sex through the contrived linkage of anatomy with gender. But imagine a non-polarized culture without this linkage, where each person would be free to explore and express his or her own unique set of traits. So much human potential could be unleashed that both the individual and the culture as a whole might self-actualize en masse.

Therapists today acknowledge that androgyny is a healthier gender model for self-actualization and fulfillment than either of the binary genders. This entails a process of transcending social conditioning in order to more fully become ourselves. Jung's process of individuation, with its reconciliation of animus and anima, leads to "wholeness"—a word that is related to health and holiness. If most people were more honest about it, they would probably find themselves somewhere in the middle of the bell shaped curve of gender distribution rather than at the Rambo/bimbo extremes.

So while many people have androgynous potential, the traditions of alternative gender expression involve a minority within which these tendencies are much more pronounced. These are the profoundly transgendered, who have real difficulty conforming to the polarized codes of gender, and whose gender identities stray far beyond the normal expectations of their biological sex. This has always been so.

Despite all the new advances in hormonal and surgical procedures, many of us are choosing to customize the program to suit our individual self-definitions and expression (Mackenzie 1994). This hearkens back to the many "two-spirit" traditions throughout human history (though some of these did involve castration) and enlivens a growing awareness among transgendered people that passing is becoming passé. Only within the last few decades have transgendered people become so seduced by the ability to assimilate, made possible by recent hormonal and surgical advances (Feinberg 1992). This has relieved society of its responsibility to recognize more than two genders. All of us—transgendered and otherwise—continue to live under the constant "tyranny of passing" (Williams 1985), of questioning our sense of belonging against our self-worth. Are we living up to the societal roles and expectations that are imposed on us? Are we accepted and valued by others? How much should we care? How much societal rejection can we endure to achieve honest self-expression before we are undermined or destroyed in the process?

Diverse manifestations of transgender, however, are certainly not new. We have existed throughout history all over the planet (Williams 1986; Roscoe 1993). We are a normal, recurring expression of human nature. As a Lakota shaman explained, "To us a man is what nature, or his dreams, makes him. We accept him for what he wants to be. That's up to him." Various cultures in the past have honored our unique ability to make special contributions to society as shamans, spiritual leaders, visionaries, healers, mediators, counselors, teachers, and in other specific ways. Within these value systems, weeds don't exist. Every being has its sacred purpose, and none are to be wasted (Swifthawk 1992). Anthropologists are continually unearthing more evidence of such multifarious traditions as the *berdache* in native North America, shamans in Siberia and the Arctic, *hijiras* in India, *xanith* in the Middle East, *gallae* in the Roman Empire, certain Druid priestesses in Old Europe, the *mahu* of Polynesia, one-breasted Amazons, and many more. Ancient goddess religions, and other natural spiritual world-views, respected men and women as equals, regarded Nature as divine, revered diversity, and loved all manifestations of life. But since the replacement of Mother Nature with God the Father (about five thousand years ago), the constructs of gender have been defined more narrowly and rigidly to suit the purposes of those in control of each particular society.

So what impact does all this have on the transgender community and all of us as human beings? Because of Western civilization's emphasis on materialism and its inherently polarized value system, most transgendered people have been manifesting as their assumed opposite, either through cross-dressing or sex reassignment surgery. This is often motivated more by a need to assimilate than a quest toward truly becoming oneself, which would otherwise support the notion of gender as a many-splendored thing. Whereas cross-dressing may vicariously lead to gender insights, and transsexualism appropriately correct those who see their gender/anatomy variance as a problem, the newly emerging paradigm of gender will lead to a potent activation of healthy and renewable alternative gender expression.

Yes, this shift is new. Never before have we had so many options, yet chosen to manifest—despite our culture—our *true selves.* We are choosing to define ourselves outside of our cultures, and virtually outside of the very system of gender as we have known it. Transgendered people are redefining gender. This will no doubt be perceived as a radical course by the prevailing cultural consciousness for perhaps another generation or so, but it will be increasingly embraced on a personal level as the simple, honest human expression of Nature that it ultimately is. Gender liberation is a crucial key to human evolution, promoting the idea that we should strive to be *whole gendered,* cultivating all our gender traits to meet the critical challenges of our time.

Is this not a timely universal message, emanating deeply from within our collective consciousness? Are we not connected by our "continuous common humanity" (Bolin 1994), in exploring fully what it is to be ourselves—infinitely unique, yet united by the undeniable commonality of our human experience? This is the very bridge of transgender: connecting the myth of polarity into a whole, healing the illusions of our separateness, and celebrating the diversity of what it is to be fully human.

The mass media, especially cinema—after TV talk shows ad nauseam—

seem to be acknowledging the revelatory human truth of transgender. This needs little documentation. Professional caregivers are gradually becoming more educated about the breadth and depth of transgender phenomena, and how they might more appropriately help their transgendered clients. This is happening at the pervasive grassroots level, and now even more extensively at this first International Congress on Gender, Cross-Dressing and Sex Issues, February 1995. There has also been an increasing influx of updated educational programming at certain annual transgender conferences, such as Southern Comfort, International Foundation for Gender Education (IFGE), and International Conference on Transgender Law and Employment Policy's (ICTLEP) law conference.

With all this newly emerging awareness comes new resolve among transgendered people to be honest, to be "out," to endeavor to educate, to be politically active, to support young people joining our ranks with new issues, to venture into the cyberspace of "virtual gender," and to gather into our own circles for the intimate, spiritual processing of who we are truly becoming (Boswell 1994).

All this is very exciting and ought to serve as a catalyst to inspire the rest of humanity. Becoming truly oneself, on any level, is a most beautiful and worthwhile process. Yet how few actually venture into this territory? Transgendered people can serve as a bridge to help others find their own way. As avid students make the best teachers, we are living advocates for the profound experience of exploring one's true humanity—nothing less. And as we are each in need of healing ourselves on this essential level, we may then be able to hope for a world that reflects the dazzling rainbow of our immense wholeness, along with our long sought harmony, and the true beauty of our natural grace.

References

Bolin, A. 1994. Transcending and transgendering: Male-to-female transsexuals, dichotomy and diversity. In *Third sex, third gender: Beyond sexual dimorphism in culture and history,* edited by G. Herdt, 448–85. New York: Zone Books.

Bornstein, K. 1994. *Gender outlaw: On men, women and the rest of us.* New York and London: Routledge.

Boswell, H. 1991. The transgender alternative. *Chrysalis Quarterly,* 1, no. 2.

———. 1994. New berdache circling. *Tapestry,* 68.

Feinberg, L. 1992. Transgender liberation. New York: *World View Forum.*

Mackenzie, G. 1994. *Transgender nation.* Bowling Green: Bowling Green University Popular Press.

Roscoe, W. 1993. *Priests of the goddess: Gender transgression in the ancient world.* Palo Alto, Calif.: Stanford University Women's Studies.

Rothblatt, M. 1995. *The apartheid of sex.* New York: Crown.

Swifthawk, R. 1992. *We have a duty to the earth.* Houston: International Foundation for Gender Education.

Williams, C. 1985. TIGC newsletter: Albany, N.Y.

———. 1995. Why transgender? *Gender Quest* (March-April).

Williams, W. 1986. *The spirit and the flesh.* Boston: Beacon Press.

Beyond Appearances: Gendered Rationality and the Transgendered

Michael A. Gilbert

Issues in Gendered Rationality

For some time now my research interests have been centered in the areas of argumentation and rationality. I am concerned to explore ways in which people may disagree more effectively, and, especially, with a greater possibility of ending in agreement. Part of this research has brought me to examine different ways in which men and women think, reason, communicate, and argue. This, combined with my long-time connection to cross-dressing, led me naturally to wonder about the relationship between the diverse ways in which men and women reason and communicate and how the transgendered do so. Is it possible for a person to be socialized or learn the socialization patterns of an opposite gender? Alternatively, can one intentionally adopt a rationality that is different from that which one might be expected to develop at birth? These are the questions that motivate this paper.

The term "transgendered" covers a wide group of individuals ranging from the occasional heterosexual cross-dresser at one extreme to the born-knowing-it transsexual at the other. To try and generalize about the thinking patterns of such diverse subgroups is impossible. Still, there is little science and no philosophy without generalization, so I will try not to let the mere impossibility of the task slow me down.

I will begin by briefly discussing the very important book *In a Different Voice* by Carol Gilligan (1982). This book's prime motivation was an investigation of the generally accepted idea that the moral development of females was different and not as sophisticated and advanced as their male counterparts of the same age. This conclusion was reached by first presenting young men and women with a moral problem, and then observing how they reasoned from problem to solution. Pre-teen males would begin to use rules and principles that could be applied to all persons in the situation or, for that matter, similar situations. Females would have difficulty doing so, and would be deeply concerned with details of context, consequence, and situation. The former, male, approach, dubbed by Gilligan the "ethics of justice," was deemed by researchers to be more mature than the mode of thought used by women. The latter mode, called by Gilligan the "ethics of care," focused on connectivity, responsibility, and personal relationship. As a result, the conclusion of the women's reasoning was only as generalizable as the contextual parameters permitted.

The reasoning patterns (one might better say "values") preferred by women, according to Gilligan and her followers, mean that women are far more focused on their attachments to others, their place in the web of human relationships, and their connectedness to the people with whom they interact. In play, for example, while boys will argue furiously over rules and decisions, girls tend to avoid dispute and change to a different game rather than alienate one of the players. This fits in with the psychoanalytic view that boys, but not girls, must go through a separation from their mothers in order to find their own independence. Gilligan writes:

> From the different dynamics of separation and attachment in their gender identity formation through the divergence of identity and intimacy that marks their experience in adolescent years, male and female voices typically speak of the importance of different truths, the former of the role of separation as it defines and empowers the self, the latter of the ongoing process of attachment that creates and sustains human community. (156)

Where women are concerned with the needs of specific individuals, men, on the other hand, are more concerned with rules and a sense of fairness that is founded on people being accorded the same treatment. Where women's first priority is to remain connected and involved with those with whom they interact, men are more concerned with their place in a hierarchy of power and control.

It is important to understand just how far-reaching Gilligan's hypothesis is. It concerns nothing less than the different ways in which individuals view and organize the world. It shapes and colors one's entire world vision and permeates all of one's relationships. What one literally "sees" in a situation is determined as much by one's moral and psychological point of view as it is by one's geographical location. And, this learning to see, to identify what is important in a situation, begins at a very young age. Research into dispute techniques in preschool children shows that there are marked differences in approaches to play conflict before the age of four (Sheldon 1993). Since we can already identify this behavior at four, we know that one begins accumulating the values with which one goes through life at a very early age.

If Gilligan is correct (and she does not have to be 100 percent dead on), then there are differences between men and women at the basic cognitive level. That is, the way in which information is processed and evaluated is different between the two gender groups, and one result of this difference may well be a frequent lack of understanding across the divergent perspectives, as well as an undervaluation of the female perspective by the dominant male perspective. Indeed, historically the female outlook has been systematically devalued and derogated by, for example, being described as morally immature. For our purposes, though, the crucial fact is that differences in the cognitive processing of situations and problems begin quite early in a child's development.

A similar situation exists in the realm of communication. Gilligan's conclusions about, if you will, thinking are mirrored by Deborah Tannen's conclusions about speaking. People who think a certain way also speak in ways that illustrate and support those forms of thought. Some communicative differences between the sexes are stylistic but still reflect the cognitive differences. One classic example is the different ways in which words like "yeah" or "uh huh" are used in conversation. For women, the words serve as an indicator that one is following the conversation, is still there, connected to the speaker, as in "Yeah, I follow you." For men, the terms signal agreement with the statements uttered by the speaker as in, "Yeah, I agree with you." The import is simply that for women the most important thing in a conversation is to be along with the speaker, not to be assessing whether the speaker is right or wrong. For men, the rightness and wrongness is crucial; agreement and disagreement are ultimately what matters, not the story itself.

The very object of conversation is different, according to Tannen, for men and women. "For most women," she writes, "the language of conversation is primarily a language of rapport: a way of establishing connections and negotiating relationships," while "For most men, talk is primarily a means to preserve independence and negotiate and maintain status in a hierarchical social order" (1990, 77).

It should be no surprise that these questions of rationality as expressed in evaluative and communicative practice mirror classic suppositions about gender differences. If we think of the traditional culturally conditioned differences such as women are more gentle, nurturing, family-oriented, and so on, then we might expect rationality to fit the mold as well. These differences do not come merely from mimicking mummy, but from learning to be mummy, to embrace her modes of thought as well as behavior. Even to the extent that language patterns and intonations can be imitated, they do not necessarily represent an underlying female structure that naturally gives rise to them. One might well adopt the speech patterns of the opposite gender such as the questioning intonation women add at the end of many declarative sentences, or the tendency to interrupt and dominate a conversation common to many men. But, and this is the nub of my concern, what can be done about adopting the underlying rationality, the substructure of thinking, examining, relating, feeling, and communicating that is absorbed, developed, and inculcated from birth?

Generalizations about people are at best tricky, and at their worst they are nothing but disastrous apologetics for stereotypes. And this is nowhere more problematic then when discussing gender. Gilligan has been criticized both within and without the feminist community for generalizing from her particular sample to women at large. The girls and women she interviewed for her study were all white, middle class, and educated. The characteristics she describes may, therefore, only apply to socioeconomic groups with a similar profile. Not only that, but cultural factors enter as well. Within North American society there are distinct groups with quite different characteristics. A Chicano woman in Los Angeles grows up in an extraordinarily different environment than a white, Radcliffe-educated woman from Connecticut. Not only will their experiences and outlooks be different, but, to a very large extent all of the social influences on them will also be dramatically different. Even when exposed to public modes of socialization such as television, rock videos, and popular magazines, their identification capabilities and their assessments of their own ability to fit the model will differ. Other examples offered in opposition to Gilligan's generalizations include, for example, the way African-American females and males differ (Kerber et al. 1986).

There are other considerations that are also relevant to this discussion, and that bear upon questions of identity even within a cultural group. These have occurred primarily within the feminist community and concern issues of essentialism. Are there "essential" characteristics that define being a woman or by virtue of which one is a woman, or are they all (or practically all) culturally acquired? If the essentialists are correct (and Gilligan is considered an essentialist), then one can only be a woman if one has the essential characteristics. If one does not have them, then these characteristics cannot be acquired through socialization or learning. However, even if the essentialist is correct, it does not mean that only nature determines gender. No one denies that the essential characteristics are still and always going to be heavily influenced by social constraints; even, by the way, if there are major hormonal factors—but that's another discussion.

There is also a style of essentialism that might be called sociological essentialism. By this I mean that the essential conditioning that is required to be a woman with a classical outlook, and to have the perspectives, values, and reactions a woman has, requires that one has gone through a certain process of acculturation. That, too, can be an understanding of essentialism. I believe that Raymond falls into this category (1979), and that many others subscribe to it to various degrees (Nicholson 1994).

As a result of such considerations one must be careful in drawing broad generalizations from Gilligan's work. Naturally, the same holds true of Tannen's work. Indeed, when it comes to cultural diversity we expect linguistic conventions to be different, so both authors' conclusions must be used guardedly. On the other hand, the group Gilligan does identify and study fits many, though certainly not all, members of at least this transgendered community. Moreover, her conclusions may allow us to consider that, regardless of group, we can reasonably expect to find gender differentiation with respect to rationality in ways described by Gilligan, though not necessarily with the same characteristics they have identified. Similarly with Tannen: communicative styles will differ according to gender within a given group even if we cannot say how without detailed study. Questions of, for example, directness, volubility, and turn-taking need to be examined for each group in question.

The issue of generalization does not only impact within gender groups, but within the transgendered as well. At the very beginning of my talk I mentioned the vast divergences that exist among the almost arbitrary collective known as the transgendered. Some of the T* community (to use the Internet expression) have identified strongly as female (or, conversely, male) virtually from birth. Others have come to it in early adolescence, and still others even late in life. For some the identification amounts to a clear certitude that one simply is of the opposite to one's assigned gender, while for others it is a question of garnering pleasure, sexual or psychological, through simple cross-dressing. To generalize about such a diverse group is not merely impossible, it is beside the point. There is nothing true of them all, so why generalize?

The reason for doing so, and forgive me as I use male to female as the exemplar, is that there is a commonality. That commonality, that common ground, is an attraction to the feminine. It is a drive, a desire, a need to be associated with, included in, connected to the female spirit, psyche, or anima. Certainly, it is vastly different as it ranges over the T* continuum. So different that some at the ends do not recognize any differentiation between the masculine and the feminine. At one end the infrequent cross-dresser may have no sense of femininity and might perceive himself as strictly male with a peculiar hobby. Such persons can even be aggressively masculine in a compensatory way. At the other end are

birth-identified males who are completely and wholly women without any significant sense of masculinity. And, yet, the drive, no matter whether the smallest
spark of the most overwhelming compulsion, is there in both groups.

Transgenderism and Gendered Rationality

A great deal of the discussion about transgenderism focuses on questions of
socialization. Even if we suppose that gender differentiation is primarily social,
we still need to ask, to what degree can one join a social group in which one was
not born? The answer given by some commentators (Greer 1989; Raymond
1979) is that it is impossible. That one must, first, have the biological base, and
second, the thorough and unrelenting conditioning that works to govern every
aspect of one's life, thought, and emotions. Of course, the more we know about
genetics and the vast number of aberrations and variations nature produces, the
less stable becomes that once secure biological base for a gender dichotomy
(Money 1993). But this just means that cultural conditioning becomes more
important in drawing a sharp line between male and female; it must, indeed,
become essential.

When we think about socialization we think of the differences and the separation. Some even go as far as Maltz and Borker (1982) and describe the two
genders as every bit as distinct as two separate cultural groups. But there are
aspects of acculturation that are being ignored here. Yes, it is likely the case that
for many people the gender socialization process is largely univocal, which is to
say that boys receive male socialization and girls receive female socialization.
However, I want to claim that no socialization is ever wholly univocal, and,
moreover, that this is even more so in a modern technological society with a
heavily electronic culture. Let me explain what I mean by this.

It has always been the case that boy children will have been exposed to the
rules and procedures of female socialization by observing the young girls who live,
play, and go to school with them. Even though socialization is as directed as it is,
so that virtually the first thing we learn is which instruction set is designed for us,
there is still exposure to the alternate stream. But in our modern age there is vastly
more than there was in earlier times. Watching television, youngsters from a very
early age gain instruction in role behavior and demeanor. While there will surely
be a great deal of selective attention with regard to observing the "proper" role,
there is still a great deal of exposure to the opposite role. As a result, there is more
social information coming in at a very impressionable age then ever before.

Remember please that I am not concerned here, nor am I suggesting,
causative agency. Rather, the question is, to what degree can a birth-assigned

male expect to enter the female socialization milieu in later life? What I am suggesting is that the bifurcation of socialization by gender is not nearly so dichotomous as one might think. Moreover, the availability of cross-gender information is certainly there; in fact it is everywhere, and it may be very easy to absorb if one has the correct self-identification. An individual who, possibly at a very young age, cross-identifies and is attracted to the information could begin absorption very early on. In other words, if there is some disposition, no matter how minimal, to absorb the alternate socialization information, then that information is certainly there and readily available. A strongly identified cross-gendered person could virtually train in alternate social practices through the medium of film and television.

Let us take a hypothetical example. Consider a transsexual who has awareness of cross-gender identification at a very young age. This individual might well pay more attention to the female-directed messages in mass media than to the male-directed instructions. The situation is perfect. In the playroom or schoolyard one might observe cross-gender clues, but one must be careful not to become too involved, not to forget that failure to maintain the birth-assigned role will lead to censure. On television there is no such difficulty. Sitting passively and staring into the tube one can identify with whichever characters seem right. And that information will be absorbed, processed, and retained.

Later in life, as one slowly comes to realize that there are more gender choices and options than were first announced, this training can be brought to the fore. Where previously it either lay dormant or was kept hidden, now it can be nurtured and cherished. Now what would have brought censure from peers and adults is either encouraged or, at least, perceived as within the realm of the acceptable. For the transsexual there comes a time when the roots of feminine socialization can form the basis for the flowering of a fuller female personality and rationality.

The degree of absorption of an alternate socialization will differ markedly from individual to individual. The later in life one becomes aware of a cross-gender identification, the more difficult will be the absorption of the desired socialization. In addition, the actual availability of cross-gender socialization in the form of playmates, electronic media, and so on, will all play a major role in determining the internal availability of the alternate social role. So where one lives, the milieu in which one exists will all make a difference. Nonetheless, there is no reason to believe that the female conditioning cannot have some sort of impact upon which one might draw later in life.

With the transvestite, as opposed to the transsexual, we can expect the situation to be somewhat different, though we must be careful here. Many transsexuals first identified as transvestites, and did so quite young. One who envies girls their clothes, watches wistfully (if secretly) as they play games, will, perforce, take in some if not all of the values cherished by the envied group. Indeed, one of the very attractions to a young person might be the way in which games are played, conversations conducted, and/or social groups run. Yet these are just key points in social conditioning. Consequently, an awareness of them, of the differences, of the simple fact that there are differences, may be a foundational factor in the construction of a later cross-gender identity.

On the other hand, a fetishistic transvestite beginning at early puberty may not have spent a great deal of time absorbing alternate socialization, or might have begun quite late in life. The classical over-made-up and tartily dressed transvestite who offers no overt feminine behavior that is not caricature may well have missed out on the time when it was naturally possible to absorb social mores and methods. Such a person might focus almost exclusively on clothing and not be at all concerned with psychological verisimilitude or value the alternate gender mode of thought or process. (Neil Cargile, recently written up in *The New Yorker,* would seem to be such an individual; vide, Berendt 1995.)

The answer, then, to what might be expected is "almost anything." However, we can say that the earlier cross-gender identification or, at least, sympathy, began, the greater is the likelihood that the alternate rationality was able to insert itself. The factors that would then influence this are diverse and might include the degree of self-recognition as cross-gendered, availability of support groups, and, I expect, a sense of self rich enough to encompass the awareness of alternate ways of thinking, feeling, and being. In other words, and I think this is very important, one must have, learn, or acquire the insight that being a woman goes beyond appearances and includes the ways in which one relates to others, speaks, thinks, and, in short, lives.

I want briefly to compare these theoretical considerations to my own personal experience in interacting with other transgendered individuals. Today the first mode of contact with other T*s for many individuals is computer communication either intentionally or (as in my case) by accident when one discovers the electronic community. From the early days of CompuServe Citizen's Band channel A 13, to the present when there are numerous regional and national BBSs (bulletin board systems) as well as the Internet lists, news groups, and forums, electronic communication has been the single greatest force in opening lines of communication. That it seems that the closet door is opening a bit is in no small part due to this phenomenon, and the consequent awareness among the T*s that they are not alone.

However, to get back to our topic, in examining the communications one comes across on the Internet, one finds a broad diversity of exhibited rationality. Some correspondents seem to be almost wholly feminine in their style of argument and communication, while others, though they sign their missives with a femme name, seem decidedly masculine. One can identify the pickiness, aggression, and lack of concern for person as opposed to position that is classically male. Moreover, many responses to postings are highly analytical and show little desire to examine more contextual or personal issues. This is especially true when anger enters the arena. In so-called flame wars (exchanges of angry e-mail), individuals with names that are extraordinarily soft and sweet exhibit the kind of intolerance and positional certitude archetypical of a patriarchal stereotype.

There is, on the other hand, a great deal of support, especially as evidenced in a willingness to expose and share emotions, that is certainly not typical of mainstream males. There is an openness, an awareness of pain, and a sense of connection that one simply does not find except between the most intimate of male friends. More, the amount of time devoted to the discussion of family, children, and relationships is disproportionate for a male group. In fact, when anger is not a factor in the communications, there is evidence of a great deal of concern for others that fits well with the notion of relationship maintenance as being paramount.

Attendance at club meetings and other events provides further glimpses into the T* community and the degree to which it is more than externally feminized (or masculinized as the case may be). Here as well there is a range, from those who seem to think they have acquired the sought-after character once the makeup is on, to those for whom the external is only one component, perhaps not even an important one. Jan Morris, for example, writes that she never cared much about clothing until she transitioned (1974).

Before I move on to the next section, it is important that I reiterate one basic point. There are birth-designated women who have identified as women all their lives and who do not meet some or all of the classical or traditional criteria for female personality characteristics. They may be aggressive, argumentative, solution-providing, hierarchical, power-conscious, and extremely status aware. (There are, after all, female lawyers.) In other words, the characteristics that define femininity may be just as much absent in a given woman as in a given transvestite. We must be wary of the broad brush.

Implications for the Transgendered

If the goal of a T* individual is to come closer to or join the chosen gender, then it is important to comprehend what that goal entails. The adoption of a cross-gender life or role, permanently or temporarily, can be a mimic or an existence. To make it an existence one must aim to incorporate into one's life the rationality of the chosen gender as well as the accoutrements.

Learning gendered rationality is not a simple undertaking. This is especially true of the male-to-female (MtF) crossover. For the FtM the literature on "How to Think" is vast and most certainly slanted to the male model practically to the exclusion of the female. (See, for example, Gilbert 1994, 1995.) All texts on critical thinking and argumentation tout the highly analytical mode of reasoning comfortable to most males (and quite a few females, especially academics). It is also important to realize that some people seem to be able to switch from one mode to another. (This can come in very handy, for example, for a woman who works in a high-powered or male-dominated environment but still wants to maintain contact with her more natural or basal modes and responses.)

For a male who wants to learn the female approach to communication and rationality the best resource is fiction. Certainly there are some writings extolling and amplifying the nature and texture of female perspectives. These include the texts mentioned above, as well as others. (See, for example, Ruddick 1989 and Lakoff 1990). But, these few exceptions aside, the main source for how women think, feel, and communicate is fiction. The reason is simply that for generations women were excluded from academic writing, and women's concerns were excluded from the academic purview. The only outlet for the expression of ideas and feelings was fiction. In fact, if you read contemporary feminist authors you will see vastly more references to fiction in their works than in the works of their male academic contemporaries.

Reading a range of books and seeing a diversity of films can provide one with a kind of insight that might otherwise be difficult to find. Films like *Waiting* and *Enchanted April,* which are about women being women, are great resources. One can also learn a great deal about being a woman from Virginia Woolf, Marge Piercy, Margaret Laurence, and (even) Danielle Steele.

This is not to denigrate the extremely important works by contemporary female scholars writing on femininity and gender differences (and, *mutatis mutandis,* male scholars writing on masculinity.) Deborah Tannen's book is a major source of information for the transsexual, whether trying to learn or trying to pass.

It is also, and as always, imperative to avoid stereotypes. This means, at the least, that one must read a range of books. There is nothing wrong with reading romances and sagas, but one should also pay attention to the lives of women as described by authors such as Marge Piercy and Anne Beattie, women whose lives are more ordinary, more routinized, more oppressed than in glamorous romance novels.

Further, we shouldn't think that being a woman means never disagreeing, never contesting, never asking for evidence. This is just not true. Similarly, being a man does not mean always being belligerent, aggressive, and disagreeable. That too is just not true. Just as a typical woman sometimes wears full makeup, a fancy dress, and heels, and sometimes does not, so a typical woman is sometimes empathic and compassionate, and sometimes analytic and withholding. It is the circumstances that dictate behavior, not only the gender. If we realize this we will be no more tempted to confuse a real female personality with a jail matron than a real female persona with an overly made-up tart.

Professionals in the field of gender dysphoria would be well advised to consider modes of thought as one of the panoply of treatment programs they advise. Certainly many, if not most, transsexuals have a sense of womanhood (and manhood for FtMs) that includes ways of perceiving the world. Nonetheless, the readings recommended tend to foster the attitude that gender is far more than appearance or even feeling.

I want to be very careful here. I said above that for some T* persons, the awareness of cross-gender identification comes at a very early age. When considering the biography of Jan Morris or Leslie Feinberg's novel, one sees people whose acculturation was heavily cross-gendered. Many others have realized early on that being a woman (or a man) is not a question of making life better, but of making it right, making it fit. Many cross-gendered persons become committed to feminism and causes of liberation. Many have a very rich sense of what womanhood is. But there are some who would be female without understanding that it requires an ethos, a perspective, a conceptual framework. To be female (or to be male) involves an entire way of viewing the world, of relating to people, of thinking, of communicating. That difference must be taken seriously.

I would also, as long as I'm being hog-wild normative here, urge the informal counselors we all rely on so much, the friends, the frequent posters to forums and groups, the activists in organizations, the opinion leaders in clubs, to be sensitive to and aware of these issues. They are difficult issues. But they are important issues.

As an individual, as a heterosexual cross-dresser who is not transsexual, I have often thought that the goal of my journey, the outcome of my own queerness, must be some sort of integration, some sort of coming together in a pan-gendered whole that will combine the best of both worlds. I have yet to come anywhere near that goal, and I am not even vaguely sure it is within reach or that I really understand it. But that integration, that combination of the male and female into a blended pan-gendered whole, is nonetheless my goal. Wish me luck.

References

Berendt, John. 1995. High-heel Neil. *The New Yorker* (January 16): 38.
Feinberg, Leslie. 1993. *Stone butch blues.* Ithaca: Firebrand Books.
Gilbert, Michael A. 1994. Feminism, argumentation and coalescence. *Informal Logic,* 42.
————. 1995. Arguments and arguers. *Teaching Philosophy.*

Gilligan, Carol. 1982. *In a different voice.* Cambridge: Harvard University Press.

Greer, Germaine. 1989. Why sex-change is a lie: On why men can never become women. *The Independent Magazine* (July 22): 16.

Kerber, Linda K., Catherine G. Greeno, Eleanor E. Maccoby, Zella Luria, Carol B. Stack, and Carol Gilligan. 1986. On *In a Different Voice*: An interdisciplinary forum. *Signs* 11, no. 21: 304–33.

Lakoff, Robin T. 1990. *Talking power: The politics of language.* New York: Basic Books.

Maltz, Daniel, and Ruth Borker. 1982. A cultural approach to male-female communication. In *Language & Social Identity,* edited by John Gumperz, 196–216. Cambridge: Cambridge University Press.

Money, John. 1993. *The Adam principle: Genes, genitals, hormones, and gender: Selected readings in sexology.* Amherst, N.Y.: Prometheus Books.

Morris, Jan. 1974. *Conundrum.* New York: Harcourt Brace Jovanovich.

Nicholson, Linda. 1994. Interpreting Gender. *Signs* 20, no. 1: 79–105.

Raymond, Janice. 1979. *The transsexual empire: The making of the she-male.* Boston: Beacon Press.

Ruddick, Sara. 1989. *Maternal thinking: Towards a politics of peace.* New York: Ballantine Books.

Sheldon, Amy. 1993. Pickle fights: Gendered talk in preschool disputes. In *Gender and conversational interaction,* edited by Deborah Tannen, 83–109. Oxford: Oxford University Press.

Tannen, Deborah. 1990. *You just don't understand.* New York: Ballantine Books.

———, ed. 1993. *Gender and conversational interaction.* Oxford: Oxford University Press.

2

TRANSSEXUAL RESEARCH AND COMMENT

Introduction

Since the case of Christine Jorgensen became a media sensation in 1952, transsexualism has dominated both popular and scientific discussion of cross-gender behavior. Though Jorgensen was not the first person to undergo a surgical change of sex, it was not just the surgical techniques that were important in her case, but the availability of hormone supplements to make the change realistic. In fact surgical attempts to deal with gender problems date from late in the nineteenth century, but simply removing a penis or testicles, as was originally done with Jorgensen, does not a female make. In fact, Jorgensen could then have been simply defined as a eunuch since attempt to create a vagina for Jorgensen date from a later period in her history (Bullough and Bullough 1993).

In 1910, long before Jorgensen underwent her surgery, the phenomenon of transsexualism, persons convinced that their body did not correspond with their mental or spiritual image of themselves, had been described by Magnus Hirschfeld (1991). David Cauldwell had begun using the term in 1949 (Cauldwell 1949), and Harry Benjamin in 1953 (Benjamin 1964). It was Benjamin who did the most to popularize the term (Benjamin 1966) and his work has been continued by the Harry Benjamin International Foundation. The fact that surgery was involved meant that transsexualism from Jorgensen on was highly medicalized and surgeons, fearful of being sued by a repentant transsexual patient, insisted from the first that psychologists and psychiatrists be involved in deciding who was to have surgery.

These medical obstacles have been a sore point with the transsexual community. Many of them simply got around it by lying, since the answers expected by the psychiatrists or psychologists became well known to those desiring to change their sex. Many individuals were in fact coached by others on what they were to say and how they were to respond. The barriers, most seriously insisted upon by university-affiliated clinics, rapidly led to the rise of surgical entrepreneurs who were not quite so demanding. Nevertheless, the fact that transsexuals of both sexes (males seeking sex change in the United States still outnumber females seeking sex change about three to one) made it more difficult to do serious research on the topic. It has only been in the last decade, as those of the transgender community have become better organized and willing to confront what they felt were standards for surgery that forced them to lie, that there have been changes and a general loosening up. Interestingly this same period has seen many people who might well have sought SRS in the past now choosing to simply adopt the clothing and role of the opposite gender, many with hormones, others without.

As we have done more serious study of transsexuals, we find that though they usually felt they had the genital organs and body of the wrong sex, the would-be male-to-females (MtFs) nevertheless often went through a period of hypermasculinity, that is, trying to show to themselves and others that they were really machismo males. Undoubtedly some of the same efforts took place on the part of the would-be female-to-male transsexuals (FtM) but this has been less studied and researched.

Moreover, even though transsexuals proclaim after their surgery that they are now real females or real males, certain segments of the public have been unwilling to accept this. Often the hormone treatments make it impossible for an outsider to know who was born female or male and who has changed their sex, but this process of effeminization or masculinization often takes several years before individuals can pass fully. Some never do. Interestingly the most vociferous in their rejection of the new transsexual identity have been militant feminists. They have been particularly upset by the MtFs since they feel somehow that these individuals have never really experienced what it is to be a woman and are attempting to pass under false circumstances. They are only slightly less critical of the betrayal of FtMs who desert the female sex. Since radical feminists are very vociferous and literate, in some ways they have dominated much of the recent discourse.

The contributors to this section represent the cutting edge of current discussion about transsexuals and transsexualism.

References

Benjamin, Harry. 1964. Clinical aspects of transsexualism in the male and female. *American Journal of Psychotherapy* 18 (July): 458–69.

———. 1966. *The transsexual phenomenon.* New York: Julian Press.

Bullough, Vern, and Bonnie Bullough. 1993. *Cross dressing, sex, and gender.* Philadelphia: University of Pennsylvania Press.

Cauldwell, David. 1949. Psychopathia transsexualis. *Sexology* 16 (December): 247–48.

Hirschfeld, Magnus. 1991. *Transvestites: The erotic drive to cross-dress.* Translated by Michael Lombardi-Nash. Amherst, N.Y.: Prometheus Books.

Narrating Ourselves:
Duped or Duplicitous?

Karen Nakamura

Unlike various liberated groups, transsexuals are reactionary, moving back
toward the core-culture rather than away from it. They are the Uncle Toms of
the sexual revolution. With these individuals, the dialectic of social change
comes full circle and the position of greatest deviance becomes that of greatest
conformity. (Kando 1973, quoted in Shapiro 1991)

As a social phenomenon, transsexualism has been heavily critiqued in the past
two decades by numerous scholars in queer theory and women's studies. It has
been labeled "conservative" or "essentialist." Some scholars have accused transsexualism of not living up to its radical potential as a political movement and that
it has functioned to reinscribe rather than deconstruct the gender boundaries that
it transgresses (Irvine 1990). Transsexual women themselves have been portrayed as either the unconscious "victims" of the medical profession that
"serves" them—or as accomplices to a patriarchal institution (Raymond 1979).

It has been hard to determine what the ideologic relationship between the
transsexual community and medical science is because most of the research has
focused on transsexual women's public voices—in particular, the narratives that
transsexual women give to gain access to medical services they desire, and the
autobiographies that they publish to explain themselves.

This paper differs from previous analyses by using the private voices of
transsexual women, material written within the transsexual women's community
for their own consumption. Analyzing privately shared autobiographies and fiction, I draw out some of the primary themes of lack of agency and choice that

have marked the genre of transsexual writing for the past three decades—and that have also served as the target of feminist/queer critique.

This paper then problematizes the relationship between biomedicine and social identity. Are transsexual women the victims of a hegemonic or ideologic medical perspective? Why have there been so few overt forms of resistance from within the transsexual community? And why have the narratives that have emerged generally reinforced the notion that transsexual women are handmaidens to the medical community? Responding to these questions, the final section of this paper will explore new articulations that have come out of the transsexual community in the past three years, narratives that challenge and explore some of the issues raised by feminist and queer scholars. Using recent forms of transsexual expression, it challenges the perspective that transsexual experiences are formed in a simple ideologic relationship to medicine. Using new voices from the transsexual/transgender community, this paper explores how one constitutes resistance to a hegemonic sex/gender ideology and whether such resistance is feasible in a post-modern world.

Coming Out in Cyberspace

Transsexual women participating in on-line computer "forums" often publish autobiographies (bios) on-line for the entire community. These autobiographies serve to introduce the newcomers to the rest of the community and to integrate them into the transsexual social milieu. Looking at these private autobiographies, we can see that many members of these communities share an experience of having as their earliest memories those of feeling "not right," a feeling that they were "born into the wrong body." This theme is often the note on which these authors begin their autobiographies:

> Hello all, My name is Rebecca. I am 24 years old, and I decided 20 years ago that I preferred to be a girl. Back then it was something intangible. I couldn't put my finger on it. Back before any inhibitions had set in though, I delighted in doing "girl's" things. I'd play with my Mum's doll, even play with the next door girl's make-up 'n things.
> —"Rebecca" (alt. transgendered, 2 June 1994)

> I have some vague memories of feeling that I wanted to be a girl when I was very young. When I started school, I felt strongly that I fit in much better with girls than with boys. I was very attracted to girls and at the same time wanted to be a girl. From when I was five, I would spend a great deal of time, every day, wishing or fantasizing that my body would change. Most often, the trans-

formation was accomplished by a girl putting her clothes on me and then I would wake looking like her. There was never anything sexual or erotic about this fantasy. I think that the clothing was significant only in that, for children, clothing is the most apparent indicator of gender.

—Paula (alt. transgendered, 10 March 1994)

These transsexual women both experienced the same feeling that they had always been transsexual—or more accurately (in their perspective), that they had been female inside all along, a common experience expressed by many transsexual women. By representing themselves as women trapped inside men's bodies, these transsexual women give up their sense of agency and control over their situation and set themselves up for medical science to reveal their inner "truth."

The published autobiographies of transsexual women also follow the same narrative structure—beginning with their earliest childhood fantasies of becoming a woman. Jan Morris's 1974 autobiography *Conundrum* begins with the following sentences: "I was three or perhaps four years old when I realized that I had been born into the wrong body, and should really be a girl. I remember the moment well, and it is the earliest memory of my life" (1–2).

Writing twenty years later, model and actor Caroline Cossey (stagename, Tula) begins the preface to her 1992 autobiography with remarkably similar words:

I now know that I was born transsexual and that I was starved of the formative experiences I needed as a little girl. It took years to fit the pieces together, to understand the past, to make the picture. I wrote this book as an honest and unadorned account of my life—a life made.[1] (xii)

Narrating Fictional Selves

Let us now compare transsexual women's fictional works with their autobiographical writing. Just as transsexual autobiographies form a genre with a set narrative structure, transsexual fiction also falls into a typical genre. Almost all of the popular stories on the commercial information service provider CompuServe follow a very similar story structure.

Prototypical Narrative Structure of Transsexual Fiction

1. Protagonist is invariably a heterosexual male (often with no inkling of transsexual desire, but occasionally a closet transvestite).
2. Protagonist is kidnapped, tricked, blackmailed, or otherwise nonwillingly

exposed to some agent ("voodoo," "magic," "radiation," "special hormones," etc.) that converts him into a woman.

3. Protagonist is then faced with the complexities of being female: having a period, having breasts, being weaker than before, having male clothes that do not fit, having to buy female clothes, having sex with a man, having sex with her formerly heterosexual female partner.

4. Protagonist discovers that after his initial distaste, he likes being a woman. Refuses treatment (etc.) that could turn her back into a man.

This genre is widespread and several medical/psychological articles have explored the thematic elements as well. Richard Docter (1988), a sexologist specializing in cross-gender behavior, summarized the findings of several analyses (Beigel and Feldman 1963, Buhrich 1976; Talamini 1982) and noted themes of fantasies of forced cross-dressing, being transformed into a full-time woman, having requirements that justify becoming a beautiful young lady or a seductive woman, and engaging in both lesbian and heterosexual relationships (Docter 1988).

The fictional stories present narrative tropes that take away the protagonists' individual agency and absolve them of blame for their condition. To illustrate the use of such tropes, here are synopses of three stories that represent three of the more popular occupations found in these stories on CompuServe:

Joe Bates. Airplane pilot Joe Bates is unwittingly exposed to radiation produced by a new device his company, Honeybone Technologies, has created. He becomes genotypically and phenotypically female. Has to explain all this to his fiancee who still remains committed to him, even if that means she has to become lesbian. Is frustrated with his weaker body. Has sex with his close (male) buddy and worries about getting pregnant, but finds "heterosexual" sex extremely enjoyable. Finds that he likes being a woman when Honeybone discovers that the sex change process might be reversible.

Not by Choice. Author is a member of a crack military troop. While on mission, he saves the Israeli Defense Minister's son from death but becomes irrevocably injured in the process. The only thing that can save him from being horribly disfigured for life is an experimental Israeli medical technique that would "regrow" his skin. The catch: it would regrow in the female form only. He agrees. He becomes a woman. The hospital staff teach him how to be a proper woman and alert him to the facts of pregnancy and menstruation. He is appropriately mindboggled by this. The rest of the story deals with his adventures as a Marine stuck in a woman's body.

Summer Pinafore. Kenny is a young boy with an older sister. He misbehaves by kicking sand too much in the sand box (typical male behavior?) and his mother forces him to wear his sister's clothes as punishment and to do girl chores with his sister. She also trains him to be a proper little girl. He is appropriately ashamed. His mother decides that this is a nice situation (having another girl in the house) and forces Kenny (who likes the idea, secretly) to remain a girl.

One fascinating aspect of most of the transsexual stories is that the proper nouns and pronouns often remain constant throughout the narrative—i.e., in the story "Joe Bates," the title character is called "Joe" and "he" even after his transformation. This leads to strange juxtapositions of sexualized bodies and gendered pronouns:

> Joe got off the bed and pulled off his top. He unsnapped his bra, and then dumped the store sack of underwear on the bed. Selecting the gray silk bra, he slipped his arms through the soft straps. He pulled it on and fastened the back clasps. It fit perfectly. He went to the mirror to examine his profile, pleased with what he observed. The gray contrasted perfectly with the tanned skin and hair, even as short as that was. He remembered the matching panties. He just had to try them. In spite of the yeast infection, he wanted to see and feel what it was like to wear them. He pulled the cotton panties off, removed the panti-liner from the little crotch, and flipped the moist pad in the trash can. (*JOE44.T*)

This use of language goes against the usual transsexual convention of calling people the gender of their choice, and it highlights a certain irony: Joe is a man's psyche trapped in a woman's body. I believe that it is this irony that appeals to the readers of these stories—a nontranssexual man had unwittingly and unwillingly achieved what they all dreamed for, to become a woman. More importantly, using this example, Joe did not choose his condition, it just happened to him. This resonates with the feelings of transsexual women—that forces beyond their control impelled them to become transsexual, they had no agency over this aspect of their lives. And so, a heterosexual man who becomes transformed into a woman and has to deal with the feelings of being a man trapped within a woman's body holds a special resonance for those individuals who feel that they are women trapped in men's bodies.

Diagnosis or Duplicity—Getting to the Truth of the Body

We have seen that two themes mark the genre of male-to-female transsexual autobiography and fiction: historical continuity and lack of a conscious agency. Perhaps not surprisingly, these were the markers used in the differential diagnosis of transsexuality as a psychopathological condition. Although the *Diagnostic and Statistical Manual* of the American Psychiatric Association has removed transsexualism from its latest edition (1994), the earlier and still extant edition (1987) described "transsexualism" (code 302.50) as follows:

> The essential features of this disorder are a *persistent discomfort* and sense of inappropriateness about one's assigned sex in a person who has reached puberty. In addition, there is *persistent preoccupation,* for at least two years, with getting rid of one's primary and secondary sex characteristics and acquiring the sex characteristics of the other sex. *Invariably there is the wish to live as a member of the other sex.* In the rare cases in which physical intersexuality or a genetic abnormality is present, such a condition should be noted on Axis III.[²]
>
> **Age at onset.** People who develop Transsexualism almost *invariably report having had a gender identity problem in childhood.* Some assert that they were secretly aware of their gender problem, but that it was not evident to their family or friends. (74–75, emphasis added)

Psychologists have found that once the mind (for whatever reason) has become gendered in a certain way, it is highly resistant to change (Irvine 1990). Therapy is only efficacious in helping people adjust to their condition and rarely is it successful in changing them back to normal.[3] Genitals have turned out to be easier to change than gender identity. What we have witnessed in the last ten years is the triumph of the surgeons over the psychotherapists in the race to restore gender to an unambiguous reality (Kessler and McKenna 1978).[4]

The similarity between the medical diagnosis of transsexuality and what we see in transsexual communities is not surprising if we assume that the 1987 diagnosis was correct, and that it accurately described what it is to be transsexual—it revealed the "truth." This model is based on the assumption that floating out there in the universe of human sexuality is a coherent sexual form known as "transsexuality" and that psychiatry had simply found the way to label and diagnose this condition.

Duped or Duplicitous?

There are some alternative explanations of the congruence between the medical diagnosis of transsexuality and the private writings. One of the arguments is that medical doctors—as part of our general cultural discourse on sex and gender—promote a particular sex/gender ideology. This ideology emphasizes such things as the stability of sex/gender over time and the nonelective nature of sex/gender, themes that come out in both transsexual writing and transsexual diagnosis. While we all suffer from a "false consciousness" of gender, transsexual women in particular are said to succumb to and reify this ideology by going through with sexual reassignment surgery—they are dupes of the Western sex/gender system.

Transsexual women have also been suspected of duplicity, intentionally fooling medical doctors into giving the symptoms that will lead to the diagnoses that they want. Judith Shapiro plays with the notion of transsexual women as both duped and duplicitous:

> [O]ne *cannot take at face value transsexuals' own accounts of a fixed and unchanging (albeit sex-crossed) gender identity,* given the immense pressure on them to produce the kinds of life histories that will get them what they want from the medico-psychiatric establishment. To take the problem one step further, the project of autobiographical reconstruction in which transsexuals are engaged, although more focused and motivated from the one that all of us pursue, is not entirely different in kind. We must all *repress information* that creates problems for culturally canonical narratives of identity and the self, and consistency in gender attribution is very much a part of this. (1991, emphasis added)

Shapiro's model of transsexual women is that of individuals who, through historical reconstruction, deceive both themselves and the doctors who analyze them. Shapiro argues that transsexual women, rather than challenging the gender ideology, instead either accept it and fall within the medical communities camp or use the ideology of the doctors against them—they manipulate them into performing surgery for them. In either case, transsexual women are caught in a web of ideologies spun by our Western sex/gender system and reify and reinscribe the boundaries of gender. Under her model, transsexual women are both duped and duplicitous.

Shapiro's model assumes that transsexual women are not aware of the narrative tropes that define their condition, that they are in the process of "repressing" information. But their private autobiographies often contain a note of self-reflexivity and self-awareness.

> OK here is a somewhat rambling bio of myself. I had the *usual feelings* of wanting to be a girl pre puberty but did nothing about them.
> —Colette (alt. transgendered, 18 February 1994, emphasis added)

> Hello to all. I have been reading articles in this group now for a couple of weeks and have to admit that I am pretty amazed and feel kinda good knowing that there are so many more people out there who share some of the same fantasies and desires of dressing like, or in some cases, being a woman. *As I compare myself to some of the others* in this group I find it hard to place myself in any one of the many categories which seem to have presented themselves to me over the last while. Maybe if I tell you all a little about myself you can help me out. Ever since I was about twelve I can remember having fantasies about being a woman. Not just wearing their clothes (which is something I do often and

deeply enjoy) but actually fantasizing about somehow "magically" changing into a beautiful woman.

—Jackie (alt. transgendered, 11 March 1994)

Self-reflexivity is not limited to autobiographical material. The introduction to the fictional story "Not by Choice" plays with the recognition that transsexual fiction falls within a set genre:

> I have read with interest the stories that one finds posted on the various boards devoted to the TV/TS. Most are fun to read, and include the notion of either i) what life would be like if the author was magically a woman, or ii) how much fun life would be if the author was forced into dressing and acting like a woman.
> My story is a little different. Although I appear to be a fully functional woman, I used to have a man's body. Unlike most authors, I did not plan for, wish for, or dream of this change, and in fact did not even conceive of such of thing for a guy like me. Two obvious questions arise, i) why did I have a sex change if I did not want to, and ii) why am I "lurking" on TV/TS boards. The first question will be answered in this story. The second is obvious: the advice, help, and information on transitioning is helpful, and this is one of the few places with sympathetic folks. Plus, who knows, maybe I can help someone understand the role shift.

The reflexivity found in their writings indicates that transsexual women are not simply the brainwashed victims of a sex/gender ideology. But the fact that even while being self-reflexive, they repeat the tropes in their private writings also indicates that they deeply believe in them. Transsexual women are too self-conscious to be thought of as simply "duped" and are too sincere to be labeled "duplicitous."

Furthermore, both transsexual and nontranssexual individuals participate within a hegemonic sex/gender system that shapes our language of gender. And, by and large the language of gender for everyone consists of historical continuity and lack of agency, it's only for people whose bodies don't match their gender psyches that this comes up as a problem. But I think it would be just as rare to find nontranssexual people who talk about their sex/gender as being historically discontiguous or an expression of their agency. And so it is somewhat unfair to hold transsexual women to this standard.

If we view biomedical knowledge as acting hegemonically (Gramsci 1971), then we cannot talk so simply about subversion, deception, treachery, and challenge as if ideologies were visible entities that could be grasped, tackled, and denounced. Transsexual women narrate their own sex/gender within a framework that has largely come out of the knowledge-power constructions of the medical-sexology community, something Michel Foucault has explored in great detail in his two pieces on Western sex/gender systems (1980a, 1990) and his discussion of "biopower." This system of knowledge surrounding our bodies and how we construct our understanding of our lives provides the space through which transsexual women come to identify themselves and also the ground from which they can launch their subversion. In Foucault's parlance, it embeds both oppression and resistance. Subversion operates through the same thematic genres that power does (Foucault 1973, 1979, 1980b).

Building on the ethnographic work of the anthropologist Esther Newton (1972) who explored female impersonators in Chicago, Marjorie Garber (1992) has used this notion of performativity to eloquently describe all genders as "drag." If anything, transsexual women—in breaking the link between alleged or diagnosed biological phenotypes, sex, and gender—question the gender performativity of everyone, nontranssexuals included.

New Challenges: Alternative Narratives

In part, most critics of transsexual women have not explored the communities very deeply and have relied on rather stereotypical or mainstream expressions of transsexuality. But other indigenous—and more radical—tropes have emerged from transsexual communities. One articulation has been the "outlaw" metaphor—most notably used by "gender outlaws" Leslie Feinberg, Susan Stryker, and Kate Bornstein. Through their writings and activist work, these individuals have constructed a discourse in which their "outlaw" status can be created. Their model is that of someone who belongs outside the bifurcated sex/gender system. Subtly aware of how they are embedded within a bifurcated gender system in which they do not want to commit themselves, these authors and political activists are trying to present new approaches to traditional notions of sex and gender.

The on-line transsexual community itself has also started to express new narratives. We are seeing more diversity and different types of challenges to both a coherent model of transsexuality and also how we organize sex and gender. Along with the "outlaw" (third sex/gender) narrative that Feinberg and Bornstein have created, we also see another narrative within the transsexual communities—one of "coexistence:"

> Hi All! I've been reading (and not contributing) for long enough, so I thought it might be time to introduce myself. I'm impressed by the strong-willed people here with a desire to flip the social pyramid structure on its side, no small task at that. My name is Deborah. I'm 24 (male-to-female), 5'6", 110 lb., married, hetero from Maine (US). I've been dressing femininely since I was about 8 or

so. I have built up a fair wardrobe of skirts, etc. over time. My feminine characteristics have always been stronger and more visible than masculine ones.

The line that some people have used in the past, "I'm a woman trapped in a man's body" doesn't feel right—I believe we all have feminine and masculine characteristics at our disposal, and thankfully science has given us more of the ability to show or hide as much of each as we desire. (For a price, of course.)

I haven't figured out just how I should label myself (I hate labels anyway). I see mixed definitions of "ts" and "tv," and don't understand really what each one is. Attempts by science to classify these feelings aren't working very well. Popeye said it best I am what I am!

—Deborah (alt. transgendered, 20 May 1994, emphasis added)

It would be hard for me to say that I am a "woman born in drag." This could be said to be partially true, but it would be more accurate to say that *I am a pair of twins, male and female, born in one body*—the male's. It seems to me that my heart and soul are feminine, under the influence of these I am artistic, musical, passionate, romantic, dreamy, blue, unrealistic, nurturing, sympathetic, and spiritual. Though my hands and forearms are very feminine, my face has feminine qualities and I'm regularly mistaken for a woman on the telephone (part voice, part delivery, I assume), my body is extremely masculine. I have a big strong neck, shoulders, large rib cage, big powerful legs and wide feet. This has always been kind of a "cognitive dissonance" for me; I have always had the conception of myself as this "wisp of a person," sexually ambiguous, lean, light and subtle, and I'm still (at 36) a bit surprised when I see this "hulk" in the mirror. My right brain is also very male—very analytical, judgmental, efficient, achievement-oriented, pragmatic, dogmatic and VERY overbearing toward the other voices that make up "me."

—Kris (alt. transgendered, 6 April 1994, emphasis added)

The first writer questions the applicability of the "woman trapped in a man's body" model for her own life and feels that she balances both masculinity and femininity within herself. The second author uses the metaphor of twins and it is fascinating how she genders both her psyche and her body in terms of this dualism. Other authors have used a Chinese "yin-yang" model of flowing and contrasting genders to organize and express themselves. This balanced masculine/feminine model has begun to emerge as its own subgenre of transsexual writing within on-line communities.

With more transsexual women becoming involved in queer politics and queer theory, we are starting to see deconstructed narratives of gender emerge. For example, in the published writings of academic transgendered theoreticians Susan Stryker (1994) and Sandy Stone (1991), these scholars have used postmodern deconstructed views of transsexuality to "genderfuck" or to twist our sex/gender systems in as many ways as they see possible. Susan Stryker writes:

My idea was to perform self-consciously a queer gender rather than simply talk about it, thus embodying and enacting the concept simultaneously under discussion. I wanted the formal structure of the work to express a transgender aesthetic by replicating our abrupt, often jarring transition between genders—challenging generic classifications with the forms of my words just as my transsexuality challenges the conventions of legitimate gender and my performance in the conference room challenged the boundaries of acceptable academic discourse. During the performance, I stood at the podium wearing genderfuck drag—combat boots, threadbare Levi 501s over a black lace body suit, a shredded Transgender Nation T-shirt with the neck and sleeves cut out. (237)

Being a gender outlaw, balancing masculinity and femininity, or deconstructing sex/gender are all narrative forms of expression, each with its own challenge. But even outlaws are defined in terms of the institutions they resist. Transgender and lesbian activist and author Leslie Feinberg challenges the sex/gender system, but she[5] still wears a three-piece suit (a clear gender marker) and identifies primarily as a woman (Feinberg 1993; Gabriel 1993). Transsexual lesbian performance artist Kate Bornstein (1994) says that she is neither female nor male, yet clearly prefers one style of dress and one pronoun over the other, and has undergone sex reassignment surgery. Attempting to stand outside the sex/gender system, they are still defined by it.

There is no such thing as a complete break, a totally new and revolutionary articulation that will liberate us all from the shackles of sex/gender. Even as transsexuality challenges the biological basis of gender, it comes out of the discourse created by sexologists surrounding sex. We may realize the nature of the machine that inscribes on us who we are, but we cannot escape it. Any new expressions, drawing from alternate sources, will similarly both challenge and reinscribe the values of the system in which it finds itself. Knowledge is not necessarily liberating, but it does give us new ways of organizing and it can free us from various forms of power, even as it enslaves us to others.

Notes

1. What makes Cossey's case interesting is that she was an accident of biology: a chromosomal check done as part of her sexual reassignment process revealed that she had XXY chromosomes. Is it then appropriate for us to consider her a pseudohermaphrodite and not a "real" transsexual? How do we deal with this "fact"? I operate within a particular frame of biological dialectism (Levins and Lewontin 1985; Bem 1993) that asserts that a fixed notion of biological reality is nonaccessible because at all levels it is mediated through social constructions, yet acknowledges that biology plays the role of the putative

ground in social construction. Saying that Cossey was "really" female because of her XXY chromosomes reveals much about how we organize sex on the basis of genetics (Cossey was phenotypically "male" in terms of external genitalia). That we seek a reality beneath the skin and find it in the genes is not surprising. In her book, *Made to Order: Sex-Gender in a Transsexual Perspective,* Orobio de Castro (1993) invites us to explore a totalizing view of the larger sex/gender system.

2. "Axis III" denotes physical disorders and conditions—i.e., those with a biological (bodily) cause rather than a mental/psychic one.

3. The parallel between this perspective and the psychiatric treatment of homosexuality should be noted. It is interesting that while gay/lesbian activists lobbied hard to remove homosexuality as a psychological disorder from the DSM-III, most transsexuals were quite content to have it continue to be listed, but do not object to the new terminology that substitutes "gender dysphoria" for "transsexualism."

4. One can also interpret this as the triumph of the mind over the body and thus the triumph of psychiatrists over surgeons. Even though surgeons can "correct" sex to match with gender, they no longer are the ones privileged with the ability to identify and name someone's true sex and gender. There is a long history to the power of naming sex and gender, Foucault gives an illuminating discussion of it in his introduction to *Herculine Barbin* (1980a).

5. Feinberg's preferential pronoun is "she," although she doesn't mind if people call her "he." In her speeches, she laments the lack of diversity in English pronouns and speaks of other societies where more genders exist.

References

American Psychiatric Association. 1987. *Diagnostic and statistical manual of mental disorders.* 3d ed. rev. Washington, D.C.: American Psychiatric Association.

———. 1994. *Diagnostic and statistical manual of mental disorders.* 4th ed. Washington, D.C.: American Psychiatric Association.

Beigel, H. G., and R. Feldman. 1963. The male transvestite's motivation in fiction, research, and reality. In *Advances in sex research,* edited by H. G. Beigel, 198–210. New York: Harper and Row.

Bem, S. L. 1993. *The lenses of gender: Transforming the debate on sexual inequality.* New Haven: Yale University Press.

Bornstein, K. 1994. *Gender outlaw.* New York: Routledge.

Buhrich, N. 1976. A heterosexual transvestite club. *Australian and New Zealand Journal of Psychiatry* 10: 331–35.

Cossey, C. 1992. *My story.* London: Faber and Faber.

Docter, R. F. 1988. *Transvestites and transsexuals: Toward a theory of cross-gender behavior.* New York: Plenum Press.

Fausto-Sterling, A. 1993. The five sexes: Why male and female are not enough. *Sciences* (March/April): 20–25.

Feinberg, L. 1993. *On being a gender outlaw.* Ithaca, N.Y.: Cornell University Press.

Foucault, M. 1973. *The birth of the clinic: An archaeology of medical perception.* Translated by A. M. Sheridan Smith. New York: Vintage Books.

———. 1979. *Discipline and punish: The birth of the prison.* Translated by Alan Sheridan. New York: Vintage Books.

Foucault, M. 1980a. *Herculine Barbin: Being the recently discovered memoirs of a nineteenth-century French hermaphrodite.* Translated by Richard McDougall. New York: Pantheon.
———. 1980b. *Power/knowledge.* New York: Pantheon.
———. 1990. *The history of sexuality.* Translated by Robert Hurley. Vol. 1: An introduction. New York: Vintage Books.
Gabriel, D. A. 1993. The life and times of a gender outlaw: An interview with Leslie Feinberg. *TranSisters: The Journal of Transsexual Feminism* no. 1: 4–10.
Garber, M. 1992. *Vested interests: Cross-dressing and cultural anxiety.* New York: Harper Perennial.
Gramsci, A. 1971. *Selections from the prison notebooks of Antonio Gramsci.* Translated by Quintin Hoare and Geoffrey Nowell Smith. New York: International Publishers.
Irvine, J. 1990. *Disorders of desire: Sex and gender in modern American sexology.* Philadelphia: Temple University Press.
Kando, T. 1973. *Sex change: The achievement of gender identity among feminized transsexuals.* Springfield, Ill.: Charles C. Thomas Publisher.
Kessler, S. J., and W. McKenna. 1978. *Gender: An ethnomethodological approach.* Chicago: University of Chicago Press.
Levins, R., and R. Lewontin. 1985. *The dialectical biologist.* Cambridge, Mass.: Harvard University Press.
Morris, J. 1974. *Conundrum.* New York: Harcourt Brace Jovanovich.
Newton, E. 1972. *Mother camp: Female impersonators in America.* Chicago: University of Chicago Press.
O'Hartigan, M. D. 1994. Welcome to the world of the intersexed. *TransSisters: The Journal of Transsexual Feminism* no. 3: 28–30.
Orobio de Castro, I. 1993. *Made to order: Sex/gender in a transsexual perspective.* Amsterdam: Het Sinhuis Publishers.
Raymond, J. 1979. *The transsexual empire: The making of the she-male.* Boston: Beacon Press.
Shapiro, J. 1991. Transsexualism: Reflections of the persistence of gender and the mutability of sex. In *Body guards: the cultural politics of gender ambiguity,* edited by J. Epstein and K. Straub. New York: Routledge.
Stone, S. 1991. The empire strikes back: A posttranssexual manifesto. In *Body guards: the cultural politics of gender ambiguity,* edited by J. Epstein and K. Straub. New York: Routledge.
Stryker, S. 1994. My words to Victor Frankenstein above the village of Chamounix. *GLQ* 1: 237–54.
Talamini, J. T. 1982. *Boys will be girls.* Washington, D.C.: University Press of America.

More Than Manly Women:
How Female-to-Male Transsexuals
Reject Lesbian Identities

Holly Devor

Sexology as a discipline first began to emerge in earnest during the end of the nineteenth and the early years of the twentieth centuries. One of the main projects of sexologists in those early years was the identification and classification of some of the many varieties of human sexuality. It was therefore during this period that characterizations of lesbians were first scientifically specified. A variety of authors, including such luminaries as Havelock Ellis and Richard von Krafft-Ebing, formulated pictures of lesbians as females in whom gender had become pathologically inverted to the point that they behaved sexually and emotionally like men and wanted to be men (Ellis 1918; Kraft-Ebing 1965). Thus, the earliest sexological diagnostic criteria for lesbianism were remarkably similar to today's diagnostic criteria for female-to-male transsexualism.[1]

As the ideas of sexologists commingled with those of members of the public, the image of lesbians as manly women became firmly embedded in the popular imagination. Indeed, the 1928 publication of Radclyffe Hall's *Well of Loneliness* was a benchmark in this regard. The book's protagonist, Stephen Gordon, who was a near-perfect exemplar of the style of lesbian described by the early sexologists, became and remained emblematic of prototypical lesbianism for close to half a century (Newton 1989).

The 1970s marked a major turning point in both clinical and popular North American conceptions of lesbianism. The combined efforts of the gay and women's liberation movements shifted definitions of lesbianism away from sin and sickness and toward images of health and happiness. The success of the public relations campaigns of these liberatory movements can be noted in two major changes, one clinical and one cultural: the December 1973 removal of homosexuality from the *Diagnostic and Statistical Manual II* (DSM-II) of the American Psychiatric Association (1980), and a noticeable shift from cultural representations of lesbians as mannish women who want to be men to images of lesbians as women-identified-women who revel in their womanhood (Radicalesbians 1970).

Concurrent with these changes in professional and public understandings of the nature of lesbianism was the development of the concept of transsexualism, which was popularly launched by the 1966 publication of Harry Benjamin's *The Transsexual Phenomenon.* By the end of the 1970s, there were an estimated three to six thousand post-surgical transsexuals in the United States alone, and approximately forty clinics worldwide that provided sex reassignment surgery. (Harry Benjamin International Gender Dysphoria Association 1990). In 1980, approximately six years after homosexuality was removed from the DSM-II, female-to-male transsexualism became an officially delineated diagnosis in the next edition of the DSM (American Psychiatric Association 1980). Thus, those women-who-want-to-be-men who were rapidly becoming personae non gratae among woman-identified lesbians were repatriated back into the clinical purview as female-to-male transsexuals.

Throughout the 1970s and 1980s, the older depiction of lesbianism retained currency while the newer, more radical one gained in definitional muscle. More quietly, but inexorably, the ideas and practices of transsexualism also became public knowledge during this time. Therefore, those female persons who both wanted to be men and felt sexual attractions to women during the 1970s and 1980s had all of these categories available to them as possible explanations for their feelings. However, they were not equally accessible to most people.[2]

In the earlier part of these two decades, the older idea of lesbians as women who want to be men was more widespread than the woman-identified-woman concept, which, in turn, was more readily available than the idea of female-to-male transsexualism. Toward the later end of this timespan the mannish woman concept had lost considerable ground and the idea of transsexualism was well on its way to becoming common knowledge. However, among groups of politically oriented lesbians, the idea of lesbians as mannish women became anathema very early in the 1970s.[3] Likewise, among gender-oriented clinicians, or readers of clinical literature, the diagnostic category of female-to-male transsexualism was readily at hand by the early 1970s (Pauly 1974).

Thus, female individuals who wanted to be men and found their way to self-consciously organized groups of lesbian women in the 1970s and 1980s would have been likely to find that they no longer fit the in-house definition of lesbianism.[4] Were such individuals to continue their search for identity in libraries or in clinicians' offices, they would have been likely to find that they did fit the template for female-to-male transsexualism. If by no other means, the fascination of the popular media with transsexualism that exploded in the late 1980s eventually would have introduced them to the idea of female-to-male transsexualism.

In this report, I recount some of the ways in which these social phenomena were played out in the lives of a group of female-to-male transsexuals. In doing so, I trace some of the ways in which they came to first think of themselves as lesbian women and, later, to reject that designation in favor of identities as female-to-male transsexuals.

Subjects

A total of forty-six self-defined female-to-male transsexuals were interviewed. They ranged from people who had, at the time of first contact, taken no concrete steps toward becoming men, to those who had completed their transition eighteen years before their participation in this research. All participants in this study volunteered their time as a result of hearing about this project through public advertisements or networks within the transsexual community. The sample was therefore probably biased toward those people who were less private about their transsexual status, more socially connected to other transsexuals, and more inclined to educate nontranssexual people about female-to-male transsexuals. One person declined to be included in the data set after completing one interview. He was unwilling to contribute to research conducted from an explicitly feminist perspective.

Although the participants in this study did not constitute a random sample of all female-to-male transsexuals, they did represent a relatively large and diverse group. They were probably more forthcoming than many female-to-male transsexuals, and the sample surely included a disproportionate number of individuals who had been active as transsexual advocates. Some participants had little or no contact with the therapeutic community in regard to their gender issues. Others had sampled all that gender clinics had to offer and were many years into their new lives.

This study was unusual in that it was conducted under nonclinical social relations by a sociologist who had no gatekeeping powers in the lives of any individuals who participated. As such, it seems reasonable to believe that participants' responses were less tainted by goal-oriented distortions than is usually found in clinically based research. Nonetheless, these data are subject to the usual distortions from which any retrospective account might suffer. The data presented here must be taken with some caution but might also be viewed as providing insights into the lives of female-to-male transsexuals from a perspective different from that of other researchers.

Measures

Data were obtained from responses to a detailed interview schedule that I created specifically for a research project leading to a monograph on female-to-male transsexuals.[5] General areas of questioning included (a) demographics; (b) gender issues with family members, peers, in schools, and at work; (c) child abuse; (d) sexuality and romance; (e) physical health and body image; (f) development of gender and transsexual identities; (g) transition experiences; and (h) philosophical questions about sex, gender, and sexuality. This report pertains primarily to question groups (d) and (f), although relevant information may have appeared in a variety of places throughout interviews.

Procedure

Announcements describing the project goals and my background were posted in places where transsexuals might congregate, distributed at transsexual support-group meetings, distributed by prominent members of transsexual communities, and printed in publications that might be read by female-to-male transsexuals. Potential participants were asked to contact me directly. I obtained written consent and interviewed twenty-three individuals face to face. Another eighteen people were mailed copies of interview questions and either answered the questions in writing or by speaking into an audiotape recorder. In an additional four cases, part of the interviews were conducted face to face and part were self-administered. Face-to-face interviews were audiotaped. All participants completed at least one interview; thirty-one persons completed two interviews. Each interview, when conducted in person, usually lasted between two and three hours. All names, and any other identifying information, are kept in a locked cabinet, to which I have sole access.

I also attended a number of formal and informal gatherings of female-to-male transsexuals. Field notes were taken when I was in attendance in an official capacity as a researcher. Transcribed interview materials and field notes were coded and collated for information about sexual attractions, sexual practices, sexual orientation, and transsexual identities.

Results and Discussion

All but two participants (95.5 percent) reported that they had been sexually or romantically attracted to women at some time during their lives as women.[6]

Thirty-five of the forty-three participants who had been attracted to women (81 percent) acted upon their inclinations to some degree, all but two of whom established relationships of approximately one year or more in duration. Twenty-five of those who were attracted to women (58 percent) thought of themselves as lesbian for at least a short period of time. Those participants who never took on the title of lesbian thought of their relationships with women as heterosexual ones.

Participants Who Did Not Act upon Their Attractions to Women

Seventeen participants (39.5 percent) went through periods during which they felt unable to act upon their sexual feelings for women, five of whom (12 percent) never became sexually involved with women while they themselves were still living as women. For all twelve of those participants who later went on to experiment with homosexual relations, their periods of reluctance to act upon their homosexual attractions were confined to their teenaged years. It became clear from the stories of most participants that the generalized homophobia of the decades during which they were children and adolescents (1950s, 1960s, early 1970s) played a significant role in discouraging them from acting upon the adolescent attractions that they felt for females. Homophobia acted to abort their lesbian activities and deflect them from lesbian identities mainly in two ways.

First, information about lesbianism was not readily available.[7] Thus, the only sexual model to which many girls had access was a heterosexual one. Therefore, when they felt sexual desire for other females, the only logical interpretation that they could place on their feelings was that they should be males in order to have such lusts. Furthermore, since they were not males, there was nothing that they could do about their feelings but contain them and bide their time until an opportunity arose to somehow transform themselves into men.

For example, Bruce[8] remembered that she had very explicitly sexual thoughts about women when she was a teenager, but did not act on them:

> I used to get out my parents' Sears catalogue and look at the women in their underwear. I got turned on. . . . But I thought, I can't do this the way I am. I have to be a boy because girls don't like girls. . . . So, I saw men and women together. So, I thought, that's what it's supposed to be, and all the girls liked me because I was a boy. . . . But I used to put those kinds of feelings behind me, I think, because I felt that I couldn't . . . be sexual. . . . It wasn't allowed. It wasn't right. Because, how can women be attracted to women?

The second way in which the homophobia of the times acted to deny these participants opportunities to explore their lesbian urges during their teen years was through misinformation. Those participants who had heard of lesbianism had only the most negative of perspectives on the phenomenon. They absorbed the messages that their society wanted them to believe: that lesbians were sick and dangerous people; that lesbian activity was sorely stigmatized and totally taboo. Thus, those individuals who wanted to retain some modicum of self-respect and a decent standing in their society avoided tainting themselves with the stain of lesbianism.

Peter,[9] for instance, thought that her childhood and adolescent attractions to girls meant that she must be "gay," but Peter did not want to accept that label as appropriate for herself. Peter recalled: "There's always been the social stigma about being gay. And I would think that probably, for a time when I was an adolescent, that, in that sense, that really backed me off. That kept me really under wraps."

The participants who were acting under the sway of these kinds of homophobia were left few alternatives. They simply could not act because they could only see their attractions as being heterosexual in form, if not in content. Nevertheless, three participants did think of themselves as lesbian on the basis of their unactualized attractions to women.

Minor Homosexual Involvements

Ten participants (23 percent) went through extended periods during which they had only limited homosexual experiences. These plateaus occurred during the adolescences of all but one such participant. They engaged mostly in kissing and in touching of their partners' breasts in the context of short-term infatuations. Only two participants thought of themselves as lesbians on the basis of these interactions. Most of these participants also kept their attractions for females relatively in check because of their fear of social stigma. Their anxieties about possible social retribution for transgressions were sufficient to deter them from any extensive homosexual adventures. Many participants had so absorbed the messages of their society that they held opinions that could be interpreted as indicative of internalized homophobia and misogyny.

Lee's comments illustrated this type of thinking:

> I knew that queers existed. . . . Things like that weren't talked about. . . . That was almost like Mafia. They's just dirt road people or something. So, that was a bad word. You didn't want to be that. . . . You knew it wasn't accepted. . . . You knew it wasn't right in the eyes of everybody. . . . It makes me sound stupid, but I didn't just sit down and think about things like that. I just did it. You knew that it wasn't right . . . but it's something you enjoyed.

It seems plausible that, had these participants lived in a time when information about lesbianism was both more readily available and more salutary, most of them would probably have been more homosexually active. In a climate more conducive to positive lesbian identity, many of them might well have more avidly adopted a lesbian identity and cleaved to it more persistently. Be that as it may, gender identity is a different matter from sexual orientation. Later, more extensive homosexual experience and lesbian identity did not banish, but only obscured, underlying male identities. Experimentation with lesbianism for most participants was one step in the process of clarifying that a male identity was the most suitable one for them.

Major Homosexual Relationships

Thirty-five participants (81 percent) became involved in ongoing genitally sexual relationships with other females during their pretransition years. Due to the explicitly sexual and nonfleeting nature of these unions, they could not be dismissed as merely affectionate or experimental. Thus, these liaisons forced participants to confront issues of sexual identity and, by extension, issues of gender identity.

Some of these unions were undertaken by both partners with the understanding that they were, at least in all apparent aspects, lesbian relationships. In other cases participants, but not necessarily their partners, maintained the belief that they were men, and that therefore their relationships were, de facto, heterosexual ones. A few relationships foreshadowed what was to come in that both partners agreed from the start that, in their own eyes, they were in heterosexual relationships. In other cases, particular relationships became redefined as they progressed and as participants went through stages wherein they came to have better insights into themselves and into the nature of lesbianism. As they did so, they generally moved more toward the rejection of the label of lesbian and of the womanhood implicit in that title.

When participants did think of themselves as lesbian women, they did so principally for two reasons. In the first place, they were faced the with unmistakable evidence of their own, and their lovers', bodies. They knew that the definition of lesbian therefore technically included them. Some participants were also persuaded by the popular conception that lesbians are women who want to be men. As that was precisely how participants felt, they uneasily accepted the appellation of lesbian, despite the fact that it required them to acquiesce to being women. However, only a very few participants easily accepted that their intimate relationships with women fully qualified as lesbian ones. More commonly, participants recognized a superficial similarity between their own relationships and those of lesbian women, but retained a sense of themselves as different.

As participants used their intimate relationships with women as testing grounds for their sex, gender, and sexual identities, they found that their homosexual relations did not allow them to express their identities adequately. After some initial delight at the increased tolerance for their masculinity that they found among lesbian women, participants began to encounter some limitations. They found that the social and sexual values of lesbian women did not align as well with their own as they might have wished. Eventually the disjunctures between their own self-images and the images they held of what lesbian women were like became too disquieting to them and they concluded that they were not lesbian women. When they reckoned that they were beyond the range of what constituted lesbian thoughts and deeds, they became receptive to the possibilities of transsexualism as a means of realigning themselves with their social worlds.

Avoiding Lesbian Communities

Thirteen participants (30 percent) went through periods of their lives during which they were homosexually active but stayed away from places where homosexual women congregated. During those periods of their lives, they fell in love and built relationships with women, but six of them (46 percent) resisted accepting identities as lesbian women. They conceived of their partners as being attracted to them for their manly qualities and did what they could to nurture their mutual conceptualizations of their relationships as straight ones.[10]

These participants found ways, outside of established lesbian environments, to meet women with whom they could establish sexual/romantic relationships. One result of their making contact with their lovers independently of communities of similarly disposed women was that they had only popular models of the nature of lesbianism against which to measure themselves. By the time that they were making such comparisons, lesbian-feminist definitions had begun to move definitions of lesbians away from the "mannish woman" typology popular before the 1970s and toward a "woman-loving-woman" characterization that has become more dominant since then (Faderman 1991; Sedgewick 1990). As a group, they found the latter definition less acceptable than the arguably more stigmatized former one, and so they eventually rejected the label of lesbian in favor of more obtusely acceptable identities as men.

For example, Stan feared being branded as a lesbian. Although Stan remembered always having had "feelings about [women] like guys do," as a woman she felt exceptionally guilty about these feelings even as she was having several years of otherwise satisfying relationships with women. As she tried to work through this contradiction, she became so depressed at the thought that she might be lesbian that she ended up spending several months hospitalized for mental problems. Stan also reported that she later destroyed one of her relationships with the heavy drinking and marijuana smoking that she used to help her cope with her extreme aversion to being known as a lesbian woman.

As was probably common among many homosexual women who came out in the 1970s, Stan seemed to have two different views of what it meant to be a lesbian woman. On the one hand, Stan had held a more traditional view of lesbian women as sinful and sick. On the other hand, Stan had also been exposed, through the media, to a more feminist version of lesbianism. When I asked Stan about it, he described lesbians this way:

> I knew about lesbians but it just didn't occur to me that's what it was. . . . What I knew about lesbians was that two women can be together and it's okay if you are a lesbian. . . . It was something they did on the coast in the big cities, more liberal people did. I just didn't consider myself that liberal, that open minded. . . . To get into being a lesbian, like, you have to march for things, and you gotta go to caucuses, you gotta hate men, you gotta dress butch, and you gotta get into all that stuff, and I didn't want to do that. I didn't want to get into all that stuff.

Stan, like others who were unable to accept lesbian identities as appropriate for themselves, later enthusiastically latched onto the normalizing potential of female-to-male transsexualism.

Moving through Lesbian Communities

Another twenty-two participants (51 percent) who were homosexually active as women went through stages wherein they initially threw themselves wholeheartedly into lesbianism. They became friends with other homosexual women and participated in social or political activities with them. They were thus exposed to socialization processes that taught them something of what lesbian subcultures expected from women who were lesbian.

In some cases, these communities were highly politicized ones whose members espoused lesbian-feminist ideologies concerning the nature of lesbianism. In other instances, they were communities of women who came together at bars or ball games and who were less heavily influenced by feminist political analyses of lesbian identity. Eighteen of these twenty-two participants (82 percent), at some time during their lives, accepted the label "lesbian" as descriptive of themselves, only to later reject it as inadequate to the task. They came to their conclusions after making comparisons between their senses of themselves and their visions of how they believed that lesbians thought and acted.

Aaron's story illustrated how this happened. Aaron started to think of herself as "probably gay" when she was a woman of twenty-five and her psychiatrist diagnosed her as homosexual. Aaron accepted that label as descriptive of herself because, at that time, in the early 1960s, "the only image I could think of was women that fell in love with women, and women that dressed and wanted to be men and acted masculine. I figured that was what a gay woman was." However, when Aaron became divorced from her husband three years after this diagnosis, she decided to remain celibate and separate from other gay women because "frankly, I wouldn't have kept my kids if I wasn't." Nonetheless, during that fifteen-year period Aaron recalled, "I was living primarily in male clothing . . . [people] just assumed I was a dyke."

At the end of the 1970s, two days after Aaron's youngest daughter reached legal adulthood, Aaron started having a series of affairs with lesbian women at the university where she was taking courses. A number of brief affairs and one longer relationship demonstrated to Aaron that she was not like other gay women. Aaron described two aspects of her process of discovery. On the one hand, she found herself at odds with the lesbian community in which she was situated:

> Let's face it . . . they saw the woman's body, and figured I was a gay woman, and I went along with that to the point where they expected me to be female. . . . It means sticking up for the female when you get into a discussion with a bunch of women on wife beating, or sticking up for the feminist role when you get with a bunch of women and no men around, or . . . preferring the company of women. . . . I was trying to get along with these women; I was trying to love some of these women . . . but I didn't fit. And the longer I was with them, the more I realized I didn't fit.

Although Aaron was able to integrate herself into a gay community she always felt different from the women around her. Aaron recalled how it was for her then:

> When I got involved with gay women and found out how frigging different I was it was obvious. Up until that point I thought that other gay females were the same as me, they wanted to be male. And when I found out that was not true, that no matter how masculine they acted, they had female identities, I realized I don't quite fit in here, but I fit in closer here than I ever had.

On a more intimate level, Aaron further found that she did not respond to her lesbian lover in the ways that both of them believed were characteristic of lesbians. Aaron drew this picture of the issues involved:

Basically she wanted a woman. At the nitty gritty deep level I wasn't a woman. . . . Okay, concrete example . . . our lovemaking. She would resent it when I got too masculine. . . . When I became too aggressive and too demanding, too macho, whatever, it ruined it for her. . . . Hey, I want to be on top part of the time . . . figuratively and literally. And it would turn her off more, it would slow her response down and turn her off right when mine was speeding up. We didn't match.

Aaron construed these events as evidence that she did not belong among lesbians and concluded that she was a female-to-male transsexual.

Another participant, Howie, summed up well the way in which these people deduced that they were men rather than lesbian women. At first Howie thought that she and her lover were lesbian but then,

Later . . . upon closer investigation I realized that lesbians enjoyed their womanhood and didn't want to change their bodies surgically. They were simply women who loved women. I realized I didn't fit that mould at all. . . . A lesbian is a woman, who is glad she's a woman, who happens to relate sexually to other women. She does not wish to be male. In fact, she rejoices in her femaleness and wants to be with other females. . . . I knew that wasn't for me. . . . I often wish I could have accepted myself as gay, or identified as gay, because it is infinitely easier than changing.

Ron also became embedded in a lesbian community and came to be extensively committed to lesbian-feminist activities. Like Aaron and Howie, Ron also concluded, on the basis of her knowledge of lesbian social and sexual mores, that she was neither a lesbian nor a woman, and that she was better suited to being a man. Ron remembered:

For one thing, sexual[ity] definitely played a big role. . . . I had to go through and analyze for myself whether I was just a strong female, or whether I was a male. Whether I just didn't fit into the stereotypical female sexist kind of role. . . .
    For instance, being with women . . . the love I got was toward the woman, the physical woman. And for me, that was a conflict sexually . . . I was not making love as a woman with a woman. From my heart, it was that I was a male. . . . It's a completely different dynamic. . . . There is a different approach from a woman to her man than the approach from one woman to another woman who are lovers. . . . There were a lot of needs that I could not express with lesbians, because the lesbians that I was having relationships with were not open to anything that had anything to do with males.

Hal, too, made a profound commitment to lesbianism. Even though Hal felt like "a man in a woman's body," she had a number of homosexual relationships, including a thirteen-year-long lesbian relationship. Hal called herself a lesbian and functioned well within a lesbian-feminist community. Hal discussed how she handled her co-identities as a man and as a lesbian:

> When a transsexual goes into the lesbian community it's because they get support there for wearing the clothes they want, relating to women . . . as sex partners. For being strong. . . . What happened was that I thought for a long long time that, although I knew inside that I was male, it was okay for me to identify [as a lesbian]. I never was homophobic or embarrassed about being a lesbian, so it was okay for me . . . as long as my lover understood that I was male, and some of my friends understood that I was male. . . . I went along like that for many, many years. . . . I felt the pressure of the [1970s' and 1980s'] lesbian doctrine. I was trying to be a "strong, handsome woman," and not a man in a woman's body after all. . . . I put off [starting a transition] for at least ten years out of a fear of rejection, fear of the risks, and fear of making a political mistake with respect to my lesbian-feminism.

However, Hal reached a point in her life when, despite the critique of gender roles offered to her by lesbian-feminism of the late 1980s, she could no longer find a way to see herself as a woman.

These participants entered into communities of lesbian women at times during which lesbian-feminists of the 1970s and 1980s were dedicated to a redefinition of lesbianism away from the depiction of lesbians as mannish women. Instead, lesbian-feminists promoted the idea that lesbians were "women-identified-women." Participants felt excluded by that definition and therefore were left to search in other quarters for labels that more snugly fit their self-images. When they discovered female-to-male transsexualism they embraced it as both an escape and a homecoming.

Summary and Conclusions

By far the strongest pattern that emerged from the stories offered by participants was one of participants' earnest attempts to fit themselves to the available social roles of their times. Forty-three participants (95.5 percent) had been sexually attracted to women at some point in their pretransition lives. Thirty-five of them (81 percent) established relationships of some duration with women during their pretransition years, two participants (5 percent) had only minor sexual involvements, and another six participants (14 percent) were attracted to women but never acted upon their emotions. Drawn as these forty-three participants were to being lovers of women, they were confronted with a difficult-to-deny characterization of their love as lesbian.

More than half of these participants who were sexually attracted to women (58 percent) passed through periods during which they thought of themselves as gay or lesbian women. They were originally attracted to making such identifications because of their awareness of the common social definition of lesbians as women who want to be men or as mannish women who are sexually interested in other women. However, over time, they came to make more finely sifted distinctions.

Two major issues became important to participants in their process of moving out of lesbian identities. Both of the axes on which participants judged themselves to be men rather than lesbian women were products of a particular historical period wherein the definitions of lesbianism constituted contested territory. On the one hand, all participants who once considered themselves to be lesbian ceased doing so during the 1970s and 1980s. These were years during which the proponents of lesbian-feminism were waging campaigns to supplant the idea that lesbians are mannish women with images of lesbians as women-identified-women who celebrate their womanhood with other women. On the other hand, these decades were also those during which female-to-male transsexualism was being defined as a treatable medical condition, similar to, but distinct from, lesbianism and characterized by the persistent desire of females to become males. Thus, participants searching for viable words to use to identify themselves were caught up in these shifting boundaries.

Participants who lived part of their lives as lesbian women were thus often in the position of having been drawn to lesbian identities on the basis of older definitions of lesbians as women who want to be men, only to discover that the lesbian pride movements of the 1970s and 1980s required them to reject those characterizations. When participants tried to measure themselves against the more woman-centered images promulgated by lesbian-feminists they found themselves lacking on two points. First, they were ashamed, embarrassed, or disgusted by the specifically female aspects of their bodies and therefore had little desire to join with their companions in the glorification of their womanhood. Second, they were generally not interested in having their sexual partners enjoy their femaleness or attempt to provide them with pleasures in specifically female ways. In other words, when participants compared themselves to both generalized and specific lesbian others, they were struck more by the contrasts than by the similarities. It therefore became apparent to these participants that they had more in common with straight men than with lesbian women. Eventually, their discomfort with being included in the lesbian camp was alleviated by their discovery of the increasingly socially available concept of female-to-male transsexualism, which offered them a conceptually simple, and more apt, solution to their extreme gender dysphoria. Once they knew themselves to be female-to-male transsexuals, they were eager to move beyond wishing to and into actually becoming men.

Thus, in the end, participants gradually exhausted their possibilities as women. Each probed the roles for women that were available to them. As each alternative was weighed and found wanting, the field of possibilities narrowed to that which was perhaps ultimately the most suitable but also seemingly the most unobtainable: to become men. Until participants happened upon the option called female-to-male transsexualism, they were relegated to forever feeling like bizarre misfits—even among those sexual minorities who already inhabited the fringes of society. Female-to-male transsexualism offered them a way out of their dilemmas: a path toward integration and self-actualization.

Notes

First and foremost I wish to express my thanks to the people who volunteered their time to become involved in this research project and to teach me something of their way of life. My thanks to Lynn Greenhough for helpful comments on early drafts of this paper and to my research assistants Noreen Begoray, Bev Copes, Sheila Pederson, and Sandra Winfield. Portions of this research were funded by the Social Science and Humanities Research Council of Canada and the University of Victoria, Canada.

1. I use the term "female-to-male transsexuals" rather than "transsexual men" because I do not wish to distinguish between individuals at various stages of transition. I have included in this category anyone who so designated themselves to me. I use the term "lesbian" to refer to sexual/romantic relationships between two persons who have gender identities as women regardless of their anatomical sexes. I use the term "homosexual" to refer to sexual relations between persons of the same anatomical sex regardless of their gender identities. For further discussion of my use of the language of gendered sexuality see Devor 1993.

2. Consider that Krafft-Ebing described "the extreme grade of degenerative homosexuality" as "hermaphroditism" wherein "the woman of this type possesses of the feminine qualities only the genital organs; thought, sentiment, action, even external appearance are those of the man . . . the[ir] desire to adopt the active role towards the beloved person of the same sex seems to invite the use of the priapus" (264–65). Compare Krafft-Ebing's description of mannish lesbians with the diagnostic criteria for adult Gender Identity Disorder from the DSM-IV: "a stated desire to be the other sex, frequent passing as the other sex, desire to live or be treated as the other sex, or the conviction that he or she has the typical feelings and reactions of the other sex" (1994, 537).

3. My comments on this topic are partially based upon my own recollections and partially upon my analysis of the data reported herein and elsewhere.

4. Consider this extract from Martin and Lyon:

It is those women who feel that they are "born butch" who tend to ape all the least desirable characteristics of men. In this case one may as well say to those butch, "Up against the wall, male chauvinist pig!" For to consider oneself a heterosexual, to stress that male and female are opposites which presumably, attract, is to accept the entire male-imposed doctrine that woman's place is indeed in the home serving the male (1972, 74).

5. The book is tentatively titled *Making Men: Female-to-Male Transsexuals in Society,* and is to be published by Indiana University Press.

6. All percentages subsequently reported are proportions of the forty-three participants who had been attracted to women.

7. In 1921 the English Parliament attempted to introduce a law that would make lesbianism a crime. Speaking against the proposition Lord Desart said, "You are going to tell the whole world that there is such an offence, to bring it to the notice of women who have never heard of it, never thought of it, never dreamt of it. I think that is a very great mischief" (quoted in Weeks 1989, 105) Clearly, many young women were still laboring under such ignorance more than fifty years later.

8. I have given all participants pseudonymous men's names and, for the sake of continuity and clarity, have used them when referring to participants at any age.

9. I have tried to remain true to the gender of the persons involved in this research project. When referring to a man telling a story about when he was a girl or woman, I have used gender pronouns that reflect the gender of the subject in each time frame, e.g., "He remembered that as a girl, she was a tomboy."

10. In addition, two participants who had been involved with lesbian communities also took this tack. One other participant was involved in a more-than-twenty-year homosexual relationship that both parties framed as a relationship between two gay men.

References

American Psychiatric Association. 1980. *Diagnostic and statistical manual of mental disorders.* 3d ed. Washington, D.C.: American Psychiatric Association.

———. 1994. *Diagnostic and statistical manual of mental disorders.* 4th ed. Washington, D.C.: American Psychiatric Association.

Benjamin, H. 1966. *The transsexual phenomenon.* New York: Julian Press.

Devor, H. 1993. Toward a taxonomy of gendered sexuality. *Journal of Psychology and Human Sexuality* 6: 23–55.

Ellis, H. 1918. *Studies in the psychology of sex.* Vol. 2. Sexual inversion. Philadelphia: F. A. Davis.

Faderman, L. 1991. *Odd girls and twilight lovers: A history of lesbian life in twentieth century America.* New York: Penguin.

Hall, R. [1928] 1986. *The well of loneliness.* London: Hutchinson.

Harry Benjamin International Gender Dysphoria Association. 1990. *Standards of care.* Available from The Harry Benjamin International Gender Dysphoria Association, Inc., P.O. Box 1718, Sonoma, CA 95476.

Krafft-Ebing, R. von. [1906] 1965. *Psychopathia sexualis with especial reference to the antipathic sexual instinct. A medico-forensic study.* Translated by F. S. Klaf. New York: Stein & Day.

Martin, D., and P. Lyon. 1972. *Lesbian/woman.* San Francisco: Glide.

Newton. E. 1989. The mythic mannish lesbian: Radclyffe Hall and the new woman. In *Hidden from history: Reclaiming the gay and lesbian past,* edited by M. Duberman, M. Vicinus, and G. Chauncey, Jr., 281–93. New York: NAL.

Pauly, I. 1974. Female transsexualism: Parts I and II. *Archives of Sexual Behavior* 3: 487–525.

Radicalesbians. 1970. The woman identified woman. In *Radical feminism,* edited by A. Koedt, E. Levine, and A. Rapone, 240–45. New York: Quadrangle.

Sedgewick, E. 1990. *The epistemology of the closet.* Berkeley: University of California Press.

Weeks, J. 1989. *Sex, politics and society: The regulation of sexuality since 1800.* 2d ed. London: Longman.

Self-Testing: A Check on Sexual Identity and Other Levels of Sexuality

Milton Diamond

For most persons the typical everyday life situations of growing up provide ample test of their sexual selves. Masculinity or femininity is measured by comparing oneself with societal images provided by family, peers, media, educational and religious institutions, and other social forces. These external measures provide one with a *gender identity*. A gender identity is how one sees him- or herself relative to society's expectations. To be emphasized is that *gender* is related to society, and many aspects of it differ from one culture to another.[1]

Also, for most individuals the private, *internal, personal* view and feeling he or she has of himself or herself, "I am a male" or "I am a female," his or her *sexual identity,* is—more or less—the same as society's gender identity. Typical XY-chromosome individuals see themselves as males and are seen as such by the surrounding society. Similarly XX individuals see themselves as females and are seen as such. But, *sexual* identity as a private phenomenon may be in direct conflict with gender identity. One can recognize society's gender attribution and not see it apply personally; individuals seem to come to "know" if they are male or female by a different process. The usual processes of social reinforcement as associated with sex-typing (e.g., Huston 1983) do not appear to hold. Were it simply by accepting familial, societal, and cultural dictates, the phenomenon of transsexuality would not exist. Almost without exception, males are reared as boys and females are reared as girls, but for transsexuals this is a cruel hoax.

A version of this paper was presented at the First International Congress on Cross-Dressing, Sex, and Gender, 23–26 February 1995. This is an expansion of that paper.

103

In considering gender identity a scale of options is available. One might consider him- or herself an appropriate or inappropriate representative of the culture's boys or girls, e.g., a sissy or tomboy. This is true regardless if the individual considers himself or herself socially appropriate as an adequate male or female, or if questions remain: "Am I masculine enough? or "Am I feminine enough?" or even if he or she makes the decision "I am not a good male or female." This last set of statements reflects on the individual's *gender patterns*[2] of behavior. Patterns of behavior are basically culturally appropriate sex-linked activities: the stereotypical playing with frilly dolls or playing house versus playing with toy soldiers, guns, or trucks (Diamond 1977, 1979, 1980, 1992). With an individual's male and female gender patterns a whole range of maleness and femaleness is on offer. For sexual identity, however, there are only two possible, mutually exclusive, choices: male or female (Diamond 1979).[3]

With most people, sexual and gender identity are sufficiently concordant to satisfy ego needs and overcome any doubt as to one's own sex and appropriate role in society. In certain cases, however, internal and external cues are not in concert or are only partially so; sex and gender are not congruent. In these uncommon cases, one's internal sexual identity signals one sex while society signals the other. Suffice it to say that intense feelings of conflict and discomfort develop from this dichotomy. This is the case with the transsexual (TS) individual.[4] How this identity supposedly comes about is debated (for reviews see, e.g., Bolin 1987; Bullough and Bullough 1993; Diamond 1965, 1993, 1995; Docter 1988; Green and Money 1969; Stoller 1969).[5]

Early in life, the transsexual becomes aware that society is reacting to her or him in a manner felt as inappropriate. In some subtle way transsexuals come to realize they would be more comfortable treated as are their opposite-sexed siblings or peers. The developing TS (male or female transsexual) realizes he or she is being treated not in accordance with internal feelings but rather in accordance with external anatomy; the presence of a penis and scrotum or vulva and vagina. This is usually signaled during childhood by the dependent wearing clothing that is offered by parents but is not in keeping with the sex in which the transsexual feels at peace, and by parental expectations of behaviors in accordance with the birth gender even though the child feels more appropriately associated with expectations of the opposite gender. With experience, the longing for mental calm and comfort drives the transsexual to the conviction that only by living not as reared, but as a male or female according to her or his inner dictates, only by living the "core" identity (Stoller 1968), will inner peace be obtained.

This disparity between the personal view of self (identity) and society's view (gender) are quite unsettling. The transsexual wishes his or her external body would match the internal psychic feelings. Basically, and eventually, the transsexual says to the world: "To rectify things, my body must change, not my mind."

The path to one's realization that he or she is a transsexual is variable. Most transsexual individuals, at first, seem to just have an amorphous feeling of being different quite early in life. Then slowly they *know* they are different from others in how they view themselves. Transsexual males (MtF = male to female) brought up as boys and transsexual females (FtM = female to male) reared as girls see this as a cruel mistake of fate (Blanchard and Steiner 1990; Zucker 1990; Zucker, Bradley, and Sullivan 1992). In their own minds there is no doubt they are of the opposite sex and should be reared accordingly. They become convinced so by everyday life events that they feel do not resonate well with their own image of who they are. They want to live life transformed so their anatomy fits their conviction and mental image of self. The TS then eventually presents to a physician or other professional with the urge to have sex reassignment surgery (SRS). When doing so, such individuals recount lives in which they had manifested or recognized a disposition toward cross-gender lifestyle events and behaviors. Their day-to-day social life, an experiential *living-test* as it was, told them their internal signals were not synchronized with the external ones and their internal signals won out. They typically recount many incidents where sex-of-birth appropriate behaviors were felt to be or were actually impossible or difficult to manage (e.g., Bolin 1987; Green and Money 1969; Wålinder 1967). And, quite often, these feelings have existed from preschool days.

Benjamin's (1966) original definition of transsexualism was relatively clear: "True transsexuals feel that they *belong* to the other sex, they want to *be* and *function* as members of the opposite sex, not only to appear as such" (13, emphasis in original). Since then, however, a second part has often been added. For example Ziegler in 1994 follows the practice started at least twenty years earlier (e.g., Fisk 1975; Mehl 1975) in offering a multipart definition of a transsexual. The first part is the same as offered by Benjamin. In the second part, Fisk, Mehl, and Ziegler add, in effect: the transsexual persistently engages in behaviors attempting to live as the other sex. Examples would be the male TS who cannot and would not bear to wear boy's or men's clothing and instead wears female garb and is a failure at sports or won't even attempt them. The typical female TS insists on binding her breasts, dressing as a man, and engaging in masculine pursuits. These persons are often seen by themselves and others as "failures" in their birth sex. Most often these behaviors arouse the ire of parents and siblings; hardly ever is this behavior reinforced for long. Stoller essentially defined a (male) transsexual as an XY individual who is fully identified with the female role, has as many feminine mannerisms, interests, and fantasies as a little girl his age, and openly expresses wishes to have his body turn into a female's (1968, 92).

This current paper, however, describes a phenomenon that more than a few transsexuals undergo in the process of trying to reconcile their disparity of sexual and gender identities. These are the behaviors of persons who, for an extended duration, overindulge in, rather than shun, behaviors typical of their assigned sex. I label this a process, a process of *self-testing*.

Self-testing is significantly challenging oneself to personally measure "Am I male or female?" The challenge may consist of a particularly crucial set of incidents or events or years of experiences. It has two interdependent components. The first component is the *situation*. It is subjecting oneself, consciously or unconsciously, to situations or processes personally dramatic or significant enough for them to take on the status of a sex/gender marker. The second component of the "self-test" is the *analysis*. For the male-to-female transsexual it is saying, to put it simplistically, something like: "Although all my male peers enjoy playing with guns, I don't. I tried it for a year or so and, although I am *good* at it and can outdraw my buddies and shoot more accurately, I would rather crochet. This proves to me **I am truly a female**." A nontranssexual male in the same circumstance, in contrast, might say to himself: "Although all my male peers enjoy playing with guns, I don't. . . . I would rather crochet. This proves to me **I am not a typical or good male**." Or, "Although all my male peers enjoy playing with guns, I don't. . . . I would rather crochet. This proves to me **I am probably different**." Later on, with greater age and experience this last individual might come to say **"Perhaps I'm gay**." Most individuals, never having heard of transsexualism, will not know how to identify such feelings at all. Transsexuals often think themselves unique in all the world. As they go over the possibility of being gay, that too doesn't seem to satisfy them exactly and, in fact, could repel them. For someone very young, it might be easier to contemplate, along with fictional beliefs of Santa Claus and the Tooth Fairy, growing up into the other sex or saying, without full understanding, "I am really a boy/girl [opposite sex noun]."

Self-testing calls to question the concept that an adequate self-esteem system only develops when life situations are positive vis-à-vis a developing and wanted ego (Epstein 1973). As Docter wrote: "if [for example] a male predicts, for whatever reason, that he will be likely to fail in roles requiring masculine-gender competencies and skills—then either the formation of that subsystem would be weakened (or stopped), or a feminine gender identity will develop, thereby facilitating pleasure and self-esteem" (1988, 81–82). Negative reinforcement to one's identity will supposedly lead to transsexual ideation. Feinbloom writes: "One can see transsexualism as a *career gone sour.* That is, one can examine the lives of transsexuals, both preoperative and postoperative, in terms of previous failure to . . . [resolve] issues in a life that have made one's particular life pattern untenable. It is not stretching the definition of career to say that transsexualism itself is a career constructed on the ruins of one that has failed" (1976, 149–50, emphasis in original). Put in other terms: getting reinforced as a male (or female) will supposedly establish and fix one's identity as a male (or female); not getting reinforced adequately will thwart proper development of suitable sexual identity.

Concomitant with this, when conflict or doubt as to which true sex exists, the individual might follow up with the thought: "If I do such-and such successfully [test myself] it will mean I really am a male and my thoughts of being female will pass." With the female-to-male transsexual the opposite would hold. She says to herself: "If I do thus-and-so successfully it will really mean I am a female and my thoughts of truly being male will pass." Certainly nontranssexual individuals might come away from their own self-testing with feelings of inadequacy as a boy or girl but the inadequacy doesn't challenge their basic sexual identity.

Simple self-testing events and demands occur early, usually pre-school, and are interpreted and resolved rather unremarkably for most children. For atypically developing individuals, however, the testing period can be prolonged, quite involved, and dramatic. With *convinced transsexuals*, repeated normal encounters with living, from early on, seem an affirmation that they are of the other sex. Failure in gender-stereotypic behaviors that might be accepted or rejected without fanfare or concern by nontranssexuals, is cause for internal reification by convinced transsexuals that they are "in the body of the wrong sex." They do not need or seek any self-test; their living-test convinces them early on.

Unconvinced transsexuals, while also harboring doubts from early on, nevertheless continue to question this disparity between inner and outer sex and eventually decide they are transsexuals only after a period of *direct* and usually prolonged self-examination. This process is often quite deliberate. It may, however, become apparent only in retrospect. Individuals of this second group of transsexuals are *self-tested transsexuals*.

Another matter might be considered for self-tested transsexuals. Kando (1973) found that typical transsexuals are highly stereotyped in accepting cultural ascriptions of gender. In their eyes, a good woman should be "comfortable in the kitchen and home," and "a good man should be macho and the bread-winner." Indeed, among the seventeen MtF transsexuals interviewed by Kando, almost all either considered themselves full-time housewives or worked in women-typical jobs such as secretaries, waitresses, and dancers. The self-tested transsexual is not that hide-bound. He or she feels capable in either the male or female role and can see that for others as well. But he or she, for self, believes that flexibility notwithstanding, an inner identification must be dealt with. The post surgical avocation is of minor importance as long as it can be done in the preferred sex.

For everyone, the second part of the self-test is its personal evaluation: the analysis. In this evaluation, male-to-female transsexuals inevitably conclude, to the effect, "I was tested or tested myself as a male in the most rigorous manner I can imagine and even though I was *successful* as far as society was concerned, it was insufficient to satisfy myself. I must therefore be the female I feel within."

Self-testing of *identity* is most dramatically demonstrated by transsexuals but is seen in lesser degree among transvestites, then bisexuals and homosexuals, and least by heterosexuals. Bisexuals, homosexuals, and heterosexuals might test their masculinity or femininity, so-called self-testing *gender patterns* or they might test their sexual *orientation*, their attraction toward members of the same or opposite sex or both, but rarely question if they are male or female. And anyone might self-test their *mechanisms* (e.g., *orgasmic ability* or *reproductive capacity*).

Several cases of transsexual persons will exemplify the phenomenon of self-testing identity. They are presented in detail to illustrate how extensive the self-test can be.

Male-to-Female Transsexuals

Case #1: Hank*

Some two decades ago a thirty-six-year-old XY individual presented himself with his wife of six years. They came to my office for advice and counseling regarding their marriage and the management of their future lives. The gist of the situation was that they had met and dated for about a year and married when he was thirty and she forty.

In general the couple seemed to be getting along well. They professed to loving each other and having few arguments or difficulties of consequence that typically beset couples. They reported themselves sexually compatible with a mutually satisfying frequency and intensity of genital play and coitus. There was a great deal of cuddling and physical warmth. There was, however, one major hurdle that had developed, and they sought help in its resolution. About a year before coming to see me, Hank had told his wife about his desires to cross-dress. She reluctantly accepted this. Following that revelation, he did occasionally cross-dress in her presence. Recently, however, he confided to her that he had always felt himself to be a female, at least since the age of four. He now desired sex-change surgery and the ability to live as a female.

---

*This is a pseudonym.

The wife, a highly intelligent woman, worked in an administrative position of authority. Originally she had thought the cross-dressing and female aspirations were temporary aberrations of her husband and that they would pass. The magnitude of the present situation confused her, and she wanted answers to what was happening and suggestions on how to proceed. Both husband and wife wanted to maintain the relationship if possible.

During interviews with transgendered individuals I typically ask about self-testing identity. The questions are posed as a sort of challenge and follow the gist of "You have a penis and scrotum and total body build of a male, you were raised as a male and treated as a male in all instances that you can recall. And, you appear to be in a satisfactory marriage with a comparably satisfying sex life. Yet, you nevertheless consider yourself a female. What makes you think so? Can you give me examples of how you know you are female and not a male? How did you convince yourself of the correctness of this unusual feeling?" This series of questions is tailored to fit each individual's history and circumstances.

Most XY individuals, in response to such questions, try to impress with occurrences documenting how "female" they had been all their lives. This is in dramatic contrast with the story that Hank told. Hank told a "hyper-male" story.

Hank was the eldest of twelve children in a poor and physically abusive dysfunctional family where the number of actual fathers involved was not known but father figures were consistently present. Routine beatings for even minor childhood infractions were common from his mother or any of the men around. Even as a child, Hank was expected to work at chores, doing much of the "man's work" around the house. This was even considered more important than school work. His family lived with cousins and other relatives to help defray costs. Some twenty or so children of all ages lived together with the boys in the basement, the girls in the attic, and the adults in between. This was in a very small midwestern town.

From about the age of four Hank recalled feeling as if he were a girl rather than a boy. He dates this first revelation from the time he had to wear a girl cousin's pants when his were unavailable. He remembered them having a pink bow on the side, which he felt was more in keeping with his "self." Until that experience, Hank said, "for reasons I couldn't explain, I didn't believe I was in tune with the way people were treating me. This, wearing of my girl cousin's clothes, which I took as being treated as a girl, seemed right." In private he would take to occasional cross-dressing choosing from the profusion of girls' clothes that were always available in the house. With so many people around, privacy was rare. When possible he "made do" with wearing the sexually ambiguous "boys' " clothes of his sisters and girl cousins. Fearing physical abuse and ridicule he dressed in outright female clothes only rarely and always in secret.

When Hank was about ten, he dared his one-year-younger brother to dress in girl's clothes. The brother was discovered and severely beaten and ridiculed within the family and at school; his mother made him wear a dress to school the next day. Hank vowed that would not happen to him. However, when Hank was about twelve his mother caught him cross-dressed and beat him brutally with the admonition to "act like a man." She informed the rest of the house of his behavior and most of the household joined in the ridicule.

Academically Hank did not do well although he says he tried hard. He also felt he was a "loner." This led to truancy and school fights when other kids teased him. He claims to have won all these fights and was soon accepted because of his strength and athletic ability. Indeed, sports and athleticism were Hank's strong suit. At elementary, middle, and high school Hank was known as a medal-winning athlete in track and field, wrestling, and football (middle linebacker). He definitely did not shun rough-and-tumble play.

At the age of twelve, after taking his friend's bike as a prank and riding it around town, Hank was charged as a thief—his pugnaciousness had marked him around this small town. He was placed in the local jail for two weeks to "cure him from being a problem kid." When in jail he was sent for psychological testing and counseling. Hank was found to be dyslexic but with an IQ he claims tested at 160. Teachers vouched for his willing and bright participation in class but poor test performance. This jibed with his then-unknown reading and writing dyslexia. As a result of his test scores and the psychologist's recommendation, Hank was advanced a grade but no treatment was available for his dyslexia. This led to further ridicule from his family and schoolmates (and more fights).

With puberty Hank started to masturbate. He did not like to masturbate touching his penis, however, since it reminded him he was male. He masturbated touching his thighs and nipples and fantasizing an erotic relationship in which he was a female with a heterosexual male.

To cover his burgeoning erotic and romantic interest in cross-dressing and boys, from about the age of fourteen Hank developed a relationship with a girl who lived in a distant town. The distance between the two towns reduced the opportunities for physical contact. During this period Hank didn't engage in any sexual activities. As a sports star in school he had many heterosexual advances made to him but all were declined. No homosexual advances were made; Hank attributes this to the homophobia of the community.

Although he still craved the parental love and affection he was denied, to get away from the abuse and ridicule at home and obtain a modicum of freedom and privacy, Hank left home at the age of sixteen. Heedless of the winter cold, he went to live alone in a barn outside of town. He continued in school and supported himself by working after school and weekends as an airplane mechanic's helper at a nearby airport. (Hank had, at the age of twelve, joined the Civil Air Patrol for the thrill of flying and, as a cadet, worked as an airplane mechanic's helper.)

While Hank was alone in his crude lodgings, the sheriff came to look in on him and found him fully cross-dressed. In consultation with Hank's mother, the sheriff offered Hank three choices: go to jail for breaking the local law against cross-dressing; go to a psychiatric facility to "get cured" of his fetish; join the military and leave town. Hank chose to enlist. He also saw this as an opportunity to prove that, indeed, he really was a man. His mother and the sheriff had, in fact, said to him: "Good decision; this will make a man of you."

While still sixteen Hank passed the test for Navy enlistment but had to wait until his seventeenth birthday to report for service. Hank chose and was granted training in the Navy's Aircraft Maintenance school. While in school, Hank's physical and athletic abilities so impressed his drill instructors they recommended him for additional training that could use his physical abilities.

With Hank's dyslexia still a problem he accepted the opportunity for further training after graduation from the Navy school. With this he learned he had been "volunteered" to become part of the Navy's Underwater Demolition Team and then, when it was activated, part of the Navy's first class of SEALs.[6] Hank reenlisted as a SEAL team member and served two tours of duty in Vietnam under extremely hazardous and demanding conditions; many of his activities are still considered top secret today. After seven years in the Navy, five of them as a SEAL, Hank wanted to be and was seen and accepted as a man among men. Hank had a girlfriend at home as a "cover" during much of this time, but since he was overseas and she in the United States, his lack of overt sexual activity did not arouse suspicion among his shipmates. While in the military Hank had his first homosexual experience at seventeen and first heterosexual coitus at twenty. During his military career he never cross-dressed.

One night Hank got very drunk and broke into the enlisted men's club after hours and was caught by the authorities drinking at the bar. He was charged and sentenced to the brig. While in the brig he physically fought with his cell mate to the extent that both had to be hospitalized. His injuries were such that Hank was granted a medical discharge.

Hank returned home and over the next three to four years took a series of jobs as an airplane mechanic, crewman on a tugboat, and other masculine-identified jobs: bodyguard, stud in both heterosexual and homosexual "adult" movies, commercial diver repairing ocean-going vessels, martial-arts instructor. During these years he simultaneously attended school and obtained a Master's degree in Physical Education. He then went to work as a P.E. instructor at a high school. Out of the service and in private Hank resumed cross-dressing. During this period, at the age of twenty-six, Hank first heard of the Erickson Educational Foundation and became aware of resources of possible aid to transsexuals. This to him "offered a prayer to all the problems about what I was."

Despite success in these demanding masculine situations, Hank could not displace his own doubts about his maleness or his belief that his true sex was female. Although he could meet the rigorous tests of masculinity required by the SEALs and the erotic demands of his wife, throughout these years, he still believed himself a female trapped into a muscular body. To his inner female convictions, passing these successful self-tests were insufficient to reinforce his male identity or dispel his female identity. He flunked all his tests. Despite meeting every possible challenge to "being a male," Hank nevertheless ended up feeling himself a female. His wife was sympathetic to his inner feelings but confused by the external realities with which she was presented.

Subsequently Hank had depilitation, went on estrogens, and planned male-to-female genital surgery. "Harriet" and her ex-wife presently live together as platonic sisters. Harriet appears as a muscular and masculine woman and presently, years later, stays at home and does the housework while her wife provides the major family support. Harriet is more content with life now than in the past when living as a man.

Case #2: Jan Morris

The life of Jan Morris, as presented in her book *Conundrum* (1974), further illustrates self-testing identity. After Christine Jorgensen (Hamburger, Stürup, and Dahl-Iversen 1953), Morris is perhaps the best-known male-to-female transsexual. In her book Morris offers testimony to what might be considered components of her self-testing. She writes:

- "I was three or perhaps four years old when I realized that I had been born into the wrong body, and should really be a girl." (15)

- "It is true that my mother had wished me to be a daughter, but I was never treated as one. . . . I was not . . . thought effeminate." (16)

- "[I] volunteered for the army at 17 [The ninth Lancers; a mechanized cavalry regiment] . . . and [although I was successful in my position and accepted by my colleagues in arms] far from making a man of me, it made me feel profoundly feminine at heart." (39)

  ". . . [T]he insight it afforded me of life in an entirely male adult world was curiously gentle and considerate." (40)

  ". . . The army had confirmed my intuition that I was fundamentally different from my male contemporaries." (43)

- "... [A]s to my sense of gender, I knew it to be as different from that of my friends as cheese from chalk, or thump from serenade. I could not share the urgency of the male impulse, or the unquestioning sense of manhood which bound these soldiers together. . . . I realized . . . how deeply a male sexuality lay beneath their conduct, and [although I could fake it] how profoundly I lacked it." (43)

- *"How could I be sure of my predicament? If I thought I felt like a woman, how could I know what a woman felt? What did I mean when I said I was feminine? . . . Were there confusions of identity? . . . When I left the Army I resolved to explore myself more deeply."* (55)

  "... *[W]as I sure that I was not just a suppressed homosexual, like so many others?"* (60, emphasis added.)

- Morris had heard of Harry Benjamin and went to see him. Benjamin accepted Morris's feelings but counseled: "Stick it out [as a male]. Do your best. Try to achieve an equilibrium, that's the best way. Take it easy!" "This advice I accepted." (63)[7]

- Bisexual in activity since college, Morris fell in love, married, and fathered five children, with a preference to have been mother rather than father. He described his marital relations thus: "We could scarcely call our sexual relationship a satisfactory one, since I would have been perfectly content without any sexual relationship at all. . . . But for me the actual performance of the sexual act seemed of secondary importance and interest." (68) There was, however, a great deal of affection, hugging, and erotic intimacy.

- Morris spent several years after his military stint traveling and working as a reporter covering wars and intrigue. In this capacity he jumped at the chance to join the first ascent of Mount Everest. Afterward Morris wrote: "The male body may be ungenerous, even uncreative in the deepest kind, but when it is working properly it is a marvelous thing to inhabit. . . . I think for sheer exuberance the best day of my life was my last on Everest." (96)

- "My sense of detachment [from the other climbers] was extreme. . . . I hated to think of myself as one of them. . . . A wayward self-consciousness . . . compelled me to keep up male appearances, perhaps as much for my own persuasion as for anyone else's. I even overdid it rather. I grew a beard and when at the end of the expedition I walked into the communications room at the British Embassy in Katmandu with my tin mug jangling from the belt of my trousers, the wireless operator asked acidly if I had [*sic*] to look so jungly. He did not know how cruelly the jibe hurt, for in a few words it cut this way and that through several skins of self-protection." (100)

- "Everest taught me new meanings of maleness, and emphasized once more my own inner dichotomy." (100)

- *"I have only lately come to see that incessant wandering as an outer expression of my inner journey."* (116, emphasis added.)

Despite success in the military, as a war correspondent, climbing Mount Everest, and as a father, despite social reinforcement as a male and the advice of Benjamin, Morris felt compelled to live life as a woman. His masculine experiences, rather than confirming his maleness, bolstered his hatred and resentment of his maleness and feelings of being female. Morris returned to Benjamin for sex-change advice and after prolonged endocrine therapy had the surgery in 1972. Although divorced, Morris, as did Hank and his spouse, maintained a loving and close relationship.

Case #3: Nancy Hunt

Nancy Hunt, another male-to-female transsexual, chronicled her life in a book *Mirror Image* (1978). She tells how she self-tested her identity.

- "I know by the age of four I was already aware that I had a girl's mind." (40)

- "By the day I graduated [prep school], I had achieved the status of a minor celebrity [by withstanding the physical fights and attacks of the other boys without crying]. More than that, I had survived the annealing fires of manhood. . . . I knew well enough that I was not a girl—had only to look at what my body had become: five feet ten inches tall, skinny as a fence post, muscles hard, beard growing, hair sprouting on chest and stomach. Secret dreams aside, I was locked in an undoubtedly male body, and like most adolescent male bodies it was bubbling with hormones and potent as a cocked pistol." (59)

- With puberty Hunt began to masturbate and occasionally dated. His feelings about girls he expressed thus: "I seethed with envy while at the same time becoming sexually aroused—I wanted to possess them even as I wanted to become them. In my nighttime fantasies, as I masturbated or floated toward sleep, I combined the two compulsions, dreaming of sex but with myself as the girl, my partner blanked out because I so loathed the male body, even my own." (60)

- With the start of World War II Hunt was determined to enlist. At the end of his basic training he was convinced he was a "tough, rugged, fighting Infantryman. . . . I could march twenty-two miles with a full field pack and an M-1 rifle, carry a 60-mm mortar up a mountain, chin myself fifty times with my hands the wrong way around on the bar, [and] kill a man with any of seventeen weapons, including the hand grenade, the .30-caliber light machine gun (air-cooled), and the bayonet. Now when I studied myself in the company mirror, I thought I saw a tough, dangerous, competent man. The military uniform always bolstered my masculine self-image, a fact that I suspect holds true for many men." (61)

- *"And for two blissful years of Army service I believed I had established my credentials as a man among men. I cherished this belief even as, night after night, lying on my iron cot, I dreamed of being a girl."* (62, emphasis added.)

- ". . . [A]s buck sergeant . . . those chevrons on my sleeves symbolized my membership in the community of men, my acceptance by . . . all the other soldiers whose self-assured virility I so much envied. To this day, I secretly celebrate the anniversary of my promotion to sergeant . . . though I have long since forgotten the dates of my college gradation, my two weddings, and my children's birthdays." (65)

- ". . . [H]ere was I, a former buck sergeant, tough, profane, and determined to succeed as a man." (39)

- "[Following my discharge and while going to college] I associated almost exclusively with veterans, attempting to extend the manly triumph of my Army career." (68)

- "Never having heard of transsexualism, I supposed I must be a homosexual, and the thought sickened me. . . . To contemplate homosexuality, to imagine the embrace of sinewy arms and hairy legs so like my own, dismayed me." (69)

- *"[Upon being recalled to active duty for the Korean War] military life had lost its power to assure me of my manhood. . . . I knew now that the military life was a delusion, but I had no other. . . . [After discharge] I turned my face resolutely in another direction and set out once more to prove myself a man."* (71–72, emphasis added.)

- Hunt became a reporter and then a copy-editor. "Newspaper city rooms ranked then with the locker rooms of professional football teams among the great bastions of masculinity. . . . I drew comfort from the hearty environment of the city room and felt myself to be a man among men, much as I felt in the Army." (76)

- "[Later, at twenty-nine years of age and again living at home] continuing to fantasize about being a woman, I remained a male virgin. In that depressing situation, marriage seemed a likely way to gain approval as a male and as a human being. To prove my claim . . . I married a girl." (77)

- "Until I became a parent [with two daughters and a son], I assumed that sex-typed behavior is acquired, but my own children convinced me that it arises spontaneously." (83)

- "[My wife] saw in me those male attributes she had come to hate and fear accentuated all the more by my determination to practice them and be as much of a man as I could. And to the extent that I succeeded in those efforts I failed in my marriage." (85)

- "I wormed my way into the sailboat-racing fraternity . . . crewing . . . in the big offshore boats . . . on whose sails the wind exerted terrifying forces. . . . And if a gale caught us with everything standing, my heart filled with cold fear. *But though I was often frightened, I continued to sail. It was a man's world. . . . If I could survive there I could prove myself a man.*" (85–86, emphasis added.)

- "[As a newspaper writer] I specialized in the most masculine stories I could find or devise, anything that would take me into a world where I could study and enjoy the way men conduct themselves . . . firemen, high-tension linemen, parachute jumpers, treasure divers. . . . I slept in the open with the Green Berets while snow fell on my face. . . . I spent countless nights with policemen, breaking down doors on vice raids and accompanying them into the most perilous cesspools of the city where snipers would fire on us from the windows of public housing high rises. (87)

Many exploits to prove his manhood were undertaken, including serving as a combat reporter in Vietnam. Falling in love with and marrying two different women were also part of the self-test.

- "I had made a fetish and a profession of manhood. (Indeed I had once written an article on what it means to be a man, and the United States Marine Corps [rewarded me for it].)" (150)

- "And there lay the heart of my dilemma: I could no longer endure pretending to be something I was not. Deceit is a tiring occupation, and despite all biological evidence to the contrary, despite my military record and my Yale degree, despite my swearing and my mustache, I knew my masculinity was fraudulent. If I were ever to make peace with myself, I would have to confront not the hairy, balding, tweed-clad façade that I presented to the world, but the person who lived inside—myself, Nancy, a woman." (262)

Thus, Hunt provides another example of an individual who tested himself, found social success as a male, was reinforced by his peers, family, and culture, yet goes on to transsexual surgery and life as a contented woman. Despite external clues to his masculine nature and gender identity, Nancy's internal cues to her female sexual identity were more potent.

Female-to-Male Transsexuals

Case #4: Barbara*

Barbara is my example of self-testing identity in a female-to-male transsexual. Like the cases of the MtF presented above, Barbara is unusual in the extent to which this phenomenon is seen.

Barbara first appeared in my office with her husband; she was dressed in jeans with a loose shirt and her long hair up in a tight bun. They came as a couple but each had a very separate agenda. His desire was for me to convince his wife that she really was a woman and not the man she claimed to be. Barbara wanted my advice on how to precede in her desire to live as a man. As a striking brunette Barbara was a most attractive woman in face and figure. Then in her early thirties, Barbara first became convinced she was male about the age of seven. Even at that time she recalls always being seen as a tomboy by others but as a real boy to herself.

Life events in her rearing, childhood, and adolescence were not remarkable. As she matured, the attention of the boys and men with which she came into contact continued to emphasize that indeed she was female. As a female beauty she was repeatedly the object of male attention. Barbara denied her attractiveness and explained away the focus of the males as due not to her features or reality, but just their indiscriminate lust. Men had been approaching her and, much to her dismay, touching her sexually since she was a teenager. She herself recalls being attracted to and aroused by females from her teenage years. Her first sexual encounter was with a female at twenty-three years of age.

Home conditions, in a small West Coast farming community, seemed supportive and were considered to have its "normal ups and downs." She recalls her home life and family as nurturing and caring. She had a brother eight years her junior. Barbara, at the age of eighteen, left home after completing high school to follow a career as an actress and professional fashion model. Her success as a beautiful female was in conflict with her inner feelings that she was a male. Again she felt her appeal was dependent upon males wanting sex from her. She claims she never gave in to the male advances. As she got older and modeling positions decreased and acting situations were sparse, someone suggested, with her attributes, she try stripping.

In a classic example of self-testing reasoning, Barbara rationalized that her success as a stripper would prove to herself she really was a female and remove

---

*This is a pseudonym.

all doubt as to her being a male. The men in the audience, she thought, would know she was not available to them and would thus judge her on her female merits alone. To further her career and, in her own words, "leave no stone unturned in proving myself a woman, I had a 'boob job.' " Suffice it to say she was successful enough as a stripper to achieve national stature sufficient to require a full-time manager. On a worldwide tour, she was in Honolulu when she came to see me. Her stage name was, at the time, widely recognizable to devotees of stripping.

She married her manager, her only husband, nine years prior to seeking counseling. This was his third marriage but her first. Despite the worldly success and adulation as a female, Barbara could not dispel her male feelings and had only several weeks before told her husband of her conviction she was a male despite "fighting such feelings for years" and appearances to him and the world. She thought "exotic romantic Hawaii as the appropriate location to broach the topic."

Her only bow toward masculine habits seemed to be, she had for some time been wearing men's jockey shorts as underwear. Her husband just thought that another sign of her "tomboy" nature. Barbara had also, several months earlier, met a female friend with whom she started a close sexual relationship.

Barbara's satisfactory abilities as a wife were testified to by her loving and attentive husband who thought she was "crazy" with these thoughts. He felt she was "just the woman he wanted." Before this recent revelation Barbara always wanted to be called by her real (feminine) name rather than her stage name or a male name. Her husband described her as not only beautiful and sexy but also feminine in mannerisms and attitudes. Barbara did not deny that she tried in all ways to please her husband sexually and otherwise. But now she adopted a gender-ambiguous name and wanted to be seen as the male she felt herself to be.

Barbara had a son from a previous relationship who was adopted by her present husband. Having this child was a further additional female self-test in Barbara's eyes. It simultaneously proved her femininity in the husband's eyes. The son, ten years old at the time, traveled with his parents and was interviewed alone and in private. Barbara had also told her son of her emotional conflicts. He saw his mother as appropriate in demeanor and, her occupation and fame aside, "just like other moms" in regard to female-ness. He was appropriately concerned with the future but wanted to stay with his mom regardless. Barbara's female lover came to Hawaii and was also interviewed. She claimed she had no preference for Barbara to be male or female. She "loved the person, not the shell."

Despite Barbara's success as a female, she now felt she had to live as a male. She said she had always been severely depressed every menses. Having a slight flow, she would often leave her tampon in for prolonged periods so she "wouldn't have to deal with them." Everything seemed to be coming to a head at once. She now fully realized she could not feel peace as a female and, without her husband's or female lover's knowledge, seriously considered suicide. She had also recently informed her parents of her desires and they threatened to disown her although her mother volunteered, "I always knew you were strange in that way." Barbara nevertheless wanted to proceed with her female-to-male transition.

After counseling over a three-week period the couple left Hawaii for scheduled performances in Japan but Barbara kept in touch by mail. Upon return to the United States, against her husband's wishes, the couple divorced. Barbara cut off her long tresses, gave up her lucrative stripping career, and started to live as a man. He bound his breasts to minimize them and was planning to remove the implants. He now took androgens and lived with his female lover. Several months later "Bob" wrote to tell me he was working as a salesman and made plans for sex-change surgery. He retained custody of the son. Contact was lost after that.

Although eminently successful and reinforced as a professional stripper and domestic wife and mother, Barbara felt, nevertheless, she had to live her life as Bob. His inner voice was stronger than her external reinforcement. Her self-test convinced her that although she could easily pass any test of female gender identity she could not pass her own self-test of sexual identity.[8]

Discussion

There is little doubt that the lives of transsexuals can be quite variable from each other and there is no one life that typifies all (e.g., Bentler 1976; Blanchard and Steiner 1990; Bullough and Bullough 1993; Green 1974; Meyer 1974; Pauly 1969a, 1969b, Tsoi, Kok, and Long 1977). Nevertheless, tabloid presentations of transsexuals often play up the before-and-after contrasts; the macho male becoming the feminine female, and so on. The cases presented here illustrate this to a marked degree. These cases also exemplify that even full and demonstrated success and acceptance in one's sex of birth and rearing can be insufficient to allay a feeling of mismatch between gender identity and sexual identity. Although reinforcement and success in society and concordance with social expectations exist, an individual can nevertheless feel drawn to a sexual and gender "calling" that may lead to ridicule and social opprobrium. Indeed, many have little hope of "passing" undetected in their new life yet choose this difficult social path. In all four cases presented, the individuals were engaged in loving relationships that they had to alter. By leaving their sex of birth, they all risked a substantial decrease in income. By rejecting their sex of birth they all left successful professions. There were no indications these individuals were not fully capable, rational, and sentient.

The question arises why such histories as those presented here seem rare in comparison with those for whom life was a succession of events demonstrating attempts or actual success in living as a member of the opposite sex. Part of this is believed due to the fact that indeed unconvinced transsexuals are not as prevalent or visible as are convinced transsexuals. Also believed critical are the criteria originally established for selecting candidates for the limited surgical slots available. As Fisk (1975) recounts: "we [at Stanford] went about seeking so-called 'ideal candidates,' and a great emphasis was placed upon attempting to exclusively treat only classical, or 'textbook cases' of transsexualism." Stoller (1971) proposed that only individuals who at no stage in their development showed masculine behavior be diagnosed as transsexual. Other centers, to reduce the likelihood of regrettable surgeries, did similarly. And once establishing such criteria of longstanding and continuous outright, gender-wished-for behavior, it is not difficult to see why such cases became dominant in practice and case reports.

The current DSM-IV criteria for "Gender Identity Disorder" also states: "there must be evidence of clinically significant distress or impairment in social, occupational, or other important areas of functioning." (1994, 533) The individuals described in the present report were able to function well in these areas. Their distress, however, was psychic and persistent. By the criteria mentioned above and those in the DSM-IV these four would not have been considered for surgery. Future editions of the DSM and surgical criteria should take account of self-testing and the manifestations of gender identity disorder described.

The origin of *dysphoric* male and female feelings arises from within, from the individual's endowment of emotions mixed with the daily living test confrontation with reality. For the majority of transsexuals this results in an early-in-life capitulation. For others, however, there is a prolonged self-test period during which the transsexual convinces him- or herself that how one can live is not necessarily how one desires or prefers to live.

It must also be mentioned that recommendations for transsexual counseling and presurgical treatment require the candidate to undergo a *real-life test*, usually for a period of one to two years, during which he or she lives as a member of the desired sex (e.g., Clemmensen 1990; Meyer and Hoopes 1974; Money and Wiedeking 1980). This requirement, one of several seen as crucial prior to sex change surgery by the Harry Benjamin International Gender Dysphoria Association, Inc. (Walker et al. 1985), demands a period during which the individual sees how the new life confirms or denies expectations. For the true transsexual this real-life test is much easier than the living-test or any self-test. It is seen as a relief.

Previous publications have indicated in broad terms how this inner identity is believed to come about (e.g., Diamond 1965, 1968, 1977, 1979, 1993, 1994) and other types of examples have been offered that show an innate sexual identity as a male develops despite social reinforcement as a female (Diamond 1982; Diamond and Sigmundson 1995). The details of this process of sexual identity formation are still to be elucidated. Nevertheless, it seems fairly certain that this inner voice can develop without reinforcement and social approval for the desired sex and with ample reinforcement in the nondesired sex. And it can occur in the face of a socially adverse future and provide an inner personal calm more important than any external rewards.

Lastly, while probably true that self-testing is seen most dramatically among transsexuals coming to terms with their identity, it is also seen when they have to cope with measuring themselves, before and after surgery, against their peers and social expectations on other levels. Indeed, to one degree or another self-testing is demonstrated by everyone along five *levels* of an individual's sexual profile: *gender Patterns, Reproduction, Identity, Mechanisms, Object choice (PRIMO)* (Diamond 1977, 1979). Many of these self-tests are so ubiquitous they pass as normal, as instinctual, or are seen as examples of simple experimentation and curiosity. They can, moreover, also be arduous challenges of "Is this right/wrong for me? Does this suit me or not? How do I feel when I do such-and-so?" Such self-testing is a common accompaniment to puberty and adolescence—not wanting to be different unless it is to excel—but often continues into adulthood. Part of growing up is testing one's limits. "Spreading wings" often infers moving in directions new and challenging. Such self-tests are brief or extended; they might be outwardly mundane or dramatic.

Everyone, male or female, transsexual or not, consciously or not, tests their "fit" with gender patterns offered by society; this is *self-test gender*. This is wide ranging, from the clothes one will choose to the occupations or leisure pursuits one adopts. *Self-test reproduction* occurs when one has a child to "prove" one's self. One often *self-tests mechanisms* with experimentation with orgasm, sexual arousal, and sexual performance of one type or another; e.g., "Why can Sally have multiple orgasms and I none?" or "Can I delay my ejaculation to better please my partner?" And, often dramatically, persons *self-test object choice*. Experimenting with male and female partners during puberty and adolescence can be viewed as such. And dating is often a more sophisticated example of this.

Often several levels are tested simultaneously and, unfortunately, at the expense of others. For instance, not a few marriages are entered into and children conceived in order to fulfill self-tests. Then, marriages consummated and children reared, many of these individuals admit to themselves and their partners that the relationship might have been loving and fulfilling and satisfactory on the outside, but it was unfulfilling and disappointing on the inside. They then change their life to concur with their inner feelings. All four of our examples demonstrated this. Self-testing along the other four of our five levels of sexual expression needs a detailed and full exposition of its own.

The phenomenon of self-testing is thus most clearly seen with transsexuals and identity. Considered in broadest terms, however, it is a process everyone experiences on all levels. The conclusion from this returns us to the old adage: "The most important sex organ is not between the legs; it's between the ears."

Notes

1. Gender has been defined in many ways . For this paper, as I've done in the past, I emphasize that *gender identity* is distinct from *sexual identity* and keeping this distinction is useful (Diamond 1976, 1979, 1993).

2. Five *levels* of sexual expression have been described that together present a distinct sexual profile for any individual. These five levels are: sexual Patterns (gender roles), Reproduction, sexual Identity, sexual Mechanisms, and sexual Orientation (Diamond, 1979, 1980, 1992). The acronym PRIMO is helpful in keeping these in mind.

3. It is true that some nontechnical societies conceive of a third sex. But even such a category is a modification of male or female (see Williams 1986). True hermaphroditism, and others with ambiguous genitalia, is extremely rare and not considered here (see Fausto-Sterling 1993).

4. As this area of sex and gender has developed, so too has a diverse set of terms to describe the variations that exist. Along with the term *transsexual,* one must define *transvestite*: a heterosexual individual, most usually male, who derives erotic or nonerotic personal satisfaction from dressing in the clothes of the opposite sex while not believing him- or herself to be a member of the opposite sex. A *drag queen* is a homosexual male preferring to live, at least a preponderance of the time, as a woman. The *transgenderist* is one who sees him- or herself as wanting to live at least components of the life of the opposite sex with or without sex-change surgery or other body modification. For the transvestite and the transgenderist, the desire to live as the opposite sex may be periodic and not permanent. Often, the term transgenderist is used broadly to include transsexuals, transvestites, drag queens, and others who somehow mix and match personal, social, and cultural views of what it means to be a male or female, a man or woman.

5. The term *identity* itself has many meanings, both technical and lay. For this paper it will be used only in the sense defined.

6. The SEALs (Sea, Air, and Land special forces) are recognized as requiring among the most demanding physical and diverse abilities of any military special forces units. More than half of those volunteering for this duty do not make the grade (Waller 1994).

7. This being early in Benjamin's experience with transsexuals, and with Morris so outwardly masculine, I guess Benjamin was being cautious. Had Morris been more effeminate or Benjamin seen other MtFs so masculine, perhaps he would have been more supportive of sex change.

8. Following the presentation of my talk at the conference, I was gratified to have several members of the audience come to me and relate how my presentation seemed to echo their lives. Several individuals, each in private, admitted having actually, in combat, subjected himself purposely to tests of manhood with risk of death. They emphasized the point by adding they didn't care if they lived or died in the "experiment" since life as they knew it, with the identity confusion, was not worth living anyway. Following their heroic military experiences they were able to make the transition in their lives realizing the inner strength demonstrated by their self-tests.

References

American Psychiatric Association. 1994. *Diagnostic and statistical manual of mental disorders.* 4th ed., s.v. "Gender Identity Disorder." Washington D.C.: American Psychiatric Association, 532–38.

Benjamin, H. 1966. *The transsexual phenomenon.* New York: Julian Press.

Bentler, P. M. 1976. A typology of transsexualism: Gender identity theory and data. *Archives of Sexual Behavior* 5, no. 6: 567–84.

Blanchard, R., and B. W. Steiner, eds. 1990. *Clinical management of gender identity disorders in children and adults.* Washington, D.C.: American Psychiatric Press.

Bolin, A. 1987. *In search of Eve: Transsexual rites of passage.* South Hadley, Mass.: Bergin & Garvey.

Bullough, V. L., and B. Bullough. 1993. *Cross dressing, sex, and gender.* Philadelphia: University of Pennsylvania Press.

Clemmensen, L. H. 1990. The real-life test for surgical candidates. In *Clinical management of gender identity disorders in children and adults,* edited by R. Blanchard and B. W. Steiner, 121–35. Washington, D.C.: American Psychiatric Press.

Diamond, M. 1965. A critical evaluation of the ontogeny of human sexual behavior. *Quarterly Review of Biology* 40: 147–75.

———. 1968. Genetic-endocrine interaction and human psychosexuality. In *Perspectives in reproduction and sexual behavior,* edited by M. Diamond, 417–43. Bloomington: Indiana University Press.

———. 1974. Transsexualism. *Medical Journal of Australia* (January 12): 51.

———. 1977. Human sexual development: Biological foundations for social development. In *Human sexuality in four perspectives,* edited by F. A. Beach, 22–60. Baltimore: The Johns Hopkins Press.

———. 1979. Sexual identity and sex roles. In *The frontiers of sex research,* edited by V. Bullough, 33–56. Amherst, N.Y.: Prometheus Books.

———. 1982. Sexual identity, monozygotic twins reared in discordant sex roles and a BBC follow-up. *Archives of Sexual Behavior* 11, no. 2: 181–85.

———. 1993. Some genetic considerations in the development of sexual orientation. In *The development of sex differences and similarities in behaviour,* edited by M. Haug, R. E. Whalen, C. Aron, and K. L. Olsen, 291–309. Dordrecht/Boston/London: Kluwer Academic Publishers.

———. 1994. Sexuality: Orientation and identity. In *Encyclopedia of psychology,* edited by R. J. Corsini, 399–402. New York: John Wiley & Sons.

Diamond, M., and A. Karlen. 1980. *Sexual decisions.* Boston: Little, Brown.

Diamond, M., and K. Sigmundson. 1995. Sexual identity and sex reassignment. In preparation.

Docter, R. F. 1988. *Transvestites and transsexuals: Toward a theory of cross-gender behavior.* New York: Plenum Press.

Dörner, G. 1988. Neuroendocrine response to estrogen and brain differentiation in heterosexuals, homosexuals, and transsexuals. *Archives of Sexual Behavior* 17: 57–75.

DSM-IV. 1994. See American Psychiatric Association, 1994.

Epstein, S. 1973. The self-concept revisited: Or a theory of a theory. *American Psychologist* 28: 404–16.

Fausto-Sterling, A. 1993. The five sexes: Why male and female are not enough. *The Sciences* (March/April): 20–25.

Feinbloom, D. H. 1976. *Transvestites & transsexuals: Mixed views.* New York: Delacorte Press/Seymour Lawrence.

Fisk, N. M. 1975. *Gender dysphoria syndrome (The how, what, and why of a disease).* Stanford, Calif.: Division of Reconstructive and Rehabilitation Surgery, Stanford University Medical Center.

Green, R. 1974. *Sexual identity conflict in children and adults.* New York: Basic Books.

Green, R., and J. Money, eds. 1969. *Transsexualism and sex reassignment.* Baltimore, Md.: The Johns Hopkins Press.

Hamburger, C., G. K. Stürup, and E. Dahl-Iversen. 1953. Transvestism, hormonal, psychiatric and surgical treatment. *Journal of the American Medical Association* 152: 391–96.

Hunt, N. 1978. *Mirror Image.* New York: Holt, Rinehart and Winston.

Huston, A. C. 1983. Sex-Typing. In *Handbook of child psychology,* 4th ed., edited by P. H. Mussen. New York: John Wiley & Sons.

Kando, T. 1973. *Sex change: The achievement of gender identity among feminized transsexuals.* Springfield, Ill.: Charles C. Thomas.

Mehl, M. C. 1975. *Transsexualism: A perspective.* Stanford, Calif.: Division of Reconstructive and Rehabilitation Surgery, Stanford University Medical Center, 15–24.

Meyer, J. K. 1974. Clinical variants among applicants for sex reassignment. *Archives of Sexual Behavior* 3: 527–58.

Meyer, J. K., and J. E. Hoopes. 1974. The gender dysphoria syndromes: A position statement on so-called transsexualism. *Plastic and Reconstructive Surgery* 54: 444–51.

Money, J., and C. Wiedeking. 1980. Gender identity/role: Normal differentiation and its transpositions. In *Handbook of human sexuality,* edited by Barbara Wolman and J. Money, 269–84. Englewood Cliffs, N.J.: Prentice-Hall.

Morris, J. 1974. *Conundrum.* New York: Harcourt Brace Jovanovich.

Pauly, I. B. 1969a. Adult manifestation of male transsexualism. In *Transsexualism and sex reassignment,* edited by R. Green and J. Money, 37–58. Baltimore, Md.: The Johns Hopkins Press.

———. 1969b. Adult manifestation of female transsexualism. In *Transsexualism and sex reassignment,* edited by R. Green and J. Money, 59–87. Baltimore, Md.: The Johns Hopkins Press.

Stoller, R. J. 1968. *Sex and gender: On the development on masculinity and femininity.* New York: Science House.

———. 1969. Parental influences in male transsexualism. In *Transsexualism and sex reassignment,* edited by R. Green and J. Money, 153–69. Baltimore, Md.: The Johns Hopkins Press.

———. 1971. The term "transvestism." *Archives of General Psychiatry* 24: 230–37.

Tsoi, W. F., L. P. Kok, and F. Y. Long. 1977. Male transsexualism in Singapore: A description of 56 cases. *British Journal of Psychiatry* 131: 405–409.

Wålinder, J. 1967. *Transsexualism: A study of forty-three cases.* Göteborg: Scandinavian University Books.

Walker, P. A., J. C. Berger, R. Green, D. R. Laub, C. L. Reynolds, Jr., and L. Wollman. 1990. *Standards of care: The hormonal and surgical sex reassignment of gender dysphoric persons.* Palo Alto, Calif.: The Harry Benjamin International Gender Dysphoria Association.

Waller, D. C. 1994. *The commandos.* New York: Simon & Schuster.

Williams, W. L. 1986. *The spirit and the flesh: Sexual diversity in American culture.* Boston: Beacon Press.

Ziegler, D. J. 1994. Transsexualism. In *Encyclopedia of psychology,* edited by R. J. Corsini, 550–51. New York: John Wiley.

Zucker, K. J. 1990. Gender identity disorders in children: Clinical descriptions and natural history. In *Clinical management of gender identity disorders in children and adults,* edited by R. Blanchard and B. W. Steiner, 3–23. Washington, D.C.: American Psychiatric Press.

Zucker, K. J., S. J. Bradley, and C. B. Sullivan. 1992. Gender identity disorder in children. *Annual Review of Sex Research* 3: 73–120.

Multiple Personality *Order*: A Response to Trauma and the Development of the Cross-Gender Experience

William A. Henkin

As we collectively search for a better understanding of the cross-gender experience, I would like to propose the term "Multiple Personality Order" as an approach to describing the phenomenon. Let me use myself as an example. A few months ago I had a telephone call from a prospective client who wanted to know why, considering how important I find Juliette, my own principal femme persona, I was not transsexual. I explained that, important as she is and important as her contributions are to the whole structure of my personality, Juliette does not control a large enough portion of my inner life to command my outer life effectively.

Perhaps because I spoke of Juliette so readily, as if she were a separate person, the caller asked if I had multiple personalities. I answered that I did, but not the way I thought he meant; and I explained that as I understand the process, there is a continuum of dissociation ranging from Dissociative Identity Disorder at one extreme, or what used to be called Multiple Personality *Disorder,* to what I've come to call Multiple Personality *Order* at the other. Multiple Personality Disorder, or MPD, is a relatively rare condition. Multiple Personality Order, or MPO, on the other hand, seems to me to be extremely common.

Classically, someone whose multiple personalities are disordered has "two or more distinct identities or personality states (each with its own relatively enduring pattern of perceiving, relating to, and thinking about the environment and self) . . . at least two of [whom] recurrently take control of the person's behavior" (American Psychiatric Association 1994, 487, Diagnostic Criteria A and B). This individual has an "inability to recall important personal information that is too extensive to be explained by ordinary forgetfulness" (American Psychiatric Association

126

1994, 487, Diagnostic Criterion C). This form of amnesia is generally experienced as lost time, or as blanks in the person's life, that may, for example, cover a year or two in her history, or may cover a particular time of day over a period of months or years, or may cover a particular event or series of events. She might not remember her ninth year, for instance, or she may remember getting up in the morning and going to school, being in school, and going to bed at night, yet she may *not* remember ever coming home from school in the afternoon.

In addition, although it is not stipulated as a diagnostic criterion, at least one personality generally does not know about the existence of some or all of the others (American Psychiatric Association 1987, 270). A conservative, church-going adult who wears only tailored clothes and neither smokes nor drinks may feel bewildered to one morning find at the foot of her bed a gaudy gown, stained with whiskey and smelling of cigarettes, along with a picture of her in the gown on the arm of a disreputable playboy at the bar of a well-known nightclub.

When someone's multiple personalities are *in* order he technically may meet the first two diagnostic criteria (A and B) for MPD, but typically his memory is not unusually compromised thereby; and with increasing awareness of the process of his own dissociation, similar to the awareness we all can have of our own processes on a moment-to-moment basis, he experiences *co-consciousness*: the various sides of himself are at least somewhat aware of each other, they may converse with one another, and they can come to align themselves so that the single entity in which they are all contained—the individual—functions as an integrated team.

It is well documented in both the clinical and the popular literature that MPD is a creative survival response to what the individual experiences, usually early on, as some kind of trauma (Ross 1994; Chase 1987; Castle and Bechtel 1987; Coons 1986; Kluft 1985; Putnam 1985; Schreiber 1973). It is traumatic *because* it is too much to accommodate, too much to adapt to, and more input to process than someone is really equipped to handle.

Though it is generally acknowledged by students of dissociative disorders that alternate personalities "as they are originally developed are involved directly in survival and thus their modes of operation are necessarily severely focused in order to guarantee survival" (Sliker 1992, 31), I am using severe dissociation only as a model here so that we can see in its boldest relief a process I believe is entirely normal. I am not now talking about the multiple personalities of MPD, but rather of the alternate personalities of Multiple Personality Order (MPO), whose development is also a creative survival strategy.

The process of dissociation as I experience it in myself and observe it in other people both in and out of the consulting room is so common that phrases in our colloquial language attest to our individual diversity. For example:

- I'm of two minds about this.
- I'm beside myself with anger.
- Why don't you act your age?
- I don't feel like myself today.

Not only our language, but even our behavior expresses the most basic forms of dissociation: we do not bring the same personalities to interactions with our parents as we bring to interactions with our children. We do not bring the same personalities to work as we bring to play. We do not bring the same personalities to our spouses as we bring to our golfing buddies, or knitting buddies, or anyone else we pal around with. Perhaps the very fact that we're so different with different people reflects our need to allow our multiple parts to emerge, to breathe, and to grow. If so, our different personalities only become problematic when the process by which they come and go is not conscious or when it is out of control.

Since I am suggesting that we literally live multiple lives at once, it may not be surprising that my remarks are consonant with the explanation of reincarnation provided by the Buddhist scholar Walpola Rahula:

> It is a series that continues unbroken, but changes every moment. . . . It is like a flame that burns through the night: it is not the same flame nor is it another. A child grows up to be a man of sixty. Certainly the man of sixty is not the same as the child of sixty years ago, nor is he another person. Similarly, a person who dies here and is reborn elsewhere is neither the same person nor another. It is the continuity of the same series. (1959, 34)

Rahula's words apply equally well to the idea of reincarnation over many lifetimes, to our progress through one lifetime from birth to death, and to what any of us does on any single day.

It is possible, however, for these multiple personalities to be out of control. Back when I was working in a community mental health facility with a population described as "severely disturbed," I had a client who had just turned eighteen. He was tall, handsome, athletic, and newly diagnosed as schizophrenic. While I was chatting with him in the office one evening, he suddenly jumped up and started climbing the wall. Literally. He ran at the wall and ran up four or five feet before he fell down, then ran up the next wall and fell down again. He quickly became enraged and threatening.

We didn't have any tools to deal with an athletic young man who was out of control in that facility, so I followed protocol and called the police. Two minutes later a couple of officers ran into the house and wrestled the boy to the ground, and as they sat on him and handcuffed him he started to talk in voices. First some loud, angry male voice yelled, "Get your fucking hands off me!" Then a young, girlish voice asked, "What's happening? Please tell me what's happening! I don't understand!" Then a child cried and somebody else pled to let him go, and all the while the boy's face was changing right along with his voices.

As I read some of the literature about dissociation, I thought about his situation. One afternoon I found myself driving on the freeway in a most unseemly manner. I was speeding, swerving, passing other cars recklessly, and in general endangering myself and dozens of other motorists. Putting to use what I'd been learning, I asked myself who was driving. The image that immediately appeared on my personal mental screen was of a terrified little boy about two years old clutching the steering wheel that was too high for him, stretching for the gas pedal that was too low for him, and driving for all he was worth, trying desperately to follow the orders a young man was barking at him from the passenger seat: "Drive here! Go there! Pass that car! Go faster!" The baby, who wanted nothing but to gain the young man's love, was doing his best to obey, but nothing would really satisfy and I was in fear for my life. "Get in the back seat," I told them both: "I'll drive." And in my mind's eye I saw them both clamber over the seat back as I felt myself take conscious control of the car. The remainder of the journey was made safely, with no upset either internal or external.

When I concluded that the boy in my facility was not schizophrenic but was, rather, a multiple whose internal alignment had cracked under some kind of stress, I also realized that his personalities and mine had some generic similarities. The way multiples are supposed to develop—from severe, unremitting, unavoidable trauma, usually in very early childhood—then seemed to me to be a paradigm for how all personalities develop. For some people who become classically multiple the trauma was more severe, less remitting, less escapable, than it was for me, but the structure was the same.

After all, even in the very best of families, with the most ideal childhoods, we all had to do things we didn't want to do. We had to go to bed when we didn't want to, to learn to use the toilet instead of our diapers, learn to eat our Brussels sprouts, okra, or spinach—there was always some kind of nonconsensual domination that was more than a little kid could tolerate.

I am *not* saying that the process of socializing children is bad or wrong, and I am not saying we should avoid growing up. I am also not saying the development of alternate personae must be a wholly psychological process, or that there might not be a strong genetic or biochemical basis for it: sometimes I am sure there is.

I *am* saying that when people are confronted with circumstances that seem to threaten them in some way they cannot accommodate, they tend to split off facets of themselves to deal with them until their minds resemble cut gemstones: one heart with many faces.

The personae with whom I spoke in my car were Baby Billy and the Executive, whom I sometimes call the Psychopath. Like Juliette, they had been making their influences felt in my life for decades before I met them. The Executive's need for control, for example, coupled with his barely contained anger, had kept my friends from riding in my car during several volatile periods in my life. The Baby's profound need for acceptance, coupled with his inability to judge other people's trustworthiness, had led me into romantic and business liaisons everyone around but me could see were doomed. And Juliette had not only trimmed my tweed- and corduroy-filled closet with cashmeres and silks: she had given me an early career in music and helped me to gain and maintain my independence with her serenity and strength.

As time went on I learned to identify a dozen major and perhaps two dozen minor players on my internal stage. Arguably, each began as simply a limited ego state. But as I let them talk to me and to each other they fleshed out into satellite personalities around my organizing center. And as they took on lives of their own, they began to inform me about the nature and meaning of my interests, desires, and fears. The more real they became, the fuller and more satisfying my whole life became. The more real they became, in a sense, the more real I became.

Not surprisingly, one of the first tacit discussions of Multiple Personality Order—tacit because it did not have any such label at the time—came from within the gender community. When Virginia Prince founded the organization that became the Society for the Second Self in the early 1960s and acknowledged "the woman within" some morphological males, she anticipated by thirty years "the child within" that many people would discover in their quests to recover from childhood trauma. Where Prince and the recovery movement parted company—or, more properly, where they never met—was that she did not accept the conventional psychiatric definitions of her own experience as pathological, even as she sought to understand that experience with the help of psychotherapy. In other words, she was among the very first modern people to recognize the possibility of nonpathological multiplicity, or what Roberto Assagioli called a "pluridimensional conception of the human personality" (1965).

Docter (1988), Fraser (1991), and others have noted people in the gender communities who talk about their cross-gendered personae as alternate "selves." In her study of transsexualism Bolin (1988) specifically notes that "personal identity is envisaged as a hierarchy of identities such that one identity is primary and others are subidentities around which one organizes the self" (70).

Whether transvestites, transgenderists, transsexuals, gender benders, or shape-shifters of any sort, many people in the gender paraculture experience themselves somewhat differently in their variant than in their usual gender roles. While at first blush the differences may sometimes seem superficial, upon further examination they often turn out to encompass "relatively enduring pattern[s] of perceiving, relating to, and thinking about the environment and one's self . . . exhibited in a wide range of important social and personal contexts" (American Psychiatric Association 1987, 269).

In other words we experience all the components needed to satisfy the psychiatric designation of an alternate personality state, replete with variations from our baselines in feeling, thought, memory, posture, belief system, attitude, behavior patterns, and social relationships that are usually associated with a severe dissociative disorder. Yet unlike the experience reported by people with Multiple Personality Disorder, transes do not generally forget their customary identities while in their cross-gender personalities. Unlike people with Depersonalization Disorder, who report experiences of unreality, transes rarely feel unreal while in their cross-gender identities and are ordinarily quite able to recall important personal events of their usual personalities. In other words, despite having a full experience of living in an alternate personality, they satisfy none of the *pathological* hallmarks of dissociation.

The Society for the Second Self evokes by its very name the reality of alternate personalities, but if a man can have an inner woman, as Virginia Prince proposed, or if a woman can have an inner man, as Lou Sullivan asserted (1988), and if anyone can have an inner child or even multiple inner children, as some theorists have proposed (Pearson 1991), why can't one have a whole inner family?

Myth and religion provide intimations that multiple personalities have been common throughout history, because the many goddesses and gods of every pluralistic pantheon can be understood to represent different aspects of their cultures' people. For instance, a person can be dominated by the rational characteristics thought of as Apollonian or the passionate ones we call Dionysian, and still exhibit others relating to the virginal qualities of Artemis, or the sexually seductive ones of Aphrodite. Similar patterns reflect different aspect of human personality and are expressed in tarot, astrology, past-life regression, channeling and spirit guidance, palmistry, and any discipline that breaks the incorporeal human entity into component parts. In the modern West we've accommodated this process in the psychological tradition.

Dissociation was a fairly common notion in the West during the nineteenth and early twentieth centuries. It underlay the development of mesmerism, hypnosis, and various other trance-induced cures for mental and emotional problems (Ellenberger 1970). Around the turn of the last century Alfred Binet and William James both described cases of multiple personality, and both regarded dissociation as a likely model by which the enigma of the human mind might be understood and studied (James [1890] 1980; Binet 1886).

Jean Charcot, a seminal figure in Freud's development even though they worked together for only five months, saw features of dissociation in hysteria, but his mechanical view of the human being would not admit principles of non-physiological psychology (Ellenberger 1970). Another of Freud's teachers, Pierre Janet, was among the very first to examine dissociation and wrote about "secondary personalities" alternating with or operating behind what Assagioli calls the "everyday personality," and what I call the "front" personality (Janet 1889, cited in Assagioli 1965; Janet 1907). Some dozen additional cases of multiple personalities were written up in the United States before World War I; in all, some ninety cases of what we would understand today as Multiple Personality Disorder were reported in the *Index Medicus* and *Psychological Abstracts* between 1820 and 1960 (Baldwin 1984).

Not everything about dissociation was considered pathological a century ago. In the *Principles of Psychology* James ([1890] 1980) described a hierarchy of selves whose multitude constituted the "empirical me." As a boy Carl Jung was aware of having two personalities, and in his middle years he discovered several more, including a female named Salome (Sliker 1992). Roberto Assagioli, whose theories of psychosynthesis underlie a great deal of subpersonality work today, claimed that "Everyone has different selves—it is normal" (Allesandro Berti, as quoted in Sliker 1992, 13).

We know that in Multiple Personality Disorder some personalities display allergic reactions to substances that other personalities in the same body do not exhibit. I have seen eye color change from persona to persona, and I have a client whose chiropractor reports that while the male host personality's legs are of unequal length, the legs of his leading female personality are quite even (Berry 1993).

Despite the interest of his teachers and colleagues, Freud based his work on a model of repression rather than pursue dissociation (Freud [1900] 1955). Although first regarded as outrageous and radical, his views soon became psychological orthodoxy, and less attention was paid to dissociation. There were almost no cases of dissociation or MPD reported in the literature between 1920 and the 1950s. Even though one of the most important psychological texts of its day, William McDougall's *Outline of Abnormal Psychology* (1926), contained references to numerous cases of "coconscious personalities," the dissociative model had already fallen into a state of clinical disregard from which it did not begin to emerge for more than thirty years, when two psychiatrists, Corbett Thigpen and Hervey Cleckley, published *The Three Faces of Eve,* a popular account of their treatment of an MPD patient (1957).

For the next sixteen years isolated reports of multiplicity once again trickled into the professional journals. In 1973 a second popular book, *Sybil* (Schreiber 1973), alerted the public to this most dramatic dissociative condition. At about the same time other psychologists began to acknowledge the possibility of MPD, and cases started to be reviewed again in the journals (Baldwin 1984).

In the 1920s and 1930s, Jacob Moreno developed psychodrama, a theatrical approach to psychotherapy that assumes that the protagonist contains all her antagonists psychologically; and the late 1950s and early 1960s are the years when Fritz Perls brought forth Gestalt therapy, many of whose techniques are closely related to psychodrama. In "empty chair" work, for example, the client talks to parts of herself imaginatively seated in a chair across from her, then moves over to the formerly empty chair and talks back to the part of herself that she was to begin with. In Gestalt dream work Perls asserted that the client was everything in a dream: not only all the people, but all the animals and all the objects as well, including the kitchen sink. If you are that kitchen sink in your dream, what do you feel as the sink?

In 1964, Eric Berne, the founder of Transactional Analysis, published a simplified explanation of his theories called *Games People Play,* which became a popular best-seller. In his book Berne provided dramatic examples, with explanations, of ways two people typically interact when they are expressing three major components of their personalities, demonstrating how those interactions typically emerged as manipulations rather than clear communication. The component parts of the personality, in his model, were the parent, adult, and child; this was not dissimilar from Freud's model using the superego, ego, and id.

Also in the 1960s, Gregory Bateson, Virginia Satir, Jay Haley, and the other members of what came to be known as the Palo Alto group started to work with family systems. One exemplary technique they developed was Family Sculpting, in which the client uses human or clay models to display the members of his family, talks about his issues with them, and moves the pieces around to change the outcome of his own story. In this way Family Sculpting works very much like psychodrama.

The Three Faces of Eve, Sybil, and the other developments in clinical psychology brought new attention to multiplicity and dissociation as psychological and pathological experiences. In the 1970s alone, about fifty cases of Multiple Personality Disorder were reported in the clinical literature. By 1980, the DSM-III included MPD as a diagnostic category; today, some controversy about the nature of the disorder notwithstanding, thousands of cases have been documented.

In 1895 Freud and Josef Breuer, following Charcot, had identified as hysteria behaviors that might also have been understood as dissociative, and psychiatrists still diagnosed dissociation as a form of hysteria more than seventy years later (American Psychiatric Association 1968). By the time dissociation was recategorized as a disorder on its own it encompassed depersonalization, psychogenic amnesia, psychogenic fugue, and multiple personality (American Psychiatric Association 1980). In its next revision the DSM-III-R acknowledged that MPD may also be present when someone does not exhibit fully-rounded personalities, but only exhibits two or more "personality states" or fragments that may or may not be aware of one another, if they are amnestic and aware of having lost time (American Psychiatric Association 1987). We are closer and closer to acknowledging a form of dissociation that does not meet diagnostic criteria for psychopathology.

There's an ongoing debate in parts of the gender community that I encounter particularly with some of my own clients who are exploring transsexuality. The question is "Where does the man go when the woman takes over?" or "Where does the woman go when the man takes over?" I never want to answer this question for anybody else, but in my own experience and observation nobody disappears. I've never met a persona who died or really vanished, though I have come across some who seem to have gone to sleep.

Rather, one seems to recede as the other steps forward, or in Billy Milligan's image one steps into the spotlight and the other steps out (Keyes 1981).

Going back to the conversation I had with my prospective client, if Juliette were larger in my inner pantheon, if she carried more weight than she does, she'd be out a lot more than she is and merely advising me a lot less. If she were very large I might have been transsexual. As it is, she comes out now and then, and from behind the scenes she influences all my other parts one way or another. Of course she conveys considerable insight to the therapist when he works with gender clients.

One of the things Juliette's been best at reminding me about has been the utter normalcy of alternate personalities, including those who cross gender lines. Another is the vital importance of their being accompanied, within the system, by co-consciousness: of being simultaneously self-aware and aware of other personalities, as well as discovering how all the system's parts are aligned so that each one contributes to the purposes of the whole, and recognizing the individual doesn't have to suffer the kind of anxiety that results from feeling torn in many directions at once. Just as in "real" life or family systems, this alignment results in teamwork, with every part working toward a common goal, even if all parts don't fully agree with it.

I don't mean that everybody has a vote: this is not a matter of democracy. Otherwise I might have a majority minus one on many of my life decisions, leaving me unhappy with much I did. What we seek is consensus: a weight of support from the people inside agreeing with what the system is doing, while those parts that don't agree, agree to support the team and not to get in the way. When that happens, in my experience, anxiety diminishes, because I'm not being pulled, I'm not being torn in different directions.

In this way, instead of defining cross-gender and other alternate personalities as examples of psychopathology, I find evidence of their original expressions as creative strategies, and as very living testimony to the richness of the human spirit.

Note

A more detailed coverage of this topic will be included in Dallas Denny, *New Concepts on Cross Gender Identity,* New York: Garland Publishers, 1997.

I am grateful to Rebecca Auge, Ph.D., and Howard Devore, Ph.D., for their critical evaluations of this paper; and I am profoundly indebted to my partner, Sybil Holiday, with whom I explored my own personae in a deeply experiential fashion, and with whom I worked out some of the concepts presented here.

References

American Psychiatric Association. 1952. *Diagnostic and statistical manual of mental disorders.* Washington, D.C.: American Psychiatric Association.

———. 1968. *Diagnostic and statistical manual of mental disorders.* 2d ed. Washington, D.C.: American Psychiatric Association.

———. 1980. *Diagnostic and statistical manual of mental disorders.* 3d ed. Washington, D.C.: American Psychiatric Association.

———. 1987. *Diagnostic and statistical manual of mental disorders.* 3d ed. Rev. Washington, D.C.: American Psychiatric Association.

———. 1994. *Diagnostic and statistical manual of mental disorders.* 4th ed. Washington, D.C.: American Psychiatric Association.

Assagioli, R. 1965. *Psychosynthesis.* New York: Penguin.

Baldwin, L. 1984. *Oneselves: Multiple personalities, 1811–1981.* Jefferson, N.C.: McFarland.

Berne, E. 1964. *Games people play: The psychology of human relationships.* New York: Grove.

Berry, L. 1993. Personal communication.

Binet, A. 1886. *Alterations of personality.* New York: Appleton.

Bolin, A. 1988. *In search of Eve: Transsexual rites of passage.* South Hadley, Mass.: Bergin & Garvey.

Castle, K., and S. Bechtel. 1989. *Katherine, it's time.* New York: Harper & Row.

Chase, T. 1987. *When rabbit howls.* New York: Dutton.

Coons, P. M. 1986. Child abuse and multiple personality disorder: Review of the literature and suggestions for treatment. *Child Abuse & Neglect* 10: 455–62.

Docter, R. 1988. *Transvestites and transsexuals: Toward a theory of cross gender behavior.* New York: Plenum

Ellenberger, H. 1970. *The discovery of the unconscious.* Boston: Basic Books.

Fraser, L. 1991. *Classification, assessment and management of gender identity disorders in the adult male: A manual for counselors.* Ph.D. diss. University of San Francisco.

Freud, S. [1900] 1955. *The interpretation of dreams.* New York: Norton.

James, W. [1890] 1980. *Principles of psychology.* New York: Dover.

Janet, P. 1889. *L'automatisme Psychologique.* Paris: Alcan.

———. 1907. *The major symptoms of hysterics.* New York: Macmillan.

Keyes, D. 1981. *The minds of Billy Milligan.* New York: Random House.

Kluft, R. P. 1987. An update on multiple personality disorder. *Hospital and Community Psychiatry* 38: 363–73.

———, ed. 1985. *Childhood antecedents of multiple personality.* Washington, D.C.: American Psychiatric Press.

McDougall, W. 1926. *Outline of abnormal psychology.* New York: Scribner's.

Pearson, C. 1991. *Awakening the heroes within: Twelve archetypes to help us find ourselves and transform our world.* San Francisco: HarperCollins.

Putnam, F. W. 1985. Dissociation as a response to extreme trauma. In *Childhood antecedents of multiple personality,* edited by R. P. Kluft.Washington, D.C.: American Psychiatric Press.

Ross, C. A. 1994. *The Osiris complex: Case-studies in multiple personality disorder.* Toronto: University of Toronto Press.

Rahula, W. 1959. *What the Buddha taught.* New York: Grove.

Schreiber, F. R. 1973. *Sybil.* Chicago: Henry Regnery.

Sliker, G. 1992. *Multiple mind: Healing the split in psyche and world.* Boston: Shambhala.

Sullivan, L. 1988. Personal communication.

Thigpen, C. H. and. H. M. Cleckley. 1957. *The three faces of Eve.* New York: McGraw-Hill.

Dissociation as a Defense against Ego-Dystonic Transsexualism

David Seil

Transsexualism, or Gender Identity Disorder (GID), as defined in DSM-IV (American Psychiatric Association, 1994, 537–38), exists in two fairly distinct clinical subtypes. The first, named Primary Transsexualism in the literature, has an earlier age of onset, and a more direct course leading to transition at an earlier age (Stoller 1968). Primary transsexuals also, almost without exception, have a sexual orientation toward members of the gender opposite their own chosen gender, i.e., heterosexual, or heterogenderal, if you prefer (Seil, unpublished data, February 1994). The other subtype has been named Secondary Transsexualism, with a later age of onset and transition and a more varied sexual object choice (Verschoor and Poortinga 1988).

However, upon closer clinical examination, what in fact distinguishes these two groups is not age of onset. During treatment, secondary transsexuals are able to overcome the amnesia of their early years and recall awareness and behavior indicative of gender dysphoria in the same developmental period reported by the primary transsexuals, i.e., around age five. The amnesia for early indications of GID is a dissociative defense against recognition of gender dysphoria, and the deployment by the ego of such defensive mechanisms is what distinguishes the secondary transsexual from the primary transsexual, not age of onset.

Primary transsexuals report knowing about their internal gender state from the age of four or five, and they relentlessly adopt the gender roles opposite to their anatomic gender throughout childhood. Parental, peer, and other societal attitudes make it painfully clear to them that such a situation is not acceptable to the world around them, but while these individuals are aware of the disapproval toward what they are doing, they rarely make any attempt to live in the appropriate gender and sex roles. For them, their internal gender state is ego-syntonic, that is, integrated into the personality structure, in spite of the fact that their gender wishes are clearly at odds with society, as well as being contrary to the physical reality of their own bodies.

Secondary transsexuals report a different struggle. For them the conflict is not only with the world around them. Early in their development they internalize society's disapproval and accept the physical evidence that their bodies present to them. Their feelings of being the gender opposite to their anatomic gender are unacceptable to the ego, and therefore ego-dystonic. The ego needs defense mechanisms to master this internal conflict and contain the unacceptable urges. It is these defenses that delay the emergence of cross-gender wishes and behavior. Among such defenses are denial, isolation, hypermasculinity (Brown 1988), and later drug and alcohol abuse. This paper focuses on the process of dissociation, as well as the use of dissociation as a defense against ego-dystonic transsexuality. Amnesia, common among ego-dystonic transsexuals, has already been mentioned, but as it is observed clinically, it is a defensive survival mechanism that does not meet the criteria for being Dissociative Amnesia (American Psychiatric Association, 1994, 481). I will present clinical illustrations of the dissociative disorders that are seen in transsexual patients. For clarity I will use the gender pronouns appropriate to the patients' current gender role, not the genetic gender or previous gender role.

Case Report #1

A is a 45-year-old genetic female who has been living as a male for several years. Many years previously he entered treatment for drug and alcohol dependence and, later, for severe dissociative states. *A* reported no sexual or physical abuse as a child, in spite of extensive attempts in psychotherapy to recover such memories. His relationship with his mother was angry and conflict-ridden but not abusive. He married upon completing high school and began drinking and using prescription medications abusively during his first pregnancy. After another child was born, *A* left the marriage because his spouse was abusive and alcoholic. However, he soon entered a second marriage and had a third child.

This marriage collapsed for the same reasons as the first and *A* developed a career of his own while continuing to drink and drug. He joined the lesbian community and eventually entered a relationship that was instrumental in bringing him to treatment for drug and alcohol dependence. With sobriety came an inability to hold a job because *A* began to experience alterations in awareness that would last for days. He was severely depersonalized during these states and remembers little about them, except that he would have to be led around during these episodes. As he put it, "When I stepped out the door, I felt like a piece of Swiss cheese." At this point, *A* sought psychotherapy.

Because of the severity of his dissociative states, the issue of child abuse was explored. This was never validated, but during therapy, long-standing feelings of internal maleness began to be uncovered. Early memories of resisting feminizing by his mother emerged, which explained many of the conflicts within their relationship. For example, he remembered being given a little girl's purse at the age of five and not knowing what to put in it. He began to read his extensive personal journals and found references to cross-gender wishes at age twenty-five, which he had previously let himself recognize only fleetingly. He made the choice to have his internal gender identity recognized by society and began to transition. During early transition, *A*'s sexual orientation fluctuated widely, as seems to be the case with many ego-dystonic transsexuals. Although his attraction to other males predominated, he also occasionally entered into relationships with females as well.

The dissociative experiences disappeared upon beginning transition, with one notable exception. For a time, *A* roomed with a female who was unaware of his actual genetic status. When the roommate found out about *A*'s status through an Alcoholics Anonymous connection, she viciously attacked *A* verbally. *A* regressed to a previous defense mechanism and entered a state of dissociation similar to what he had previously experienced. The depersonalization lasted only several hours and subsided spontaneously.

A has received mastectomy and lives successfully as male. With the one exception noted above, the dissociative states have not returned.

Case Report #2

B was a genetic male living as a female when she was seen in evaluation for hormone therapy. *B* was born with severe hypospadias* and micropenist† and was inappropriately designated female at birth. When she was examined for school at age five, the error was uncovered, and from that point on she was expected to adopt the male role. During the ensuing ten years she underwent over thirty surgeries to create an approximation of normal male genitalia.

During adolescence she began to have lapses of memory for periods of time as long as two weeks. She might "awaken" in a place or town and not remember

---

*A congenital malformation of the penis in which the urethra opens on its underside.
†A condition characterized by an abnormally small penis.

how she got there. She was told by her peers that at times she appeared as a female with a different name who had a reputation for drinking and partying. She claimed to have no memory of these episodes. In her conscious male persona, she considered herself homosexual.

Without the aid of psychotherapy, *B* slowly realized and owned her previously ego-dystonic gender wishes and began to transition. As she developed into the female gender role, the alter faded, as did the male persona that she had defensively adopted. She began a relationship with a male and moved into his mother's house with him. At that time she sought hormone therapy and chromosomal studies revealed XXY on 46. Unfortunately, *B* was HIV-positive and was lost to follow-up.

Case Report #3

C was a forty-eight-year-old genetic male living as a female who was referred for evaluation by her therapist because she wished to begin hormone therapy. When *C* had entered psychotherapy several years earlier, she was diagnosed as suffering from Dissociative Identity Disorder (DID) (American Psychiatric Association 1994, 487). She had more than twenty alters, most of whom were female.

C's father abandoned the mother when *C* was an infant. Because the mother had desired a female child, she decided to raise *C* as a female. There were evidently no anatomic abnormalities: the mother answered *C*'s question about having a penis by reassuring her that it would fall off in time. This situation was discovered during a routine examination in third grade when a school physician exclaimed, "This is a boy!" From that time on, *C*'s mother reversed her determination to raise *C* as a girl and began being physically abusive whenever *C* showed any inclination to express femininity. The mother was severely abusive in punishing *C* in general. *C* was also severely sexually abused by older males.

C valiantly tried to adopt the male persona, mainly in an attempt to please her mother. She joined the military and married. She also became morbidly obese. It is unclear when the DID developed, but *C* clearly had a variety of psychological complaints and conditions that eventually led to disability. When the DID was uncovered, it was found that most of the alters were female, and during treatment *C* integrated several of these into a conscious female personality that she began to live out with a great increase in her internal comfort and a loss of two hundred pounds. She is actively pursuing transition with electrolysis and hormones and remains in treatment for residual DID.

Case Report #4

D was a self-referred twenty-year-old genetic male college student who complained of transvestitism, which interfered with her relationship with a girlfriend. Two months into treatment, she revealed her secret, which was that she suspected that she had other personalities of which she was not directly aware. She found clothing and objects in her room that she did not remember obtaining. In class she had appeared as a little girl and had no memory of this. People she did not know left her messages on her computer, evidently knowing her password.

D was an only child who had been selected for adoption because the adoptive parents wanted a male. Both *D* and her parents recounted much teasing by peers as *D* had always been thought a "different" child, but there was no obtainable history of abuse of the magnitude needed to explain DID.

A consultation and psychological testing were obtained. There was no evidence of psychosis on the testing, and the consultant equivocated regarding the existence of DID. *D* began to display alters in the office. There was a little girl who was very frightened, a female teenager who liked to have fun, and a thirty-year-old hairdresser who was very confident and stylish. A male alter was known by the others to be a troublemaker who had been hospitalized many times for depression and violence, and they were afraid he might appear. *D* became aware of the alters, but could not directly interact or speak with them.

During summer vacation *D* entered therapy with a therapist experienced in treating DID. Alters began to multiply, and a brief hospitalization was necessary when the hostile and threatening male appeared. Upon return to school, *D* started therapy with another therapist experienced in treating DID. During a session, an alter told the therapist that *D* really wanted to be a woman. The therapist suggested that *D* be made aware of this, and with painful tears, *D* acknowledged the truth of that wish.

The DID abruptly disappeared when *D* decided to become a woman and began transition. Memories returned of expressing her female self through cross-dressing and play throughout childhood. The parents recalled that an evaluation by a child psychiatric clinic was done at age eight. These records were obtained and they indicated a working diagnosis of GID of childhood. Possibly because of a move to a different state and peer pressure, *D*'s gender dysphoria was temporarily repressed. Obviously, *D*'s parents also repressed not only their memory of *D*'s early, frequent, cross-gender expressions, but the psychiatric consultation regarding this behavior as well. In the past seventeen months, seven of which *D* has lived as female, the DID has not recurred.

Discussion

Dissociation as a process describes a variety of mental states, from absorption to the most complete and severe manifestation of dissociation, DID. Dissociation enables us to "space out" during a dental cleaning, to block out distractions as we study, or to lose ourselves in a movie or a play. For dissociation to be called a dissociative disorder, it must cause "significant distress and/or dysfunction" (American Psychiatric Association 1994, 481, 484, 490). As a process it can be described as "a structured separation of mental processes (e.g., thoughts, emotions, conation, memory and identity) that are ordinarily integrated" (Spiegal and Cardena 1991), or "disruption in the usually integrated function of consciousness, memory, identity, or perception of the environment" (American Psychiatric Association 1994, 477). All four patients displayed a dissociative disorder: *A* suffered from depersonalization ("a sense of physical fragmentation or separation from part of one's body" [Steinberg 1993, 62]). *B* suffered from DID, in that there was a history of dual personality (Ross 1989, 120). *C* and *D* suffered from DID. For all four, the dissociative disorder disappeared or at least was ameliorated when the suppressed gender wishes were made conscious and the patients took steps to reintegrate physical with mental identity. The history of abuse that is seen in 72 percent to 98 percent of cases of the dissociative disorders (Steinberg 1993, 64) was clearly present in only one of these cases, unless multiple surgical procedures during childhood is sufficient abuse to account for *B*'s dual personality. These patients were able to recover the memory of early experiences of having a gender identity that did not match physical reality. Memories of cross-gendered behavior were also recovered. The internalized social unacceptability of their inner identity and the awareness of the incongruity of that with their anatomic gender necessitated the defensive maneuver of dissociation.

Two of the questions on the Structured Clinical Interview for DSM-IV Dissociative Disorders (SCID-D) relate to identity confusion. Question number 102 is "Have you ever felt as if there was struggle going on inside you about who you really are?" and question number 105 is "Have you ever felt confused as to who you are?" (Steinberg 1993). The ego-dystonic transsexual would answer affirmatively to both. The ego-syntonic transsexuals, who see their struggle as being between themselves and the outside world, and have no internal confusion about who they are, would answer in the negative. But both groups might be considered to be in a state of dissociation because the unity of the identity of the mind and body is grossly disrupted. Both groups use a variety of mechanisms to alleviate internal distress about this situation and restore unity.

Other patients with GID report experiences that can be considered signs that the dissociative process is employed to increase internal comfort. For example, male-to-females (MtFs) regard their genitals as not belonging to them or as tumors, indicating a dissociation of those organs from the ego's representation of the body, enabling the ego to maintain a more unified representation. A transsexual often avoids the lack of integration between mind and body by maintaining a low-level dissociation for long periods of time, which increases a sense of inner integration. A glance at a mirror or the experience of being "read" in public interrupts this defensive dissociation and brings back an acutely disturbing dissociative state. The following vignette illustrates this.

Patient *E*, a genetic male, related going out to dinner with a girlfriend early in transition. Although *E* was not cross-dressed, she was interacting with her friend as one female to another. When she went into the bathroom to wash her hands, she looked up at the mirror and saw her unmistakably male face. "I felt a strong blow, so much sadness. It was like a curtain going up and seeing myself. I felt 'No, that's not who I am!' " The mild dissociation she had achieved while being with a woman friend had been replaced by the severe dissociation between her internal and her anatomic state.

By the same means, dissociation, transsexuals can increase intrapsychic unity and experience relief from mental and physical tension by putting on opposite-sex garments, by introducing cross-dressing into a marriage, and finally, by undergoing gender transition and sexual reassignment surgery. The following vignette illustrates the importance of cross-dressing.

F, a genetic male, was coming to terms with her gender yearnings in her mid-forties. She attended a cross-gender convention, where for the first time in her life she appeared in public in female clothing. The night of the final banquet, *F* borrowed an evening gown from a new friend and had her face made up by a professional. Upon returning to her room at the end of the evening, she looked into the mirror and burst into tears. "For the first time in my life, I saw myself as I really was—a woman. I felt relief, I felt joy and I felt sadness that I had wasted so many years trying to be something I was not!" The appearance of the female in the mirror dissociated the reality of her anatomy temporarily from her consciousness, and she was able to finally establish a unity within her mind.

The dissociative state used by the transsexual to cope with anatomic reality is not the defense of denial in the true sense of the word because the reality is readily available to consciousness. Instead, this state of mind might be likened to reverie. It does not fall into the category of a disorder because it is not associated with dysfunction or distress. To the contrary, a certain level of comfort is achieved by the process of dissociation. However, this state is easily disrupted by reality, at which time an acute sense of detachment and division occurs that is severely distressing and that does fall into the category of depersonalization. I do not think that there is a transsexual who has not experienced that pain. If the pain of GID can be considered a constant state of dissociation between inner experience and the reality of the body, increasing relief is experienced as the disparity between mental identity and physical reality narrows, as it does during transition.

Ego-syntonic transsexuals experience the same amount of abuse at the hands of society regarding their gender expression as do ego-dystonic transsexuals. But early in life, the ego-dystonic transsexuals internalize these attitudes, compounding their distress and necessitating further defensive, coping ego mechanisms, in order to appear "normal" and live an apparently normal approvable life. For some this may mean developing another disorder, for example, alcoholism. Then they can attach their low self-esteem and shame to the label "alcoholic," evidently a status preferable to being a transsexual.

Why some transsexuals develop internal conflicts around their gender feelings and others do not is not clear. In some, perhaps, gender identity may be of a strength that cannot be repressed, as is the case with psychological-anatomic concordant gender identity. These individuals with ego-syntonic GID do not undergo the delay in opposite gender role development that the ego-dystonic transsexuals impose upon themselves, and therefore they tend to transition earlier.

Even for the primary transsexual, GID is a state of distress and discomfort regarding the disparity between internal identity and anatomy. In addition, society's disbelief and disapproval create social distress and disability for these people. However, when the unacceptability is internalized, creating an ego-dystonic state, the ego-dystonic transsexual can develop a wide variety of disorders, among them the dissociative disorders. It may be that because GID is in fact a dissociative state, dissociative defenses may be more available to these individuals than to others.

Conclusion

Gender Identity Disorder is seen as including two related entities, ego-syntonic transsexualism and ego-dystonic transsexualism. Four cases of the latter are presented in which the patients used the process of dissociation as a defense against recognition of their gender dysphoria to an extent that they suffered from a dissociative disorder. Whereas GID is a dissociation in itself, sudden experiences of depersonalization will commonly occur during the course of the disorder. Some patients will develop full-blown dissociative disorders that result from internalization of societal disapproval. A certain percentage of dissociative disorders is not associated with childhood abuse, and in these instances, an underlying GID must be considered as a possible etiology.

References

American Psychiatric Association. 1994. *Diagnostic and statistical manual of mental disorders.* 4th ed. Washington, D.C.: American Psychiatric Association.

Brown, G. R. 1988. Transsexuals in the military: flight into hypermasculinity. *Archives of Sexual Behavior* 17: 527–37.

Ross, C. A. 1989. *Multiple personality disorder.* New York: John Wiley and Sons.

Spiegal, D., and E. Cardena. 1991. Disintegrative experience: The dissociative disorders revisited. *Journal of Abnormal Psychology* 100: 366–78.

Steinberg, M. 1993. *Interviewer's guide to the structured clinical interview for DSM-IV dissociative disorders (SCID-D).* Washington, D.C.: American Psychiatric Association.

———. 1994. Systematizing dissociation: symptomatology and diagnostic assessment. In *Dissociation culture, mind and body,* edited by D. Spiegel. Washington, D.C.: American Psychiatric Association.

Stoller, R. J. 1968. *Sex and gender.* New York: Science House.

Vershoor, A. M., and J. Poortinga. 1988. Psychological differences between Dutch male and female transsexuals. *Archives of Sexual Behavior* 17: 173–78.

Feminist and Lesbian Opinions
about Transsexuals

Monica Kendel, Holly Devor, and Nancy Strapko

What is a woman? Both feminist activists and feminist theorists of the past two and a half decades have often been influential in debates about meanings of womanhood. Transsexualism as a state of being and transsexual women and men themselves have periodically presented thorny issues to those involved in such discussions. As a result, the boundaries of womanhood have become more blurred, and previously uncontested territories have become more frequently challenged by both feminists and transsexuals. Briefly, the controversy centers on when, if ever, sex and gender statuses change for transsexuals. When do female-to-male transsexuals cease to be women (if ever)? When do male-to-female transsexuals become women (if ever)? Exclusion of transsexuals from women-only events has been one manifestation of the conflicts that have been brewing in feminist movements since the early 1970s. Because women-only events are largely organized and attended by lesbians, lesbians have often been at the forefront of feminist debates about the womanhood of transsexuals.

A variety of feminist commentaries have been written on the topic of trans-sexualism (Daly 1984, 1990; Eichler 1987; Greer 1986; O'Leary 1994; Raymond 1977, 1979; Steinem 1977; Sturgis 1979; Walsh-Bolstad 1993), many reflecting a negative attitude toward transsexuals. Probably the most popular and most hostile text is Janice Raymond's *The Transsexual Empire: The Making of the She-Male,* originally published in 1979 (with a new edition released in 1994), which continues to set the terms of feminist debate. However, feminists are far from united on this issue (Baynes 1991; Califia 1980; Dworkin 1974; Rubin 1992; Siegal 1994). As a result, there are divisions among feminists that sometimes

146

result in differing camps working against each other (Douglas 1979; *Lesbian Connection* 1992a, 1992b, 1994; *Lesbian Contradiction* 1992; Lindau 1992). Furthermore, members of transgendered and transsexual communities have been caught in the crossfire and have suffered from discrimination and hostility directed at them by some feminists (Burkholder 1991, 1992; Riddell 1980; Stone 1991; *TransSisters* 1993a, 1993b, 1994a, 1994b, 1994c, 1994d, 1995).

There has been much lively debate in the feminist communities on the topic of transsexualism; however there has been little research looking specifically at feminist attitudes about transsexuals (Walworth 1993). To address this gap in our knowledge, we have conducted a study of feminist opinions about transsexuals by means of a questionnaire. The survey (see Appendix A) was developed by Dr. Holly Devor in consultation with Monica Kendel and Dr. Nancy Strapko. This paper describes some preliminary findings based on 100 of 1,400 surveys returned thus far.

Method

One major site of confrontation between feminists and transsexuals has been at the Michigan Womyn's Music Festival, which has a policy of offering entrance to "womyn-born-womyn only." For this reason, a large portion of our surveys were distributed at the Michigan festival. From June 1994 through February 1995, approximately 6,000 surveys were distributed by hand by Monica Kendel and Dr. Nancy Strapko. Three thousand surveys were distributed at the Michigan Womyn's Music Festival including Camp Trans.[1] The remainder were handed out at feminist and lesbian gatherings such as academic conferences, women's dances, and music festivals in the North Eastern United States (approximately 1,000) and western Canadian urban settings. From this distribution approximately 1,200 surveys were returned. A second distribution went out over the Internet to feminist and lesbian bulletin boards. An additional 200 surveys were returned from that distribution. To date approximately 1,400 surveys have been returned.

Our preliminary data are from a random selection of fifty self-identified lesbian feminist responses and fifty non-lesbian feminist responses out of the 1,400 returned surveys. Since many of the women-only spaces are organized and attended by lesbian feminists, we were interested in establishing if there were any differences in opinion between the lesbian and non-lesbian feminists in their attitudes toward transsexuals. For this initial examination, we chose responses from a selection of general questions that examined concepts of sex and gender and membership into womanhood. Because the survey answers allowed for multiple choices and comments, we have a very rich data set that however offers some challenges for coding and traditional statistical analysis. We have not at this time attempted significance tests. We offer only an exploration of some of the data from the full data set.

Sample

The average respondent was Caucasian, twenty-five to thirty years of age, urban, non-medical professional with a university degree, earning an income average of 30,000 U.S. dollars, U.S. citizen with no stated religion. The weakness of our sample lies in its underrepresentation of people from diverse ethnic and racial backgrounds, its fairly narrow age representation, and its overrepresentation of lesbians who attended the Michigan Womyn's Music Festival.

Results

The responses from questions 15, 16, 26, 27, 28, 29, and 30 probe respondents' potential for empathy with the idea of sex change or gender dysphoria.

Q15—Have you ever wanted to be the other sex?
     In the total sample, 30 percent stated that they had wanted to be the other sex at some time. However, 40 percent of lesbian feminists wanted to be the other sex compared to 20 percent of non-lesbian feminists.

Q16—Have you ever thought that you might be a transsexual?
     Overall 5 percent have thought that they might be transsexual. Eight percent of the lesbian feminists compared to 2 percent of non-lesbian feminists have thought that they might be transsexuals.

Q29—How many male-to-female (MtF) transsexuals do you know?
     See Figure 1.

Q30—How many female-to-male (FtM) transsexuals do you know?
     See Figure 2.
     The entire sample knew more MtF than FtM transsexuals. Approximately 40 percent of the respondents knew at least one MtF transsexual, and 15 percent knew at least one FtM. Lesbians knew more transsexuals than non-lesbians. Most lesbians knew from one to five MtFs and/or only one FtM. Most non-lesbians know only one MtF and/or FtM. Sixty percent of the whole sample did not know any MtF transsexuals while 85 percent did not know any FtM transsexuals.

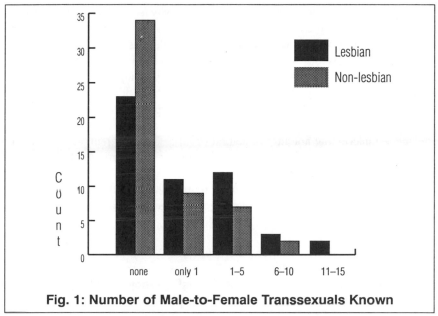

Fig. 1: Number of Male-to-Female Transsexuals Known

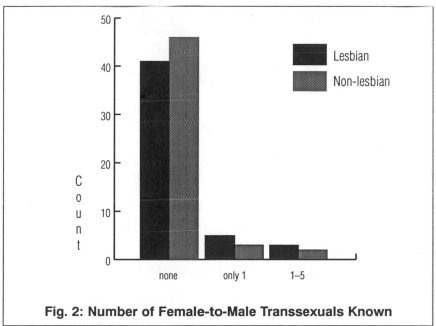

Fig. 2: Number of Female-to-Male Transsexuals Known

Q26—If you do not know any transsexuals, how do you feel about them in general?

Sixty percent of the whole sample did not know any transsexuals. For question 26, these respondents were asked to choose the answers that best fit their experience of "how do you feel about transsexuals in general?" They could choose one or more from: "revolted," "hostile/angry," "unaccepting/not angry," "confused," "indifferent," "curious," "fascinated," "accepting," "ally/defender," "turned on," "don't know," and "other." For the purposes of this examination we grouped the responses into three general categories: negative (revolted, hostile/angry, unaccepting/not angry), neutral (confused, indifferent, curious, fascinated), and supportive (accepting, ally/defender, turned on). At this time we excluded responses of "don't know" and "other."

There were only five responses in the negative category. The largest collection of responses were in the neutral category; the second popular response was in the supportive category.

Q27—If you do know any transsexuals, what was your first reaction to meeting them?

Comparing answers from question 26 and question 27 we noted that the respondents who did know one or more transsexuals (40 percent of the sample) initially had more negative opinions about transsexuals than those who did not know any transsexuals. Among those who did know at least one transsexual, thirteen selected negative responses. The highest negative rating was among non-lesbian feminists, six of whom stated that they felt "hostile/angry" when they first met a transsexual. For both groups, however, the responses in the neutral category were the predominant selections.

Q28—How do you feel about the transsexuals that you know?

The answers to this question reveal a shift of attitude from respondents' first reactions upon meeting transsexuals to the time when this survey was answered. There was a trend toward more acceptance. In response to question 27, thirteen responses in the negative category were chosen, compared to only two in response to question 28. The neutral category has shrunken, while the supportive category has grown. Most noteworthy may be that the "ally" selection grew from three to thirteen responses.

The responses from questions 32, 33, 34, 35, and 36 relate to the respondents' interpretations about the sex and/or gender of transsexual people.

Q33—What is the physical sex of a MtF? (female, male, both, neither, other)
Q34—An MtF is a: woman, man, both, neither, other?

Q35—What is the physical sex of a FtM? (*female, male, both, neither, other*)
See Figures 3 and 4.

Q36—An FtM is a: woman, man, both, neither, other?
See Figures 5 and 6.

Questions 33 through 36 deal with concepts of sex and gender. Respondents' interpretations about the sex and gender of transsexuals appeared to be consistent whether about FtM or MtF, therefore the FtM charts will be used to represent the findings. The responses by *non-lesbian feminists* (see figures 3 and 5) indicate that 60 percent of the respondents believed that transsexuals change sex and gender. On the other hand, 6 percent believed transsexuals do not change sex, and 10 percent believed that transsexuals do not change gender. Eighteen percent believed that transsexuals are both male and female. And 22 percent believed that transsexuals are both men and women. The non-lesbian feminists did not seem to make a strong distinction between the concepts of sex and gender when applied to transsexual people.

Lesbian feminist respondents (see figures 4 and 6) seem to have made more of a distinction between the concepts of sex and gender. Thirty percent believed that transsexuals change physical sex, whereas 60 percent of non-lesbian feminists believed transsexuals change sex. Forty-six percent of the lesbian feminists believed that transsexuals change gender. Therefore, among the lesbians who were surveyed, 46 percent believed that transsexuals change gender, while only 30 percent believed that transsexuals change sex. Compared to the non-lesbian feminists, the lesbians were less likely to believe that transsexuals change sex and gender.

The third preferred response for non-lesbian respondents when asked about transsexuals' sex and gender was the "both" category. In this case, "both" meant that a transsexual's sex is male and female, and that the gender is both man and woman. The lesbians had a larger "other" category. When qualified, the lesbians identified "other" as "transsexual sex" and "transsexual gender."

Q32—When do transsexuals change sex?
See Figure 7.

The respondents were able to choose one or more of the following answers: when they say so, when they are cross-living, when they take hormones, after surgery, when the law says, never, other. Overall, 8 percent believed that transsexuals never change sex. Six percent of the lesbians said that the transsexuals never change sex, compared to 2 percent of the non-lesbian feminists. Fifteen percent of the overall sample chose the "other" category, which when qualified included a combination of options stated above. The most popular answer chosen was "after surgery." Twenty-two percent of non-lesbians and 21 percent of

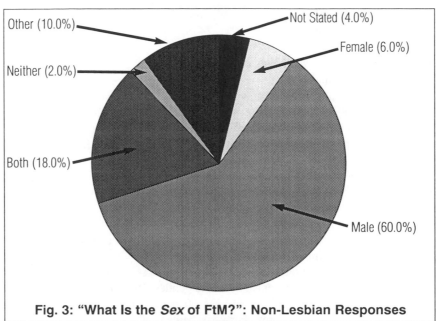

Fig. 3: "What Is the *Sex* of FtM?": Non-Lesbian Responses

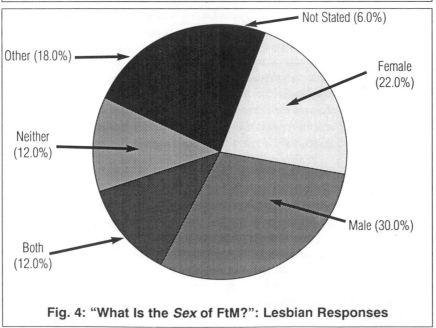

Fig. 4: "What Is the *Sex* of FtM?": Lesbian Responses

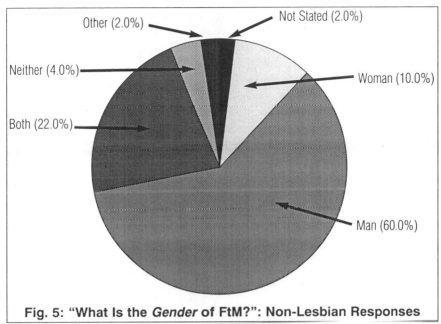

Fig. 5: "What Is the *Gender* of FtM?": Non-Lesbian Responses

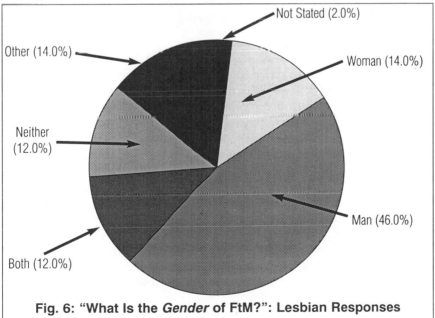

Fig. 6: "What Is the *Gender* of FtM?": Lesbian Responses

lesbians stated that transsexuals change sex after surgery. The second largest category chosen was "when transsexuals say so" with 10 percent of lesbians and 15 percent of feminists making these choices.

The responses to questions 39, 40, 43, 44, and 60 relate to the inclusion and acceptance of transsexuals in women-only activities/organizations.

Q40—If you are feminist . . . would you include male-to-female transsexuals in women-only activities/organizations?
Q44—If you are lesbian . . . would you include male-to-female transsexuals in women-only activities/organizations?
   Overall 60 percent of the respondents indicated that they would include MtFs in women-only events. Seventy-two percent of non-lesbians would include MtFs, although only 60 percent believed that transsexuals change gender. Forty-eight percent of lesbians would include MtFs in women-only events, which closely corresponds with the percentage (46 percent) who believed that transsexuals change gender. These findings would suggest that non-lesbian feminists are more welcoming of male-to-female transsexuals into women-only events than are lesbian feminists.

Q39—If you are a feminist . . . would you include female-to-male transsexuals in women-only activities/organizations?
Q43—If you are lesbian . . . would you include female-to-male transsexuals in women-only activities/organizations?
   Eighty percent of non-lesbian and 82 percent of lesbian feminists were in agreement that they would not let female-to-male transsexuals into women-only events. Eight percent of non-lesbian feminists indicated that they would include FtMs in women-only events compared to 12 percent of lesbians who would include FtMs. Looking back to figures 3 and 4, we can see that the non-lesbians are consistent in their interpretation of transsexuals' sex and gender—6 percent to 10 percent do not believe that transsexuals change sex or gender. Consequently, these non-lesbians would include female-to-male transsexuals in women-only events. Looking back at figures 5 and 6, we can see that a larger number of lesbians (22 percent) believed that transsexuals do not change sex, compared to 14 percent who believed that transsexuals do change gender. Nevertheless, a smaller number (12 percent) would include female-to-male transsexuals in women-only events. These findings suggest that non-lesbian feminists are more consistent in their interpretations of sex and gender, and in their application of those interpretations to their acceptance of transsexuals, than are lesbian feminists.

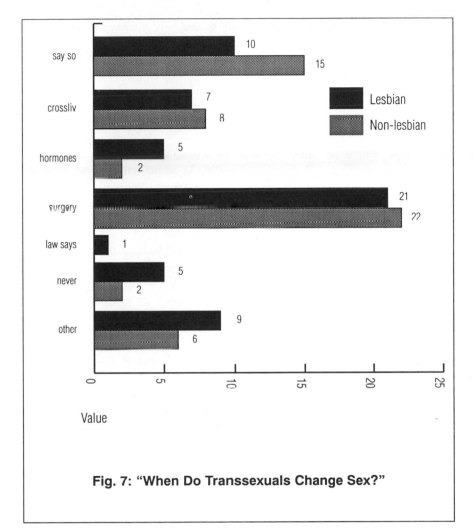

Fig. 7: "When Do Transsexuals Change Sex?"

Q60—Do you think that transsexual people should have the same human rights protection as everyone else?

One hundred percent of those polled agree that transsexuals should have the same human rights as everyone else.

Conclusion

On the basis of these preliminary results, we suggest some possible trends. Lesbian feminists were more likely to have wanted to be the other sex at one time and to have thought that they might be transsexual than were the non-lesbian feminists. As well, lesbians knew more transsexuals than did non-lesbian feminists. Despite this potential for empathy, lesbians were more apt to limit transsexuals' inclusion in women-only space. Perhaps this tendency by lesbians to exclude transsexuals is related to the fact that lesbian feminists make more of a distinction between sex and gender than do non-lesbian feminists. However, lesbian feminists have been the main organizers of women-only events, and have used the membership into womanhood as a foundation for political organizing against patriarchal oppression. Further analysis is required to understand what relationships, if any, exist between these issues. However, the preliminary results of our research are more encouraging than the feminist literature about transsexuals might suggest. A majority (60 percent) of the respondents were in favor of including male-to-female transsexuals in women-only events, 26 percent were opposed, and 14 percent were undecided. The trends also seem to indicate that once feminists know transsexuals, their attitudes shift in a positive direction. It is our hope that these findings may lead to better understanding and improved relations between feminist and transsexual communities.

Note

1. Camp Trans was a protest camp stationed outside the gates of the Michigan Womyn's Music Festival to protest the "womyn-born-womyn" policy. Guidelines of the camp stated, "During the past several months it has become clear that our actions here have much larger implications than protesting the festival policy against admitting transsexuals—it is the right of all individuals to self-define their sex and gender" (*Guidelines* 1995, 34).

References

Baynes, Sylvia. 1991. Trans-sex or cross-gender? A critique of Janice Raymond's *The Transsexual Empire. Women's Studies Journal* 7: 53–65.

Burkholder, Nancy. 1991. Transsexual at Michigan. *Off Our Backs* 21: 17.

———. 1992. Transsexual rights. *Off Our Backs* 22, no. 1: 28.

Califia, Pat. 1980. *Sapphistry. The book of lesbian sexuality.* Tallahassee, Fla.: Naiad.

Daly, Mary. 1984. *Pure lust: Elemental feminist philosophy.* Boston: Beacon Press.

———. 1990. *Gyn/ecology: The metaethics of radical feminism.* Boston: Beacon Press.

Douglas, Cad. 1979. Transpersons transcendent. *Off Our Backs* 9: 9.

Dworkin, Andrea. 1974. *Woman hating.* Vancouver: Clarke, Irwin.

Eichler, Margrit. 1987. Sex change operations: The last bulwark of the double standard. In *Gender roles: Doing what comes naturally?* edited by E. D. Salamon and N. Robinson, 67–78. Toronto: Methuen.

Feinbloom, Deborah Heller, Michael Fleming, Valerie Kijewski, and Margo P. Schulter. 1976. Lesbian/feminist orientation among male-to-female transsexuals. *Journal of Homosexuality* 2, no. 1: 59–71.

Guidelines. 1995. *TransSisters* (Winter): 34.

Greer, Germaine. 1986. Review of *Conundrum* by Jan Morris. In *The madwoman's underclothes: Essays and occasional writings, 1968–85,* 189–91. London: Picador.

Lesbian Connection. 1992a. Responses. 14, no. 5 (March/April): 9.

———. 1992b. Responses. 14, no. 6 (May/June): 8–10.

———. 1994. Festival Forum. 16, no. 4 (January/February): 8.

Lesbian Contradiction: A Journal of Irreverent Feminism. 1992. *Boy Girl?—Special Issue on Sex and Gender!* vol. 39.

Lindau, Rebecka. 1992. Transsexuals. *Off Our Backs* 22, no. 5: 22.

O'Leary, Claudine. 1994. Commentary—Queer politics. *Off Our Backs* 24, no. 1: 3, 8.

Raymond, Janice. 1977. Transsexualism: The ultimate homage to sex-role power. *Chrysalis* 3: 11–23.

———. 1979. *The transsexual empire: The making of the she-male.* Boston: Beacon Press.

Riddell, Carol. 1980. *Divided sisterhood: A critical review of Janice Raymond's "Transsexual Empire."* Liverpool: News From Nowhere.

Rubin, Gayle. 1992. Of catamites and kings: Reflections on butch, gender, and boundaries. In *The persistent desire: A femme-butch reader,* edited by Joan Nestle, 466–82. Boston: Alyson.

Siegal, S. 1994. Call for transgender tolerance. *Off Our Backs* 24, no. 1: 23.

Steinem, Gloria. 1977. If the shoe doesn't fit, change the foot. *Ms.:* 76–86.

Stone, Sandy. 1991. The empire strikes back: A posttranssexual manifesto. In *Body guards: The cultural politics of gender ambiguity,* edited by J. Epstein and S. Straub, 280–304. New York: Routledge.

Sturgis, Susanna. 1979. An interview with Jan Raymond. *Off Our Backs* 9: 14–15.

TransSisters: The Journal of Transsexual Feminism. 1993a. September/November.

———. 1993b. November/December.

———. 1994a. Summer.

———. 1994b. Winter.

———. 1994c. Spring.

———. 1994d. Autumn.

———. 1995. Winter.

Walsh-Bolstad, Beth. 1993. The new, improved (surgically constructed) woman/lesbian? *Off Our Backs* 13, no. 10: 14, 23.

Walworth, Janis. 1993. Results of 1992 gender survey conducted at Michigan Womyn's Music Festival. *TransSisters* (November/December): 13–14.

3

MEN WHO CROSS-DRESS

Introduction

Although men who cross dress have appeared cross-culturally and through time, the incidence seems to be much higher in the twentieth-century world (Bullough and Bullough 1993). After the initial work by Magnus Hirschfeld and Havelock Ellis, study of the phenomenon was dominated by psychiatrists who studied their patients. As the therapy field expanded, psychologists and other therapists continued to add to the literature with examples from their own clients. The emphasis was on causality in early childhood experiences in order to provide a rationale for treatment. Since the 1970s surveys of transvestite club members or readers of magazines aimed at cross-dressing audiences have been done, usually by behavioral scientists. These broader-scale studies provided new insights about the larger group of cross-dressers who did not need psychotherapy. Such studies, however, like the therapy studies that preceded them, have been biased toward the middle- and upper-income cross-dressers, because they are the ones who can afford psychotherapy, participate in cross-dressing clubs, and subscribe to the magazines.

In spite of this, two of the surveys included in this section, based on organized cross-dressing, have new insights to offer. Our own study, for example, identifies the growing group of transgenderists within the cross-dressing population, confirming the findings of Richard Docter (Docter and Fleming 1992). Hogan-Finlay, Spanos, and Jones used a control group and found few differences between them and the cross-dressing group except for their cross-dressing. Even here, in their control group of 108 persons, they found five men who reported experiences typical of the cross-gendered person. While this sample is much too small to indicate any kind of incidence of cross-dressing in the general population, it hints that this is a rare phenomenon.

The cross-cultural approach to the study of male cross-dressers emphasizes this finding and points out that there are large transvestite communities in many countries outside of Western Europe and North America. Though in many ways these cross-dressing individuals are similar to the cross-dressing club members, there are also major differences. They often live on the edge of poverty and earn their living in the entertainment world, by hair dressing, or as prostitutes. The prostitute group is described by Shifter and Madrigal. It is clear that most of their clients, and even their lovers, are men, although the clients call themselves heterosexual and think of the transvestite prostitutes as women because they allow penetration.

These four chapters in juxtaposition suggest that a more comprehensive model is needed to understand the cross-dressing phenomenon in men as it relates to gender identity and gender role. This model must reckon with other causalities besides childhood experience and expand to include genetic, prenatal, and other biological factors. Cultural settings are only beginning to be explored, and what we have found only emphasizes how important cultural assumptions are in influencing how cross-dressing is accepted by any community and what role the cross-dresser might play. Any model must also look carefully at the relationship between gender and sexuality. While it is reasonable to separate sexuality and gender for purposes of definition, the two factors cannot be seen in isolation and seem somehow to be intertwined, with each influencing the other. Future studies must also study how men and women relate to each other. The fact that in the past most people who passed as the opposite sex were women impersonating men while today the opposite seems to be true, at least in the United States and Europe, only hints at the importance of gender roles in society. In short, there is still much to be done, even though we know more about the topic than we did even a few years ago.

References

Bullough, Vern L., and Bonnie Bullough. 1993. *Cross dressing, sex, and gender.* Philadelphia: University of Pennsylvania Press.

Docter, Richard F., and James S. Fleming. 1992. Dimensions of transsexualism: the validation and factorial structure of the cross-gender questionnaire. *Interdisciplinary Approaches in Clinical Management,* 15–37.

Development of the Cross-Gender Lifestyle: Comparisons of Cross-Gendered Men with Heterosexual Controls

Mary Hogan-Finlay, Nicholas P. Spanos, and Bill Jones

Our interest in cross-gender research originated with the work of one of us as a psychotherapist in general practice. Several male clients, who initially presented with problems in relationships, anxiety, drinking, or depression, gradually revealed their gender conflict and need to cross-dress. None of these men were interested in further assessment by a specialized clinic though they wanted to learn more about how the lifestyle develops. For the therapist, it was obviously necessary to understand how the cross-gender lifestyle develops and how mainstream therapists determine the needs of these men. Although it is possible to identify early, middle, and late phases (e.g., Docter 1988), there has been little empirical investigation of the way in which the lifestyle typically develops. Equally, there are few studies that have investigated differences between cross-gendered and heterosexual men with respect to such important variables as family background or psychological functioning, gender identity, sexual behavior or sexual fantasies (see, e.g., Beatrice 1985; Bullough, Bullough, and Smith 1983), though it is commonly held that transvestite behavior should be understood in clinical terms. Consequently the aims of our study were (1) to examine retrospectively the development of the cross-gender lifestyle, and (2) to investigate the similarities and differences between cross-gender men and a control group of heterosexual males.

Development of a Cross-Gender Lifestyle

It was hypothesized that cross-gendered men move through the following invariant age-related phases during the development of a cross-gender lifestyle:

1. fetishism and cross-dressing;
2. fantasies of the "woman within," with or without sexual arousal;
3. public expression of female persona, e.g., cross-dressing in public, using a femme name, etc.; and,
4. in the case of transsexuals, permanent steps toward feminization and full-time life as a woman.

Each of these phases should be characterized by particular patterns of fantasy activity as well as particular behaviors and reasons for cross-dressing. According to our hypothesis, the temporal sequence of cross-gendered activity should remain invariant.

Comparison of Cross-Gender Men and Heterosexual Controls

Hypotheses tested under this rubric were exploratory and based on theoretical suppositions about the family background and childhood activity of individuals who are cross-gendered. The literature (e.g., Buhrich and McConaghy 1985; Person and Ovesey 1974a, 1974b; Stoller 1975) suggests that the childhood backgrounds of men who become transvestites are characterized by (1) parents who had wished their son to be a girl, (2) being frequently dressed as girls by family members or by others, (3) being considered "sissies" by themselves or others, (4) fathers who were either physically or emotionally absent from their son, (5) mothers who had a conflicted or overly close relationship with their son, (6) the adoption of female gender roles and female identity compared to traditional male roles and identity, and (7) psychological disturbance. The present study compared cross-gendered men with a control group of heterosexual men on a number of variables including (1) demographics, (2) childhood and family background, (3) current psychological functioning, and (4) gender issues, sexual fantasies, and activities.

Method

Participants

CONTROL GROUP

Male participants identified their sexual orientation as "heterosexual." A broad sample of men who were similar to the cross-gender group in age, geographical area of residence (Canada and the United States), as well as education and employment status was obtained. A total of 231 questionnaire packages were mailed out. Forty-six percent (108) were returned. Seven of the packages were eventually not included in the control data. Two packages had substantial missing data, while five other respondents (4.6 percent) reported experiences typical of cross-gendered men, and it was decided to include their data with the cross-gender group.

CROSS-GENDERED GROUP

The criterion for acceptance into the cross-gender group was acknowledgment of at least one of the following activities: (1) having experienced cross-dressing with or without sexual excitement; (2) having experienced fantasies of being a woman, with or without sexual excitement; and (3) having experienced sexual arousal to articles of female clothing or toiletries. Transvestite clubs were approached to recruit participants. The presidents of transvestite clubs in both Canada and the United States were contacted either by telephone or through correspondence or both, and given details of the study. Those interested in having their members participate in this study distributed the research packages to club members. A number of questionnaires were also distributed through an establishment that catered to support and grooming for the cross-gender community in an urban center.

We should note possible sources of bias in the sample. Obtaining participants through transvestite clubs excluded cross-gendered men still "in the closet," as well as those who cannot financially afford to participate in a transvestite club and cross-gender men who live in centers without such clubs.

A total of 256 questionnaire packages were mailed to transvestite clubs in Canada or the United States. Thirty-eight percent (98) were returned. Data from two respondents were ultimately excluded because of extensive missing data. As noted, five individuals who had been contacted as potential members of the control group were included in the cross-gender sample.

Table 1

Summary of Questionnaires

1. **Personal History Questionnaire** (Hogan-Finlay, unpublished)
   Demographics, childhood and family background, etc.

2. **Cross-Gender Lifestyle Inventory** (Hogan-Finlay, unpublished)
   Cross-gender activities and age first initiated.

3. **Reasons for Current Cross-Dressing** (Hogan-Finlay, unpublished)
   Reasons and frequency for current cross-dressing.

4. **Autogynephilia Scale** (Blanchard 1989)
   Fantasies of being a woman.

5. **Cross-Gender Fetishism Scale** (Blanchard 1985)
   Current erotic arousal to wear women's clothing, perfume, etc.

6. **Pure Gender Dysphoria Scale** (Blanchard 1993)
   Level of gender conflict related to early desire to be female.

7. **Feminine Gender Identity Scales** (Freund et al. 1977)
   Early feminine behaviors and cross-gender activity.

8. **Androphilia Scale** (Freund et al. 1977)
   Sexual interest in mature males by males.

9. **Gynephilia Scale** (Freund et al. 1977)
   Sexual interest in mature females by males.

10. **Heterosexual Experience Scale** (Freund et al. 1977)
    Level of actual heterosexual experience.

11. **The Bem Sex Role Inventory** (Bem 1974)
    Femininity, masculinity, androgyny, and social desirability.

12. **Traumatic Symptom Checklist** (Briere and Runtz 1989)
    Depression, anxiety, dissociation, sexual, and sleep problems.

13. **Inventory of Childhood Memories and Imaginings** (Wilson and Barber 1981)
    Past and current imaginative ability.

In order to test the hypotheses outlined earlier in this study, a number of pre-existing scales were used. For other variables of interest, measures were specifically constructed. Table 1 lists the scales administered to participants.

Results

Demographic Comparisons

Cross-gendered men and controls were both modally between thirty and forty-five years of age. Both groups were likely to have been raised in a two-parent family (84.0 percent in the case of controls, and 87 percent in the case of cross-gender participants). Current relationship status was not associated with the transvestite lifestyle, although more cross-gendered men remained single (26 percent) compared to controls (18 percent). Cross-gendered men were more likely to be affiliated with a conventional religious denomination. Both groups were on average highly educated compared to the general population in the United States and Canada, although controls were more likely to have obtained a university degree (54 percent to 31 percent) and perhaps in consequence to enjoy higher salaries and higher occupational status. The relationship between social class, religious affiliation, and the cross-gendered lifestyle would warrant further investigation.

Development of a Cross-Gender Lifestyle

The Cross-Gender Lifestyle Inventory asked respondents to report whether they engaged in specific behaviors and/or fantasies and at what age they first initiated those activities. Factor analysis reduced the sixteen-item inventory to four factors, each of which represented a phase of the cross-gender lifestyle. Phase I (Private Cross-Gender Identity) included cross-dressing, fetishism, and fantasies of being a woman. Phase II (Fantasies of a Female Body) involved such specific fantasies as pregnancy or menstruating. Phase III (Public Cross-Gender Identity) includes activities such as having electrolysis, passing in public as a woman, using a "femme name," socializing with other cross-dressers. Phase IV (Permanent Cross-Gender Identity) encompasses activities such as taking hormones, surgical intervention, or living as a woman.

The participants were grouped according to the phases through which they

Table 2
Mean Age Associated with
Each Phase for Each Cross-Gender Group

	MEAN	SD
Group 1: Transsexuals (n = 27)		
Phase I	18.5	11.1
Phase II	24.2	12.3
Phase III	36.8	10.3
Phase IV	38.1	7.6
Group 2: Transvestites (n = 51)		
Phase I	17.2	7.3
Phase II	20.2	10.1
Phase III	35.0	9.2
Group 3: Transvestites (n = 13)		
Phase I	20.5	9.5
Phase III	38.1	9.5

had progressed. The age at which participants proceeded through the phases is shown in table 2. Men who proceeded through all four phases will be referred to as Group 1 (n = 27) and were considered transsexuals. They have either taken steps toward sex reassignment or currently live as women. Men who proceeded to Phase III were considered transvestites as they engaged in cross-gender activities both in private and public but had not taken steps to live permanently as a woman. The fifty-one men who proceeded in sequence through Phases I through III will be referred to as Group 2. Thirteen men who proceeded to Phase III without reporting activities typical of Phase II will be referred to as Group 3.

Specific age periods were found to be reliably related to the different phases of the cross-gender lifestyle. Private cross-gender activities typical of Phases I and II (cross-gendered men who are still "in the closet") occurred on average during the teenage years and early twenties, respectively. Public cross-gender activities typical of Phases III and IV occurred modally during the mid to late thirties. Each of the first three phases of the Cross-Gender Lifestyle were initiated at the same average age whether men were classified as transsexuals or transvestites. Transsexuals reported coming out publicly and obtaining feminization therapy (Phase IV) during the same age period that transvestites were satisfied to enjoy "passing in public" as a woman (Phase III).

The age at which activities defining the phase were first initiated was calculated for each member of the cross-gender group. This analysis indicated that 74 percent of the Group 1 participants and 71 percent of men in Group 2 moved through the first four or three phases, respectively, with increasing age.

Childhood Influences on Cross-Gender Activities

Group membership could not be predicted based on relationships with either parent, the relationship of parents to each other, familial abuse (physical, sexual, or emotional), reported happiness during childhood, being considered a sissy, or imaginative ability. The only variable related to childhood experiences to differentiate the groups was that transsexuals were slightly more likely than transvestites to report having been dressed or as having dressed themselves as a girl during childhood while such activities were almost never reported by the control group.

Psychological Functioning

Transsexuals were found to report above average levels of psychological distress, though no differences were found between controls and transvestites in this regard (see table 3). The implications of this finding will be discussed below.

Gender Issues, Sexual Behavior, and Fantasies

Transsexuals compared to transvestites reported significantly higher levels of gender dysphoria, of feminine gender identity, and the lowest levels of heterosexual fetishism (see table 4). Different aspects of feminine gender identity were associated with different phases for the two groups. For transsexuals only, wanting to be a woman and gender dysphoria were both positively correlated with Phase II ($r = 0.46$ and $r = 0.43$, respectively) and Phase IV ($r = 0.43$ and $r = 0.53$, respectively). For transvestites (Groups 2 and 3) only, fetishism and being sexually aroused by the thought of being admired by another while dressed as a woman were correlated with Phase I ($r = 0.45$ and $r = 0.54$, respectively).

Table 3
Psychological Functioning

	Mean	SD
Depression		
Group 1	8.80	4.5
Group 2	5.66	4.0
Group 3	6.15	4.4
Control	5.02	3.3
Dissociation		
Group 1	3.80	3.0
Group 2	3.04	2.9
Group 3	3.46	2.4
Control	2.31	2.3
Anxiety		
Group 1	6.56	4.2
Group 2	3.72	3.0
Group 3	4.84	3.2
Control	3.66	3.4
Sexual Abuse Trauma Index		
Group 1	4.16	2.8
Group 2	2.83	2.6
Group 3	3.61	2.9
Control	2.26	2.6
Sexual Problems		
Group 1	4.76	3.3
Group 2	4.55	2.6
Group 3	3.69	2.8
Control	2.81	2.4
Sleep Disturbance		
Group 1	8.32	4.8
Group 2	5.70	3.2
Group 3	5.07	3.1
Control	5.83	3.6

Table 4
Gender Identity and Erotic Preference Variables
(FGIA and FGIBC = Feminine Gender Identity in
Males and Homosexual and Bisexual Men,
PGD = Pure Gender Dysphoria; FS = Fetishism)

Variables		Group 1	Group 2	Group 3	Control Group
FGIA	M	18.0	10.8	10.6	5.0
	SD	6.2	5.3	3.1	2.9
FGIBC	M	14.0	10.1	8.0	0.6
	SD	4.0	3.8	3.5	1.4
PGD	M	6.8	4.6	3.5	0.1
	SD	2.3	2.0	2.1	0.4
FS	M	5.6	8.8	7.8	0.3
	SD	4.2	3.1	2.0	0.8

Discussion

The results are immediately relevant to theories of the development of cross-gender behavior. Theories that are based on the idea of radical differences in treatment or situation during childhood (e.g., Buhrich and McConaghy 1985; Person and Ovesey 1974a, 1974b; Stoller 1975) find no support in the present results. Essentially, cross-gender men and men in the control group reported the same pattern and the same quality of upbringing. The only difference was relatively minor. Transsexuals were likely to report having been dressed as a girl during childhood, though even here the frequency of the behavior was low. Moreover, we need to keep in mind that retrospective reports may be colored by present contingencies. Transsexuals seeking gender reassignment by surgery or other means may feel it in their interest to report the feeling of being female or having been considered female as ever-present.

The results also lead us to question the notion that transvestite activities per se should be considered as pathological behavior. In general, cross-gendered men in Groups 2 and 3 were not differentiated from controls on measures of psychological distress. Transsexuals reported higher levels of distress and, as expected, higher levels of gender dysphoria. However, it is not known precisely what caused elevated levels of distress in this group. The effect may have resulted from the stress that must accompany any major lifestyle change and may, therefore, be a transient, not a permanent, effect. Equally, it may be that the regimes associated with gender reassignment including hormone therapy result in increased distress and sleeplessness. Again, the results may be transitory. We should note in passing that while transsexuals and transvestites engage in many of the same activities at the same period in their lives, the meaning of these activities may be different for the two groups, reflecting fundamentally different ways of living. Plausibly, the groups may have differed throughout development though the evidence on this point is less direct. Transsexuals feel like women all the time and endeavor to obtain permanent physiological changes; transvestites continue to exercise their option to adopt a male or a female role at their discretion.

The development of the cross-gender lifestyle was shown to develop in an orderly manner for most of the participants from private fantasy and behavior in the early teens to public expression in the mid-30s. Typically we found a gap of approximately twenty years between initial private cross-gender activities and eventual public enactment. This finding has a number of implications. First, clinicians or researchers working with cross-gendered men may be better able to understand the degree to which the cross-gender activities are fantasized about or actually lived out according to phase and in consequence understand the further implications of the phase of the lifestyle for other aspects of their clients' lives. For example, a cross-gender client who is in the initial phases of this lifestyle and is still "in the closet" may feel relief upon learning that others like himself have experienced similar fantasies and behaviors that typically occur in an orderly fashion. Participants, many of whom belong to transvestite clubs, often expressed relief and pleasure at having the opportunity to take part in this study and respond to questions about their fantasies or behaviors that are usually kept secret. Others who were confused about whether they are transvestite or transsexual may also benefit from understanding both the similarities and differences between these groups. A Phase I client who has chosen to keep all cross-gendered activities secret from his spouse, friends, or colleagues may need to deal with guilt and with marital problems encountered when intimate details of one's lifestyle are not disclosed to an intimate partner. Alternatively, if he is moving in the direction of public disclosure of his lifestyle and is not in contact with a cross-gender support group, he may require guidance to explore the negative consequences of his decision related to his marital, family, and legal status.

The rationale for time delays between private and public cross-gender lifestyle is unclear. Docter (1988) has suggested that the twenty-year period between initial cross-gender fantasies and behavior and coming out publicly is related to the need to develop a cross-gender identity or feminine self-identity. An alternative position, which we support, is that many social factors (family, marital relations, dress codes at work or in public, gender roles, etc.) restrict living more openly as a cross-gender person. Overcoming these restrictions is in itself time-consuming. It is possible that while the cross-gender identity is established during the teenage period, societal rejection of the lifestyle is the primary reason for the delayed public expression, not the need to practice or develop the cross-gender identity. The twenty-year time frame is similar to what many homosexual women and men encounter in coming out as they often face realistic fear of reprisal by employers or rejection by family members (e.g., Coleman 1985). An example of the latter possibility was given by Kane (personal communication, 1995). He indicated that a primary reason for long delays in "coming out publicly" for cross-gender individuals is related to the socialized need for men to be successful in their work as well as being financially secure. "They [cross-gender men] take every precaution not to jeopardize their success."

Narrative reports of participants in this study emphasized as some reasons for maintaining secrecy the aspect of "fear of being caught," of being ostracized by their original families or divorced by their spouse, of losing their jobs, and the financial burden involved in the practice of the lifestyle. The following citations from written comments by participants in the study confirm these perspectives. Two examples must suffice:

> I have to continue to be seen as a "strong" male to those around me, except for the few [who] also know my true feelings. Fear of being ostracized and financially ruined has played a key role in my not acting on this at age 20. (Transvestite)

> I married. . . . I was forced to dress secretly. . . . This gave me an extreme guilt complex . . . specially because I thought myself "queer" I did not know there were other men who had the same desires. (Transsexual)

In short, the explicitly stated reasons given by cross-gender men for the delay in "coming-out" include a broad range of needs to conform to social mores related to marital, parental, financial, or professional obligations rather than to any need to learn aspects of the lifestyle over a period of two decades.

The Cross-Gender Lifestyle Inventory (C-G LI) developed for this study clearly distinguished between transsexuals and transvestites according to the phases of their lifestyle. Transsexuals by definition moved through all four phases and transvestites potentially moved through the first three phases. An instrument such as the Cross-Gender Inventory may be a useful measure for psychologists in general practice who encounter men with cross-gender issues. The inventory may be self-administered in five minutes and could be included as part of a larger test battery that assesses overall gender dysphoria. A clear indication of whether the client reports activities characteristic of the first two phases (private cross-gender activity), the third phase (public cross-gender activity), or wants to take steps toward feminization may assist professionals to counsel the uninformed, gender-conflicted man.

The measure could also be used to determine if referral to a specialized clinic is appropriate or whether counseling to adapt to the stresses inherent in the lifestyle is sufficient. It has been the experience of one of us that men in transvestite clubs or men in the early phases of their cross-gender career are cautious about approaching professionals, particularly professionals at clinics specialized in gender disorders. Moreover, psychologists in general practice may not normally be equipped to assess objectively the needs of cross-gendered men, or to identify the phases of the lifestyle. An instrument such as the C-G LI may therefore serve as an objective means for therapists new to this area to evaluate the situation of their cross-gendered clients.

References

Beatrice, J. 1985. A psychological comparison of heterosexuals, transvestites, preoperative transsexuals, and postoperative transsexuals. *Journal of Nervous and Mental Disease* 173: 358–65.

Bem, S. L. 1974. The measurement of psychological androgyny. *Journal of Consulting and Clinical Psychology* 42: 155–62.

Blanchard, R. 1985. Research methods for the typological study of gender disorders in males. In *Gender Dysphoria: Development, research, management,* edited by B. W. Steiner, 227–57. New York: Plenum Press.

———. 1989. The concept of autogynephilia and the typology of male gender dysphoria. *Journal of Nervous and Mental Disorders* 177: 616–23.

———. 1993. Varieties of autogynephilia and their relationship to gender dysphoria. *Archives of Sexual Behavior* 22, no. 3: 241–51.

Briere, J., and M. Runtz. 1989. The traumatic symptom checklist scale (T.S.C.-33): Early data on a new scale. *Journal of International Violence* 4, no. 2: 151–63.

Buhrich, N., and N. McConaghy. 1985. Preadult male behaviors of male transvestites. *Archives of Sexual Behavior* 14: 413–19.

Bullough, V., B. Bullough, and R. Smith. 1983. A comparative study of male transvestites, male to female transsexuals, and male homosexuals. *Journal of Sex Research* 19, no. 37: 238–57.

Coleman, E. 1985. Developmental stages of the coming out process. In *A Guide to psychotherapy with gay and lesbian clients,* edited by John C. Gonsiorek, 31–43. New York: Harrington Park Press.

Docter, R. F. 1988. *Transvestites and transsexuals: Toward a theory of cross-gender behavior.* New York: Plenum Press.

Freund, K., R. Langevin, J. Satterberg, and B. W. Steiner. 1977. Extension of the gender identity scale for males. *Archives of Sexual Behavior* 6: 5507–19.

Person, E., and L. Ovesey. 1974a. The transsexual syndrome in males. I. Primary transsexualism. *American Journal of Psychotherapy* 28: 4–20.

———. 1974b. The transsexual syndrome in males. II. Secondary transsexualism. *American Journal of Psychotherapy* 28: 174–93.

Stoller, R. J. 1975. *The transsexual experiment.* Toronto: Irwin & Co.

Wilson, S. C., and T. X. Barber. 1981. Vivid fantasy and hallucinatory abilities in the life histories of excellent hypnotic subjects ("somnambules"): Preliminary report with female subjects. In Vol. 2 of *Imagery: Concepts, results and applications,* edited by E. Klinger, 133–49. New York: Plenum.

Men Who Cross-Dress: A Survey

Bonnie Bullough and Vern Bullough

This chapter reports findings from a study of 372 persons who answered a questionnaire constructed by the authors. All of the members of the study sample started life as men, and all cross-dressed at some time in their lives. The two major purposes of the study were (1) to continue to describe male cross-dressers as a totality, filling in the gaps in the knowledge base about the phenomenon of cross-dressing, and (2) to furnish empirical data to better differentiate the several different subgroups of men who cross-dress now or have cross-dressed at some time in their lives.

Literature Review

There are two major bodies of research literature related to cross-dressing: the older studies and opinions were medical/psychiatric with the more recent approach the behavioral science (Bullough and Bullough 1993). The pioneer in the study of cross dressing was Magnus Hirschfeld, a German physician, who was an avowed homosexual, a reformer, and a specialist in the study of sexuality. Hirschfeld coined the term *transvestism—trans* (across) and *vestis* (dress)—to describe the key behavior of transvestites, although he indicated that this was only the most obvious characteristic of the condition he described. In 1910 he published what may well be the key work on cross-dressing, *Transvestites: An Investigation of the Erotic Drive to Cross-Dress* (in English: 1991). He reviewed the cases of sixteen men and one woman, most of whom were patients. The others were located through newspaper stories, correspondence with people he heard about, and referrals from colleagues. He described cross-dressing as starting in early childhood, increasing during puberty, and remaining almost unchanged after that. Although most of the persons he studied were heterosexual in their orientation, Hirschfeld noted there were a few homosexuals, but argued that the dominant sexual urge among transvestites was focused on themselves dressed in the women's finery rather than other persons of either sex. The one woman in the group indicated some attraction to women, but eventually she was married and had children. In her history she focused on the freedom and lifestyle that a man's identity provided her more than on erotic pleasure (Hirschfeld 1991).

Richard von Krafft-Ebing included four cases that we can now identify as cross-dressers in his comprehensive list of conditions he called "pathological" (1933). Havelock Ellis, another early-twentieth-century sex researcher, also collected case histories of men who cross-dressed, but he did not consider transvestism to be a serious problem because those who practiced it were able to live normal lives (Ellis 1913, 1936).

After Hirschfeld and Ellis, those who studied the phenomenon for the next sixty years were treatment-oriented psychiatrists who characterized cross-dressing as psychopathology and sought to cure it with psychotherapy. They searched for key elements in the history that would help them understand and treat their clients. Castration anxiety and homosexual panic emerged as the major early explanations for transvestism (Gutheil 1930; Fenichel 1930; Hora 1953; Peabody et al. 1953; Randall 1959; Lukianowitz 1959). Eventually other experiences were considered important, with the investigator Stoller focusing on the powerful mother as the major factor in the transvestite pattern (1971). More recently the psychiatrists and psychologists have sought understanding using a broader range of variables but have continued to use an illness model to conceptualize all types of cross-dressing (Person and Ovesey 1978; Brierley 1979; Beatrice 1985; Fagan et al. 1988).

The codification of the thinking of the psychiatric community on transvestism is reflected in the definition of the term in the fourth edition of the *Diagnostic and Statistical Manual* (DSM) of the American Psychiatric Association (1994). The current definition of "transvestic fetishism" reads as follows:

> A. Over a period of at least six months, in a heterosexual male recurrent intense sexually arousing fantasies, sexual urges, or behaviors involving cross-dressing.
>
> B. The fantasies, sexual urges, or behaviors cause clinically significant distress or impairment in social, occupational or other important areas of functioning.

This definition is essentially the same as the one in the third revised edition of the DSM (1987). However in the discussion section of the current edition new research is acknowledged with statements that (1) although transvestism is considered a heterosexual condition, some individuals are on occasion attracted to males, and (2) the fact that levels of eroticism change over time so some people lose the fetishism and continue to cross-dress to lessen anxiety or depression (American Psychiatric Association 1994). The basis for including "transvestic fetishism" as a definition however remains the same, namely, that it is an illness that is amenable to treatment by the psychotherapeutic community.

The survey research approach to studying cross-dressing developed after the emergence of the transvestite clubs in the 1960s. A major difference in the two approaches is the fact that the survey researchers do not gather their samples from patient populations. The first survey was done by Virginia Prince, the organizer of the first transvestite club. She worked with P. M. Bentler, a psychologist, to gather data from 504 readers of the magazine *Transvestia* between 1964 and 1966 although the study was not published until 1972 (Prince and Bentler 1972). Other surveys were done by Buhrich and McConaghy using Australian transvestite club members (1977a, 1977b, 1978, 1979, 1985), and by Buhrich and Beaumont using both Australian and American club members (1981). Bullough, Bullough, and Smith used sixty-five Los Angles transvestite club members and compared them to transsexual, homosexual, and an undifferentiated control group (1983a, 1983b, 1985). Newcomb also used comparison groups to study childhood patterns (1985). Richard Docter gathered data at transvestites' meetings to study 110 transvestites (1988). His more recent study includes 692 cross-dressers (1993). Richard L. Schott used the personal advertisements in the magazine *Tapestry* as a sample source of eighty-five transvestites (1995).

These surveys have concentrated on three areas: (1) childhood experiences, often with a goal of searching for causality; (2) current patterns of cross-dressing, to see if the DSM definition and the popular beliefs about cross-dressing are accurate, and to see if the patterns change over time; and (3) data to use to develop classification systems to separate the various types of cross-dressers.

The first classification scheme was developed by Buhrich and McConaghy, who noted they could divide club members they were studying into two groups: those who were satisfied with cross-dressing, and those who desired at least partial feminization with hormones or surgery. Some of these people wanted sex reassignment surgery but desisted from seeking it for family reasons. The first group, which fits the traditional definition of transvestism, was called "nuclear" while the other group, which seemed closer to the model of transsexualism, was called "marginal." Members of the marginal group shared many characteristics with transsexuals; they often did not experience erotic arousal with cross-dressing and they showed more homosexual interest (Buhrich and McConaghy 1977).

Having differentiated these two subgroups of transvestites, in 1985 Buhrich and McConaghy added a third category titled "fetishistic transsexualism." They identified a group of five men who had requested sex reassignment surgery, had lived as women for at least six months, considered themselves to be women even when they were nude, but they reported erotic arousal to cross-dressing. Two of the group had ejaculated spontaneously while cross-dressed during adolescence, and all reported fetishistic arousal at some time (Buhrich and McConaghy 1985).

Richard Docter developed a longitudinal classification system. He divided the group according to five stages and showed that with the passage of time and experience there were marked increases in the frequency of cross-dressing and that more items of clothing were added. After starting with a few items of clothing, individuals progressed to stage 3, which was complete cross-dressing; stage 4 includes taking on a femme name, and stage 5 is transsexualism (Docter 1988, 195–227). In Docter's more recent study he noted a significant group of cross-dressers who progressed to living full-time as women but did not seek sexual reassignment surgery (1993).

Some of the survey researchers were very much influenced by the psychiatric definitions. The Australian team, Buhrich and McConaghy, followed the DSM definition and excluded from their study sample people who had no sexual arousal related to cross-dressing. This is probably because Buhrich and McConaghy were psychiatrists even though they did survey research. Similarly Richard Docter, a psychologist, excluded people who did not fit the definition in two areas; if they had never experienced excitement in association with cross-dressing, or if they were homosexual (Docter 1988, 135). Buhrich and Beaumont, who compared American and Australian transvestites, indicated that they excluded 9 percent of their American respondents and 11 percent of their Australian respondents because they did not report fetishism. The Prince and Bentler study, the early Bullough studies, and the Schott study (1995) did not exclude these groups.

Methodology: Data Gathering

Questionnaires were sent to out to the members of Tri-Ess, a national cross-dressing organization, by enclosing the questionnaire with the association's magazine, *Femme Mirror.* In addition the American Educational Gender Information Service (AEGIS) sent questionnaires to its mailing list of five hundred, which includes persons who identify as transvestites, transgenderists, or transsexuals, as well as members of the helping professions and related support groups. News of the study also spread through other newsletters and friendship networks, which prompted people to write to the researchers to secure questionnaires. These sources yielded approximately forty individual requests for the questionnaires.

An ad in the *Advocate,* a gay newspaper published in Los Angeles, yielded no responses. Although there are many gay persons who cross-dress, apparently the readers of the *Advocate* did not perceive this study of cross-dressing as something in which they wanted to participate.

Data gathering started in the summer of 1994, and analysis was done in 1995. The study group of 372 includes respondents from every state in the Union, eight from Canada, and eight from other countries. Structured questions were answered carefully and the answers to open-ended questions were often answered at length. Some subjects indicated they had never told anyone all of their background before. Many people sent their names so we could contact them for additional data.

The Questionnaire

The questionnaire asked about childhood experiences, current patterns of cross-dressing, demographic facts, and attitudes and opinions. Scales were used to measure attitudes regarding sexuality, homosexuality, and cross-dressing as sexual stimuli. In addition a short screening scale was used to identify obsessive-compulsive behavior patterns.

Findings

The sample was made up of older, upwardly mobile men, with a median age of forty-eight and a range from nineteen to eighty-nine years of age. Although all occupational levels were represented, including 3 percent who were laborers, 42 percent of the group indicated they were employed in professional or technical occupations, 10 percent were managers and 14 percent were in clerical or sales positions. Their families of origin were not as affluent, with only 29 percent of the parents being in professional or technical positions, and 22 percent of them being laborers.

Early Cross-Dressing

The median age at which cross-dressing started was 8.5, which is a year or two younger than found in most of the other studies. Thirty-four percent of the sampled men reported their first cross-dressing incident took place by age six and 91 percent by age fourteen. After age fourteen the age of the first incident varied widely, with the oldest reported taking place at age fifty-five.

Table 1
Early Cross-Dressing as a Clandestine Activity

	%
Were you afraid of being caught?	
Yes	93
No	7
Why were you afraid?	
Rejection	45
Sissy label	25
Crazy label	25
Sin	5
Were you caught?	
Yes	44
No	56
If caught, what happened? (n = 149)	
Big problem, crisis at home	33
Minor problem	44
No problem	21
Sent to therapy or counseling	5
Whose idea was the cross-dressing? (n = 363)	
Subject's own idea	79
A female's idea	15
A male's idea	2
Group	4
Who were you with the first time you cross-dressed? (n = 321)	
Alone	71
With a female	11
With a male	3
In a group	13

CROSS-DRESSING WAS CLANDESTINE

Cross-dressing was, for most, a clandestine activity. As indicated in table 1, 93 percent of the group indicated that they were afraid of being caught cross-dressed. When asked why they were afraid, most answered an open-ended question indicating one of four fears: they were afraid of rejection by family or others, afraid of a sissy label, a mental illness (crazy) label, or that what they were doing was a sin. Some of the respondents further defined the sissy label to indicate homosexuality, but for many "sissy" seemed to mean a weak or girlish person.

Fifty-six percent of the group were never caught. Given the young age of these boys, the fact that a slight majority was able to keep the activity clandestine is very interesting. Among the 149 persons who were actually caught, the outcome varied; 33 percent faced what they described as a big problem or a major family crisis, and 5 percent were sent for psychotherapy or counseling. However, 42 percent indicated that their punishment was minor, and 20 percent said that being caught caused no problem.

The clothing used for the first cross-dressing experience usually belonged to the mother, sister, or other young female relative. Those who did not use mother's or sister's clothes tapped a wide variety of sources including costumes for Halloween or school plays, or if the incident occurred at an older age, wives' or purchased clothing was often utilized. Cross-dressing was usually done in isolation, and for 79 percent of the subjects it was their own idea. If someone else did influence them it was usually a female.

Normal Childhoods

Against this backdrop of clandestine cross-dressing, the subjects in the study seemed to have had more or less normal childhoods. Selected questions related to childhood are shown in table 2. Only 12 percent of the subjects described their childhood as unhappy. The majority associated mostly with boys and participated in sports. Most said they were considered good children and they tried to please the adult authority figures in their lives. However, many of them reported they envied girls and clothing was an important symbol of this envy.

Sexual Excitement

As indicated, a point of controversy in the literature is the extent to which cross-dressing is a related to sexual excitement. The first question that probed this behavior did not use the word "sexual." Subjects were asked whether or not their first cross dressing experience excited them. As indicated in table 3, the major-

Table 2
Childhood Patterns

	%
Happy	42
Somewhat	46
Unhappy	12

Associated mostly with

Boys	73
Girls	17
Both about equal	10

Sports

Full participation	33
Occasional participation	44
No participation	23

Were you considered a "good" child or did you get in trouble and get a "bad" label?

Good	67
Neither label	29
Bad	5

Did you envy girls?

Yes	70
No	30

Why? (n = 245)

Their appearance	33
Their role	12
People nicer to girls	6
No reason given	20

Table 3
Sexual Excitement as a Part of Cross-Dressing

	%
Did your first cross-dressing experience excite you?	
Yes	73
Somewhat (qualified answer)	14
No	9
No answer	4
Age first ejaculated with cross-dressing?	
Age 10 or younger	11
Age 13 or younger	50
Age 21 or younger	85
No ejaculation reported	14
Current cross-dressing linked to sexual excitement?	
75% of time (or more)	21
50% to 74%	11
10% to 49%	16
Less than 10% or rarely (but excitement happens)	21
No sexual excitement with CD	30

ity of the subjects found it exciting. The next question was clearly sex related; subjects were asked the age at which they first ejaculated with cross-dressing. They reported ejaculation at a later age than simple excitement: only 11 percent ejaculated by age ten, but 85 percent ejaculated by age twenty-one. Note however, that 14 percent reported they never ejaculated in connection with cross-dressing. While 2 percent of this sample are transsexuals who have had sex reassignment surgery, this does not account for the whole group of men who consider themselves to be cross-dressers but have never ejaculated with CD. Among the forty-nine persons in the sample who reported not having ejaculated as a part of their cross-dressing experience, there were some who had strong emotional feelings on this topic. They felt that the popular link between cross-dressing and sex-

Table 4
Sexual Orientation Now

	%
Heterosexual	68
Bisexual	10
Homosexual	2
Sex not a part of my life now	20

ual excitement or a fetish, as it is labeled in the DSM, is erroneous. Several people wrote notes indicating they found this and similar questions that asked about sexual practices and attitudes objectionable; they believed that cross-dressing is unrelated to eroticism, and this belief was in fact very important to them.

CURRENT EXCITEMENT LEVELS

When subjects were asked about their current patterns of cross-dressing, answers were quite varied, with 31 percent of the group reporting that at the present time they experience no sexual excitement with cross-dressing. This suggests that the DSM definition of transvestites as having sexual excitement is wrong for almost one-third of the men in this study sample. However, at the other end of the continuum 21 percent of the group indicated they experience sexual excitement at least 75 percent of the time they cross-dress, with each of the other respondents reporting his individualized pattern.

Sexual Patterns

Sexual orientation is the other issue that is not clear in the literature, even though the label "heterosexual" is widely used. The current sexual orientations of the subjects who answered the questionnaire are shown in table 4. While the majority (68 percent) were heterosexual, 10 percent were bisexual, and 20 percent of the sample were celibate. This last group checked the alternative, "Sex is not a part of my life now."

Table 5
Current Cross-Dressing Patterns
(Full Dress or Selected Items)

	%
All of the time	55
Half the time	19
Once a week	17
Once a month	8
Less than once a month	1

Cross-dressing seemed to be a more enduring activity than sexual intercourse. As shown in table 5, 55 percent of the sample dress fully or partially all of the time. For some, this means they wear female underpants, but for others it is complete cross-dressing, with wide variation in between. Only 1 percent of the sample dress less often than once a month.

The Transgenderists

The emergence of the transgenderists is a phenomenon that has often been mentioned in the gender community in the last decade, and is discussed in several selections in this book. It was reported in the most recent article by Richard Docter (1993). This trend was again confirmed in this study. Eleven percent of the study sample members are living full time as a woman. Since only 2 percent had sex reassignment surgery, the percentage of transgenderists in this sample is 9 percent. At least two of these people have firm plans for transsexual surgery, but the rest are more-or-less adjusted to their female status with or without the aid of hormones.

Twenty-five percent of the total group took hormones at some time, although most of the time hormone use was under two years, which is long enough to stimulate breast development but short enough to avoid some of the other side effects.

The transgenderists and transsexuals are less likely to be heterosexual than the rest of the sample. Table 6 shows a cross-tabulation of the men who indicated they were living full time as women with sexual orientation. Among the thirty-seven persons included in the table who are living full time as women, twelve are heterosexual, twelve are bisexual or homosexual, and thirteen are asexual. The

Table 6

Cross-Tabulation of Living Full-Time as a Woman with Sexual Orientation Now

Living Orientation

	hetero	*bi-homo*	*asexual*
Yes	12	12	13
No	227	31	56

Pearson: 26.51: Sig .0000

division of the rest of the sample, which focuses on men who do not live as women, is loaded in the heterosexual category, although all three lifestyles are represented.

Discussion

No effort was made to direct this study toward a new classification system. However, the emergence of the transgenderists as a permanent part of the gender spectrum is a pattern clearly to be reckoned with by the system builders. They fit into the patterns devised by Buhrich and McConaghy and with Docter's scheme, but not with schemes that were focused on sexual reassignment surgery (SRS) as the endpoint. Many of these men seem to be reevaluating the necessity of surgery for gender change.

Eleven percent of the sampled group are living full time as women, with 2 percent having had SRS. The transgenderists tend to be divided on sexual orientation, with one-third being heterosexual, one-third being bisexual or homosexual, and one-third considering sex not a part of their life now. They are a very interesting subgroup of the population, which has become much more obvious in the last decade.

As indicated, cross-dressing was an early clandestine activity, carried out primarily in the home. Since most of the subjects were afraid of being caught, they took great pains to keep the activity secret. These boys had obviously absorbed the norms of society at that early age, even though they secretly violated those norms.

A pattern noted recently by Schott positing causality in the family system, with mothers fostering cross-dressing (1995), is not supported by these data because most of the subjects themselves did the cross-dressing and kept it a secret from their mothers. Eleven percent of the first-time cross-dressing was done with a female present, but that female figure included girl cousins, sisters, and friends, as well as mothers.

Although most of these men cross-dressed from an early age, they lived outwardly normal and happy lives and were thought of as good boys. They associated mostly with boys, even though many of them envied girls for either their appearance or their roles. Although the age at which cross-dressing started is earlier than in the other behavioral science studies, this picture is not unlike childhood patterns that are similar to most of the past surveys of cross-dressers. (Prince and Bentler 1972; Buhrich and McConaghy 1977, 1978; Buhrich and Beaumont 1981; Bullough, Bullough, and Smith 1983a, 1983b; Bullough, Bullough, and Smith 1985; and Docter 1988). The clandestine characteristic of the activity and the almost unanimous fears of being caught have not been reported previously in the literature.

Most of the subjects found cross-dressing exciting, and 91 percent ejaculated as a part of cross-dressing. As they grew older they cross-dressed more, but the activity became less erotic. Thirty-five percent of the current sample live alone, and 20 percent lead a life that does not include sexual activity.

A limitation of this study is the fact that the sample is drawn from organized groups and people who read the literature of the gender community. Missing from this sample are the less affluent cross-dressers, many of whom are transgenderists. These people are described later in this volume by Schifter and Madrigal, who studied a small group of prostitutes in Costa Rica, and by Whitam, who has studied the transvestite communities in Pacific Rim countries and South America. Usually these men are entertainers, prostitutes, hair dressers, and persons in related occupations, and they tend to be bisexual or homosexual.

The cross-dressing-club members and readers who have made up the study sample in all of the surveys are more affluent and are very often professional people. It may be that the search for causality has been premature, particularly when it is tied to a need to guide or even justify therapy. Probably the best next step in understanding the phenomenon of cross-dressing is to assess its parameters more completely, including the whole socioeconomic spectrum, and then to follow the lead of the gay community, which in 1973 declared itself cured of its psychiatric diagnosis. This declaration freed up the energy of researchers to investigate the whole phenomenon of sexual orientation, including its physiological parameters. The gender community could similarly make the point that the totally dimorphic conception of gender is out of date, and by so doing open up possibilities to think new thoughts about old gender patterns.

References

American Psychiatric Association. 1987. *Diagnostic and statistical manual of mental disorders.* 3d ed. rev. Washington, D.C.: American Psychiatric Association.
———. 1994. *Diagnostic and statistical manual of mental disorders.* 4th ed. Washington, D.C.: American Psychiatric Association.
Beatrice, James. 1985. A psychological comparison of heterosexuals, transvestites, preoperative transsexuals and postoperative transsexuals. *Journal of Nervous and Mental Disease* 173: 358–65.
Brierley, Harry. 1979. *Transvestism: A handbook with case studies for psychologists, psychiatrists, and counselors.* Oxford: Pergamon Press.
Buhrich, Neil, and Trinia Beaumont. 1981. Comparison of transvestism in Australia and America. *Archives of Sexual Behavior* 10: 269–79.
Buhrich, Neil, and Neil McConaghy. 1977a. The clinical syndromes of femmiphilic transvestism. *Archives of Sexual Behavior* 6: 397–412.
———. 1977b. The discrete syndromes of transvestism and transsexualism. *Archives of Sexual Behavior* 6: 483–95.
———. 1977c. Can fetishism occur in transsexuals? *Archives of Sexual Behavior* 6: 223–35.
———. 1978. Parental relationships during childhood in homosexuality, transvestism and transsexualism. *Australian and New Zealand Journal of Psychiatry* 12: 103–108.
———. 1979. Three clinically discrete categories of fetishistic transvestism. *Archives of Sexual Behavior* 8: 151–57.
———. 1985. Preadult feminine behaviors of male transvestites. *Archives of Sexual Behavior* 14: 413–19.
Bullough, Bonnie, Vern L. Bullough, and Richard Smith. 1985. Masculinity and femininity in transvestite, transsexual and gay males. *Western Journal of Nursing Research* 7: 317–32.
Bullough, Vern L., and Bonnie Bullough. 1993. *Cross dressing, sex and gender.* Philadelphia: University of Pennsylvania Press.
Bullough, Vern L., and Bonnie Bullough, and Richard Smith. 1983a. A comparative study of male transvestites, male to female transsexuals, and male homosexuals. *Journal of Sex Research* (19 August): 238–57.
———. 1983b. Childhood and family values of male sexual minority groups. *Health Values: Achieving High Level Wellness* 7: 19–26.
Docter, Richard F. 1988. *Transvestites and transsexuals: Toward a theory of cross-gender behavior.* New York: Plenum Press.
———. 1993. Dimensions of transvestism and transsexualism. *Journal of Psychology and Human Sexuality* 5: 15–37
Ellis, Havelock, 1913. Sexo-aesthetic inversion. *Alienist and Neurologist* 34, pt. 1 (May 1913): 3–14; pt. 2 (August 1913): 1–31.
———. [1906] 1936. Eonism. In *Studies in the psychology of sex,* vol. 2, pt. 2, 1–120. New York: Random House.

Fagan, Peter, J., Thomas Wise, Leonard J. Derogotis, and Chester W. Schmidt. 1988. Distressed transvestites, psychometric characteristics. *Journal of Nervous and Mental Disorders* 176: 214–17.

Fenichel, Otto. 1945. *The psychoanalytic theory of neuroses.* New York: Norton.

Gutheil, Emil. 1930. An analysis of a case of transvestism. In *Sexual aberrations; the phenomenon of fetishism in relation to sex,* edited by Wilhelm Stekel, 345–51. New York: Liveright Publishing Co.

Hirschfeld, Magnus. 1991. *Transvestites: An investigation of the erotic drive to cross-dress.* Translated by Michael Lombardi-Nash. Amherst, N.Y.: Prometheus Books (Originally, Leipzig: Medical Publishing House Max Spohr Publishers, 1910).

Hora, T. 1953. The Structural Analysis of Transvestism. *Psychoanalytic Review* 40, 268-74.

Krafft-Ebing, Richard von. 1933. *Psychopathia sexualis: With especial reference to the antipathic sexual instinct: A medico-forensic study.* Translated and adapted from the twelfth German edition by F. J. Rebman. Brooklyn, N.Y.: Physicians and Surgeons Book Co.

Lukianowicz, N. 1959. Survey of various aspects of transvestism in light of our present knowledge. *Journal of Nervous and Mental Disorders* 128: 36–64.

Newcomb, Michael. 1985. The rule of perceived relative parent personality in the development of heterosexuals, homosexuals and transvestites. *Archives of Sexual Behavior* 14: 147–64.

Peabody, G. A., A. T. Rowe, and J. M. Wall. 1953. Fetishism and transvestism. *Journal of Nervous and Mental Disease* 119: 339–50.

Person, Ethyl, and Lionel Ovesey. 1978. Transvestism: New perspectives. *Journal of the American Academy of Psychoanalysis* 6: 304–22.

Prince, C. Virginia, and P. M. Bentler. 1972. Survey of 504 cases of transvestism. *Psychological Reports* 31: 903–17.

Randall, J. B. 1959. Transvestism and trans-sexualism : A study of 50 cases. *British Medical Journal* 2: 1148–52.

Schott, Richard L. 1995. The childhood and family dynamics of transvestites. *Archives of Sexual Behavior* 24: 309–27.

Stoller, Robert J. 1971. The term "transvestism." *Archives of General Psychiatry* 24: 230–33.

Culturally Universal Aspects of Male Homosexual Transvestites and Transsexuals

Frederick L. Whitam

Some confusion exists within the psychiatric and sex research communities with regard to the nature of transvestites and transsexuals. Some of this confusion can be traced to an effort some thirty years ago to have the term "transvestite" refer exclusively to heterosexual transvestites, only one of the two main groups of transvestites. Before this change in terminology the term transvestite and its cognates or equivalent terms were used historically and cross-culturally to refer to homosexual transvestites. Male homosexual transvestites and transsexuals exist as a group in homosexual communities in all societies. While lesbian transvestites and female-to-male transsexuals probably exist in all societies as well, it is male homosexual transvestites and transsexuals who appear to be most conspicuous and most common. If one works cross-culturally, it is the male homosexual transvestite/transsexual whom the investigator is most likely to encounter first. The following summary highlights the culturally universal characteristics of male homosexual transvestites/transsexuals:

1. Homosexual TVs/TSs are highly cross-gendered as children.
2. Homosexual TVs/TSs exhibit low levels of athletic interest as children.
3. Homosexual TVs/TSs often are highly feminized, with early appearance of "sissy" behavior and early interests in highly sex-typed "feminine" activities.
4. Homosexual TVs/TSs do not cross-dress fetishistically.
5. Manner of dress of homosexual TVs/TSs tends to be theatrical and "glamorous."

6. All male homosexual TV/TS communities of any size produce a conspicuous entertainment form(s).
7. The most appealing occupations for homosexual TVs/TSs are entertaining, singing, dancing, acting, and related performances.
8. Homosexual TVs/TSs often work in traditionally female or "gay" occupations such as prostitution, hair styling, seamstress, maids, manicurists.
9. Homosexual TVs/TSs have high levels of genital sexual interest.
10. The sexual partners of male homosexual TVs/TSs tend to be heterosexual or bisexual men.

These conclusions are based on ethnographic observation of and interviews with homosexual TVs/TSs in Brazil, Guatemala, the Philippines, Indonesia, Thailand, and the United States from 1975 through the present.

Sociologists and anthropologists tend to emphasize the variability of human behavior in order to call attention to the role of culture in the shaping of human existence. In so doing they have often ignored the importance of cultural invariability. One of the most remarkable aspects of gay communities is the striking similarity in the behavior of subgroups of male homosexual transvestites and transsexuals that exist within the larger gay communities in culturally different societies. Each time I have entered a new gay subculture, it is with remarkable predictability that I have found not only the existence of a subgroup of homosexual transvestites and transsexuals, but also that these groups tend to resemble each other in considerable detail. Their general appearance is similar, including behavior that is difficult to quantify (such as gestures, facial expressions, and mannerisms). These groups use cross-gendered pronouns among themselves, using the equivalent of "she" and "her" in respective languages and giving themselves female names.

Much of the research on transsexualism is clinically based and tends to emphasize the notion that transsexuals are a markedly different class of people from transvestites. Observation of these people in the field, and attending their social functions, beauty contests, performances, and other social events suggest a somewhat different picture—and I emphasize that I refer only to homosexual transvestites and transsexuals. In all the societies where I have observed such people, the most important distinction within the homosexual communities is between conventionally masculine gay men on the one hand and transvestites/transsexuals on the other, not the distinction between transvestites and transsexuals. The homosexual transvestites and transsexuals tend to form a single social group, somewhat apart from more masculine gay men, and do not ordinarily draw strongly demarcated lines between the transvestites who cross-dress less frequently and the transsexuals who tend to live as women, feel they should have been women, and may desire sex reassignment surgery. There exists a complex continuum of cross-gendered behavior within this group. Some homosexual transvestites have fleetingly or seriously considered sex reassignment surgery. Some are very close to being transsexual. Even if the transvestites do not desire surgery themselves, they understand the transsexuals' desires and vice versa. Even after surgery many transsexuals of this type continue to be friends with the transvestites, attend their shows, bars, and social functions. Even post-operative transsexuals of this type, despite marriage or relationships with heterosexual men, often remain in close contact with the "drag queens," frequently attend drag shows, and give advice to young "drag queens" and transsexuals.

Obviously points 1, 2, and 3 are interrelated. transvestites and transsexuals of the homosexual type are highly cross gendered as children, exhibit low levels of athletic interest, and are often highly feminized, characterized by extensive "sissy" behavior and interest in highly sex-typed female activities. There appears to be a strong association between adult sexual orientation and overt femininity in homosexual men, with the more overtly feminine reporting the most extensive early-childhood cross-gendered behavior. It is unfortunate that the discussion of "gender identity disorders" in DSM-IV (1994) blurs the distinction between transvestites and transsexuals of the homosexual type and transvestites and transsexuals of the heterosexual type. In ignoring this fundamental distinction DSM-IV has grouped all transvestites and transsexuals together as a single behavioral entity, when in fact, the two groups can and should be separated for purposes of analysis and for meaningful understanding of the behavior of the two groups. This blurring between the two groups is especially misleading in the discussion of childhood manifestation of "gender identity disorder." The DSM-IV reads as follows:

> In boys, the cross-gender identification is manifested by a marked preoccupation with traditionally feminine activities. They must have a preference for dressing in girls' or women's clothes or may improvise such items from available materials when genuine articles are unavailable. Towels, aprons, and scarves are often used to represent long hair or skirts. They particularly enjoy playing house, drawing pictures of beautiful girls and princesses, and watching television or videos of their favorite female characters. Stereotypical female-type dolls, such as Barbie, are often their favorite toys, and girls are their preferred playmates. When playing "house," these boys role-play female figures, most commonly "mother roles," and often are quite preoccupied with female fantasy figures. They avoid rough-and-tumble play and competitive sports and have little interest in cars and trucks or other nonaggressive but stereotypical boys' toys. They may express a wish to be a girl and assert that they will grow up to be women. They may insist on sitting to urinate and pretend not to have a

penis by pushing it in between their legs. More rarely, boys with Gender Identity Disorder may state that they find their penis or testes disgusting, that they want to remove them, or that they have, or wish to have, a vagina. (1994, 530)

This excerpt from DSM-IV is not an accurate description of the childhood behavior of transvestites and transsexual of the heterosexual type, who tend to exhibit considerably less cross-gender behavior. Often their only cross-gender behavior is cross-dressing, which may not appear until just before, during, or after puberty and is often done in secret. Many transvestites and transsexuals of the heterosexual type have childhood experiences indistinguishable from those of boys who later become nontransvestic heterosexual men. On the other hand, it is rare to find homosexual transvestites/transsexuals whose childhood behavior resembles that of boys who as adults are heterosexual. The DSM-IV uses the childhood profile of the homosexual transvestite/transsexual, misleading the reader to believe that this description is accurate for the transvestites and transsexuals of the heterosexual type as well.

Such complex cross-gender behavior in childhood is to be found in all the societies. The notion suggested for example by Gagnon (1987, 742) that cultures differ so markedly in social definitions and meanings of gender, femininity, masculinity, and sexual orientation or that non-Western languages differ so completely from "Western" languages that it is impossible to accurately translate and infer meanings of these and related terms and concepts is simply not correct. All homosexual transvestites and transsexual informants in the various societies in which I worked were able to discuss intelligently their cross-gendered childhood experience and were able to understand without the help of psychiatrists that they were indeed transvestites or transsexuals. This is true even of the least Westernized society studied—Indonesia. For example, Rina and Rini revealed in interviews childhood experiences remarkably similar to those experienced by homosexual transvestites/transsexuals in Western societies and their experiences are consistent with the description of the childhood behavior of such people as described in DSM-IV. For example, Rina, a twenty-four year-old *waria,* is from a lower-middle-class family in which the father is a minor government official. Rina remembers being a "sissy" boy and wanting to be a little girl as early as four years of age. For several years his parents sent him to a doctor because he was so effeminate, but at age fourteen gave up trying to change him when he started to cross-dress regularly. His parents presently respect him as he is and allow him to live at home cross-dressed. Another *waria,* Rini, was born into a middle-class family in which the father is an air force officer. Rini also was a highly effeminate boy who felt like a girl at age five and liked cooking and girls' activities and games. Both Rina and Rini cross-dress full time, live with their families, and are known in the neighborhood. They report that attitudes are generally tolerant, though some people don't like *waria.* They are attracted to men and work as prostitutes in the evenings.

All or nearly all societies have words in their language to refer to such people. For example, the term *bayot* in Cebuano (Philippines), *louca* or *travesti* in Portuguese, *loca* in Spanish, *kathoey* in Thai, *banci* or *waria* in Indonesian, and "queen" or "drag queen" in English mean very much the same, referring to effeminate male homosexuals, homosexual transvestites, or transsexuals. Terminology in each of the societies tends to be more complex than suggested here, often including more than one word for these persons. For example, two commonly used terms for Javanese transvestites/transsexuals are *banci* and *waria. Banci* is the older, more traditional and familiar term while *waria,* coined from *wanita* (woman) and *pria* (man), is the newer and, from the point of view of emerging Indonesian homosexual and *waria* organizations, more politically correct term. Both terms are sometimes used by non-homosexual Indonesians to refer to all homosexuals. Members of the homosexual community use the terms *waria* and *banci* to refer to the transvestite/transsexual subset of their group. While both *banci* and *waria* are used by Javanese transvestites/transsexuals, *banci* seems to be more frequently used in West Java and *waria* is more common in East Java.

Point number 4 states that transvestites and transsexuals of the homosexual type do not cross-dress fetishistically, unlike the transvestites and transsexuals of the heterosexual type, who often report cross-dressing fetishistically at least for a period of time, usually in the late teens or early twenties. With more complete and regular cross-dressing this often stops by the mid-twenties except for persons whose cross-dressing is primarily fetishistic. Apart from these, a few cross-dressers continue to cross-dress fetishistically occasionally throughout their lives.

The cross-dressing of transvestites and transsexuals of the homosexual type seems to hold different meanings from those of the heterosexual type. It is commonly held by individuals of the heterosexual type that "drag queens" cross-dress just for the "fun of it" or "to attract men," with the implication that transvestites/transsexuals of the heterosexual type are the "real" transvestites/transsexuals while the cross-dressing of individuals of the homosexual type is "superficial" and of a purely volitional nature.

In reality, the cross-dressing of both groups is characterized by a strong element of complusivity. The cross-dressing of individuals of the homosexual type often emerges earlier in childhood, is usually more complete, and is more apt to be conducted publicly than that of individuals of the heterosexual type.

Transvestites and transsexuals of the heterosexual type usually dress conventionally so as to pass and blend. Homosexuals, on the other hand, as suggested by point 5, dress in a more unconventional manner so as to call attention to themselves and to project an image of glamour, sensuality, and theatricality. Their dressing merges with the costuming for shows and other performances that some members of this group give. They seem to be drawn toward cross-dressing and related activities such as grooming and make-up quite naturally and at an early age. Janice, an American post-operative transsexual, for example, reports that at the age of twelve or thirteen (as an effeminate boy), she gave advice to her junior-high girlfriends who sought her help about their make-up, hair, and dress style when dressing for proms and parties. Tata is a Native American who lives full time as a woman, has boyfriends, but does not desire sex reassignment surgery. She started sewing at a very early age and now makes many of the costumes for drag shows in Phoenix although she does not perform herself.

Not unrelated to cross-dressing is interest in performing—dancing, acting, singing, and related activities, as suggested by points 6 and 7. In all observed communities of homosexual transvestites/transsexuals, giving performances occupies a conspicuous place and is probably the single most important behavior that distinguishes this group from not only heterosexual men in general but from heterosexual transvestites/transsexuals as well, who rarely are involved in performances. The particular cultural form through which performances are presented varies from society to society, and the specific content depends upon the cultural context. Yet the underlying impulse to perform exists regardless of the culture. In the Philippines, for example, several types of performances have emerged. An important social event in Cebu City is an annual expensive dinner-and-fashion show held at a leading hotel and attended by many well-to-do Cebuanos. The entire event is planned and executed by the *bayot* with the full knowledge of those attending that this is a *bayot* event. At the same hotel on Sunday afternoons, the *bayot* may be seen at the swimming pool camping and laughing, putting on make-up and teasing hair. The heterosexual Filipinos who work or swim at the Magellan Hotel hardly react at all to what is regard as highly innocent behavior. Even Gigi, a stunning pre-operative transsexual, hardly caused an eyebrow to be lifted when she used the women's locker room to change clothes.

In Bacolod, also in the Viasayas, the *bayot* are conspicuous in the Christmas Eve festival, the town's major event held in the "Sea-Breeze," Bacolod's leading hotel. The Christmas Eve festival consists of traditional Filipino folk dancing, singing, caroling, feasting, and midnight Mass, followed by partying until dawn. Most of the folk dancing is done by *bayot* who take both male and female parts. The queen of the Christmas festival—crowned by the leading matrons of Bacolod—is also a *bayot*. Midnight mass is said to all participants of this celebration including the *bayot,* who take mass cross-dressed.

Perhaps the best-known and most popular of the *bayot* activities, however, is the "beauty contest." These are female impersonation shows in which *bayot* typically pretend to be representatives of various countries participating in an international beauty pageant. They are organized and presented all over the Philippines in both large and small towns. No town's annual fiesta is complete without a *bayot* beauty contest, and it is one of the favorite events of the fiesta. A remarkable aspect of the Philippine beauty pageant is that it is not regarded as a decadent, sub-rosa activity, suitable only for a third-rate gay club, as in the United States, but rather is viewed as family entertainment. The beauty contest I attended was held in a barrio near a military base and was sponsored by the Philippine military base for the entertainment of the families of the base and the general public, with prizes donated by the base commander and presented by local civic leaders. Local residents paid a small fee to attend, and many children were in the audience and delighted by the performances. *Bayot* contests are often sponsored by the Rotary or Kiwanis Clubs in various parts of the Philippines as luncheon entertainments.

Female impersonation is a popular activity of the *kathoey* of Thailand, where attitudes are also quite tolerant. Female impersonation shows are presented in gay clubs as well as in special theaters built for female impersonation. Bangkok, Pattaya, Chiang Mai, and Phuket are the major centers for female impersonation. In the resort city of Pattaya three extravagant palaces of female impersonation have been built as commercial enterprises—Simon Show, Alcazar, and Tiffany. Tiffany, for example, is a multimillion dollar building, lavishly furnished with chandeliers, elegant staircases, plush seating, deep carpet, and splendid outside fountains lit by night. Every evening extravaganzas are presented mainly for tourists, both Thai and foreign. The cast consists of some one hundred performers who range from gay men who want to perform to *kathoey* who are the equivalent of "drag queens" to *kathoey* who live full time as women and may or may not have sex reassignment surgery. The music, choreography, and costumes are handled by members of the *kathoey* community. These performances are considered a part of the larger gay community.

The Thai *kathoey* also perform a camp version of classical masked dance-drama called the "kön" that is normally performed in Buddhist temples. Allyn and Impardith describe this camp performance as follows:

Li'gay . . . is a popular earthy form of performance. Performers are usually made up in flamboyant costumes, and painted with grotesque make-up. The songs are bawdy, there is lots of slapstick, and the accompanying music is jarring. Audiences spontaneously interact with performers, resulting in more mirth. A number of gay bars throughout the country put on such shows but with transvestite performers, many of whom are nationally known. Many of these shows could be described as "high camp." (1993, 26)

Indonesia, predominantly Muslim, is a more conservative society than either the Philippines or Thailand with regard to attitudes toward both homosexuals and female impersonation. Surabaya, Java, the second city of Indonesia, is said to be the most tolerant city in the country for female impersonation. In Indonesia modern drag shows can be found simultaneously with female impersonation in centuries-old traditional theatrical forms. There are an estimated 450 *waria* in the Surabaya area. Of these, two hundred are members of a *waria* organization officially called Persatuan Waria Kotamadya Surabaya (Transvestite Organization of Surabaya) and commonly known as "Perwakos." Seventeen of these two hundred have had sex reassignment surgery. Many Surabayan *waria* have breast development from ingestion of a birth control pill called Pil Keluarga Berencana containing estrogen. Surabayan *waria* carry on a lively trade in prostitution in homemade huts made of branches and pieces of wood along a river bank in central Surabaya. They are also to be found in the beauty salons, and their performances center on public singing and roles in traditional *ludruk* drama.

Waria singers perform every Thursday night in the well-known Taman Hiburan Rakyat (People's Amusement Park) in central Surabaya. The venue consists of an open-air bandshell stage with a concrete dance area in front. As many as twenty *waria* singers perform on Thursday evenings accompanied by *dangdut* music, a kind of Indonesian rock. The non-*waria dangdut* group occupies the stage with the *waria* singers who, in contrast to female impersonators in many countries, do not lip-synch but actually sing with a microphone while several hundred young men and women dance to the musical performance. Non-singing *waria* are conspicuous in the audience, as well as many non-*waria* gays and a few lesbians. This Thursday night event is known in the Surabayan gay community as "gay night" and is very popular, especially with working-class gays and lesbians.

The most glamorous roles played by East Javanese *waria* are those of singers and actresses in *ludruk*. According to Peacock (1986, 29) the *ludruk* drama is found in Java as early as the thirteenth century. *Ludruk* was quite popular in East Java until the 1970s when the advent of television and other aspects of modernization contributed to its decline. While it is not known at what point in its history the *waria* began taking women's roles in *ludruk*, their presence in this drama form has been documented by eyewitness accounts and reported in Pigeaud (1938, 32) as early as 1822.

Ludruk is usually performed on Friday evening in villages in the Surabaya area. The rather large traveling troupe consisted of about thirty actors, including the owner who played a leading male role. Half of the company were *waria* playing women's roles. One ordinary female actress was also a member of the cast. Another ten or so people performed tasks such as wardrobe lady and stage hands. The performance took place in the village of Sawo Cangkring some fifteen miles south of Surabaya. The Javanese language, not Bahasa Indonesian, was used because the audience was mainly working-class village people.

The performance itself consisted of three parts: (1) a musical prologue sung by *waria*, (2) a comic prologue, and (3) the main event titled "Chinese Romeo and Juliet" accompanied by a *gamelan* orchestra. All singing and female parts except for one were taken by *waria*.

As suggested by point 8, the occupational interests of homosexual transvestites/transsexuals appear to be similar in all societies observed and include highly sex-typed "female" or "gay" occupations such as hair styling, sewing, manicure, domestic workers and the like. Better-educated persons of this group may work as social workers, nurses, clerks, and even teachers where permitted. Laura de Vison is a fifty-year-old, 250-pound, Brazilian *travesti* who by night performs in the famous gay club Boêmio in Rio de Janeiro, and by day is Norberto Chucri Davi, a social studies teacher in a public school. Norberto uses female impersonation in his teaching, dressing, for example, as Cleopatra or other famous women in history while he lectures. Some Filipino *bayot* are public school teachers and wear light make-up to school, though they do not cross-dress at work. It is unusual to find transvestites/transsexuals of this type in traditional masculine occupations such as mechanic, engineer, or airplane pilot. Their occupational interests contrast sharply with those of the heterosexual transvestites/transsexuals whose occupational interests are much wider in scope and include traditionally masculine occupations. It is rare to find persons of this latter type employed as beauticians or manicurists.

All groups of homosexual transvestites/transsexuals seem to contain conspicuous numbers of prostitutes. Some individuals hold jobs such as beautician by day and work as prostitutes by night. In Bandung, West Java, for example, there are reported to be about one hundred *waria*, all of whom are more or less known to each other. About twenty-five of the more affluent *waria* own their hairdressing salons and another twenty-five work for them in the salons. Another fifty work as prostitutes, some of whom have part-time jobs in the hair salons. The prostitutes are divided into two groups—a middle-class group of about thirty that frequents Taman Malaku (Malaku Park) and a lower-class group of about twenty that works near Taman Tagallega (Tagallega Park). The Bandung *waria* occasionally give shows in rented halls or discos.

These respondents stated that all Bandung *waria* would like to have sex reassignment surgery, although at present only two have had the expensive surgery. Many have had hormonal breast development or implants. Oetomo and Emond (1990, 2) dispute the notion that all *waria* wish to have sex reassignment surgery, contending that some *waria* are content to cross-dress. This contention is consistent with my observations in Indonesia and other societies where transvestites and transsexuals tend to form a single cross-gendered group consisting of some members who wish surgery and some who do not.

While prostitution is illegal in Indonesia, laws against prostitution are not usually enforced as long as prostitutes work in designated areas. *Waria* prostitutes in Bandung are treated much the same as female prostitutes and report that they are well-treated as long as they stay in the two designated parks. Police sometimes advise *waria* prostitutes to stay out of the parks on certain holidays such as Independence Day or during Ramadan.

The local Bandung government uses a social work approach rather than criminalization, fostering a *waria* organization that meets twice a year and provides the *waria* classes in hair dressing, clothes-making, and photography in an effort to increase marketable skills and discourage prostitution.

The *travestis* of Brazil are quite famous as prostitutes. They cater mainly to heterosexual and bisexual men with exotic sexual tastes and are equivalent to persons who are called "she-males" in the United States. Such tastes seem to be more highly developed in Brazil and other Latin countries than in the English-speaking world. Reliable sources in São Paulo (such as social workers who interview infected *travestis* at São Paulo's main AIDS facility, the Centro de Referencia e Treinamento AIDS) report that in 70 percent of their sexual contacts the *travestis* take the *ativo* role, performing anal sex on their clients. Relatively few Brazilian *travestis* have sex reassignment surgery, partly because they are regarded by some Brazilian men as desirable secondary sex objects even without surgery and because surgery would put an end to their careers as prostitutes. A *travesti* in São Paulo told me that she would like the surgery, but it would cut off her income as a prostitute because so many clients request *ativo* anal sex performed by the *travesti*.

A highly publicized and dramatic event in recent years was the exodus in the late 1970s and early 1980s of large numbers of *travesti* prostitutes to Europe, especially to Paris and Rome. Trevisan writes:

> Since the end of the 1970's a large number of [transvestite prostitutes] have arrived in Paris, considered the paradise of transvestite prostitution. There, it is said, they have managed to make small fortunes on the street or, more rarely, in cabaret shows. At the peak of this unexpected migration there were even special charter flights for transvestites from Brazil to Paris. Of the 700 transvestite prostitutes working in France 500 are reckoned to be Brazilian—and very successful. (1986, 165)

Some of the early arrivals made considerable amounts of money and returned to Brazil with their savings. Many also became infected with AIDS, having arrived in Paris just as the AIDS virus was making its appearance there. *Travestis*, shuttling among Paris and Rio de Janeiro and São Paulo, became an important conduit for the introduction of the AIDS virus into Brazil. By 1985 the French police began to harass and even beat and rob them, according to Sander, who writes that they then moved to Milan where

> The meeting place became the cemetery called the Alberto Algentário Cemetery, which at the time was frequented by female prostitutes until there was a fight in the cemetery between the *travestis* and the female prostitutes. The *travestis* won because the real women had other places to go. In the mid-80's the Brazilian *travestis* began to move *en masse* from France to Italy. The Italian men were very susceptible to the Brazilian *travestis'* charms and the Italian media gave them enormous attention. (1993, 41, translated by F. Whitam)

One of the most famous *travestis* in Brazil presently is "Brenda Lee," who was one of the early arrivals in Paris. After a few years in Paris she returned to São Paulo and bought a large, three-story house which now has been turned into a hospice for *travestis* with AIDS. Brenda Lee administers the hospice, called "Casa de Brenda Lee," from her private quarters under the direction of public health authorities. The color theme, gold and white, is carried throughout the house. The outside of the building and even her car are painted gold and white. Brenda Lee lives cross-dressed but has not had nor does she desire sex reassignment surgery.

As suggested by point 9, homosexual transvestites tend to have high levels of genital interest—after all, they are genetic males. The use of camp humor and explicit sexual references are immediately obvious in all these groups. Sex and especially sexual references to men are prominent in their conversation. Female impersonation shows typically utilize bawdy, sexually explicit humor and sometimes even props such as oversize dildoes and other toys.

Chita, an American twenty-seven years of age, has neither breast development nor sex reassignment surgery but lives most of the time cross-dressed. However, she manages to dress in such a way as to give the appearance of having breasts and works as a part-time street prostitute, specializing in active anal sex with heterosexual or bisexual men. She also specializes in servicing ex-cons and is said to have her telephone number written on all the prison walls in Arizona. She receives and responds to masturbatory phone calls from prisons, likes to have ex-cons stay with her after their release, keeps a written record of her sexual adventures, and claims to have had sexual relations with 2,500 men.

Some homosexual transvestites/transsexuals report impersonating women as telephone sex workers on 900 numbers. Employees, of course, realize they are not real women, but telephone customers do not. Transsexuals of this type often do not live conventional married lives even after marriage to heterosexual men. Candace, an American post-operative transsexual, is married to a prosperous businessman with whom she has an active sex life. Even so, she frequents hustler bars, sometimes picking up tricks or accepting money from men for sexual encounters.

The most sexually explicit academic presentation I have witnessed was a panel of *bayot* at the Roman Catholic University of San Carlos in Cebu City, Philippines. In front of an audience consisting of many teachers, priests, and nuns, as well as students, the *bayot* told ribald jokes and stories that included graphic descriptions and references to anal sex, fellatio, and other unconventional sexual acts. Their outrageous performance was encouraged by calls from the engineering students who sponsored the event.

A Native American Apache transvestite, Cara, presenting in one of my classes, recently talked mainly about her sexual exploits with men, evoking from the class the criticism that she was "man-crazy."

I am aware of a strain of thought that emphasizes the spirituality of such people and the notion that they are often shamans and healers. I have failed to find any *intrinsic* connection between spirituality and these transvestites/transsexuals. There are undoubtedly individual transvestites and transsexuals of this type who are shamans and healers. There are societies where cross-gendered people are considered to have special powers, but I have neither seen nor heard anything suggesting that this behavior is typical of such people. On the contrary, this group seems to be quite carnal and explicitly sexual rather than spiritual.

Whether within the context of prostitution or otherwise, the sexual partners of homosexual transvestites and transsexuals tend to be heterosexual or bisexual men, as suggested by point 10. Conventionally gay men are not usually sexually attracted to such people, nor do the transvestites and transsexuals seem to be interested in gay men.

Homosexual transvestites have long occupied a role in Brazilian sexuality. Brazil maintains the custom of the beautiful and elegant *travesti* as a secondary sex symbol for men. The position occupied by Rogeria and Valeria a generation ago, in the 1980s and early 1990s was occupied by Roberta Close, one of Brazil's most celebrated *travestis*, who frequently appeared on television and in well-known nightclubs. Heterosexual men often expressed admiration for Roberta Close's beauty and some desired sexual relations with her. It is said that recently Roberta Close underwent sex reassignment surgery in Germany and married a wealthy German man. At a different social level many lower-class *travestis* work cross-dressed as street prostitutes and may be found in all large Brazilian cities. Their clients are usually heterosexual and bisexual men, often married, who pay the *travesti* to perform sexually. It is commonly said that most houses of prostitution in Brazil, even in small towns in the interior, keep at least one *travesti* on hand to meet clients' needs. With regard to Brazilian *travesti* prostitutes in Italy the *Journal Do Brasil* (1986, 12) reports that ". . . Lucy says that she earns up to 430 dollars a night, going out with 10 or 12 men. Her clients are not gays but heterosexual men in search of the exotic."

Heterosexual men in the Philippines commonly use *bayot* as substitutes for women. Teen-aged girls and young women from poor families are encouraged to maintain their virginity intact so as to make the best marriage possible in order to pull themselves and their families out of poverty. Most Filipinos are aware of the frequent *bayot*-heterosexual male liaisons and many approve such contact as a way of controlling pre-marital pregnancies.

Stage door johnnies—heterosexual men—customarily gather back-stage during the *bayot* beauty contests where they await the outcome of the contest, flirting and joking with the contestants. By tradition, the winner selects her man and spends the prize money on him. It is not unusual in the Philippines to see heterosexual men on dates with their *bayot* "girlfriends," who usually pay the bills for the dinner and discos and may even give their boyfriends spending money or buy him clothes.

One of the few brothels in the world featuring transvestites and transsexuals exclusively is located in Pattaya, Thailand. All have breast enhancement and some have had sex reassignment surgery. Bangkok has become the center for such surgery in the Southeast Asian region. The English language newspaper the *Nation* (1995, C1) estimates that some five hundred sex reassignment surgeries are preformed on *kathoey* each year. A public controversy has emerged, however, because the surgery is performed by plastic surgeons, many of whom are not properly trained for sex reassignment surgery. Moreover, there is little regulation of and psychological preparation for such surgeries. A significant number of cases of post-operative emotional problems have been reported. The *kathoey* prostitutes undergo surgery in part to attract more customers or in hopes of snaring a "husband." In Chiang Mai lower-class *kathoey* prostitutes are conspicuous in the evenings soliciting near The Pae Gate in the city center. Their customers tend to be heterosexual men on whom they perform fellatio or whom they allow to perform active anal sex for five dollars.

American transvestites/transsexuals have relationships almost exclusively with heterosexual or bisexual men. When post-operative transsexuals marry, it is almost always with heterosexual men. Most drag shows have a following of heterosexual men who attend the shows to admire the drag queens and ask for dates. Lower-class drag queens often form quasi-marital relationships with street hustlers, ex-cons, or other heterosexual men who may be drug users or otherwise unemployable.

The clients of *waria* prostitutes in Indonesia are mainly heterosexual males consisting of three types: (1) young, single men, not yet married, who use *waria* as a substitute for women and who will eventually marry and forget about *waria*; (2) men who like women most of the time but who pick up *waria* occasionally for fun or extra kicks; (3) men who seem to be attracted mainly to *waria*. Most common sexual activities are hugging and fondling, kissing, performing oral sex on the client, and playing the passive role in anal intercourse. Rates are 10,000 to 20,000 rupiah ($5.00 to $10.00 U.S.).

In contrast to the strong, overt sexuality of the homosexual transvestites/transsexuals, the heterosexuals seem to manifest significantly lower levels of sexual interest, despite the fact that they are also genetic males. While many, no doubt, privately maintain active sexual lives, within this group norms emerged which discourage sexual conversations and contacts. By definition, the sexual partners of the heterosexual group are women, and it is well known that sex reassignment surgery does not change sexual orientation. Despite this fact, a few post-operative transsexuals from this group enter into relationships or even marry heterosexual men, usually from within the transgender community. It is not clear whether this is related to the fact that these individuals were somewhat bisexual pre-operatively or whether estrogen treatment has lowered sexual interest to the point where such an adjustment is possible, or whether other factors are involved. Nonetheless, the sexual partners of this group are generally heterosexual women, though a few may be lesbian.

It is obvious to all who have worked with transvestites and transsexuals that their behavior is quite complex. This present discussion has focused on male homosexual transvestites and transsexuals, with some reference to heterosexual transvestites and transsexuals. It should be kept in mind that there are also female-to-male transvestites and transsexuals, hermaphroditic transvestites and transsexuals, and probably other types of individuals who do not fit neatly into any of these categories. Yet most transgendered people—perhaps 90 percent—fall into one of the two main categories discussed here. It is indeed unfortunate that DSM-IV has failed to delineate and describe the differences between these two main groups in any meaningful way. This retrogressive move by DSM-IV will add to, rather than resolve, the confusion and misunderstanding that already surrounds transgendered people.

Note

In connection with conducting field research I gratefully acknowledge the invaluable help of the following persons—in Brazil: Celeste Cerviño Rivas, Léa Maria Fonsêca, Maria de

Lourdes Motta, Hédimo Rodrigues Santana, Aroldo Assunção, and Dr. Luiz Mott of the Federal University of Bahia; in Peru: Gaby Cáceres Girón, Octavio Gerónimo Pérez, and members of the Movimiento Homosexual de Lima (MOHL); in the Philippines: Professors Agapito G. Tiu and Lourdes Cedeño of the University of Jose-Recoletos and Dr. Resil Mojares and Father Theodore Murnane of the University of San Carlos, and Weenie Cedeño of Manila; in the United States: scores of women who wish to remain anonymous. In Indonesia I thank Dr. DéDé Octomo, lecturer in anthropology, University of Airlangga, Surabaya. I am also grateful to Ruddy Mustapha, Jusup Rianto, and Mbak Ratana, all of Surabaya. In Yogyakarta I am indebted to André Susanto and Sindhu Suyana. For his excellent interpretative skills I thank Bruce Emond.

Grateful acknowledgment is made to the College of Liberal Arts and Sciences at Arizona State University for research and travel grants in connection with data collection in Brazil, Peru, and the Philippines.

References

Allyn, E., and S. Inpradith, eds. 1993. *The men of Thailand: 1993 guide to gay Thailand.* 4th ed. San Francisco: Bua Luang Publishing Company.

American Psychiatric Association. 1994. *Diagnostic and statistical manual of mental disorders.* 4th ed. Washington, D.C.: American Psychiatric Association.

DSM-IV. 1994. See American Psychiatric Association.

Gagnon, J. 1987. Review of *Male homosexuality in four societies: Brazil, Guatemala, the Philippines and the United States,* by F. Whitam and R. Mathy. *American Journal of Sociology* (November): 742.

Journal Do Brasil (Rio De Janerio). 1986. Travestis brasileiros animam a "dolce vita" romana. Terca-feira 23 de Setembro: 12.

The Nation. 1995. A cosmetic crossing. (May 31): C1, C3.

Oetomo, D., and B. Emond. 1990. Homosexuality in Indonesia. Translated by S. Suyana. Unpublished manuscript.

Ponooolt, J. L. 1968. *Rites of modernization. Social aspects of Indonesian proletariat drama.* Chicago: The University of Chicago Press.

Pigeaud, T. 1938. *Javaanse Volksvertoningen.* Batavia: Volkslectuur.

Sander, M. 1993. A saga dos travestis Brasileiros na Europa. *Travestis,* Edição No. 240, Ano IX, No. 12-C, 41–43.

Trevisan, J. S. 1986. *Perverts in paradise.* Translated by M. Foreman. London: GMP.

The Transvestite's Lover: Identity and Behavior

Jacobo Schifter and Johnny Madrigal

Although transvestites in Costa Rica are exploited by mass media, the police, and sex magazines, very little is known about their sexual partners or lovers. The clientele of the transvestite dedicated to prostitution (because there are quite a few who are not) is very hidden and difficult to interview. Most of the clients are married men who do not feel comfortable exposing their identity to an interviewer. The same can be said about the transvestites' lovers. Nevertheless, in 1990, with the idea of studying transvestite culture, the Association for the Fight against AIDS, known by its Spanish acronym, ILPES, decided to perform an ethnographic study and in-depth interviews, as well as a survey about attitudes and knowledge of AIDS among the transvestite population of the red light districts of San Jose and of other areas such as the "La Clinica Biblica." Transvestites who did not already live in these zones were also visited in their homes throughout different areas of the city. An interviewer who knew many of them personally was selected for this task. During the next three months he did twenty-two closed-ended interviews and twenty in-depth interviews. One thousand colóns was paid to each prostitute for the interview. Each interview was taped and the name of the respondent was kept in total confidence.

In order to broaden the knowledge of the transvestite culture, 1,000 colóns was also offered to each partner in exchange for an interview. The interviewer was a gay male who as a young boy had sold lottery tickets to transvestites. They felt comfortable with him and the partners or lovers agreed to participate with little hesitation. The names used when transcribing the interviews are not the real names of either the transvestites or their lovers.

204

Who Are They?

All of the lovers were men who think of themselves as heterosexual but for one reason or another decided to try a transvestite relationship. Their lifestyle is similar to that of any other Costa Rican heterosexual male: married, with children, and attracted to feminine qualities. They do not remember, as children, feeling attracted to their own sex or having any feeling of being "different," as occurs with many men who are gay. In their replies, there is no evidence that they feel attraction toward men other than the transvestites. Most of the men interviewed are blue-collar workers with very low incomes and little schooling. Juan Carlos sells Jell O at a local market and makes about 400 colóns a day; he used to work as a mechanic and a shoe repairman. Delio is a construction worker who finished the sixth grade, and who is not working at the present time. Pablo was an accountant for a warehouse but lately he has been out of work and has turned to petty theft. Luis is a hardware store clerk who earns 3,600 colóns per week. Moises is a hair dresser who only finished second grade; he presently works at a restaurant and makes 3,200 colóns a week; he has two sons but does not support them. David, who has finished his second year of high school, works as a butcher and earns 5,000 colóns a week. Miguel only made it through second grade and works at a bus stop where he makes 500 colóns a day. Jorge is a factory supervisor who makes 5,000 colóns a week. Daniel is a construction worker with no schooling who makes 3,400 colóns a week. Jose is an accountant who finished three years of high school and later took the equivalency test and graduated. Melvin finished second grade and works in a bingo parlor where he makes 800 colóns a day. Jorge is an office boy who finished the fifth grade. Others, such as Moises, who says he is with Monique "for the money," are being supported by the transvestites. Pablo lives on what Paula makes but feels bad about this and states that he used to support her also. Ricardo lives on what Felicia makes. Delio also receives money from Corina because he is unemployed.

   Not all live off their transvestite partners. David gives 1,000 colóns to his transvestite lover. Daniel and Miguel both live with Rita and they help her by giving her part of their wages. Jorge and Shasta share salaries and house expenses. Juan-Carlos helps Monica with the money made from the Jell-O sales. Melvin gives his entire salary to Lina and has nothing to live on. Pablo drinks beer, uses marijuana and coke, and lives off Paula. Delio spends 5,000 colóns on beer, coke, and marijuana even though he is unemployed. Corina, his partner, gets him the money. Juan Carlos consumes coke, marijuana, and beer and spends 500 colóns a day on marijuana alone, despite the fact that he makes only 400 a day. Only Laura's partner, Jose, does not use drugs, although he does recognize that he has bouts of alcoholism.

For Some, Drifting Away from Heterosexuality Is Easy

The history of the men who are the transvestites' lovers shows that they were predominately heterosexual until their relationship with a transvestite. Some, such as Jose, are married and have children. Miguel had five heterosexual relationships before he met Rita. Daniel has been with transvestites for the past two years but before that had heterosexual relationships. David is twenty-nine and has been in a transvestite relationship for five years; prior to that, he had only heterosexual encounters and has two children from them. Luis is twenty-nine and has been with a transvestite for a year and a half. Previously, he had been only with women. This is also the case with Melvin, who initiated his relationship with Lina a year ago but had only been with women before that. Delio is nineteen and has been with Corina for a year—this is his first relationship. Juan Carlos began earlier, at seventeen, and Jorge started at eighteen, but both began with the person they are still with. Moises had his first relationships with women although now he has been with two transvestites. Despite this past heterosexual activity, all are very satisfied with their transvestite relationship and most, with the exception of Delio and Luis, no longer have any relationships with women. All expressed their preference for the transvestite over the woman and give the following reasons: the transvestite is warmer, more passionate, sexier, and tighter than most women.

In the Transvestites' World, the Penis Does Not Make the Man

Even though transvestites are men and their sexual partners are men, this does not mean that their culture is similar to that of the gay community in Costa Rica. In reality, the transvestite and his clients or lovers participate in a sexual culture where gender takes on a very particular meaning. Transvestites feel like women and are perceived, with few exceptions, as such by their clients and lovers. Being a "woman" means being "feminine" and their male sexual organs present no obstacle. The sexual partner of the transvestite regards himself as a man and his partner a woman. In sexual intercourse the partners report that they play the active role during anal sex, with very few exceptions. Paula's partner Pablo says that "he is the man in the relationship"; Melvin says that he is so masculine he does not even want to see the penis of his partner Lina; Luis says the same thing about his partner Salom, who stated that he avoided "seeing the penis." In the minds of these men, seeing the transvestites' penis could signify that they were like their clients or that they are homosexual. However, Ricardo, who says that he is the active partner in anal sex, states that it does not bother him that Felicia has a penis; on the contrary, he likes it because it is different. Shasta's partner Jorge states that "I play the role of the male and she the female"; Moises states that he "screws Monique" and that is why he is the male. Delio recognizes that Corina has tried penetration but "she has never screwed me." Miguel says the same thing, his partner Rita agrees that he screws her, since when she tried to screw him, it only led to fights. Juan Carlos, who makes love to his partner every day, feels the same way. The only exception was found with Daniel, who admitted that Rita has penetrated him.

Being a man is defined as penetrating a woman or another man. Since this is the case, the transvestites' lovers do not feel they are gay or homosexual and do not participate in gay social activities or AIDS prevention. Some see themselves as bisexual, others as homosexual, and some as heterosexual, but most of see themselves as *cacheros. Cachero* can mean many things. Pablo sees himself as a man and Paula as a woman; he does not see himself as a man who likes other men, even though he considers himself to be bisexual. Jorge also defines himself as a man and his lover Shasta as a woman. Ricardo is the only one who considers himself to be homosexual, since he interprets that word as someone who likes other men. Moises defines himself as a *buga* which means heterosexual; all the rest define themselves as *cacheros,* although the meaning of the word varies. Juan Carlos defines *cachero* as a person who has sex with homosexuals but he himself is not one. Delio defines it as the person who gives pleasure to someone of the same sex. Melvin defines it as a homosexual who acts like a man; Luis interprets it as a man who sleeps with both men and women; David, as a "a man that screws a queer"; and finally, Miguel, who defines it as a man who makes love to other men.

It is not only the sexual partners of transvestites who do not consider themselves homosexual, but most of the transvestites do not consider themselves homosexual either. Ninety-one percent of transvestites (and only 13 percent of gays in bars) are in total agreement with the following statement: "It is better that one's lover be heterosexual." Another, smaller group, 4 percent, is somewhat in agreement with this statement. In other words, transvestites prefer men who consider themselves heterosexual, and it is possible that this is how they do see their partners. The fact that they do not consider themselves homosexual or bisexual could define why they do not feel they belong to a group at risk for acquiring HIV/AIDS.

Partners' or Lovers' Knowledge of AIDS

The transvestites' partners are aware of the danger of AIDS. Juan Carlos knows that AIDS is a threat "because one is close to the problem" and that the only protection is the use of a condom. Jorge knows that AIDS is transmitted through sexual contact and through blood, and that it has no cure. Moises is just as clear and knows that AIDS is fatal and condoms are the only protection. Ricardo, Pablo, and Luis are aware that AIDS is a worldwide plague and that it is important to use condoms. Jose knows all the details of AIDS and how it can affect him because of the life he leads with Laura; even so, he does not use a condom. The same thing happens with David: he perceives AIDS as another venereal disease, and that, like all the rest, nothing can be done to avoid it. Although the lovers of the transvestites know about AIDS, their low income and education have deprived them of the knowledge of preventive medicine.

In the National AIDS Survey (Madrigal et al. 1991), it became evident that the groups most opposed to condoms in Costa Rica are precisely those with little education and low income. However, in addition, the problem is complicated by the drug addiction of the transvestites' partners. The fact that most of the transvestites' partners are addicted to one or more drugs and that their cost is high—between 1,000 and 12,000 colóns a week—make the partners dependent on the transvestites, since their wages would be insufficient to supply them, especially those who support another household and who have children. This drug addiction places them at additional risk, because of the levels of intoxication under which they practice their sexual activities and because they become dependent on others. They depend not only on the transvestite for their drugs but also on her sexual customers. This is not really a paradox, for although they know the risks involved in prostitution, they must consent to them. Miguel, who earns 3,000 colóns a week, spends 1,000 on marijuana alone; David does not use drugs but spends between 2,000 and 3,000 colóns a week on beer. Moises spends 1,000 colóns a day on drugs and does not even have a job. Luis spends about 14,000 colóns a week on cocaine and beer and this does not include the money he spends on marijuana; his salary is 3,600 colóns a week, and he gives 1,000 colóns a week to his family.

The sexual partners of the transvestites also define themselves as "macho" but must consent to being dependent on other men, the transvestites or their clients, in order to satisfy their needs. This disempowerment leads them to control and to express their jealousy by establishing different rules for jealousy and socialization; jealousy is not directed toward clients, but toward other *cacheros,* or other transvestites, and this breaks all ties of solidarity.

The transvestites' lovers have to accept that their partners must prostitute themselves. This makes them feel jealous. Pablo says that he feels bad when Paula is with other men, but he knows why she does it. On the other hand, Paula is very jealous if Pablo talks to other women. Ricardo admits that he "is not jealous" because if he were "she would not sell herself that way"; but he does admit that Felicia is jealous of other transvestites. He knows that with others she does it for money and with him it's for love. Jose is also bothered by Laura's sleeping around: "She does it because she wants to." Miguel and Daniel, who live with Rita, are also bothered by prostitution; Miguel recognizes that he is more jealous than the transvestite and Daniel does not like it when Rita prostitutes herself, but "there is nothing we can do about it." This case is very special because although they share the same transvestite, they do not feel jealous toward each other. David knows that Cristina prostitutes and steals but he is not jealous. "Cristina would not do it if I were there, and I also do not like it when she talks about what she did in the 'district.' " Luis is bothered when Salom sleeps with other men; so he just refuses to visit the place where he knows she works. Salom says that "it's the only thing she can do well" and that "it gives them money for their vices." Delio recognizes that he is jealous but not of Corina's prostitution, rather, it's her relationships with other *cacheros* that distresses him and Corina is jealous of his relationships with other transvestites.

Since the jealousy of the transvestites' lovers is directed toward men like themselves, there exists little communication between the *cacheros*. They see themselves as rivals, and friendships between them are rare. This lack of solidarity characterizes the transvestites and their partners as a group and sets them apart from the gays, who establish very close social relationships. In the case of AIDS, the isolation of transvestites from general society makes them less exposed to information about safe sex and patterns that reinforce it, in contrast to the case of gays who go to bars and follow the norms of the gay community. Transvestites are left more exposed to the ramifications of their personal decisions and those of their clients and *cacheros* who many times do not consider themselves as a group at risk.

Most of the transvestites' lovers prefer not to use a condom, even though they are aware that the transvestites practice prostitution. All of the partners felt that the condom diminishes the level of pleasure and view it as something negative. The transvestite views it in a more positive manner but must abide by what the partner wants. This, of course, creates a great obstacle to its use. Laura's partner Jose says he does not use the condom because "if we are faithful it does not matter. It has been three years and we are still not seropositive." Even so, he does recognize that it bothers him that Laura gets involved with other men for money and is aware that she does it. Rita's partner Miguel says that he does not like condoms and uses them every once in a while but he admits he prefers to "stick it in raw without anything." Cristina's partner David does not use them either: "I protect myself, I don't use a condom. I see AIDS like any other venereal disease, like syphilis, gonorrhea, or cancer; one can catch it at any moment. We all have to die some time; a lot of people take care of themselves and they get sick sooner. I don't like to use condoms." Moises does not use a condom with his partner Miriam, and although he doesn't like how it feels, he does use one with other transvestites. Jorge, Shasta's partner, does not use one because he does not like it and because he is faithful. If he did not know the person he would use one. The only two exceptions are Felicia's partner Ricardo, who uses condoms but does not like it, and Delio, who doesn't like them either, but uses them.

In view of the fact that these sexual relationships can turn into sources of infection with the AIDS virus, it is important to discuss the factors that could explain why the transvestites' partners do not use condoms. First of all, their low income and educational level place them in the group that most dislikes the use of condoms. In the same fashion, the use of drugs and alcohol places them at a disadvantage for prevention due to the fatalism and intoxication linked to these. Another factor is the need to regain power and control. Since the transvestite works as a prostitute, and this is beyond the partner's control, the lover looks to create different love symbols. He associates prostitution with condom use and love with unsafe sex. In this way, the lover makes a distinction not only in his sexual role (he is the penetrator), but also in his sexual practice (he doesn't use a condom). The fact that they do not use a condom becomes an act of love that the couple practices in order to differentiate theirs from other relationships. The transvestite is not bothered by the condom, but the *cachero* is and he is the one who pressures against its use.

This decision goes beyond physical feelings. To not use a condom demonstrates love and trust, and in terms of these relationships, both take on an important significance. A necessary aspect to understand is that the lovers do love the transvestites. The fact that many of them are not afraid to go out into the streets with the transvestites, even though they suffer both physical and verbal onslaughts on the street, shows that the *cacheros* are willing to take risks. There is more to the relationship than simple curiosity.

Many of them admit that it hurts when people make fun of their partners and that has led to fights more than once. However, a few do not want to be seen with the transvestites at all for fear of losing their jobs, although they are in the minority. Others who are bolder, like Daniel and Miguel, live openly with their transvestite partner. It is clear then that for both the *cachero* as well as the transvestite, love is manifested by the actions and risks that each takes to have a relationship. For them AIDS is just one of many risks that they face. People who love each other do not use condoms, and for people who have almost no power, this risk is what little they have to offer as a sign of love. Katia recognizes that "with her lover she did not use it." Laura also reports: "Since my lover did not use it, both of us trusted that we would not harm each other." Her partner states: "I don't protect myself when I am with her, because if we are faithful it doesn't matter." Paula and her partner came to an agreement that she use it with clients but not with him: "I protect myself against AIDS. I trust Paula in that she uses condoms with other clients since I don't do it with a shirt [condom]." Since he is bisexual he does not always do it only with women: "If I sleep with a woman, I use a condom as long as I have one with me, if I don't, I just don't. I always use it with other 'homosexuals.' " Susy uses a condom with everyone, especially with her lover, whom she does not trust: "Let's say I don't trust him because he has lived on the seacoast." Of the eleven transvestite lovers interviewed, only two always use condoms.

Note

Adapted and reprinted from Jacobo Schifter and Johnny Madrigal, "The Transvestite's Lover: Identity, Behavior and Prevention." *Iconoclasta* 2, no. 3 (June 1994).

Reference

Johnny Madrigal. 1992. *Men who love men.* Costa Rica: Ilep-Sida.

4

INSIGHTS FROM HISTORY AND ANTHROPOLOGY

Introduction

Transgender behavior is ubiquitous throughout history. It has played a prominent part in religious ritual in the ancient Near East and elsewhere, including American Indian culture. In its western Judeo-Christian setting, it was most easily sanctioned among females, and history provides thousands of cases of men who were only discovered to be female when they died. Many such women become saints (Bullough and Bullough 1993). A traditional explanation for the greater number of female transgenderists in the past was found in the efforts of such cross-dressers to gain status and freedom in male society.

This is not to say that males did not cross-dress. They did, and their cross-dressing was often institutionalized. A good example is the stage, regarded as a place not suitable for proper women, and so in much of European history males played the female roles until well past Shakespeare's time. Even more contradictory was that they also did so in opera where the voice power of the *castrato* was prized until the nineteenth century. Japanese society still has its traditional Kabuki in which the women's roles are played by males.

It seems as if even Western society recognized that the traditional roles of both men and women were confining because there were many festivals in the calendar in which cross-gender behavior was permitted. Some of these "holidays" have been perpetuated in segments of our society such as the Mummer's parade in Philadelphia and the Mardi Gras festival in New Orleans. Cross-dressing on Halloween is ubiquitous.

Only rarely have scholars made detailed studies of cross-dressing. Often such studies have been made by amateurs, such as Winnie Brant, who are members of the transgender community. Their research is no less valid than that of the professionals such as Mildred Dickemann, who explores a topic that has rarely made its way into the anthropological literature. Similarly, Linda Heidenrich, by looking at contemporary accounts of Christine Jorgensen, throws new light on one of the key persons in the transgender community. Professionals from almost every discipline can add their own insights to the phenomenon as Michael Saffle, a historian of music, does. The section also includes a long, analytical, historically oriented paper on shamanism by William Dragoin, who teaches in a combined department of psychology and sociology.

Reference

Bullough, Vern L. and Bonnie Bullough. 1993. *Cross dressing, sex and gender.* Philadelphia: University of Pennsylvania Press.

The Gender Heresy of Akhenaten

Winnie Brant

Early in the last century, explorers of Egypt came across a desolate, ruined city on the eastern bank of the Nile. At the boundaries of this place, they found a number of stelae depicting what appeared to be two queens worshipping the sun in the form of a disk with rays ending in human hands. But when they deciphered the hieroglyphs, they found that one of the "queens" was a king! His name was Akhenaten, and the other queen was his wife Nefertiti. The name of the sun-god was Aten, and the city was Akhetaten, "The Horizon of the Sun," which the king had founded. Since that time, much more has been unearthed about this intriguing couple through excavations of the city and other sites in Egypt. Akhenaten is now famous as the "Heretic Pharaoh" who abandoned all the old gods in favor of Aten as the sole God. He reigned for seventeen years circa 1360 B.C.E. and was succeeded by an ephemeral king Smenkhkare and then by Tutankhamen, whose tomb was discovered in 1923.

The religious revolution was accompanied by an artistic revolution, particularly in the portrayal of the royal family. The most extreme examples of the new art coincide with the first appearance of the god Aten as a rayed sun-disc, making it virtually certain that there is a direct connection. Queen Nefertiti was portrayed with the exaggerated figure of a female fertility goddess, a common theme in prehistoric art. Astonishingly, Akhenaten had himself portrayed in the same manner! Pointing to the phrase *Ankh em Maat* ("living in truth") that Akhenaten often used in describing himself, the usual explanation is that he had a passion for telling the truth, and suffered from a condition that rendered him epicene. The gender confusion extends to the succeeding king Smenkhkare, who was married to Akhenaten's eldest daughter Meritaten. Smenkhkare is known to have used an alternative feminine name, Nefernefruaten, and Egyptologists have been puzzled by this.

Historical Outline

Toward the end of the Eighteenth Dynasty, Egypt was at the height of its power, ruling over an empire of vassal states in Canaan, Lebanon, and Syria, and the pharaohs worshiped Amen-Re, "King of Gods." About 1375 B.C.E., Amenhotep IV ascended to the throne, married his chief queen, Nefertiti, and immediately began a family. There are a few portrayals of Amenhotep IV as a conventional pharaoh paying homage to traditional gods, but he soon began a new temple at Karnak devoted to Re-Herakhte, the god of the rising sun portrayed as a falcon-headed man with a sun-disc on top of his head.

Surviving evidence of such a temple includes new titles and epithets of Re-Herakhte identifying him as the Aten (the sun itself), which were placed in a pair of cartouches like the names of pharaoh. No other god of Egypt was ever recognized as "Heavenly King" in this way. Very soon after, the anthropomorphic representation was abandoned and the Aten sun-disc became self-suspended above the heads of the worshipping royal couple. Many rays descend from the disc, ending in human hands. Once this icon appears, the king is never shown worshipping any other god. He changed his birth-name from Amenhotep to Akhenaten and began a campaign of iconoclasm against the old gods, especially Amen, defacing their names and images throughout the land.

Akhenaten wished his new cult to replace the old, and expanded his building project at Karnak to encompass several new temples. But he had a problem: how to compete with the huge temple of Amen, which had been a-building for centuries? The compromise solution adopted by his architects was novel. Instead of massive, hard limestone blocks, requiring a crew of workmen with a sledge to move, use small, soft sandstone blocks cut at the quarry to a size (52 × 22 × 26 cm) that could easily be carried by one man. This strategy enabled Akhenaten to complete his temple complex at Karnak in about five years.

However, it was equally easy to tear down these temples after the old religion was restored. Later pharaohs used many of the blocks as fill in the construction of more pylons extending the temple of Amen-Ra. Over time, these pylons have tumbled down, revealing the re-used blocks inside. In restoring the pylons, archaeologists have removed the blocks, today called talatat, and stacked them in row upon row at several locations in the area. The disjointed scenes carved and painted on the talatat have long intrigued Egyptologists, who have called it the world's biggest jigsaw puzzle, with over 35,000 pieces and many more missing. In 1966, they began a computer-aided attempt, known as the Akhenaten Temple Project, to put it together on paper (Redford 1976, 1978). One finding that surprised them was the importance of Nefertiti in the Aten cult.

Other relics from these temples, including fragments of fifteen colossal statues of Akhenaten and the remains of twenty-eight rectangular pillars before which the statues had stood, were discovered in 1925 during excavation of a ditch. The king's statues were executed in the highly exaggerated art style characteristic of the early years of his reign, notably with an elongated face and broad feminine hips. Only two statues were found complete down to the knees; in one of these, the king is wearing a kilt, but in the other he is completely naked and without genitalia (Aldred 1973, figs. 9 and 10).

In the fifth year of his reign Akhenaten decided to move his capital to a new city, Akhetaten, built on a virgin site in the middle of Egypt and dedicated to Aten (Murnane and Van Siclen 1993). By the twelfth year of his reign, the city was near completion and ready for the "official opening." On the wall of a tomb, he is shown side-by-side with Nefertiti, welcoming the foreign dignitaries and receiving their presents (Aldred 1988, fig. 27). The royal couple are accompanied by their six daughters. Here, and wherever the girls are mentioned, they are called "king's daughters" and Nefertiti is always explicitly named as their mother. This is highly unusual, since the mother of an Egyptian king's children was seldom named in inscriptions.

The celebration of year twelve is regarded as the high point of Akhenaten's reign. Shortly thereafter, his second daughter, Meketaten, died and was interred in the royal tomb. The final five years of the reign are obscured by confusing evidence and are the subject of much debate. Did Nefertiti die before or after Akhenaten? Who were the parents of the succeeding kings, Smenkhkare and Tutankhaten (later Tutankhamen), who married the eldest surviving daughters, Meritaten and Ankhesenpaaten, respectively? Answers to these and other questions must be reconstructed from excavations at the ruined city itself, today called El-Amarna, and the cliff tombs on the east bank of the river.

The Transgender Interpretation of Evidence

The Strange Statues

Looking at the strange statues and reliefs of Akhenaten (Aldred 1973, figs. 33 and 34), one physician diagnosed Fröhlich's syndrome, caused by a pituitary tumor. However, this and every other condition known to modern medicine

(Risse 1971) that might have given him a shape resembling these statues would have made him impotent and sterile, a possibility contradicted by his claim to have fathered six children. Others have suggested that he was a transvestite, particularly a woman (Nefertiti) masquerading as a man, since the king is always shown wearing a masculine skirt (or kilt) despite his physique, and never a feminine dress. If Akhenaten was a transgendered male, it would be inaccurate to describe him as a transvestite. In view of the religious connection, it is more appropriate to regard him as *transfigured* by the Aten. Whatever Akhenaten was or did in defiance of convention, it should be evident that he was convinced that he had the full support of the only god he recognized.

In a text inscribed on the walls of tombs at Akhetaten, the god is praised as "the father and mother of mankind," and it has been suggested that Akhenaten portrayed himself in this aspect of his divine father. However, a traditional pharaoh was expected to be the masculine role model for the entire nation, and some additional motive seems necessary to explain Akhenaten's departure from the norm. The evidence to be presented points to transgenderism as the most likely motive.

One hundred years before Akhenaten, a woman, Hatshepsut, had served as pharaoh and as such she was depicted as a man. The daughter of Thutmose I and his chief queen Ahmose, Hatshepsut had married her half-brother who had succeeded to the throne as Thutmose II. Upon the early death of Thutmose II, his minor son by a secondary wife became Thutmose III, but Hatshepsut acted as regent. Soon after, however, she abandoned her queenly titles and assumed the title of pharaoh. She claimed legitimacy by right of divine birth. The walls of her mortuary temple portrayed the god Amen entering the bedchamber of Queen Ahmose and telling her that while he may look like King Thutmose I, he is actually the god who has taken over the body of her husband in order to father a daughter who will become king.

Hatshepsut is often depicted with the physique of a male, wearing a masculine skirt and topless, but with no sign of breasts (Aldred 1988, pl. 51.) At other times she is portrayed as a woman in figure and dress. Interestingly, no one has suggested that she developed a disease that made her appear masculine. Instead it is understood that her motive was to gain political power: kingship was a man's job, and one had to act and dress the part. A pharaoh apparently had no difficulty in having himself (or herself) portrayed by artists in any manner, even if totally false.

The Desecrated Temples

So, let us suppose that a pubescent, transgendered prince Amenhotep prayed to Amen-Min: "You made Hatshepsut a girl; I want to be a girl, too; please use your magic and change me!" Of course, nothing happened, which may have turned the prince against the god and led him to question his power. In frustration, it is possible that the young prince had vandalized the ithyphallic representations of Amen in reliefs on the shrine of Senwosret I, circa 1950 B.C.E. (Fischer 1976). The mutilations are confined to the phallus, and clearly the damage is intentional. Similar desecration of the ithyphallic form of Amen is found in reliefs in the Luxor temple of Amenhotep III, where his divine conception is recorded. Again, the mutilations of Amen's figure are confined to the phallus, but his name has also been erased, along with lettuce plants that are emblems of Min's fertility. The main focus of Prince Amenhotep's displeasure in these examples is revealed by his attack on the masculinity of Amen-Min.

Reflections in the Sun

In order to come to terms with their feelings, transgendered people are forced to question numerous things taught by their elders and taken for granted by most of society. In ancient Egypt, the subject of religion would have been foremost. The gods created the world and everything in it and were responsible for defining and maintaining just and proper order, which the Egyptians called *Maat*. Egyptian religion recognized hundreds of gods and over the centuries became encrusted with layers of myth and magic ritual. The pharaoh was ex-officio high priest of all the gods and privy to the tricks performed by priests to impress an uneducated populace. The gods were represented by anthropomorphic statues, many animal-headed, which the divine spirits entered to receive offerings. Priests dressed as their gods and wore masks. The Nile god Hapi was hermaphroditic, apparently male but portrayed with breasts and pregnant; his priests must have worn appropriate forms, so Akhenaten would have been familiar with the use of padding for cosmetic purposes.

Egyptian gods of both sexes are often shown carrying an *ankh* in one hand and a *was* in the other. The *ankh* signifies the divine gift of life and has a feminine connotation in that females are the bearers of new life. The *was* (a scepter with a strange, bent animal head and a bulbous bottom, much shortened as a hieroglyph) signifies divine dominion or power and has a masculine connotation in that these are male prerogatives on Earth. The *ankh* and *was* hieroglyphs are the ancient prototypes of our modern sex symbols: the mirror of Venus and the arrow of Mars!

Disenchanted with Amen, young Akhenaten might have searched for a more helpful god. In all ancient religions, a sun-god was among the most important and often the first created as well as the creator of other gods. Egypt had such a god, and the main center of the cult was in Heliopolis (now a suburb of Cairo).

Here, the sun-god Re took various forms, including Re-Herakhte, the god of the rising sun who was self-created every day. The sun-disc itself was called the Aten and regarded as a minor god in its own right. It was the only god neither human nor animal, and the only god that needed no human-made statue; it is up in the sky for all to see. Akhenaten could conclude that it was the only real god in the Egyptian pantheon, and the only one not the product of imagination.

Aten is clearly identified as the seat of Re, the all-pervasive superhuman intelligence that is the universal requirement for divinity. Akhenaten claimed to be the only one who knew the Aten and was taught by the god. He frequently used the epithet *Wa-en-Ra,* meaning "The Only One of Re," a feeling familiar to the transgendered. Addressing the Aten, Akhenaten called himself "your son who came from your body." In view of the factual basis for many of his assertions, what could he mean by this?

The Egyptian word "Aten" was usually translated as "Disc," but more recent literature more accurately translates it as "Globe" or "Orb." In the ancient reliefs, the sun clearly has a convex shape. On the high altars of temples, such as the stela that was the focus of worship in the Great Temple at Akhetaten, the solar relief would have been gilded. It is virtually certain that there would also have been three-dimensional statues of the sun—a solid gold sphere or a larger gilded stone. Now, what would the king have seen while worshipping at the altar of the Aten, illuminated by its prototype overhead? *His own reflection!* The optical properties of convex mirrors are well-known—the mid-parts of the image are magnified and the extremities elongated, just like in the strange statues. He must have been pleased with the broad hips he saw; here was a god who answered his prayers. Akhenaten could have called his chief sculptor Bek to come and look and told the artist to portray him in the manner ordained by the god. Such an explanation is likely to dismay those who believe Akhenaten was a brilliant religious visionary ahead of his time, but it is probably closer to the truth.

Nefertiti-Nefernefruaten

Nefertiti is given a unique position of prominence during Akhenaten's reign, far greater than any other queen consort in Egyptian history. She appears beside him in scenes of offering to the Aten, denoting an equal status in religious affairs. She is presented with foreign female prisoners, arms bound behind them in the same manner that male prisoners were presented to the King; female captives were usually not bound, but followed their humiliated menfolk. She is shown with a club raised to smite the head of a female captive, a traditional pose of pharaoh; for this act, she wears a man's skirt, and is topless (Aldred 1988, pl. 41).

Egyptologists have found no evidence that Akhenaten cross-dressed; by this they mean that have found no representation of him in women's clothes. The reason for this should be evident, remembering that Hatshepsut found it necessary to have herself pictured as a man in men's clothes to call herself king. If Akhenaten dressed in women's clothes, he would not be pharaoh! If he felt the urge to appear cross-dressed in public, there was only one woman he could pretend to be and still maintain his royal authority: his chief queen, Nefertiti. The queen had two sanctuaries at Karnak, apparently for her exclusive use, with no counterpart for the king; one of them contained a Benben, the central cult object of Egyptian solar temples (Redford 1984, figs. 6 and 7).

While the construction of the Karnak temples was underway, Nefertiti was given an epithet that was incorporated into her cartouche: Nefernefruaten, meaning "The Beautiful Beauties of Aten." At the same time, she was being portrayed with a face resembling that of Akhenaten! The usual explanation is that the king regarded his supposed deformities as a gift from God and allowed his wife the "honor" of being portrayed in like manner. For any man married to a beautiful woman, this seems quite unlikely, and even less likely for a cross-dresser: one would more likely expect to find her pretty face upon his body.

Akhenaten was clearly fascinated by beauty. He incorporated *nfr,* meaning "beautiful" or "good" into his throne name Neferkheprure ("The Beautiful Transformations of Re") and made a woman named Nefertiti ("The Beautiful Woman Comes") his Great King's Wife. He then bestowed beauty in plural upon her—Nefernefruaten—and upon two of his daughters, Nefernefruaten-tasherit (tasherit meaning "the little") and Nefernefrure. The king's own self-selected name change must surely be another indicator of how he felt about himself. "Akhenaten" means something like "Effective Spirit of Aten" (Friedman 1986), but "Akh" also has the connotation of a transformation (Aldred 1968, note 33).

Both king and queen wore similar styles of wigs, particularly the so-called Nubian wig that was popular at the time. They also wore similar crowns, which came in great variety. There are a number of royal portrait heads that have become detached from their bodies and any inscription, and art critics have difficulty in deciding whether they represent he or she. There is a relief of the queen in the Ashmolean Museum (Aldred 1973, no. 31), in which her head and crown are practically identical to a relief of Akhenaten in Cairo. But her dress and inscribed name make it clear that Nefertiti is the subject, so Aldred is confident in pointing out the erotic femininity of her portrayal.

When Akhenaten is pictured in similar fashion, the reaction of art critics is quite different, and "epicene" is the most polite term applied; others are "hideous," "appalling," "misshapen," "grotesque," "bizarre," "weird," "peculiar," "disturbing," "extraordinary," etc. But there is an unusual feature in the Ashmolean relief of Nefertiti: she has *two navels!* Perhaps, a simple mistake by the artist, who carved the first one in the wrong place and was told by his over-seer to fill in the hole with plaster (none now visible) and re-carve it in the proper location; but, in view of the general distortion, neither spot seems aesthetically more pleasing. Or, is the duplication intentional, to indicate the merging of two bodies, which is betrayed by a slight imperfection?

Smenkhkare

Smenkhkare is the most ephemeral monarch of the Eighteenth Dynasty, yet this king has left the most puzzling evidence of his identity and aroused more con-troversy among Egyptologists than even Akhenaten. He sat on the throne be-tween the reigns of Akhenaten and Tutankhamen. It is believed that both he and Tutankhamen must have been "king's sons" because they were too young to have gained the throne without right of birth. But which king, and which mother? While there are some inscriptions mentioning a "king's son, Tutankhaten" before he ascended the throne, there is no hint of the existence of Smenkhkare until he appears on the scene as pharaoh, married to Meritaten. On the wall of a private tomb at Akhetaten, the new royal pair are shown together worshipping the Aten, in the same pose familiar from the previous reign.

The interpretation of the reign of Smenkhkare depends crucially upon whether one believes he was merely a co-regent of Akhenaten or had an inde-pendent reign, the position which I take. The evidence for a co-regency is simi-lar to that postulated for a co-regency between Amenhotep III and Akhenaten and is open to alternative scenarios in both cases. There are a few uninscribed objects apparently showing two kings together, one of whom has the characteristic fea-tures of Akhenaten portrayed in intimate poses familiar from scenes of Akhen-aten and Nefertiti. Since it is known that Smenkhkare also used the feminine name Nefernefruaten, previously given to Nefertiti, some assumed that Nefertiti had been abandoned and disgraced by her husband in favor of a homosexual affair with their son-in-law, who was also supposed to be Akhenaten's younger brother. Another view was that since Nefertiti might well have been co-regent with her husband (Aldred 1973, no. 57), she adopted the masculine name Smenkhkare and ruled as king, like Hatshepsut, after the death of her husband (Samson 1978). While this relieved Akhenaten of the stigma of homosexuality, it put Nefertiti into a lesbian relationship with her own daughter, Meritaten. To avoid this complication, it was then suggested that Nefernefruaten and Smenkhkare were two different persons, one female (formerly Nefertiti) and one male (of unknown origin), both using the same throne name, Ankhkheprure, "The Mirror (or Living?) Transformations of Re."

Much of the inscriptional and pictorial evidence for these confusing names and events during the later years at Akhetaten is fragmentary, and we must rely on expert philologists for translation, each of whom fills the gaps according to personal preconceptions. Writers usually call this uncertain person(s) "Smenkhkare," no matter which of the three names are actually written in hieroglyphs, so it is difficult to determine which version was used without a photograph of the original. But like Akhenaten, Smenkhkare was also depicted with a figure resembling a naked woman.

The Mysterious Mummy

In 1907 Theodore Davis discovered a small tomb in the Valley of the Kings near the spot where Tutankhamen was later found. The tomb, now numbered KV 55 (Bell 1990), had been violated in ancient times through a low tunnel dug through the fill of the entrance corridor. Laying in the tunnel was one side of a gilded funerary shrine decorated in Atenist style, featuring Akhenaten (whose figure and names had been hacked out) worshipping the Aten, and followed by his mother Queen Tiye, for whom he had made the shrine. Inside the small tomb chamber, they found the other sides of the dismantled shrine laying against the walls and a single coffin made in a style typical for a woman. The gold face on the coffin had been ripped off and the name of the deceased had been cut out wherever it appeared (Davis 1990).

In Cairo, the remains of the mummy, now reduced to a disarticulated skeleton, were examined by a pathologist. Expecting to see the skeleton of a middle-aged woman, he was surprised to find instead the bones of a young man in his early twenties! Too young to be Akhenaten, the consensus has focused on Smenkhkare as the most likely candidate, but some have insisted that it must be Akhenaten and his "disease" made his bones immature. However, the remains have now been re-examined and X-rayed several times and there is no sign of any disease. Also, the mummy shares a common blood group with Tutankhamen, so they could be closely related and may be brothers. In 1963, one pathologist estimated the age at death to be between nineteen and twenty-four, with age twenty the most likely (Harrison 1966). Others have recently suggested the age at death to be thirty-five to thirty-seven years, much higher than any earlier estimate, and old enough to make Akhenaten a possibility.

The coffin and its hieroglyphic texts have also been examined a number of times (Aldred 1988, pl. 53). The original name of the owner appears to be that of a woman closely associated with Akhenaten, but it was not enclosed in a cartouche; this and a uraeus were later added to make it signify a king or queen. Determinatives were altered from the feminine (a seated woman) to a king (a seated person with an artificial beard), but one instance was overlooked and escaped the change. However, all the names were cut out by the mutilators of the tomb. Some experts believe the woman was a daughter of Akhenaten, probably Meritaten, but others suggest she was Kiya, a secondary wife of that king. The name erased from the canopic jars could also have been Kiya. Experts have also examined the coffins and other funerary equipment of Tutankhamen (Aldred 1988, pl. 54) and discovered that much of it was originally made for Smenkhkare and inscribed with his name, which was altered to his alter ego Nefernefruaten before the final change in favor of Tutankhamen. Why, if Smenkhkare had some very nice funeral furniture made for him in the traditional style of a masculine pharaoh, was he not buried in it?

The only known date from the reign of Smenkhkare-Ankheprure is in his third regnal year, written in graffiti on the wall of a private tomb by a priest from the mortuary temple of King Ankheprure. But if Ankheprure was building his mortuary temple in Thebes, he must have planned to be buried in Thebes and likely had moved back there from Akhetaten. Egyptologists have further specu-lated that Smenkhkare must have abandoned Atenism and returned to the old religion, thereby severing his gay relationship with Akhenaten, assuming that they were co-regents. However, if this mummy discovered in a tomb in Thebes is Smenkhkare, as most believe, why do Egyptologists almost unanimously declare this to be not an original burial, but a re-burial following a move from Akhetaten after that city was abandoned? Although the funeral goods are sparse and appear to have been originally made for several different people, it seems likely that the body and viscera would have been kept in their original contain-ers during any move. How can all this be explained? What the Egyptologists fail to note as significant is that all this miscellaneous equipment is *feminine!* I argue that a transgendered male, frustrated in life and believing in life after death as did the ancient Egyptians, would do his best to secure eternal life in the desired gen-der, even foregoing a funeral on the lavish scale of Tutankhamen. This person was buried as she wished.

Smenkhkare is usually thought to be a younger brother of Akhenaten fathered by Amenhotep III or one of his sons by a secondary wife or concubine, the latter being more likely because Tutankhamen could only have been a son of Akhenaten (unless there was a long co-regency with Amenhotep III, a theory which is now rejected) and would otherwise have succeeded first. However, if Smenkhkare had an independent reign of two or more years and died at age twenty, he would be essentially the same age as Meritaten. In one letter to the king of Egypt, the vassal ruler of Tyre calls himself "the servant of Mayati" as well as the king and refers to Tyre as the "city of Mayati, my mistress" (Moran 1992, EA 155). Together with the other evidence cited, it seems possible that the king and Mayati (Meritaten) are the same person. This means that Akhenaten must have raised his eldest son as a girl. But if Akhenaten regarded his feelings as a gift from god, and had felt strongly enough to establish a new religion on this account, then he may have believed that his son would inherit similar feelings and fostered them, remembering the problems he had faced as a child.

If this scenario is adopted, certain evidence must be regarded as having been intentionally falsified. Meritaten was depicted with her parents as an infant, naked and obviously female (Aldred 1973, fig. 2, no. 16); here, the artist would have been told the child was a girl, and she always wore a dress when appearing in public. The "marriage" between Meritaten and Smenkhkare must have been a fabrication. Although they could well have appeared individually in public, they could never have appeared together, as in the picture in the tomb. Certain fragmentary inscriptions have been interpreted to indicate that Meritaten (as well as Ankhesenpaaten) was the mother of a daughter; this might mean that, after the death of Nefertiti, the two eldest surviving daughters were given the responsibility of caring for their younger sisters, as adoptive mothers.

Tutankhaten (Tutankhamen)

If Meritaten was indeed Smenkhkare and male, then we can seek the infancy of Tutankhaten among the other daughters of Akhenaten and Nefertiti, and the youngest, Setepenre, seems most likely on chronological grounds. Setepenre appears to have been born about year eleven of Akhenaten's reign and would have been about nine years old upon the death of Smenkhkare. Tutankhaten reigned for nine years and died at about eighteen years of age, so he would have been about nine at his accession.

The Egyptian priest Manetho wrote a history of Egypt in Ptolemaic times, some extracts of which have survived through notations in other ancient writers, including Josephus. He quoted a king-list of the Eighteenth Dynasty, which reads in part:

> Tethmosis, for nine years and eight months; after him came Amenophis, for thirty years and ten months; after him came Orus, for thirty-six years and five months; then came his daughter Acenchres, for twelve years and one month; then was her brother Rathotis, for nine years. . . . (Josephus 1974, 4:165)

Tethmosis, Amenophis, Orus, his daughter Acenchres, and her brother Rathotis correspond to the order of succession of Thutmose IV, Amenhotep III, Akhenaten, Smenkhkare, and Tutankhamen. Despite the corruption of names and years of rule, the stated filiation indicates the relationship between Akhenaten, Meritaten, and Tutankhaten that I propose here. It can be shown that the distortions in Manetho's king-list are the plausible result of erroneous deletions of the heretics, followed by a later attempt to reconstruct the true list.

Conclusion

This paper has examined the archaeological evidence in the light of transgenderism as the most likely motivation for Akhenaten's actions and proposes a consistent history of his reign and family situation. It suggests a link to his selection of the Aten as god and concludes that the world's first monotheistic religion was founded by a transgendered king, precisely because of this aspect of his personality. Most authorities believe that his revolutionary religion perished with him but it is possible, as Sigmund Freud argued, that Moses was an Egyptian and the religion he gave the Hebrews may have been derived from the Aten religion (Freud 1939).

References

Aldred, Cyril. 1968. *Akhenaten: Pharaoh of Egypt.* London: Thames and Hudson.
———. 1973. *Akhenaten and Nefertiti.* New York: The Brooklyn Museum.
———. 1988. *Akhenaten: King of Egypt.* London: Thames and Hudson.
Bell, Martha R. 1990. An armchair excavation of KV 55. *Journal of the American Research Center in Egypt* 27: 97–137.
Davis, Theodore M., et al. [1910] 1990. *The tomb of Queen Tiyi.* San Francisco: KMT Communications.
Fischer, Henry G. 1976. An early example of Atenist iconoclasm. *Journal of the American Research Center in Egypt* 13: 131–32.
Freud, Sigmund. 1939. *Moses and monotheism.* New York: Vantage.
Friedman, Florence. 1986. Akh in the Amarna Period. *Journal of the American Research Center in Egypt* 23: 99–106.
Harrison, R. G. 1966. An anatomical examination of the pharaonic remains purported to be Akhenaten. *Journal of Egyptian Archaeology* 52: 95–119.
Josephus. 1974. *The works of Flavius Josephus.* Translated by William Whiston. 4 vols. Reprint. Grand Rapids, Mich.: Baker Book House.
Moran, William L. 1992. *The Amarna letters.* Baltimore: The Johns Hopkins University Press.
Murnane, William J., and Charles C. Van Siclen III. 1993. *The boundary stelae of Akhenaten.* London: Kegan Paul.
Redford, Donald B. 1978. The razed temple of Akhenaten. *Scientific American* 239, no. 6: 136–47.
———. 1984. *Akhenaten: The heretic king.* Princeton: Princeton University Press.
Redford, Donald B., and Ray Winfield Smith. 1976. *The Akhenaten temple project,* vol. 1, *Initial discoveries.* London: Aris & Phillips.
Risse, Guenter B. 1971. Pharaoh Akhenaton of ancient Egypt: Controversies among Egyptologists and physicians regarding his postulated illness. *Journal of the History of Medicine and Allied Sciences* 29: 3-17
Samson, Julia. 1978. *Amarna: City of Akhenaten and Nefertiti.* London: Aris & Phillips.

The Gynemimetic Shaman:
Evolutionary Origins of Male Sexual
Inversion and Associated Talent

William Dragoin

Many who concern themselves with sexual and gender behaviors are inclined to structure their questions in terms of what Money has called an "obsolete nature-nurture fence . . . unmindful of the fact that there is a biology of learning and memory, albeit mostly undiscovered as yet" (1987, 380). There are varied explanations of sex role acquisition that derive from attempts to consider gender/sexual behavior in terms of natural selection and the processes of evolution having produced a nervous system that inclines males and females readily to acquire culturally prescribed behavior patterns (Archer and Lloyd 1982; Buss 1989; Daly and Wilson 1983; Symmons 1979). Within this framework of evolution and biological preparedness, an interesting problem presents itself in the form of sexually inverted male children. The term "sexual inversion" is used here instead of homosexuality or transsexualism for two reasons: first, to emphasize the fact that effeminacy, "sissy boy syndrome" (Green 1987), or gynemimesis (Money and Lamacz 1984; Money 1986), likely emerges developmentally prior to sexual orientation or gender identity; and second, while this boyhood inversion correlates with adult homoeroticism, the relationship is by no means perfect. Simply put, sexual identity, sexual orientation, and sexual behavior are not identical. At the outset let us emphasize that there is considerable variation in the personality, abilities, and behavior patterns of those labeled homosexual, and the hypothesis developed below applies, at least in its strongest form, only to that minority of young males typified by those in Green's long-range study whose cross-gendered behavior persists to adulthood (Harry 1983). These sexually inverted boys manifest a variety of behaviors that are described as "effeminate," often including

227

cross-dressing, choosing toys judged gender inappropriate, avoiding rough-and-tumble play and sports, and displaying gender identity sometimes not in agreement with their chromosomes and genitals. As adults, the majority are homosexually oriented (Green 1987; Lebovitz 1972; Zucker 1985; Zucker et al. 1992; Zuger 1966, 1989; Zuger and Taylor 1969). Additionally, and of central importance to this paper, is the observation that many of these inverted males often demonstrate prodigious interest in and talent for theater arts (Barr et al. 1972; Green 1987; Green and Money 1966; Hoffman 1968; Kiefer 1968; Money and Lamacz 1984; Whitam 1987).

That there may be a biological basis for male sexual inversion is argued on the basis of several different kinds of data.

Nonhuman Animal Studies

An increasing number of experiments with nonhuman animals have clearly demonstrated that gonadal steroids administered to pregnant females or given perinatally to individuals will produce in the offspring of the mothers, or in neonates so treated, morphological effects in their brains (MacLusky and Naftolin 1981; McEwen 1981). These modifications in the nervous systems have been typically discussed in the literature as "masculinizing, demasculinizing, feminizing, and defeminizing" (Ellis and Ames 1987; Money 1981, 1987; Money, Schwartz, and Lewis 1984; Pillard and Weinrich 1987) and are correlated with modification of sex-dimorphic, species-specific behaviors such as sexual mounting, lordosis, frequency of aggressive play, emotionality, nest building, and other maternal behaviors. And finally, these morphological traits are likely lateralized in the mammalian brain (Nordeen and Yahr 1982). For reviews and discussion, see Goy and McEwen (1980), Money (1981), Ellis (1982), Hines (1983), and Hines and Collaer (1993).

Human Analogues to Animal Research

There are many complex problems in generalizing to humans data based upon experimentally induced sexually dimorphic features of bird, rodent, and monkey brains. However, there are a variety of "natural experiments" (all subject to the nurturist's criticism) that result in clinical syndromes (hermaphroditic and intersexed subjects) that approximate and mimic the variables of the animal experiments and point toward a conclusion that certain types of sexual and gender behaviors are more readily acquired by people whose nervous systems have been hormonally differentiated in specific ways (Ehrhardt and Meyer-Bahlburg 1979; Ellis and Ames 1987; Gladue 1987; Money and Ehrhardt 1972; Money 1987; Money, Schwartz, and Lewis 1984; Swaab and Fliers 1985).

And recent research (Swaab and Hofman 1990; LeVay 1991; Allen and Gorski 1992) continues to report morphological differences in the brains of heterosexual and homosexual men, strengthening the hypothesis that the neurohormonal substrates of the two groups differ.

Genetic and Familial Studies of Sexual Orientation

While Zuger (1989) finds little in his data to support the hypothesis of a genetic basis for inversion (effeminacy) per se, there is some evidence to indicate that the concordance rate for homosexuality is higher in monozygotic twins than in fraternal twins (Bailey and Pillard 1991; Kallman 1952; Heston and Shields 1968; Whitam, Diamond, and Martin 1993), and family studies of homosexual subjects indicate higher incidence of homosexuality among their siblings than for heterosexuals and higher among more distant relatives than would be expected by chance (Pillard, Poumadere, and Carretta 1981; Pillard and Weinrich 1986). There are, to be sure, methodological problems and other sources of bias in family studies that limit the interpretation of these data; however, even when such problems are taken into consideration, these data, combined with recent DNA linkage analysis (Hamer et al. 1993), still supply evidence that homosexuality (particularly male homosexuality) tends to run in families and may manifest genetic predispositions.

Ubiquity and Antiquity of Homosexuality and Inversion

Homosexual behavior and/or cross-gendered behavior have been and continue to be institutionalized in many societies throughout the world, and the institutionalization is manifested in various forms (Ford and Beach 1951; Bullough 1976, 1979). In some instances this socially institutionalized homosexual pattern involves noninverted males serving as passive partners in fellatio and/or anal intercourse for noninverted older males, and the behavior may be concurrent with or precede a heterosexual behavior pattern by one or both of the participants and may or may not involve "limerence" (Tennov 1979) or romantic involvement. Typical of this pattern are the tribal rites of the Sambia (Herdt 1981; Stoller and

Herdt 1985) and the Keraki (Ford and Beach 1951), both indigenous peoples of New Guinea. Institutionalized pederasty of ancient Greece (Bullough 1976) and the Samurai "comrade-love" of medieval Japan (Carpenter [1919] 1975; Watanabe and Iwata 1990) could also be similarly described.

That homosexual behavior is probably a cultural universal is attested to by recent studies of Whitam (1980, 1983, 1987). His cross-cultural research conducted over a ten-year period examines homosexual behavior in nonclinical settings in Central and South America, the Philippines, Thailand, and among native Hawaiians. He concludes that about 5 percent of the male population is predominantly homosexually oriented and that approximately one-fourth of them may be described as inverted or effeminate. However, the ethnographic record also indicates that gynemimesis (i.e., effeminacy and cross-gendered behavior) in and of itself has also been institutionalized socially; and while it almost always involved homoeroticism, gynemimesis was the identifying characteristic of the young male selected and the salient quality of the social roles named below. The best known examples are the "berdache" among Native Americans (Callender and Kochems 1983; Devereux 1937; Forgey 1975; Whitehead 1981; Williams 1986). However, Ford and Beach (1951) mention similar social roles among the Lango of Uganda; they also note the "sarombauy" of Madagascar, and Levy (1971) calls attention to the "Mahu" of Tahiti. The "Xanith" of present day Oman (Wikan 1978) and the "Hijra" of India (Nanda 1984, 1990) are contemporary examples of the social institutionalization of male inversion wherein a biological male adopts a female social role, and his effeminate behavior is recognized and tolerated, if not always condoned and supported, by other members of society.

European anthropologists have emphasized (see commentary by Signorini and Hultkrantz following Callender and Kochems 1983) that the social institutionalization of inversion is an age-old phenomenon with its roots in the prehistorical practice of primitive people selecting effeminate young males for the position of tribal shaman. The early Greek historian Herodotus (circa 484–425 B.C.E.), who traveled as far north as the Dnieper, described the barbaric Scythians of that area whose soothsayers were "Enarees, or woman-like men" (1952, 256). Others have noted that sexual inversion has long been a part of human history, prehistory, and mythology (Green [1966] 1977; Bullough 1974; Steiner 1981; Taylor 1965). Indeed, it is probable that the Judeo-Christian taboo regarding cross-gendered behavior (Deut. 22:5) derives from a rejection by the Hebrews of the custom of the other early Mediterranean peoples, whose worship of the fertility goddess variously called Ishtar, Ashtoreth, Ashtaroth, Ashirah, Anaitis, Astarte, or Aphrodite included altars and temples attended to by sexually inverted priests called hieroduli (LaBarre 1970; Carpenter 1975; Bullough 1976; Steiner 1981; and Hoffman, 1983–84). European Catholic conquistadors routinely executed the ever-present, cross-dressed, "sodomite," priests among the Central American Indian peoples they vanquished (Williams 1986; Flaherty 1988b). Furthermore, this practice of institutionalizing cross-gendered priests seems likely to have been a vestige of a much older fertility worship and presents the distinct likelihood that, at an even earlier time, paleolithic Eurasian hunter-gatherers had, like Herodotus's Scythians, institutionalized male inversion in their shamanism. (A map depicting the historical and geographical distribution of the gynemimetic shaman is provided by Baumann 1955, 352). Indeed, this practice continued into modern times among Central Asian and Arctic hunters and herders and was widespread among preliterate peoples in varied parts of the world (Eliade 1964). Why this is so is examined below, but that it was so is convincingly demonstrated by an examination of the ethnographic data tabulated by Weinrich (1976) that indicates twenty three of twenty-seven (85 percent) "primitive" peoples upon which he could find information institutionalized homosexual males as shamans.

Resistance to Change

Effeminacy and homosexuality are stigmatized in the United States, but in societies where moral judgments are not as severe, numbers of overtly effeminate male homosexuals increase (Whitam 1987), suggesting that repressive social control of cross-gendered behavior is not without some effect. Nevertheless, a heated debate still continues regarding the efficacy of various psychotherapies in "treating" cross-gendered behavior in children. Zucker (1985) doubts the effectiveness of UCLA behavior modifier George Rekers (1982) to do so. Most therapists agree with Pinkava (1987), who calls for models of variant sexuality other than social learning or psychodynamic, because techniques of change based upon these models do not work.

Interestingly enough, heterosexual orientation is not as malleable as some predict. Herdt (1981) and Stoller and Herdt (1985) find that considerable experience with fellatio among pubescent Sambian boys has little effect upon their adult heterosexual preference. Despite the best efforts of numerous psychotherapists of various theoretical persuasions and despite exceedingly punitive social control, cross-gendered behavior and homosexuality endure, and one interpretation of this recalcitrance may be that unique or particular neurohormonal mechanisms undergird its etiology and persistence.

Early Developmental Appearance

Retrospective studies (Bell, Weinberg, and Hammersmith 1981; Saghir and Robbins 1973; Harry 1982) of adult men with homosexual orientation indicate that the majority of them recall a childhood and adolescence typified by cross-gendered toys, play, and dress. Whitam's (1983) cross-cultural observations of homosexuals also point to cross-gendered behavior in childhood as a precursor of adult sexual orientation.

Again, the recent longitudinal study by Green (1987) shows a strong relationship between childhood effeminate behavior and adult homosexual orientation. Green reminds us that sex differences in identity, attitudes, and behaviors emerge early, as do parental and societal expectations. Early developmental appearance of inversion in and of itself may not be taken as evidencing biological predisposition to learn gender role behavior; however, when placed against the backdrop of the other kinds of data cited above, it seems to add weight to that argument.

Sexual Inversion and Associated Talent

Singularly, none of the data sources above leads to a firm conclusion regarding the etiology of inversion. However, the most enigmatic of the behavioral correlates of male sexual inversion is the personality's prodigious and continuing interest in and talent for theatrical and performing arts. Many researchers (Harry 1983; Hoffman 1968; Green and Money 1966; Tripp 1975; Green 1987; Peschel and Peschel 1987; Whitam 1987) have commented upon the engrossing interest shown by many male homosexuals in careers in the entertainment industry and the performing arts.

Hoffman, in his early study of San Francisco's "Gay World" (1968) offered: "My experience in conversations with homosexuals has been that they show an especial interest in the arts." Hooker notes the same phenomenon: "I also have observed that homosexuals are particularly attracted to professional careers in the arts, especially in the performing arts, and a number of other writers have noted that there seems to be an unusual percentage of homosexuals who have taken up acting as an occupation" (1957, 70).

Barr et al. posted a notice at the New York office of Actors Equity to recruit subjects for an experiment and ended up with a sample of fifty male aspiring actors. "About two-thirds were evaluated as lacking adequate masculine identification and about one-half had strong homosexual tendencies. Overt homosexuality was quite common and several were bisexual" (1972, 17). This preoccupation with performing arts is not limited to Western society (Kiefer 1968). Whitam (1987) notes after studying homosexual groups cross-culturally that a strong interest in the arts, dance, and theater is a salient core feature of inversion in all of the societies observed and, while many social scientists assume that such behavior results from cultural transmission, these behaviors seem to appear spontaneously, predictably, and indigenously in different societies. Green and Money studied cross-gendered young boys, many of whom "displayed an exceptional interest in theatrical stage acting, dramatic role-taking in childhood play" and "demonstrated considerable resourcefulness in the improvisation of facilities for staging plays, as director, producer, casting director, costumer, or role player" (1966, 536) And, in Green's (1987) more recent study of the "sissy boy syndrome," he again finds an interest in acting as a career to be strong discriminator between his "feminine boy" group and his "masculine boy" controls, with *all sixteen boys* (italics in original, 256) who had such aspiration belonging to the former. Moreover, if our inference from reading Green's summary of this is correct, he would agree with Whitam, who concludes that among the universal core elements of homosexual subculture is "The more overtly feminine the individual, the greater is his interest in entertainment and the arts . . ." (1987, 181).

It is easy to account for these observations by noting that the milieu of the theater and the entertainment world provides a haven for the sexually inverted male, but the early developmental appearance of such interests poses a more difficult problem. Green commented, "And again, in this new group, interest in acting as a career began early in life, before the social sanctuary of such a career would be apparent to most boys" (1987, 257).

Money and Lamacz acknowledge that the exaggerated interest in performing arts shown by gynemimetic males around the world is not the result of "cultural borrowing" and that it is "presumed to be a feature of the gynemimetic syndrome itself," and put forth a social learning hypothesis regarding the "unusual talent" phenomenon: "Thus it is that gynemimesis, being itself a feminine identification, manifests itself as an impersonation of women in cosmetics, dress and mannerisms. Being a manifestation of acting, it lends itself to musical, theatrical, film, or television entertainment as an occupation" (1984, 402).

We submit that this often observed penchant for theater should also be considered in terms of how it fits the widely cited Geschwind and Galaburda (1985a, 1985b, 1985c, and 1987) model of cerebral lateralization, disability, and exceptional talent. These Harvard neurologists have summarized data and devised a theory of talent and disability based upon anomalous brain dominance and lateralization that they assert result from hormonal influences upon fetal brain development. Essentially, Geschwind and Galaburda postulate that unusual amounts of testosterone present in the fetal system results in a unique cluster of neuro-immuno-endocrinological attributes that correlate with cerebral lateralization, pituitary/hypothalamic organization, left-handedness, and unusual behavioral abilities and disabilities. Homosexual orientation is one of the behavioral attributes postulated by Geschwind and Galaburda (1985b, 546) and the hypothesis here is that *"acting" or showmanship as described below is another Geschwind-Galaburda type talent.*

Prodigious talent in sports, language acquisition, musical ability, and mathematics is easily defined, recognized, and measured. Individuals with these "exceptional brains" are now the subject of serious study (Obler and Fein 1988). Acting, however, as a talent is like literary art in that it is less easily defined and recognized in children, but the evidence cited above suggests that many effeminate males have such propensity.

One further note here. Geschwind and Galaburda think many disabilities associated with anomalous brain differentiation may be offset by an exceptional talent and the trade off leads to superior group fitness (1985a, 455). This "pathology of superiority" leads to natural selection of special talents. Below, it is posited that institutionalized shamanism of nonliterate peoples depends upon exceptional theatrical talent for its success and the theatrical talent exhibited by shamans depends upon some unusual brain and endocrine functioning (cf. Raymond Prince [1982], *Ethos* 10: 4; the entire issue is devoted to neuropsychology of shamanism). We argue also that the reproductive success of early man depended upon his breeding group's containing talented shamans. Our hypothesis is not an inclusive theory of homosexuality but one that may aid in the understanding of male-to-female transsexuals and effeminate male homosexuals. The author agrees with Hoffman who, reflecting on this topic, says ". . . there are certain connections here which have been noted repeatedly by different observers and deserve thoughtful consideration. It is clear, at any rate, that there is very probably some early tendency toward an interest in those kinds of activity which lead to later interest in the arts and in acting. Such a tendency appears to exist well prior to puberty and therefore prior to the age at which sexual orientation becomes a conscious part of the homosexual's life" (1968, 71–72).

Altruistic Shamans and Their Kin

For all but the smallest portion of the evolutionary history of *Homo sapien sapien,* people have lived, reproduced, and developed cultural patterns as social groups of hunter-gatherers. In such a society the male's ability to hunt and fight typically accord him status, wealth, and, most importantly (from the biological standpoint), mating opportunities (Symmons 1979). Consequently, it seems difficult to offer a biological (i.e., genetic or hereditary) explanation of a behavior so obviously reproductively disadvantageous as gynemimesis and/or homoeroticism. However, several proposals have been offered to explain how such a biogenetic mechanism might be maintained in a breeding population (Weinrich 1976, 1987; Ruse 1981, 1988; Kirsch and Rodman 1982). One is that genes for homosexuality could be maintained if they, using the analogy to sickle cell anemia, conferred some survival advantage to the heterozygotic carrier, like the enhanced resistance to malaria. Of course, in the homozygotic individual, either sickle cell or sexual inversion would be reproductively unfit; the former would cause fatal anemia, and the latter would result in fewer offspring as compared with noninverted males.

Another way biogenetic predisposition toward inversion could be preserved in a breeding group is if the phenotypic manifestation of the underlying genes in some way enhanced the inclusive reproductive fitness of the invert's close relatives with whom he has great genetic commonality or even of his clan with whom he has some. Since the basic unit of natural selection is at the level of the gene, it matters not if the particular gene(s) are transmitted to the next generation by the invert or by his kinfolk (Dawkins 1976). The idea that the homosexual or sexually inverted male might confer reproductive fitness upon others is an example of what sociobiologists refer to as "altruism," a very different use of that word from common parlance, but an idea that has sound mathematical logic behind it and substantial empirical support when applied to the social and sexual behaviors of animals (Daly and Wilson 1983; Eberhard 1975; Alexander 1974). Sociobiologists (Buss 1984; Crawford, Smith, and Krebs 1987; Wenegrat 1990) find much merit in applying evolutionary logic and principles of population biology to human behavior and problems of clinical psychology and psychiatry also, and one variation of this idea of genetic altruism has been termed the Kin Selection Hypothesis of Homosexuality (Ruse 1981).

Several aspects of this hypothesis require further clarification and elaboration. First, the point needs to be made that there is evidence to suggest that seers, shamans, artists, and keepers of tribal knowledge were among hunter-gatherer peoples throughout European prehistory often the same individual, and this person was quite frequently an inverted male (LaBarre 1970; Baumann 1955). Second, the evidence indicates that it was inversion, or effeminacy, and not homoeroticism per se that was institutionalized in shamanism; an important aspect of shamanism of which Wilson, Williams, Weinrich, and Ruse fail to take note. Indeed, a close reading of the anthropological literature indicates that boyhood effeminacy, as opposed to homoeroticism, was the probable basis for many individual males becoming shamans (see Callender and Kochems 1983, and commentary). Additionally, another point needs to be made if one is to understand fully the kin selection hypothesis. One must completely grasp the critical importance of shamanism to the culture of early man. So important was this religious institution to our ancestors that, if one equated its impact upon their way of life to that of the combined influences of religion, science, and art upon contemporary industrialized peoples, one would not be exaggerating or hyperbolic. The hypothesis as developed here asserts a relationship, an interconnectedness of socially recognized male inversion, shamanism, and primary theatrical talent based upon brain organization.

Shamanic Religion

The anthropological literature on shamanism is immense, and this treatment of it owes much to Mircea Eliade's (1964) authoritative *Shamanism: Archaic Techniques of Ecstasy,* M. A. Czaplicka's (1914) *Aboriginal Siberia,* and to Weston LaBarre's (1970) *The Ghost Dance: Origins of Religion*; the last containing extensive description of shamanistic influences on primitive society and offering a psychoanalytic perspective of the widely diffuse transvestism/effeminacy shown by these spiritual technicians. However, none of these authors indicates familiarity with those data that point toward a biogenetic interpretation of cross-gendered behavior, nor do they anticipate latter efforts to specify the neurochemical and neuropsychological mechanisms involved in shamanistic phenomenon (Prince 1982).

Ancientness of Shamanic Religion

Shamanism is a form of primitive religion that focuses upon a particular individual who is said to possess tremendous supernatural powers with which he (or she) can control phenomena (weather, animals, illness) of critical importance to the survival of hunter-gatherer peoples. Ample evidence exists in the form of physical artifacts, common elements of widely diffuse ceremonial practices, ritual, and mythology to support the contention that shamanism was a major part of the cultural life of Eurasian stone-age peoples and is continuous with and still manifested in altered form in virtually all hunter-gatherer peoples today; in its classical form among the recent Arctic, Siberian, and Central Asian tribes (Chukchee, Tungus, Yakuts, Eskimos), and with similar elements clearly evident across the Bering Strait among American Indian cultures from Alaska to Patagonia (Czaplicka 1914; Eliade 1964, 1965; Hultkrantz 1967; LaBarre 1970).

Additionally, Williams's (1986) treatment of the berdache tradition among American Indians also supports the notion that the berdache is probably derived from shamanistic traditions, and its New World diffusion indicates to Williams that the relationship existed prior to the migration of the Asians to North America between fifteen and thirty thousand years ago.

Shamanism and Gynemimesis: Co-Evolution of Culture and Mind

That male sexual inverts were part of the pattern of religious behavior over such a substantial part of time is more problematical than the ancientness of shamanism alone, but the argument is most frequently advanced by European scientists who tend to make more of the association between transvestism/effeminacy and the ancient religious complex than do their American colleagues.

The age of the institution can be argued on the basis of the following evidence.

Again, the geographical diffusion of this cultural pattern points toward an origin of great antiquity, and the sexually inverted shaman is a fixture of primitive society, not only among transarctic peoples and American Indians, but also among the peoples on the African and South American continents and in Australia and Oceania as well (Eliade 1964; Baumann 1955). While to anthropologists this speaks of the great age of the institution, for the sociobiologist it is a behavior pattern to suggest a co-evolution of genes, culture, and cognitive functioning (Lumsden and Wilson 1981). The effeminate shaman represented a behavior pattern that correlated with other mental characteristics that were interpreted by early humans as being of supernatural origin and that modern man would characterize as showmanship or theatricality. Furthermore, if the kin selection hypothesis as presented here is correct, by examining the behavior patterns of shamans, one can not only discern ways in which these individuals aided in the survival of their kinsmen, and thereby maintained their own genes in the pool, but additionally, one can also make some predictions regarding the way in which the effeminate boys of Green (1987), Zuger (1966), and Zucker (1985) differ from noninverted controls (i.e., one can perhaps identify the psychological characteristics of "sissy boys" that led nonliterate peoples everywhere to select them as technicians of the sacred).

Trance as Talent

Typical of the practices of these folk is that some special person is chosen, usually around puberty, to learn those skills and techniques that will allow him or her to interact with the supernatural. While the "specialness" may be some mental characteristic, an illness, or infirmity, the defining quality of shamanistic ability everywhere is that the individual must be able to alter ordinary modes of consciousness and enter an ecstatic trance state. This "special talent" comprises the common thread of hunter-gatherer shamanism (Eliade 1964). Margaret Mead suggests that this propensity to alter states of consciousness "may trigger sex role assignment" (1973, 1453). What is proposed here is the exact opposite! We argue that "trance-proneness" or the ability to learn or otherwise respond to ecstatic techniques is the psychology underlying the near-universal selection of effeminate males as shamans and that this is a *"Geschwind-Galaburda-type talent"* and directly related to the widely observed penchant for the performing arts observed in homosexual subcultures in the modern world; furthermore, the development of trance-proneness is based upon a specialized neurobiological organization (Prince 1982), and is passed across generations by the mechanism of kin selection.

The anthropological literature suggests the following as an accurate summary of the common elements of culturally institutionalized shamanism among hunter-gatherer peoples.

A shaman undergoes certain experiences that alter ordinary states of consciousness and his people believe that he is possessed by supernatural entities who torture him until he accepts his role as shaman. While in trance state he displays an ability to communicate with the transcendent world, to bring forth ceremonially and dramatically spiritual personalities from that world, and to sing and chant mythically or socially important messages. He magically and most dramatically (cf. Charles 1953) heals the sick, improves the hunt, and increases fertility, all critically important rituals for hunter-gatherer folk. Both Kirby (1974) and Flaherty (1988a) note that the shaman's role often required talent as a ventriloquist, a magician, singer, dancer, musician, prestidigitator, bard, panegyrist, or hypnotist. He could literally mesmerize his people and, as a consequence of doing so, bond them together and enhance the solidarity of the group. They in turn would function more effectively and have more offspring in the process. In the critical business of hunting, fishing, herding, and having babies, those folk who had a powerful shaman functioned more effectively than those without one. In sociobiological terms, the powerful shaman enhances the inclusive fitness of the breeding population. He aids in keeping all genes—including his own—replicated. The mathematics of kin selection as an evolutionary mechanism is such that if it is in fact the process that allowed the genes of altruistic, relatively nonreproductive, gynemimetic males to be transmitted to the next generation, it would be necessary to demonstrate that they differentially enhanced the reproductive advantage of their closer kin over their more distant relatives. All of our authorities indicate that the powerful hunter-gatherer shaman was a source of pride, prestige, and even wealth for his family, factors likely to enhance his reproductive fitness. A dramatic talent for ceremony and ritual makes the shaman powerful; however, the key to that talent seems equivalent to the ability to respond to techniques of trance induction. We predict that effeminate males may show this *special talent* also.

Techniques of the Ecstatic Trance

The hypothesis is that sexually inverted males frequently became the most powerful shamans because they have a hormonally differentiated and uniquely organized nervous system that, in addition to predisposing them toward the development of cross-gendered behavior and homosexuality, manifested itself in a differential sensitivity to those stimulus situations that are known to alter ordinary states of consciousness and/or induce ecstatic trance states.

It is the trance that allows the shaman to experience and demonstrate all of the phenomena that have fascinated scientists and lay observers of shamanistic performances. As presented later, trance-proneness is correlated with the inordinate talent for and interest in acting displayed by many young effeminate males. Ruse (1981) emphasizes acting ability in the selection of inverted males as shamans, but we wonder whether or not the notion of theatrical role-taking (acting) and religious role-taking (shamanism) should be considered as the same psychological process. Is theatrical role-taking an accurate or valid description of the hunter-gatherer shaman's ecstatic behavior? *Is the modern Pentecostal glossolalic or Catholic stigmatic acting?* The hypnotic trance state of the ecstatic visionary, one can argue, is based upon role-taking (see Sarbin 1950 and following text); however, it may or may not be identical with what we ordinarily call acting. That primitive religion seemed to be the product of artistic showmen is attested to by many anthropologists. Charles reviews the healing ceremonies of shamans from over one hundred cultures recorded in Yale University's Human Relations Area Files and argues convincingly that *primitive religion is theater* and that successful healing by the shaman depends upon his displaying the "ecstasy or frenzy which may be considered a supreme example of dramatic impersonation" (1953, 96).

Differential sensitivity of effeminate males to trance-inducing techniques is exactly what is predicted here, and this hypothesis differs from that of other theorists who have considered the sexually transformed shaman. To digress just a bit, Weinrich (1976) summarizes a number of studies to argue that homosexuals were selected as shamans because they are more intelligent. However, this possibility seems unlikely as Finegan et al. (1982) find no difference between overall IQ scores of preadolescent boys who met DSM-III criteria for Gender Identity

Disorder when they were compared with siblings and other controls. What is suggested here is that if effeminate boys were subjected to psychological variables that are modern analogues of primitive ecstatic and trance techniques and compared with noneffeminate controls, that the probability of response differences is high and that such differences relate to brain organization.

Music and Trance Induction

Shamans use long periods of singing, chanting, dancing, and drumming to alter the consciousness of themselves and members of their audience. Perhaps the effect is another form of hypnosis? How this is accomplished is not well understood, but the interested reader will find Gilbert Rouget's (1985) *Music and Trance* to be a stimulating piece of ethnomusicological scholarship. This work leaves little doubt that throughout history and prehistory shamans have altered consciousness with music and dance. The neurological substrates of musicality have not been frequently investigated but are known to be complex and distinct from those underlying language (Neher 1962; Gates and Bradshaw 1977; Critchley and Henson 1977). And given the "widespread incidence of cross-sex identification among musicians in our own and other cultures" (Kiefer 1968, 107), could it possibly be that R. Hoffman's (1968) gay males are more readily "possessed" by music and drama (opera), not in the archaic, but rather in a neurohormonal sense of the word "possessed"? An informed speculation is that the observed aesthetic sensibilities of these individuals may biologically based.

Summary and Conclusions

Perhaps a comment upon criticism of an evolutionary analysis of inversion and homosexuality is presently in order.

Several critical papers (Ricketts 1984; Dannecker 1984) place emphasis upon Foucault's (1978) contention that the homosexual as "pathology" or a "special person" arises conceptually as the disciplines of medicine and psychology produce a scientization of sexuality. Foucault is an "archaeologist of scientific knowledge," and his diggings may well indicate that the homosexual as "pathology" is a nineteenth-century construction of science, but the effeminate male as a "third sex" or as a "special person" is a part of the language of nonliterate peoples everywhere (Czaplicka 1914; Williams 1986; Flaherty 1988b). That these special people can be identified by folk around the world does, for this author anyway, produce a meaningful question regarding the etiology of their "specialness."

Futuyma and Risch reject the kin selection hypothesis and imply that the question of the etiology of sexual orientation is a trivial one. ("It requires no more explanation than a preference for blondes or brunettes or for music or sports" [1984, 16]), and Coleman, Gooren, and Ross (1989) criticize gender transposition theories based upon evolutionary biology because they are reductionistic and give insufficient weight to social, cultural, and familial variables. While one may ultimately prefer social learning or psychodynamic explanations of gender dysphoria, one must remember that social learning (i.e., conditioning and imprinting-type early experience) is also based upon a biology and the contention here is that the question of the cause of sexual orientation (homosexual and heterosexual) is meaningful and a scientifically valid and important one, and why primitive religion found its priests among cross-gendered males will continue to intrigue.

Other critics (e.g., Birke 1981) reject a biological approach to the study of homosexuality and seem to believe that such an approach is tantamount to stating that the homosexual is somehow defective, ill, or otherwise abnormal. Homosexuals have every right and much reason to be wary of all who would "cure" or correct their "defects"; however, it should be plain that the thrust of the sociobiological hypothesis is that gynemimesis and homosexuality arise from the same natural selective pressures and mechanisms that have led to the evolution of heterosexual orientation and behavior. Asserted here is that sexual inversion may be a natural result of kin selection, and, contrary to the idea of "illness" or "defect," this variation and extension of the hypothesis proposes that such an individual might better be considered "talented" or "gifted," with a readiness to learn to enter a trance state or a native ability to readily alter ordinary states of consciousness, and in so doing to become the ecstatic visionary. . . . *To become the shaman for one's people, or in a secular modern world, a stage personality.* If indeed this ability to alter consciousness relies upon some biogenetic aspect of the individual's nervous system, then male inversion, institutionalized in hunter-gatherer shamanism, may come to exemplify the premise put forth by Lumsden and Wilson (1981). These sociobiologists argue that cultural and genetic evolution are interrelated with biologically based developmental processes that lead to variation in cognitive functioning and that these processes are in turn modified by cultural learning. With this thought in mind we would offer our hypothesis that the gynemimetic personality is maintained by natural selection because such individuals provided a reproductive advantage to ancestral groups.

Anthropologists have shown that such individuals have been a part of the nonliterate societies for many millennia and the author is inclined toward the view expressed a half century ago by the eminent scientist Ruth Benedict, who after considering the Indian berdache and the transformed shamans offered this thought:

It is clear that culture may value and make socially available even highly unstable human types. If it chooses to treat their peculiarities as the most valued variants of human behavior, the individuals in question will rise to the occasion and perform their social roles without reference to our usual ideas of the types who can make social adjustments and those who cannot. Those who function inadequately in any society are not those with certain fixed "abnormal" traits, but may well be those whose responses have received no support in the institutions of their culture. The weakness of these aberrants is in great measure illusory. It springs, not from the fact that they are lacking in necessary vigor, but that they are individuals whose native responses are not reaffirmed by society. (1934, 270)

A different culture with a different psychology, perhaps even American or Western culture at some point in the not-too-distant future, may view the sissy boy not as "syndrome" but as child prodigy . . . an individual, a personality with a savantlike talent for emotional communication so highly regarded in theater.

References

Allen, L., and R. Gorski. 1992. Sexual orientation and the size of the anterior commissure in the human brain. *Proceedings of the National Academy of Science* 89: 7199–202.

Archer, J., and B. Lloyd. 1985. *Sex and gender.* Cambridge: Cambridge University Press.

Alexander, R. 1974. The evolution of social behavior. *Annual Review of Ecology and Systematics* 5: 325–83.

Bailey, J., and R. Pillard. 1991. A genetic study of male sexual orientation. *Archives of General Psychiatry* 48: 1089–96.

Barr, H., R. Langs, R. Holt, L. Goldberger, and G. Klein. 1972. *LSD: Personality and experience.* New York: Wiley-Interscience.

Baumann, H. 1955. *Das doppelte geschlecht: ethnologische studien zur bisexualitat in ritus and mythos.* Berlin: Reimer Company.

Bell, A., M. Weinberg, and S. Hammersmith. 1981. *Sexual preference: Its development in men and women.* Bloomington: Indiana University Press.

Benedict, R. 1934. *Patterns of culture.* Boston: Houghton Mifflin. Sentry Edition, 1959.

Birke, L., 1981. Is homosexuality hormonally determined? *Journal of Homosexuality* 6, no. 4: 35–49.

Bullough, V. 1974. Transvestites in the middle ages. *American Journal of Sociology* 79 no. 6: 1381–94.

———. 1976. *Sexual variance in society and history.* Chicago: University of Chicago Press.

———. 1979. *Homosexuality: A history.* New York: New American Library.

Buss, D. 1984. Evolutionary biology and personality psychology: Toward a conception of human nature and individual differences. *American Psychologist* 39: 1135–47.

———. 1989. Sex differences in human mate preferences: Evolutionary hypothesis tested in 37 cultures. *Behavioral and Brain Sciences* 24: 1–49.

Callender, C., and L. Kochems. 1983. The North American berdache. *Current Anthropology* 24, no. 4: 443–70.

Carpenter, E. [1919] 1975. *Intermediate types among primitive folk: A study in social evolution.* New York: Arno Press.

Charles, L. 1953. Drama in shaman exorcism. *Journal of American Folklore* 66: 95–122.

Coleman, E., L. Gooren, and M. Ross. 1989. Theories of gender transpositions: A critique and suggestions for further research. *Journal of Sex Research* 26, no. 4: 525–38.

Crawford, C., M. Smith, and D. Krebs, eds. 1987. *Sociobiology and psychology: Ideas, issues, and applications.* Hillsdale, N.J.: Lawrence Erlbaum.

Critchley, M., and R. Henson. 1977. *Music and the brain: Studies in the neurology of music.* London: Heinemann Medical Books.

Czaplicka, M. A. 1914. *Aboriginal Siberia: A study in social anthropology.* Oxford: Oxford University Press.

Daly, M., and M. Wilson. 1983. *Sex, evolution, and behavior.* Boston: Willard Grant Press, PWS Publishers.

Dannecker, M. 1984. Toward a theory of homosexuality: Socio-historical perspectives. *Journal of Homosexuality* 9, no. 4: 1–8.

Dawkins, R. 1976. *The selfish gene.* New York: Oxford University Press.

Devereux, G. 1937. Institutionalized homosexuality of the Mohave indians. *Human Biology* 9: 498–527.

Domjan, M., and B. Galef. 1983. Biological constraints on instrumental and classical conditioning. Retrospect and prospect. *Animal Learning and Behavior* 2, no. 2: 151–61.

Dorner, G. 1976. *Hormones and brain differentiation.* Amsterdam: Elsevier Scientific Publishing Co.

———. 1988. Neuroendocrine response to estrogen and brain differentiation in heterosexuals, homosexuals, and transsexuals. *Archives of Sexual Behavior* 17, no. 1: 57–75.

Eberhard, M. 1975. The evolution of social behavior by kin selection. *Quarterly Review of Biology* 50, no. 1: 1–33.

Ehrhardt, A., and H. Meyer-Bahlburg. 1979. Prenatal sex hormones and the developing brain: Effect on the psychosexual differentiation and cognitive function. *Annual Review of Medicine* 30: 417–30.

Eliade, M. 1964. *Shamanism: Archaic techniques of ecstasy.* New York: Bollinger Foundation/ Pantheon Books.

———. 1965. *Mephistopheles and the androgyne.* New York: Sheed and Ward.

Ellis, L. 1982. Developmental androgen fluctuations and the dimensions of mammalian sex with emphasis upon the behavioral dimension and the human species. *Ethology and Sociobiology* 3: 171–79.

Ellis, L., and M. Ames. 1987. Neurohormonal functioning and sexual orientation. A theory of homosexuality-heterosexuality. *Psychological Bulletin* 101, no. 2: 233–58.

Finegan, J., K. Zucker, M. Bradley, and R. Doering. 1982. Patterns of intellectual functioning and spatial ability in boys with gender identity disorder. *Canadian Journal of Psychiatry* 27: 135–39.

Flaherty, G. 1988a. The performing artist as the shaman of higher civilization. *M.L.N.* 103, no. 3: 519–39.

———. 1988b. Sex and shamanism in the eighteenth century. In *Sexual underworlds of the Enlightenment,* edited by G. Rosseau and R. Porter, 261–80. Chapel Hill: University of North Carolina Press.

Ford, C., and F. Beach. 1951. *Patterns of sexual behavior.* New York: Harper.

Forgey, D. 1975. The institution of berdache among North American Plains Indians. *Journal of Sex Research* 11, no. 1: 1–15.

Foucault, M. 1978. *The history of sexuality,* translated by R. Hurly. New York: Random House.

Futuyma, D., and S. Risch. 1983–1984. Sexual orientation, sociobiology and evolution. *Journal of Homosexuality* 9, nos. 2 and 3: 157–68.

Gates, A., and J. Bradshaw. 1977. The role of the cerebral hemispheres in music. *Brain and Language.* 4: 403–31.

Geschwind, N., and A. Galaburda. 1985a. Cerebral lateralization: Biological mechanisms, associations, and pathology: 1. A hypothesis and a program for research. *Archives of Neurology* 42: 428–59.

———. 1985b. Cerebral lateralization: Biological mechanisms, associations, and pathology: 2. A hypothesis and a program for research. *Archives of Neurology* 42: 521–52.

———. 1985c. Cerebral lateralization: Biological mechanisms, associations, and pathology: 3. A hypothesis and a program for research. *Archives of Neurology* 42: 634–54.

———. 1987. *Cerebral lateralization: Biological mechanisms, associations, and pathology.* Cambridge, Mass.: MIT Press.

Gladue, B. 1987. Psychobiological contributions. In *Male and female homosexuality: Psychological approaches,* edited by L. Dimant. New York: Hemisphere Publishing Corp.

Gladue, G., R. Green, and R. Hellman. 1984. Neuroendocrine response to estrogen and sexual orientation. *Science* 225: 1496–99.

Goy, R., and B. McEwen. 1980. *Sexual differentiation of the brain.* Cambridge, Mass.: MIT Press.

Green, R. [1966] 1977. Transsexualism: Mythological, historical and cross-cultural aspects. In *The transsexual phenomenon,* edited by H. Benjamin, 206–21. New York: Warner Books.

———. 1987. *The "sissy boy syndrome" and the development of homosexuality.* New Haven, Conn.: Yale University Press.

Green, R., and J. Money. 1966. Stage acting, role-taking and effeminate impersonation during boyhood. *Archives of General Psychiatry* 15: 535–38.

Hamer, D., S. Hu, V. Magnuson, N. Hu, and A. Pattatucci. 1993. A linkage between DNA markers on the X chromosome and male sexual orientation. *Science* 261: 321–27.

Harner, M. 1980. *The way of the shaman.* New York: Harper & Row.

Harry, J. 1982. *Gay children grown up: Gender culture and gender deviance.* New York: Praeger.

———. 1983. Defeminization and adult psychological well-being among adult homosexuals. *Archives of Sexual Behavior* 12: 1–19.

Herdt, G. 1981. *Guardians of the flute: Idioms of masculinity.* New York: McGraw-Hill.

Herodotus. 1952. The history of Herodotus, translated by G. Rawlinson. In *Great books of the western world,* vol 6. Chicago: Encyclopedia Britannica and the University of Chicago.

Heston, L., and J. Shields. 1968. Homosexuality in twins: A family study and a registry study. *Archives of General Psychiatry* 18, no. 2: 149–60.

Hines, M. 1983. Prenatal gonadal hormones and sex differences in human behavior. *Psychological Bulletin* 92: 56–80.

Hines, M., and M. Collaer. 1993. Gonadal hormones and sexual differentiation of human behavior: Developments from research on endocrine syndromes and studies on brain structure. In *Annual review of sex research,* edited by J. Bancroft, 1–48. Mt. Vernon, Iowa: SSSS Publishers.

Hoffman, M. 1968. *The gay world.* Toronto: Basic Books Inc. Reprint, Bantam, 1969.

Hoffman, R. 1983–1984. Vices, gods, and virtues: Cosmology as a mediating factor in attitudes toward male homosexuality. *Journal of Homosexuality* 9, nos. 2 and 3: 27–44.

Hooker, E. 1957. The adjustment of the overt male homosexual. *Journal of Projective Techniques* 21: 18–31.

Hultkrantz, A. 1967. *The religions of the American Indians,* translated by M. Setterwall. Berkeley: University of California Press.

Kallman, F. 1952. Comparative twin study on the genetic aspects of male homosexuality. *Journal of Nervous and Mental Disorders* 115: 283–98.

Kiefer, T. 1968. A note on cross-sex identification among musicians. *Ethnomusciology* 12: 107–109.

Kirby, E. 1974. The shamanistic origins of popular entertainments. *Drama Review* 18 (T-61): 5–15.

Kirsch, J., and J. Rodman. 1982. Selection and sexuality. The darwinian view of homosexuality. In

Homosexuality: Social, psychological, and biological issues, edited by W. Paul, J. Weinrich, J. Gonsiorek, and M. Hotvedt. Beverly Hills: Sage.

LaBarre, W. 1970. *The ghost dance: Origins of religion.* New York: Doubleday. Reprint, Delta book/Dell edition, 1972.

LeVay, S. 1991. A difference in hypothalamic structure between heterosexual and homosexual men. *Science.* 253: 1034–37.

Levy, R. 1971. The community function of Tahitian male transvestism: A hypothesis. *Anthropological Quarterly* 44: 12–21.

Lebovitz, P. 1972. Feminine behavior in boys: Aspects of its outcome. *American Journal of Psychiatry* 128, no. 10: 103–109.

Lumsden, C., and E. Wilson. 1981. *Genes, mind, and culture: The coevolutionary process.* Cambridge, Mass.: Harvard University Press.

MacLusky, N., and F. Naftolin. 1981. Sexual differentiation of the central nervous system. *Science* 211: 1294–303.

McEwen, B. 1981. Neural gonadal steroid action. *Science* 211: 1303 11.

Mead, M. 1973. Cultural determinants of sexual behavior. In *Sex and internal secretions,* edited by W. Young, vol. 2. New York: Kreiger Publishing Co.

Money, J. 1981. The development of sexuality and eroticism in humankind. *Quarterly Review of Biology* 56, no. 4: 379–404.

———. 1986. *Lovemaps: Clinical concepts of sexual/erotic health and pathology, paraphilia, and gender transposition in childhood, adolescence, and maturity.* New York: Irvington.

———. 1987. Sin, sickness, or status? Homosexual gender identity and psychoneuroendocrinology. *American Psychologist* 42, no. 4: 384–99.

Money, J., and A. Ehrhardt. 1972. *Man and woman: Boy and girl.* Baltimore: The Johns Hopkins University Press.

Money, J., and M. Lamacz. 1984. Gynemimesis and gynemimetophilia: Individual and cross-cultural manifestations of gender-coping strategy hitherto unnamed. *Comprehensive Psychiatry* 25, no. 4: 392–403.

Money, J., M. Schwartz, and V. Lewis. 1984. Adult erotosexual status and fetal hormonal masculinization and demasculinization: 46,XX congenital virilizing adrenal hyperplasia and 46,XY androgen-insensitivity syndrome compared. *Psychoneuroendocrinology* 9, no. 4: 405–14.

Nanda, S. 1984. The hijras of India: A preliminary report. *Medicine and Law* 3: 59–75.

———. 1990. *Neither man nor woman: The hijras of India.* New York: Wadsworth Publishing.

Neher, A. 1962. A physiological explanation of unusual behavior in ceremonies involving drums. *Human Biology* 4: 151–60.

Nordeen, E. and P. Yahr. 1982. Hemispheric asymmetries in the behavioral and hormonal effects of sexually differentiating mammalian brain. *Science.* 218: 391–93.

Obler, L., and D. Fein, eds. 1988. *The exceptional brain. Neuropsychology of talent and special abilities.* New York: Guilford Press.

Peschel, E., and R. Peschel. 1987. Medical insights into the castrati in opera. *American Scientist* 75: 578–83.

Pillard, R., J. Poumadere, and R. Caretta. 1981. Is homosexuality familial? A review, some data, and a suggestion. *Archives of Sexual Behavior* 10: 465–75.

Pillard, R., and J. Weinrich. 1986. Evidence of familial nature of male homosexuality. *Archives of General Psychiatry* 43: 808–12.

———. 1987. The periodic table model of gender transpositions: Part I. A theory based on masculinization and defeminization of the brain. *Journal of Sex Research* 23, no. 4: 425–54.

Pinkava, V. 1987. Logical models of variant sexuality. In *Variant sexuality: Research and theory,* edited by G. Wilson, 116–41. Baltimore: The Johns Hopkins University Press.

Prince, R. 1982. Shamans and endorphins. *Ethos* 10, no. 4: 409–23.

Rekers, G. 1982. *Shaping your child's sexual identity.* Grand Rapids, Mich.: Baker Book House.

Ricketts, W. 1984. Biological research on homosexuality: Ansell's cow or Occam's razor? *Journal of Homosexuality* 9, no. 4: 65–93.

Rouget, G. 1985. *Music and trance: A theory of the relations between music and possession,* translated by B. Biebuyck. Chicago: University of Chicago Press.

Ruse, M. 1981. Are there gay genes? Sociobiology and homosexuality. *Journal of Homosexuality* 6, no. 4: 5–34.

———. 1988. *Homosexuality.* Oxford: Basil Blackwell.

Saghir, M., and E. Robbins. 1973. *Male and female homosexuality: A comprehensive investigation.* Baltimore: Williams and Wilkins.

Steiner, B. 1981. From Sappho to sand: Historical perspective on cross-dressing and cross-gender. *Canadian Journal of Psychiatry* 26, no. 7: 502–506.

Stoller R., and G. Herdt. 1985. Theories of the origins of male homosexuality. *Archives of General Psychiatry* 42: 399–404.

Swaab, D., and M. Hofman. 1990. An enlarged suprachiasmatic nucleus in homosexual men. *Brain Research* 537: 141–48.

Swaab, D., and E. Fliers. 1985. A sexually dimorphic nucleus in the human brain. *Science* 228: 1112–15.

Symmons, D. 1979. *The evolution of human sexuality.* Oxford: Oxford University Press.

Taylor, G. 1965. Historical and mythological aspects of homosexuality. In *Sexual inversion,* edited by J. Marmor, 140–64. New York: Basic Books.

Tennov, D. 1979. *Love and limerence: The experience of being in love.* New York: Stein and Day.

Tripp, C. 1975. *The homosexual matrix.* New York: Signet Books.

Watanabe, T, and J. Iwata. 1990. *The love of the samurai: A thousand years of Japanese homosexuality,* translated by D. Roberts. New York: GMP publishers/Distributed by Alyson.

Weinrich, J. D. 1976. *Human reproductive strategy. I. Environmental predictability and reproductive strategy: Effects of social class and race. II. Homosexuality and non-reproduction; Some evolutionary models.* Ph.D. diss., Harvard University, 1976. Ann Arbor Mich.: University Microfilms, no. 77–8348.

———. 1987. A new sociobiological theory of homosexuality applicable to societies with universal marriage. *Ethology and Sociobiology* 8: 37–47.

Wenegrat, B. 1990. *Sociobiological psychiatry: Normal behavior and psychopathology.* Lexington, Mass.: Lexington Books/D.C. Heath.

Whitam, F. 1980. The prehomosexual male child in three societies: The United States, Guatemala, and Brazil. *Archives of Sexual Behavior* 9: 87–99.

———. 1983. Culturally invariable properties of male homosexuality: Tentative conclusions from cross-cultural research. *Archives of Sexual Behavior* 12, no. 3: 207–26.

———. 1987. A cross-cultural perspective on homosexuality, transvestism, and transsexualism. In *Variant sexuality: Research and theory,* edited by G. Wilson, 176–201. Baltimore: The Johns Hopkins University Press.

Whitam, F., M. Diamond, and J. Martin. 1993. Homosexual orientation in twins: A report on 61 pairs and three triplet sets. *Archives of Sexual Behavior* 22: 187–206.

Whitehead, H. 1981. The bow and the burden strap: A new look at institutionalized homosexuality in native North America. In *Sexual meanings: The cultural construction gender and sexuality,* edited by S. Ortner and H. Whitehead. Cambridge: Cambridge University Press.

Wikan, U. 1978. The omani xanith. *Man* 12: 314–19.

Williams, W. 1986. *The spirit and the flesh: Sexual diversity in American Indian culture.* Boston: Beacon Press.

Zucker, K. 1985. Cross-gender identified children. In *Gender dysphoria: Development, research, management,* edited by B. Steiner, 75–174. New York: Plenum Press.

Zucker, K., S. Bradley, and C. Sullivan. 1992. Gender identity disorder in children. In *Annual review of sex research,* edited by J. Bancroft, 73–120. Mt. Vernon, Iowa: SSSS Publishers.

Zuger, B. 1966. Effeminate behavior present in boys from early childhood. I. The clinical syndrome and follow-up studies. *Journal of Pediatrics* 69: 1098–1107.

———. 1989. Homosexuality in families of boys with early effeminate behavior: An epidemiological study. *Archives of Sexual Behavior* 18, no. 2: 155–66.

Zuger, B., and P. Taylor. 1969. Effeminate behavior in boys from early childhood. II. Comparison with similar symptoms in non-effeminate boys. *Pediatrics* 44, no. 3: 375–80.

The Balkan Sworn Virgin:
A Traditional European Transperson

Mildred Dickemann

There lived—and still live—in one small region of Europe, transgendered indi-viduals who are genetic females become social men, living masculine lives. Most current researchers learned of the existence of these individuals through reading the works of Mary Edith Durham, a British traveler who spent many years in the Balkans during the early twentieth century and provided descriptions and pho-tographs of these "Balkan sworn virgins" (Durham 1928, 1987).

These transpersons, so named because they customarily swore lifelong celibacy and chastity when assuming masculine identity, are known from the mountain regions of South Serbia, including Montenegro, Macedonia, and Alba-nia, from the early 1800s. Some still live in all these areas. Scandinavianist Carol Clover (1986) proposes that these are the last exemplars of a role and identity once widespread in pre-Christian Europe.

Modern data are fragmentary, coming from travelers, journalists, geogra-phers, and anthropologists, with the best sources to date being Durham's work and René Grémaux's (1989, 1994) brief summaries of interviews, his own and others, with living and recently deceased individuals. Karl Kaser (1994) has recently analyzed the context and functions of the role. No long-term fieldwork is currently in progress, though British investigator Antonia Young (1995) main-tains that far from dying out, this gender change may be undergoing a revival, at least in Albania. The Balkan sworn virgin role occurs in mountain regions where a mixed pastoral-agricultural economy supported patrilineal extended and frater-nal households (the Yugoslav zadruga, Hammel 1972), organized into lineages of several hundred individuals, which again formed named tribes many generations deep. At each level, from family upward, a head or chief had absolute authority, was shown great deference, but could be deposed by members. Tribal councils and courts of adult men existed; the latter adjudicated disputes, declared war and made peace according to elaborate oral legal codes. Feuding was continual, to avenge family and lineage honor, defend territory, and raid livestock. Conflict was often provoked by the seductions, rape, capture, or elopement of women, which were seen as slights to the patriline that possessed the women. Blood revenge was a primary masculine duty, demonstrating bravery: at puberty a boy received from his father a rifle, pistol, and knife, and his head was shaved in the tribal pattern. Enemy heads were taken, so a topknot was left for ease of carrying. Feuds might last for years, forcing women to assume all the agricultural and herding duties while men hid during daylight. A variety of fortified housing styles resulted (Boehm 1984; Coon 1950; Filipović 1982; Hasluck 1954; Shyrock 1988).

There is regional variation in the sworn virgin role. Data from outside Albania are too fragmentary for adequate description. In South Albania, sworn virgins often retained feminine dress and might become priests' assistants or lay sisters or even nuns attached to the few lowland monasteries (Coon 1950; Durham 1928, 195). The most completely cross-gendered identity occurred among the Gheg-speaking North Albanians, in Kossovo (now Serbian but heavily Albanian in population) and in Montenegro. There is no correlation with language or religion: the ceremony before elders occurred among Eastern Orthodox, Roman Catholic, and Muslim lineages and among Serbo-Croatian and Albanian speakers.

In North Albania, after receiving approval of twelve tribal elders, with consent of her father if living, the young female now cross-dressed, associated with men rather than women, socializing, smoking, and drinking with them, thus separating herself from social interaction with women other than close relatives. She now assumed masculine labor roles in agriculture, herding, hunting, and sometimes feuding, though some declined to carry a rifle due to personal inclination or poverty. This transformation generally occurred at puberty, when boys became men and women were sent off to other patrilines in marriage (Boehm 1984; Coon 1950; Durham 1910; Filipović 1982). The status had various names, of several local and regional terms, I give the most commonly cited: Albanian *vergjineshe* (virgin, unmarried); Serbo-Croatian *harambaša* (woman-man), *muskobanja* (manlike woman); *tybeli* or *tombelije* (from Turkish, one bound by a vow); *ostajnica* (one who stays, i.e., in the natal household). The identity was generally life-long, although in rare cases it was abandoned in midlife for marriage (Durham 1987, 57; Grémaux 1989, 162–63).

These social men were, I believe, generally chaste. The violation of the oath was punishable by stoning or burning to death, traditional sanctions against female infidelity, but no actual case is known to my authors. Some early travelers charged the sworn virgins with heterosexual promiscuity, but there is only one recent case of a sworn virgin engaging in such sex (Coon 1950). There is also little evidence of same-sex involvements. A few lifelong blood sisterhoods between sworn virgins are recorded, and Grémaux (1989, 1994) gives accounts of individuals who expressed physical attraction to women without consummating their desire. In addition he records two recent cases of locally acknowledged relationships with feminine women, one of which earned the label "lesbian" from neighbors. Grémaux's cases make clear that at least some sworn virgins shared the misogynist attitudes held by mountaineer men. Durham (1987, 81) reports of one, "She treated me with the contempt she appeared to think all petticoats deserved—turned her back on me, and exchanged cigarettes with the men. . . ." Montenegran Stana Cerovic, who lived into the 1980s, "denounced women for their chatter and preoccupation with clothing" (Grémaux 1994, 256–62).

Most, though not all, of these individuals assumed a masculine cognomen. Most were addressed with masculine terms of address: husband's brother, father-in-law, godfather (a term of respect for elder men), uncle. Most referred to themselves with masculine terms of reference. But things are not simple: the two individuals described by Grémaux, Stana Cerovic and Tonë Bikaj, who never adopted masculine first names, nevertheless referred to themselves and were referred to with masculine pronouns and terms of address. Grémaux errs in using the expression "male disguise" (Grémaux 1994, 270): these were social men who were known to be female-bodied. There was no need for deception, so names could be a matter of personal preference, and less consistency in attributes was required than in our own society. (Grémaux [1994, 270–71] does record a case of a daughter raised in disguise by parents, but that is not a sworn virgin, *sensu stricto,* though such deception may have been made easier by the existence of the sworn virgin role. This individual married in her twenties.)

In the anthropological and derivative literature, there are two canonical rationales for the adoption of this role and identity. One is to escape an unwanted marriage; the other is to serve as surrogate son, preserving the existence of the patriline. These seem to be half-truths, the product of the dominant masculine ideology, perpetuated uncritically by visitors. All marriages were arranged, often at or before birth. There was much marriage resistance by women, attempts at elopement, and physical coercion by male relatives (Durham 1987, passim). But many women must have opposed not only a specific bridegroom but also marriage in general. Significantly, the girl in question had often been cross-gendered in dress, activities, and identity since early childhood. (None of Grémaux's cases involves marriage avoidance.) Thus the social category of "sworn virgin" seems to include transpersons of several different motivations.

While male relatives ratified the transition, close female relatives played determining roles. A widow without sons was returned to her natal home, remarried or sent to her dead husband's brother as a second wife, all demeaning fates. But with a surrogate son, she could remain in her marital home (Filipović 1982, 49; Nopcsa 1910, 90). In at least one case, even sisters avoided marriage (while remaining women) and remained in their natal home because they had a sworn virgin to act as a social brother (Grémaux 1994, 261). In a few cases, a mother's or grandmother's encouragement to her daughter's assumption of masculine identity is recorded, while others recount father and mother cooperatively allocating the daughter to the role in infancy or childhood, or validating her personal choice.

For the men of the family and lineage, a critical issue must have been the number of adult fighters. A shortage of men was expressed by residents, and deaths by homicide were fearsome. Coon (1950) estimated about 50 percent of all male deaths in North Albania in the 1920s were homicides. A distorted childhood sex ratio and great differential adult height of men and women were surely signs of female infanticide and differential neglect. Thus it seems likely that at least local shortages would have caused men of the group to welcome another warrior.

It seems implausible that a chaste celibate could serve to perpetuate the patrilineal unit, since the extension could only be for one generation. In fact, we are only looking at the failure of investigators to penetrate the customary rationales of natives. Grémaux attempts to address this problem in his 1994 essay (278), stating that the sworn virgin "was expected to safeguard the property until his final hour, as it was to be handed down to the legal male heirs. . . ." But why not hand it to them immediately on the death of the male head of household (usually the sworn virgin's father)? As in all kin-based societies, families were obsessed with the perpetuation of the line and its holdings, and so expressed that perpetuation in lineal terms, that is, through directly descending generations of males. But case histories reveal (as they do in all kin-based societies) that flexibility permits perpetuation through several other avenues and means of recruitment. Thus Tonë Bikaj (1901–1971), who decided to become a son at nine years of age, her two genetic brothers having died in infancy, retained sworn virgin status when, eleven years later, another son was born and survived. This placed Tonë in the role of elder brother: he remained head of the household, which included the married brother and the latter's offspring, until his fifties, when he formally passed that role to his younger brother, though continuing to participate in councils of household heads (Grémaux 1994, 253–56). Thus preservation of the patriline could be achieved by the mature virgin's ascendancy during the immaturity of a later-born son, and most likely by the accretion of sisters and their husbands, or of other male relatives. The details of this process have gone unaddressed by the investigators I have read.

That a female should wish to escape not only marriage but also women's life altogether is not hard to understand, given women's role in these societies. For the male-dominated patriline, women had three values. They were "sacks for carrying," that is, gestational vessels that contributed nothing to the fetus's development. Those who could not bear or bore no sons were sent home. In addition, they were the primary laborers, doing all agricultural labor except the heaviest plowing and haying (and even that, in extremis); most carrying of wood and water; all dairying; some herding; some marketing in the lowland markets; all preparation of wool; weaving, sewing, and embroidering of linens and garments; all food processing and cooking; and of course childbearing (with high mortality) and childrearing.

In these only marginally monetary economies, there were no specialist roles for men or women, other than the unpaid, nonexclusive vocations of epic singer and caravaner, assumed by some men and some sworn virgins, and the household and lineage leadership roles. Thus all division of labor was sexual division of labor: for a female wishing to escape the standard reproductive woman's role there was no alternative to becoming a man. Finally, women brought bridewealth into the family through their sale in marriage: these brideprices were needed to buy brides for the family's sons. But women from outside the exogamous lineage served the functions of labor (as wives) and the production of offspring. Only natal daughters could be sold for wealth. Thus any individual family's choice for its own daughter was between sale in marriage, a gain of bridewealth and perhaps alliance with another family, versus sworn virgin status, a gain of a fighter and support in old age, and possible perpetuation of the family through recruitment of other relatives. (The above summary relies primarily on Durham 1928, 1987; Hasluck 1954; and Whitaker 1976, 1981.)

Also essential is the recognition of women's demeaned status, in contrast with that of the transgendered man. Women were viewed as rebellious chattel: men deemed them stupid, sexually untrustworthy, strong, and insensitive to pain. They required regular beatings to ensure compliance, were secluded from visitors, and segregated from family men in eating, socializing, and work. Since they did not usually participate in feuding, they could not defend the group's honor. Nevertheless, in the poor north of Albania, women were often sassy and uncooperative (Durham 1910, 461; 1987, 37, 63, 184). In contrast, the transformation to a sworn virgin resulted in marked rise in status. They seem usually to have enjoyed respect and even high esteem for doing what women were believed incapable of doing. Further, because they were classed as men, they automatically received the expressions of deference in speech and behavior regularly accorded to adult males by women and junior men. They sometimes acceded to leadership status in the family, in lineage and tribal councils (though this seems to have varied regionally), and became heads of all-man feuding and guerrilla bands.

This is not to deny that there was some ambiguity in their status, and that ambiguity seems to have found differential expression. They were, for example, buried in man's dress with a man's funeral but denied the ritual mourning accorded genetic males; addressed alternately with male or female pronouns; teased by children (Grémaux 1994, 251); able to inherit but unable to bequeath property except to surviving kinsmen; and protected from feudatory homicide by the code of honor as were other genetic females (though this varied from region to region). These social men occupied a borderline position. They existed in a zone of contestation: their own self-definitions as well as society's views of them vary not only by locale but also by family and person. Such a contested, ambiguous status is understandably subject to the prevailing winds of definition as well, including recent influence of Western notions of homosexuality and lesbianism.

These are not, however, "manly women" as recognized in some Plains Indian societies (Medicine 1983, 271). Such women certainly existed in the Balkans: adults fully feminine in role and aspect who temporarily enacted masculine revenge for the death of a husband or male relative, or temporarily assumed leadership roles in government or warfare, and were respected for their bravery and competence (Durham 1928, 170–71; Filipović 1982; Hasluck 1954, 223–24). Such women probably occur in all intensely patrilineal societies. But their transgression of gender boundaries is not sufficient, and not formally adequate, to their classification as men.

Nor are sworn virgins "passing women" as we know them in our own society (cf. Sullivan 1990), since they were recognized as transgendered by family and community.

Are we dealing, then, with a third gender? I think not. Our classificatory difficulty is that some attributes, such as the special term given them, or their legal and political status, distinguish them from most other men, whereas others reflect a total assimilation to masculine behaviors, attitudes, and appearance, producing masculine status and privilege. Our analytic problem stems in part from our own difficulty in conceiving of individuals who are acknowledged to have achieved a gender by an alternate route, rather than entered a disguise or developed the more usual sex-conforming gender from birth. But if "man" is a social category, which it appears to be, then these sworn virgins must be a species of man, in Jason Cromwell's term, a femalebodied man.

One telling evidence of this is the importance of dress in defining gender. It appears in all accounts as an essential attribute of the transformation. I quote one striking example from Durham's conversation with the head of a large extended family. "Only if a woman were sworn to virginity did he allow her equal rights with a man. He knew one who was forty now. Her only brother had been shot when she was ten. Since then she had always worn male garb. . . . I asked if the men ate with her. He slapped his thigh and said: 'Of course! she has breeches on just like mine and a revolver.' " (1987, 63). It seems to me we must listen to the signals of the society in question. The Balkan sworn virgin—however we label its adherents—was and is a subcategory of men.

Many problematic areas remain, however, in our understanding of these traditional transpeople. Better comprehension awaits investigators who control the literature in Serbo-Croatian and Albanian, undertake long-term fieldwork in the native tongues, attend to the socioeconomic and political context of these people's lives, and finally, are possessed of more awareness of and sensitivity to gender issues than is revealed in the published literature so far. Let us hope that such research will soon be undertaken.

Acknowledgments

I thank Deborah Amory, Evelyn Blackwood, Alan Bray, and Stephen Murray for discussion and assistance with sources. Especial thanks to Jason Cromwell for long talks and help in rethinking genders.

References

Boehm, Christopher. 1984. *Blood revenge: The anthropology of feuding in Montenegro and other tribal societies.* Lawrence: University Press of Kansas.

Clover, Carol J. 1986. Maiden warriors and other sons. *Journal of English and Germanic Philology* 85, no. 1: 35–49.

Coon, Carleton. 1950. The mountains of giants: A racial and cultural study—the North Albanian Mountain Ghegs. *Papers, Peabody Museum of American Archaeology and Ethnology* 23, no. 3. Cambridge, Mass.: Harvard University.

Durham, Mary Edith. 1910. High Albania and its customs in 1908. *Journal of the Royal Anthropological Institute* 40: 453–72.

———. 1928. *Some tribal origins, laws, and customs of the Balkans.* London: George Allen & Unwin.

———. [1909] 1987. *High Albania.* Reprint, Boston: Beacon Press.

Filipović, Milenko S. 1982. *Among the people: Selected writings of Milenko S. Filipović,* edited by Eugene Hammel et al. Papers in Slavic Philology no. 3, Department of Slavic Languages and Literature, University of Michigan. Ann Arbor, Mich.: The Department.

Grémaux, René. 1989. Mannish women of the Balkan mountains: Preliminary notes on the "sworn virgins" in male disguise, with special reference to their sexuality and gender-identity. In *From Sappho to de Sade,* edited by Jan Bremmer, 143–72. London: Routledge.

———. 1994. Woman becomes man in the Balkans. In *Third sex, third gender: Beyond sexual dimorphism in culture and history,* edited by Gilbert Herdt, 241–81. New York: Zone Books.

Hammel, Eugene. 1972. The zadruga as process. In *Household and family in past time: Comparative studies on the size and structure of the domestic group over the last three centuries in England,*

France, Serbia, Japan and colonial North America, with further materials from Western Europe, edited by P. Laslett, and R. Wall, 335–73. Cambridge: Cambridge University Press.

Hasluck, Margaret. 1954. *The unwritten law an Albania.* Edited by J. H. Hutton. With a preface by Mrs. J. E. Anderson. Cambridge: Cambridge University Press.

Kaser, Karl. 1994. *Die Mannfrau in den patriarchalen Gesellschaften des Balkans und der Mythos vom Matriarchat. Z. für feministische Geschichtswissenschaft,* Vol. 4.

Medicine, Bea. 1983. "Warrior women"—Sex role alternatives for Plains Indian women. In *The hidden half: Studies of Plains women,* edited by P. Albers and B. Medicine, 267–80. Lanham, Md.: University Press of America.

Nopcsa, Baron Franz. 1910. *Aus Sala und Klementi: Albanische Wanderungen. Zur Kunde der Balkanhalbinsel: Reisen u. Beobachten, H.* 11. Sarajevo: D. A. Kajon.

Shyrock, Andrew. 1988. Autonomy, entanglement, and the feud: Prestige structures and gender values in Highland Albania. *Anthropological Quarterly* 61, no. 3: 113–18.

Sullivan, Louis. 1990. *From female to male: The life of Jack Bee Garland.* Boston: Alyson Publications.

Whitaker, Ian. 1976. Familial roles in the extended patrilineal kin-group in northern Albania. In *Mediterranean family structures,* edited by J. Peristiany, 195–203. Cambridge: Cambridge University Press.

———. 1981. "A sack for carrying things": The traditional role of women in Northern Albanian society. *Anthropological Quarterly* 54: 146–56.

Young, Antonia. 1995. Personal communication, January 28, 1995.

Wagner's "Letters to a Seamstress": Cross-Dressing, Egoism, and Polymorphous Perversity

Michael Saffle

On June 16 and 17, 1877, the *Neue Freie Presse*, Vienna's leading daily newspaper, published a series of letters addressed by composer and author Richard Wagner (1813–1883) to a seamstress named Bertha Goldwag. Secured without his complicity or approval, rival composer Johannes Brahms (1833–1897) had a hand in the sordid business of ensuring that the stolen documents were published (Karpath 1934; Newman 1941, 567–69). They prove that during the mid-1860s Wagner purchased on credit from Goldwag large amounts of cloth, chiefly satin, and large numbers of finished garments, chiefly dressing-gowns and other intimate apparel. Reprinted on several occasions (Spitzer 1906; Liebling 1941), these documents have come to be known as the "Putzmacherin-Briefe" or "Putzmacherin letters"—i.e., the "Letters to a Seamstress" or simply "Letters."

The letters do not *prove* Wagner was a cross-dresser. They do not even prove he wore female clothes—the items sewn by Goldwag having been, technically speaking, *men's* dressing-gowns. On the other hand, they testify to Wagner's lifelong fascination with fabrics and costumes, one which served him in good stead as a sometime producer and director of opera. They also suggest that his infatuation with silks and satins was part and parcel of his love life during the 1860s, if only because he used these fabrics to decorate his love nest in Penzing. Moreover, Wagner's fondness for dressing-gowns affected his relationship with Cosima Liszt von Bülow (1837–1930), his second wife, and must be related, however peripherally, to the "androgyny" that permeates his literary and musical works (Nattiez 1993).

256

Background

The material Wagner purchased from Goldwag during the 1860s may have had something to do psychologically with the midlife crisis he experienced during that decade (Stanway 1988, 47). In 1861 he witnessed the catastrophic reception accorded his *Tannhauser* in Paris, and two years later he was forced to abandon plans for a Viennese performance of his *Tristan und Isolde*. To make matters worse, he was estranged from his first wife, Minna Planer, and his financial affairs were in ruins. His desire to flee from this world into another must have been intense. In May 1863 (the month he turned fifty), in a frenzy of self-indulgence, he set up housekeeping in an attractive apartment in Penzing outside Vienna and decorated it lavishly, a luxury he could not afford. Some forty years later historian Julius Karpath (1866–1936) interviewed Goldwag, then an old woman, about her relationship with Wagner during the 1860s. Describing her employer's Penzing retreat, she stated that

> [t]he walls were festooned with silk; from the ceiling hung a wonderful chandelier giving out a soft light; the floor was covered with a very heavy, unusually soft carpet, into which your feet literally sank; the furniture consisted of a small sofa, armchairs and a table, all covered with the most costly rugs and cushions. . . . I made them all! (Chancellor 1978, 189)

Sometime opera director and radical politician August Röckl (1814–1876) left a more detailed description of the apartment Wagner decorated for himself several years later on Munich's Briennerstrasse:

> The so-called "Grail" or satin room . . . was about eleven feet six inches high, fourteen feet six inches broad, and sixteen feet long. The walls were covered with fine yellow satin, finished off with yellow vallances [*sic*] of the same material. The two blunt corners of the long wall . . . were broken by iron galleries; the resulting recesses, about 27 inches deep, were covered with pink satin in folds. Each of the iron galleries was marked by two wings of white silk tulle, trimmed with lace. The white curtains and their draperies were also adorned with delicate artificial roses. . . . The curtains of this window were of pink satin, interlaced with pink and white satin draperies. . . . The cornice of the window curtains, the frame of the mirror [opposite] and that of the picture [of Murillo's *Madonna*] were puffed out with pink satin and tied back with white satin bows. The ceiling was also bordered on all four sides with similar pearl-grey ruches strewn with artificial roses. The centre of the ceiling was adorned with a rosette of white satin about 12 inches in circumference and 10 inches in depth, trimmed with narrow blond

lace and with roses like those on the ceiling. The floor was covered with a soft
Smyrna carpet [and in] the middle of the floor was a soft and springy couch, covered with a white flowered moire. (Newman 1941, 438–39)

At first Wagner lacked a consort for his satiny Penzing kingdom. He invited
his close friend Mathilde Maier to join him in Penzing and "remedy [his] deficiency in a becoming manner" (Chancellor 1978, 189). She declined, however,
because they could not be married (Newman 1941, 185–86). Thus a certain Marie,
the younger daughter of a local pork butcher, became for a time the mistress of his
household. "Dearest Marie," Wagner wrote to her on one occasion in 1864,

> see that my pretty [Penzing] study is in apple-pie order . . . perfume it nicely. Buy
> the best perfumes so that it will really be fragrant . . . look pretty and charming
> [yourself]. . . . I deserve to have a really good time. (Chancellor 1978, 189)

Wagner may have been greedy, but he was rarely stingy, and he hastened to
share with his friends the luxury goods he purchased ever more carelessly on
credit. The outspoken composer Peter Cornelius (1824–1874) says that, for the
holidays at the end of 1863,

> Wagner had [prepared] a huge Christmas tree, with a royally opulent table
> beneath it for me! Just think: a wonderful heavy overcoat, an elegant grey dress-
> ing gown, a red scarf, a blue cigar case and lighter, fine silk handkerchiefs, mag-
> nificent gold cuff links, the *Struwwelpeter*,[1] a stylish pen wiper with a gold
> motto, several fine cravats, a meerschaum cigar holder with [Wagner's] ini-
> tials—in short, presents such as only an oriental imagination could devise. It
> made my heart heavy, so next day I gave half of them away. At last I was happy.
> (Sabor 1987, 146)

By April 1864, however, Wagner's fortunes reached their lowest ebb. Heavily in debt, yet pledged to support Minna, he found himself unable to borrow more
money from his friends or secure additional advances on any of his works. Mirac-
ulously, he was rescued at the eleventh hour by Ludwig II (1845–1886), Bavaria's
youthful ruler who had recently come to the throne. A lifelong devotee of Wagner's music, Ludwig brought the composer to Munich, heaped money and gifts
upon him, and paid off many of his creditors, including Goldwag.

These favors, conjoined with his lust for what Cornelius called "satrapic"
luxury (Newman 1941, 207) and his controversial political opinions, resulted in a
scandal that finally drove Wagner into self-imposed exile. Among wags, especially in Bavaria and Austria, he acquired the nickname "Lolus"—after Lola Mon-
tez (1816–1861), the notorious Irish dancer who married Bavaria's Ludwig I

(1786–1868), was raised to the rank of Baroness von Rosenthal and Countess von Landsfeld, and in 1848 brought about her husband's abdication. Innumerable aspects of Wagner's personal life and habits also served as grist for the newspapers; among them were his illicit affair with Cosima, who had not yet divorced her husband Hans von Bülow (1830–1894), and Wagner's virulent anti-Semitism.

The "Letters to a Seamstress" present Wagner at his worst: selfish, ridiculously self-obsessed, and ripe for mockery. One selection from these documents must suffice: at the end of a letter addressed to Goldwag on February 1, 1867, Wagner appended the following postscript and an illustration of a dressing gown he had designed himself:

> Pink satin. Filled with eiderdown and sewn in checkered squares, like the gray and red blanket which I have from you. . . . Lined with light, white satin. The width of the bottom of the coat to be six feet, therefore very wide. Extra attachments, not to be sewn onto the quilting!—a scaled frilling of the same material, all around; from the waist on, the frilling should go down and become wider and wider, with a fitting in front. . . . On the side three or four pretty bows made of material. . . . Look to the [enclosed] illustration for exact specifications. (Hirschfeld [1910] 1991, 168)

In his satiric comments upon this letter's first publication, editor Daniel Spitzer (1835–1893) largely ignored effeminacy as an issue. Instead, he attacked the composer for proclaiming himself Germany's "artist-savior," and for his anti-Semitism:

> [Wagner's] drawing of the dressing-gown betrays an extraordinary knowledge of the best out of the fashion magazines. The "sewn on checkered squares" are drawn with light lines and betray a noble feeling of gentility. The "scaled frilling and bows" are shown to us in broad strokes and with an energetic hand. . . . And what life is in the whole; the love of the master brought it to life; the eiderdown pulsates in the quilted squares; these frillings are not scaled, feeling puffs them up; these bows breathe. In this dressing-gown there is a striving that knows its goal; it is as if it is storming forwards, and a voice in it is calling triumphantly: "I am no ordinary dressing-gown; there is no bosom of a thoroughly bad Jewish banker's wife heaving under me; in me beats the heart of a great reformer of German art; Wagner is wearing me. I . . . know that I must soon die and perhaps have to make room for a white-flowered satin dressing gown; but what is that to me? Better to be worn for a week by the great, serious man who discovered and understood me, than to be worn year in and year out by that "ridiculous Rossini up to his ears in luxury," that "lascivious son of Italy, whose lustful roaming eyes leave me cold."[2] When the Wagnerians have placed the master as musician above all musicians before and after him and as poet next to Sophocles, then they

will place him, after his having made this picture, as a dressing-gown Rafael among the ranks of the great painters. (Hirschfeld [1910] 1991, 169)

Wagner and Cross-Dressing

During his lifetime there must have been many people who suspected Wagner cross-dressed. And with reason. The "Letters to a Seamstress" could only have been written by a man obsessed with effeminate (although, strictly speaking, not necessarily feminine) attire. True, a few prosperous and eccentric men dressed more lavishly during the mid-nineteenth century than they might today. However, those who knew him considered Wagner's tastes "womanly." Spitzer prefaced his edition of the "Letters" with the satirical words "How like the woman he looks!"—a line borrowed (out of context, it should be noted) from Wagner's own *Die Walküre*. After October 1864, when she twice trundled her bales of satins and silks to Wagner's Briennerstrasse apartment, Goldwag avoided customs duties by claiming, as Wagner himself instructed her, that the finery in her possession belonged to a countess in Berlin (Karpath 1907, 29).

Wagner must also have impressed his contemporaries as the *kind* of man who might enjoy dressing up as a woman—or pretty much anything else, for that matter. His fondness for costumes was legendary, his "everyday" sartorial sensibilities extraordinary. On one occasion in Prague, for example,

> the fifteen-year-old Lilli Lehmann [(1848–1929) was shocked by] Wagner's manner of dress. He had appeared in a yellow damask dressing gown, pink tie, and voluminous black velvet cape lined with rose satin. Thoroughly frightened by this apparition and its impetuous hugs and kisses, she had to be quieted by Mamma Marie, who later joked with her old friend about Wagner's bantering proposal to adopt the talented young charmer. (Gutman 1968, 227)

This is only one example of Wagner "coming on" to a woman he scarcely knew, in this case a young girl. Perhaps his costume sharpened his erotic appetite. On another occasion, Natalie Planer, the illegitimate daughter of his first wife Minna, reported with astonishment that Wagner's costume consisted of

> snow-white trousers, a sky-blue tail coat with large gold buttons, projecting cuffs, an extremely high black top-hat with a narrow brim; carried a [walking] stick as high as himself with a huge gold knob, and topped it all off with bright saffron-yellow glacé kid gloves, thus providing [according to two of his critics] an admirable costume for the tenor who will play his part when his works are perverted into a popular musical comedy on his life. (Hurn and Root 1930, 89)

Wagner's childhood and family history resembled that of some of the cross-dressers and "feminine boys" studied by psychiatrists like Robert Stoller (1974). Wagner grew up surrounded by women in a family that lacked an assertive father figure, for example, and as a boy he showed unusual interest in theatrical productions (Nattiez 1993, 181ff.). Yet Wagner did not become homosexual like certain effeminate nineteenth-century men, among them the notorious, London-based Ernest Boulton and F. W. Park (Bullough and Bullough 1993, 189–91). Instead, he went on to live a thoroughly heterosexual life and fathered several children.[3] Wagner's circumstances, of course, do not *prove* he was a cross-dresser, but they are suggestive. Among other things they lend support to the hypothesis that, as a boy, Wagner must have tried on his sisters' clothes, if only during the course of "amateur dramatics" (Nattiez 1993, 186).

Satins and silks were part and parcel of Wagner's erotic wardrobe, at least on certain occasions. Even if some of the dressing-gowns Goldwag sewed for him were worn *only* by "little Marie," the pork butcher's daughter, for instance, they would have taken on sexual significance. Nor was Wagner interested in satiny things only as an adult. As a boy he was fascinated by his sisters' dresses; these, he stated in his autobiography *Mein Leben*, ex.rcised a "subtly exciting effect" on his fancy; merely touching them caused his heart "to beat wildly" on several occasions (Wagner [1870] 1983; Nattiez 1993, 185–86). Wagner's second wife Cosima, who all but worshiped him, came to dislike his predilection for fabrics and gowns and indicated as much on January 24, 1869, when she confessed that silks and satins had come between them (Wagner 1980, 1:47). Cosima's confessions about Wagner's interests are especially important, because she rarely wrote down anything that acknowledged or even implied criticism of her husband. Later she grew more cautious; in her entries for June 22–23, 1877, she said the *Neue Freie Presse* planned [*sic*] to publish some letters "from R[ichard] to a milliner" (Wagner 1980, 1.969). This is disingenuous; Cosima knew Goldwag personally because she herself had written to the woman. Later, some of her own correspondence was included in "Letters" reprints. Finally, on July 20, 1881, Cosima mentions that Wagner punned on the concluding lines of Goethe's *Faust*, Part I, to the effect that silky things are delightful to wear (Wagner 1980, 2:693).[4]

On the other hand, Wagner is not known *ever* to have cross-dressed; even Goldwag confessed she never saw him wear dresses or other unmistakably feminine clothes (Karpath 1907, 26). Furthermore, Wagner's fondness for silks and satins may have even had a medical explanation: he suffered for years from shingles and throughout his life had sensitive skin. He wore silk underwear whenever he could afford it (as many men of his generation did), and Goldwag tells us he "wore satin trousers . . . [because] he needed an inordinate amount of warmth if he was to feel well. All his clothes which I made for him," she added, "had to be heavily padded with cotton wool, for he was always complaining of the cold" (Karpath, 1907, 30–31; Sabor, 144). Wagner also claimed on several occasions that the silks and satins with which he surrounded himself helped him compose music. Newman went so far as to affirm that Wagner's "imagination dwelt as lovingly on fabrics and shades as ever it did on the harmonies and colours of his orchestra" (Newman, 1941, 438). The extravagant richness of his harmonic and orchestral vocabularies can be compared to the richness of his surroundings in Penzing or Munich or even Bayreuth—where Cosima saw to it that he behaved somewhat more sensibly and decorously than before, at least while company was present.

Egoism and Polymorphous Perversity

I believe the basis of Wagner's extraordinary fondness for fabrics, frills, and costumes of all kinds was not fetishism, at least in the original sense of that psychosexual term (Freud, [1905] 1953, 151–53), but unbridled egoism and appetite. His foremost biographer Ernest Newman asserted time and time again that Wagner was prone neither to hiding his light under a bushel nor to doing anything by halves:

> Nowhere and at no time was a middle course possible for him. It was all or nothing. . . . He knew no law of life except the full realisation of himself at the moment. He was by turns Christian and Freethinker and Christian again, republican and royalist, lover of Germany and despiser of Germany, anti-Semite (in theory) and pro-Semite (in practice); but in each of his many metamorphoses he was sincerely convinced that he was not only right as against all the world, but right as against the Wagner of earlier years. . . . In later life he becomes a vegetarian; it therefore went without saying that all mankind should forthwith abjure meat. He has the sense to recognize that a flesh diet is imperative for most people in a climate like that of Northern Europe. But a little difficulty of this kind does not daunt him; all that European humanity has to do, he tells us, is to migrate into other parts of the world. (Newman 1946, 128–29)

Self-importance of this kind borders on megalomania. In the middle of composing *Die Meistersinger von Nürnberg*, Wagner is supposed to have made the suggestion that the government of Bavaria be transferred to Nuremberg because, after all, *he* was living there at the time. In other words, he was a "narcissist," if only in the everyday, rather than pathological, sense of that term. Cornelius once said:

[Wagner] has to talk about himself, he has to sing and read from his own works, or he is unhappy. That's why he always wants to be surrounded by a small, intimate circle, because he can't have what he wants with other people. (Millington 1992, 99).

A long line of psychologists and biographers have diagnosed Wagner's "illness" in terms of more-or-less scientific mental disorders. Some, like Theodor Puschmann, have claimed he suffered from megalomania as well as from persecution mania and "moral insanity." Others, including Magnus Hirschfeld (1868–1935), a pioneering figure in sex research, considered him a fabric fetishist ([1910] 1991, 158–70). Still others—among them Eduard Fuchs and Erich Wulffen—have suggested that Wagner suffered, respectively, from "effeminacy" and "homosexuality" or from "narcissism" (Vetter 124ff.). A number of debunking biographers have capitalized on these diagnoses and making fun of Wagner. Some of the monographs written by debunkers are not always reliable (e.g., Hurn and Root 1930). Other volumes that lay stress on the "Letters to a Seamstress," however, are among the best studies ever published of Wagner's life and character (e.g., Gutman 1968; Millington 1992; Newman 1941; Watson 1979). Other debunking studies remain comparatively little-known (e.g., Karpath 1914).

Wagner may have cross-dressed, but he was also fascinated with other forms of sexual behavior. Newman explained he paid so much attention to Wagner's appetites and affairs "not only because of the enormous part the erotic played in his life and in the shaping of his character, but because to know him thoroughly from this side is to have the key to his whole nature" (1946, 128). Virtually everything—fame, riches, clothing, the women he knew, the women he didn't know (including the teenaged Lehmann, who later sang at his first festival at Bayreuth)—served as food either for Wagner's sexual fancies, including works like *Tristan und Isolde*, or his aesthetic sensibilities. Nor did he merely daydream; he acted on his impulses as often as possible. His lack of shame, sexual irregularities, and willingness to do whatever might be necessary to achieve his goals call to mind Freud's definition of the "polymously perverse disposition" ([1905] 1953, 191).

The "Letters to a Seamstress," then, document Wagner's extraordinary penchant for self-indulgence as well as his attachment to fabrics and frills. Not surprisingly, they have been slighted or ignored altogether by many of his supporters, just as they have been used by many of his detractors as a stick with which to beat him. Thus, in one groundbreaking but entirely "orthodox" early Wagner biography, it was claimed that

Wagner's "Sybaritic life" in his little house in Penzing . . . supplied the newspapers with inexhaustible matter for moral indignation against the great poet. We hear of silk and velvet, of champagne suppers and so on. Supposing these accounts to have some foundation, they would still, at most, only bear out what has already been said [about his sufferings]. . . . [I]n Vienna, in the capital of "real frivolity," as Wagner afterwards called it, there was nothing—no comfort, no worthy diversion, no "asylum" for the poor tortured heart, for genius driven almost to the verge of despair; there was nothing—except frivolity. . . . [H]e needed another atmosphere. He fled from Vienna. (Chamberlain 1900, 82-83)

In point of fact, Wagner pursued frivolity with a vengeance in Penzing; contemporary accounts of his "silks and velvets" seem to be thoroughly reliable; and it was creditors, not "asylum for his tortured heart," that forced him to flee Vienna, just as he was forced to flee half-a-dozen other towns and cities during his checkered financial life. In December 1865, for example, he was ordered to leave Bavaria by a regime weary of his excesses. Baron Ludwig von Pfordten (1811–1888), Cabinet Minister to Ludwig II at the time, described them somewhat prejudicially as "overweening and vicious luxury and extravagance" (Newman 1941, 498–501)—as well as his insupportable egoism and meddling in politics.

After World War I Wagner became so important to so many Germans, including Hitler, that he was all but deified. Everything he had done *had* to have been right; unsavory attitudes or episodes, like his anti-Semitism, were either justified ideologically or ignored insofar as possible. Moreover, "true Wagnerites" have in all times and places been loath to admit that the man who gave the Western world the *Ring des Nibelungen* and *Parsifal* could have written so much claptrap about aesthetics and published so many hateful words against the French, the English, the Italians, and especially the Jews. Even in recent years the authors of otherwise fine Wagner studies have either ignored the "Letters" altogether (e.g., Westernhagen 1978), or denigrated those who refer to them as the "silks and satins brigade" (Vetter 1992).

Today it is difficult to speak about Wagner dispassionately, in large part because those who continue to defend him against every slander have muddied the waters, members of his own family included. Those who have sought to understand him, "warts and all," continue to struggle toward a more-or-less objective evaluation of his propensities for remarkable extravagance, ruthless self-indulgence, and outright dishonesty. Wagner may not have been a cross-dresser or fetishist, but what I've called his polymorphous perversity knew few bounds. When people interfered with his pleasures or prevented him from slaking his appetites and thirsts, he all too often treated them with considerably less affection and respect than he treated the dressing-gowns so carefully made for him by Berthe Goldwag more than 130 years ago.

Notes

A preliminary version of this article was presented at a chapter meeting of the American Musicological Society (Saffle 1994). The author wishes to thank Virginia Polytechnic Institute and State University for the financial support that helped him complete this study.

1. *Der Struwwelpeter, oder, lustige Geschichte und drollige Bilder,* a book of children's stories by Heinrich Hoffmann (1809–1894), was published in many editions during the nineteenth and twentieth centuries.

2. On several occasions Wagner ridiculed the Italian operatic composer Gioacchino Antonio Rossini (1792–1868), whom he attacked for his artistic "frivolity" (Watson 1979, 122). His reputation for animosity toward Rossini was exaggerated during the 1860s, however, by newspaper hacks looking for a good story (Watson 1979, 163). Snide remarks about non-German artists were typical of Wagner throughout his life.

3. "The style of Wagner's correspondence with Ludwig, at a first glance, might give a misleading impression of their exact relationship. . . . [But] apparent expressions of ardent love did not imply [at that time] the connotations of physical attachment that we are tempted to read into them" (Watson 1979, 200). Today it is generally accepted that Ludwig II was homosexual; his tastes, however, seem to have run to men younger than Wagner who, at the time the two men first met, was fifty-one.

4. Goethe's original lines, a hymn of praise to the "Eternal Feminine" (*das Ewig-Weibliche*), are among the most familiar in German literature: *Das Unbeschreibliche, / Hier ist's getan, / Das Ewig-Weibliche / Zieht uns hinan*—or, in Robert Macdonald's translation, "All that's mysterious / Here finds the day, / Woman in all of us / Shows us the way." Wagner's pun reads: *Das sanft Bestreichliche / Hat's uns getan / Das angenehm Weichliche / Zieht man gern an* (Vetter 1992, 128)—or, roughly, "We all love what's gently strokable and what feels good to wear."

References

Bullough, V. L., and B. Bullough. 1993. *Cross dressing, sex, and gender*. Philadelphia: University of Pennsylvania Press.

Chamberlain, H. W. 1900. *Richard Wagner*. Translated by G. A. Hight. London: J. M. Dent.

Chancellor, J. 1978. *Wagner*. Boston: Little, Brown.

Freud, S. [1905] 1953. Three essays on the theory of sexuality. In *The standard edition of the complete psychological works of Sigmund Freud*, edited and translated by J. Strachey, Vol. 7, 135–243. London: Hogarth.

Gutman, R. 1968. *Richard Wagner: The man, his mind, and his music*. New York: Harcourt, Brace & World.

Hirschfeld, M. [1910] 1991. *Transvestites: The erotic drive to cross dress*, translated by M. A. Lombardi-Nash. Amherst, N.Y.: Prometheus Books.

Hurn, P. D., and W. L. Root. 1930. *The truth about Wagner*. London: Cassell and Co.

Karpath, L. 1907. *Zu den briefen Richard Wagners an eine putzmacherin. Unterredungen mit der putzmacherin Bertha: ein beitrag zur lebensgeschichte Richard Wagners* [On Wagner's letters to a seamstress. Conversations with seamstress Bertha: A contribution to the life of Richard Wagner]. Berlin: Harmonie.

———. 1914. *Richard Wagner, der schuldenmacher.* Vienna and Leipzig: Kamönenverlag.

———. 1934. *Begegnung mit dem genius: Denkwürdige erlebnisse mit Johannes Brahms—Gustav Mahler—Hans Richter . . . und viele anderen bedeutlichen Menschen.* Vienna and Leipzig: Fibs.

Liebling, L., ed. and trans. 1941. *Richard Wagner and the seamstress; First publication in the English Language of a collection of letters by Richard Wagner.* New York: F. Unger.

Millington, B. 1992. Appearance and character. In *The Wagner compendium: A guide to Wagner's life and music,* edited by B. Millington, New York: Schirmer Books.

Nattiez, J. J. 1993. *Wagner androgyne: A study in interpretation.* Translated by S. Spencer. Princeton, N.J.: Princeton University Press.

Newman, E. 1941. *The life of Richard Wagner.* Vol. 3, *1859–1866.* Cambridge and New York: Cambridge University Press.

———. 1946. *Wagner as man and artist.* New York: Tudor.

Sabor, R. 1987. *The real Wagner.* London: André Deutsch.

Saffle, M. 1994. Wagner, crossdressing, and "gender dysphoria." A paper presented at the annual fall meeting of the Southeast Chapter, American Musicological Society, Duke University, Durham, North Carolina, 12 November 1994.

Spitzer, D., ed. 1906. *Briefe Richard Wagners an eine putzmacherin.* Vienna: C. Konegan.

Stanway, S. 1988. *A woman's guide to men and sex.* New York: Carroll and Graf.

Stoller, R. 1974. *Sex and gender.* 2 vols. New York: Jason Aronson.

Vetter, I. 1992. Wagner in the history of psychology. In *Wagner handbook,* edited by U. Müller and P. Wapnewski, translated by S. Spencer, 118–55. Cambridge, Mass.: Harvard University Press.

Wagner, C. 1980. *Cosima Wagner's diaries.* Vol. 1, *1869–1877*; and Vol. 2, *1878–1883.* Edited by M. Gregor-Dellin and D. Mack, translated by G. Skelton. London: Collins.

Wagner, R. 1983. *My life.* Edited by A. Gray, translated by M. Whittall. Cambridge and New York: Cambridge University Press. (Opening volume originally published in 1870)

Watson, D. 1979. *Richard Wagner: A biography.* London: J. M. Dent.

Westernhagen, C. V. 1978. *Wagner: A biography.* Translated by M. Whittall. 2 vols. Cambridge and London: Cambridge University Press.

A Historical Perspective of Christine Jorgensen and the Development of an Identity

Linda Heidenreich

"Charming, Humorous Woman"

It was extraordinary to sit across a luncheon table from Christine Jorgensen and try to realize that nineteen years ago this charming and humorous woman was a man.

Anyone over thirty will have no trouble recalling the earth-shaking news of the first sex-change surgery with which the name Christine Jorgensen became synonymous. . . . She makes her fame sound hard to swallow. But when you consider that she was the first person in the history of the world to successfully change her sex, it's quite understandable that her story made lasting headlines.

(*San Francisco Chronicle,* June 12, 1970, p. 50)

In May 1950, George William Jorgensen set out for Sweden. He planned to stay with friends and relatives in Denmark while attempting to contact sympathetic physicians in Sweden who might treat him with hormones and/or perform an early form of what is now called sex reassignment surgery. His trip to Sweden soon became unnecessary because the friends with whom he was staying informed him that there were endocrinologists doing similar work in Denmark. It was through those friends that Jorgensen came to know Dr. Hamburger, who after two years of experimentation and treatment saw to it that Jorgensen received sex conversion surgery. The year of the surgery was 1952, and while Jorgensen was still recovering in a hospital in Copenhagen, the news of the surgery was leaked to the American press (Jorgensen 1968).

So began the history of Christine Jorgensen. But it was not the beginning of the history of the transsexual. Before the sex reassignment surgery of Christine Jorgensen, there was transsexuality. This is apparent in the work of Richard von Krafft-Ebing, whose work was published in 1893. It is also apparent in the work of Karl Heinrich Ulrichs who died in 1896, and in the reports of sex reassignment surgery recorded from as early as the 1930s. The purpose of asserting such a history is not to challenge Christine Jorgensen as a significant historical figure, rather, it is to challenge how we look at the life of Christine Jorgensen and why her life was significant in the history of transsexuality.

In discussing the histories of "homosexuals" living in the early twentieth century, Allen Berube suggested that a question more appropriate than "Who were the homosexuals?" is "What were people doing with their homosexuality?" (1991). To investigate a history of transsexuals, similar questions are useful. Instead of looking for a history of transsexuals, it is more useful to begin with questions such as "Where was the transsexuality?" and "What were people doing with their transsexuality?" One looks for those instances where people assigned the gender of male asserted that they were not male, instances where people assigned the gender of female asserted that they were not female, and instances where individuals attempted to alter the primary signifier on which society had based their assignment (in this case, their genitals).

In the history of transsexuality, the experience of Christine Jorgensen marks a lasting shift in the modern sex taxonomy. Her experience served as a catalyst by which the press, medical communities, and the American public defined a modern public identity. The new identity was given a name: Transsexual. Such an identity distinguished transsexuality from homosexuality, with which it shared a rich history.

The study of transsexuality in the West emerged in the late nineteenth century with the work of Richard von Krafft-Ebing and his work *Psychopathia Sexualis* (1893). As noted by Vernon Rosario, many of Krafft-Ebing's cases bore a striking resemblance to the modern transsexual (1995). In *Psychopathia Sexualis*, sex and gender deviants were described, analyzed, and categorized. Under the broad rubric of "Homo-sexual" (the term that Krafft-Ebing used), Krafft-Ebing placed both individuals who asserted an attraction to persons of their same assigned sex, and individuals who asserted that their sex assignment was wrong. If one had mild homosexuality, one was attracted to persons of the same sex. If one came from a very sick family, or masturbated excessively, one would eventually degenerate to a point where one believed oneself to be a person of the other sex (Krafft-Ebing 1893, 188–216). The paradigm that he established was that which we today would call a "slippery slope."

The first stage of the process strongly resembles modern homosexuality or, perhaps, bisexuality. With Eviration (stage two), "the [male] patient undergoes a deep change of character, particularly in feelings and inclinations, which become those of a female"—or the "(Congenital) Urning of high grade" (Krafft-Ebing 1893, 197).

Krafft-Ebing took his term "Urning" from the nineteenth-century activist Karl Heinrich Ulrichs who described himself as such. For Ulrichs, male Urnings demonstrated same sex attraction, but they also had feminine identities to varying degrees. The presence of attributes of both same sex attraction, or what we today might call homosexuality, and the feeling that he was not a male, or what today we might call transsexuality, is apparent in several of his writings. In his writing, Ulrichs sometimes referred to Urnings as a "third sex," "Built like a man, not a man, to yourself a riddle and a wonder" (Kennedy 1988, 13, 50, 57).

The third level of Krafft-Ebing's model presents us with a "woman" who would have bodily sensations of a *transmutio sexus,* feeling that she was physically male. "Men," at this stage believed they had female bodies. It was Krafft-Ebing's case 99, a level-three "male" homosexual, who wrote, "I feel like a woman in man's form; and even though I often am sensible of the man's form, yet it is always in a feminine sense" (Krafft-Ebing 1893, 209). Such an assertion is indicative of the role that gender played in case 99's biography. At the age of fifteen, case 99 found riding in the male style "painful," and found relief when able to dress as a woman (Krafft-Ebing 1893, 206–14). While the biography contained information related to sexual orientation, the above citations demonstrate the issues of gender identity that the individual addressed. Identified as a male by family and by Krafft-Ebing, she asserted "The constant feeling of being a woman from top to toe" (Krafft-Ebing 1893, 214). What the individual "did with [her] transsexuality" does not seem extraordinary. At times the person wore female attire, but usually, she expressed herself as a man while "feeling only like a woman" (Krafft-Ebing 1893, 213–14).

Krafft-Ebing had yet another level of acquired homosexuality; this was the fourth level—*Metamorphosis Sexualis Paranoica* and it was "a final possible stage . . . the delusion of transformation of sex" (Krafft-Ebing 1893, 216).

Of case 105 it was written

> . . . she believes herself a man, and flies angry if she is addressed as "madam." Once, when male clothing was placed at her disposal, she was beside herself with joy. . . . She expressed her delusion of being a man until shortly before her death. (Krafft-Ebing 1893, 221)

Here the object of case 105's sex attraction was not discussed. In other cases of fourth-level inversion, Krafft-Ebing also discussed gender identity to the exclusion of sexual orientation. He informed us of what individuals did with their transsexuality. Case 103, like case 105, was identified by Krafft-Ebing as a woman. Case 103, like case 105, preferred to dress as a man and referred to himself as a man. In addition to this, he cut his hair short and "parted it on one side in the military fashion" (Krafft-Ebing 1893, 220–21).

For the most severe cases of acquired homosexuality, then, the distinguishing factor between the homosexual and other men and women was not that they experienced same sex attraction but that they claimed that the sex assigned to them by their physicians, family, or peers was wrong. It was their transsexuality that caused Krafft-Ebing to categorize them homosexual. The way that such individuals dealt with their transsexuality was by cross-dressing. Sex conversion surgery does not appear to have been an option.

Transsexuality did not disappear after 1898. Beginning in the 1930s, there were instances of people seeking sex conversion surgery, or attempting to alter the primary signifiers upon which society had based their sex assignment.

Among these was a Danish "male" painter who became Lili Elbe after her surgeries. Her story was published in the book *Man into Woman* in 1933 (Bullough 1993, 254; Raymond 1979, 21). From Switzerland, there were at least two cases of sex conversion surgeries. Among these was that of Margrith Businger (from Niklaus Businger) in 1931 and Arlette-Irene (from Arnold-Leon) in 1945 (Savitsch 1958, 61–78). Many of these cases found their way into the work of Eugene de Savitsch, where once again, people who insisted that the gender assigned to them on the basis of their genitals was wrong were categorized as homosexual.

There was the case of Mlle. Leber who in the early 1940s was admitted to the psychiatric clinic in Berne, where he announced to the doctors that he would commit suicide if they did not turn him into a woman. Leber was certain that this was possible because he "had read about the procedure in a Prague newspaper. . . . The doctors did not sanction the operation and dismissed him. . . . [Eventually] Dr. Wolf . . . agreed to operate and the operation was carried out in three stages" (Savitsch 1958, 70–71).

In 1951 and 1953, surgery was performed on "J."

Every cent of the money that J could earn, and anything he could borrow from his wife, was spent on different doctors who were reputed to be specialists in these matters. Finally, he heard about Dr. Wolf, who was referred to him as one of the greatest experts and pioneers in this field. Without wasting any time he abandoned his work and rushed to Dr. Wolf, . . . secured an appointment under a false name and finally convinced the doctor, by threats of suicide, that the operation ought to be performed. (Savitsch 1958, 80)

In the first case the patient was successfully integrated into her community and found employment as an office worker (Savitsch 1958, 75–76). The second was initially unable to change the name and gender on her passport, but had an understanding wife with whom she maintained her relationship. Eventually, "in spite of being married and the father of a son, [he] was none the less granted permission to change his [*sic*] civic status" (Savitsch 1958, 83).

Such individuals demonstrate that as early as the 1940s, some individuals who had the characteristic or trait of transsexuality successfully sought out surgeons who performed sex conversion surgery. They then integrated into society as persons of their self identified gender. The occasions of their surgeries did not prompt news reporters to harass their parents, neither do they appear to have been thrust into a life of notoriety.

It is useful to speak of such individuals, both those found in the cases of Krafft-Ebing and in the work of Eugene de Savitsch, as having transsexuality rather than having the *identity* of transsexual. This is because at the time of their experiences, the identity of transsexual was not distinguished from that of transvestite or homosexual. They did, however, all share a common *trait*, or *characteristic*. They felt and asserted that they were or should be of the gender opposite that assigned them at birth. A decade later, the experience of an American individual who had transsexuality was central to the shift from transsexuality as a trait to the identity of transsexual as one distinguished from that of homosexual.

In 1949, George William Jorgensen went to a medical library in Manhattan to find information about himself. The information he found led him to believe that there were physicians in Sweden who performed sex conversion surgery (Jorgensen 1968, 80). Given the paucity of information available prior to the experience of Christine Jorgensen, it is probable that the materials encountered reflected the experiences of those early cases discussed above. Male individuals who were desperate for surgery, convinced physicians to operate, and then resumed their lives as women.

In 1952, Jorgensen underwent one of a series of uncommon operations then called sex change surgery. While she was still in Denmark, Ben White, of the *New York Daily News,* received information of Jorgensen's surgery and tracked down her parents in New York. White interviewed the parents, obtained photos and correspondence, and then gave the public a story which sent reporters rushing to Copenhagen where Jorgensen was still recovering in the hospital (*Time* 1952, 58). Within twenty-four hours, according to a historian of the New York *Daily News*, Christine Jorgensen "had become a national figure" (Chapman 1961, 96). Jorgensen, in his first formal press conference in this country, refused to affirm or deny recent American newspaper reports that suggested his highly publicized "man-into-woman" operation was nothing more than surgery to remove his masculine organs (Silverman 1953, 1).

The articles entitled "Charming, Humorous Woman" were still far in the future. The immediate media attention could often be cruel, as the press and the public attempted to understand the phenomenon of Christine Jorgensen. Articles wavered back and forth on pronoun choice. Writers interviewed physicians and psychiatrists, and people who had spoken with physicians and psychiatrists—in an effort to perhaps explain, perhaps understand, while selling more papers.

The *San Francisco Chronicle,* perhaps unsure of how it should treat the issue of gender, printed a two-paragraph announcement of her engagement at the Orpheum Theater without using any pronouns (*San Francisco Chronicle* 1953, 16). Two weeks later it printed another article, "Christine Talks: But is He or Isn't She?" In it, "science writer" Milton Silverman decided upon the masculine pronoun: "The tall, blond, heavy-featured, flat-chested Jorgensen insisted on his rights to privacy, and claimed he had done everything possible to avoid publicity. . . ." The article took an angry tone. Photographs of women featured in other news articles and in advertisements of the decade clearly demonstrate a media preference for full-busted women. Silverman's comment was not meant to flatter.

At the same time, the science writer attempted to identify Jorgensen. Her physical features, clothing, and words were scrutinized. The article contained a brief explanation of transvestism as explained by "medical experts" and "one psychiatrist," as the American press and public began to push medical communities to explain and define what, to their experience, was a new phenomenon.

Initially, *Time* magazine decided upon the female pronoun. In an article which relied heavily on the New York *Daily News*, in its "Manners and Morals" section *Time* announced

> The [New York *Daily*] *News* . . . no longer had Christine to itself. At New York's International Airport to welcome home the blonde who used to be George Jorgensen were some 350 curious citizens and a phalanx of photographers and reporters. When Christine appeared, a woman in the crowd turned to her little girl and said: "Look, Ruthie. She used to be a man." Wrote the *News* with high disdain: "Ruthie stared popeyed. All she needed was a bag of peanuts and a bottle of soda."

The assembled reporters could have done with some peanuts and soda themselves. No sideshow mermaid ever got closer scrutiny than Christine (*Time*, February 23, 1953, 28).

"Curious citizens," and the press, came to view Jorgensen. The press described her in detail—once again, the reader was informed of her clothing, her manners, her words. They were also informed of how the press and public interacted with her—as with a mermaid, at a sideshow.

Time ran another article on April 20. Like earlier articles it attempted to explain the identity. While the article's main theme was that Jorgensen was not a real woman, only an altered male, it also discussed hormone treatment, ran a definition of transvestite, and contrasted the opinions of Dr. Georg Stürup with that of American psychotherapists concerning the treatment of what the press was still calling transvestism (*Time*, April 20, 1953, 20).

With the experience of Christine Jorgensen, a discourse was manifestly active as she, the American press and public, and medical communities struggled to understand and define an identity. Initially, it appeared that the media attention received by Christine Jorgensen had a negative effect on both herself and other people seeking sex change surgery. An article appearing in *Time* magazine announced, "The Danes have decided never to perform it [the surgery] again on a foreigner. Too much excitement" (*Time*, April 20, 1953, 84).

Jorgensen's pictures—sometimes flattering, sometimes unflattering—were featured in papers as diverse as the tabloid the New York *Daily News* and the more conservative *New York Times*. Prior to the release of her story to the press, Jorgensen had been working on a travel film of Denmark. The National Tourist Association had supported her work by taking care of her travel expenses while she worked on the film. She had intended to show the completed project to schools and small towns both in Denmark and in the United States (*Time* 1952, 58–59; Jorgensen 1968, 123–132). This was no longer a possibility.

Initially Jorgensen was displeased with the rash of publicity, but then she decided to cooperate with a reporter from Hearst Publishing, in an effort to "bring courage and understanding to others" (Jorgensen 1953, 4). In a series of articles appearing in the *American Weekly* from February through March 1953, Jorgensen told her story to the American public.

The Hearst articles mark a divergence from the earlier narratives of transsexuality. Like the individuals of whom Krafft-Ebing wrote, Jorgensen had sometimes cross-dressed in order to reduce the tension she experienced due to her transsexuality. Like the individuals of whom Savitsch wrote, Jorgensen had sought out physicians who performed sex conversion surgery and convinced them to perform such surgery for her (Hamburger, Stürup, and Dahl-Iverson 1953). The rash of publicity which followed Jorgensen's surgery added a variable to her story that was different from those which preceded her. Jorgensen first turned away from the press, and then embraced it. Like the early homosexuals of whom Foucault wrote (1980), Jorgensen took the language of those who attempted to categorize her and used it to define herself. Jorgensen, with the press and the medical establishment, brought the identity of transsexual to the American public.

An immediate result of the publicity surrounding Christine Jorgensen was that both Jorgensen and Hamburger were inundated with mail. Within five months of Jorgensen's surgery, Drs. Christian Hamburger and Georg Stürup had received over 600 letters from people desiring sex conversion surgery. By mid-1953 (less than one year after the initial publicity) Jorgensen had received "some 20,000 letters," some "merely addressed to 'Christine Jorgensen, United States of America' " (Jorgensen 1968, 189; Fogh-Anderson 1956, 135; *Time* April 20, 1953, 84). One of the letters that Jorgensen received was from Dr. Harry Benjamin. It was the first of many letters that would be exchanged between them (Jorgensen 1968, 190–91).

Benjamin began using the word transsexual in his publications immediately following the media attention surrounding Jorgensen (Benjamin 1966, 16). He presented work at a symposium on Transsexualism and Transvestism for the Association for the Advancement of Psychotherapy in December 1953 (*American Journal of Psychotherapy* 1954, 219). Articles presented at the symposium, which were later published in the *American Journal of Psychotherapy*, contained some similarities to the articles written in the popular media. Many attempted to explain or understand the new identity. Benjamin's article, which was included in the collection, presented a definition of transsexual that remains dominant in our modern sex and gender taxonomies.

Other articles such as that written by Emil A. Gutheil, M.D., while attempting to explain, asserted that the surgery should not have been performed. Gutheil too began to use the word transsexual to describe people who claimed to be of the gender opposite to that assigned them at birth. Regarding Jorgensen, he asserted: "The Danish physicians who recently operated on a much-discussed case, accepted the patient's demands uncritically, and 'did something about it.' They proceeded from the (unsupported) supposition that they had to correct 'an error of nature' " (1954, 232).

Without venturing into the field of prophecy one can say that the patient's guilt feelings, unresolved, but temporarily stilled by the fact that an illegal situation has been turned into a sanctioned one, may "catch up" with the patient one day—and there is nothing left to castrate away (Gutheil 1954, 238).

Gutheil voiced the concern of other psychotherapists that transsexualism was due to "psychopathologic factors." Because of this, sex conversion surgery could be a mistake—one which those requesting the surgery might later regret.

While the response both from the press and from the psychiatric community was often negative, the experience of Christine Jorgensen continued to shape modern sex and gender identities. The well integrated life that she lived while under the scrutiny of the American press and public demonstrated to many that sex conversion surgery was a viable option for transsexual people. Dr. Harry Benjamin continued to work and to be influenced by Jorgensen's experience. In 1966 he published *The Transsexual Phenomenon* and thanked Jorgensen: "without Christine Jorgensen and the unsought publicity of her 'conversion,' this book could hardly have been conceived" (Benjamin, viii).

In addition to the work of Benjamin, Dr. Hamburger published his work for the *Journal of the American Medical Association*. The negative publicity he received from the media and a request from the American Medical Association prompted him to publish the article in an effort to reestablish his professional reputation (Jorgensen 1968, 209–10). In 1966 the Johns Hopkins Gender Identity Clinic was opened and began to offer therapy and surgery. Other universities and major hospitals throughout the United States followed suit (Jorgensen 1953, 324; also Raymond 1979, 22).

Following from a long history of transsexuality, then, the experience of Christine Jorgensen served as a catalyst for the creation of the modern transsexual identity. Cross-dressing and sex conversion surgery were not new strategies for people who had transsexuality. Yet while Jorgensen shared such strategies with earlier people who had the trait of transsexuality, her experience was dramatically different. By using the press to educate and inform the public, Jorgensen fueled a new discourse and played an active role in defining herself. While the publicity surrounding her experience dramatically altered the course of Jorgensen's life, it also altered our country's understanding of "the transsexual phenomenon."

Note

Throughout this paper I use both the terms sex reassignment surgery and sex change surgery when speaking of those surgeries performed in a deliberate effort to alter the genitals of an individual. While the political implications of both terms are still being argued in the 1990s, I argue that because American culture bases gender identity primarily on the genitals, to alter or change the genitals is to change one's sex, the primary signifier of one's gender. Whether or not this is a 180-degree turn can be argued; the sex, however, is definitely *changed*. John Money and Anke A. Ehrhardt, in *Man and Woman Boy and Girl* (Baltimore: The Johns Hopkins University Press, 1972) assert such, but even on a more basic level, it should be noted that in simple events such as the birth of a child, as noted by Susan Stryker in "My Words to Victor Frankenstein" (*GLQ*, 1, no. 3 [1994]) the child is identified as boy or girl on the basis of its genitals at the time of delivery.

References

American Journal of Psychotherapy. 1954. Vol. 8.
Benjamin, Harry. 1967. *The transsexual phenomenon.* New York: Paul D. Erikson, Inc.

Berube, Allen. 1991. Lecture given at Lesbian, Gay, Bisexual Student Leadership Conference, University of California at Santa Cruz.

Bullough, Vern L., and Bonnie Bullough. 1993. *Cross dressing, sex and gender*. Philadelphia: University of Pennsylvania Press.

Chapman, John. 1961. *Tell it to Sweeney: The informal history of the New York* Daily News. New York: Double Day & Co.

Fogh-Anderson. 1956. Transvestism and trans-sexualism: Surgical treatment in a case of autocastration. *Acta Medicinae Legalis et Socialis* 9: 33–40.

Foucault, Michel. [1978] 1980. *The history of sexuality,* Vol. 1, *An introduction*. New York: Vintage Books.

Gutheil, Emil A. 1954. The psychologic background of transsexualism and transvestism. *American Journal of Psychotherapy* 8: 231–39.

Hamburger, C., G. K. Stürup, and E. Dahl-Iverson. 1953. Transvestism: Hormonal, psychiatric, and surgical treatment. *Journal of the American Medical Association* 12, no. 6: 391–96.

Jorgensen, Christine. 1953. The story of my life. *American Weekly* (February 22): 4–12.

———. 1968. *Christine Jorgensen: A personal autobiography*. New York: Bantam Books.

Kennedy, Hubert. 1975. *Ulrichs: The life and works of Karl Heinrich Ulrichs, pioneer of the modern gay movement*. New York: Arno Press.

Krafft-Ebing, Richard von. 1893. *Psychopathia sexualis, with especial reference to contrary sexual instinct: A medico-legal study*. Philadelphia: F. A. Davis and Co.

Raymond, Janice. 1979. *The transsexual empire: The making of the she-male*. Boston: Beacon Press.

Rosario, Vernon. 1995. Paper presented at Queer Studies Conference, University of California, San Diego, California, January.

San Francisco Chronicle. 1953. Christine to star in L.A. review, April 24, 16.

———. 1970. Charming and humorous woman, June 12, 50.

Savitsch, Eugene de. 1958. *Homosexuality, transvestism and change of sex*. London: William Heinemann Medical Books Ltd.

Silverman, Milton. 1953. Christine talks but is he or isn't she? San Francisco *Chronicle*. May 5, 1.

Stryker, Susan. 1994. My words to Victor Frankenstein above the village of Chamounix. *GLQ* 1, no. 3: 237–54.

Time. 1952. The great transformation, December 15: 58.

———. 1953. Manners and Morals: Homecoming. February 23: 28.

———. 1953. Medicine: The case of Christine. April 20: 20, 84.

5

LITERARY TREATMENT OF THE PHENOMENON OF CROSS-DRESSING

Introduction

Literature, from lyrics to the novel to drama to criticism, and from the ancient classics to contemporary popular songs, contains a vast record of transgender behavior. Interestingly, except for studies of the boy actors who played women's roles during the age of Shakespeare, the subject traditionally has been little explored. In the past three years, however, in large part due to the success of Marjorie Garber's (1992) book on the subject, it has become a popular topic among specialists in literature. It is almost as if the topic had not been regarded as suitable for exploration by literary specialists, regardless of their language, until Garber wrote. Though psychologists, sociologists, anthropologists, and historians had been exploring the topic in some detail since the 1970s (and in a few cases before), none of these investigators were members of the Modern Language Association and therefore were not usually read or cited by literary specialists. This emphasizes in a sense how compartmentalized modern literary scholarship has become and how once a barrier has been broken, and a new topic such as transgenderism has been authenticated, graduate students find much to explore in what had previously been ignored.

In a sense, however, Garber was only taking the next logical step in gender studies, a field pioneered by the current generation of feminist scholars (both men and women). One of the obvious ways to explore gender is by looking at those who do not conform, and transgender people are the best example of this in real life as well as in literature.

If members of the transgender community sometimes complained in the past that only physicians and psychiatrists studied cross-gender behavior, and then only to classify such behavior as pathological, they will soon find that there is now almost an open season on investigating the topic. The literary specialists represent the most numerous group of scholars in an academic setting, and as such will add much to the quantity of literature being turned out. Fortunately, there is much to explore, and we hope it will also add to the quality through many new insights. This section gives a good sampling of the material beginning to appear and how scholars are treating the subject.

Reference

Garber, M. 1992. *Vested interests: Cross dressing and cultural anxiety.* New York: Routledge.

Saving Their Own Selves: Female-to-Male Cross-Dressing as a Means of Survival for Married Women in Two English Plays

Keith Dorwick

Gender and sexuality, always difficult issues to read in the Renaissance and seventeenth century, are complicated enough in the plays that use cross-dressed boys to play a Juliet or a Cleopatra. However, when the plot of the play requires a female character to further cross-dress as a male (thus layering male assumed identity on a female character who is a boy actress), that act of multiple or reversed cross-dressing—in which the boy appears as a boy and yet is not a boy—requires us to do an even more complicated act of critical reading, one that allows the gender implications of women's roles in English Renaissance drama to resonate. In his 1992 *Sodometries*, Jonathan Goldberg notes that the feminist Shakespearean scholar Jean Howard questions "whether a potential, liberation for women, can be glimpsed in cross-dressing." He reads Howard as answering with a qualified "no" (Goldberg 1992, 107). But I would like to respond with a resounding "Yes!" In fact, cross-dressing conventions in the Renaissance are usually a guarantee of success.

Of all the cross-dressed women in Renaissance plays, however, I would like to contrast the cross-dressing strategies of Dorothea in Robert Greene's *James the Fourth*, and of Imogen in Shakespeare's *Cymbeline*. There are many similarities between these women—both are unjustly accused of adultery by jealous husbands, both use a male disguise to escape their husbands' wrath, and both end with their names restored and their marriages healed, an archetype borrowed from a folklore character known as Patient Griselda. What draws me to these two texts is the way in which Dorothea and Imogen effect their own restoration and how cross-dressing, successfully or otherwise, is used to that end.

The power of both these plays stems in no small part from the isolation of the two women once their husbands' accusations of infidelity remove them from the accustomed pattern of their lives. Let me start by discussing a case of failed cross-dressing: Dorothea's assumption of male garb in Greene's *James the Fourth*. Dorothea's husband, the king of Scotland, has fallen madly and unreasonably in love with Ida, a young woman in his court. As a result of this "effeminate" behavior, that is, behavior driven by the inordinate love of women, the king falls under the evil influence of one Ateukin, who convinces him that Ida will return his love only if Dorothea is removed; the king agrees to her murder. In order to escape and save her own life, Dorothea flees dressed as a man, complete with sword.

Dorothea is Greene's free adaptation of the lead female, Arenopia, from the fifteenth century Italian Cinthio's *Hecatommithi* (Sanders 1970, xxix–xxxi); her name is derived from the Greek word for "warrior," but ends in the feminine ending "ia." Arenopia is, unlike Dorothea, a skilled warrior. Thus, her name represents her character—the warrior who is somewhere between male and female. In Renaissance terms, she is the "hic mulier, or the man-woman." As Norman Sanders has put it, "Dorothea's . . . behavior in disguise . . . shows none of the Amazonian qualities and martial efforts displayed by the soldierly and self-sufficient Arenopia" (Saunders 1970, xxxi) who successfully passes as male.

Though, like Arenopia, she lives, her efforts to pass as a man fail, at least in part. For unlike most female characters who cross-dress as men, whose alter ego and that alter ego's gender are accepted by those who are not confidantes of the cross-dresser, Dorothea is immediately recognized as female by her would-be assassin. She survives, but only after being grievously wounded, and then only because she was left for dead by an incompetent assassin.

Note the following lines from act 4, scene 4:

JACQUES: Ah you *calletta*, you *strumpetta, Maitressa* Doretie *etes-vous surprise?* Come, say your paternoster, *car vous etes morte, par ma foi.*

DOROTHEA: Callet? No strumpet, caitiff as thou art,
But even a princess born, who scorn thy threats.
Shall never Frenchman say, an English maid
Of threats of foreign force will be afraid.

Though Jacques is identified throughout as French, and speaks in a mixture of French and English, he also uses Italianized versions of English insults that are then translated by Dorothea. Thus, the English *callet* and *strumpet* become *calletta* and *strumpetta*, both of which mean whore. *Calletta*, by the way, is an actual word in Italian: Jacques is actually calling Dorothea "a small street in Venice," when he means "drab" or "slut." His use of pseudo-Italian serves to mark him as one who is aligned with Italy, land of Catholics and thieves in Renaissance literature. In fact, the use of foreign languages is an important part of his characterization, if not the only characterization for Jacques that Greene has bothered with.

What is of note for this paper is that it is Jacques, the foreigner, who immediately recognizes and names his opponent and does so correctly. In calling her *calleta* and *strumpetta*, he is not only insulting her, but he is also gendering her, given that Italian is a gendered and inflected language, as English is not. He also calls her by her own name, Doretic, even if that name is transmitted through his language. Now, this violation of the conventions that surround cross-dressed women characters may simply represent the fact that the use of cross-dressed characters is a novelty for Greene.

But I do not think it insignificant that Dorothea's male counterpart is unnamed. This is especially noteworthy given Greene's source, in which Arenopia renames herself Arenopio. At the very least, Greene had a precedent for naming the male alter ego even as Imogen takes on the name Fidele. In effect, he has suppressed her other self. Her inability to pass successfully pass is nearly her death.

In Shakespeare's *Cymbeline*, the dramatic situation is similar to that of *James the Fourth*. Imogen not only must contend with her husband, Posthumus, who is out to have her killed as a result of the machinations of the villain, Iachimo, but she must also contend with her stepmother, the queen, a figure of evil described by David Bevington as "Snow White's step-mother" (Shakespeare 1980). When Posthumus loses his faith in his wife, his decision to have her executed leaves her without any companionship in the world she knows. Her only option is to become the boy, Fidele (that is, Faithful), and thereby disappear as Imogen.

In analyzing *Cymbeline*, the critic David Daniell (1986) has argued ". . . the faithfulness of Imogen ('Fidele') carries the play's principal charge. . . . Imogen is not an abstraction, but a living and brave girl who . . . causes the final peals of truth to ring out." Of course, this is certainly true, but what is also interesting in Daniell's comment is the refusal to see Imogen as Fidele, the name of the boy's role that she takes on in self-defense: for Daniell, she remains a "girl." It is "Fidele" who remains only an "abstraction." The tension between Imogen and Fidele and between cross-dressed boy actress and female character (and, for that matter, between female character and female character reverse cross-dressed as a boy or man) is glossed over by his analysis, indeed, by his use of single quotation marks to set off Fidele's name and identity. Imogen's cross-dressing and her display of courtly artistic skills (notably singing) allow her to reveal her true nature, but only by becoming a "man" caught between two aspects of the courtier: while she can sing and has good breeding, she cannot fight. She is a warrior of virtue, not of war.

It is for this reason she takes on male attire: it is her only protection in a hostile world. As Jean MacIntrye states, even major characters in Renaissance plays "change costume only when the play requires them to change in some way" (1987, 12). By dressing as Fidele, Imogen puts on a man's prerogatives without actually possessing the skills of battle: as she says, "Best draw my sword; and if mine enemy / But fear the sword like me, he'll scarcely look on it" (25–26). Yet as the play continues, we find that Imogen is loved not for her martial skills but for courtly arts—the exiles from court, Belarius and his two supposed fostersons, who are in reality heirs to the English crown, all cherish Fidele for it "appears he hath / Good ancestors," and sings "angel-like," and, most importantly, "yokes / A smiling with a sigh" (4.2.50–62). This cheer in adversity is a sign of Imogen/Fidele's character and breeding.

The total devotion to Fidele by these men, and by his (or her, as you will) employer, Caius Lucius, shows us Imogen's true worth and value in spite of all the lies we have heard, and in the face of her husband's loss of faith. We can see this pattern of loyalty in the sources for Imogen's character in *Cymbeline*, which Shakespeare adapted from Boccaccio[1] and from the anonymous *Frederyke of Jennen*. In Boccaccio's *Decameron*, Genevra, Imogen's counterpart, is betrayed by Ambrogiulo so that he may win a bet placed with her husband, Bernado. To save herself, Genevra (or Zinerva, depending on translation and editor) takes on the male guise of Sicurano da Finale—in Italian, roughly safe (or sure, proven trustworthy) in the end—and draws the Soldan's attentions by her skill in languages, again a sign of her inner virtue. As Boccaccio puts it, "her service proved so pleasing and acceptable to [Enchararcho, her first protector], that he liked her care and diligence beyond all comparison" (Bullough 1975, 58). In *Frederyke of Jennen*, the pattern is repeated: here it is Frederyke's skill with falcons that draws the attention of the king (Bullough 1975, 72).

And, in both these sources, Sicurano and Frederyke confront "his" accuser and trip him up in his own lies by purchasing the tokens stolen from the nuptial bedroom that had served to prove her infidelity (Bullough 1975, 59, 74–75). The women in these tales confound a man on his own ground (in a marketplace in both versions) thus proving her worth both to her own husband and to the representative of secular power (the soldan and the king, respectively).

In the same way, though Posthumus receives a tablet that confirms Imogen's innocence, it takes Imogen's confrontation with her accuser, Iachimo, and her recognition of the ring on his finger to finally prove her chastity. It is in this manner that she acts as her own protector. Her innate strength, seen through the lens of a male disguise, allows her to be happy once again. As in Boccaccio and in the

Frederyke, her fortitude causes both her husband and her king to honor her. Imogen must take on men's clothing to show her energy and domination of events—it is not possible for her to remain a woman and survive in the situation she must brave alone.

There is one more thing I would like to point out. What is very interesting in the two plays is the heroine's choice of male alter ego— -man or boy. Arenopia and Dorothea appear about the same time and are both soldiers. According to the French edition of Cinthio's *Hecatommithi*, published in 1583–1584 (133), an edition which Greene apparently knew (Sanders 1970, xxx), Arenopia had been "taught in her father's house to manage and use arms in such a way as to be able to hold her own against any knight" (136). However, Arenopia does not initially intend to take on a man's role: instead, she is mistaken for a man by her rescuer, an errant knight who happens by and thinks she is "a knight and not a woman, because having been very ill a few days before, it had been necessary to cut off all her hair, so that she looked like a young man of fifteen or eighteen years." She then takes advantage of the situation by calling herself Arenopio thus abrogating male privilege and power (Sanders 1970, 137).

Likewise, the Dorothea of Greene's 1590–1594 play must be taught to fight by her servant, Nano, who says "I'll teach you, madam, how to ward a blow" (3.3.116). However, Nano only teaches Dorothea the art of defense, or warding off a blow, not the art of offense, of attacking. Though she is an ineffectual soldier who can only act in defense, she remains a man by costume. Clearly, Dorothea intended to be recognized as male, following Nano's advice to wear clothes that will make Dorothea appear to "seem a proper man" (3.3.100). Nano later describes her in terms that make her liminal nature clear: she is "[i]f not a man, yet like a manly shrew" (4.4.10).

Contrast these two mannish or manly women to the gracious singer and courtier Fidele, who does not appear until 1609–1610. In Shakespeare, women tend not to cross-dress as men but as boys. Witness Fidele: he is known and loved, but not as a man: Belarius describes him as "an angel; or, if not / An earthly paragon. Behold divineness / No elder than a boy" (3.6.42–44).

In any case, man or boy, it is necessary for Imogen and Dorothea to take on men's clothing in an attempt, whether successful or not, to show their virtue, dominate the plot, and save their own lives—in the contexts of *Cymbeline* and *James the Fourth*, it is not possible for these characters to remain women and to survive in the situation that they must brave alone.

Note

1. This was not translated into English until 1620, ten years after *Cymbeline*, but was available to Shakespeare in a French version (Bullough 1975, 16).

References

Bullough, Geoffrey. 1975. *Narrative and dramatic sources of Shakespeare.* Vol. 8, *Romances.* New York: Columbia University Press.

Daniell, David. 1986. Shakespeare and the traditions of comedy. In *The Cambridge companion to Shakespeare studies.* Vol. 2. Edited by Stanley Wells. New York: Columbia University Press.

Goldberg, Jonathan. 1992. *Sodometries: Renaissance texts, modern sexualities.* Stanford, Calif.: Stanford University Press.

Greene, Robert. 1967. *The Scottish history of James the Fourth.* Edited by J. A. Lavin. London: Ernest Benn Limited.

MacIntrye, Jean. 1987. "One that hath two gowns": Costume change in some Elizabethan plays. *English Studies in Canada* 13, no. 1.

Sanders, Norman, ed. 1970. *The Scottish history of James the Fourth,* by Robert Greene. London: Methuen & Co., Ltd.

Shakespeare, William. 1980. *The complete works of William Shakespeare.* 3d ed. Edited by David Bevington. Glenview, Ill.: Scott, Forseman and Company.

———. *Cymbeline.* 1988. Edited and with an introduction by Richard Hosley. New York: Penguin Books. Signet Classic, 1968.

"This Strange Way of Meeting": Theatricality and the New Woman in Hardy's *Return of the Native*

Lisa Nakamura

The mummer's play in Hardy's *The Return of the Native* is an exceptionally rich site of category crises; it is a "fossilized" relic performed during carnival time in a late-nineteenth-century house, and all of its performers are village men dressed in extravagantly feminine outfits except for one, the English lady Eustacia Vye, who disguises herself as a boy performing the part of a Turkish knight. In Marjorie Garber's words, "the time is carnival, the liminal, festive period in which inversion is not only permitted but valorized. As Terry Castle, among others, has pointed out, carnival and masquerade were often directly associated in the European public mind with transvestism" (1992, 381). Though Eustacia's cross-dressed performance is not socially validated—we are to read it as a measure of her lack of "moral training" that her grandfather does not reproach her more strongly for her exploit—it is certainly and puzzlingly tolerated. This is because gender inversion in the context of the mummer's play is in keeping with the dynamics of carnival.

While theater depends upon delineation between performer and audience, carnival depends upon the eliding of these categories. As Mikhail Bakhtin writes:

> carnival does not know footlights, in the sense that it does not acknowledge any distinction between actors and spectators. Footlights would destroy a carnival, as the absence of footlights would destroy a theatrical performance. Carnival is not a spectacle seen by the people; they live in it, and everyone participates because its very idea embraces "all the people"; carnival is "life itself," but life shaped according to a certain pattern of play. (1984, 7)

285

Rural English practices, such as skimmity-riding, charivari, May-Polings, market festivals, gipsying, and mummery figure largely in *The Return of the Native* and *The Mayor of Casterbridge* and perform some of the functions mentioned by Bakhtin.

Mummery's status as both spectacle and performance position it in a liminal space between carnival and theater. The appearance of these carnivalesque rituals signals something quite different in Hardy than it does in Rabelais, the subject of Bakhtin's study, of course; by the nineteenth century these rites had become "survivals," just like the barrows and roads left in Hardy's Wessex by the Romans. Though they were still *used,* they had acquired a different character. Critics have long debated the question of the significance of folk ritual in Hardy, though surprisingly few have engaged with Bakhtin's theories on the topic. Some attribute a certain type of cynicism to Hardy's treatment of ritual, classing it as "dead" and therefore merely quaint, a remnant or souvenir of the past but otherwise "no longer accessible to contemporary man" (Squillace 1986, 172) while others envision it as a potent, if latent, force in the modern world. No one has yet analyzed the significance of carnival in Hardy's treatment of gender. I maintain that carnival's subversive power, its licensing of social inversion and parody, definitely includes gender inversion and gender parody. In contrast to Rabelais's world, in which carnival was omnipresent, robust, an essential part of life rather than merely its adjunct, in late-nineteenth-century England carnival had been relegated to isolated incidents in modern life. Keeping this crucial difference in mind, one can see how carnival incidents in Hardy mediate between the antique and the modern world, and how they provide opportunities for gender inversion and other transgressive gender behavior while yet containing this behavior in a bracketed-off theatrical space.

Bakhtin claims that carnival constructs a "second world" in which people lived during a given time of year; he by no means intends to understate its importance in the lives of its inhabitants by emphasizing its "secondness." It presents a potent alternative to "officialdom" by "celebrating temporary liberation from the prevailing truth and from the established order; it marked the suspension of all hierarchical rank, privileges, norms and prohibitions" (1984, 10). Both the sensuous and pleasure loving Wildeve and the ascetic bachelor Clym Yeobright succumb to Eustacia's dangerous charm and social unconventionality and daring. Though she only cross-dresses once, the act has such transgressive significance that it sets the tone for the rest of the narrative.

Eustacia lacks a coherent feminist ideology, and cross-dresses not to protest for political reform, but rather as part of a romantic plan to capture the attention of the interesting young bachelor Clym Yeobright. In 1878, the year the novel was written, Hardy too lacked a coherent position on feminism and the "Woman

Question." He was later to resolve his doubts in favor of feminism, and in fact admitted to having been sympathetic to feminism for many years prior to the publication of the archetypal New Woman novel *Jude the Obscure.* Hardy's views on the Woman Question follow a continuum of development toward an increasingly radical gender politics that can be traced through the novels. While his novels of the 1870s, such as *Far from the Madding Crowd* and *Return of the Native*, were warmly received as pastoral novels of rural life that dealt with the issue of feminism obliquely, in the 1890s his novels *Tess of the d'Urberbilles* and *Jude the Obscure* were read by scandalized readers as works endorsing free love and the abolition of conventional marriage. *Jude* was attacked by the press as immoral, and as Hardy later remarked, was "burnt by a bishop—probably in despair at not being able to burn me" ([1896] 1961, vi). *Jude* was not the first New Woman novel,[1] though some modern critics consider it the "greatest" of his novels, and it is the most widely read today.

In 1909, Hardy and "hundreds of other male advocates, such as William Archer, Arthur Wing Pinero, and James M. Barrie, signed a petition favoring suffrage which was published in the *Times,*" and in 1922 Hardy finally revealed that "I have for a long time been in favor of woman-suffrage" (quoted in Beckson 1992, 157, 147). In fact, many of Hardy's ideas concerning the enlargement of women's spheres appear, though less explicitly, in his novels published twenty years or so before this pronouncement. Though feminist discussions of Hardy focus upon his later novels, which are more overtly concerned with the Woman Question, and to some contemporary readers became identified with it, early novels like *The Return of the Native* and *The Hand of Ethelberta* contain a type of feminine heroine for which there was not yet a name. Though Eustacia Vye is not a New Woman (the term wasn't coined until 1894), she is certainly a new *kind* of woman whose rebelliousness, ambition, and transgressive antisocial acts make her a threat to the commonwealth of both local community and nation, just as the New Woman was to be perceived twenty years later.

Bakhtin identifies carnival as a politically subversive practice that, by temporarily licensing various forms of social inversion, parodies of existing structures of authority, and indulgences in bodily pleasure, enabled an authentic form of resistance to an increasingly centralized, oppressive state apparatus. It is important to distinguish between Bakhtin's notion of carnival and the theater. Carnival is a genuinely egalitarian experience that involves every member of a community in play, and theater more closely resembles a commodity that is produced by one group of people for consumption by another.

Mummery occupies a uniquely liminal space between carnival and theater. As Squillace notes, "the plays originated in a pagan ritual, performed around the time of the winter solstice" and "the rural poor . . . maintained the mummers' play long after it lost fashion at court in the sixteenth century" (1986, 173). Though the play differs from true carnival in the sense that there are some who play and others who watch, there the resemblance to theater ends. The play is performed by local lads, known by all, rather than professionals from outside the village, and its preparation includes literally everyone in the community. Performance occurs in a private house during Christmas festivities rather than a theater, and the source of illumination is the hearth rather than footlights. Most importantly, the repetition of the St. George mummer's play constitutes a "traditional pastime," of which not a word changes from year to year; it is a "fossilized survival" rather than a "mere revival" (Hardy 1958, 129).

Depictions of mummery are quite rare in nineteenth- or twentieth-century fiction. This antique practice is seldom written about; while there is George Moore's *A Mummer's Wife* and Charlotte Yonge's *The Christmas Mummers*, *The Return of the Native* is by far the most famous novel that features a mummer's play. The Fifth Edition of the Oxford *Companion to English Literature*'s entry under mumming mentions only Hardy's novel as a source of references to the practice.

There are, on the other hand, many Victorian novels that deal with both public and private theater. Jane Austen, George DuMaurier, Wilkie Collins, Mary Braddon, Henry James, Louisa May Alcott, Charlotte Brontë, George Eliot, and of course Charles Dickens all wrote novels dealing with modern performance, theater, and actresses. While references to the theater in the novels of this period are so common as to be almost commonplace, references to mummery are strikingly rare. This can be accounted for by the fact that mummery was an outmoded form of performance, no longer practiced in most parts of England, while the theater was an extremely popular form of entertainment that enjoyed a great deal of visibility. It is more difficult, however, to explain why Hardy revived this moribund practice and placed it at the center of his novel. Though some critics have cited Hardy's well-known fascination with rural practices and customs as the most likely reason, and tend to lump mummery in with skimmity-riding and gipsying as occasions for "local color," the particular type of performance characteristic of mummery requires that it be considered separately from other forms of theatrical performance.

Women were absolutely barred from mummer's plays, a theatrical form whose status as a marginal and practically dead practice had afforded it immunity against change. E. K. Chambers notes that "Mummers' Plays, Plough Plays, and Sword Dances are exclusively male performances. I owe to Dr. Marett the saying of an Oxfordshire participant, 'Oh, you wouldn't have women in that; it's more like being in church' " (1966, 5). Thus, the appearance of Eustacia Vye in drag in the St. George play signifies the crossing of a gender boundary that had already been partially overcome in the modern theater. By placing a performing woman in the context of mummery Hardy reinvests the performance with transgressive import. While many fictional representations of professional actresses both denied and affirmed Victorian conceptions of "proper" womanhood by showing that women could indeed excel as artists on the stage, if sometimes at the expense of their virtue, they always posed the debate as one between privacy and propriety. Could a "public" woman be a good one as well? The appearance of a cross-dressing heroine in an exclusively masculine form of theater poses a different but closely related question, that is, could that "man" up there on the stage be . . . a woman? The emphasis has shifted from the issue of feminine propriety to the nature of gender itself.

Eustacia's actresslike ability to appear in different guises through the use of costume and performance sets her apart from the stable, respectable citizens of Egdon. This type of self-transformation and mobility of character and role are aligned with the theatric. In *Private Theatricals* Nina Auerbach identifies mobility and transformativity as the primary elements of theatricality responsible for its demonized status in Victorian culture, which valued "sincerity" as the most important—indeed constitutive—element of character. As she puts it, "reverent Victorians shunned theatricality as the ultimate, deceitful mobility. It connotes not only lies, but a fluidity of character that decomposes the uniform integrity of the self" (1984, 4).

The idea that character is something that can be seen by observing the play of the face close-up constructs the world as a stage upon which players both constantly enact themselves, and observe the performances of others. During the performance of the mummer's play gazes circulate between players and audience, effectively erasing the distinction between the two positions, as in carnival. The presence of drag performance in this arrangement subverts the notion of a knowable, essential gender that can be apprehended by the eye. Drag confounds the eye's "search for truth" in appearances.

Impressive claims have been made regarding the social subversiveness of the transvestite. S. Gilbert and S. Gubar identify female cross-dressing as an important part of the modernist woman's larger project to "define a gender-free reality behind or beneath myth, an ontological essence so pure, so free that 'it' can 'inhabit' any self, any costume" (1989, 332). They argue that for these women, "cross-dressing became a way of addressing and redressing the inequities of gender categories" (347). They assert that though female cross-dressing is "radically revisionary," male modernist costume imagery and transvestitism is "profoundly conservative" (332). Elaine Showalter, in her article "Critical Cross-Dressing: Male Feminists and the Woman of the Year," makes more cautious, if more confusingly historicized, claims about the conservative function of the cross-dressed man. Though she acknowledges that in "nineteenth century feminist literature, cross-dressing is the redressing of an emotional debt owed to women, and dressing like a woman is the hero's penitential and instructive immersion in humility, impotence, and subordination," she ultimately appeals to psychoanalytic theory to confirm her point that, for men, "cross-dressing is a way of promoting the notion of masculine power while masking it. . . . The male transvestite is not a powerless man . . . he is a 'phallic woman' " (1987, 123).

Marjorie Garber, while affirming and extending the subversive function of transvestitism for *both* genders, asserts that the transvestite was often conceived of as a "third sex," or the "third term" that disrupts *all* binary arrangements, including, but not limited to, gender. She asserts that "one of the most consistent and effective functions of the transvestite in culture is to indicate the place of what I call 'category crisis,' disrupting and calling attention to cultural, social, or aesthetic dissonances" (1992, 16). Garber's impressively flexible formulation embeds transvestitism in a larger epistemological discourse, as does Eve Sedgewick (1990) in *The Epistemology of the Closet,* linking the figure of the transvestite/homosexual to the structures of knowledge and revelation in any text. If, as in the case of *The Return of the Native,* transvestitism only appears in one or two seemingly peripheral episodes, the possibilities for "reading" the transvestite as a sign of category crises elsewhere proliferate rather than contract. As Garber puts it:

> The apparently spontaneous or unexpected or supplementary presence of a transvestite figure in a text (whether fiction or history, verbal or visual, imagistic or "real") that does not seem, thematically, to be primarily concerned with gender difference or blurred gender indicates a *category crisis elsewhere*, an irresolvable conflict or epistemological crux that destabilizes comfortable binarity, and displaces the resulting discomfort onto a figure that already inhabits, indeed incarnates, the margin. (1992, 17)

Garber's formulation, which situates the transvestite as a marker of a category crisis not necessarily overtly related to gender roles, clarifies the relation between two very uncomfortably paired terms in *The Return of the Native,* that is, modernity and antiquity, whose instability is revealed in cross-dressed ritual performance. The tensions between and competing claims of the antique and modern worlds constitute the "epistemological crux" in this text that is displaced onto its most marginal and theatrical figure—the modern New Woman.

Although the mummer's play in general is "fossilized," several modifications to the play occur that call attention to its potential for category subversion. Though the play partakes of the antique tradition of prohibiting women from the stage, the mummers are totally dependent upon local "sisters and sweethearts" to create the costumes, which are called "dresses." These costumes, which the women decorate with "loops and bows of silk and velvet in any situation pleasing to their taste," defy "tradition" (Hardy [1878] 1958, 129), both by making it impossible to distinguish one knight from another, and by feminizing them with the addition of "brilliant silk scallops and ribbon tufts" (130), thus ensuring that each player appears in a form of drag. This category confusion on the level of clothing effectively confuses other categories as well: "Saint George himself might be mistaken for his deadly enemy, the Saracen" (130). The mummers' plays often included, according to R. J. E. Tiddy's 1910 study, a grotesque character called the "man-woman, which is now played by a boy in woman's clothes" (76), thus indicating that though women did not perform in the plays, gender confusion was a distinctive feature of the ritual. Distinctions between pagan and Christian, antique and modern, traditional and innovative, and masculine and feminine are all temporarily confounded as a result of theatrical dress. The mummer's play is an occasion of "category crisis," a play of transgressive behaviors and carnival excesses.

As Jann Matlock puts it, "transvestism is, after all, dressing across gender boundaries, not just disguise *(Verkleidung)*. In its most subversive moments, female cross-dressing *plays* on the boundaries between gender, translating the lines that divide into sources of excitement, teasing difference into desire" (1993, 58). Certainly, Eustacia Vye signifies desire in the novel. She is its most desirous character (her last name, "vie," homonymically indicates this quality) and she "teases" desire into others. Eustacia's performance is "modern" in that it depends upon the contrast between the self and the role it chooses to perform. Shock at transgressive cross-dressed performance carries a charge of erotic titillation; while Clym Yeobright's sense of convention is chagrined at seeing "a cultivated woman playing such a part as this," simultaneously "his eyes lingered on her with [a] great interest" (Hardy [1878] 1958, 152), an interest inseparable from this "strange way of meeting."

The transgressiveness of her cross-dressed performance is foregrounded in his question, "do girls often play as mummers now? They never used to." She replies, despite the fact that she is wearing the Turkish knight's outfit and has just performed his part in the play, that "they don't now." Her adventure is figured as a masculine one, something that a "young buck" might do. This sartorial transgression does not truly shock her grandfather, but it does cause him to characterize the exploit as something one of the "buck[s] I knew at one-and-twenty" might do, while he warns her "no figuring in breeches again" (Hardy [1878] 1958, 155). Male fears that women who took over the prerogatives of male status, such as masculine dress or breeches, would pose a threat to established sexual categories surface in these dialogues but are deflected by the presence of a carnival frame around Eustacia's cross-dressing episode.

It is astonishing how ineffective her male garb is; everyone who has extended or even brief contact with Eustacia finds her out in short order. The permeability of her disguise heightens what Garber calls the "transvestite effect"; in contrast to "passing" for male undetected, drag depends upon the revelation of artifice; the "doffing of the wig" after a male drag performance, for example.[2] Drag's subversive effect "put[s] in question the 'naturalness' of gender roles through the discourse of clothing and body parts" (Garber 1992, 151). In addition, drag is a theatrical mode that exposes some of the mechanisms of gendered reading and misreading on and off the stage, and thus possesses political significance as well. The fact that any of the men are deceived even momentarily by Eustacia's theatrical ability calls into question their ability to read gender accurately, and identifies gender at least initially as a function of clothing rather than of essential qualities.

Hardy envisioned this tension created by drag performance as central to the entire novel. When the Dorcester Dramatic Society dramatized *The Return of the Native* in November 1920, Hardy's "respected alderman Mr. Tilley" sought advice from him regarding the representation of the novel as a performance. Though the letters reveal that Hardy was flattered and amused by this scheme, his only correspondence to Tilley regarding his wishes relates specifically to the drag performance. In a letter to Tilley, dated November 1920, Hardy writes: "Reminder: To tell Clym and Eustacia to *speak* up very *clearly* when they first exchange words ('Are you a woman?' & etc.) as it is the key to the whole action—" (Hardy 1978, 45). The fantastic guise of female drag performance provides the occasion for calling into question notions of gendered "presence" and quality by introducing the shadow of a doubt, a momentary disbelief, about "the sex of the creature."

The situating of the drag performance in a carnivalesque setting licenses and contains it in a finite space and time, bracketed off from everyday life. As Garber puts it:

> Cross dressing can be "fun" and "functional" so long as it occupies a liminal space and a temporary time period; after this carnivalization, however, whether it is called "Halloween" (in Provincetown) or "green world" (in Shakespeare), the cross-dresser is expected to resume life as he or she was, having, presumably, recognized the touch of "femininity" or "masculinity" in her or his otherwise "male" or "female" self. (1992, 70)

Drag performance plays on the threshold of two terms, "male" and "female," by revealing the performative nature of these categories, and in so doing blurs them. Thus, life cannot be resumed as it was afterwards, especially not in this novel, whose singular heroine's desires are so far out of the ordinary as to constitute a major disruptive force in the commonwealth.

It is worth restating that the New Woman did not appear in Hardy's fiction until the 1890s, about twenty years after *The Return of the Native*. At this time, women who were neither spinsters nor the angel in the house did not yet have a name. Eustacia's otherness in her community, along with her drag performance and singular ambitions, figures her as an "other" woman—the New Woman's precursor. Comparing protofeminist heroines, with their desire for "direct actions forbidden to the . . . proper lady" (Poovey 1984, 43) to their proper sisters, enables Hardy to create female characters who deviate from the proper. And of all these deviations, the most striking is their propensity for the theatrical, a quality long figured as "improper" in other fiction of the period. Theatricality marks one of the differences between the "old" woman and her "new" sister, since it emphasizes the difference between the self and the roles it plays, rather than the identity between a woman's role and her self, and thus establishes a space for a new conception of womanhood that displaces pure domesticity as the only privileged term.

Theatricality in Hardy's novels can occur in both overt and covert forms, and Eustacia's performances occupy several different registers. Her drag performance in the mummer's play overtly situates theatricality in a recognizable, if anachronistic and thus problematic, dramatic setting. Her other performances, such as the mock marriage with Charley, dramatic unveiling at Wildeve's wedding, and final death-bed tableau as a close-up sublime image, occupy various positions on a continuum of significant theatrical behavior.

While Hardy's doomed but fascinating heroines such as Tess and Eustacia are characterized as theatrical, presenting themselves to be seen by diverse audiences, their "homespun" sisters occupy the opposite pole. Their abhorrence of performance, often described as part of a becoming feminine modesty, was part and parcel of the cult of domesticity that gave rise to the figure of the "angel in the house." Eustacia's affinity for drag, for performance, and for visibility sets her apart from the Victorian ideal of the proper lady. Her rebellion against conventional roles for women and the marriage contract enacts itself by theatrical cross-dressing because this type of performance radically critiques gender roles through parody and role reversal.

Eustacia's change of gender during her drag performance at the mummer's play, where she appears "changed in sex, brilliant in colors, and armed from top to toe" (Hardy [1878] 1958, 135) challenges sexual hierarchies without entirely dismantling them by depicting cross-gender mobility in a ritual setting. Theatricality signifies something far more complicated than simple bad faith or duplicity, and operates in this text in far more subversive ways. Keeping Hardy's views on suffrage, marriage reform, and feminism in mind, one can see how the transgressive adoption of differently gendered theatrical roles both on the stage and in everyday life constructs Eustacia as a multiply selved, performative subject whose engagement in play temporarily removes her from the sequestered world of traditional womanhood. The transgressive adoption of forbidden roles both on and off the stage constitutes a defensive reaction against having to act a part dissonant with the self in everyday life, and more importantly indicates the existence of a self, a New Woman, unrepresentable by traditional Victorian codes of femininity.

Notes

1. Although many critics imply that Hardy (1961) and George Robert Gissing (1893) created the category of New Woman novels by writing *Jude* and *The Odd Women*, respectively, in fact the first, and most popular, New Woman novels were written by women. Sarah Grand's (1893) *The Heavenly Twins* and George Egerton's (1893) *Keynotes* were both widely read and enjoyed in their day, but in ours, have been relegated to, in E. P. Thompson's words, "the lost continent of the female tradition" (quoted in Showalter 1987, 11).

2. Julie Andrews's doffing of the wig in the film *Victor/Victoria,* in which she plays a woman passing as a man who does female drag performance, complicates this gesture in a way that illustrates my point here about the distinction between passing and drag. Another Blake Edwards film, *Switch,* depicts the ultimate female cross-dressing narrative—its fantastic premise asks the viewer to believe that the actress Ellen Barkin is playing a man sent back to earth to inhabit a woman's body as *punishment.*

References

Auerbach, N. 1984. *Private theatricals.* Cambridge: Harvard University Press.
Bakhtin, M. 1984. *Rabelais and his world.* Bloomington: Indiana University Press.
Beckson, K. 1992. *London in the 1890's.* New York: W. W. Norton.
Chambers, E. K. 1966. *The English folk-play.* New York: Haskell House.
Garber, M. 1992. *Vested interests: Cross dressing and cultural anxiety.* New York: Routledge.
Gilbert, S., and S. Gubar. 1989. *No man's land 2: Sex changes.* New Haven: Yale University Press.
Hardy, T. [1878] 1958. *The return of the native.* New York: St. Martin's Press.
———. [1896] 1961. *Jude the obscure.* New York: Signet.
———. 1978. *Collected letters of Thomas Hardy.* Edited by R. Purdy and M. Millgate. Oxford: Clarendon Press.
Matlock, J. 1993. Masquerading women, pathologized men: Cross-dressing, fetishism, and the theory of perversion, 1882–1935. In *Fetishism as cultural discourse.* Edited by E. Apter and W. Pietz. Ithaca: Cornell University Press.
Poovey, M. 1984. *The proper lady and the woman writer.* Chicago: University of Chicago Press.
Sedgewick, E. K. 1990. *Epistemology of the closet.* Berkeley: University of California Press.
Showalter, E. 1987. Critical cross-dressing: male feminists and the woman of the year. In *Men in feminism.* Edited by A. Jardine and P. Smith. New York: Methuen.
Squillace, R. 1986. Hardy's mummers. *Nineteenth Century Literature* 41 (September): 172–89.
Tiddy, R. J. E. 1923. *The mummers' play.* Oxford: Clarendon Press.

The Boys Don't Count: Or Why Won't Shakespeare Put His Men in Dresses?

Lynn M. Thompson

It does not take long for even a casual reader of Shakespearean drama to notice how frequently the image of the cross-dressed woman appears. At times, the cross-dressing either involves a secondary character or else occurs only briefly as in *Cymbeline* or *The Two Gentlemen of Verona*, but at other times it is the central character who cross-dresses, her disguise becoming the crux upon which the solution to the play's central problem rests, as in *Twelfth Night*, *The Merchant of Venice*, or *As You Like It*. In these plays, it is the female characters who cross-dress—always female characters. But, where are the cross-dressed men in Shakespeare?

At this point, one is likely to recall that boy actors portrayed all of the female characters on the early modern English stage: *here* are the cross-dressed men. Here is the male manifestation of transvestism. (In the study of Renaissance literature, it is the practice to use the terms cross-dressing and transvestism as synonymous.) However, these cross-dressed boys are not characters within the play, but only the actors creating the performance. A close examination of Shakespeare's plays will reveal a few cross-dressed male characters, but these characters—save one—are nearly identical and tangential to the plot in that they are usually cross-dressed pages or children. It also becomes necessary to consider the implications of transvestism occurring on stage and compare such cross-dressing with the transvestism occurring within the dramatic plot.

The complexities and ambiguities are compounded when both forms of cross-dressing occur at the same time. For example, how does one discuss the transvestism of a boy actor who portrayed a female character in male disguise?

295

In such cases, there was no *actual* cross-dressing, for the boy actor on stage was dressed in male attire. However, the actor who played the part of a woman was accepted as a woman by the spectators for the duration of the play. Because of this acceptance, transvestism was called to the audience's attention: the actor represented a woman dressed as a man. By contrast, the more frequent occurrence of *actual* transvestism—where cross-dressing boy actors played all the female roles—was *not* called to the attention of the audience.

The absence in drama of male characters in women's clothing is a curiosity—adult male transvestism occurs on stage only once in all of Shakespeare's plays—and briefly at that—in *The Merry Wives of Windsor*. One might argue that a playwright would see no advantage for his male character in giving up male status and privilege just to solve the type of plot complications one finds in comedies such as *The Merchant of Venice*. As a mere woman and wife of Bassanio, Portia cannot help Antonio except by masquerading as a lawyer, and so disguise is necessary for her where it may not be so for a male character. But this argument loses force when one considers the situation that occasionally arises in nondramatic romances such as Sidney's *The Countess of Pembroke's Arcadia*. In order to approach and woo Philoclea, Pyrocles assumes the name and dress of an Amazon. Similarly, in Spenser's *The Faerie Queene*, Artegall is conquered by the Amazon Radigund and forced to dress in women's clothes. Considering the ubiquity of disguise and female cross-dressing in plays, whether comedy, romance, history, or tragedy, why did the playwrights—and Shakespeare in particular—rarely, if ever, incorporate a transvestite plot involving a male character?

Although we must be careful not to project assumptions and practices into the past, the absence of cross-dressed males becomes even more odd in light of their frequent appearance in our contemporary age. In fact, it is the cross-dressed woman who has become rare by comparison, though she still exists. Does the absence of this representation on Shakespeare's stage mean that the idea never occurred to him or that it was up to a later age to invent this comedic image? Or is it that there was something so unsettling to an Elizabethan audience about the sight of a man in women's clothing that it was too disturbing to portray on stage? And if that *is* the problem—and I think it is—then what are we to think about all those boy "actresses," as Stephen Orgel (1989) calls them? Why are transvestite boys acceptable, but men in drag are not? And is the problem that one cannot show a male *character* in a dress or, rather, that one cannot show an adult male *actor* in a dress? Or both? If the idea of a cross-dressed man is so dangerous, then how do we explain Falstaff's transvestism in *The Merry Wives of Windsor*?

I believe the restriction on this particular form of dramatic transvestism can be explained by the anxiety in early modern England over a commonly held belief in the fluidity of sex differences and the conviction that the spectacle of cross-dressing on the stage could corrupt and subvert the masculinity of men both on stage and in the audience. Anti-theatrical writers of the time believed that stage portrayals of male transvestism undermined male identity and privilege by suggesting that any man could be effeminized or even transformed into a woman. Laura Levine, paraphrasing a 1583 tract by Phillip Stubbes, states: "male actors who wore women's clothing could literally 'adulterate' male gender" (1986, 121). If a man could so easily become a woman or like a woman, then was there a significant, fundamental difference between a man and a woman? And if the line between male and female was so thin, it became possible to ask why men had all the power and privilege in society and women had none. To maintain and protect traditional gender roles, it was vital to forestall or eliminate any threats. Because of the potential for subversion, stage portrayals of cross-dressing adult males were more threatening than the sight of juvenile males cross-dressing. The effeminization of a boy posed less of a threat to society because, in the hierarchy of sex, a boy was less perfect than a man and, therefore, more like a woman than a man was. By contrast, any adult male wearing feminine attire jeopardized not only his own place in the social hierarchy, but also the place of every other male.

Thus society policed and reinforced male gender status through social taboos against violating the rigid boundaries of masculinity, even in the theater. Shakespearean drama sharply limited and contained male gender transgressions—evidence that these plays more closely adhered to cultural laws—to satisfy society's anxious need to fix masculinity despite its belief that biological sex, and therefore gender, was ever-shifting. On the other hand, the nondramatic *Arcadia* and *Faerie Queene* allowed their male characters greater freedom from legal and cultural gender restrictions, primarily because the gender transgressions were not actually represented on stage but, additionally, because society's gender roles are invariably upheld in the end. For example, Pyrocles eventually sheds his female garb and marries his princess, suffering no permanent consequences from his transvestism; on the contrary, for him, cross-dressing becomes a tool to maintain male privilege and power, instead of a destabilizing force.

The need for early modern English society to fix masculinity in place was further complicated by beliefs about human physiology. While apparently supporting society's construction of gender roles, these biological views also suggested that an individual could change potentially from male to female or female to male. As Thomas Laqueur (1990) explains in *Making Sex*, female and male genitalia were thought to be essentially the same in form and function, different only in position within or without the body. The vagina was the mirror image of the penis; the ovaries, the testes; and the womb, the scrotum. There were not two sexes, but only one. As a result, it was believed that vigorous activity could cause a woman to transform into a man; likewise, a man who was too "womanish" in behavior and appearance could become a woman. Stephen Greenblatt (1988) tells of a young French woman who, while chasing her pigs, spread her legs too far leaping over a ditch, spontaneously turning into a man. Stories like this were taken very seriously by Elizabethans because they verified beliefs about sexual development—that women were simply a lower order of men—and seemed proof that it was possible for men to regress, to turn back into women (Orgel 1989). Thus, all qualities that contributed to a man's social position could be given up or taken from him. According to Greenblatt, "A man in Renaissance society had symbolic and material advantages that no woman could hope to attain, and he had them by virtue of separating himself, first as a child and then as an adult, from women" (1988, 76).

Renaissance medical authorities also believed that a child forever carried within it the intermingled male and female "seed" and that the child's sex and gender was determined by which seed predominated. Problems arose when the predominance of one seed or the other was sufficient to sex the child, but not sufficient to subdue all traits of the opposite gender. Thus a man became effeminate and a woman too masculine (Greenblatt 1988; Orgel 1989). Another important ingredient in establishing a child's sex was heat. The heat of male seed made the child stronger and more vigorous and so the child was able to push its genitals outside its body and become male. Female seed was colder and weaker and, therefore, created a less perfect female child with internal genitalia (Greenblatt 1988; Orgel 1989).

Stage portrayals of male transvestism create an enormous unease in the mind of the Elizabethan man about the instability of his gender. No man could be sure just what it would take to push him "down" into femaleness. In light of this pre-occupation with the ambiguity of gender, the anxiety over the transvestite theater and the plays produced upon its stage is understandable. If there is not that much difference between a man and a woman, there is even less difference between a boy and a woman. In a patriarchal society concerned with preserving male status and privilege through the control and restriction of women, boy "actresses" are logical. According to most scholars, the transvestite theater arose in order to eliminate woman as spectacle and to exert control over women both as performers and spectators. Women were expected to be chaste, silent, and obedient. An actress is not silent, and by performing on stage, she risks her chastity by making herself the erotic object of the gaze of spectators. A transvestite theater was constituted to avoid such problems. However, this solution created new problems of gender ambiguity, for now the transvestite boy actor became the eroticized object of the spectators' gaze; although the women were no longer at risk of gender transgressions, the men were. Not only were the boy actors effeminized, it was feared that the adult actors who performed with them, as well as the male spectators who gazed at them, were also effeminized. According to the anti-theatrical writers, cross-dressed boy actors, because they were eroticized, would cause men in the audience to be sexually attracted to boys instead of to women. Fears that theatrical cross-dressing would lead to widespread homosexual activity underlay many of the arguments against the theater. (According to Alan Bray and other scholars, the term "homosexual" did not exist at the time, nor did early modern English society conceive of the idea of a person who had a *permanent* sexual preference for those of the same sex.) Arguments grew more shrill after cross-dressing became a fad among the citizens of London; it appeared that the predictions about the subversion of the social order were coming to pass.

Because of the theory that human anatomy was mutable and thus threatened individual gender identity, the transvestite theater, as well as the plays performed on its stage, becomes the locus of anxiety over gender transgressions. If maleness was not fixed, then a society concerned with the rank and privilege of males needed to set up gender boundaries to protect male status. Maleness needed to be defined, redefined, and reinforced by signs of masculine identity. By constructing and adhering to rigid gender boundaries, society could guard against the erosion of power and privilege that would occur should a man become unsexed and "slip" from his superior position or, indeed, should a woman "rise" from her subordinate rank. Laura Levine, in her article on anti-theatricality, discusses the idea of the fluid self as it pertains to actors in and spectators of plays:

> If we locate a self whose chief characteristics are its abilities to be carried, programmed, poured out of its container into something else, we begin to see how it would be possible to maintain the kinds of claims [the anti-theatricalists make in their tracts], the claim that the spectator could be made compulsively to replicate the actor. If you believe the self is so tenuous that it can be altered at the slightest touch, then the slightest touch becomes magic, witchcraft, capable of radical, constitutive, mysterious change. (1986, 127)

With this concept of the self, cross-dressing by either sex, even by actors performing in a play, becomes an activity full of risk. For if a woman is strong, independent, and dresses as a man, what is the difference between her and a man? Similarly, if a man dresses in female attire, how does he differ from a woman? For the Elizabethans, the lines become disturbingly fuzzy, biological sex notwithstanding. A man dressed as a woman causes other men to react to him just as though he were a woman. The cross-dresser, through the magic of the instability of the self, becomes another self, and can lead others to similar instability. The man in women's clothing becomes an effeminizing influence on himself and others, leading men away from their natural roles as husbands to women. Lisa

Jardine, in *Still Harping on Daughters*, quotes from Dr. John Rainoldes's 1599 anti-theatrical tract *The Overthrow of Stage-Players*:

> The appareil of wemen is a great provocation of men to lust and leacherie. . . .
> A womans garment beeing put on a man doeth vehemently touch and moue him
> with the remembrance and imagination of a woman; and the imagination of a
> thing desirable doth stirr up the desire. (1983, 9)

Thus, the absence of adult male cross-dressing in the plays becomes understandable. Indeed, it is the frequent male cross-dressing within the nondramatic texts that, at first, seems at odds with social gender restrictions. A look at nondramatic texts shows, however, that they are not entirely insensitive to these anxieties regarding gender transgressions. Both Spenser's *The Faerie Queene* and Sidney's *The Countess of Pembroke's Arcadia* portray cross-dressed men: Artegall, who is held captive by an Amazon, and Pyrocles, who is in disguise as an Amazon. The Amazon, a figure originating in classical Greek texts, was a problematic one both in antiquity and in early modern England. Spenser most clearly reflects this ambivalence, for the representation of his Amazonian characters, including Britomart, Knight of Chastity and avatar for Queen Elizabeth, and Radigund, the Amazon queen who defeats Artegall, is not wholly positive. In Sidney's *Arcadia*, Pyrocles takes on the disguise of the Amazon in order to woo Philoclea, much to the consternation of his friend Musidorus. Sidney acknowledges fears about emasculation through the horrified words of Musidorus, who warns Pyrocles that he risks letting "himself slide to viciousness" by donning female attire, and that his action "subverts the course of nature in making reason give place to sense, and man to woman" (1977, 133). However, Pyrocles is certain that, because he takes on his disguise in the name of love, his masculinity will be strengthened, not weakened. Although deployment of the figure of the Amazon by both Sidney and Spenser captures perfectly the anxiety about male gender transgressions of early modern English society, male cross-dressing is used more extensively in these romances than in dramatic texts because there is no actual performance or enactment of transvestism as there would be in a dramatic performance.

Now, what are we to make of Falstaff's appearance in *The Merry Wives of Windsor*, the sole example of an adult male appearing on stage in women's clothing in all of Shakespeare's plays? It should come as no surprise that Shakespeare chooses Falstaff. Patricia Parker in *Literary Fat Ladies* points out Falstaff's feminine nature as he appears in the *Henriad*, speaking of the "tongues of women" and his "womb"; his fat is "compared to the image of the pregnant earth" (1987, 21). Feminized in the history plays, by the end of *The Merry Wives of Windsor*,

Falstaff has little left to him besides a weary and resigned sense of humor about his humiliation at the hands of the merry wives: "I do begin to perceive that I am made an ass" (Evans 1974, 5.5.119). First, the wives strip Falstaff of his noble status by having him tossed in the river; next, they peel away his male status when he must dress as a woman to escape the wrath of Master Ford; finally, the wives deprive him even of his humanity when Falstaff is persuaded to dress as the spirit of Herne the Hunter, wearing the head of a buck. It is also likely that because Falstaff's transvestism is brief and ritualized, it poses little risk, either to the actor portraying him, or to the audience watching him. Indeed, Falstaff is the cause of the disruption to the social order by attempting to seduce two honest wives, thereby creating two cuckolded husbands. Because the cross-dressing episode occurs at the urging of the wives, it becomes a means to reassert the proper social order, not subvert it. Thus, this episode of cross-dressing carried little risk to the actor playing Falstaff. It is also significant that Falstaff dresses up as a specific woman: the witch of Brainford. Witches were the most masculine of women; they were thought to be sexually wanton, and they were outside male control because they did not fulfill acceptable roles such as daughter, wife, or mother. In fact, witches often had thick beards and controlled others through their magic. If an actor *had* to play a woman, he would want to play the most masculine kind of woman possible for his own safety: what better role than the witch of Brainford? Also, Falstaff's transvestism is very brief. It is not comparable in either duration or scope to a role such as Viola's in *Twelfth Night* or Rosalind's in *As You Like It*, where the female character is cross-dressed for most of the play.

In the comedies, Shakespeare permits his female characters much latitude to resolve complications successfully through cross-dressing. Males who try to do the same are punished by humiliation. It is not permissible for a male character to relinquish his gender privilege, even temporarily, because the cross-dressed male undercuts the authority of all men. Thus, Falstaff receives a beating for cross-dressing because his act devalues not only male privilege, but also his noble status as a knight. The comic undercutting of males who fail to uphold society's standards of masculinity also occurs through other types of transformations besides cross-dressing: Malvolio's absurd attire and Bottom's ass's head are examples of such undercutting. Male behavior permissible in the comedies is not, however, possible in the tragedies. Although these plays do not deploy cross-dressing on stage, there are numerous instances of male characters who exhibit some gender ambiguity either through their language or their behavior. Antony, for example, is effeminized by his love for Cleopatra and turns against Octavian's Rome. Similarly, Hamlet's tragedy is the result of what he perceives as his "womanish" reliance on language and inaction. These characters transgress male gender codes by failing to think or act in socially acceptable masculine ways. In the tragedies, such language or behavior on the part of these characters could be defined as "metaphorical transvestism," and a "metaphorical transvestite" would be any male character who takes on feminine qualities and consequently creates the very tragedy he tries to avoid. In Shakespearean tragedy, a male character's failure to embody "proper" masculine characteristics threatens his society with chaos or disintegration; order can return only with the arrival of a conventionally masculine leader, as occurs in *Hamlet* or *Antony and Cleopatra*. In the case of Hal, in *Henry IV, Part 2*, he is able to free himself from the influence of the weak, "womanish" Falstaff to assume his proper role as prince and, later, king. Through such metaphorical transvestism, Shakespeare defines and limits acceptable masculine behavior.

It is no surprise that the fascination with gender and sex exhibited by early modern English society coexisted with considerable anxiety over the possible impermanence and artificiality of sex and gender distinctions. Because one's place in the social hierarchy was determined by sex, and because men and women had widely disparate roles and identities, any suggestion that one's sex could change abruptly was disturbing. The texts of Shakespeare, Sidney, and Spenser are preoccupied with the place of the individual in the social order and, naturally, gender is a primary concern. By defining and reinforcing the roles of men and women, and by fixing sex and gender in place, these texts reassured readers and audiences of the permanence of the individual's place in society, regardless of the many political, economic, or religious changes that were occurring at the time.

References

Bray, A. 1988. *Homosexuality in Renaissance England*. Boston: Gay Men's Press.

Evans, G. B., ed. 1974. *The Riverside Shakespeare*. Boston: Houghton Mifflin Company.

Greenblatt, S., ed. 1988. *Shakespearean negotiations: The circulation of social energy in Renaissance England*. Berkeley: University of California Press.

Jardine, L. 1983. *Still harping on daughters: Women and drama in the age of Shakespeare*. New York: Columbia University Press.

Laqueur, T. 1990. *Making sex: Body and gender from the Greeks to Freud*. Cambridge: Harvard University Press.

Levine, L. 1986. Men in women's clothing: Anti-theatricality and effeminization from 1579–1642. *Criticism* 28: 121–43.

Orgel, S. 1989. Nobody's perfect: or why did the English stage take boys for women? *South Atlantic Quarterly* 88, no. 1: 7–29.

Parker, P. 1987. *Literary fat ladies*. New York: Methuen.

Sidney, Sir P. 1977. *The countess of Pembroke's Arcadia*. New York: Penguin Books.

Spenser, E. 1977. *The faerie queene*. Edited by A. C. Hamilton. London: Longman.

"Just Man Enough to Play the Boy": Theatrical Cross-Dressing in Mid-Victorian England

Ellen Bayuk Rosenman

This paper began with a glancing reference in an article by Martha Vicinus, in which she mentioned a cross-dressing heroine in a mid-Victorian novel, George William MacArthur Reynolds's *The Mysteries of London* (1848). I was fascinated; although I knew that cross-dressing was a theatrical tradition, I had not encountered any equivalent treatment in Victorian novels. A look at *Mysteries* itself convinced me of its originality and, at the same time, made me wonder where, ideologically and iconographically speaking, this character had come from. The illustration on its very first page depicts a slim, attractive young man facing the reader squarely: extending the line of his body with a flourish of his hand, he is foregrounded and articulated against the dim, sketchy figures in the background. Nothing, it seems, could speak an upper-class male youth more directly. Except, of course, that he is "really" a woman. (These quotation marks, it should become clear, are the real subject of this paper.) What, I wondered, did this image mean? How would it have been received by its Victorian audience? If gender is a "reiterative and citational practice" (Butler 1993, 2) what is this body citing?

These questions sent me back to the theatrical tradition on which Reynolds clearly drew. I want to delineate this context, to read this provocative image and its attendant narrative, and to pursue the radical take on gender identity that the novel suggests. *Mysteries of London* is significant because it was, as it happens, the best-selling novel of mid-century, selling over a million copies in serial form before it was bound and republished, and remaining in print for several decades thereafter. In *Mysteries of London*, cross-dressing is not an aberration or deviance—although it is a crime. Rather, it is a particularly explicit performance that clarifies the status of femininity throughout the novel.

I want to begin with a caveat about historical and contextual specificity. In my research, I found many different versions of theatrical cross-dressing and many different responses to them. Critics in the early part of the century severely censured this phenomenon as a violation of sexual propriety. In a famous review published in 1821, the *British Stage and Literary Cabinet* attacked Mme. Vestris, the most famous performer of breeches parts, for being "utterly offensive" in male attire, claiming that such parts "depend solely on the prostitution of . . . actresses" because they invited the "libidinous criticism of debauchees" in exchange for money (Fletcher 1987, 14). Because male breeches exposed the shape of the legs and buttocks, such display has sometimes been characterized as entirely pornographic (Davis 1991). Yet, by the mid-1840s, such vitriolic criticism of legitimate theater was rare. Indeed, in Christmas and Easter extravaganzas, cross-dressing was literally unremarkable; a staple of such entertainment, it was mentioned only rarely, and then with a matter-of-factness quite at odds with earlier diatribes. For instance, in 1848 the *Times* declared the same Mme. Vestris "a most princely King of the Peacocks" and left the matter there. What this means is not that theatrical cross-dressing has lost its ideological charge, but that it has lost this charge in extravaganzas in the 1840s. It would be surprising indeed if these entertainments depended so exclusively on the pornographic meanings sometimes ascribed to all cross-dressed roles, since women and children comprised the main portion of the audience (as they do now at performances of *The Nutcracker*, probably the closest modern equivalent). My point is that a cross-dressed body does not automatically mean any one thing. Its meaning changes over time and in context. Even then, its meanings may be multiple and confusing, as spectators attempt to make sense of its unfamiliar semiotics.

This was certainly the case with breeches roles in Shakespeare in the 1840s, which form the most relevant context to Reynolds's novel. My aim in examining critical responses to these roles, along with Cushman's Romeo, is not to construct a comprehensive, global account of them but to follow some of the different implications that these bodies supported. Cross-dressed performers were difficult to interpret, and attempts to categorize them reveal, as much as anything, the difficulty of describing a phenomenon composed of ideologically opposed qualities. If "masculine" and "feminine" are polarized and mutually exclusive terms—if "masculine" is everything "feminine" is not, and vice versa—how can one talk about their intersection? This apparent impasse, rhetorical and ideological, results in a re-theorizing of gender difference—implicit, inadvertent, incomplete, and sometimes inconsistent—as reviewers cope with cross-dressed bodies.

Several reviewers make arguably the most predictable response to cross-dressed bodies: to "look *through*" the disguise and insist upon the female identity beneath (Garber 1992, 9). In a review of *Twelfth Night*, for example, Mrs. Kean is praised for retaining her femininity in spite of her male clothing (*Morning Chronicle* 1848). Such responses assume that cross-dressing is a simple disguise—and an unsuccessful one at that, which never actually complicates the actress's underlying identity, to the reviewer's obvious relief. But in many instances, the challenge to binary gender oppositions was not so easily averted.

Indeed, the role of the principal boy—that is, a woman playing an adolescent boy—implies the necessity of complication. Its conventional status as a fixture of theatrical history masks the subversiveness of its assumptions: that women make better boys than men do. To make such an assumption is to question the organization of gender into two opposing categories. The quotation with which I title my paper, "She was just man enough to play the boy," applied to Charlotte Cushman's legendary portrayal of Romeo, suggests instead a configuration of gendered qualities in which a woman's femininity leavens or dilutes masculinity, and in which gender characteristics reorganize themselves at different point in the life cycle (Ludlow 1880, 316). Instead of a single opposition, masculine and feminine, we have two constitutive categories, gender and age. Although the male impersonator has been placed in an imaginary no-person's land between genders (Rowland 1989–1990), it is also worth noting that such a figure is understood as existing, already gendered, in real life, in the form of the adolescent boy. The notion of masculine and feminine intermingling in male youth recurred in such descriptions, as in a performance of Olivia in which masculine and feminine characteristics are "blent" in the portrayal of the page (*Mirror Monthly Magazine* 1848). This is not to deny the enormous fantasy component of such bodies, but it does suggest that they also depend on a socially sanctioned intermingling of masculine and feminine.

Cushman's Romeo (which she plays opposite her sister's Juliet, for the added spice of lesbian incest) was justified in precisely these terms. Romeo was understood as a boy, not a man—in fact, as a boy masquerading as a man: "a youth who begins to imagine he is a man because he has some hair on his upper lip" (Ludlow 1880, 316). Romeo himself is a male impersonator. We now have a double crossing: a woman imagining herself as a boy imagining himself as a man. In both cases, it goes (almost) without saying, the impersonation is sustained by the semiotics of visible appearance: clothing, gesture, and facial hair—all of which are assumed for the performance—and so calls into question the notion of an absolute natural gendering. The role succeeds in establishing its credibility because of the overlay of identities rather than by asserting a single, univocal presence. Here, the "identity" of male youth is a complex composite, construed from both actual and imagined masculinity and femininity.

It may be that the relative social marginality of the boy, in relation to the man, also made such intermingling safe.

Thus, Romeo presented a problem because of his importance in the play and the seriousness of his experience (compared to, say, Orlando's in *As You Like It*). The role of Romeo lent him a maturity that made the impersonation disturbing. Such a violation of theatrical decorum might be tolerated this once because of Cushman's extraordinary talent, her alleged motivation of securing a first-rate part for her sister, and the dearth of other good Romeos in the season, but the reviewers clearly worried about the effect of such gender complications, especially on actresses:

> Assuming her possession of a masculine mind and a correspondent style, may not their results be mischievously exaggerated, for want of a counteracting influence in the characters embodied, and thus, at lengths, the feminine attraction which should soften and dignify the severed traits, gradually disappear? (*Athenaeum* 1846, 19)

In this bizarre formulation, the already-masculine Cushman is in danger of becoming even more masculine because she plays only male parts; she needs to impersonate women in order to maintain some femininity from which to construct an appropriate bisexuality—the combination of "severer traits," implicitly defined as male, and female softness. The *Athenaeum*'s attempt to normalize Cushman's potential deviance posits an even more deviant solution, the "disciplining" of a woman's inherent masculinity by a feigned femininity for a doubling of masculine and feminine. Equally interesting is the power of performance: neither "mere" acting nor the expression of an interior essence, it is itself a discipline that genders not only bodies but personalities, a kind of gender therapy.

Such a claim is only a step away from the arguments of modern theorists such as Garber, Butler, and Joan Riviere, that all gender is performative or, in Riviere's famous phrase, a "masquerade" (Riviere 1929). Rejecting the idea of an essential gender expressed through the body, these theorists argue that clothing, gestures, and behaviors make gender happen. While the *Athenaeum*'s account posits an interior self to be shaped and corrected by performance, modern accounts argue that this interiority is an effect produced by the masquerade, and that status as "woman" or "man" is achieved not by being born with a particular anatomy but by performing gendered behaviors successfully in accordance with prevailing social norms.

Now I want to turn to *Mysteries of London*, the most sustained account I have found of the subversive energy of cross-dressing. *Mysteries of London* both draws on and extends some of the problematics I have just described in a truly unorthodox fashion. The novel is not well known now, so I want to describe it briefly and summarize the plot of Eliza Sydney, the central practitioner of cross-dressing. Published serially from 1846 to 1848, *Mysteries of London* (first series), is a sensationalistic, melodramatic, multiplot novel aimed at a popular audience. Its central plot pits a good and bad brother against each other, culminating in the predictable victory of virtue over vice, a resolution that has led the few modern critics who have noticed it to dismiss it as formula fiction. But around this central action, Reynolds weaves fifty or so other plots that are not as predictable, especially when they involve women. Reynolds grants his female characters extraordinary autonomy and agency, leading them through a series of adventures, both sexual and otherwise, that leave them gasping but still, somehow, respectable. Reynolds's intentions are partially pornographic, as he repeatedly displays his female characters half-dressed and in male clothes that reveal the contours of the female body as women's clothes did not. But he is also fascinated with the mysteries of female identity: while male characters have secrets, which are invariably discovered before the end of the novel, female characters present less easily resolved difficulties of interpretation, implying that femininity is more complicated, shifting, and enigmatic.

Eliza Sydney is one such character. Her commanding, dramatic presence appears on the novel's first page. Reynolds draws her pose, in fact, from a prominent handbook on acting (Barnett 1987, 156). Young and beautiful, she is persuaded by an unscrupulous friend to dress as her dead twin, Walter, for four years in order to collect his inheritance. In representing this disguise, the novel is both conventional and unorthodox. In some ways, it insists that Eliza is really a woman. In male guise, she is "a walking lie" (Reynolds 1848, 1:3), implying a true gender identity behind the facade of male clothing. She has a well-guarded and "voluptuous" boudoir in which she discards her male clothing and revels in femininity. She is described in conventional fetishizing terms, with emphasis on her "luxuriant" hair and "polished ivory . . . flesh" (1:17). Once again, we see the "looking *through*" described by Garber to deny the challenge of the cross-dressed body. In case the reader misses the point, an engraving depicts her lounging in bed with one nipple showing: the naked truth indeed. Here, in the female body, is the foundation of sexual identity. "The masculine attire and habits which the lady had assumed," the novel assures us, "had not destroyed the fine and endearing characteristics of her woman's heart" (1:52).

But in other descriptions, it certainly complicates her woman's body. The disguise itself calls into question the opposition of masculinity and femininity. Eliza achieves her masculine body through the traditional feminine device of stays, and her military frock coat is particularly well-suited for accommodating the female anatomy because it "is invariably so prominent about the chest"

(1:19). This surprising adaptability of male dress, noted before, and military dress at that, suggests a secret collusion between gender identities—a closet interdependence, if you will. Even the boudoir presents a complicated image. On the one hand, it is a sanctuary of femininity, the one place where Eliza can take off her disguise and be her feminine self. On the other, it also expresses the complexity of her crossing:

> [It] contained articles of male and female use and attire strangely conmingled [*sic*]—pell mell—together . . . it seemed as if some cunning hand had purposely arranged them all so as to strike the eye in a manner calculated to encourage the impression that this elegant boudoir was inhabited by a man of strange feminine tastes, or a woman of extraordinary masculine ones. (1:16)

The feminine retreat is itself cross-dressed. Its ambiguous signs suggest that it might be the home of a man or a woman—indeed, or a feminine man or a masculine woman, a double disruption of gender identity, as in the *Athenaeum*'s description of Charlotte Cushman. Moreover, it is a self-conscious visual object, as if constructed intentionally to puzzle the observing eye. Like the masquerade of gender itself, it implies an audience.

The question of Eliza's real identity is raised most dramatically by a moment in which she attempts to recover her femininity. Significantly, the scene takes place before a mirror. Within what the narrator calls, accurately enough, "the impenetrable mystery of this boudoir" (1:19), Eliza reports, she sometimes dresses in women's clothing "just to see myself reflected in the mirror" (1:18). The experience of being a woman or of wearing women's clothes is somehow not enough; Eliza needs to *see* herself as a woman to fully *be* one. Here, the body alone is not sufficient as the bedrock of identity. Eliza's need to see herself in women's clothes suggests a certain uncertainty about what is really there, about how gender is constituted and stabilized.

Like Cushman, the woman who needed to play women's roles, Eliza needs to perform femininity to achieve it. As in her male disguise, her femininity involves the self-conscious, italicized donning of the markers of gender rather than the unveiling of the naked truth. It is not a "real" alternative to her dishonest masculinity but a parallel identity, performed in costume and before an audience. There could hardly be a more graphic illustration of Riviere's formulation of femininity—even "normal" femininity—as masquerade. Thus, the novel both offers Eliza's body as the naked truth about her gender and simultaneously implies that gender enjoys no such absolute grounding. The image of a person surrounded by the trappings of both masculinity and femininity, and making her selection—of a woman dressed like a woman in the midst of her bisexual boudoir—suggests an arbitrariness about gender identity, as if it were simply a style. When she changes her clothes, Eliza tries on both masculinity and femininity, depending on which suits her purposes at the moment. She seems to choose a gendered self from a range of available signifiers, revealing a single gender identity as a temporary point of focus amid more fluid possibilities.

And, as in descriptions of the principal boy, the gender identities which are "so strangely conmingled . . . pell mell" in Eliza's boudoir engage each other in her self-understanding as well. When Eliza stands before the mirror dressed as a woman, it seems that her cross-dressing has heightened her femininity, has made it a role as well, and, in doing so, makes it into a sensual pleasure—an eroticism present in many such masquerades (Garber 1992). In Eliza's case, this eroticism extends to her re-appropriated femininity as well. She "loves" and even "adores" the accoutrements of women (Reynolds 1848, 1:19), which she enjoys in the "soft voluptuousness" of her private, perfumed boudoir (1:18). The pleasures of womanliness are enhanced when they are denaturalized. When it enters the realm of representation, the body realizes its erotic potential; it is intensified and objectified so that it can be better and more consciously enjoyed.

Eliza's male masquerade is discovered in the nick of time, by the police and the law courts, social authorities who implicitly discipline and punish her gender fraud as well as her economic one. The formulas of the detective story and the courtroom drama, each representing the quest for a single truth, appear to shut down the possibilities of her masquerade and deny its fluid notion of identity. Her appearance in court returns her to her proper place as a true woman: tastefully and unambiguously dressed, her "moist red lips" and expression of "soft and bewitching melancholy," she is the very picture of feminine distress upon whom all eyes are turned (1:91). Eliza is sentenced to two years in Newgate Prison; upon her release, she returns, apparently unscathed, to her (relatively) normal life. For the rest of the novel, she appears as a woman, captivating an Italian duke and exerting her moral influence through many plots.

But the masquerade has not completely ended. Every time Eliza appears, her body becomes plumper and more luscious. Indeed, Eliza's come-hither figure threatens to get out of hand, as it were; her growing curves "gave to her beauty a voluptuousness that was only tempered by the chaste glances of her melting hazel eyes" (2:109). It is as if, after her early bout with gender ambiguity, her metabolism feels obliged to overcompensate. Or perhaps it would be more accurate to say that masculinity is absorbed or sublimated into Eliza's body as "voluptuousness," a hyperbolic gendering and eroticization of her plentiful female flesh. Her masculinity was a performance, a masquerade, and the erotics of self-representation are borrowed from masculinity to supplement and italicize her "real" gender. Inflated to the bursting point with womanliness, Eliza is the Dolly Parton of *Mys-*

teries of London. Her career seems to take her from male disguise to female impersonation, exposing the means of by which gender is constructed and the limitations of its categories, which she overflows no matter what she wears.

Thus, Reynolds's deliberate citation of stage tradition theatricalizes not only cross-dressing but the return to "true" femininity, implying the performative nature of gender itself. And, reading *Mysteries of London* along with reviews of dramatic performances, we can see that, in particular and circumscribed contexts, Victorian ideology implicitly sustained several different "theories" about sex and gender. Whether or not cross-dressing as I have explored it challenged or subverted the prevailing ideology is another question. These instances did not constitute any official perversion, and, although they clearly provoked some anxious responses, they had no noticeable effect on the central Victorian discourses of gender: conduct books, medical texts, journalistic constructions of the Woman Question. Instead, in their very local manifestations, they reveal the "give" in ideology when, seeking to rationalize gender anomalies, writers momentarily and strategically change the rules of the game.

References

Athenaeum. 1846. January 4.
Barnett, Dine. 1987. *The art of gesture: The practices and principles of 18th-century acting.* Heidelberg: Carl Winter.
Butler, Judith. 1993. *Bodies that matter: On the discursive limits of "sex."* New York: Routledge.
Davis, Tracy. 1991. *Actresses as working women: Their social identity in Victorian culture.* London: Routledge.
Fletcher, Kathy. 1987. Planche, Vestris, and the transvestite role: Sexuality and gender in Victorian popular theatre. *Nineteenth Century Theatre* 15: 9–33.
Garber, Marjorie. 1992. *Vested interests: Cross-dressing and cultural anxiety.* New York, Routledge.
The Mirror Monthly Magazine. 1848. No. 4 (December).
Morning Chronicle. 1848. November 15.
Ludlow, N. M. 1880. *Dramatic life as I found it.* St. Louis: G. I. Jones and Co.
Reynolds, G. W. M. 1848. *The mysteries of London* (first series). London: George Vickers.
Riviere, Joan. 1929. Womanliness as masquerade. *International Journal of Psycho-Analysis* 10: 303–13.
Rowland, Andrea. 1989–1990. Tilley and Menken: Male impersonators in the popular theater of nineteenth-century England. *Theatre Annual* 44: 11–20.

6

THE CHANGING FACE OF THE TRANSGENDER COMMUNITY

Mariette Pathy Allen

As a photographer and chronicler of the transgender community, I have focused on the re-interpretation of the community to itself and to the outside world. I have produced a body of work with a vision of people leading productive lives, replete with relationships with partners, children, friends, and co-workers, and I have offered an alternative to past images of the transgendered as lonely, sick, freakish, criminal, or lewd.[1]

This chapter, with the help of a few photographs, summarizes in a more formal way the rollicking journey of the slide show I presented at the First International Congress on Gender, Cross-Dressing, and Sex Issues. It represents images of transgender people taken over the past sixteen years, with an emphasis on recent developments in the community.

It is equally important for people who work with the transgendered to be familiar with the tremendous variety of people who fall within this spectrum, as it is for them to be aware of the evolution in the lifestyles and attitudes of this community. Some of the changes I depict concern political activism, new ideas about spirituality, increased visibility for female-to-males, the burgeoning numbers and variety of transgender gatherings, and the loosening of the bi-polar cross-dresser versus transsexual gender model.

Until fairly recently, most transgendered individuals grew up believing they were the only ones in the world to have the particular feelings and needs that they had. For that reason, my first few pictures portray the individual and his identity.[2] How does he present himself in his masculine image as compared to the feminine persona he creates? How do his clothes represent him? How does his body

311

image change? His facial expression? Which image is more self-confident? More at peace? Some of the later pictures present several individuals who are comfortable enough with their feminine selves to be able to play with that image, to vary it, give it moods, so that they are no longer limited to a single, or simple, image of their femme. I believe this is a sign of maturity.

A major change in self-acceptance occurs when the (usually closeted) individual is fortunate enough to come into contact with a local transgender support group or attend a cross-dressing convention. In 1980, when I went to Fantasia Fair in Provincetown, Massachusetts, there were few national conventions. Provincetown provided Fantasia Fair with a safe, friendly environment, in large part because of the city's large gay/lesbian population. For a transgendered person to be welcomed at church was to many an overwhelmingly moving experience. Being able to participate in a "pajama party" (a uniquely female experience), model in a fashion show, perform as a woman on stage, and attend workshops where the emphasis was on the improvement of their skills and development of greater understanding of their "femme side" were tremendous antidotes to lifelong guilt and shame.

Other cross-dressing conventions held earlier were usually held at hotels in rural retreats. Within the hotel, there was little mixing with other guests, and when participants went into the city for shopping or other reasons, it was on a bus, as a group. In effect, the convention was a giant, cozy closet, where most of those who attended were self-defined heterosexual cross-dressers.

Over the past fifteen years, the numbers, variety, and locations of conventions have grown tremendously. Although some conventions are very carefully hidden from the public, many inform the media in advance of the convention in the hope that their stories will educate the public and reach local transgendered people who might still be isolated. In recent years, a downtown hotel location is likely, making interaction with the public more casual, and sight-seeing easier.

Because there are now so many conventions, some have come to specialize. "Southern Comfort" focuses on transsexuals and transgendered people, with the recent addition of a strong female-to-male presence. The summer of 1995 witnessed the first convention of just for female-to-males and their partners. "Spice," a conference held in the summer (the worst time of the year for crossdressing), is limited to female partners of cross-dressers; their husbands may only attend "in drag." The highlights of "The Texas T.," which caters to couples, is the "renewal of vows" ceremony at which both members of the couple may dress as they choose while expressing their vows. The annual "Transgendered Law Conference" seeks to involve as many lawyers as possible from within and outside of the community to work on changing laws that discriminate against the transgendered.

Paul

Paul as Constance

Pajama party at a convention for cross-dressers

"Daddy" Chrysis with daughter Nicole

James, a female-to-male transsexual

Members of "Camp Trans" (All photographs © Mariette Pathy Allen.)

Parallel to the growth in transgender gatherings has come the growth in self-acceptance of the individual. He emerges gradually from complete isolation to communication with his partner, children, other family members, friends, and in some cases, even co-workers or the general public, via the media. This enormous trip out of the closet sometimes occurs within only a few years of active cross-dressing, and may range from a traumatic to a giddy, euphoric experience, and anything in between. Some experience all these feelings in a single conference. This struggle over issues of identity and self-acceptance is not unique to the transgendered: it occurs to many of us as we attempt to come to terms with whatever haunts us.

Once free of their "deepest, darkest secret," some look for the next step in the journey out of themselves and into the world. Many of those who have solved their own issues feel a need to help other transgendered people and empathy turns to action. For others, action substitutes for self-acceptance and is used as an outlet for "sustained tantrum."

Political activism provides the opportunity for the formation of new alliances. People who spent years working to define (and separate) themselves, now look for common goals and mutual benefits in allying with the whole transgender spectrum: cross-dresser, transgenderist, transsexual, drag artist, et al. Some look beyond the United States and start thinking globally, traveling to Europe for transgender events, or attempting to connect with transgendered people in parts of the world where being transgendered may prove to be fatal.

After years of depending on gay and lesbian bars, restaurants, discos, and drag shows as safe havens, while at the same time often expressing discomfort with the "lifestyle" in these safe places, transgendered people are attempting more and more to build bridges with the gay/lesbian/bisexual community. Both the drag and the gay communities claim the Stonewall Riots. In fact, a transgender group threatened to picket the New York City Pride Parade of 1995, if transgendered people were not included in the parade banner group. They also objected to the separation of the drag and transgender contingents in the parade line-up. In other areas, transsexual and intersexed women have attempted to participate in "Womyn's" festivals. Other transgendered people feel strong alliance with feminists and join organizations like the National Organization of Women (NOW).

Lagging many years behind the Women's, the Gay, and the Civil Rights Movements in organizing for political change, the transgender community, by forming alliances, is learning and growing quickly. Groups of transgendered people have fought successfully against local laws that discriminate against gays and transgendered and assembled in Washington D.C. in October 1995, to lobby their congresspeople for health-care reform and the passage of federal antidiscrimination laws that would include them.

Unfortunately, the transgender community is particularly vulnerable in the area of negative publicity or misrepresentation by the media. Their visibility tends to make them an easy target if only because their very existence brings into question the meaning of identity and the logic of opposites. Inevitably many people tend to react with fear or titillation. From the movie *Psycho* to the average talk show, there is almost no escape from negative attitudes. In addition, those members of the community who have not yet gained self-acceptance, and confuse attention with acceptance (or even admiration), bend over backward to participate in whatever media morsel is offered, or collude in other ways with negativity.

Since many transgendered people cannot, and others choose not to, hide who they are, the issue of "passing" has become political. A small, activist group, probably among the most "passable in the community," wear "transsexual menace" jackets in public in order to attract media attention to their causes. Growing numbers of transgendered people are reacting to media bashing by becoming media savvy, blitzing advertising agencies over thoughtless ads, learning to use talk shows to make their own points, and responding to newspaper articles by letters or calls. They publish books, start their own radio talk shows, create performance pieces. A transsexual artist, was, for example, exhibited in the Whitney Museum Biennial.

While some people confront the political status quo that allows discrimination against transgendered people, others question the appropriateness of religions that seem based on patriarchal values. The study of anthropology offers a view of cultures that recognize and, in some cases, honor and revere transgendered people as healers and shamans. Although it seems like a tremendous stretch of imagination to many, there are some in the community who practice Wicca, and others who see themselves in the long tradition of the "berdache." The study of Native American practices and healing circles has led to the creation of "Kindred Spirits," a gathering in nature, open to transgender people as well as other searchers. The "Open Door" group in New York City, led by a transgendered minister, meets every Sunday to create or find its own spiritual traditions.

The final development in the transgender community that I would like include was dramatically in evidence at the "First International Congress": the partnership of the transgendered and the doctors, therapists, scholars, and others who work with them. The vision of "consumers and providers" allows the creation of joint lectures and workshops such as the Congress and the first annual "Transsexual and Transgender Health Conference" held in April 1995. Others, I am sure will follow, inspired by these.

By refusing to give the "provider" sole or ultimate authority, the "consumer" hastens the acceptance of the transgendered (mixed) body as a viable alternative to the old polarizing choice: "transvestite or transsexual?" "Provider" and "consumer" dance a duet, creating a one-of-a-kind-person each time, and the body is transformed from battleground to *tabula rasa*.

As a "provider," my work with individuals involves creating a dialogue between the body and the mind or soul in the exploration of identity. An example: a cross-dresser stands in front of me, trembling in anxiety and joy: this is the first time he has allowed himself to appear as his femme self in front of another person. Later, we study the photographs, to learn about the woman who lives inside of him. The information that emerges teaches the man. When he cross-dresses the next time, more has changed than the surface appearance.

Just as the use of photography facilitates the individual's communication between his inner and outer self, so does it work in establishing a sense of history, or identity, for the transgender community. In presenting slide shows of the community, I offer it a vision of itself and its evolution. The vision gets absorbed in myriad bits and pieces and is reflected back as history. The empowering sense of shared history enables further developments upon which we can only speculate, which, in turn, will need the nurturance of new images.

Notes

1. See my *Transformations: Crossdressers and Those Who Love Them* (New York: Dutton, 1989).

2. I say "he" because most of my early work was with male-to-female cross-dressers.

7

STANDARDS OF CARE

Introduction

The role of a gatekeeper is never an easy job since by definition not every one can be let in. Those who are excluded are inevitably critical of the reasons given for exclusion while even those admitted are often upset at what they had to do to enter. For those seeking transsexual surgery, there are at least two gatekeepers who have to be satisfied. A person wanting to undergo sexual reassignment surgery (SRS) has to find a surgeon who is willing to do such surgery. In a less complex world, this might well be enough, but in today's world where liability insurance (at least in the United States) is astronomical, surgeons like to protect themselves as much as possible by operating only on those who have been recommended as good candidates, i.e., who have undergone some sort of psychiatric or psychological evaluation.

In a sense a good candidate from a psychological point of view is an oxymoron. How can any male in his right mind want to have his penis and testes removed and a vagina constructed or conversely how can any female want to undergo a hysterectomy, an ovariectomy, and the removal of both breasts, and be given a penis of some sort or another? We see nothing wrong with a person having his or her nose remade, her breasts augmented through surgery, or his penis lengthened, but sex reassignment surgery touches at the core of our concept of maleness and femaleness. No sane person would want to change, but sane people do. The best a psychiatrist or psychologist can do is to see if the client under-

317

stands what the change entails. But how can one predict outcomes? It is understandable that some professionals regard the task as awesome, and we know of cases where therapists have held up their surgical recommendation for years because they did not want to assume such responsibility. There are also good reasons for refusing permission if the therapist is convinced the client does not know what is involved. Some people who have undergone SRS have later become disenchanted with their new "sex" and sued the therapist or the surgeon for his or her participation in their SRS.

The difficulty is that there is also money involved (at least in the United States), not only for the therapist but for the surgeon as well. Some individuals want the surgery so intensely that they will literally pay everything they have to get it. In this situation, medical hustlers appear. We know of one who shall be nameless who, though having lost his license in California and been refused licensure in other states, simply did the surgery for anyone who would pay his price. He even operated on kitchen tables. When the police threatened to intervene, he simply moved across the border into Mexico where he recruited candidates from the United States. Unfortunately his surgery was not very good and he operated under conditions where infection was rampant.

We also know that clients often lie to their therapist. They know what answers they are expected to give, and there is an informal group of pre-operative transsexuals feeding them information. Though this might get them the surgery, it is not conducive to the best adjustment in their new life.

It was to set a guide both for clients and professionals that what is now called the Harry Benjamin International Gender Dysphoria Association issued standards of care in 1979. These have since been revised four times in response to the growing knowledge and changing standards for treating transsexualism. (See the Appendix for the 1990 version.) The standards are undergoing further revision now, considering how long a therapist should refuse to approve surgery before either giving permission or advising the client to find another therapist.

One of the standards that both sides tend to agree on is the willingness of the person seeking SRS to spend some time, at least six months, sometimes a year, in the anticipated gender role, and many are advising increasingly longer periods. They need to know and experience what the opposite gender does and how they are treated. During this period the subject might well be taking hormones and, in the case of males, undergoing electrolysis. Beyond this, however, there is nonagreement and even disagreement between therapist and the individual wanting SRS on how long the experimental lifestyle should be and how much hormones should be given. Still, in many places having the HBIGDA Standards actually facilitates the client obtaining surgery, and it certainly makes for easier public acceptance.

Unfortunately, we are still not fully certain of the factors involved in transsexualism and, as articles in this section as well as those in section 2 demonstrate, some of the early barriers were due to erroneous ideas about transsexualism. Fortunately, both professionals and past and would-be consumers are involved in drawing up standards, and as a new proposed revision is under study, the debate presented here is a timely one.

Results of a Questionnaire on the Standards of Care of the Harry Benjamin International Gender Dysphoria Association

Dallas Denny and Jan Roberts

There is strong evidence that transgendered individuals have existed panculturally and throughout history (cf. Ford and Beach 1951 and Herdt 1994 for cross-cultural information; and Feinberg n.d., Money 1992, and Roscoe 1994 for historical evidence). Ritual emasculation and castration have been practiced in the West (Roscoe 1994), and in the East (Nanda 1989), but only in the second half of the twentieth century has it been possible for large numbers of transgendered persons to change their primary and secondary sex characteristics and come to function in society as members of the other sex. This process is called sex reassignment (Green and Money 1969), and it has created a medicalized class of people known as transsexuals.[1]

Sex reassignment has been considered by some to be palliative, as it does not do away with the "problem" (a term which unfortunately presupposes illness or pathology), but rather eases the pain and suffering of the individuals concerned by allowing them to live in the other gender role (Meyer 1973). The procedure was once very controversial, and has been attacked by medical (cf. Socarides 1976) and feminist (Raymond 1994) scholars, and defended as appropriate in some cases by other scholars (cf. Money 1971).

Interestingly, the one characteristic shared by almost all of the attackers is that their knowledge of and actual experience with transexual people is limited or even nonexistent. To give but one example, Janice Raymond interviewed only fifteen transexual people before writing her antitransexual manifesto, *The Transsexual Empire* (1994), in which she concluded that transsexualism (and no doubt transexual people) should be "morally mandated" out of existence.

320

The obvious willingness of Raymond and others to use transexual bodies for political purposes while purposefully remaining ignorant about transexual people as human beings has made their voices, once very influential, increasingly marginal. The sheer volume of people who have successfully undergone sex reassignment, the popularization of the subject in the popular press and on television talk shows, and the maturation of the scientific literature have made it clear that sex reassignment is the treatment of choice for many persons with chronic distress about their sex of assignment. Despite the often-lamented problem with keeping track of people following surgery, follow-up studies tend to show high rates of both positive subjective satisfaction and objective outcomes by those who have had the procedure (cf. Blanchard and Sheridan 1990). The only study that showed "no objective advantage" (Meyer and Reter 1979) was so seriously flawed as to be discredited (Blanchard and Sheridan 1990); recently, one of the conspirators has admitted in print that it was a plot perpetrated for political rather than scientific motives (McHugh 1992; Ogas 1994).

As we approach the millennium, sex reassignment has become a realistic goal for those who are seriously unhappy about their sex of assignment and primary and secondary sex characteristics. That is not to say that it is the proper treatment for everyone with questions or doubts about their bodies or their social roles, but it is considered the treatment of choice in some cases. And so far as we know, this point has not been broached in the scientific literature, but we will put it to you here: Within very broad limits, it is the right of informed persons to do what they please with their own bodies. The ultimate decision to pursue sex reassignment should and does rest with the individual, and not with the mental health or medical professional. Only when the individual seeks medical treatment is it appropriate for the professional to serve as a gatekeeper.

Sex reassignment is not an experimental procedure. The hormonal, surgical, and other medical techniques that facilitate an individual's changing of social role have a history dating back more than forty years (Hamburger, Sturup, and Dahl-Iversen 1953), and can reasonably be said to have matured, in the same way that, say, the management of diabetes has matured. The social techniques of sex reassignment have long lagged behind, outpaced by medical technology (see Rothblatt 1994, for a discussion of this). However, it is clear that a paradigm shift (Kuhn 1962) has occurred, with the old model, in which persons with transgender or transexual feelings are viewed as unfortunate victims of a disorder, changing to a model in which it is the society that is seen as pathological (Bornstein 1994; Denny, in press; Rothblatt 1994).

Before about 1980, sex reassignment was available in only two ways: extralegally and extramedically, by purchasing services on the black market (often with disastrous results); or by going to a university-based gender program.

The black market had no rules and the gender programs, most of which were overly controlling and judgmental, required compliance with too many rules, and tended to turn away the majority of those who sought sex reassignment (Denny 1992).[2] There were, to be fair, a few private practitioners who offered ethical services to transgendered and transexual persons (Harry Benjamin was a prime example), but they were few and far between, and difficult to locate by those not privy to the transexual grapevine (Stone 1991).

To provide guidance to both practitioners and consumers alike, a group of concerned professionals came together in the late 1970s to form the Harry Benjamin International Gender Dysphoria Association, Inc. (HBIGDA). Named for Harry Benjamin, a pioneer in the field, the organization straightaway set about formulating minimal standards of care (Berger 1990).

The HBIGDA Standards of Care for Hormonal and Surgical Reassignment of Gender Dysphoric Persons were released in 1979. They consisted of a series of principles and standards that defined a professional ethic for treating transgendered and transexual persons, suggesting constraints on both the caregiver and consumer. They were and are a road map, as it were, to sex reassignment. As such, they have served admirably. However, there is usually more than one path to a destination, and the route mapped by the HBIGDA Standards of Care may not be the only reasonable one. Recently, for instance, the International Conference on Transgender Law and Employment Policy (ICTLEP) formulated its own protocol (ICTLEP Health Care Standards 1993), and the American Educational Gender Information Service (AEGIS), a national clearinghouse for information about transgender and transexual issues, is preparing to publish *Recommended Guidelines for Transgender Care*, a book by Gianna Eveling Israel and Dr. Donald Tarver.

The HBIGDA Standards of Care set minimum guidelines for access to medical procedures. They mandate ongoing involvement of mental health professionals (defined as "clinical behavioral scientists"), who provide authorization for medical procedures like hormonal therapy and sex reassignment surgery (SRS). The standards also require a minimum one-year period of real-life test, in which the individual must live and work (or go to school) twenty-four hours a day in the new gender role before he or she is eligible for irreversible genital sex reassignment surgery.

The HBIGDA Standards of Care have been used for more than fifteen years. They are widely accepted by helping professionals and are discussed and disseminated by the transexual grapevine. They have been revised on a number of occasions, most recently in 1990, and are currently being revised yet again. Dr. Friedemann Pfäfflin discussed the proposed revisions and asked for input in the same session at the International Congress on Cross-Dressing, Sex, and Gender at which this paper was originally presented (Pfäfflin 1995). However, the HBIGDA

Standards have changed relatively little in fifteen years, and, while there has been much grumbling about them from transexual people over the years, they have recently begun to be seriously questioned by transexual scholars.

In 1993, alternative standards of care were proposed by ICTLEP, the International Conference on Transgender Law and Employment Policy (ICTLEP Health Care Standards 1993). The ICTLEP standards were written without input from mental health or medical professionals. They consider it unethical for a medical professional who does hormonal therapy or sex reassignment surgery on transgendered and transexual persons to refuse a procedure to any individual who asks for it, subject only to informed consent and to the absence of counterindicating medical conditions. Quite frankly, in our opinion, they make very little sense as standards of care. However, as a transexual and transgender bill of rights, they make a great deal of sense, and they must be taken seriously as such.[3]

It is at the points of conflict between the HBIGDA Standards of Care and the ICTLEP standards that effort must be placed. What is the obligation of the caregiver to do no harm versus the right of the individual to self-determination? Why is access to hormones and genital surgery more tightly regulated than other medical treatments? Is it because of a legitimate concern about the well-being of transexual people (of course it is), or because sex reassignment violates cultural norms (of course it does), or because tight regulation decreases the threat of provider liability (certainly it does), or because the pathology-based model on which these treatments are based colonizes transexual people and trivializes our decision-making abilities? (It certainly does.)

In our opinion, the HBIGDA (that is, the original) Standards of Care, although far from perfect, have served well, despite having been and continuing to be used as roadblocks by some caregivers. We are frankly concerned by the ICTLEP (new) standards, which were written because of a supposed widespread dissatisfaction with the Benjamin Standards. Certainly, the right of the individual to freedom of his or her body and the ethical duty of psychological and medical professionals to do no harm provide fertile ground for conflict. Certainly, the wisdom of having special standards for transgendered and transexual persons is questioned by some in the transgender community, who find them patronizing and paternalistic. Certainly, much work needs to be done, and a reasonable starting place would seem to be to begin to examine the opinions about the HBIGDA Standards of Care by those who are most directly affected by them: transgendered and transexual persons. To our knowledge, no one has ever looked at the HBIGDA Standards to determine whether those who are most directly affected by them even know about them, much less how they feel about them.

Method

Since we consider the time ripe for a major revision of the standards, and since we were alarmed by the ICTLEP standards, and since we had access to large segments of the transgender and transexual community, we formulated a questionnaire which attempted to determine whether transgendered and transexual consumers knew of the Benjamin Standards, whether they have followed various standards, and how they felt about the standards. The questionnaire asked for demographic information and treatment history and solicited opinions about individual HBIGDA Standards and about whether the HBIGDA Standards of Care were seen as serving a useful purpose.

The questionnaire was included in a mailing of more than five hundred copies of *Chrysalis* (a journal that deals with transgender and transexual issues), as well as to various helping professionals, support groups, and publications. Several newsletters and magazines reprinted the questionnaire, and it was distributed at various support group meetings and to the clients of the Program in Human Sexuality at the University of Minnesota. The questionnaire ended up posted on several electronic bulletin boards (BBSs) and on the Internet as well. Completed questionnaires were mailed to our post office box, and over a period of several months, responses were entered into a MS-DOS database program called RapidFile.

Results

We are now ready to present our findings. Let us say that these results should not be considered final. There are a variety of additional analyses which could be done. However, we have learned from our survey most of what we wished to learn, and are unlikely to do further analysis unless called upon to do so.

We received a total of 340 completed questionnaires. One was discarded because it contained only demographic information. That left 339 questionnaires, of which 270 were from persons who reported having been designated as males at birth, and 69 by individuals designated as females at birth. This breaks down to 79.6 percent born male, and 20.4 percent born female. Because the terms male transexual and female transexual are confusing and are offensive to many transexual people, we prefer in the context of this paper to use the terms born male and born female to refer to the original sex assignment of the individual. This is in contradiction to the bulk of the literature.

The age of respondents ranged from 18 to 88 years, with an overall mean of

Table 1. Demographic Information

n = 339

	n	%
Born M	270	79.6
Born F	69	20.4
Total (Born M + Born F)	339	100.0
Born M, living F	163	60.4
Born F, living M	56	81.2
Total cross-living (M + F)	219	64.6
Born M, SRS	61	22.6
Born F, SRS	15	21.7
Total number SRS (M + F)	76	22.4
Born M, plan SRS	137	50.7
Born F, plan SRS	47	68.1
Total planning SRS (M + F)	184	54.3
Born M, plan or had SRS	198	73.3
Born F, plan or had SRS	62	89.9
Total, plan or had SRS (M + F)	260	77.0

	Age Range	Mean Age	Age of those with	
			SRS	No SRS
Born M	18–88 years	44.3	43.9	44.4
Born F	20–69	36.7	39.7	35.8
Total (M + F)	18–88	42.7	41.4	42.5

42.7 years. Mean age of born males was 44.3 years, and mean age of born females was 36.7 years. The mean age of those who had had SRS was 41.4 years, and the mean of those who had not was 42.5 years (table 1).[4]

What sort of people returned our survey? Well, mostly transexual. Of the 270 born males, 163, or 60.4 percent, were living full-time as women. Fifty-six of 69, or 81.2 percent of born females, were living full-time as men. That is 64.6

percent of the total sample. These people had made major strides along the road to sex reassignment.

Sixty-one of 270, or 22.6 percent of born males, had had SRS. Fifteen of 69, or 21.7 percent of born females, had had SRS. Seventy-six, or 22.4 percent of the total sample, had had SRS. One hundred and thirty-seven born males and 47 born females indicated that they planned to have surgery. This is 50.7 and 68.1 percent of total born males, and born females, respectively, or just more than one-half of the total sample.

When those who already had SRS are added to those who plan to have it, we see that nearly three-quarters of the born males and nearly 90 percent of the born females either had or plan to have surgery. This shows a great deal of commitment to the process of sex reassignment by the sample population.

How Did Respondents Self-Identify?

Respondents were asked how they self-identified as transgendered persons. Item 4 of the questionnaire allowed them to check off boxes for transexual, cross-dresser, transgenderist, or other. There was an additional space so that "other" could be explained. The breakdown is shown in table 2.

One hundred and eighty-four, or 54.3 percent of respondents self-identified as transexual. Twenty-eight, or 8.3 percent, identified as cross-dressers, and forty, or 11.8 percent, identified as transgenderists (someone who retains characteristics of both genders). The remaining 25.7 percent of the respondents did not indicate any of the three preprogrammed choices but checked "other," in many cases writing in their self-identification. There were more than forty terms used by respondents to describe the ways in which they identified themselves.

Knowledge of HBIGDA Standards of Care

Table 3 shows that 269 of the 339, or 79.4 percent, of the respondents had heard of the HBIGDA Standards of Care. Of these, 125, or 46.5 percent, had learned of them from professional sources (physicians; therapists; gender clinics; information services like the American Educational Gender Information Service and its predecessor, the Erickson Foundation; and the professional literature). These are listed in table 4. Seventy-five, or 27.9 percent, had learned of them from the transgender community (from other transgendered or transexual persons, at support groups, on computer BBSs, and through transgender publications). Of the remaining sixty-nine, twenty-three (8.6 percent of the 269) did not know or did not remember how they had heard of the Standards of Care, and forty-six (17.1 percent) gave responses like "book," "reading," or "library," which did not specify the nature of the material in which they found information.

Table 2. Self-Identification of Respondents

n = 339

184 (54.3%) ts (transexuals)
 28 (8.3%) cd (cross-dressers)
 40 (11.8%) tg (transgenders)

18 woman	1 female with transsexual past
8 female	1 human
6 male	1 human being
5 ts/tg	1 labels harmful
4 blank	1 man wanting to live/love with
4 ts/woman	breasts
3 man	1 Merissa
2 cd/tg	1 metamorph
2 tg/cd	1 normal
2 ts (non-op)	1 other
2 ts/cd	1 sex-reassigned
2 new woman	1 testicular feminization
1 androgyne	1 tg/bisexual
1 bigenderal (completely both)	1 tg/male
1 bigendered	1 tg/man
1 cd/sissy	1 ts/androgyne
1 cd/tg?	1 ts/gay
1 cd/ts	1 ts (tg maybe)
1 confirmed correct gender	1 ts/tg/cd/other
1 ex-transexual: woman	1 don't know
1 female-bodied man	1 uncertain

Table 3. Had Respondents Heard of HBIGDA Standards of Care?

n = 339

	n	%
Born M	213	78.9
Born F	56	81.2
Total, M + F	269	79.4

Table 4. How Did Respondents Learn of HBIGDA Standards of Care?

n = 269 respondents had heard of HBIGDA Standards of Care

Professional

Personal	54		
Clinics	30		
Info Svc.	29		
Literature	7		
Conferences	3		
Other	2		
Total	125 (46.5%)		

Transgender Community

27	Personal
25	Support Groups
11	Literature
10	BBS
1	Conference
1	Other
Total 75 (27.9%)	

Unspecified

10	Book
10	Magazine
7	Unspecified Reading
7	Library
6	Unspecified Friend
2	Personal Research
1	Television
1	Word of Mouth
1	College
1	Popular Literature
Total	46 (17.1%)

Blank/DK

5	Blank
18	Don't Know
Total	23 (8.6%)

Table 5. Respondents' Compliance with the HBIGDA Standards of Care

n = 339 respondents

How many respondents have had therapy for a gender issue?

	n	*%*
Born M, been in therapy	218	80.7
Born F, been in therapy	63	91.3
Total M + F, been in therapy	282	83.2

Number of respondents who had been to a gender clinic

n = 133 (39.2% of total respondents)

Compliance with the HBIGDA Standards of Care

Therapy is an important part of the HBIGDA Standards of Care. We wondered how many of our respondents had been in therapy at some point because of their gender issues. The answer was that 218 of 270 or 80.7 percent of born males, and 63 of 69 or 91.3 percent of born females had been in therapy because of their gender identity (table 5). The percentage was even higher for those who self-identified as transexual or transgendered. Of the 242 respondents on hormones, only 18 (7.4 percent) reported not having contacted a therapist.

One hundred thirty-three, or 39.2 percent of total respondents, had at some time contacted a gender program or clinic in regards to their gender identity.

Disclosing the Existence of the HBIGDA Standards of Care

The respondents reported that only about half (136 of 282, or 48.2 percent) of the therapists (psychologists, psychiatrists, counselors, social workers) whom they first contacted disclosed the existence of the HBIGDA Standards of Care (table 6). Sixty-five, or 23.0 percent of these respondents reported having told a therapist about the standards. One hundred twenty-five (44.3 percent) of respondents reported knowing about the HBIGDA Standards upon entering therapy for the first time.

Table 6. Data on Disclosure

(Who Told Whom about the HBIGDA Standards of Care?)

	n	%
n = 282 respondents who reported having seen a therapist		
Therapist* told respondent about SOC (Standards of Care)	136	48.2
Respondent told a therapist about SOC	65	23.0
n = 245 respondents who consulted a physician for hormones		
Physician told respondent about SOC	77	31.4
Respondent told physician about SOC	52	21.2
n = 257 respondents who had joined a support group at some time		
Someone at support group told respondent	153	59.5
n = 269 respondents who had heard of HBIGDA the Standards of Care		
Respondents who had told another transgendered persons about the standards of care	182	67.7

*The first therapist contacted.

Two hundred forty-five respondents (72.3 percent of the total sample) reported having consulted a physician for hormonal therapy. In seventy-seven (31.4 percent) of these instances, the physician told the respondent about the HBIGDA Standards. In fifty-two (21.2 percent) instances, the respondent reported telling the physician about the standards of care.

Two hundred fifty-seven (75.8 percent) respondents reported having at some time joined a transgender or transexual support group. In 153 cases (59.5 percent), the respondent reported having been told of the standards of care by someone in the support group. One hundred eighty-two of 269, or 67.7 percent of those who knew of the standards, had told another transgendered person about them.

Opinions about the HBIGDA Standards of Care

Did our respondents think the Benjamin Standards serve a useful purpose? Two hundred ninety-eight of 339, or 87.9 percent of total respondents, did think so. In

Table 7. Respondents' Opinions about the HBIGDA Standards of Care

Question	Overall n = 339		Previous Knowledge of SOC (n = 269)	
	Yes	%	Yes	%
29	256	75.5	216	80.3
31	265	78.2	224	83.3
33	245	72.3	209	77.7
34	298	87.9	256	95.2
35	116	34.2	97	36.1
36	103	30.4	87	32.3

Key

29. The Standards of Care require a ninety-day evaluation period by a therapist before referral for hormonal therapy. Do you think this standard is a good idea?

31. The Standards of Care require a one-year (minimum) period of full-time living in the new gender role before sex reassignment surgery. Do you think this standard is a good idea?

33. The Standards of Care require a letter from a therapist for authorization of hormonal therapy and two letters from therapists for sex reassignment surgery. Do you think this standard is a good idea?

34. Do you think the Standards of Care serve a useful purpose?

35. The Standards of Care require that the individual wish to be rid of the genitals in order to receive hormonal therapy. Do you agree with this standard?

36. Do you believe that breast reduction/contouring of a male chest in genetic females should be considered genital sex reassignment surgery (i.e., should require approval letters)?

fact, when we eliminated those who had no knowledge of the standards of care prior to our survey, 256 of 269, or 95.2 percent thought so.

Standard 6 requires a ninety-day evaluation period by a therapist before referral for hormonal therapy. Two hundred fifty-six of 339, or 75.5 percent of total respondents, thought this was a good idea. Two hundred sixteen of 269, or 80.3 percent of those who had previous knowledge of the standards of care, thought it was a good idea (table 7).

Standard 9 requires a one-year period of full-time cross-living before the individual is eligible for genital sex reassignment surgery. Two hundred sixty-five of 339, or 78.2 percent of total respondents, thought that this standard was a good idea. Two hundred twenty-four of 269, or 83.3 percent of respondents who had previous knowledge of the standards of care, thought it was a good idea.

Two hundred forty-five of 339, or 72.3 percent of total respondents thought that it was a good idea to require letters for hormonal therapy and SRS. Two hundred nine of 269, or 77.7 percent of respondents with previous knowledge, thought that it was a good idea. In their comments section, many individuals discussed the prohibitive expense involved with therapy, and especially with the necessity of having multiple therapists in order to obtain medical treatment.

We asked respondents whether they agreed with the standard that requires that one must desire to have SRS in order to initiate hormonal therapy. Only 116 of 339, or 34.2 percent of total respondents, and 97 of 269, or 36.1 percent of respondents with a previous knowledge of the standards of care, thought so.

We also asked respondents whether they thought breast reduction surgery/contouring of a male chest in born females should require approval letters from therapists. Only 103 of 339, or 30.4 percent of total respondents, and 87 of 269, or 32.3 percent of respondents with previous knowledge of the standards of care, thought so.

Discussion

Although our survey does not indicate the widespread dissatisfaction with the HBIGDA Standards of Care that is claimed by ICTLEP, both the solicited and unsolicited comments on the questionnaires indicate that at least some respondents were vehemently opposed to the standards. However, the overwhelming majority of respondents believes that the standards of care serve a useful purpose. Perhaps the "widespread dissatisfaction" about the HBIGDA Standards is instead the loud voices of a few dissatisfied persons.

It is clear from our results that most transgendered and transexual persons are in favor of some sort of regulation of hormonal therapy and SRS. It should be noted, however, that most respondents noted in their comments that they felt there are problems with the HBIGDA Standards of Care, and that further work is indicated. Many respondents commented that the standards lack flexibility and should acknowledge the differing needs of individuals seeking sex reassignment.

Our survey clearly reached the population most affected by the standards of care (those who identify as transsexual), and clearly shows that there is widespread knowledge of and dissemination of the standards in the transgender community. The data clearly show that therapists and especially physicians have not been as active in informing their clients about the standards as they might have been. No doubt some therapists deliberately withhold this information from their transgendered and transsexual clients, but these data are more likely due to the fact that many therapists and physicians do not themselves know about the standards of care. This is borne out by the fact that many of the respondents reported having told their therapists and physicians about the standards.

It is also clear that the survey population was highly compliant in regard to the standards of care. Most of the respondents had been in therapy (some, for many years), and of 242 respondents on hormones, only 18 (7.4 percent) reported not having been in therapy.

We were especially intrigued by the variety of ways in which respondents self-identified. It is clear that many transgendered and transsexual people are not willing to limit themselves to the "traditional" categories of transsexual and crossdresser, or even transgenderist, going to the trouble to write in their individual self-identifications rather than checking the pre-programmed boxes. For this reason, it is important that any future revisions of the standards uncouple hormonal therapy and SRS, making it clear that one need not desire or request surgery in order to be eligible for hormonal treatment. The relatively low number of respondents who believed that one should wish to be rid of one's genitals in order to have hormonal therapy suggests that many of the respondents already understand the distinction between transgenderism and transsexualism. We believe that as this distinction becomes more clear, more members of both the transgender and professional community will come to realize that genital surgery is not the inevitable goal of sex reassignment.

A relatively low percentage of respondents agreed that breast reduction/contouring of a male chest in persons born with female bodies should be considered genital sex reassignment surgery. Comments indicated that some respondents strongly feel that this standard is the result of objectification of the female body, and that it should be removed or rewritten.

In the past, Jude Patton was the "consumer" representative on the HBIGDA Board of Directors. There are currently not, to our knowledge, any transgendered or transsexual persons on the HBIGDA Board, or on the committee to revise the standards of care. Considering the large number of transgendered and transexual physicians, psychologists, and other professionals, many of whom are members of HBIGDA, in our opinion this shows a serious lack of judgment on the part of HBIGDA. One need only reframe this to imagine an analogous organization comprised of professional persons who intimately affect the lives of gay and lesbian people, or black people, but without gay or lesbian or black professionals intimately involved in the running of that organization, to realize that transgendered and transexual persons are still stigmatized by nontransgendered people, even by those who are trying hardest to help them.

Conclusion

The results of our survey indicate that our largely transexual sample believes the Benjamin Standards to be useful. This suggests that most transgendered and transexual people understand that sex reassignment is serious business and support some limitations on access to medical treatment. The written comments of the respondents, however, indicate considerable desire for changes in the standards.

Future revisions of the standards of care should include input from transgendered and transexual professionals.

Notes

In keeping with the emerging transexual sentiment that those who are transexual have the ultimate right of self-definition, throughout this paper we have used the word *transexualism* rather than the more commonly used *transsexualism*.

1. Bullough and Bullough (1993) have noted that the term "transsexual" was first used by Hirschfeld ([1910] 1991). However, the term did not come into common usage until after the publication in 1966 of Harry Benjamin's *The Transsexual Phenomenon*.

2. The first author had a personal experience with one of these clinics. In 1979, she (then he) applied to the Gender Identity Clinic at Vanderbilt University, asking for sex reassignment. After evaluation, she was told by Dr. Embry McKee that since she had a history of being able to function in the male role (i.e., she had finished college and graduate school and had a respectable job) and since her primary erotic attraction had been toward women, the clinic would not help her to feminize herself; they would not offer hormonal therapy or surgery. Dr. McKee offered no alternatives except for her to relocate to San Francisco, where there was another gender program, and where, he let it be known, she would likely be told the same thing.

3. This is not to denigrate the spirit in which the ICTLEP standards were formulated, or the excellent things that ICTLEP does. The ICTLEP has done groundbreaking work in

the areas of law and employment policy, and their concerns about gatekeeping and their belief in the autonomy of the individual are valid.

4. We have not done statistical analyses of these data for several reasons. First, we feel that they are clear as presented, without statistical manipulation (as were Pavlov's [1926] data, which were similarly presented). Second, as applied behavioral analysts, we are aware that statistical analyses are often unwarranted, and needlessly complicate articles such as this, while adding very little to (and sometimes even obfuscating) the understanding of the phenomenon being studied. Is it really critical in this context to know whether the less-than-one-year age difference between respondents who have and have not had SRS are significant beyond the .05 level? We think not.

References

Benjamin, H. 1966. *The transsexual phenomenon: A scientific report on transsexualism and sex con version in the human male and female.* New York: Julian Press. Currently available in reprinted form from The Human Outreach and Achievement Institute, 405 Western Avenue, Ste. 345, South Portland, Maine 04106.

Berger, J. C., et al. 1990. *Standards of care for the hormonal and surgical sex reassignment of gender dysphoric persons.* Harry Benjamin International Gender Dysphoria Association, P.O. Box 1718, Sonoma, California 95476.

Blanchard, R., and P. M. Sheridan. 1990. Gender reorientation and psychosocial adjustment. In *Clinical management of gender identity disorders in children and adults*, edited by R. Blanchard and B. W. Steiner, 159–89. Washington, D.C.: American Psychiatric Press.

Bornstein, K. 1994. *Gender outlaw: On men, women and the rest of us.* New York: Routledge.

Bullough, V. L., and B. Bullough. 1993. *Cross dressing, sex, and gender.* Philadelphia: University of Pennsylvania Press.

Denny, D. 1992. The politics of diagnosis and a diagnosis of politics: The university-affiliated gender clinics, and how they failed to meet the needs of transsexual people. *Chrysalis Quarterly* 1, no. 3: 9–20.

———. 1997. Transgender: Some historical, cross-cultural, and contemporary models and methods of coping and treatment. In *Gender Blending*, edited by Bonnie Bullough, Vern Bullough, and James Elias, 33–47. Amherst, N.Y.: Prometheus Books.

Feinberg, L. N.d.. *Transgender liberation: A movement whose time has come.* World View Forum, 55 W. 17th St., 5th Floor, New York, New York 10011.

Ford, C. S., and F. A. Beach. 1951. *Patterns of sexual behavior.* New York: W. W. Norton.

Green, R., and J. Money. 1969. *Transsexualism and sex reassignment.* Baltimore: The Johns Hopkins University Press.

Hamburger, C., G. K. Stürup, and E. Dahl-Iversen. 1953. Transvestism: Hormonal, psychiatric, and surgical treatment. *Journal of the American Medical Association* 12, no. 6: 391–96.

Herdt, G., ed. 1994. *Third sex, third gender: Beyond sexual dimorphism in culture and history.* New York: Zone Books.

International Conference on Transgender Law and Employment Policy, Inc. 1993. *Health Care Standards.* Available from ICTLEP, 5707 Firenza Street, Houston, Texas 77035-5515.

Hirschfeld, M. [1910] 1991. *Transvestites: The erotic drive to cross-dress.* Translated by Michael Lombardi-Nash. Amherst, N.Y.: Prometheus Books.

Kuhn, T. S. 1962. *The structure of scientific revolutions.* Chicago: The University of Chicago.

McHugh, P. R. 1992. Psychiatric misadventures. *American Scholar* 61, no. 4: 497–510.

Meyer, J. K. 1973. Some thoughts on nosology and motivation among "transsexuals." In *Proceedings of the second interdisciplinary symposium on gender dysphoria syndrome,* edited by D. Laub and P. Gandy, 31–33. Stanford, Calif.: Stanford University Medical Center.

Meyer, J. K., and D. Reter. 1979. Sex reassignment: Follow-up. *Archives of General Psychiatry* 36, no. 9: 1010–15.

Money, J. 1971. What are your feelings toward sex-change surgery? *Medical Aspects of Human Sexuality* 5, no. 6: 135.

———. 1992. Transsexualism and homosexuality in Sanskrit: 2.5 millennia of Ayurvedic sexology. *Gender Dysphoria* 1, no. 2: 32–34.

Nanda, S. 1989. *Neither man nor woman: The Hijras of India.* Belmont, Calif.: Wadsworth Publishing.

Ogas, O. 1994. Spare parts: New information reignites a controversy surrounding the Hopkins gender identity clinic. *Baltimore City Paper,* March 9: cover, 10–15.

Pavlov, I. P. 1926. *Conditioned reflexes: An investigation of the physiological activity of the cerebral cortex.* Translated by G. V. Anrep. New York: Dover Publications, Inc.

Pfäfflin, F. 1995. Revision of Standards of Care in progress. Paper presented at the International Congress on Cross-Dressing, Gender, and Sex Issues, Van Nuys, Calif., 24–26 February 1995.

Raymond, J. 1994. *The transsexual empire: The making of a she-male.* Boston: Beacon Press, 1979. Reprint, New York: Teacher's College Press.

Roscoe, W. 1994. Priests of the goddess: Gender transgression in the Ancient World. Presented at the 109th Annual Meeting of the American Historical Association, San Francisco, Calif.

Rothblatt, M. 1994. *The apartheid of sex: A manifesto on the freedom of gender.* New York: Crown Publishers.

Socarides, C. W. 1976. Beyond sexual freedom: Clinical fallout. *American Journal of Psychotherapy* 30, no. 3: 385–97.

Stone, S. 1991. The empire strikes back: A posttranssexual manifesto. In *Body guards: The cultural politics of gender ambiguity,* edited by J. Epstein and K. Straub, 280–304. New York: Routledge.

Revision of the Harry Benjamin Standards of Care in Progress

Friedemann Pfäfflin

The late Paul Walker, founding president of the Harry Benjamin International Gender Dysphoria Association, Inc., Jack Berger, Richard Green, Don Laub, Charles Reynolds, Jr., and Leo Wollman have to be credited for having achieved a consensus on minimal requirements for the indication of hormonal and surgical sex reassignment, which was accepted at the Sixth Gender Dysphoria Symposium in San Diego, California, sixteen years ago in February 1979, and which were named the Harry Benjamin Standards of Care. After revisions in 1980, 1981, 1983, and 1990, these standards are now under revision again. I coordinated a committee that prepared a new draft that was approved by the membership at the Fourteenth Harry Benjamin International Gender Dysphoria Symposium in Germany in September 1995. Still, this discussion is pertinent.

As we have heard in many discussions at this conference, quite a few people are dissatisfied with the Harry Benjamin Standards, but there seemed to be more who are satisfied, and I am pleased to hear that. Once, when inviting people to give their comments on the Harry Benjamin Standards, I received a consumer's letter saying: "The requirement of real-life-test is an unreasonable and even irresponsible imposition by the Harry Benjamin International Gender Dysphoria Association." The writer addressed one of the most controversial control and boundary aspects.

In contrast, I think the Harry Benjamin Standards are useful and a necessary instrument to promote cross-gender living on an international platform. In discussions with beginners in transsexualism and the transgender business, it is easily forgotten that without the Harry Benjamin Standards of Care, hormonal and surgical treatment and the legal acknowledgment of the new gender status for those who need it would never have been achieved in many countries of the world. This is so because they include boundaries and control issues. The United States may be the place where it is easiest to cross-live, to get hormones, and to get surgery. This is often forgotten. I just want to remind you of the Islamic countries. Some ten years ago two patients arrived from Teheran with a letter of recommendation from the University of Teheran. That was still in the times of the Ayatollah Khomeini, and the letter said that these two people had cross-lived for five years, had hormone treatment, had all the evaluations, but could not be operated on in their country. The letter also stated that they would not be able to return if they were not operated on abroad. You can imagine that a normal clinical team would not accept such travelers if they just dropped in without announcement and brought such a letter. But it was very helpful that the University of Teheran had applied the principles of the Harry Benjamin Standards of Care, and thus the University of Hamburg accepted those patients and operated on them. The individuals also returned to Hamburg one year later for follow-up.

You may also consider the situation in socialist countries, such as the former East Germany, where a government committee decided on sex reassignment surgery. The committee was not very democratic and nobody really could control it. In most of the Catholic countries, and some of the totalitarian countries, transsexuals, cross-dressers, and transgenderists still have great difficulties. A couple of years ago colleagues from Communist China visiting our institution in Germany secretly confessed that they had operated on the son of a general. They could not publish it because they had promised to keep silence about it. They had received special permission to perform surgery on this prominent patient, but the Party would never accept such Western methods. This has changed, with a lot of thanks to a growing body of international expert exchange. So, it is very important to have standards on an international level.

I was involved in the formulation of standards of care for the treatment of sex offenders a couple of years ago at a conference in Minneapolis, and the colleagues in Minneapolis included a paragraph saying that the death penalty is not an appropriate means to treat sex offenders. I found that ridiculous and suggested that they delete the paragraph, but they were quite right in emphasizing that we wanted to have these standards of care for an international audience because in many countries people don't know about certain standards of treatment.

Need for Revision

Having said this, I agree that there is need for revision of the Harry Benjamin Standards of Care for several reasons:

1. Knowledge of gender dysphoria, of transgenderism, of cross-dressing, etc., has increased tremendously in the last decade. A lot of the information given in the Harry Benjamin Standards of Care is outdated.

2. The Harry Benjamin Standards are somewhat confusing to read, with their thirty-one principles, sixteen standards, and some explications. Some of the explications are really principles and some of the standards are explications. They are too long and are not conducive to reading. The standards are also inconsistent in some parts.

3. A number of countries have issued legal regulations governing name and sex change, the requirements of which vary from almost nothing, e.g., in Turkey (at least as it is put down in law—in practical terms it is quite different), to very high legal standards. Some of these standards conflict with the Harry Benjamin Standards of Care.

4. The International Conference on Transgender Law and Employment Policy has issued "Standards of Care" of their own that counteract the intentions of the Harry Benjamin Standards of Care and that propose sex reassignment therapy on request only, which is still unfeasible in many countries.

Again, I want to emphasize the international perspective here because with such standards as ICTLEP's one could not petition parliaments of other countries to change their laws in favor of sex reassignment. The liberal-sounding ICTLEP recommendation attracts the support of many people who do not reflect at all on its consequence for the public health care system, and who do not consider that such politics may provoke a severe conservative backlash. At the International Congress on Cross-Dressing, Gender, and Sex Issues, in her paper "SRS Tomorrow—The Physical Continuum," and in her statement in the discussion, Nancy Nangeroni compared the access to sex reassignment surgery with free access to abortion.* I just want to remind you that in some of the former socialist countries in Eastern Europe, where abortion used to be freely available, the liberation has brought new abortion laws, and it has become very hard to get an abortion. We always have to consider the political context of statements. It might be appropriate to discuss SRS in this way in the United States, but it is not so everywhere in the world, and even in the United States one may not be sure that there will be free access to abortion forever.

Areas of Revision

Time is short, and what I can offer here is just an outline of the main areas of the Benjamin Standards needing revision, according to suggestions sent in by mem-

---

*See pp. 344–51.

bers of the Harry Benjamin Association and from experts in the field working in gender identity clinics and other institutions with longstanding experience in handling gender dysphoria issues.

To Whom Should the Harry Benjamin Standards of Care Be Addressed?

In the statement of purpose it says that the Benjamin standards are addressed to prospective consumers, to "applicants for sex reassignment," which is undoubtedly very important, but certainly not enough. Consumers should know what they can expect. It should be made explicit, however, that the standards were formulated to address providers as well. In the commentaries I received there were several complaints about colleagues who did not respect a minimum of criteria for informed consent or readiness of patients for reassignment treatment. I just learned that there are members of the Board of Directors of the Harry Benjamin Standards who do not do so. Generally accepted standards will safeguard providers against unfounded claims arising out of poor performance of sex reassignment procedure, actual negligence, of course, excepted. It will protect consumers against inadequate providers as well. In addition to consumers and providers, standards are important for health care providers such as hospital administrations, insurance companies, courts and other legal agencies that are involved in procedures of sex change. They have the right to know if a treatment is performed *lege artis*. For colleagues from the United States it may be interesting to hear that hormonal and surgical sex reassignment and epilation are also accepted treatments, provided certain criteria are met, in several European countries that are covered by Medicare and health insurance. This was achieved only because the patients appealing to the courts had demonstrated that they had been treated according to methods accepted by the scientific community.

What Diagnostic Areas Should Be Covered by the Harry Benjamin Standards, and Should They Cover Diagnostic Areas at All?

The DSM-IV has dropped transsexualism as a distinct diagnostic category in favor of the broader category "Gender Identity Disorder." This choice reflects the growing clinical evidence that a remarkable portion of persons presenting with gender dysphoria, and even with intense gender dysphoria in the sense of the classical transsexualism, will give up their wish to cross-live in the course of time with or without psychotherapeutic support. The tenth edition of the *International Classification of Diseases,* ICD 10, of the World Health Organization, a national diagnostic manual binding in many more countries than the DSM, links the diagnosis of transsexualism with somatic measures of treatment, thus suggesting that there be no alternative.

It is obvious, however, that there are a lot of transgendered people, and even classical transsexuals, who will finally give up their wish for sex reassignment surgery and live in their former gender role, or in the new gender role without wanting surgery anymore, or exist somewhere in between the two gender roles. With this in mind, it seems as if the authors of the DSM-IV have poured out the baby with the bathwater when they rescinded the diagnosis of "transsexualism" and replaced it with "gender identity disorder." Within that broader category there will always be a subgroup of persons with intense gender dysphoria in the classical sense of transsexualism as used by Harry Benjamin. The Harry Benjamin Standards of Care should address the diagnostic and therapeutic issues of this specific subgroup, but perhaps not the broad spectrum of gender dysphoric persons, in order to provide adequate and effective treatment.

When talking politically, when talking to employers, families, schools, etc., it might be totally adequate to picture even intense gender dysphoria as just a way of life and to fight against its association with illness and disorder. In the clinical context, however, it is obvious that almost everybody who seeks sex reassignment suffers or has suffered distress for some time due to his or her condition. When offering treatment, diagnosing is fundamental because there can hardly be an adequate therapy without a proper diagnosis. To associate diagnosis with negative discrimination seems inappropriate. It is not a fault or a defect if somebody suffers and he or she cannot be blamed for taking refuge in medical support. But medical support has to follow certain rules, otherwise it is malpractice.

Readiness

This is a crucial issue for consumers as well as providers and diagnostic clarification seems essential. The Harry Benjamin Standards of Care should not consider sex reassignment for persons who have not clearly shown intense gender dysphoria. To say that every applicant may make as many mistakes as he or she wants and it will be his or her own fault, as was said in one of the discussions at the congress, to me resembles adopting a nihilistic position.

Almost none of the national laws for legal sex change contains regulations concerning the minimum age. Clinical work with children and adolescents with gender identity disorders suggests that sex reassignment should not be performed on minors, but only on persons who have attained maturity. And that is what the Harry Benjamin Standards say. This age restriction is now debated in England and in the Netherlands, and in September 1995 there was a one-day satellite conference bringing together people from the child and adolescent sectors to discuss this issue. I think it is very important, and how one should decide remains an open question.

The most controversial issue, not in the literature, but in clinical practice, is the minimum time span that should be required for experience in the opposite gender role before hormonal treatment or sex reassignment surgery should be allowed, i.e., the duration of the real-life test. The votes submitted up until now show a broad spectrum of choices, from leaving it as it is (twelve months minimum) to suggesting cancellation of this requirement to recommending that the time required be lengthened to two years. This is something that has to be debated. The results of follow-up studies suggest that regrets over SRS clearly correlate with poor performance in the real-life test, but this does not necessarily have to be like that; there are also exceptions. Some individuals see the real-life-test requirement as an undue imposition. Most, however, retrospectively acknowledge that it helped them greatly to have the experience of a long real-life test, even though they had opposed its imposition when starting their treatment.

It is hard to regulate psychotherapy, and the Harry Benjamin Standards of Care do not regulate psychotherapy. They are standards of care for hormonal and surgical treatment. Just as an aside, it may be mentioned that discussing the alternatives of psychotherapy and social support on the one hand, and sex reassignment surgery on the other, is outdated. The opposition of many transgenderists to psychotherapy is to a great deal due to such an ill-advised discussion of alternatives, which is often supported in the medical and psychological literature.

Who Is in Charge of Selecting Patients for Sex Reassignment?

Of course, it is exclusively and primarily the person himself or herself who will decide for sex reassignment. It is not the task of the counselors or clinicians to do so for the patient. It is not even their task to recommend such treatment; their task is primarily to inform the patient fully about the possibilities and risks of SRS. This information is very closely connected with intensive support during the real life test.

The qualifications of the person called "clinical behavioral scientist" in the Harry Benjamin Standards of Care should be discussed from an international perspective. It is an important and also difficult issue because the Harry Benjamin Standards of Care are very much adapted to the North American situation and mention many professions that either do not exist in other countries or are not legally qualified to refer individuals to hormonal or surgical treatment.

What Procedures Should Be Applied?

Hormonal treatment and surgical procedures are in a permanent process of revision and invention of new techniques or schemata. Restrictive standards of care may impede new developments. On the other hand, standards of care should include provisions against experimenting without consideration or against infinite re operations, the demand for which may reflect an acting out of inner tensions rather than an objective necessity. You may all know such cases.

Some teams still apply procedures in genital reconstruction that more advanced teams abandoned many years ago. Maybe it would be useful if the endocrinologists and the surgeons would issue additional standards of care reflecting the technical procedures of their special fields. I would rather not include these aspects in the outline of the general Harry Benjamin Standards of Care, which should only regulate (1) the access to sex reassignment for applicants, (2) the qualifications of those giving permission for SRS, and (3) the formal prerequisites to give permission.

Summing Up

The intention of the Harry Benjamin Standards of Care is to provide minimal standards for the best care possible and to protect consumers against providers who are not up to date. Standards are guidelines that have exceptions, just like all other rules. Janis Walworth's paper in this book* has emphasized that the practical procedures are often different from what is suggested in the literature. Everybody knows that it is very easy to bypass the Harry Benjamin Standards of Care, but that should not be a reason to abolish them.

I like the constructive atmosphere at this conference, although there were some very harsh attacks upon the Harry Benjamin Standards of Care that I think are not really justified. Some people may have had poor and unsatisfactory encounters with professionals in gender identity teams or clinics. The Harry Benjamin Standards of Care allow individually planned proceedings for sex transformation.

---

*See pp. 352–69.

SRS* Tomorrow:
The Physical Continuum

Nancy Reynolds Nangeroni

I will present for your consideration a single idea, a thesis. I will attempt to justify the thesis, and then explore its ramifications, including potential benefits and drawbacks. Few, if any, of the ideas in this presentation are new. Rather, this is to the best of my ability a synthesis based on the excellent work by others that I have encountered to date. Here is my thesis.

If a woman's body is her own, and she gets to decide whether or not to abort her fetus, then why is it that I do not have the right to decide for myself whether to invert my penis?

A woman's right to decide has been established for some time in this country. Yet if I wish to obtain SRS, I must undergo a process of extensive psychological evaluation and obtain letters of permission, as defined by the Harry Benjamin Standards of Care. Though this requirement is not set in law, the standards of care have the effect of law by providing the surgeon with a standard for defensibility against potential lawsuits. Even I would not be so foolish as to engage the services of a surgeon who ignores prevailing standards. The Benjamin Standards of Care rule the day, and they need to be changed. It is my body, and I'm the *only* one who *must* live with the consequences of the decision either way. Therefore it *must be my decision.*

---

*Sex reassignment surgery

Why Is There a Demand?

If we are to relax restrictions on SRS, we must first consider why access to the procedure is restricted. We also need to consider why there is a demand for SRS. Historically, our culture has erected enormous barriers between male and female through male domination of women and intensely polarized stylizing of gender. To allow flexibility of gender and sexual identity would be to breach this longstanding divide. Most of us were raised in an environment where male meant masculine, female meant feminine, and we have been effectively excluded from one or the other since birth.

Throughout history there have been individuals who transgressed gender norms, yet for the most part they did so in secret. The communications revolution is changing this. Today's media take advantage of our fascination with the subject. Mobility of gender and sexuality, in concept if not in practice, is widely accessible for perhaps the first time in our culture.

Meanwhile, our notions of what is proper with respect to gender and sex have been evolving, thanks in large measure to the feminist and gay liberation movements. Public acceptance of alternative perspectives is growing. Men and women are seeking better balance between the sexes. Barriers separating the two are melting away, slowly but surely. Personal freedom with regard to gender-determined roles is on the rise. Transgender liberation is, in the words of Leslie Feinberg, "a movement whose time has come." Its seed has always been here, but the environment is newly fertile.

Sex reassignment surgery is a relatively recent product of technology. It allows an individual to more closely approximate in intimate physical detail the characteristics of an idealized opposite sex. The identity of *transsexual* justifies SRS and helps provide escape from a burdensome role, and/or entry to a role that seems preferable. In some minds transsexualism displaces transgenderism altogether as the only legitimate cross-gender lifestyle choice. Elements of the medical profession have embraced this somewhat self-serving viewpoint.

Objections

There are a variety of objections to the practice of SRS. Some people feel that SRS is a violation of the body that should be avoided unless absolutely necessary. I cannot hope to justify desire for SRS any more than I can justify the desire for body piercing, tattoos, cosmetic surgery, liposuction, or extreme muscle development. All of these violate some sense of propriety, yet all fall within the bounds of individual discretion and acquisition of preferred body and role.

Sex reassignment surgery has less potential impact on my life than would the birth or abortion of a child on the life of someone else. The surgery does not change my gender; I have already done that without its help. The change that the surgery makes is so easily hidden, so personal, that very few people will be able to say for sure whether or not I have had it. Only those very close to me will really know. It is really not such big deal.

Some people would object to my SRS on the grounds of "morality" or concern for my well-being. Their objections, though, are essentially the same as those leveled against abortion, and just as poorly founded. I don't care how good your intentions may be, they do not justify denying my right to decide for myself. This is my body, they're my genitals, and it's my choice.

Some folks argue that post-surgical transsexuals are no better off then before the surgery. It has been observed that for many patients, the levels of post-op depression and paranoia were essentially undiminished, compared to pre-op levels. Some professionals reasoned that, since the surgery does not always seem to fix things, we should be more restrictive of who gets it. Some even go so far as to discourage SRS entirely. Their reasoning is flawed, though, because most transsexuals were routinely encouraged to violate their own integrity by lying about their past. Passing themselves as women forced them to hide their uniqueness and construct fake pasts. Their lifestyle required deception as a prominent feature of day-to-day life. Their paranoia arose out of fear of being found out. Their depression grew from the continued isolation of their intimate self. Their post-op blues were due to breach of integrity, not failure of the surgery.

As most transsexuals learn sooner or later, the surgery is a cosmetic change that can be helpful in some ways, but that cannot by itself change some aspects of one's mental state, including paranoia and depression.

Ramifications

If we make the decision to have SRS the right and responsibility of the individual, certain things are bound to occur. Probably the most obvious, and most feared, is that some people will undergo SRS and later decide that they made a mistake. I would propose two approaches to dealing with this issue: education and assignment of responsibility.

When a person *requests* SRS, he or she should be exposed to a *divulgence* of information about the procedure designed to highlight potential pitfalls and expose weaknesses in the requester's resolve or reason. Such information might take the form of questions requiring a response or an interview process. However, it should be made clear that the informing of the requester is not a test, rather a suggested part of the process of making his or her own decision. The requester would assume all responsibility for determining the suitability of the procedure for him- or herself by signing comprehensive waivers and release forms.

In support of an effective divulgence, surgeons should be required to do follow up on all patients and make resulting statistics known to *all* patients beforehand. Standards for such follow up should be developed by independent organizations such as the Harry Benjamin Association.

Despite careful education, there will still be those who regret their choice. Such is the case with all elective surgery. It is an accepted fact that regrets sometimes occur, and transient regret is not uncommon. The holding of SRS as a special case reflects, in my opinion, our discomfort with our own sexuality. Making a mistake with our organs of sexuality carries a special fear, because these parts themselves arouse fear for many of us. There are good reasons for that: we discourage learning about this part of our bodies, and far too many of us experience genital abuse by others. Our fear is understandable, but can be conquered by exposing it to the light of day and the treatment of reason. The fear that I might make a mistake with my genitals is no reason for denying my right to own my body, any more than a fear that a woman might abuse her right to abortion allows you to deny her right to choose.

The best teacher is experience, and her primary tool is the mistake. Success teaches little; failure teaches realms. I regret every mistake I've ever made, and yet, I would take back not a single one, including the terrible motorcycle accident that crippled me. Were it not for that accident, I'd probably still be cowering in a closet somewhere. Protecting me from that accident would have robbed me of what I sought and needed most, and relegated me to a state of even greater ignorance than the one that I currently occupy.

End of Insurance

A significant consequence of allowing individual choice will be the reclassification of SRS as an elective procedure. This will probably lead to the end of insurance coverage. Such eventuality will cause some serious problems for individuals who do not have the means to pay for the surgery, and who are currently expecting their insurance to pick up the tab. These people tend to be adamant opponents of de-pathologizing transsexuality, since doing so could prevent them from ever having the surgery.

I would propose two ways to help these people. First, we should recognize that some pre-op transsexuals need special help in developing the skills they need to earn good money. By focusing on a path to SRS via becoming productive first, we would empower them both to pay for the surgery and to be more successful afterward.

Second, I would propose the establishment of a fund for providing financial assistance to transsexuals. Clearly, such a fund could not satisfy all of the need, but it could reduce the obstacle for some, and provide a means for the rest of us to help these folks. By structuring assistance as loans, the fund could regenerate itself in time. Like student loans, this fund would provide a way for those for whom lack of surgery is particularly troublesome to defer payment until after their productivity is facilitated.

Re-Locate Pathology

If we are to vest authority in the individual to make her or his own decision, we need to accompany this with a revision to our philosophy. We presume that it is wrong to want to change sex or gender, so we bully and badger and pathologize anyone who so desires. Then, lo and behold, we find that lots of transgender folk are traumatized, so we're justified in pathologizing them. We're like the mechanic who convinces you that your car needs a tune-up, then leaves it running worse than before.

The simple truth is that it is our society that is sick. We mistreat each other, particularly our children, who cannot stand up for themselves against the overwhelming power of adults. We use our greater power to train them like pets, to behave in ways that we find satisfying. We give them toys instead of attention, lies instead of love. And we squeeze them into one of two molds, depending on whether they've got a penis or not. When they don't fit exactly, we figure we screwed up somehow. Instead of questioning the mold, we figure either we or our kids just are not working hard enough to fit in.

This is the pathology of a sick society. The sickness rests not in the individuals who sense discord between themselves and the mold, but rather the system that produces the molds. Let us recognize the mechanism that shapes our desires. Let us manage for ourselves the shaping of our desires. Let us end the unconscious manipulation that traps us in a system of fear and prejudice. Let us teach our people to appreciate our children, all of them, in their variety of self-expression. Let us teach our parents that good parenting is measured not in performance, appearance, and manner, but in autonomy, creativity, and smiles. Let us teach our children to appreciate each other, and to lose the fear of nonconformity that we've burned into their brains. Let us show tough love for all forms of bullying, whether by parent against child or child against child. Let us tolerate no violation of autonomy, period.

Promote Acceptance of Transgender Roles

Medically sanctioned transsexualism based on SRS, with no similarly sanctioned transgender or non-SRS transsexual option, skews the emerging desire of transgender people. The young person who feels such desire is blocked from exploring it by the fact of his or her body type. He or she comes to see his or her body as the agent of imprisonment, and SRS as the only visible cure. In other words, sanctioning of a non-op transsexual or transgender alternative will likely reduce demand for SRS in a healthy way. Today, many transsexuals are choosing to change some elements of their physical sexuality without undergoing SRS. It's time our helping professionals took an active role in promoting transsexualism and transgenderism *without* SRS.

It we accept that it is my right to decide if I want SRS, it follows that, if I do so, there must be some good reason. There must be some aspect of SRS that is healthy for me or I would not desire it. Likewise, there must be some positive force behind all transgenderism and transsexuality. We were not created by some cosmic mistake. We are a variation of the human condition that is normal and natural, part of the continuing health of humanity as a whole. We have a unique contribution to make to the world. Our uniqueness is something to be respected, for it contributes to the fullness of human expression and enriches all whose lives feel its touch.

If transsexualism and transgenderism are to be respected, they cannot be promoted as something that must be hidden. Rather, we must develop a respectable social role for those who change either gender or sex over the course of a lifetime. The notion of changing one's past is inherently dishonest and robs us of integrity, community, and a healthy role in society as people gifted with a powerful perspective. I and my "out" brothers and sisters are living proof that it is healthier not to hide. It is time for the helping professionals to recognize this simple truth and help us eliminate institutionalized paranoia by publicly declaring the health benefits of being "out." Enough causality, already. Let's compare efficacy of solutions.

Advantages and Drawbacks

The changes that I've described would convey a variety of benefits to both individuals and society. The most significant benefit would be the fostering of individual integrity and responsibility. The knowledge that our desires will be respected, and that nobody else will try to make our decisions for us, cannot help but buttress our self-esteem and confidence. The absence of a gatekeeper role will simplify our self-exploration by encouraging greater honesty with both helping professionals and ourselves. Removing the fear that we will not be allowed to follow our hearts will eliminate one more obstacle to clarity of desire. The vesting of authority in the individual will promote diversity while supporting the growth of personal dignity.

The recognition of the natural participation of transgenderism in society will facilitate social gender reform. More people will come to view gender as *bimodal* rather than binary or bipolar. The extreme polarization of our society along sex and gender lines will soften as gender display becomes more a matter of discretion than expectation. Sex and gender role oppression will diminish as mobility among the roles is facilitated. Our culture will see, for the first time, the rise of a spirit that transcends sex and gender polarity.

We are already seeing a new flowering of transgender and transsexual spirituality. The loosening up of constraints on the personal search for sexual and gender fulfillment will further encourage such activity.

Perhaps most challenging to our sensibilities, bodies that do not exactly fit the expected types will become more commonly visibly. Already, many people elect to develop breasts without ridding themselves of their penis, and some people obtain mastectomies with no intention of hysterectomy or phalloplasty. Also, many people are gifted with sexually variant body types at birth. When we lose our fear of body variation, and instead see a cornucopia of opportunity and diversity, it's easy to see a future unfolding of richly variant human sexuality.

A difficult aspect of this change might be greater conflict with traditional sensibilities. Such conflict, if ignored or taken lightly, could lead to hatred and acts of violence. Although it is clear that our European-derived culture is founded on a tradition of violence and bigotry, our tradition is not without its positive aspects. Moreover, there will always be those who seek solace in an imagined past and wishful beliefs. Conflict with such persons can be minimized by intercommunication with an approach of mutual respect and accommodation. As the old saying goes, you catch more flies with honey than with vinegar. As a community, we will have to be proactive in such pursuit, or risk playing the role of respondent to someone else's agenda.

Conclusion: Implementing the Solutions

We challenge our health services professionals to be astute observers of social change, and to design our medical, psychological, and sociological support systems to best fit the evolving needs of our people. The Harry Benjamin Standards of Care have served well as guidelines to caring for those needs. Yet, as with all processes, nature demands that life evolve to meet changing need.

So I challenge our helping professionals to act out of courage, trust, and compassion, for it is the spirit of our actions that guides our future. Have the courage to expand the vision of your practice, to recognize and nurture within us this nascent self-esteem. Trust that individual responsibility for self is the starting point for effective healing technique. Have the compassion to allow others to make the mistakes that they need to make in order to move ahead with their lives.

The day will come that we no longer sort our children by sex, when sexual polarity is no longer a boundary for restriction. However, this is not currently the case. To be born male or female today imposes on most people an entire set of expectations and restrictions based entirely on presumption and that may be entirely inappropriate in virtually any aspect. Under such a repressive system, with well-developed avenues for transgender and transsexual mobility, there's no good reason why any individual should not be allowed to have SRS if that's what she or he wants. For any person other than myself to exert final authority over decisions of what to do with this physical body is a violation of my personal autonomy. This is *my* body, and it is the one thing that I own from the day I'm born until the day I die. To paraphrase a famous American, I may not agree with what you choose to do with it, but I will defend to the death your right to make your own choice.

Sex Reassignment Surgery in Male-to-Female Transsexuals: Client Satisfaction in Relation to Selection Criteria

Janis R. Walworth

In the forty years since Christine Jorgensen underwent male-to-female sex reassignment surgery (SRS), thousands of individuals have presented themselves to surgeons, psychiatrists, and gender identity clinics requesting SRS. It is agreed that those who present themselves as candidates for SRS constitute a heterogeneous group and that not all of them should be approved for surgery (Freund, Steiner, and Chan 1982; Leavitt and Berger 1990; Meyer 1974). However, little solid empirical evidence or theoretical ground has been developed that can help clinicians predict which candidates for SRS are most likely to be "successful" (Benjamin 1971). Professionals who enter this field are nonetheless in a position where they must make these decisions, because in order to obtain surgery from a reputable surgeon, a transsexual must have two letters of approval from mental health clinicians. In this environment, a profile of the "nuclear" (Buhrich and McConaghy 1978), "primary" (Person and Ovesey 1974), or "classic" (MacKenzie 1978) transsexual emerged; the closer a candidate matched this picture, it was presumed, the greater the chances of a successful outcome after SRS (Lundström, Pauly, and Wålinder 1984; Randell 1971).

Transsexuals as a group are well informed (Stoller 1973) and highly motivated. It is not surprising, therefore, that as this stereotype was elaborated in the medical literature, more and more of the transsexuals who presented themselves as candidates for SRS fit the stereotype (MacKenzie 1978; Stoller 1973). This circumstance not only impairs the clinician's ability to decide who should be approved for surgery, but it also confounds research results based on presurgical interviews of these clients by clinicians.

Once SRS has been performed, transsexuals have no need to distort their personal histories to fit a preconceived stereotype. Therefore, a retrospective study was performed to determine how well post-operative transsexuals actually fit the profile of the primary transsexual and met other selection criteria commonly used before surgery. An attempt was also made to determine how honest subjects had been with clinicians who were in a position to grant approval for SRS. Several outcome measures were used in an attempt to differentiate more successful from less successful outcomes. Finally, correlations were sought between the pre-surgical variables and the outcome measures.

The Primary Transsexual

The profile of the primary, or classic, male-to-female transsexual includes a sense of inappropriateness about one's initial sex that begins in childhood (Benjamin 1971; Hastings and Markland 1978; MacKenzie 1978). Childhood characteristics found in one study to be most predictive of transsexualism are wishing one had been born a girl, imagining oneself as the female character in stories, and preferring girls' games and toys (Freund et al. 1974).

Primary transsexuals also experience gender dysphoria in adulthood, evidenced by a disgust for (male) secondary sex characteristics (Leavitt and Berger 1990), eagerness to part with the penis (Person and Ovesey 1974), a conviction that the patient is really a "woman trapped in a man's body" (Stoller 1973), and feeling like a woman even when not wearing women's clothes (Freund et al. 1974).

A prominent feature of the classic transsexual is lack of sexual pleasure derived from the male genitals (Fisk 1974; Leavitt and Berger 1990), lack of genital erotic focus (MacKenzie 1978), and avoidance of using the male genitals in sex or masturbation (Leavitt and Berger 1990; Lothstein 1979). It is believed that the true transsexual cannot achieve erection or orgasm during intercourse with a woman (Stoller 1973), that orgasm can be reached only by fantasizing that one is a woman, and that the transsexual must take a passive role in sex (Sorensen and Hertoft 1982).

The primary male-to-female transsexual is sexually interested in men and is not aroused by cross-dressing. Attraction to women and fantasies of lesbian relationships have been considered a contraindication to SRS (Benjamin 1971; Leavitt and Berger 1990; Lothstein 1979; Meyer 1974; Tsoi, Kok, and Long 1977). Interest in sadomasochistic practices and erotic arousal in response to handling or dressing in women's clothes have usually been felt to be adequate reasons for refusing SRS (Fisk 1974; Leavitt and Berger 1990; Lothstein 1979; Randell 1971). A single episode of cross-dressing associated with sexual arousal has been considered sufficient for excluding a diagnosis of primary transsexualism (Baker 1969; Person and Ovesey 1974; Stoller 1973)

Feminine behavior and manner of dress have been used as an important factor in selection of patients for SRS (Benjamin 1971; Hastings and Markland 1978; Lothstein 1979; Stoller 1973). Randell (1971) believed that candidates for male-to-female SRS should be weak, submissive, timid, and shy, and more recently Leavitt and Berger (1990) identified as most suitable for surgery those candidates who had more feminine sex-typed behavior.

Other Selection Criteria

Although not part of the psychological profile of the primary transsexual, the ability to pass as a nontranssexual woman has been viewed as one of the most important factors in determining who should be approved for SRS (Fisk 1974; Randell 1971; Stoller 1973). Benjamin (1971) believed that too many masculine features, such as a heavy beard, deep voice, height over six feet, and heavy frame, constituted a contraindication to SRS and that the best candidates were those whose physical build and general appearance were so feminine as to be a cause of constant torment.

Various aspects of social functioning have been included as factors in treatment decisions. The ability to support oneself has been used as a selection criterion (Fisk 1974; Ross and Need 1989) and has been thought to be an important factor in satisfaction with SRS (Abramowitz 1986; Blanchard et al. 1989; Wålinder, Lundström, and Thuwe 1978). Most investigators agree that criminal records militate against approval for SRS (Hastings and Markland 1978; Hoenig, Kenna, and Youd 1971; Randell 1971; Ross and Need 1989; Wålinder, Lundström, and Thuwe 1978). Serious abuse of drugs or alcohol is usually regarded as a contraindication (Hoenig, Kenna, and Youd 1971; Sorensen 1981; Wålinder, Lundström, and Thuwe 1978).

Mental health has been found to predict good outcome of SRS (Lindemalm, Körlin, and Uddenberg 1987; Stein, Tiefer, and Melman 1990), whereas psychopathic tendencies and severe feelings of inadequacy (Randell 1971), psychosis and severe depression (Stoller 1973), history of psychosis (MacKenzie 1978), immature personality (Benjamin 1971), multiple or intensive neurotic symptoms (Fisk 1974), and personality disorders, affective psychoses, and schizophrenia (Hoenig, Kenna, and Youd 1971) have been regarded as conditions that disqualify candidates for SRS.

MacKenzie (1978); Hoenig, Kenna, and Youd (1971); and Fisk (1974) regarded a patient's familial support or social support system as one of the main factors to be considered in making a decision to approve SRS, and Ross and Need (1989) deemed such support to be central to post-operative functioning.

Investigators agree that surgery should not be performed on transsexuals under eighteen years of age, and many are reluctant to approve SRS for those in their early twenties (Hastings and Markland 1978; Randell 1971). Most are also wary of approving surgery for "older" transsexuals, most often defined as patients beyond their early to mid-thirties (Lindemalm, Körlin, and Uddenberg 1987; Lundström, Pauly, and Wålinder 1984; Stein, Tiefer, and Melman 1990; Wålinder, Lundström, and Thuwe 1978). On the other hand, some investigators have had good results with much older patients (Benjamin 1971; Docter 1985; Randell 1971).

Outcome Measures

Outcome measures have focused on a wide variety of areas, including cosmetic appearance of the genitals after surgery (Lothstein 1980; Stein, Tiefer, and Melman 1990), functionality of the genitals for sexual purposes (Fisk 1974; Hastings and Markland 1978; Lothstein 1980), ability to pass undetected as a (nontranssexual) member of the chosen sex (Ross and Need 1989), criminal record (Hastings and Markland 1978; Hoenig, Kenna, and Youd 1971; Money 1971), acceptance by family (Hoenig, Kenna, and Youd 1971; Hunt and Hampson 1980), "appropriate" sexual object choice (Hunt and Hampson 1980; Lindemalm, Körlin, and Uddenberg 1987; Meyer and Reter 1979), socioeconomic status (Hunt and Hampson 1980; Meyer and Reter 1979; Stein, Tiefer, and Melman 1990), gender-appropriate job (Hoenig, Kenna, and Youd 1971), and psychiatric contacts (Meyer and Reter 1979).

The value of subjective data in the evaluation of transsexuals has been emphasized by Kuiper and Cohen-Kettenis (1988), who note that SRS can be evaluated only on the basis of subjective data because SRS is intended to solve a problem that cannot be observed objectively. Outcome studies that use external measures find more unsatisfactory results than those that rely on subjective evaluation (Abramowitz 1986; Lief and Hubschman 1993). The current study relies on subjects' reports of both their inner states and outer realities.

Methods: Subjects

Subjects were post-operative male-to-female transsexuals who voluntarily filled out a survey distributed through transsexual networks, including conference mailing lists, gender-related electronic mail networks, gender organizations, and participants themselves. This meant that the number of people who had an opportunity to participate, and therefore the response rate, would be unknown; however, confidentiality required that some names and addresses not be given to the investigator.

It was expected that this sample would be unrepresentative of post-operative male-to-female transsexuals for several reasons: Those who have maintained contact with other transsexuals would be more likely to receive surveys than those who have severed their contact with this community. Those who are financially successful would be overrepresented because they can afford to come to conferences and receive E-mail. Those who have been so unhappy with the results of SRS that they have committed suicide, been institutionalized, or become dysfunctional would not be available for survey.

On the other hand, this group would be diverse in ways that previously studied groups were not. They have not all had surgery performed by the same surgeon or seen the same psychiatrist. They have been subject to a variety of criteria for approval, and some may never have received approval. They are not limited to a small geographic area, and they may have had surgery over a longer period of time than other groups studied.

Materials

The independent variables this study focuses on are characteristics identified by previous researchers as important in making decisions about which applicants should receive SRS, as outlined above. Besides age at SRS and at first request for SRS, these characteristics fall into the following areas: history of childhood gender dysphoria, symptoms of adult gender dysphoria, gender role behavior, sexual functioning, erotic orientation, psychiatric status, social integration, physical appearance, and supportive relationships. Three questions were asked in each area and were selected to reflect each concept as fully and concisely as possible.

The questions used in this study to measure successful outcome of SRS were designed to examine patient satisfaction with the decision to have SRS, success in achieving their primary objective in undergoing SRS, alleviation of symptoms for which SRS is indicated, losses sustained due to transition, and improvement in functioning in areas of life identified as problematic before SRS.

Questions were modified after in-depth discussion with a post-operative male-to-female transsexual and pilot testing with two transsexuals.

Procedure

Subjects were informed about the purpose of the study, how their data would be used, the time required to fill out the survey, and how confidentiality would be handled. Informed consent was obtained from all participants. This study meets the ethical standards of the American Psychological Association.

Data were entered on a Macintosh computer using StatView + Graphics software. Correlations were sought using Pearson's correlation coefficient for ratio and interval data and Spearman's for ordinal data. The Mann-Whitney U test was used as a test of difference. P values of less than .05 were considered significant.

Results

Fifty-two surveys were returned. Thirty-six (69.2 percent) out of fifty-two surveys that had been sent directly to transsexual women were returned. In addition, sixteen completed surveys were obtained from people to whom they were not sent directly: five of these were via e-mail, and eleven had been copied and distributed by other participants. Forty respondents (77 percent) were from the United States, from twenty-one different states. Eleven (21 percent) were from Canada, with four provinces represented, and the remaining subject was from Finland.

Subjects had undergone genital SRS between 1976 and 1993. Eight had surgery prior to 1987, thirteen in 1988 through 1990, fourteen in 1991, ten in 1992, and six in the first half of 1993. One subject would not say when she obtained surgery. The mean interval between surgery and follow-up for the other fifty-one was 4.2 years (± [SD] 3.9 years; range, one month to seventeen years).

Pre-Surgical Variables

Mean age at surgery for fifty-one subjects was 41.1 years (± 10.2 years), with a range from twenty-four to sixty-five years. Subjects stated that they first sought surgery from ages four to sixty-two years, with a mean of 34.3 years (± 13.1 years; n = 49). Subjects' age at surgery was correlated with year of surgery (r = 0.45, p < 0.01), with no surgeries before 1988 being performed on subjects over fifty years of age at the time of surgery, and none of those before 1984 performed on those over thirty-five years old.

For most subjects, surgery was obtained within three years of first seeking it; however, there were three who first sought surgery before their teen years, all

Table 1. Distribution of Scores for Characteristics of Primary Transsexualism and Suitability for SRS

Total Scores	Childhood Gender Dysphoria	Adult Gender Dysphoria	Sexual Practices	Erotic Orientation	Femininity	Physical Characteristics	Social Functioning	Psychological Health	Social Support
0	4 (7.7)	15 (28.8)	5 (9.6)	3 (5.8)	0 (0)	1 (1.9)	28 (53.8)	10 (19.2)	2 (3.8)
1	11 (21.2)	14 (26.9)	8 (15.4)	15 (28.8)	2 (3.8)	12 (23.1)	14 (26.9)	15 (28.2)	2 (3.8)
2	11 (21.2)	10 (19.2)	18 (34.6)	18 (34.6)	14 (26.9)	11 (21.2)	7 (13.5)	16 (30.8)	15 (28.8)
3	7 (13.5)	9 (17.3)	5 (9.6)	9 (17.3)	12 (23.1)	19 (36.5)	2 (3.8)	8 (15.4)	8 (15.4)
4	2 (3.8)	2 (3.8)	10 (19.2)	3 (5.8)	12 (23.1)	7 (13.5)	0 (0)	1 (1.9)	14 (26.9)
5	7 (13.5)	0 (0)	1 (1.9)	3 (5.8)	8 (15.4)	1 (1.9)	0 (0)	2 (3.8)	8 (15.4)
6	0 (0)	0 (0)	0 (0)	1 (1.9)	1 (1.9)	1 (1.0)	0 (0)	0 (0)	1 (1.9)
Missing data	10 (19.2)	2 (3.8)	5 (9.6)	0 (0)	3 (5.8)	0 (0)	1 (1.9)	0 (0)	2 (3.8)

Note: Data shown are number (percent) of respondents; $n = 52$ in all categories except Sexual Practices, for which $n = 48$. Higher scores show more deviance from the profile of the primary transsexual and most suitable candidate for SRS.

Table 2. Areas in Which Subjects Lied or Misled Their Therapists

Area	Number
Sexual arousal in response to women's clothing	7
Sexual attraction to women	6
Preferring girls' games and toys as a child	6
Childhood wish to have been born a girl	5
Identifying with female characters as a child	5
Obtaining sexual pleasure from male genitals	5
Sadomasochistic practices or fantasies	5
Sexual attraction to men	4
Primary motivation for having SRS	3
Doubts about undergoing SRS	3
Abuse of drugs or alcohol	3
Wearing women's clothes when living as a man	3
Feeling like a woman when not dressed as a woman	3
Suicide plan if rejected for SRS	2
Experiencing orgasm during sex with a woman	2
Living as a woman for at least 6 months	2
Being ridiculed for being effeminate	2
Family supportive of transition	2
Attempts to remove own genitals	1
Unhappiness with secondary sex characteristics	1
Spouse or partner supportive of transition	1
Suicidal tendencies	1
Engaging in criminal activity	1

$n = 52$

of whom actually had surgery in their forties. Three others first sought surgery in their late teens or early twenties and obtained it seventeen to twenty-four years later. The mean time that elapsed between first seeking surgery and obtaining it was 6.5 (± 9.8) years (range, < 1 to 40 years).

Respondents answered questions regarding their feelings of gender dysphoria during childhood and about eight areas of their lives during the two years before surgery. Answers to individual questions were ranked according to the degree of approval they usually receive from clinicians, based on the literature reviewed above, and scores were summed for each subject. Results are shown in table 1.

All but three of the respondents had lived as women for at least six months before surgery and had obtained at least one letter of approval from a qualified mental health professional. Of the three who did not, one switched back and forth between living as a male or female due to an employment situation, one lived only two months as a woman, and the third did not obtain letters of approval.

When asked whether they had lied or given a false impression about themselves when talking to a mental health professional in order to increase their chances of obtaining approval for SRS, thirty-nine (75 percent) said they had not, ten (19 percent) said they lied about between one and six items, and three (6 percent) said they had lied in eleven to thirteen areas. The topics lied about, with numbers of subjects identifying those areas, are shown in table 2. The number of areas about which subjects lied was negatively correlated with year of surgery ($r = \pm0.41$, $p < 0.05$).

Outcome Measures

When asked whether they regretted undergoing SRS and whether they would undergo surgery if they had it to do over again, all but one subject said they had no regrets and would definitely do it again. One subject said she had occasional regrets and was not sure whether she would do it again.

The questionnaire attempted to assess subjects' current level of gender dysphoria using questions about satisfaction with reassigned sex, whether subjects' feelings were more typical of men or of women, whether their bodies matched the way they felt inside, whether they felt like frauds as women, and whether they had lived as men since having SRS. A complete absence of gender dysphoria was reported by twenty-eight respondents (53.8 percent); another nineteen (36.5 percent) reported low levels of current gender dysphoria; and data were missing for the remaining five subjects.

Subjects were asked to identify their primary motivation for undergoing surgery, and whether they had met these goals. Of the forty-five who had surgery so their body would match they way they felt inside, forty-one (91.1 percent) had completely met their goal. One of the two who had surgery so she could participate in society as a woman met that goal. The remaining five subjects partially met their goals. An additional five subjects had given other or multiple reasons for obtaining SRS.

Table 3. Number of Subjects Reporting Losses Due to Transition

Area	Painful loss	Minor loss	Total
Friends	18	24	42
Parents	14	10	24
Partner/spouse	20	5	25
Children	10	3	13
Other relatives	9	18	27
Community	8	13	21
Job	10	10	20
Profession	4	12	16
Income	11	8	19
Church	3	3	6
Sexual function	6	17	23
Residence	7	8	15
Privacy	5	17	22

$n = 52$

Subjects were questioned about losses suffered because of transition in thirteen areas; results are shown in table 3. More losses were sustained in the area of friendships than in any other single area. Many losses were felt in relationships with relatives, including partner or spouse. Community relations, job, income, and privacy also suffered. Notably, nearly half the subjects said they had a loss of sexual function; some commented that this was minor compared to the satisfaction of completing surgery, but comments from others were bitter. Two respondents added that they suffered a financial loss of savings because surgery was not covered by insurance.

Subjects were asked to identify areas of their lives in which their functioning before surgery was poor and to rate whether their functioning in those areas was currently better, unchanged, or worse (table 4). Of eighteen areas listed, subjects identified a mean of 8.6 (± 4.0) as areas of poor functioning, with a range of 0 to 17. Of the fifty subjects who identified at least one area of poor functioning, forty-nine had a net improvement in those areas.

Table 4. Change in Functioning in Areas Considered Poor before SRS

Area	Better	Unchanged	Worse	Total
Satisfaction with your body	44	0	1	45
Peace of mind	38	2	0	40
Overall happiness	38	0	0	38
Anxiety level	29	5	0	34
Self-esteem	29	2	0	31
Sexual satisfaction	20	7	4	31
Self-confidence	21	4	0	25
Ability to handle stress	17	7	0	24
Partner/spouse relationship	14	7	3	24
Belonging to community	16	3	2	21
Social skills	17	3	0	20
Spiritual connection	16	4	0	20
Career advancement	9	6	4	19
Job satisfaction	7	6	4	17
Quality of friendships	16	1	0	17
Suicidal thoughts	15	1	0	16
Relationships with family	6	3	6	15
Income	6	3	2	11

n = 52

Predictors of Successful Outcome

There were few statistically significant correlations of presurgical variables with outcome measures. Current level of gender dysphoria was correlated with feeling like a woman only when dressed in women's clothing before SRS (Spearman's = 0.38, $p < 0.05$), with physical build making it difficult to appear feminine (= 0.30, $p < 0.05$), and with deepness of voice (= 0.33, $p < 0.05$). The amount of loss sustained due to transition was correlated with lack of support from friends (= 0.33, $p < 0.05$).

Five of the fifty-two subjects scored suboptimally on more than one measure of successful outcome. All five had not completely met their primary goal in undergoing surgery. Three were the respondents with the highest levels of gender dysphoria after surgery. Three were among the five subjects showing the least improvement in areas in which they functioned poorly before surgery. One was the subject who felt the greatest amount of loss because of transition, and one was the only respondent to have any regrets about surgery.

These five subjects were compared with the remaining forty-seven respondents on pre-surgical variables. Significant differences were found for psychological health before SRS (Mann-Whitney $U = 40.5$, $p < 0.05$) and for two of the three questions making up that score: treatment for psychological problems other than transsexualism ($U = 69.5$, $p < 0.05$) and suicidal tendencies ($U = 57.5$, $p < 0.05$). Differences were also found in the area of social support ($U = 41$, $p < 0.05$) and in particular for support from friends ($U = 61$, $p < 0.05$). A significant difference was also found for abuse of drugs or alcohol ($U = 59.5$, $p < 0.05$).

Discussion: The Transsexual Stereotype

Most subjects reported a high degree of gender dysphoria in childhood, although few completely conformed to the profile. All three of the questions asked about childhood gender dysphoria were among the topics most often lied about. Ten subjects had missing data on one or more of these questions due to not remembering childhood feelings, which may lead to more fabrication of data in this category than in those referring to adult life.

In the category of adult gender dysphoria, the majority of respondents showed complete or almost complete conformity with the classic profile. One of the questions was correlated with current level of gender dysphoria, suggesting the possibility that the stronger gender dysphoria is before surgery, the more likely SRS is to alleviate gender dysphoria.

Over four-fifths of respondents had obtained sexual pleasure from their male genitals occasionally or frequently. Over half had had orgasms while having sex with a woman. Both of these areas were among those most frequently lied about. Most subjects fit the profile of primary transsexual sexual practices only moderately well. This finding is in agreement with the recent assessment by Leavitt and Berger (1990) that erotic pleasure in the penis among male-to-female transsexuals is more common than previously assumed.

Male-to-female transsexuals who admit being attracted to women before surgery have often been denied SRS. Those who have had SRS have been reported as rare cases (Feinbloom et al. 1976; Gottlieb 1978; Oles 1977). The 50 percent

Table 5. Sexual Orientation before and after SRS

	Men	Women	Both	Neither	Total (%)
Before SRS					
Men	6	1	0	0	7 (13.5)
Women	4	18	3	1	26 (50.0)
Both	1	3	9	0	13 (25.0)
Neither	0	2	2	2	6 (11.5)
Total	11	24	14	3	
(%)	(21.2)	(46.2)	(26.9)	(5.8)	

Above "Men / Women / Both / Neither / Total (%)" spans the heading **After SRS**.

Note: Number of respondents attracted more to men than to women (Men), more to women than to men (Women), about equally to men and women (Both), and not attracted to anyone (Neither).

who said they had been more attracted to women than to men before SRS and the 25 percent who were equally attracted to men and women in the present study are unlike figures previously reported. Current sexual object choice was reported to be different from that prior to SRS by nearly one-third of subjects, but the overall pattern was about the same (table 5). Lesbians and bisexuals may be overrepresented in this study due to the fact that subjects were recruited through networks; it is likely that heterosexual transsexuals more often cut their ties with these networks. On the other hand, sexual attraction to women and to men was frequently lied about, so the impression of other investigators that the vast majority of operated transsexuals was attracted to men before (and after) SRS (Leavitt and Berger 1990) may be based on misinformation. The strong attraction to men and lack of attraction to women described in the classic transsexual were present in only a few subjects in the current study.

Occasional or frequent sexual arousal in response to women's clothing was reported by well over half of the subjects, with some commenting that as transition progressed, this erotic response diminished. Over one-quarter of respondents had experienced sexual arousal in response to sadomasochistic practices or fantasies. These two areas were among those most frequently lied about, lending support to the contention that fetishism is underreported (Blanchard et al. 1989).

Only three subjects completely conformed to the expected profile, that is, were attracted more to men than to women, had no fetishism for women's clothing, and had no interest in sadomasochism.

Few respondents could be considered very feminine in behavior, and the majority conformed only moderately to the transsexual profile in this area. Most subjects held jobs that were not gender-specific; only three had jobs they characterized as unusual for a man. Nearly half had never been ridiculed or attacked for being effeminate. However, almost all had worn women's clothing some or all of the time during the two years before SRS when they were not living as women.

Other Selection Criteria

Regarding physical characteristics, most subjects felt that their physical characteristics presented a small to medium challenge to achieving an acceptable appearance as a woman. Two of the questions about physical characteristics were correlated with feelings of gender dysphoria after surgery, suggesting that masculine physical characteristics may interfere with the resolution of gender dysphoria after SRS.

The subjects in this study gave very desirable responses in the area of social functioning. Almost all were self-supporting and did not engage in criminal activity. Two-thirds said they never abused alcohol or drugs. Overall, more than half were in complete conformity with the demand for high social functioning, and only a few subjects had lied about this area.

The psychological health before SRS reported by these subjects was moderate to good. Most had not undergone treatment for any other psychological problem. Half of respondents had thought about suicide, but only four had attempted it during the two years before SRS.

Most subjects had a moderate amount of social support before SRS. Support came mainly from friends, much less from families, and very little from partners. Support from friends was correlated with the amount of loss subjects felt they had suffered due to transition, reinforcing the impression from the literature that social support makes transition smoother.

Age of subjects at time of SRS or at the time they first sought surgery was not related to any outcome measure. The correlation of age at SRS with year of SRS suggests that the upper limits of age criteria are becoming more relaxed, which would appear to be justified in light of the satisfactory outcomes in subjects in this study who were in their forties, fifties, or sixties when they had surgery.

Despite warnings in the literature that transsexuals often alter their histories and current profiles in order to obtain surgery (Benjamin 1971; Blanchard, Clemmensen, and Steiner 1987; Leavitt and Berger 1990; Lundström, Pauly, and Wålinder 1984; Meyer 1974; Money 1978; Pauly 1965), only 25 percent of respondents said they had misinformed a mental health professional. Two subjects volunteered that they had been rejected for SRS by the first therapists they had seen, and felt that their honesty was the reason. The areas most often lied about—sexual arousal to women's clothing, sexual orientation, sadomasochism, pleasure from male genitalia, and symptoms of gender dysphoria in childhood—show a sensitivity to the prevailing requirements for surgery. The correlation of lying with year of surgery indicates that lying is becoming less frequent, perhaps because criteria for obtaining SRS are becoming less restrictive.

Outcome

None of the fifty-two subjects in the present study had definite regrets about surgery, and only one expressed occasional regrets. This finding is consistent with those obtained in most other outcome studies, in which no (Hastings and Markland 1978; Lothstein 1980; Meyer and Reter 1979; Money 1971; Stein, Tiefer, and Melman 1990) or few (2 percent to 8 percent) regretful subjects have been found (Benjamin 1966; Blanchard et al. 1989; Kuiper and Cohen-Kettenis 1988). Pauly (1981) estimated that, overall, 5 percent to 6 percent of patients had regretted undergoing SRS.

None of the fifty-two subjects had failed to meet their stated primary objective in having surgery, although five of the forty-seven who endorsed one of the listed choices had not fully met their goal. This question has rarely been asked of subjects in other studies. Sorensen (1981) reported that 75 percent of a group of twenty-three transsexuals had achieved the state of mind at which they had aimed pre-operatively, although what that state of mind was is not made explicit.

Assessment of subjects' current level of gender dysphoria again showed a high level of success, with all forty-seven of the respondents for whom complete data were available showing absent to low levels of gender dysphoria. Of the pre-surgical variables investigated, only physical characteristics and adult gender dysphoria were related to post-surgical gender dysphoria.

A large amount of variation was found in losses incurred due to undergoing a change of sex. Some subjects experienced almost no loss and others, a great deal. No assessment was made of how much subjects had to lose before beginning the process of transition, so few losses in some subjects might have been due to not having much to lose. Degree of loss was correlated with lack of support from friends.

Finally, all subjects but one reported a net improvement in areas of life identified as areas of poor functioning before surgery. As in studies that have reported both subjective and objective outcome measures, a wide variation in losses sustained and change in functioning were compatible with respondents' satisfaction with SRS.

Five subjects whose outcome could be considered less than ideal based on suboptimal scores on more than one of the five outcome measures were different from the other forty-seven subjects in having a poorer psychological adjustment, less social support, and more drug or alcohol abuse before SRS. The measures of classic transsexualism were not different in these subjects. Age at first request, age at surgery, and physical characteristics were also not different in this group. Lying was not more prevalent in these subjects.

These five subjects cannot be considered to be treatment failures because most had no regrets about having had SRS and would choose to do it again. Thus, variables found to be significantly different in this group cannot be considered to be predictors of unsatisfactory outcome. Rather, these results suggest that improved counseling services and the recruitment of more support from friends, family, and support groups could help to ease transition.

Conclusions

Because the subjects in the current study are not representative of the entire transsexual population, conclusions cannot be drawn about how well transsexuals generally fit the stereotype often employed by clinicians to determine who is most appropriate for SRS. Although this survey used many questions similar to those used in other studies, its validity has not been tested. Only a few questions were asked in each area because of the broad nature of the research question; therefore, the results can be considered only suggestive and further studies are needed before firm conclusions can be reached.

Because there were no treatment failures among the subjects in this study, no conclusions can be reached regarding which of the components of the classic transsexual profile might be associated with success versus failure. However, in those areas where there was sufficient variation among fifty-two subjects with satisfactory outcomes, it can be said that deviating from the classic profile is not incompatible with success. Thus, considerable variation in the areas of childhood gender dysphoria, sexual practices, sexual orientation and other erotic responses, and femininity, as measured by the questionnaire employed, are not incompatible with a successful outcome of SRS. Furthermore, lack of social support, moderately masculine physical characteristics, and advanced age both at first seeking surgery and at surgery do not preclude a successful outcome. A reevaluation of the relevance of these variables to outcome should be addressed by future research.

References

Abramowitz, S. I. 1986. Psychosocial outcomes of sex reassignment surgery. *Journal of Consulting and Clinical Psychology* 54: 183–89.

Baker, H. J. 1969. Transsexualism—Problems in treatment. *American Journal of Psychiatry* 125: 118–24.

Benjamin, H. 1966. *The transsexual phenomenon.* New York: Julian Press.

———. 1971. Should surgery be performed on transsexuals? *American Journal of Psychotherapy* 25: 74–82.

Blanchard, R., L. H. Clemmensen, and B. W. Steiner. 1987. Heterosexual and homosexual gender dysphoria. *Archives of Sexual Behavior* 16: 139–52.

Blanchard, R., B. W. Steiner, L. H. Clemmensen, and R. Dickey. 1989. Prediction of regrets in postoperative transsexuals. *Canadian Journal of Psychiatry* 34: 43–45.

Buhrich, N., and N. McConaghy. 1978. Two clinically discrete syndromes of transsexualism. *British Journal of Psychiatry* 133: 73–76.

Docter, R. F. 1985. Transsexual surgery at 74: A case report. *Archives of Sexual Behavior* 14: 271–77.

Feinbloom, D. H., M. Fleming, V. Kijewski, and M. P. Schulter. 1976. Lesbian/feminist orientation among male-to-female transsexuals. *Journal of Homosexuality* 2: 59–71.

Fisk, N. M. 1974. Gender dysphoria syndrome—The conceptualization that liberalizes indications for total gender reorientation and implies a broadly based multi-dimensional rehabilitative regimen. Editorial comment. *Western Journal of Medicine* 120: 386–91.

Freund, K., E. Nagler, R. Langevin, A. Zajac, and B. Steiner. 1974. Measuring feminine gender identity in homosexual males. *Archives of Sexual Behavior* 3: 249–60.

Freund, K., B. W. Steiner, and S. Chan. 1982. Two types of cross-gender identity. *Archives of Sexual Behavior* 11: 49–63.

Gottlieb, A. 1978. Three atypical results. *Archives of Sexual Behavior* 7: 371–75.

Hastings, D., and C. Markland. 1978. Post-surgical adjustment of twenty-five transsexuals (male-to-female) in the University of Minnesota study. *Archives of Sexual Behavior* 7: 327–36.

Hoenig, J., J. C. Kenna, and A. Youd. 1971. Surgical treatment for transsexualism. *Acta Psychiatrica Scandinavica* 47: 106–33.

Hunt, D. D., and J. L. Hampson. 1980. Follow-up of 17 biologic male transsexuals after sex-reassignment surgery. *American Journal of Psychiatry* 137: 432–38.

Kuiper, B., and P. Cohen-Kettenis. 1988. Sex reassignment surgery: A study of 141 Dutch transsexuals. *Archives of Sexual Behavior* 17: 439–57.

Leavitt, F., and J. C. Berger. 1990. Clinical patterns among male transsexual candidates with erotic interest in males. *Archives of Sexual Behavior* 19: 491–505.

Lief, H. I., and L. Hubschman. 1993. Orgasm in the postoperative transsexual. *Archives of Sexual Behavior* 22: 145–55.

Lindemalm, G., D. Körlin, and N. Uddenberg. 1987. Prognostic factors vs. outcome in male-to-female transsexualism: A follow-up study of 13 cases. *Acta Psychiatrica Scandinavica* 75: 268–74.

Lothstein, L. M. 1979. The aging gender dysphoria (transsexual) patient. *Archives of Sexual Behavior* 8: 431–44.

———. 1980. The postsurgical transsexual: Empirical and theoretical considerations. *Archives of Sexual Behavior* 9: 547–65.

Lundström, B., I. Pauly, and J. Wålinder. 1984. Outcome of sex reassignment surgery. *Acta Psychiatrica Scandinavica* 70: 289–94.

MacKenzie, K. R. 1978. Gender dysphoria syndrome: Towards standardized diagnostic criteria. *Archives of Sexual Behavior* 7: 251–62.

Meyer, J. K. 1974. Clinical variants among applicants for sex reassignment. *Archives of Sexual Behavior* 3: 527–58.

Meyer, J. K., and D. J. Reter. 1979. Sex reassignment: Follow-up. *Archives of General Psychiatry* 36: 1010–15.

Money, J. 1971. Prefatory remarks on outcome of sex reassignment in 24 cases of transsexualism. *Archives of Sexual Behavior* 1: 163–65.

———, moderator. 1978. Open forum. *Archives of Sexual Behavior* 7: 387–415.

Oles, M. N. 1977. The transsexual client: A discussion of transsexualism and issues in psychotherapy. *American Journal of Orthopsychiatry* 47: 66–74.

Pauly, I. B. 1965. Male psychosexual inversion: Transsexualism. A review of 100 cases. *Archives of General Psychiatry* 13: 172–81.

———. 1981. Outcome of sex reassignment surgery for transsexuals. *Australian and New Zealand Journal of Psychiatry* 15: 45–51.

Person, E., and L. Ovesey. 1974. The transsexual syndrome in males. I. Primary transsexualism. *American Journal of Psychotherapy* 28: 4–20.

Randell, J. 1971. Indications for sex reassignment surgery. *Archives of Sexual Behavior* 1: 153–61.

Ross, M. W., and J. A. Need. 1989. Effects of adequacy of gender reassignment surgery on psychological adjustment: A follow-up of fourteen male-to-female patients. *Archives of Sexual Behavior* 18: 145–53.

Sorensen, T. 1981. A follow-up study of operated transsexual males. *Acta Psychiatrica Scandinavica* 63: 486–503.

Sorensen, T., and P. Hertoft. 1982. Male and female transsexualism: The Danish experience with 37 patients. *Archives of Sexual Behavior* 11: 133–55.

Stein, M., L. Tiefer, and A. Melman. 1990. Followup observations of operated male-to-female transsexuals. *Journal of Urology* 143: 1188–92.

Stoller, R. J. 1973. Male transsexualism: Uneasiness. *American Journal of Psychiatry* 130: 536–39.

Tsoi, W. F., L. P. Kok, and F. Y. Long. 1977. Male transsexualism in Singapore: A description of 56 cases. *British Journal of Psychiatry* 131: 405–409.

Wålinder, J., B. Lundström, and I. Thuwe. 1978. Prognostic factors in the assessment of male transsexuals for sex reassignment. *British Journal of Psychiatry* 132: 16–20.

8

COUNSELING AND TREATMENT

Introduction

Therapy for gender nonconformity is a twentieth century phenomenon; before
that time it was either ignored or thought of as sin or crime. With the emergence
of the medical model departures from the strict dimorphism represented by
"masculine" and "feminine" were reconceptualized as illness. This opened up the
opportunity for treatment, and psychotherapy emerged as the major treatment
modality, although surgery, including castration and clitoridectomy, was used
experimentally, usually against the patient's will.

Following the publicity about the surgical treatment of Christine Jorgensen,
at mid-century, the surgical treatment of transsexualism emerged and, although
it has been criticized in this book and elsewhere, it brought a welcome measure
of relief to many transsexuals. Stanley Biber, who is credited with having done
the largest number of male-to-female operations in the United States and a lesser
number of female-to-male operations, describes the procedures he developed
over the years.

Xia Zhaoji and Wang Chuanmin describe their work developing transsexual
surgery in China, where female-to-male surgery outnumbers male-to-female.
This ratio is reversed in North America and Europe, emphasizing the importance
of the cultural variable in shaping the response to gender dysphoria.

With the changing climate of opinion and more acceptance by the public,
many people whose gender identity is not completely male or female have real-

ized that they can live with this situation without surgery. Most notable among this group are the transgenderists who are described in other sections of this book. However, there are still a significant number of people who seek counseling or psychotherapy in addition to surgery or instead of surgery. The professional community, especially the clinical contingent, must also deal with the interaction and dynamics of the family with its issues of discovery, blame, triangulation, and accommodation.

In the past therapists tried to remedy the situation by attempting to cure the disorder. The classic psychoanalytic approach conceptualized the female cross-dresser as a victim of the Electra complex, and the male as a latent homosexual. Those who treated sexual issues considered transgender behavior a perversion caused by childhood trauma or arrested development. That approach was not very fruitful, however, and the individual usually simply endured the treatment as he wandered through the morass of stigmatized opinions resting on the framework of perversion.

While there is still significant distance to be traveled before persons exhibiting transgender behavior encounter more than limited acceptance, the understanding and approach by the therapeutic community have undergone significant change in recent years. The shifting area of "gender disorders" both in and out of the sexuality chapter in the *Diagnostic and Statistical Manual of Mental Disorders* put out by the American Psychiatric Association (APA) suggests ambivalence on the part of the APA as to how to label transgender behavior and questions whether it should be included in a manual of disorders. For example, if we trace the explanations given for transsexualism and transvestism through the last two editions of the DSM (1987, 1994), it is possible to note significant changes. Transsexualism has been removed from the list of psychiatric diagnoses and replaced by "gender dysphoria." The discussion in the section on "transvestic fetishism" suggests that not all cross-dressing is pathological.

We see the building of an extensive data base about the phenomenon of gender as a crucial step in helping professionals. In this section and throughout the book up-to-date information about transgender behaviors and roles is provided so the professionals can better understand what they are dealing with. As the number of informed gatekeepers grows and information disseminates, then a fuller awareness and understanding of transgender behavior can occur.

The articles in this section also move beyond the traditional treatment modalities to address issues of self-acceptance and acceptance by others of a wider range of gender identities and gender roles. As data is gathered and conceptual frameworks established new and more effective means of providing counseling and support can be found. The triage system described by Yvonne Cook-Riley is one such approach. Another experimental approach suggests the use of dance and movement in learning to adjust to a new gender role.

Counseling by an informed clergyman can be very important in helping remove the burden of guilt from the shoulders of transgendered people. Unfortunately the medical/psychiatric institutions are not the only ones lagging in their understanding of transgender behavior. Religious groups vary, but many are still unable to resolve issues of gender roles at the level of what should be masculine and what should be feminine, much less deal with the transgendered person. Many use the model of the attitude toward homosexuality of the Catholic or Mormon churches, which argues that it is not a "sin" or offense to have feelings as long as nothing is done to act out those feelings; thus denial is the only acceptable answer. However, some of the Protestant churches take a much more conciliatory view and in this situation the clergy can be of significant help to the transgendered individual and the family.

Whatever the approach, the importance of bringing the knowledge and understanding of the therapeutic community up to date remains important, and the Gender Attitude Reassessment Program (GARP) described by Ariadne Kane provides one framework for doing that.

References

American Psychiatric Association. 1987. *Diagnostic and statistical manual of mental disorders.* 3d ed. rev. Washington, D.C.: American Psychiatric Association.
———. 1994. *Diagnostic and statistical manual of mental disorders.* 4th ed. Washington, D.C.: American Psychiatric Association.

Current State of Transsexual Surgery: A Brief Overview

Stanley H. Biber

Over the years various techniques have developed for vaginal construction or, technically, neocolporrhaphy in the male-to-female transsexual patient. At the Mt. San Rafael Hospital in Trinidad, Colorado, we ourselves have adopted many refinements in the technique during our twenty-six years of operation, and what I report here are our current practices.

It is necessary, however, to point out that the procedure is not exactly the same for everyone since the size of the penis and scrotum along with perineal measurements determine the exact type of procedures utilized. For example, if the penis is small we usually will resort to utilizing a split-thickness skin graft taken from the buttock or thigh, which is wrapped around an air-filled stent and inserted in the cavity. In some operations, depending upon the perineal dimension, we might also use a posterior flap to aid in forming the orifice of the newly created vagina. In my consideration, the key to the operation is to do what is necessary to make a vagina of sufficient depth. This requires utilization of a technique that will allow a minimum depth of five inches, and preferably six.

Our preference, and the procedure followed in about 95 percent of the cases, is the penile inversion technique in which we line the newly created vaginal cavity with inverted penile skin. We attempt to carry a dorsal nerve root into the cavity along with the inverted glans to form a cervixlike structure at the apex of the vagina, and usually, but not always, we succeed.

Early operations attempted to make vaginas out of a bowel segment but this has fallen into disrepute in our group. This not only adds another major procedure to an already extensive one but makes for other complications. The patient

374

suffers from the normal problems of any case of bowel resection, but in vaginal reconstruction efforts there is constriction at the orifice and discharge of variable amounts of mucus depending on stress factors in the patient's life. There is also bleeding during vaginal intercourse since the bowel mucosa is easily irritated and probably also provides easier access to infection, including HIV virus, when compared to the use of skin barrier. Approximately six months ago, I had to remove a colon segment from such a vagina when more conservative management failed to deal with the patient's severe ulcerative colitis resulting in very bloody mucus discharge.

In our technique, we not only form a vagina in a normal female position, but also construct a urethral orifice in the natural female position so that our patient can pass urine directly downward into the bowl while sitting on a toilet like a normal female, instead of over the top of the bowl as a male does. We also form a clitoris from the remaining corpus spongiosum. This is rolled on itself after careful hemostasis and brought out through an opening created approximately two centimeters above the urethral orifice. This erectile tissue maintains its blood and nerve supply and responds to tactile simulation by tumefaction and sensation, thus aiding in orgasm.

We also create, depending on the amount of scrotal tissue available, a set of inner and outer lips. If tissue is sparse we try to make at least a facsimile of inner lip as well as the outer lip. Because of the nature of the blood supply in the scrotal tissue, the lips usually emanate from the lateral position and do not form an interior fourchette. Approximately 40 percent of the patients upon whom we do this procedure come back after six months for a labioplasty procedure (requiring one further day of hospitalization) where we form an interior fourchette over the now well-healed clitoris. Cosmetically the resulting perineum mimics the one in the normal female.

During this same period in the hospital, we often perform other cosmetic procedures to enhance femininity, if the patient so desires. This includes rhinoplasty (nose surgery), a tracheal shave, breast augmentation, blepharoplasty (eyelid surgery), face lift, brow lift, or various other cosmetic procedures, singly or in combination.

Our goal, of course, is to satisfactorily to convert an anatomic male physique to its female counterpart as visualized by the patient's gender concept of "herself." A happy, satisfied patient who has made an excellent transition means that surgically we have accomplished our purpose. A bad surgical outcome usually leads to an unhappy patient and distorts negatively the patient's psychological outcome as well.

We have also done female-to-male surgery but much less frequently. We tried various abdominal skin flaps with the hollow-tube technique, turned to the

Gracilis musculocutaneous flap from the thigh, and are now back to the advanced midline hollow-tube flap procedure but now it also includes scrotum formation and the insertion of silicone testicles. With the advent of the new electrolysis machines and the capability of developing a midline patch of lower abdominal skin without hair and without fibrosis and scarring, we can now form a hollow tube with skin lining that can be attached to the original female urethra without fear of hair growth, obstruction, infection, and fistula formation that made the old procedures so disastrous. Using a staged perineal build up and with the aid of a vaginal mucosal flap, we now form this connection and the patient can pass his urine through the shaft. The procedure still has its complications, but not as many as before. The capability of erection and sensation is still poor, and this will be worked upon by us and others during the next few years. We also do clitoral advancement (metadioplasty), and for some this is sufficient.

Transsexualism in China in 1995

Xia Zhaoji and Wang Chuanmin

Reported by Vern L. Bullough

In 1989, when Ruan and Bullough reported on transsexualism in China, there was only one known case of actual sex reassignment. By the beginning of 1995 there were 1,524 individuals diagnosed as transsexuals, although only a few had undergone sex reassignment surgery. The authors reported on the summary analysis they had made of these cases as well as on the twenty-five surgical cases in which they themselves had participated. This last included four cases in which vaginas, penises, ovaries, and testes were exchanged from two sets of patients.

Those diagnosed as transsexuals came from nineteen provinces, municipalities, and autonomous regions of China. Some of the patients came to their clinic for consultation, while another segment of the patient population wrote them letters detailing their cases. Diagnoses of transsexualism were made utilizing the criteria in the third revised edition of the *Diagnostic and Statistical Manual of Mental Disorders* (American Psychiatric Association 1987). To be included in the study, patients had to (1) be dissatisfied with what they regarded as their erroneous sexual anatomy, (2) desire to change their sexual organs through surgery and be reassigned to the opposite sex, (3) express such ideas over a two-year period without any change in their attitudes, (4) have had other diagnoses of mental and physical illnesses ruled out (such as schizophrenia, hermaphroditism, or genetic defects), and (5) have reached puberty.

Interestingly, of the 1,524 patients, 570 were male and 954 were female. These results are different from those observed by others, where the male-to-female rate is roughly three (MtF) to one (FtM) (Wålinder 1971; Hoenig and Kenna 1974; Lund 1988; Tsoi 1988). We believe that this difference is due to

377

Table 1. Age of Transsexuals

Age group (years)	MtF n	%	Cumulative Total %	FtM n	%	Cumulative Total %
Under 18	31	5.4	5.4	97	10.2	10.2
18–25	357	62.6	68.0	619	71.2	81.4
26–30	106	18.6	86.6	146	15.3	96.7
31–35	38	6.7	93.3	24	2.5	99.2
36 and over	38	6.7	100.0	8	0.8	100.0
Total	570	100		954	100	

Chinese tradition, which emphasizes the importance of the male. The overwhelming majority of parents wants and desires a son in the one-child ideal of contemporary China. Often when a girl is born they try to bring her up as a boy. Moreover, because of the emphasis on the male it remains more difficult for the female to get employment and housing than it is for the male, and young girls learn about their inferior status very early in their life.

The age range of those desiring surgical reassignment of their sex extends from fifteen to sixty-two years for the males, with an average of 24.2, and from fifteen to thirty-eight years for the females, with an average of 21.7. See table 1 for the breakdown. Note that the overwhelming majority of females, 81.4 percent, have been diagnosed as transsexuals before their twenty-sixth birthday, compared to 68 percent of the males.

The etiology of transsexualism was investigated in 810 of the 1,524 patients. To diagnose patients and explain causal factors a number of approaches to data gathering was utilized, including interviews, oral histories, and physical examination. Clients were also given the MMPI (Minnesota Multiple Personality Inventory), and they scored quite differently from other Chinese who had taken the test. Male transsexuals turned out to be more effeminate than the average for other Chinese males (48 points difference) while females scored higher on masculine values (51 points) than the average female (Fang 1993). Before being recommended for surgery, patients also went through psychoanalysis, a procedure that was reported as accentuating their transsexualism. Patients had to apply in written form for SRS and be approved by their legal representative (mostly their parents). The local safety department also had to approve, and *densi* (the political group to which they were assigned) had to agree as well.

Causal factors were broken down by the researchers into seven basic ones. The first they called imitation, defined as childhood gender dysphoria where the patient demonstrated cross-gender behavior early, living and playing in an environment of the opposite sex. Such children had come to think of themselves psychologically as belonging to the opposite sex and their behavior conformed to this belief. We classed a second category as "intensiting," what might be called "encouraged" gender dysphoria. These children were brought up, dressed, and treated by their parents as children of the opposite sex, and encouraged to adopt the manners of talk of that sex. In our minds these feelings intensified over time and the psychology of the patients tended to be of the opposite sex.

The third group was a combination of the above two; the confused imitation of the opposite sex was encouraged and intensified by parental support. A fourth type, which existed only among females who wanted to change their sex, was called the business type. These subjects believed that only the male could succeed in society and only by changing their sexual organs and becoming a male could they use their natural talents to achieve long dreamed-of success. A fifth group, whose desire to change their sex gradually evolved into transsexualism, we called the "homosexual type." For a sixth type of transsexuals, a "cause" could not be found, but it was thought these persons subjectively grew to believe they belonged to the opposite sex. These we called primary transsexuals. The seventh and last type we called the sex unconscious, patients who lacked sex consciousness until they reached puberty or began to live in collectives, and then identified with the opposite sex. For numbers and percentages see table 2.

Questions asked of potential SRS individuals included some about their education. The replies were broken down into two groups: those who had been classified and tested and those who had not yet received such attention. See table 3 for the summary. Nearly half of those classed as transsexuals and whose etiology was known had either received or were enrolled in higher education. See table 4 for numbers and percentages.

Questions were also asked about what subjects had done to themselves to deal with their condition. Some 35 percent of them had attempted suicide at least once; others had turned to self-mutilation of their genitalia. Females who felt plagued by their breast development tried to avoid bringing attention to their breasts, many of them by bending over so their breasts would not stick out, and some had become severely hunchbacked as a result. Some patients took hormones to gain the secondary sex characteristics more appropriate to the opposite

Table 2. Etiology of Transsexualism

Type	n	%
1. Imitative Gender Dysphoria	390	48.1
2. Encouraged Gender Dysphoria	120	14.8
3. Combination Gender Dysphoria	66	8.1
4. Business Gender Dysphoria	90	11.1
5. Homosexual Gender Dysphoria	72	8.9
6. Primary Gender Dysphoria	48	5.9
7. Unconscious Gender Dysphoria	24	3.0
Total	810	100.0

Table 3. Educational Status of Transsexuals

Level	Completed School		Current Students		Total	
	n	%	n	%	n	%
Higher Ed.	180	11.8	153	10.0	333	21.9
Middle Ed.	37	2.4	253	16.6	290	19.0
Primary Ed.	11	0.7	74	4.9	85	5.6
Not evaluated	816	53.5	0	0	816	53.5
Total	1,044	68.5%	480	31.5	1,524	100.0

Table 4. Educational Background of Evaluated TS Patients

Level	Completed School		Current Students		Total	
	n	%	n	%	n	%
Higher Ed.	180	25.4	153	21.6	333	47.0
Middle Ed.	37	5.2	253	35.7	290	41.0
Primary Ed.	11	1.6	74	10.5	85	12.0
Total	228	32.2	480	67.8	708	100.0

Table 5. Some Reported Coping Mechanisms

Mechanism	n	%
Attempted suicide or often suicidal	528	35.0
Attempted or contemplated mutilation	66	4.3
Took hormones	24	1.6
Married	42	2.8
Divorced	30	2.0
Had children	24	1.6

sex. While some had married and attempted to deny their desires, even giving birth to children, they usually divorced when they found this did not "cure" them. Answers to their "daily life" situation are given in table 5. Overall, male patients diagnosed as transsexuals were an average age of 24.1 while female patients were 21.7, lower than that reported in Western countries (Wålinder 1971; Hoenig and Kenna 1974; Lund 1988; Tsoi 1988; Ross, Wålinder and Lundström 1981; Pauly 1968)

Of the twenty-five cases of surgical sex reassignment performed in the Beijing Center in the past two years, ten were male to female and fifteen female to male. In the male cases the age distribution was twenty to thirty years with an average of 23.7 while the females ranged from twenty-two to thirty-six years with an average of 26.5 years. In the follow-up done so far, all patients remained satisfied with the sex change, and they do not appear to have undergone the postoperative effect reported by Lundström, Pauly, and Wålinder (1984) or Abramowitz (1986). This might be due to the short time available for follow-up.

One of the problems in transsexual surgery is inappropriate application of exogenous sexual hormones. To see if this difficulty could be overcome by surgical means, we experimentally attempted to do sex exchange surgery on four patients in 1992 and 1993, implanting testes from the male into the female, and the ovaries from the female into the male. The operations were carried out under spinal anaesthesia. Blood supply of the grafts were reconstructed by end-to-end anastomoses of graft surgery and vein to the inferior abdominal artery and vein separately with 9-0 nylon sutures. Regular transsexual surgery was then done.

After re-establishment of blood circulation, all grafts were satisfactorily supplied with blood except for one ovary that had severe blood stasis in a vein. All patients were under regular immunosuppression treatment. Level of testosterone (T), estradiol (Ez), and follicle-stimulating hormone (FSH) in the serum were assayed by radio immuno analysis method. All grafts were functioning after the operation. The mean value of T in female to male was 7.29 ng/dl preoperative to 288 ng/dl postoperative. The mean value of Ez in male to female was 3.24 pg/ml preoperative to 50.6 pg/ml postoperative. The values of FSH were slightly increased in all four post-operative patients. In a three-month follow-up an acute rejection had developed in a female-to-male patient where only one testis had been transplanted due to cessation of immunosuppression treatment by patient himself. Immunosuppressant assault treatment was begun and the symptoms of rejection disappeared but the testis had been damaged severely, and in further follow-up it was found to be fibrotic, hard and small, and had ceased functioning. The other grafts in one female-to-male and two male-to-female patients at this writing are still functioning. The longest survival time of the transplanted ovary is one year and the testis is nine months. Desired physical changes that take place in the usual transsexual surgery through administration of exogenous hormones have been taking place through the functioning of endogenous hormones.

Whether this method will be useful in SRS in the long run is still not clear, since follow-up time is short and rejection remains a major problem.

References

Abramowitz, S. 1986. Psychosocial outcomes of sex reassignment surgery. *Journal of Consulting and Clinical Psychology* 54: 183–89.

American Psychiatric Association. 1987. *Diagnostic and statistical manual of mental disorders.* 3d ed. rev. Washington, D.C.: American Psychiatric Association.

Bullough, V. L., and F. F. Ruan. 1989. First case of transsexual surgery in China. *Journal of Sex Research* 25: 546–47.

Fang, Mingzhao. 1993. Clinical analysis of 40 transsexuals. *Journal of Chinese Sexology* 3: 20.

Hoenig, J., and J. C. Kenna. 1974. The prevalence of transsexualism in England and Wales. *British Journal of Psychiatry* 124: 181–90.

Lund, E. K. 1988. Prevalence of transsexualism in the Netherlands. *British Journal of Psychiatry* 152: 636–40.

Lundström, B., I. Pauly, and J. Wålinder. 1984. Outcome of sex reassignment surgery. *Acta Psychiatrica Scandinavica* 70: 189–94.

Pauly, I. B. 1968. Current status of change of sex operation. *Journal of Nervous and Mental Disease* 147: 460–71.

Ross, M. W., J. Wålinder, B. Lundström. 1981. Cross-cultural approaches to transsexualism. *Acta Psychiatrica Scandinavica* 63: 75–82.

Tsoi, W. F. 1988. The prevalence of transsexualism in Singapore. *Acta Psychiatrica Scandinavica* 78: 501–504.

Wålinder, J. 1971. Incidence and sex ratio of transsexualism in Sweden. *British Journal of Psychiatry* 119: 195–96.

Patterns in and Treatments for Gender Dysphoria

Gretchen Fincke and Roger Northway

This paper describes our work as clinicians with clients with gender dysphoria. Our program started in 1983 and since that time we have seen approximately 194 people who presented with some form of gender dysphoria.

Philosophy

Based upon experience with the programs at Johns Hopkins and the University of Minnesota and consultations with gender professionals and consumers of program services, it appeared that in the early years of sex reassignment surgery people presenting to a clinician or program saying they were transsexual were forced to prove it. Gender service consumers, being fairly bright and determined to get their needs met, learned to speak the jargon and to tell clinicians what they thought the clinicians wanted to hear. This meant that the clients did not get the real service, therapy, or support they needed. Since the professionals had to authorize hormones and surgery, they became authoritarian permission-givers.

While we may not have completely escaped those past dilemmas, we make an effort in our program to design an individual therapy program for each person. It may be minimal attendance at a group session once a month, or it may be involve intensive weekly therapy. Our program provides client-centered treatment where people can obtain whatever therapeutic services they need.

Fig. 1. Overall Schemata of Identity

IDENTITY

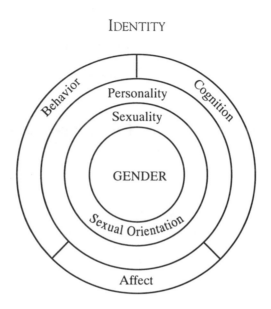

Identity Schemata

We use the above diagram as an overall schemata of identity. We see cross-dress-ing behavior showing up in each of these areas, depending on the function of the cross-dressing.

Patterns and Treatments

We have seen the following patterns in our clients and developed treatment approaches for each. The categories and treatment modalities are not exclusive.

Category 1: Cross-Dressers

These persons are exclusively male, as neither society nor the medical profession defines females who wear masculine clothing as problematic. These males periodically enjoy wearing female clothing, wigs, and make-up as a recreational activity, not for the purpose of sexual gratification. The men involved do not totally disavow their masculine identity, rather, they enjoy the expression of a "feminine identity." This periodic behavior may take place only in times of complete privacy or may extend to public settings or to social clubs organized to meet their needs for a safe social setting.

A majority of cross-dressers are heterosexual and many are married. Cross-dressing behavior may be accompanied by a marked release of tension and anxiety or may be a pleasurable, leisure-time activity. The cross-dresser's desire to cross-dress may be occasionally compulsive, but is not exclusively so. Cross-dressing behavior may begin in childhood or adulthood. It often accelerates in middle age, as the men lose early feelings of self-consciousness and have more resources, money, and leisure time.

Men who are married or partnered often wish their partners were part of the cross-dressing experience. Some partners are willing and supportive; a majority know their mates cross-dress, but do not participate. Some partners are kept in complete ignorance. The male cross-dresser rarely has other psychopathology or gross personality dysfunction. He has a masculine gender identity and masculine behaviors when not cross-dressed. He may be sexual when cross-dressed, but is also sexual when not so dressed.

This pattern is connected to the personality portion and, to some extent, to the gender portion of the identity schemata.

TREATMENT

Treatment consists of an individual evaluation and exploration of exactly what the person wants. By far the most requested treatment involves couple counseling aimed at helping the spouse understand and develop some tolerance for the cross-dressing behavior. Some also want referrals to social groups.

Category 2: Cross-Dressing Utilized as a Major Defensive Pattern

This pattern is also seen exclusively in men. Many come from severely dysfunctional families where there was physical abuse and/or emotional neglect severe enough that the child learned it was unsafe to have feelings at all or to have certain kinds of feelings. There was a family climate that promoted a sense that it is unsafe to be who they were. At some point, they made a defensive decision that incorporated being the other gender and dressing accordingly in time of stress in order to either feel anything at all or to numb out particular feelings. There are distinct elements of compulsion in this pattern, but no acceleration, progression, or necessarily ritualistic aspects of cross-dressing behavior. There is usually other significant psychopathology and/or other addictions. He does not want to change genders in a permanent way.

This pattern is connected to the behavior/affect/cognition portion of the identity schemata.

TREATMENT

Intensive individual psychotherapy utilizing insight therapy is used to help such persons learn individual emotional safety. They may also have to deal with accompanying addictions.

Category 3: Homosexual with Homophobia

The subject fitting this pattern is a male, homosexual in sexual orientation, who has an almost insurmountable homophobia about himself and other homosexuals. He does not want to admit the orientation to himself, nor does he want to be seen as partaking in the gay lifestyle. In a particularly convoluted/delusional way, he cross-dresses to obtain desired sexual behavior, while "pretending" the behavior is "heterosexual." This is not as common as when more gays were closeted. There is often a strong religious component to the homophobia.

This pattern is connected to the sexual orientation portion of the identity schemata.

TREATMENT

Intensive individual psychotherapy is used to get the person to accept his sexual orientation. Sometimes we make referrals to coming out groups.

Category 4: Cross-Dressing as Part of a Compulsive/Addictive Pattern

This is seen in those who use cross-dressing as a part of, or as a necessary condition to, sexual arousal. In addition, the behavior involves progressive acceleration to the point where the person's life becomes unmanageable in key areas. He or she may have trouble with family relationships, work, socializing, or have legal problems. The behavior is often solitary, ritualistic, and, coupled with sexual release, mood altering. Acting out is followed by revulsion towards cross-dressing, guilt, and anxiety. This population is primarily male, but not exclusively.

This cross-dressing pattern is connected to the behavior/affect/cognition part of the identity schemata.

TREATMENT

The treatment program for people with an addictive problem includes an intensive evaluation, individual psychotherapy, and attendance in a group that helps the person develop an abstinence contract and a 12-step program. We often see spouses and family members for co-dependency work as well.

Category 5: Transvestites

These people use cross-dressing or fantasizing about cross-dressing as part of, or as a necessary condition to, sexual arousal. It differs from the addictive cross-dressing pattern in that it is not progressive and does not make the person's life unmanageable. It is "kinky fun" and rarely do those involved seek treatment to change their behavior. The men may be homosexual or heterosexual in orientation and seek partners who will go along with or enthusiastically support the behavior. The women are straight or lesbian and may be involved with the S-M leather dominatrix scene. Occasionally, we see heterosexual women who like to involve cross-gender dress in sex play with a partner.

This pattern is connected to the behavior/affect/cognitive portion of the identity schemata.

TREATMENT

These people rarely ask for treatment beyond the initial assessment and then they usually want to learn comfort with what is, rather than change. They often want referrals to social groups.

Category 6: Transgender-Transsexual

This pattern is seen in both men and women. It is identified by a lifelong sense of gender confusion. It is rarely identified before adulthood and is marked by an understanding that what is needed is to change to the gender other than that of rearing. It is most often articulated by a description of a continual feeling that they are/should be the gender other than the one the world perceives them to be. It is often characterized by a long history of other-gender-dressing, behaviors, and feelings. These people are willing to go through a process of gender change, socially, hormonally, legally, and physically. This pattern occurs in about equal numbers in men and women; however, more men present for formal treatment. Sexual orientation can be gay, straight, or bisexual in conformation with the gender that is felt internally.

This pattern is connected to the gender portion of the identity schemata.

TREATMENT

Treatment starts with four hours of psycho-social-sexual history. We use the MMPI (Minnesota Multiphasic Personality Inventory) as our major psychological test and occasionally use the Bem gender test as well. This is followed by a psychiatric evaluation, where warranted. The range of therapeutic services offered includes individual psychotherapy and couple, family, and group work. We have two male-to-female groups and one female-to-male group. We use the Benjamin Standards, with occasional exceptions. The most useful part of the standards states that a person must cross-live for one year prior to any unalterable surgeries. We continually hear from people in the program that this is a fundamentally important learning time. In addition, we offer advice on legal name/gender change procedures, employer inservices for those who transition on their job, and referrals for hormone therapy and surgical procedures.

Category 7: Multiple Personality Disorder

This pattern is very recent and we are not entirely sure how to respond. Two people have been referred to our program by their treating psychiatrists, and another was in the program for a significant period before becoming symptomatic. The first two carry a diagnosis of multiple personality disorder. They all seem to be coalescing into a dominant female personality. They are all biologically male. We are not clear whether their psychiatrists misdiagnosed or simply did not know what to do, so referred their patients on to us. Both psychiatrists are comfortable and supportive of the female personality, and the people seem most comfortable in the female gender.

TREATMENT

We are proceeding very slowly and cautiously through the normal steps of gender reassignment, although at this point no surgeries have been done.

Conclusion

It is important to remember that people often do not fit neatly into categories. We take our cues from the client and use the categories as a way of clinically sorting them for appropriate treatment. The majority of people we work with are in category 1 or 6. We do not insist that people live their lives in a certain way, but help them become clear about decisions they make. Our clients tell us, "Please give us credit for what we know about ourselves." This we do.

The Hotline Call,
or, "How to Do a Year's Psychotherapy in Thirty Minutes or Less"

Yvonne Cook-Riley

The International Foundation for Gender Education (IFGE) operates a telephone hotline serving people with gender concerns. The hotline is useful not only for the help it gives, but also as a source of data about the gender community. There are four big questions the hotline operator must answer in order to maximize the usefulness and the value of the call to the caller.

1. What is the caller's sex or gender issue?
2. What is the appropriate action for the caller to take at this point?
3. Is the caller ready to take this next step or action? If not, how can the operator help him or her to get ready? If he or she is ready, how can the operator get the caller to actually take that step?
4. How can the operator water the garden of the caller instead of letting the problem fester?

The real teacher in the hotline call is the person who is calling in, but it takes a skilled operator to bring out the caller's knowledge about himself. The operator must ask questions of the caller to learn who and what the caller is, and then use more questions to help the caller teach himself. I have discovered that by using a specific series of questions it is possible to gain significant insight into the individual and his issues, his level of self-knowledge, and his level of self-acceptance. In so doing, we gain insight into how to help direct the caller into taking positive action to address his personal concerns.

This chapter summarizes the conclusions I have drawn, based on my talks on the phone with members of the transgendered community.

Since April 1988, I have answered well over 2,000 calls from people who were making their first contact with anyone regarding their own transgendered issues. The callers obtained the telephone number from other hotlines, an issue of the *TV/TS Tapestry* magazine, the media, or some other gender community publication. They were almost exclusively male, and were seeking information about their transgendered issues.

Our foundation's policy is to begin by getting an address from the caller, so that we can send the caller information about publications that are available, for example, *Tapestry,* and about transgendered events, activities, and support groups. We then ask the caller a series of questions that help to classify his gender issues.

Let us review the spectrum of the transgendered community. The fetishistic cross-dresser, the marginal TV (or what I will refer to as cross-dresser), the transvestite, the transgenderist, the secondary transsexual, the primary transsexual. I am basing these categories of this spectrum on Richard F. Docter's research, as reported in his book entitled *Transvestites and Transsexuals: Toward a Theory of Cross-Gender Behavior* (1988).* You can refer to his book if you need any more breakdown. As you know, the spectrum is a spectrum: in other words, it is just not one, little, simple box that everybody is going to fit into, nor a guidepost that everybody is going to follow. The categories are important because the clients' information needs and possible interventions vary from one category to another.

Records of the hotline calls are a valuable source of data about the transgender community. Those data are presented here along with findings from IFGE's first marketing research on the transgendered community and the gender community's demographics. This was executed by Laura Caldwell, the chair of our budget committee. The survey respondents and the charts presented here represent 891 people responding to a questionnaire that was sent to 9,000 people on IFGE's mailing list. The built-in bias of the sample is the fact that it is made up of activists who belong to and support IFGE and the callers to the hotline who were willing to give an address. The people who make up this population had a safe mailing address, like a post office box, for instance, or were "out" enough themselves that they could receive mail from us at home without fear of life-destroying discoveries. Nevertheless, it provides important information about the cross-dressing community.

---

*(New York: Plenum).

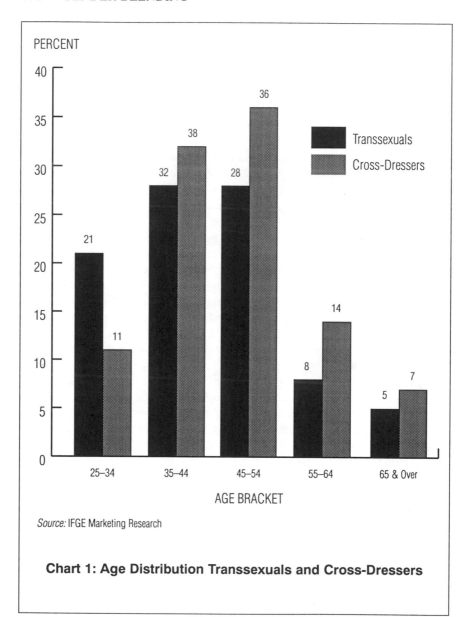

Source: IFGE Marketing Research

Chart 1: Age Distribution Transsexuals and Cross-Dressers

Chart 1. Age Distribution, Transsexuals and Cross-Dressers

Let's look at age distribution and how persons classify themselves as compared to their age. You will notice on the first chart that younger persons are more likely to classify themselves as transsexuals. The older persons will more than likely classify themselves as cross-dressers. I will refer to this chart again later.

Chart 2. Age Comparison, U.S. Population vs. Sample Research

The second chart compares the ages of the men in our study group with the age distribution of the male population in 1992. When the percentages are compared, it is clear that most people do not come out or identify themselves as being transgendered until they are older. Also, there is a great number of transgendered people as compared to the general population, so it is not a phenomenon that is buried and affects only a small percentage of the total male population. It is exciting to find out that we are really beginning to get a handle on just how many transgendered people there are.

Getting back to my telephone conversations, I use three questions to sort where the caller is in the gender spectrum, and where he is in his self-acceptance. My first question is "How old are you?" Again, referring back to chart 1, if the caller is younger I will suspect that transsexual issues are the main focus of his inquiry. If the caller is older, I will work on the basis that cross-dressing or marginal transvestism is the emphasis and probably where this caller could be on the spectrum at this time.

The key question that really lets me know what's going on is the second question I use. "After you masturbate, do you keep the clothes on or do you take them off?" I use this question very simply because I make the assumption that most males masturbate. How they interact with that activity and the clothing can make a big determination of where they fall in the transgender spectrum.

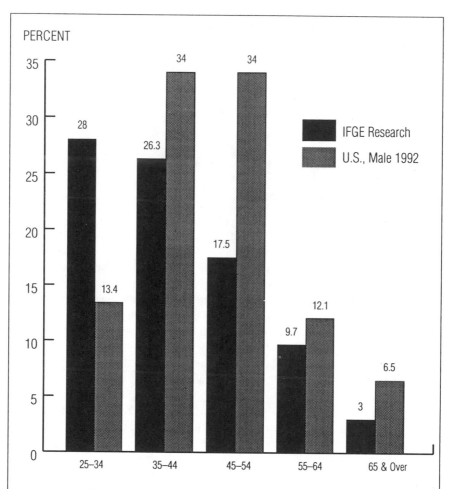

Source: U.S. Bureau of Labor Statistics, Bulletin 2307, and Employment Earnings

**Chart 2: Age Comparison U.S. Population (Male/1992)
vs. IFGE Research**

Chart 3. Transgender Spectrum, Whether or Not Clothes Are Kept On

In my chart you will see that when the clothes are taken off right after masturbation, this person falls more into cross-dressing and fetishistic, or marginal, transvestite activity. When the clothes are *sometimes* left on after masturbation, you will see that this activity includes the fetishistic and marginal transvestite and moves into the transvestite category. When the caller masturbates little and leaves the clothes on, this indicates to me that this person is out of the fetishistic range and is into trying to realize that the cross-dressing is more than just gratification through masturbation. Answering "No masturbation but dresses most of the time" strongly indicates the issues are moving in the direction of gender identity, and will place him somewhere in the transgenderism, secondary transsexualism, and primary TS spectrum bar.

Again, age is an important factor here. The younger the person is, the more likely he is to be a primary transsexual, while the secondary transsexual is a person who has had life male experiences and would, of course, be older. When there is no masturbation, after I ask the question, they immediately get into asking *me* questions about sexual reassignment surgery (SRS), which leads me to categorize them as transsexual or transgenderist. These answers get right down to identifying what their issues are very quickly.

Chart 4. Transgender Spectrum, Whether or Not Caller Has a Femme Name

After that, to help me again nail it down just a little better, I ask my third question, "Do you have a femme name?" It is a simple question. I use it after the masturbation question because it again deals with self-esteem issues and identity.

On the transgendered spectrum, where the answer is no, 99 percent of the time this person is into cross-dressing and fetishistic cross-dressing and probably has never gone out in public, and probably has never worn all the clothing or put on full make-up. When the answer is yes, this person has moved from fetishistic cross-dressing and is dealing with identity issues, is using full make-up and has some street experience, or has gone out at night to take the mail to the mail box, or a similar activity.

Where do we end up and what are the results that I am hoping for? Basically, I want to increase the caller's personal investigation into his own identity through

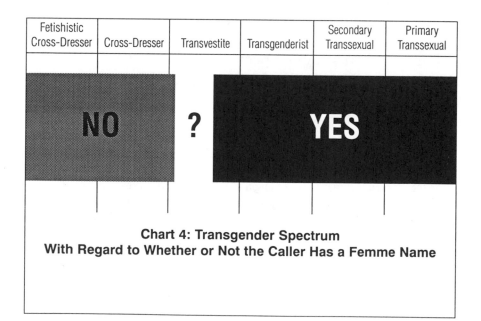

Fetishistic Cross-Dresser	Cross-Dresser	Transvestite	Transgenderist	Secondary Transsexual	Primary Transsexual
Takes off clothes after masturbation					
Sometimes leaves them on					
	Leaves on, little masturbation				
			No masturbation, dresses most of time		
			No masturbation, asks about SRS		

**Chart 3: Transgender Spectrum
Related to Whether or Not Caller Keeps Clothes on
after Masturbating**

Fetishistic Cross-Dresser	Cross-Dresser	Transvestite	Transgenderist	Secondary Transsexual	Primary Transsexual
NO		?	YES		

**Chart 4: Transgender Spectrum
With Regard to Whether or Not the Caller Has a Femme Name**

publications and support groups. Also, I offer him a reality check—bringing home to him that SRS is not a weekend cure to life's problems, and getting him to contact a support group and to learn for himself about his own issues. I encourage the caller to look for a therapist or counselor and, again, find the support.

The hoped-for result from the telephone conversation, and my responses to the caller's answers, is more insight on the part of the caller. We try to get the caller to move toward greater self-discovery and self-acceptance. The nontranssexual caller will often come to see this process as a positive approach to becoming comfortable with himself.

As a footnote, I would like to bring to your attention a support group in Michigan called Cross Roads that has published an outreach manual on phone calls. It is an excellent manual. I have not used any of the material from their manual, but I have reviewed it and recommend it highly to any support group that is going to have phone contact with the transgendered person and for follow up on inquiries to the support group.

Religion and Cross-Gender Behavior: Wellspring of Hope or Swamp of Despair?

Kathryn J. Helms

Religion is defined as a primary means by which individuals and groups give meaning to life, create visions of life beyond death, organize behavior to sustain faith and serve others, and show honor to their concept of the divine through some form of worship. Cross-gender behavior is defined as assuming the dress, role, and attitude of the gender opposite to one's biologically determined sex. Cross-gender behavior and religion may be in partnership, harmony, or inimical.

Because religion is concerned with all aspects of human life, it has an interest in cross-gender behavior as well. Depending on its self-understood revelatory insight from its divine source(s), religion may manifest itself through cross-gender behavior, recognize it but not approve, or reject such behavior as demonic (counter-religious). The impact of religious belief on persons who practice cross-gender behavior can be either health producing or health destroying. The outcome depends on whether integration of religion and cross-gender behavior is possible within a particular belief system.

My Background

I have been consciously aware of my own cross-gender feelings since age three. I was encouraged in expressing these feelings by my mother and generally accepted by my father. Thus for all practical purposes, I have always had a strong sense of what I now call a "feminine gender identity" woven into my masculine identity and my male sexual identity. Balancing the masculine and the feminine has not been easy and at times I have struggled with serious depression. However, my religious faith as a committed Christian has helped me cope with the complexities of my life. I came to my own commitment to Jesus Christ as a youth of fourteen. During those same teen-age years, I experienced a sense of calling to prepare for ordination as a minister in my Protestant denomination.

After undergraduate and graduate studies I began my work as a clergyperson. For over twenty-five years I have fulfilled that calling as a pastor, program administrator, and teacher.

As a young child I did not understand that many people disapprove of cross-gender behavior. As a teenager, I began to learn and "went underground." As an adult I began to be open again, although with a selective group of people.

I am married and deeply appreciate the wonderful support and love I receive from my spouse, a love that I happily reciprocate. Since 1988 I have been a member of the board of directors of Tri-Ess, a national support group for heterosexual cross-dressers and their wives and partners. I am also president of ALPHA, the mother chapter of Tri-Ess. I function as a peer counselor in the transgender community providing crisis counseling, referrals to licensed psychotherapists, and pastoral care.

Every month or so I receive a phone call from a cross-dresser, whom I'll call "Tom" (not his real name). Tom lives in a remote part of the United States and works on a rugged job that does not permit him to cross-dress much, although he often thinks about it. Tom is a recovering alcoholic and an evangelical Christian within the community of charismatic churches. His faith has been an integral part of his recovery process for the last thirteen years.

Tom's cross-dressing, on the other hand, has been a source of dissonance for him. He feels his community of faith would censure him if they knew. His wife knows but is unhappy about the cross-gender feelings Tom expresses. Tom is in a quandary. He is a lifelong cross-dresser. He does not believe his feelings will go away. Though his community of faith has a strong belief in "deliverance" and Tom has experienced significant positive behavior modification with regard to his alcoholism, yet his cross-gender feelings and behavior remain a deeply felt need. Tom is not fully comfortable with those cross-gender feelings. He wrestles spiritually, emotionally, and mentally with them. He is not sure they are "morally right," but he acknowledges they have remained constant even though he has experienced dramatic changes in most other areas of his life.

What is the answer to Tom's dilemma? Is the tension between his cross-gender behavior and his faith a hopeless problem? Must Tom choose between his religion and his cross-gender feelings? This Hobson's choice is like being asked to choose between food and water.

Much of Tom's struggle grows out of the fact that he is a Christian and takes his faith's scripture and tradition seriously. It may be painful for him to wrestle with the issues of his faith and his cross-gender behavior, but he believes he cannot give up one for the other and remain at peace with himself. I empathize with Tom. As a Christian I share some of the same tensions that he experiences. And I carry an additional burden. As an ordained minister I am responsible to help provide others with the means to understand their faith. Just as a medical doctor vows to "do no harm," so I too must strive to do no harm by my teaching and counsel.

To me this is an awesome responsibility. My struggle to find answers to the questions posed by Tom's dilemma lies behind the subtitle of my presentation: "Wellspring of Hope or Swamp of Despair?"

While my own existential struggle is informed by and played out against a Christian faith, I am fully cognizant that many people who express cross-gender feelings and behavior come from other faiths or share no organized religious feelings at all. However, since the focus of my paper is the interaction between religious attitudes and cross-gender behavior, I have not attempted any apologetic for religion versus nonreligion, but rather began by accepting that very large numbers of people hold deeply felt religious beliefs and that many of these are persons in the "transgender community." The question is "How does religion affect these 'gender gifted' individuals" (a term coined by Ms. Linda Peacock, a wife and leader in this community) and conversely, "How do these persons in the gender community affect their religions?"

By necessity this paper is only a starting point for discussions on these issues. As in any discussion there is the need for a definition of terms. Delineating these terms leads to assessing the role of religious belief in the context of cross-gender behavior. In the body of this paper, I have briefly surveyed the ways the major faith systems such as Christianity, Islam, Judaism, Hinduism, and Buddhism address cross-gender behavior.

Exploring the interaction between religious belief and the disciplines of psychology, sexology, and sociology as they address cross-gender behavior adds warp to the woof of my tapestry. My conclusions, drawn from this weaving, point to health-giving elements in religious behavior as well as illness-producing ones.

What do we really mean by the term cross-gender behavior? I define it as assuming the attitudes, role, and dress of the gender role that is opposite to one's biologically determined sex and typical gender role expression. This definition is concise but embraces a spectrum of behavior and attitudes from occasional cross-dressing to transsexual identity. While more typical definitions focus on the "costume" of cross-gender behavior (as witness "cross-dressing") or on sexual identity (as in "transsexual") reality is far more complex.

The great ethnologist Clifford Geertz in his book *Local Knowledge* (1983, 10ff.) speaks of "thick" definitions and "thin" ones. "Thick" definitions take into account the significance of specified behavior for the persons within the culture being studied. "Thin" definitions are external constructs given significance from the culture of the "expert" without tapping the essential self-understanding of those being studied (see also Geertz 1968, 17ff.).

Especially in the context of religious behavior the words "cross-dresser" or "transsexual" (or even "transgendered") become thin, one-dimensional statements, inadequate to define the complexities of cross-gender behavior patterns. It is only when the complexities of these patterns are acknowledged and wrestled with that fair assessments may be made and accurate conclusions drawn.

How, then, does religious behavior relate to the complexity of cross-gender behavior? In its essence, religious behavior is the patterned behavior that enables individuals or groups to give meaning to life, to express their visions of life after death, to organize behavior to sustain faith and serve others, and to show honor to their concept of the divine through some form of worship.

For religions that view the universe from a monistic viewpoint, cross-gender behavior is but an affirmation of the essential continuity of all life and a natural expression of the spectrum of life. Religions such as animism (primitive), pantheism, and Hinduism/Buddhism all embrace a monist view of life (Kinsley 1982, 86–87).

Examples abound of shamanist priests who practice cross-gender behavior in tribal societies (e.g., berdache). Hindu rituals historically include cross-gender behavior (Kinsley 1986, 92–94). (Such behavior continues today in some areas in Indonesia as well as in devotion to some goddesses in India in certain entertainment *jatis* of certain castes [cf. Kinsley]).

Buddhism also has stories of cross-gender behavior among the gods and goddesses. There is even a saying of Buddha, "All things are neither male or female" (Kit 1989, 42–43). Indeed, both Hinduism and Buddhism embrace an incarnational theology/metaphysic that accepts cross-sex rebirths on the "wheel of life" and the "eightfold path."

Religions that have a strongly transcendent view of the separation of the divine and creation such as Judaism, Christianity, and Islam offer no formal place for cross-gender behavior in their rituals. In fact they share a common mistrust of blurring of lines between the sexes (perhaps drawn from their understanding of *Kadash* [Hebrew for holiness] as both separation from uncleanness and separation for service to God).

The complexities of cross-gender behavior were little understood or discussed in Hebrew Scripture such as the Torah (which is the same in the Al Koran and in the Christian Pentateuch). Only one verse—Deuteronomy 22:5—addresses the matter. It is set in the midst of other verses about not yoking an ox and an ass together, about not mixing kinds of cloth, and about doing justice in small matters.

The actual text asserts that women are not to wear "that which pertains to a man." (The words "that which pertains to a man" [*keli geber*] translate as "battle gear.") It further asserts that men are not to wear women's garments. I believe the most thoughtful explanation for this passage is that male temple prostitution was commonly practiced by the Canaanite peoples around Israel and that this was forbidden—therefore the prohibition (Driver 1951, 250–51). Several biblical commentaries, including Catholic, Protestant, and Jewish, affirm that "social transvestism" is not the topic of discussion in this passage (see Thompson 1974, 234). However, orthodox Judaism, strict Islam, and conservative Christianity tend to assess cross-gender behavior in negative ways based on this passage and on shared mores.

On the surface a more serious issue might be seen to be the phrases, "God detests" or "it is an abomination." In reality, though, this phrase is not only used for serious moral issues but also for ritual cleanness/uncleanness on matters dealing with handling corpses, menstruating women, and other issues not generally embraced as binding today (Rad 1956).

One might ask, "What fears and anxieties does cross-gender behavior raise among the conservative points of view?" Many writers suggest the following (see Cairns 1992, 194):

1. It is contrary to the natural order of things.
2. It confuses the distinctions between the sexes.
3. God has said it is wrong.
4. Our tradition does not approve of it.

All of these arguments are rather circular and certainly fail to stand up to exegetical analysis of the whole of the scriptures involved. In every one of these transcendent religions, there are records of cross-gender behavior, whether approved or not. Accounts of generals like Deborah (who led Israel into battle, Judges 4–5) among the Jews, Christian saints who were discovered at death to be women (Bullough 1974), occasional men such as the Abbe de Choisy, and so on.

What then can we say in a general way about the integration of religion into cross-gender behavior and vice versa? For persons in monistic religions, integration comes easily. They have little moral struggling and there is a relative acceptance of cross-gendered individuals by these religions.

For persons in transcendent religions there are more difficulties. If their religious scriptures are regarded as prescriptive and morally binding on adherents in all cultures under all circumstances, then the Deuteronomy passage becomes a major stumbling block, as do the "traditions of the fathers" that establish patterns of behavior that cannot easily be changed. Perhaps even more serious is their lack of awareness that sex and gender are not the same thing. Therefore all cross-gender behavior is considered "cross-sexual behavior" and is thereby loaded with unnecessary connotations.

Thankfully for those of us in these transcendent religions, there are other "hermeneutical" (interpretive) filters that are more friendly toward cross-gender behavior. Scriptures may still be honored as revelatory without being prescriptive. Religious traditions may be respected without being unchanging. The complexities of modern life and scientific studies need not force religious people to retreat to fundamentalism or to cultural isolation such as that practiced by the Amish.

When scriptures are treated as enculturated expressions of valid truths that must be freshly integrated into each generation's time, they become less rigid and more practical. Thus a balanced hermeneutical filter of Scripture, reason, tradition, and experience provides a means to wrestle with the question of cross-gender behavior and to find ways to integrate it into religious belief and practice.

In my own journey of faith I have concluded that it is possible to be a practicing Christian and express cross-gender behavior. In fact many emphases of my faith on behavior that embraces love, joy, kindness, patience, gentleness, and self-control are generally regarded as "feminine." Metaphors that attribute feminine relationships between Christ and the church (His bride) place me in a cross-gender role. Paul affirms that the only clothing that matters is that one be "clothed with Christ" (Gal. 3:27). Added to this is the Pauline understanding that in humanity's new relationship to God in Christ there is now neither male nor female, Jew nor Greek, bond nor free, but all are one in him (Gal. 3:22). I conclude from this that essentially there are no sex or gender role status issues with Christ.

There are clear biblical witnesses to the inclusiveness of God's gender as embracing (and indeed as transcending) both masculine and feminine. All biblical language about God must by necessity be expressed by metaphors and similes. Therefore while the common biblical metaphor for God is Father, there are also images of God as "mother eagle" (Deut. 32:11) and "mother hen" (Matt. 23:37). In creation, Genesis affirms that God created "male and female in his own image" (Gen. 1:27). This suggests to me that God embraces the feminine as well as the masculine. One of the names of God in the Pentateuch is "El Shaddai" (Gen. 17:1). This word, which means "The one who provides," has as its root the word for "nursing and giving milk." There are many more metaphors and similes using feminine imagery for God (Smith 1993, 64).

Returning to our paradigm of Scripture, reason, tradition, and experience, I would point out that reason offers us access to the best of scientific insight on the question of cross-gender behavior. There is a need to integrate our best human effort into understanding these behavior patterns. Our creation as persons of intelligence suggests that we are entrusted with our intellects and must use them.

Even tradition has a place for cross-gender behavior. It is clearly present in every cultural and religious history. Its expression today may be more varied but its roots are in the past.

Experience also argues for the place of cross-gender behavior in religion. This behavior's universality suggests that it must be addressed by religion. Its persistence in individuals' lives who have remarkably thrown off a variety of unhealthy behaviors suggests that it is as integral to the persons expressing it as eating and sleeping. Cross-gender behavior is morally neutral and takes on the moral characteristics of the belief system of the person expressing it.

References

Bullough, Vern L. 1974. Transvestism in the Middle Ages. *American Journal of Sociology* 79: 1381–94.

Cairns, Ian. 1992. *Word and presence, a commentary on Deuteronomy.* Grand Rapids, Mich.: Eerdmans Publishing.

Craigie, Peter C. 1976. *The Book of Deuteronomy.* Grand Rapids, Mich.: Eerdmans Publishing.

Driver, S. R. 1951. *A critical and exigetical comment on Deuteronomy.* Edinburgh: T. and T. Clark.

Geertz, Clifford. 1968. *Islam observed.* Chicago: University of Chicago.

———. 1983. *Local knowledge.* New York: Basic Books.

Grossfield, Bernard, trans. and comp. 1988. *Targum of the book of Deuteronomy.* Wilmington, Del.: Michael Glazier.

Holy Bible, The. 1989. New Revised Standard Version. Nashville, Tenn.: Cokesbury.

Kinsley, David R. 1982. *Hinduism.* Englewood Cliffs, N.J.: Prentice-Hall, Inc.

———. 1986. *Hindu goddesses.* Berkeley: University of California Press.

Kit. 1989. A Buddhist's view of transvestism. *Tapestry* 53: 42–43.

Smith, Paul R. 1993. *Is it okay to call God "Mother?"* Peabody, Mass.: Hendrickson Publishers.

Thompson, J. A. 1974. *Deuteronomy.* Leicester, England: Intervarsity Press.

Rad, Gerhard von. 1956. *Studies in Deuteronomy.* London: SCM Press.

Weinfeld, Moshe. 1992. *Deuteronomy and the Deuteronomic school.* Winona Lake, Ind.: Eisenbrauns.

The Use of Dance/Movement
in the Adjustment to a New Gender Role

Jayne Thomas and Annette Cardona

The following is a discussion that preceded a demonstration of dance/movement therapy techniques that can be used with individuals who cross-dress and/or are transitioning gender roles.

JAYNE: Let us first introduce ourselves. I am Jayne Thomas, a psychologist and a reassigned person. I have this somewhat unusual background, having lived a number of decades as one sex (a male) and now completing my first decade living as a woman and female. In my professional life I am a professor and I instruct at a number of colleges in southern California. Through my son I came to know his acting and dance teacher.

Several years ago when Jonathan trained as an aspiring actor and, as such, was involved in a number of acting programs, I met Annette Cardona. Annette, why don't you introduce yourself and tell them a bit of your own background.

ANNETTE: My name is Annette Cardona. I come from the world of the performing arts and my many years as an actor, dancer, teacher of acting and dance/movement, as well as the work which I have done with at-risk teenagers, have all inspired a tremendous interest in utilizing my creative experience as a means of healing and promoting positive self-examination and esteem. Originally from Los Angeles, I am at present working and living on the East Coast. Jayne and I had the pleasure of meeting about eight years ago. At that time, I was teaching aspects of musical theater at the Los Angeles Music Center and Jayne's son, Jonathan, was an aspiring thespian.

Jonathan had a wonderful presence on stage, was extremely bright and energetic, and his potential for being a wonderful actor and performer were definitely present. Although he did struggle with a particular area of concern that I felt would, if not nipped in the bud, hinder his full potential and affect the quality of his overall performance.

Jonathan had a tough time being thoroughly convincing when scenarios involving mother-father, father-son, mother-son issues, for instance, were being expressed. I sensed struggle and resistance in this area. His delivery was slick, intellectual, and somewhat controlled; and the depth of his interpretations was not as honest and heartfelt as it could be. With Jonathan, these parental areas seemed inaccessible and I simply could not pinpoint what was wrong. I tried everything to stir a breakthrough; even improvisation work failed to bring out the issues and release them. I knew that in order to portray the human condition with true empathy and significant relevance, he would need to confront and come to terms with these obstacles.

Human beings communicate more effectively when their bodies and minds are compatible, comfortable, creative, and honest. Martha Graham coined the phrase, "movement doesn't lie." It is very tough to fool our audience.

One afternoon, as I was packing up at the end of class, Jonathan came to me with a request to share something important. I listened. He said the reason that he was having difficulty being completely honest in his work was because he had a very "unusual" home situation. His father was now living as Jayne—his dad was now a woman.

Coming from the show business community, for the most part nothing is unusual. However, I must tell you I was a little thrown by this revelation. I remember telling Jonathan how much I appreciated him sharing this delicate issue with me. Yet, at the same time, I wondered how to handle and interject this sensitive information into the classroom work. Thankfully, the first step had been taken. We could now communicate more openly and would find a way to overcome this challenge.

Shortly thereafter, Jonathan told me that Jayne had asked if I could work with her privately. She wanted to get "in touch" with her body, to experience dance and other aspects of the performing arts. I agreed to take her on, honestly not knowing how I could help. We made arrangements to meet at the dance studio for an initial session. Moments before her arrival, I was wondering what I was going to do with my first transgendered student. How would I handle this new situation emotionally, and how would I approach the first lesson?

Jayne showed up in these ugly sweats, looking rather dumpy and kind of . . . oh dear. I thought, Aha! We will simply begin with getting her in better physical shape. There is enough here to get started. I then realized, as we worked, that "a body is a body." The sex, one's orientation, is not the issue if the body is not working to the best of its capabilities. The physical body must have the flexibility to project whatever it desires to be, whatever it wishes to communicate. If the body is in conflict, struggling and cannot get out of its own way, one will feel very uncomfortable.

Jayne had taken on this new identity, a monumental task in and of itself. Her body seemed to be lagging behind, imploring, "Wait a minute, where are we going, what are we?" feeling very disoriented. So we worked. We worked hard and I employed the same techniques I use with my dancers and actors, opening up the body with various exercises, taking her to the dance barre, stretching her capacities both physically and creatively.

Soon, within weeks, I asked Jayne to join one of my dance classes. She expressed concern about joining a regular dance class; "Wait a minute, what are the other students going to think?" I said I did not foresee any problems and would like to give it a try. Truthfully, I too harbored the same curiosity.

As it turned out and as my instincts expected, everybody was so busy tackling their own work that our "new guest" never became an issue. There was great camaraderie in that all the participants were striving to be the best that they could be. I believe when goals are in communion there is more acceptance. Jayne ended up expanding her participation to include two classes a week, plus continuing our private sessions for the next five to seven years. This group of students became friends and, interestingly, went on to do projects together in various areas. Jayne encouraged me to begin a class expressly for the transgendered community. I actually benefitted the most from the challenge. Working with this special population inspired and motivated me to discover new and innovative ways to improve and better articulate my dance/movement instruction.

A natural progression from loosening the body through movement is that it allows for the emotions to surface. For the gender conflicted, this freedom releases the courage to dialogue more honestly in front of others.

My students come from all walks of life; the gender people were now finding acceptance and understanding from the other students. We learned that common needs, wanting to be loved, wanting to look our best and be proud of ourselves, are universal themes. The differences meshed and the prejudices diminished. Jayne and I have gone on to expand this work with other communities and areas of concern, applying these highly successful techniques.

JAYNE: One of the things I have found fascinating about working together with Annette has been the way in which each of us has learned from the other during the development of our programs. While working together we have become most aware and attuned to a body of literature that uses techniques gleaned from the performing arts in therapeutic ways.

I remember discussing dance/movement therapy with Annette, telling her that what the pioneers of dance therapy, such as Mary Whitehouse, Trudy Schoup, and Joan Chodorow, were doing was based on well-founded psychological principles and then hearing Annette tell me that their techniques were incorporated in exercises she had been using for years. Now she felt a camaraderie with the pioneers of dance/movement therapy that had gone before her.

ANNETTE: The godmothers of dance/movement therapy were primarily from the creative arena, many of them former dancers. As all dancers eventually experience, once you reach a certain age, the poor body simply cannot take the rigors of intense rehearsing and the demand of multiple performances. Often dancers are forced to go into other fields. Early on, a number of these artists started working as movement specialists in hospitals on the East Coast. At the time, a professional degree or licensing in the area of dance therapy was not a requirement. The medical and psychological communities were discovering that what movement had to offer was proving successful and patients were being helped.

JAYNE: I find dance/movement particularly appropriate for use in the transgender community. Just think of the enormousness of the problem faced by those who have spent a great part of their life in a role that didn't feel right, that they knew was not right, where their entire existence had been spent pretending to be someone they were not. However they had to live that sham role for an extended period of time. Finally, a decision was made to change to the preferred role without any of the preparation that one normally gets from childhood and adolescence. I myself did not live in society as a female child, a small girl, an adolescent, or an adult woman. I did not receive the training that society provides, training that teaches us how to become women.

ANNETTE: Well, this brings us to a critical issue. When Jayne and I met for our first session, she shared that she had done some work with feminine movement. I reacted surprisingly. Feminine movement? The concept was alien to my experience. As artists, our bodies are trained to express diversity of roles, emotions, and ideas, be it male, female, animate, or inanimate in nature. We are prepared to meet the demands of the theatrical message and its expectations.

Jayne showed me a videotape of an instructor teaching feminine deportment, only to find that what the instruction consisted of seemed a caricature of how females walk. Being very comfortable in my female identity, I have never, ever, in my life walked as was being demonstrated in this video, with pelvis thrust forward and hips swinging in a most exaggerated manner. Only as an actor, portraying a certain type of character, would I ever walk in such a manner. I told Jayne that exterior kind of stereotypical imaging and movement was not what I taught. I found this interpretation uncomfortable to watch and limiting in its message. It was not real, not authentic, so we discarded that idea and started from scratch.

Being truly feminine is in your thoughts, feelings, and experiences, which of course manifests and finds expression through the body. Only when you are "comfortable in your skin" will you project a naturalness and compatibility with your chosen identity. Attaining this takes work. Many people are imprisoned in a specific role and have not given themselves permission to explore options.

How does one begin to discover his or her full potential? This is where the performing arts can be a wonderful vehicle for that process. Particularly with challenges facing the transgendered, these techniques can help expand their true capabilities and assist in achieving a greater positive presence and authenticity.

JAYNE: Investigators have long known that 75 percent to 90 percent of the meaning of what gets transmitted between two people is in the nonverbal component of the message. For example, we know that when someone walks into a room and we sense their unhappiness, even though their words may try to convince us everything is "okay," we disregard the words and continue to be convinced that there is a problem. We invariably believe the nonverbal messages over the verbal message. Each of us has become expert at reading the nonverbal communication of others. It therefore follows that when we go out in public trying to present ourselves as who we really are without those appropriate life experiences for our preferred gender role, we may have a problem. If we aren't coming across in an authentic way, with a natural attitude and bearing (and the nonverbal channels of communication convey attitude wonderfully), we will have a problem. Much of the unacceptance we initially experience in trying to live a new gender role stems from such non-authenticity. Annette and I state emphatically: Our program does not teach you to act the part of a specific gender role. We do not teach someone to develop a gender act. Rather, we teach the individual to become comfortable and in touch with who he or she really is. To do this requires a lot of work. It does not come easily; but the payoff is great and doing the actual work can be, and often is, a lot of fun.

ANNETTE: Another aspect of working with this population has to do with the difficulty of unlearning lifelong habits. Many people transitioning from one gender role to another have a tendency to approach this unknown territory intellectually. We are all guilty of sabotaging new possibilities by overanalyzing.

I remember one student, Jennifer, a gifted individual and medical professional who, at the time, was struggling tremendously with her transition. Jennifer would enthusiastically show up for the lesson, ready to attack this new experience like a research project. It was very difficult for someone of this nature and background to trust the guidance of another's teaching. Dance/movement is not an intellectual concept. It is a visceral adventure. This discipline requires physical and emotional involvement.

Throughout our work, Jennifer would continually stop the flow of the movement and ask:

"Annette, what is the meaning behind these steps?

"How are these moves structured?

"What is the theoretical approach to this choreography?

"How far should I move my arm? I can't pick up my foot, it doesn't want to move."

I would say, "Jennifer, just do it. Give it a whirl."

"But, I have to understand where it comes from."

"Simply let go and give the process a chance."

I could not stress enough how important it was to move first, to allow the experience to live in the body. In the sheer doing of it, we receive answers. And, most importantly, we begin to move past our fears. Jennifer found comfort and safety remaining locked up in her intellectualizing.

Change requires using a new set of muscles. The minute she took a risk and really began moving, there was such a release of emotion. She shared, "I'm feeling so terribly vulnerable and out of control . . . this is all so hard for me to handle. Secretly, I've always wanted to dance . . . but as a man, I have never been given permission. I have not been allowed to dance like this. A few social occasions have been my limit."

JAYNE: I am convinced that women know their bodies better than men do; they know and have become more comfortable with their abilities and limitations. Like it or not, a woman in a social situation gets looked at and judged by how she appears and presents herself. Therefore, women get to know better how they are being perceived. When someone is making such a profound change in their life as in gender role, they are doing so without complete knowledge of what lies ahead. Consider this, I had my final surgery nine or ten years ago. The medical establishment pretty well said that since I had completed all the steps necessary, complied with the "Benjamin Guidelines," I qualified for surgical sexual reassignment. Following surgery, I could now go out in society and live as I had always wanted. I do not remember anyone giving me a set of instructions for the new anatomical equipment or how I should go about maintaining it. But there I was, a newly configured female without the life experiences genetic females receive growing up as a girl and becoming a woman in society. Oh, I certainly had my fantasies—I would be Marilyn Monroe, I would be desired, protected, and taken care of by a man, etc. But I soon found learning to become a woman is like learning to play basketball. You don't learn it from reading a book. You have to get out there in the fast lane and do it.

Many of my friends, including Annette, had to put up with me going through a much-delayed feminine adolescence, an adolescence occurring in my forties. Because that is the only way you get the experiences that are required in successfully growing up. What dance/movement can do is to help you become more comfortable. All of the resources we draw upon, in using techniques from the performing arts and communication, can help you explore those necessary and essential growth experiences.

ANNETTE: Creativity can be a wonderful friend to anyone choosing to embrace growth and self-reflection. We all can appreciate how difficult and challenging the road toward greater development can be. One way to motivate this challenge is through the use of dance/movement expression. Because 99 percent of the creative arts lives in one's imagination, it is a wonderful vehicle for people who spend most of their time and energy imagining they would like to be someone else. Learning to use this imagination in a positive and constructive fashion toward achieving inner growth and understanding can be one of the many rewards of an artistic process. By virtue of the subjective nature of the arts, one's participation in the experience is always reaffirming, honest, and without judgment or expectation. This type of validation has no price tag, nor does it need the outer temporary affirmations we seek from others. It is a self-valuing process . . . a gift of confidence one gives to oneself.

JAYNE: As men who have grown up in our heads and been trained to have the correct solution cognitively, we feel the pressure of having to be right and to constantly reach for perfection. As men we go for the bottom line, the logical solution.

I remember Annette struggling to try to get me to look in the mirror in my dancing. Dancers work in front of mirrors to develop a sense of seeing the correct line. I refused to look at myself until I could do the movement correctly. I did not want to see the imperfection that needed correcting.

ANNETTE: What Jayne shares about her struggles in the dance class with regards to the mirror is extremely important. Most students, at first, have difficulty facing their imperfections. Although, for anyone, the mirror can serve as wonderful metaphor for taking responsibility for all our significant issues. As dancers, we are always fine-tuning our craft, extending and stretching our full potential, reaching past our limitations, mastering the beauty of our expression.

The mirror serves as a guide and supportive partner, we hope, in teaching you to instruct so as to help the person become his or her own teacher. The goal is not to remain dependent on you. If the students can look in the mirror honestly and make corrections with the language you have given them, then they may begin to fix things independently. This is when you start to "own" your body, when the movement becomes more natural and one's unique quality begins to manifest. The mirror is analogous to what we are trying to do in dance/movement with individuals dealing with gender-related concerns, as well as other populations challenged with adversity. We want to give students the opportunity to become comfortable and authentic with their physical presence, to explore, in a safe and nurturing environment, positive ways of gaining esteem and confidence with their new identity.

> "You are unique,—and if that is not fulfilled, then something has been lost."
>
> Martha Graham

Gender Attitude Reassessment Program (GARP)

Ariadne Kane

The Gender Attitude Reassessment Program has been in evolution for fifteen years, and we have come to use the acronym GARP to describe it. It started with my efforts in the gender community but it has spread to include health care professionals. This program represents a combination of my thinking and that of my co-presenters, Marilyn Volker, a sex educator and therapist from the Miami-Ft. Lauderdale area, and David Prok, a professor of sociology at Baldwin Wallace College in Berea, Ohio. The three of us have presented to professionals several of these programs, which vary in length from four hours to a day and half. The object is to transform the current perception of gender into something different from the one the participants originally have, and it is this aspect of the program that is presented here.

Gender perception is a key to understanding since cross-dresser/cross-gender individuals often express behaviors and individual lifestyles in ways that *isolate from* rather than *integrate with* general cultural diversity. I strongly believe that such isolation is not only counterproductive, but is probably more destructive than instructive for our society.

The GARP addresses three fundamental questions: the question of perception, role playing and behaviors, and modes of presentation. Briefly, perception is what is in a person's head, role playing and behaviors are how a person acts, and modes of presentation are what a person wears and how he or she functions in a particular society. Note that I use the word perception rather than conception. This is because there is no fixed notion about gender, but instead each of us has a notion of gender and through role playing and presentation we convey our perceptions. Gender perception is interactive with gender expression, that is, the role playing and the way a person presents in any particular society including clothing, attitudes, and characteristics. Gender perceptions are not necessarily fixed. A person at age twenty has a perception of masculinity and femininity that will be different from such perceptions at age thirty or at age forty. Changes are ongoing. It is important for health care professionals to know some of the dynamics of gender perception in their efforts to understand gender shift.

In the context of the GARP certain things are assumed. One assumption is that there are at least two universes out there. The first might be called the bio-centric universe. This is the universe through which all humans have evolved into the bimorphic entities, male and female. But this universe interacts with a changing environment as soon as a person leaves the womb. Parents, relatives, friends, siblings, teachers, clergy, et al., interact with an individual in determining gender perception, and this perception changes with different influences. What the GARP attempts is to make people aware that gender perception is fluid, that it is not fixed.

We emphasize during the GARP workshop that gender is mainly a sociological construct, although set in a biological background. This opens up a vast array of tools that can be used to measure some gender ideas and allows discussion about just how feminine a feminine person is. In such discussions we raise questions about whether femininity is different from being effeminate or being a very effeminate male. What do such terms really mean, how are they used, and in what context? Such a discussion encourages participants to view gender in terms of change and interaction, that gender perception is a social pattern. A person with a Chicano-American background will have a different concept of gender role, and gender presentation will be somewhat different from that of a Euro-American. This is true of members of the Afro-American and other communities. Participants are encouraged to look at gender diversity in terms of where people come from and not just in terms of apparel and accoutrements.

One of the tools we use in GARP is the gender role inventory (GRI). We ask everyone who participates to list a set of characteristics that really represent his or her persona. These are to be divided into two parts, one part called "feminine" and the other labeled "masculine," although we are careful not to describe what we think might be feminine or masculine. The results vary tremendously since femininity for some women is quite different from femininity for other women, and similar differences are noted in the males. This leads to discussion about what these role-inventories signify, and from such discussions a consensus emerges about the diversity of gender role expressions. In going through this particular exercise, it seems evident to us that the GRI reflects how a person views himself or herself at this particular point in time.

A second major unit of the GARP is the cross-dressing, cross-gender (CD/CG) "crucible." Here, for the first time we examine the cross-dressed (CD), cross-gendered (CG), and transsexual (TS) persons, the major groups making up a conscious gender community and whose differences reflect the diversity that is within every human being. However, instead of viewing these gender options as separate and unique, the focus is on the specific behavioral social construct as a means of accessing all of the diversity in gender. This represents a different approach for most health professionals, who have become accustomed to looking at CD/CG individuals as dysfunctional in a world where the only norm is a binary one. Drawing upon films and other programs we have used at Fantasia Fair, we then explore different aspects of the CD/CG phenomena and encourage specula tion about what it would be liked to be in a different gender role or presentation. At a later point in the GARP, the props of gender, such as clothing, are intro= duced. We point out that people buy a variety of clothes for a variety of reasons. Some clothing is used to enhance erotic feelings or to satisfy other needs. For instance, there is a myriad of bra styles and types. Which type should a woman or a CD/CG pick or should a person go without wearing a bra? Similarly with pantyhose. The conditions for choice of item are important determinants. For example, during the Vietnam war, many of the American troops wore pantyhose. This is because they would slog through the marshes and swamps of the MeKong River Delta where there were mycetes that could penetrate the skin and enter the bloodstream and then end up in the liver, where they caused severe damage. Since pantyhose provided a barrier against the entry of these microbes, all troops were required to wear pantyhose to protect them. The importance of this story is that it illustrates how a specific prop, used in one context by women, were now used for a different purpose—to protect males in combat against disease.

At the GARP, there is a whole table of such props of clothing and accou-trements that women use, and similar items for men. We found that there were some items that female participants of any GARP gravitate toward when they want to define or look at a masculine gender role, and similarly some things that males gravitate to. For example, at one GARP where there were seven women, three of them opted for mustaches. They would put on authentic theatrical mus-taches and add sideburns with a magic marker and wear a hat. These three mas-culine props created an illusion of masculine visage. The six men involved had a greater variety of props to choose from since for every prop that was "masculine" there were five or six that were "feminine," and within each category there was a wide variety. Most men chose a bra, of which there was a variety. Three chose the kind of bra that is associated with Victoria's Secret while two others chose bras that are listed in sport magazines for women; one man chose the long-line bra, one with all the backing and lots of hooks. They then tried to fill them with objects at hand (such as socks) since we had only two sets of breast prostheses of the type used by women who have had mastectomies. Those men who used these underwent a notable transformation. One man who chose this prop set was so elated with the feel and weightiness on his chest that he put on a sweater and "came out" to the group as "Brenda." He wore the ensemble for the remainder of the GARP and reported that he felt very comfortable with his newly "augmented" chest and had a desire to add some other props to express his "anima" or feminine side further. Generally, in fact, the application of masculine and feminine props to access one's animus or anima is one highlight of the GARP experience.

After exploring and using the props, and discussing the CD/CG behavior model as a crucible for exploring individual gender diversity, we move into role playing in which a male accessing his anima interacts with a female and addresses her animus. The dyad role play points out some of the challenges of communication between players who typically do not relate in these roles. The imagination displayed by the participants is truly amazing although the roles played in our session have not been particularly erotic or sexual.

As the GARP participants begin to think about gender in a different way, we ask participants to generate a biosketch of their other gender persona, listing their ages, what they do for a living, their likes and dislikes, current relationship status, and so on. This exercise emphasizes the potential gender diversity within each of us, something we then try to enforce didactically.

This last is the nub of what I call the *Tao of Gender*. For this we utilize Carl Jung's concept of the anima and animus inside each of us. Most Americans probably accept this in theory but it is when they see the diversity of gender portrayals, sometimes labeled as deviations, that many people tend to become uncomfortable. The *Tao of Gender* is based on the need to balance one's anima with one's animus, or in Chinese terms getting a balance between our yin force and yang force. We ask our participants to illustrate what their anima is if they are male and their animus if they are female. Large sheets of newsprint and crayons are provided and each participant is given fifteen to twenty minutes to draw his or her anima or animus. Participants then share these with the others.

We find that there has been a considerable change in how the participants changed their perceptions, many of them quite radically, over the course of the GARP workshop. We conclude by emphasizing the ethnocentric cultural and racial diversity within American culture and the dangers of health care providers not taking these into account. We feel the GARP is an important learning experience for exploring and broadening each individual's scope of gender perception, and it gives him or her a way of developing his or her own understanding. I hope that this brief outline proves helpful to our readers.

References

Bardwick, J. M. 1979. *In transition: How feminism, sexual liberation, and the search for self-fulfillment have altered America.* New York: Holt, Rinehart, & Winston.

Bem, S. 1993. *Lenses of gender.* New Haven, Conn.: Yale University Press.

Bolin, A. 1988. *In search of Eve: Transsexual rites of passage.* South Hadley, Mass.: Bergin & Garvey.

Bornstein, K. 1994. *Gender outlaw: On men, women, and the rest of us.* London: Routledge.

Bullough, V., and B. Bullough. 1993. *Cross dressing, sex and gender.* Philadelphia: University of Pennsylvania Press.

Devor, H. 1989. *Gender blending.* Bloomington, Ind.: Indiana University Press.

Gerzon, M. 1991. *A choice of heroes.* Boston: Houghton-Mifflin,

Gill, A. 1984. *Mad about the boy.* New York: Holt, Rinehart, & Winston

Hanna J. 1988. *Dance, sex and gender.* Chicago: University of Chicago.

Herdt, G. 1994. *Third sex, third gender: Beyond sexual dimorphism in culture and history.* New York: Zone Books

Hirschfeld, Magnus. 1991. *Transvestites; The erotic drive to cross dress.* Translated by M. Lombardi-Nash. Amherst, N.Y.: Prometheus Books.

Jordan, J., et al. 1991. *Woman in connection.* New York: Guilford.

Jung, C. G. 1987. *Jung and feminism.* Edited by D. S. Wehr. Boston: Beacon Press.

Miller, J. B. 1976. *Towards a new psychology of woman.* Boston: Beacon Press.

Money, J., and M. Lamacz. 1989. *Vandalized lovemaps: Paraphilic outcome of seven cases in pediatric sexology.* Amherst, N.Y.: Prometheus Books.

Morgan, J. 1992. *Discovering men.* London: Routledge.

Nanda, S. 1990 *Neither man nor woman: The Hijrai.* Belmont, Calif.: Wadsworth Publishing.

Nelson, J. 1988. *The intimate connection.* Philadelphia: Westminster Press.

Offerman-Zuckerberg, J. 1989. *Gender in transition.* New York: Plenum.

Powell, J. 1969. *Why am I afraid to tell you who I am?* Niles, Ill.: Argus Publishers.

Richards, M. C. 1980. *Toward wholeness.* Middletown, Conn.: Wesleyan University Press.

Roscoe, W. 1991. *The Zuni man-woman.* Albuquerque: University of New Mexico Press.

Sanford, J. 1980. *The invisible partners.* New York: Paulist Press.

Sargent, A. 1983. *The androgynous manager.* New York: American Management Association.

Tanner, D. 1990. *You just don't understand.* New York: Morrow.

Thorne, L. 1993. *Gender play.* London: Routledge.

Villoldo, A., and S. Krippner. 1987. *Healing states.* New York: Fireside Books.

9

LAW AND LEGAL ISSUES

Introduction

Law is a form of social power. It regulates human relations by establishing rules, backed by sanctions, that prescribe certain lines of conduct in certain situations. What is legal, or for that matter moral, in any society is not dependent upon the inherent nature of things, but upon an act of recognition that is essentially arbitrary. Morality and law are not necessarily the same thing, however, since morality covers a wide range of informal organized opinion and deeply held convictions. Law, on the other hand, consists exclusively of those rules enacted by formally organized social power, rules that are backed by definite sanctions, the imposition and interpretation of which are normally entrusted to special officials. Laws are not necessarily concerned with what is right or good or what one thinks or how one's conscience works, but rather on external actions. Some, however, want the law also to enforce morality.

American law is based upon English common law as opposed to the Roman law to which most of continental Europe as well as Latin America adheres. Common law was originally based on custom and court decisions and is supplemented by statutory laws. Even statutory law, however, is subject to interpretation by the courts. Thus, it can change, either through court decisions or through legislative enactments.

A point of controversy in American and English law is the question of what actions should be defined as criminal. Over 150 years ago, Jeremy Bentham, the

English utilitarian philosopher and legal critic, spoke out against including in the criminal law what he called imaginary offenses and crimes unsuitable for punishment. In American popular discourse these were called "victimless crimes" and included in this category were crimes involving consenting adults, i.e., homosexuality or prostitution, and crimes for which legal prohibitions were substantially ineffective, i.e., abortion (Schur 1965).

Similar discussion took place in Great Britain, where the Wolfenden Report, the product of a government-appointed commission, in the 1950s recommended the removal from the criminal law of prohibitions against homosexual conduct in private between consenting adults and recommended that prostitution be decriminalized. The report stated that "There must remain a realm of private morality and immorality, which is, in brief and crude terms, not the law's business" (Wolfenden 1957). In the United States similar recommendations were made in the Model Penal Code of the American Law Institute.

Matters are never that easy, however, and some critics of the Model Penal Code condemned it because they felt that conduct that society thinks is wrong should be defined as criminal even if such laws cannot be enforced (Devlin 1959). It is this ongoing debate that most affects the transgender community. Large segments of the American population feel that the penal law should resemble an official code of morality, and though the majority of Americans probably believe that matters of sexual morality should be of no concern to the law as long as they take place between consenting adults, there is enough uncertainty in public opinion to allow critics of such a position to righteously proclaim a legal enforcement of morals.

Many states, for example, had legal prohibitions against cross-dressing, particularly by males, since it was assumed they would only do so for criminal purposes. Many city ordinances (including for a time those in Los Angeles) refused to license entertainment in which cross-dressing took place. However, it could be done for an educational purpose, in serious drama, and on special occasions (i.e., Halloween) without interference. Gradually many of these laws have been declared unconstitutional, removed by legislative fiat, or ignored by law enforcement officials.

Many of the legal battles have been fought by transsexuals who, after winning the right to undergo sex reassignment surgery, had to get all their records changed, including birth certificates, drivers' licenses, and passports. Many also had to challenge laws that would not have permitted them to marry in their new sexual identity. Obviously the law in the area of gender and transgender issues is changing. Three legal experts included in this section, Louis Swartz, Richard Green, and Stephen Whittle, are among the leaders in this area of law, and their overview and background information help the reader understand the shifting legal situation in both the United States and the United Kingdom. Just how pervasively legal definitions carry over into civil matters is explained by the fourth contributor, Lisa Middleton, an expert on insurance. Society has made considerable progress in coming to terms with its transgendered population, but it still has a long way to go.

References

Devlin, P. 1959. *The enforcement of morals.* Oxford: Oxford University Press.
Schur, E. M. 1965. *Crimes without victims.* Englewood Cliffs, N.J.: Prentice Hall.
Wolfenden, John, chair. 1957. *Report of the Committee on Homosexual Offenses and Prostitution.* London: Her Majesty's Stationery Office.

Law and Transsexualism

Louis H. Swartz

> The life of the law has not been logic: it has been experience. The felt necessities of the time, the prevalent moral and political theories, intuitions of public policy, avowed or unconscious, even the prejudices judges share with their fellow-men, have had a good deal more to do than the syllogism in determining the rules by which men should be governed. (Holmes 1881, 1)

The above quotation from Oliver Wendell Holmes, Jr., can be taken as stating some of the themes of this paper. American law, with all its variety, strengths, and weaknesses, tends to be pragmatic, and is not necessarily logically consistent. I see that as a potential strength. That inconsistency has oftentimes permitted piecemeal adjustment to the situation of post-operative transsexuals (post-op TSs), as with some birth certificate statutes or judicial decisions, for example, or in the case of some validity of marriage decisions (e.g., *M.T.* v. *J.T.*, 140 N.J. Super. 77, 355 A. 2d 204, cert. denied 71 N.J. 345, 364 A. 2d 1076 [1976].) On the other hand, a strong putative emphasis on deductive logic and consistency, especially in the English decision in *Corbett* v. *Corbett* (2 W.L.R. 1306, 2 All E.R. 33 [P.D.A. 1970], [1971] P. 83), led there to the conclusion that for legal purposes, including adjudicating validity of marriage, sex is fixed at birth, is tied to chromosomal makeup, and cannot be changed. In the New Jersey case we see what might be called a functional multifaceted approach; a compassionate legal accommodation based upon what might loosely be called a judicial version of situation ethics. In the English case of *Corbett* the syllogism is more in evidence, and a highly nuanced flexibility is by implication ruled out.

We are in a time of gender ferment, gender-role pluralism and change, and gender controversy. There appears to be considerable openness in the United States, both socially *and* legally, to the processes of gender ferment, but not without significant, perhaps increasing, opposition. The term openness, in this context, paradoxically includes the coexistence, on one hand, of efforts to repress or control departures from the "standard" legitimate patterns of the past. It also includes, on the other hand, behaviors and attitudes tolerant of, or favorable to, innovative or previously concealed or disparaged phenomena, including those concerning transgender.

In this short paper, I will attempt to do many things, perhaps seeking to include too much within too brief a space. Included here, in Part One, is a brief guide to legal literature pertinent to transsexualism. I focus mainly on the United States, but also include some reference to the United Kingdom, Australia, and New Zealand. This literature is substantial. The number of topics involved is large. Readers will have to turn to the references themselves for detailed analysis of particular legal problems, which may of course be resolved differently in various states, or in various geographical parts of our federal court system.

Part One

1. *Relevant legal issues.* From the outset of modern developments concerning TS, legal issues have been highlighted (Benjamin 1966; Hamburger, Stürup, and Dahl-Iversen 1953; Green and Money 1969).

2. *Literature on a wide variety of legal issues pertaining to lesbians and gay men can be relevant.* This may especially be the case for pre-op or non-operative TSs when we are talking about what the law may regard as same sex relations and interactions (Achtenberg 1985/1993; Harvard Law Review Editors 1989; Hunter, Michaelson, and Stoddard 1992; Rubenstein 1993).

3. *Freedom of expression with respect to transgender has not recently posed special legal problems in the United States.* We have broad legal freedom of expression here concerning printed and pictorial matter, although it is sometimes accompanied by police harassment, especially at the local level (Swartz 1994). Expression even in mainstream film and video has been fairly open (Bell-Metereau 1993; Murray 1994).

4. *Controversy about transgender and its therapy in professional and lay literature.* See Raymond 1994; Stoller 1985.

5. *Broad surveys.* Green (1992) is the most comprehensive, easily accessible, recent U.S. work, but the issues are sufficiently complex and varied so that this is only a start. See also Bradley 1991 (U.K.); David 1974–1975; Finlay and

Walters 1988 (Australia and U.K.); Green and Money 1969; International Conference on Transgender Law and Employment Policy 1992, 1993, 1994; McMullan and Whittle 1994 (U.K.); Richardson 1983; Smith 1971; Taitz 1987; Walz 1979. These broad surveys sometimes also include several of the specific topics listed below.

6. *Birth certificates and other vital records.* See David 1974–1975; Finlay and Walters 1988 (Australia and U.K.); Gould 1979; Kopka 1983; Phillips 1991; Taitz 1988 (U.K.); Walton 1984, 1992 (U.K.); Walz 1979.

7. *Criminal law.* See Bailey-Harris 1989 (Australia); David 1974–1975; Finlay and Walters 1988 (Australia and U.K.); Otlowski 1990 (Australia); Pace 1983 (U.K.); Smith 1971.

8. *Cross-dressing.* See Gould 1979; Haag and Sullinger 1982; Neff 1985; Twardy 1980.

9. *Custody and related issues.* See Clark 1989; Richardson 1983.

10. *Employment rights and discrimination issues.* See Annual Survey 1982; Cotton 1986; Green 1992; Hiegel 1994; International Conference on Transgender Law and Employment Policy 1992, 1993, 1994; Neff 1985; Pannick 1983 (Australia and U.S.); Richardson 1983; Schmitz 1993–1994.

11. *Funding of, or public provision of, medical services.* See Bradley 1991 (U.K.); Gordon 1991; Green 1985, 1992; Jacobs 1980.

12. *Marriage.* See Armstrong and Walton 1990 (U.K.); Bradley 1991 (U.K.); David 1974–1975; Hurley 1984; Kopka 1983; MacKenzie 1992 (New Zealand); Phillips 1991; Richardson 1983; Taitz 1986 (mainly U.K.); Twardy 1980; Walton 1984 (U.K.); Watson 1986.

13. *Prison environment.* See Haag and Sullinger 1982. Also *Farmer v. Brennan*, vol. 62 *United States Law Week*, 4446–56 in which the Supreme Court of the United States (June 6, 1994) recognized the U.S. Constitution's Eighth Amendment basis for claim (damages, injunctive relief) of female-appearing male pre-op TS federal prisoner, with respect to protection against inmate-to-inmate sexual assault and other violence.

14. *Professional liability of physicians and related professionals.* See Belli 1978; David 1974–1975; Kopka 1983; Twardy 1980.

15. *Sports.* See Bassis 1978; Green 1992.

16. *Self-help organizations: They have been gaining in legal capability and sophistication.* The value of professional and self-help organizations involved in the transgender movement in assisting with and providing guidance concerning practical law-related problems is great. One highly important development has been the activities of the International Conference on Transgender Law and Employment Policy (1992, 1993, 1994), whose published proceedings of task force reports and presentations now total about 1,000 pages. It should also be

emphasized that self-help organizations may sometimes be very helpful in suggesting practical ways of achieving important objectives, e.g., concerning making a gender transition while on the same job, or changing records of various kinds, *without* getting involved in a formal legal dispute. See, for example, McMullan and Whittle 1994 (U.K.). Legal dispute *avoidance* can be the best kind of legal dispute resolution if a constructive, practical result can be accomplished that way. For some other, early publications, see Erickson Educational Foundation 1974a, 1974b.

Part Two

I would like to continue now with a series of observations, especially with respect to law in the United States, and to a lesser extent in the United Kingdom, Australia, and New Zealand.

1. *Availability of medical and related professional services.* The outstanding fact concerning medical, surgical, and psychological interventions pertinent to gender dysphoria, including sex reassignment hormonal and surgical interventions, is that professional services have been lawfully available. I refer to the period from the 1960s onward. This has made the modern transgender movement possible. Financial provision for such services has been much more difficult, although in the United Kingdom apparently these have been available under the National Health Service. Transnational recourse to surgical services, or recourse across state boundaries in the United States, has been an important part of the picture.

2. *Medicine and related professions have had great autonomy.* For purposes of the matters under discussion here, the medical and psychological professions have been largely free to engage in self-governance. Furthermore, certainly in the United States as well as in a number of other countries, individual physicians and surgeons, or particular clusters of these professionals, have had enormous legal autonomy. Legally speaking we have had great pluralism and diversity among individual practitioners, as opposed to centralized governmental control or judicial monitoring. This has made highly innovative approaches possible.

3. *Courts have usually given great weight to medical opinion in cases involving post-op TSs.* That has not always resulted in liberal decisions, however, in part because of the position taken by the particular medical personnel themselves. The judge in the restrictive *Corbett* case had medical qualifications; some of the medical witnesses in that case took the clear position that sex reassignment surgery did *not* change a person's sex. An early medical committee advised that the law should not permit birth certificates to be changed following sex reassignment surgery (New York Academy of Medicine 1966).

4. *Legal shaping of professional medical practice by way of tort claims, or a perceived risk of tort claims, apparently has been fairly moderate.* Although actual or potential medical malpractice claims, with resultant defensive medicine, have been much commented upon in other aspects of health law, it would seem that gender dysphoria therapies and therapists have not been the target of civil tort claims to any unusual extent. This fact, if it is a fact, is an important one.

5. *Professional subspecialty self-guidance efforts concerning gender dysphoria therapy practice have been important.* Instead of detailed legal governance of medical practice in this area, by legislatures, governmental administrative bodies, and courts, we have had what I will call professional self-guidance, as illustrated by the Benjamin Standards of Care and by the American Psychiatric Association's DSM-III and DSM-IV (1980, 1994). These have been consensus guidelines and diagnostic classification schemes.

6. *Legal approaches to transsexual legal issues in the United States have been incremental and piecemeal.* We have not had in any of the American states comprehensive legislation pertaining to transsexualism, including regulation of its therapy plus legal definition of transsexualism's various possible criminal, public, and private civil consequences.

7. *It can be argued that the piecemeal legal approach, rather than a unified comprehensive legislative approach, is by far the better one for gradually bringing about constructive legal change concerning transgender issues in the United States.* Sweeping legislative arrangements concerning transgender issues seem highly vulnerable to veto-group politics. While hypothetically reasonable, efforts at comprehensive legislative change in areas pertinent to sexuality, within the American context, seem all too likely to result in no change, or retrograde change.

8. *In spite of professional and social controversy and debate concerning transgender issues, the legal response to transsexualism in the United States has been fairly receptive and accommodating.* The picture is mixed, of course, and is far from what many would like to see. Considering the profound nature of the issues sometimes involved, pertaining to the permissible scope of medical interventions on a voluntary basis, and pertaining to fundamental rearrangement of one's social gender identity, American law has shown much flexibility. The greatest achievement has been the heavy, continued reliance on legally grounded professional medical autonomy, and respect for the legal autonomy of the individual in medical and other therapeutic decisionmaking. Compassionate accommodation has been present to an important degree in some judicial decisions, e.g., concerning marriage validity, and in enactment of some statutes concerning change of birth certificates. Nevertheless, moralistic exclusion and even punitive condemnation have also been expressed by some legislatures and courts.

References

Achtenberg, R., ed. 1985/1993. *Sexual orientation and the law*. National Lawyers Guild Lesbian-Gay Rights Committee. Deerfield, Ill.: Clark Boardman Callaghan. Published 1985, with loose-leaf updates through 1993.

American Psychiatric Association. 1980. *Diagnostic and statistical manual of mental disorders* (DSM-III). 3d ed. Washington, D.C.: American Psychiatric Association.

————. 1994. *Diagnostic and statistical manual of mental disorders* (DSM-IV). 4th ed. Washington, D.C.: American Psychiatric Association.

Andrews, J., and Sherlock, A. 1991. Council of Europe, Court of Human Rights: Transsexual rights in the United Kingdom. *European Law Review* 16, no. 3: 262–66.

Annual Survey. 1982. 1981-1982 Annual survey of labor relations and employment discrimination law. Transsexuals and Title VII: *Sommers v. Budget Marketing, Inc. Boston College Law Review* 24, no. 1. 266–72.

Armstrong, C. N., and T. Walton. 1990. Transsexuals and the law. *New Law Journal* 140, no. 6474: 1384–90.

————. 1992. Transsexual metamorphoses. *New Law Journal* 142, no. 6536: 96–97.

Bailey-Harris, R. 1989. Sex change in the criminal law and beyond. *Criminal Law Journal* 13: 353–67.

Bassis, L. M. 1978. A legal conundrum—transsexuals in athletics. *COMM/ENT: A Journal of Communications and Entertainment Law* (Hastings College of Law) 1, no. 2: 369–417.

Bell-Metereau, R. 1993. *Hollywood androgyny*. 2d ed. New York: Columbia University Press.

Belli, M. M. 1978. Transsexual surgery: A new tort? *Journal of the American Medical Association* 239, no. 20: 2143–48. Reprinted 1978–1979, *Journal of Family Law* 17: 487–504.

Benjamin, H. 1966. *The transsexual phenomenon*. New York: Julian Press.

Bradley, D. 1991. Transsexualism and legal policy. *Gender Dysphoria* 1, no. 1: 25–40.

Bullough, V. L. 1994. *Science in the bedroom: A history of sex research*. New York: Basic Books.

Bullough, V. L., and B. Bullough. 1993. *Cross dressing, sex, and gender*. Philadelphia: University of Pennsylvania Press.

Clark, R. 1989. *Daly v. Daly*: The closing of a door. *Journal of Juvenile Law* 10, no. 2: 221–31.

Cotton, D. D. 1986. *Ulane v. Eastern Airlines*: Title VII and transsexualism. *Northwestern University Law Review* 80, no. 4: 1037–65.

David, E. S. 1974–1975. The law and transsexualism: A faltering response to a conceptual dilemma. *Connecticut Law Review* 7, no. 2: 288–345.

Erickson Educational Foundation. 1974a. *Guidelines for transsexuals*. Baton Rouge, La.: Erickson Educational Foundation.

————. 1974b. *Information on transsexualism for law enforcement officers*. Baton Rouge, La: Erickson Educational Foundation.

Finlay, H. A., and W. A. W. Walters. 1988. *Sex change: The legal implications of sex reassignment*. Victoria, Australia: H. A. Finlay.

Gooren, L. J. G., and F. A. van der Reijt. 1994. Transsexualism, sex reassignment, and the law. In *The handbook of forensic sexology: biomedical and criminological perspectives,* edited by J. J. Krivacska and J. Money, 184–200. Amherst, N.Y.: Promethcus Books.

Gordon, E. B. 1991. Transsexual healing: Medicaid funding of sex reassignment surgery. *Archives of Sexual Behavior* 20, no. 1: 61–74.

Gould, M. 1979. Sex, gender, and the need for legal clarity: the case of transsexualism. *Valparaiso University Law Review* 13, no. 3: 423–50.

Green, R. 1985. Spelling "relief" for transsexuals: Employment discrimination and the criteria of sex. *Yale Law & Policy Review* 4, no. 1: 125–40.

——. 1992. *Sexual science and the law*. Cambridge, Mass.: Harvard University Press.

Green, R., and J. Money, eds. 1969. *Transsexualism and sex reassignment*. Baltimore: The Johns Hopkins University Press.

Haag, J. S., and T. L. Sullinger. 1982. Is he or isn't she? Transsexualism: Legal impediments to integrating a product of medical definition and technology. *Washburn Law Journal* 21, no. 2: 342–72.

Hamburger, C., G. K. Stürup, and E. Dahl-Iversen. 1953. Transvestism: hormonal, psychiatric, and surgical treatment. *Journal of the American Medical Association* 152, no. 5: 391–96.

Harry Benjamin International Gender Dysphoria Association, Inc. 1985. Standards of care: The hormonal and surgical sex reassignment of gender dysphoric persons. *Archives of Sexual Behavior* 14, no. 1: 79–90.

Harvard Law Review Editors. 1989. Developments in the law—Sexual orientation and the law. *Harvard Law Review* 102, no. 1: 1508–1671. (Republished 1990. *Sexual orientation and the law*. Cambridge, Mass.: Harvard University Press.)

Hiegel, A. L. 1994. Sexual exclusions: The Americans with Disabilities Act as a moral code. *Columbia Law Review* no. 4: 1451–93.

Holloway, J. P. 1968. Transsexuals—their legal sex. *University of Colorado Law Review* 40, no. 2: 283–95.

Holmes, O. W., Jr. 1881. *The common law*. Boston: Little, Brown.

Hunter, N. D., S. E. Michaelson, and T. B. Stoddard. 1992. *The rights of lesbians and gay men*. 3d ed. (An American Civil Liberties Union Handbook.) Carbondale: Southern Illinois University Press.

Hurley, T. M. 1984. Constitutional implications of sex-change operations: Mind over matter? *Journal of Legal Medicine* 5, no. 4: 633–64.

International Conference on Transgender Law and Employment Policy (ICTLEP). 1992. *Proceedings from the First International Conference on Transgender Law and Employment Policy*. Houston, Tex: ICTLEP, Inc.

——. 1993. *Proceedings from the Second International Conference on Transgender Law and Employment Policy*. Houston, Tex: ICTLEP, Inc.

——. 1994. *Proceedings from the Third International Conference on Transgender Law and Employment Policy. TRANSGEN '94*. Houston, Tex: ICTLEP, Inc.

Jacobs, S. A. 1980. The determination of medical necessity: Medicaid funding for sex-reassignment surgery. *Case Western Reserve Law Review* 31, no. 1: 179–209.

Kopka, S. L. 1983. The legal status of the postoperative transsexual: The grey gelding ain't what he used to be, or the grass isn't always greener. *Medical Trial Technique Quarterly*, 456–76.

MacKenzie, G. O. 1994. *Transgender nation*. Bowling Green, Ohio: Bowling Green State University Popular Press.

MacKenzie, R. 1992. Transsexuals' legal sexual status and same sex marriage in New Zealand: *M* v. *M. Otago Law Review* 7, no. 4: 556–77.

McMullan, M., and S. Whittle. *Transvestism, transsexualism and the law*. London: The Gender Trust and The Beaumont Trust.

Money, J. 1986. *Venuses penuses: Sexology, sexosophy, and exigency theory*. Amherst, N.Y.: Prometheus Books.

——. 1988. *Gay, straight, and in-between: The sexology of erotic orientation*. New York: Oxford University Press.

Murray, R. 1994. *Images in the dark: An encyclopedia of gay and lesbian film and video*. Philadelphia: TLA Publications.

Neff, D. M. 1985. Denial of Title VII protection to transsexuals: *Ulane* v. *Eastern Airlines, Inc.* *DePaul Law Review* 34, no. 2: 553–86.

New York Academy of Medicine, Committee on Public Health. 1966. Change of sex on birth certificates for transsexuals. *Bulletin of the New York Academy of Medicine* 42, no. 8: 721–24.

Otlowski, M. 1990. The legal status of a sexually reassigned transsexual: *R.* v. *Harris and McGuinnes* and beyond. *Australian Law Journal* 64: 67–74.

Pace, P. J. 1983. Sexual identity and the criminal law. *Criminal Law Review,* 317–21.

Pannick, D. 1983. Homosexuals, transsexuals and the Sex Discrimination Act. *Public Law* no. 2: 279–302.

Phillips, S. L. 1991. Chromosome loophole: Homosexual marriages should be legalized based on transsexual marriages. *Adelphia Law Journal* 7: 73–108.

Raymond, J. G. 1994. *The transsexual empire: The making of the she-male.* Reissued with a new introduction on transgender. New York: Teachers College Press. (Original edition published 1979, Boston: Beacon Press.)

Richardson, L. A. 1983. The challenge of transsexuality: Legal responses to an assertion of rights. *Northern Illinois University Law Review* 4, no. 1: 119–52.

Rubenstein, W. B., ed. 1993. *Lesbians, gay men, and the law.* New York: New Press.

Schmitz, M. 1993–1994. *Doe* v. *Boeing*: The employer's duty to reasonably accommodate the handicapped employee. *Gonzaga Law Review* 29, no. 1: 205–23.

Smith, D. K. 1971. Transsexualism, sex reassignment surgery, and the law. *Cornell Law Review* 56, no. 6: 963–1009.

Stoller, R. J. 1985. *Presentations of gender.* New Haven, Conn.: Yale University Press.

Swartz, L. H. 1994. Laws and sex. In *Human sexuality: An encyclopedia,* edited by V. L. Bullough and B. Bullough, 347–54. New York: Garland.

Taitz, J. 1986. The law relating to the consummation of marriage where one of the spouses is a postoperative transsexual. *Anglo-American Law Review* 15, no. 2: 141–48.

———. 1987. Judicial determination of the sexual identity of post-operative transsexuals: a new form of sex discrimination. *American Journal of Law & Medicine* 13, no. 1: 53–69.

———. 1988. Transsexuals and sexual identity. *Modern Law Review* 51, no. 4: 502–508.

Twardy, S. 1980. Medicolegal aspects of transsexualism. *Medical Trial Technique Quarterly,* 249–314.

Walton, T. 1984. Why can't a woman? *New Law Journal* 134, no. 6175: 937–38.

———. 1992. A measure of appreciation. *New Law Journal* 142, no. 6566: 1202–1204.

Walz, M. B. 1979. Transsexuals and the law. *Journal of Contemporary Law* 5, no. 2: 181–214.

Watson, C. K. 1986. Transsexual marriages: Are they valid under California law? *Southwestern University Law Review* 16, no. 2: 505–31.

Legislating for Transsexual Rights: A Prescriptive Form

Stephen Whittle

Addressing the legislative needs of transsexual people who request legal recognition in their new gender roles is not such a simple and straightforward task as one might imagine. Those states that have legislated are now many and widespread, but the process of obtaining legal rights for transsexuals worldwide is by no means complete and the procedures undertaken can often be seen to provide unsatisfactory solutions in the cases of many individuals, because the legislation is either ill thought out, or has not taken into consideration what it is that transsexuals are actually seeking.

Legislation that apparently affords the transsexual recognition is in place in over forty of the states of the United States, most of Canada, South Australia, and fifteen of the states that are signatories to the European Convention on Human Rights. Ironically, one of the first countries that originally provided such legislation was that bastion of prejudice, South Africa, which legislated in 1974. Furthermore many Eastern-bloc states did provide legislative or civil procedure recognition for transsexuals prior to the fall of the Soviet bloc, but in the aftermath of the changes in the early 1990s, legislation often disappeared, and the new regimes must again look at the question. However, the legislation that exists has not always provided a satisfactory solution, in particular, in the cases of female-to-male transsexuals, but for all transsexuals as far as issues of employment protection are concerned.

The United Kingdom's government is one of the few Western states left that has not provided either a legislative, judicial, or civil procedure to enable transsexuals to obtain recognition in their new gender role. However, the British government is finding itself under increasing pressure from both individuals, and the campaign group "Press for Change," who are demanding that the state not only allow the transsexuals new status to be recognized for all legal purposes, but that that recognition afford the transsexuals full protection from the law in many aspects of their lives. They want protection from discrimination in employment, a recognition of the new families they form for welfare and policy purposes, and for the criminal law to treat them for all purposes as a member of their new gender role.

It is to what the issues are, and what should be considered by a legislative body in this area, that I wish to draw attention in this essay. Particular reference is given to the United Kingdom, but only insofar as it is my home, and it is here that I find myself campaigning for the law's change. Nonetheless, the issues themselves are not parochial and will hopefully provide some enlightenment when we consider the protection of any minority group through the law, wherever in the world this is to take place.

Rights and Freedoms

In the United Kingdom there is a common-sense assumption that this is "a free country," and we tend to think in terms of freedom rather than freedoms. It has long been considered that a person's rights and freedoms are safeguarded by a policy of minimal state intervention in people's lives, such intervention only taking place after the scrutiny of Parliament and its elected representative body: the House of Commons. Protection from corrupt administrative bodies is provided by an independent judiciary. The precept is that an individual's freedom will only be interfered with in order to protect another's freedom, and therefore you are free to do what you want to do (or not) (Feldman, 1994, 50).

Axiomatically, freedoms exist in the spaces between statutory or common laws. Every new piece of legislation or judicial precedent erodes these spaces and imposes upon some or all people either restrictions on what you can do, or duties, what you must do. Thus some particular aspect of personal freedom is reduced.

"Rights" are habitually mentioned alongside freedoms but it is difficult to conceive of freedoms and rights as having some sort of equivalency. Freedoms are aspects of personal liberty that "allow one to x"; "rights" concern what a person is fairly and justly entitled to "as of right," either as a privilege or through immunity.

Freedoms do not in themselves impose any sort of duty. Duties may be imposed on those who seek to use particular freedoms, but the essential nature of a freedom is that it is autonomous in its action, albeit not in its formation. Thus freedoms may need protection: they are not natural, inborn, or inherent; they only exist through their potential restriction. Without law, freedoms would never

be named because all human life would automatically be in a state of autonomous (anarchic) "freedom" (a lot of people just "*x*"ing). In reality, of course,
such a situation is totally unthinkable.

The essence of this unthinkability is that freedoms do not actually come into
existence without a notion of rights. Whether we are considering, for example,
rights to property, or rights to bodily integrity, the "freedom to *x*" is embodied in
the "right to *x*." It is this sense of "rights" that creates law. It is "rights" that allow
"the assistance of others in giving effect to one's autonomous choices [free-
doms]" (Feldman, 1994, 8).

Rights therefore exist before the law, and so can exist without the law. Current debates on rights generally agree on two broad fronts: first, that individuals
need protection against the state or government elected by the majority, and that
legal or moral rights are a necessary, if not necessarily sufficient, means of ensuring this protection. Second, that rights are goods which individuals have or own
(Kerruish 1991, 141).

It is this ownership that makes rights independent of law. The individual is
assumed to have "rights" regardless of law, and society looks to creating laws to
support and safeguard the freedoms embodied in those rights. Rights are independent of law, and are often seen as having some sort of universality, but as
Valerie Kerruish states, rights "have a value, like the use-value of commodities,
that is value for whoever has the right" (1991, 199).

In real terms, the use-value of any right will be circumscribed and relative,
depending upon the freedom it seeks to protect and the effectiveness of that protection. As David Feldman asks, "What types of rights are needed to protect
whatever sort of freedom is thought to merit protection?" (1994, 3).

When considering legislation for transsexual rights, we must consider not
only what such rights may be, but also what freedoms lie behind them. We must
also consider in what respects the freedoms of individual transsexuals are currently not legally protected.

Transsexual Rights

It is difficult to conceive of the idea of "Transsexual Rights." The issue of rights
for transsexuals, particularly in the United Kingdom, apparently fits in with neither of the two criteria detailed by Kerruish above (1991). First, there is apparently no need of protection from the government of the day. The United Kingdom government has often gone out of its way (as far it can without changing the
status quo concerning marriage laws and birth certificate regulations) to accommodate the needs of transsexuals for new documentation in order to minimize

any adverse effects the current legal position may have on their lives. Second, if rights exist through their ownership, then the idea that transsexuals have specific rights because of their status as transsexuals would tautologically destroy any concept of legal recognition of their new gender status. Transsexuals, as far as their relationship with the law is concerned, and as a general rule socially, seek to become "of no concern": to blend in as members of their gendered groupings in society. If special recognition were afforded to them, then their gender reassignment would have been unsuccessful. The whole point is that they become men and women in their new role, not pastiches of men and women.

However if transsexual rights as such are not at issue, what exactly is it that transsexuals are seeking? To discover that, we must look at the freedoms that they would like to be protected by law. The freedoms they seek are

1. The freedom not to have to disclose details of their gender role reassignment unnecessarily.
2. The freedom to marry a member of the opposite gender.
3. The freedom to enjoy a job without fear of dismissal or harassment because of their gender role change.
4. The freedom to use the legal process to protect themselves in all aspects of their life in their new gender.
5. The freedom to take a parental social role in their new gender.
6. The freedom to be acknowledged at death as being a member of their new gender group.

These freedoms are being asked for within the legal limitations that currently exist for the general population of men and women. Thus, though transsexuals are seeking a unique set of freedoms that are related to the process of undergoing gender reassignment or assertion, they are not seeking a new set of rights.

Transsexuals are seeking for the law to acknowledge that they have rights, not as transsexuals, but as men and women who have finally become appropriately recognizable through medical intervention. They are seeking for the law to recognize the gender assertions they have made through reassignment.

This demands a different approach to "Rights Legislation" from that which is conventionally taken. Such legislation often exists as constitutional state documents such as the American Bill of Rights, or as idealized forms of democratic process such as in the United Nations Universal Declaration on Human Rights, or the European Convention on Human Rights.

In the United Kingdom, where the constitution is unwritten, and the European Convention on Human Rights is not a part of domestic law, "rights legislation" has traditionally been undertaken through a *laissez-faire* approach. The British public have relied on the good sense of politicians to restrain Parliament from introducing legislation that might unduly interfere with people's rights. However, this liberal approach assumes that if people are left as free as possible to pursue their "rights," they will also be enabled to do so. This assumption fails to take account of the indeterminate forces that shape people's lives. As Kerruish states:

> The equality of legal persons inheres in their being conceived as autonomous actors with a capacity to make reasoned choices as to their rights and obligations.
>
> The reality of the material inequality of social relations, as well as the actual identities of people living within them is left behind in this abstract representation.
>
> Our actual being as members of and agents for classes or groups constituted by social relations, the exploitative, repressive or oppressive character of our basic social relations, and the differences between the range of choices actually available to people occupying different positions in a hierarchical social structure, are thus no part of law's "truths": not, at least, within this classical form of the laws, obligations in contract, property and tort. (1991, 196)

The United Kingdom government has at times been forced to recognize the inequalities inherent in society, and the ways in which these limit the freedom of individuals to assert their rights; for example, the structure of the welfare state partly came about through this recognition. In the 1960s, this in turn led to the idea that individuals had a right to be free from discrimination on morally irrelevant grounds such as race and sex. Anti-discrimination legislation such the 1970 Equal Pay Act, the 1975 Sex Discrimination Act, and the Race Relations Acts of 1965 and 1968 takes the form of providing particular protection or rights to groups of people who, as individuals, face discrimination or need protection in various spheres of their life because of their membership in that group.

This traditional approach to enforcing rights and ensuring freedoms would not be of benefit to transsexuals. In order for transsexuals to benefit from such legislation they would be required to make known their reassigned gender status; then potential discriminators would know that they were likely to be breaking the law, and so could avoid such situations. Thus the first freedom mentioned above —not to have to disclose their gender status unnecessarily—would be curtailed.

A legislative approach to transsexual rights must take account of the freedoms transsexuals are seeking through a process of recognition of the gender role they have affirmed. In any attempt to draft such legislation the questions must be

A. Is there an obligation to provide legal recognition to the new gender status of transsexuals? If there is, then:

B. How can legislation protect transsexuals' rights:
  i.   to be legally (and socially) acknowledged for all purposes as a member of their new gender role group?
  ii. to receive protection through the law as a member of the gender group to which they have been reassigned, in all situations where such protection is normally afforded?
C. In what way could legislation be drafted to deal with such potentially difficult areas as
  i.   transsexuals who have parented children in their former gender role?
  ii. whether allowing transsexuals to marry a member of their opposite gender group but of the same natal sex would open the way to same sex marriages?
  iii. the rights of others to have such information, concerning the transsexuals' status change, as is relevant and necessary?

Lessons from Other Legislatures

Those states that have legislated to safeguard transsexual rights have taken the path of ensuring that transsexuals will be recognized for all legal purposes in their new gender role from a specific point in time, rather than attempting to safeguard their rights as transsexuals through anti-discrimination legislation.

The types of legislation that exist take two basic forms: the first allows transsexuals to be recognized as if their new gender designation existed from the point of birth. The second allows transsexuals to be recognized as of their new gender designation from a specific point in time, after their reassignment treatment has taken place.

The first type of legislation is common in those states that have a common-law system and a public birth-registration system. The form taken is either issuing a new birth certificate (as in many states of the United States, such as Colorado, Arizona, Delaware, California, etc.) or amending the old certificate (as in Indiana, Connecticut, and Mississippi) (Sr. Mary Elizabeth 1990, 68–73). An early example of this form is the 1974 South African Births, Marriages and Deaths Registration Amendment Act. This short act allows that the

> Secretary may on the recommendation of the Secretary for Health alter, in the birth register of any person who has undergone a change of sex, the description of the sex of such person (S1 ss 1)

The secretary may call for any medical reports and instigate any investigation necessary to support this action. Thus transsexuals will from the point of alteration have a birth registration certificate as if they had always been of their new gender. Male-to-female transsexuals will be as if they had always been women, the female-to-males as if they had always been men. No conditions are laid down in respect of other aspects of their legal lives; therefore, it must be presumed that for pension purposes, retirement, marriage, etc., it is as if they always were of their new gender role; therefore such regulations as exist would automatically treat them in the same way as any other man or woman. The act also allows that:

> Any alteration of the sex description of a person who has undergone a change of sex, which has been effected in the birth register of such person before the commencement of this Act shall be deemed to have been effected in terms of section 7B of the Births, Marriages and Deaths Registration Act, 1963. (S1 ss 2)

This allows identical status for those transsexuals who had already had their birth certificates altered prior to 1974, under the mechanism previously afforded for mistakes of sex designation at birth. This clause is of particular interest, as some British transsexuals had amendments made to the sex designation on their birth certificates prior to 1968, and those individuals could in this way be accommodated in any new legislation proposed. However, this solution would fail to include those people who have undergone reassignment in the period between 1968 and any proposed legislation; unless such alteration of sex designation could be made retrospective, they could find themselves having a life period in which they were legally neither a man nor a woman.

The South African act has proved to be successful in practice, and those transsexuals who live there have been able to blend successfully into society in their new role. Various American and Canadian states have enacted similar bills. For example, in British Columbia under the Revised Statutes British Columbia 1974, chap 66, s 21a, an unmarried transsexual may apply to have the Director of Vital Statistics

> change the sex designation on the registration of birth of such a person in such a manner that the sex designation is consistent with the intended results of the transsexual surgery.

The evidential requirements are that either a doctor licensed to practice in Canada certifies that he or she has performed the surgery; or, where a transsexual has received treatment outside Canada, evidence that the doctor who performed surgery was licensed to practice medicine in that jurisdiction, and a certificate from a doctor licensed to practice in Canada that he or she has examined the patient and the surgical results are those required by the regulation. However the actual requirements for surgical procedures or results are not detailed at all.

The regulation then provides that

> Every birth certificate issued after the registration of birth is changed shall be issued as if the original registration had been made showing the sex designation as changed under this section. (s 21a, ss 3)

This, as in the South African act, creates what some would refer to as a legal fiction—that is, it is as if the transsexual had always been the gender he or she has now taken. However, according to the testimony of many transsexuals and of the doctors who treat them, this "legal fiction" is an appropriate recognition of a psychological and social reality. One needs only to think back to the comment by Harry Benjamin in his introduction to Christine Jorgensen's autobiography in which he said, "This was a little girl, not a boy (in spite of anatomy) who grew up in this remarkably sound and normal family" (Jorgensen 1967, vii).

A very interesting example of this sort of approach is that taken in Alberta, where not only can the birth certificate be changed, but also according to the regulations,

> if the sex of the person is registered outside Alberta [then the Director shall] transmit to the officer in charge of the registration of births and marriages in the jurisdiction in which the person is registered, a copy of the proof of the change of sex produced to the Director (Revised Statutes Alberta, 1973, chap 384, s 21.1, ss 2)

This suggests that a transsexual of any nationality can apply in Alberta to have a change of sex recorded, and can expect the director to inform the state in which their birth was registered, and can hope that as a result that state will automatically re-register their birth details. No doubt the situation was only meant to apply to Canadian states, but it does provide food for thought.

Other state legislatures have taken the second option: producing an amended birth certificate for the transsexual; the procedures are similar to that which took place in Britain prior to the Statutory Instrument 1968/2049 that amended the 1953 Births and Deaths Registration Act, and the 1971 case of *Corbett* v. *Corbett*. The same criteria are followed as those adopted in the situations mentioned above: it is not required that a substantive or factual error should have been made; rather, confirmation is sought of the individual's transsexual status and reassignment treatment.

In states that have a codified legal system (an exception to this is South Australia—see the following) the format generally taken is to provide a "recognition certificate" of some sort. German legislation allows for two separate procedures to accommodate the needs of the pre-operative and the post-operative transsexual. The first section of the Transsexual Law TSG (1980) provides that a German citizen, or a homeless foreigner who is stateless, or a foreign refugee or asylum seeker who is resident in Germany, can change their forenames to ones more appropriate to their gender role. The requirements are that they should be at least twenty-five years old and "it can be assumed as a great probability that their feelings of belonging to another gender are not going to change" (TSG [1980] First Section, SS 1 [ii]).

Transsexuals themselves bring the procedure to their Regional Court, and the interests of the public are represented through a state-appointed legal representative. The transsexual must submit independent reports from two experts in the field of transsexuality, which must confirm that "according to scientific evidence the applicant is unlikely to change his or her feeling of belonging to another gender with a high degree of probability" (TSG [1980] First Section, SS 4.4).

Once an order to change the forename has been made, the transsexual and his or her relatives are obliged to state only the new names, not the old, for official records and registers. Applicants can later apply for the decision to be annulled, if at some time in the future they feel that they have made the wrong choice. However this recourse is not available to anyone who adopts or has a child after the names have been changed, or who marries using the new name.

The second section of the act provides for the "establishment of belonging to a sex group." Designed for the post-operative transsexual, this section allows the court to establish that the person can now be considered as belonging to the other sex from that stated in the birth certificate. The requirements are that

    ii.   they are not married

    iii. they are continuously non-reproductive and

    iv. they have undergone an operation to alter their other sexual marks, so that a visible closeness to the appearance of the other sex has been achieved. (TSG [1980] Second Section, SS 8. 1 [ii-iv])

Transsexuals must state the forenames they are going to use, and they must produce expert reports to say that the criteria have been met. According to SS 10, from the date of the decision the transsexual is to be regarded as belonging to the other sex; this is final and any rights and duties that depend on sex are to be governed by their new sex.

The TSG (1980) in SS 11 states that parent-child relationships formed before the gender change will not be affected, so the transsexual for legal purposes will still be the parent's son or daughter as he or she was before. They would also remain as a father or mother, as they were before, of any children born or adopted before the decision is made final, and lines of inheritance due to sex will not be affected. Section 12 ensures that existing pension rights and other benefits will be untouched, and this includes the rights of a former spouse to pension benefits.

As far as the birth certificate is concerned, only government offices and the transsexual concerned may have access to the birth register. The transsexual may also be issued with a personal status certificate.

Similarly, in other states that have followed the German model, such as Quebec (which unlike other Canadian states has a system modeled on the French codified law) (Revised Statutes Quebec 1979, ch 10, s 16-22), the transsexual becomes of the new gender at a specific point in time, generally after surgery. His or her life in the former gender remains intact.

In the South Australian legislation, the provisions for transsexuals are included with the provisions to alter the sex of a child who has undergone some medical intervention to clarify its sex status (Sexual Reassignment Act [1988]). The act provides that a recognition certificate can be issued for an adult who has undergone reassignment treatment in South Australia, or for an adult who was born in South Australia. Unusually, the act requires that an adult must have "received proper counselling in relation to his or her sexual identity" (Part III, S 8, ss iii), or in the case of a child that the "magistrate is satisfied that it is in the best interest of the child that the certificate be issued" (Part III, S 7, ss 9.b).

Such a certificate is conclusive evidence that a person has undergone reassignment and is now of the sex stated in the certificate, and it will allow the Registrar of Births to register the reassignment of sex. This procedure is the same as an amendment rather than a re-issue of the certificate.

However, although the registrar can issue a copy from the register showing the new sex, the certificate cannot be used for legal purposes in another place unless the laws of that place expressly allow it and the relevant authorities are informed of the reassignment of sex (Sexual Reassignment Act 1988, Part III, S 9 , ss 4). Because of this, the transsexual cannot get married in another state where the marriage would not be recognized because of the transsexual's status.

The South Australian legislation also provides regulation for those hospitals and doctors providing reassignment treatment (Sexual Reassignment Act 1988, Part II). The requirements are that they must be licensed under the act, and that transsexuals who seek a recognition certificate must have undergone assessment at a licensed clinic, even if they have obtained treatment elsewhere.

Legislation now exists in many states to support transsexuals as they seek a change in their civil status and a recognition of their rights in their new gender role.

Legislation for the Transsexual

In considering appropriate legislation in any state, we must not only consider the freedoms that the transsexual wishes to gain, but also political expediency, potential areas of difficulty, and administrative cost. These three will all have a bearing upon whether a bill is likely to receive support from the parliamentary body of a state. Any proposed legislation must be

1. concise and simple in both its format and its effect;
2. as non-contentious as possible, and able to garner all-party support;
3. with little space for interpretation;
4. able to safeguard as many potential interests as possible.

A Legal Obligation?

I now refer back to the questions originally suggested: First, is there an obligation to provide legal recognition of the new gender status of transsexuals? Many commentators such as Feldman (1994), Walton (1992), and Taitz (1988) would consider that there is, but even if no obligation exists as such, many governments will sooner or later face a defeat either in their own or other courts because of the persistence of transsexuals themselves as they become more educated about their lack of civil rights in their new gender role. For example, the government of the United Kingdom is currently facing challenges in the European Court of Human Rights, the European Court of Justice, and its own courts.

In the meantime media and hence public sympathy is increasingly on the side of the transsexual; therefore the ever-rising cost of defending such litigation will increasingly be judged to be improvident. Legislation seems the manifestly simple resolution to this predicament.

The Functions of Any Proposed Legislation

If we consider the protections that need to be afforded to the transsexual, the legislation must enable them, at the very least, to be acknowledged as a member of their new gender role group. This can be done either by allowing a new birth certificate to be registered that gives the new sex of the transsexual, or by amending the old certificate and issuing a certificate similar to that used in adoptions, which gives the new details.

Alternatively, a certificate of recognition of the new sex could be provided. However, this is likely to be unsatisfactory, as it would tend to mark transsexuals as different and could soon become little more than an identity card and a signifier for many authorities that the individual concerned had undergone gender reassignment.

If a legal acknowledgment is made, then the question is whether it should provide retrospective legal protection or merely provide protection from some point after reassignment has taken place. Issuing a new birth certificate would allow the protection to be retrospective; amending the old certificate would not.

A new certificate would thus be preferable for those transsexuals who have been living in their new gender role for a long period but who have not to date been afforded such legal recognition, as this would give them the right in law to challenge those decisions that have been detrimental to them because of their gender change. Politically, though, this could be disastrous, as it could open a floodgate of claims for compensation for such things as unfair dismissal, judicial review of administrative decisions, and pension and insurance reviews. And who knows how many marriages would suddenly fail to have existed?

Therefore the best solution seems to be to allow some an amendment followed by an "adoption style" certificate for public use.

On Whose Authority and with What Requirements?

The next question must be "on whose authority will a change of gender be recognized?" Most acts require the transsexual to provide evidence from a medical source that reassignment treatment has taken place. But the legislation does not demand any particular sort of surgical procedure or hormone therapy. For example, the German legislation requests that the transsexual has "undergone an operation to alter their other sexual marks, so that a visible closeness to the appearance of the other sex has been achieved" (TSG [1980] Second Section, SS 8. 1 [iv]), but it does not specify that the operation be penectomy and vaginoplasty, or hysterectomy and phalloplasty. There are good reasons for following this sort of approach. For example, not all transsexuals have sufficiently good health to undergo repeated major surgery, yet they live successfully in their new role; also, genital surgery for the female-to-male transsexual still produces very poor results. To require genitals to be reconstructed could be a path to mutilation for some, and possibly a death sentence for others.

However, in Germany and Ontario in particular, the requirement in the legislation that some surgery is undergone has led to questions in the courts concerning to what extent surgical reassignment has taken place, particularly in the case of female-to-male transsexuals. Michael Wills mentions the case of OLG

Zweibruken (1992), concerning a female-to-male transsexual, which asks whether in order to achieve what the law calls a "clear approximation" to the opposite sex, will a bilateral mastectomy be sufficient, or is genital surgery that includes vaginal occlusion and phalloplasty required? The case has been decided in two lower courts in favor of the female-to-male transsexual applicant, but again the state representative has appealed (Wills 1993).

In two Canadian cases, *C(L)* v. *C(C)* (1992) and *B.* v. *A.* (1990), female-to-male transsexuals were held not to be spouses/husbands for the purposes of marriage and family law if the only surgery they had undergone was a bilateral mastectomy and a hysterectomy. The courts, both in Ontario, followed the doctrine in *Corbett* v. *Corbett* (1970). In *B.* v. *A.*, the parties had lived together for twenty years, and on that basis had applied for a motion of financial support. Though the female-to-male transsexual had had birth records changed from female to male, the courts held that the requirements for surgery of the Registrar General were not the same as those required to decide if a relationship was one of husband and wife. The failure to undergo genital surgery on the part of an FtM transsexual would mean that he continued to be female and hence could not marry another female. The case of *C(L)* v. *C(C)* (1992) followed this line of thinking, and it was held that the marriage the two parties had undergone was a nullity and was void *ab initio*.

It seems that any surgical requirement will produce this sort of difficulty. In particular, in Britain, where surgical techniques to produce a phallus are extremely poor, it would seem an absurdity to require female-to-male transsexuals to undergo such surgery in order to obtain legal recognition, whereas their male-to-female counterparts would generally have less of a problem in meeting such stringent requirements. Therefore the sensible solution would be merely to require appropriate and recommended medical treatment to have been undergone. This would leave the decision as to exactly what sort of reassignment treatment was carried out in the hands of transsexuals and their doctors, who are best placed to decide what is advisable for the individual concerned.

Licensing Clinics?

It is sensible to use medical "experts" to provide the necessary evidence for supporting legal recognition; however one must be careful of two possible dangers. First, if one insists, as in the South Australian Act, that clinics or medical practitioners undergo some sort of licensing, then the transsexual will be restricted in regard to sources of treatment. There are today "Gender-Identity Clinics" in England, controlled by psychiatrists who are out of touch with current practice and thinking in the field, as well as those that provide excellent treatment. I do not see how someone without an extensive and close knowledge of the field could judge the competence of a clinic, and those who could would be loathe to criticize one of their few colleagues in such a small field.

The second danger is that treatment prices could rise rapidly, as licensed clinics turn to private sector provision. Many transsexuals, for whom work is difficult to obtain, and who are therefore not well off financially, could find themselves having to travel long distances regularly to licensed clinics when in fact much of their treatment could be provided through their local district health structure. Patient choice could prevent a closed shop situation.

Licensing therefore does not seem desirable, but an independent opinion is still needed as regards the transsexual's medical condition. If one wished to provide more direction than that contained in the South African Act (i.e., a general provision allowing a call for information and any medical reports), the solution would be to call for two or more independent medical reports, which must also be independent of each other. Alternatively, one could appoint the duty to an already existing body, such as the independent tribunals who assess individuals for invalidity benefit.

Form and Protection of Other Parties

Protection must be provided for children, whether biological or adoptive, parented by the transsexual prior to gender reassignment. These children need to have their inheritance rights under intestacy law and other possible claims (such as for maintenance) protected. Ex-spouses' claims, such as for maintenance, should be protected. The detail provided in the German and South African Acts could provide a model here.

The Right to Marry

Legislation must also consider the politically difficult question of inadvertently opening the way to same sex marriages. In the United Kingdom, where homosexual activities are still illegal for men under eighteen, same sex marriages are very low on any political agenda. Any legislation must appear to prevent opening a back door route to this. As heterosexual marriage is possible from the age of sixteen, a reassigned transsexual could, potentially, have publicly legitimated a relationship that would be illegal if he or she had not undergone reassignment. This anomaly could be avoided by allowing recognition of a new gender role only after a certain age, for example, eighteen or twenty-one.

Nonetheless it must be accepted that legitimating transsexual marriage would certainly provide good ammunition for the "same sex marriage" lobby. One way in which legislatures have resolved this is by necessitating that extensive medical treatment undertaken, and that the transsexual who seeks legal recognition is for all purposes infertile, or completely incapable of reproduction (see the following). Such demanding requirements would certainly preclude the faint-hearted or the "political games player."

The Requirement of Sterility

The issue of sterility has arisen in German case law, in a case concerning a female-to-male transsexual who had undergone a bilateral mastectomy, but who because of a motor accident was unwilling to undergo any further hormone treatment or surgery. The German TSG (1981) requires that the transsexual be "completely non-reproductive" and this has a bearing on the discussion as to what surgery an applicant for the major solution (i.e., change of sex designation) must have undergone. The Courts granted a name change with no problem, but would not allow the change of sex designation because regular menstruation showed that the applicant was still fertile. However in obiter, the courts held that a reversible interruption of the fallopian tubes might be sufficient, because an FtM would be very unlikely to seek such a reversal (Wills 1993). Wills, like many commentators, takes the view that "sterility must be absolutely certain and permanent" (1993, 10) but he does not explain his reasoning: it is presented as a "common sense" assumption.

This sort of assumption does beg certain questions. It seems almost obsessional to demand that the transsexual is infertile. In reality, in most cases, hormone therapy will almost certainly have rendered the transsexuals infertile at the point where they might be considered to have sufficient commitment to their new role. However some transsexuals, for health reasons, cannot take the high hormone levels normally prescribed, nor can they necessarily undergo extensive surgery. Should they be denied recognition? It is a difficult question to answer, but it must be stated that the requirement of sterility smacks of eugenics and begs us to ask from whom else do we require sterilization before we allow them full citizenship before the law? Furthermore, I think, it is an issue that will increasingly be put on the agenda by transsexual people themselves.

A Right to Know

Finally, any bill must take into consideration those others who might have a "right" to know of the change in transsexuals' status in order to allow them to safeguard their own freedoms or those of the state, yet at the same time provide some sort of penalty if those people misuse the knowledge to which they have a privileged access.

Conclusion: A Draft Bill

> ... [law] fails to understand that alienated identities are creative only in a struggle for a sense of self and other that challenges the conditions of that alienation. (Kerruish 1991, 199)

Any bill must try to take into consideration all the issues discussed above without becoming too complex or controversial. It must attempt to recognize transsexuals' rights to be the men and women they are, and to enable them to enjoy those rights so that they may also take on the mantle of responsibilities that full citizenship brings. At the same time it needs to address policy needs and administrative costs and to gain political will.

References

Feldman, D. 1994. *Civil liberties and human rights in England and Wales.* Oxford: Oxford University Press.
Jorgensen, C. 1963. *A personal autobiography.* New York: Eriksson Inc.
Kerruish, V. 1991. *Jurisprudence as ideology.* London: Routledge.
Mary Elizabeth, Sister. 1990. *Legal aspects of transsexualism.* Wayland, Mass.: International Foundation for Gender Education.
Taitz, J. 1988. A transsexual's nightmare: The determination of sexual identity in English law. *International Journal of Law and the Family* 2: 139–54.
Walton, T. 1992. A measure of appreciation. *New Law Journal* 142, no. 6566:1202.
Wills, M. R. 1993. Legal conditions of sex reassignment by medical intervention—Situation in comparative law. Paper presented at the Twenty-Third Colloquy on European Law of the Council of Europe in Amsterdam.

Cases

B. v. *A.* (1990) 29 R.F.L. (3d) 258.
C(L) v. *C(C).* (1992) Ont. C.J. Lexis 1518.
Corbett v. *Corbett* (1970) 2 All E.R. 33, 48; (1970) 2 W.L.R. 1306–1324.
OLG Zweibruken (1992) 47–53.

Statutes

Births, Marriages and Deaths Registration Amendment Act, 1974. South Africa's Government Gazette, 16 October 1974, No. 4440: 3. South Africa.

Births and Deaths Registration Act 1953. Great Britain.

Legislation regarding the change of forenames and the establishment of the belonging to a sex group (Transsexual Law TSG), 10 September 1980. Germany.

Registration of Births, Deaths and Marriages Regulations, Statutory Instrument 1968/2049, 1968. Great Britain.

Revised Statutes Alberta, 1980, chap. 384, s 21.1. Alberta.

Revised Statutes British Columbia, 1974, chap. 66, s 21a, Eliz.2, 5034-5034-1. British Columbia.

Revised Statutes Quebec, 1979, chap. 10, s.16-22. Quebec.

Sexual Reassignment Act, 1988, No. 49. South Australia.

Cross-Dressing in the United Kingdom: The Law

Richard Green

In contrast to American law, a complex with fifty state jurisdictions plus a federal body of law, the United Kingdom is essentially one body of law with only minor variations among England, Scotland, Wales, and Northern Ireland.

Much of American law is statutory, made up of laws enacted by an elected body of representatives, usually addressing a specific issue. American law is less a common law, or a body of general laws that emanate over decades from court rulings. By contrast, the United Kingdom has relied extensively on the common law but recently is enacting more codified statutes.

In the United Kingdom, cross-dressing per se is not barred by law. However, the common law can be involved to curtail activities of a cross-dressed person. Such common law violations include "gross indecency." These situations will be summarized first. Then specific statutes relevant to a cross-dressing individual will be addressed. Family law is discussed next. Finally, legal anomalies that are consequence of the United Kingdom's refusal to change the legal sex of the postoperative transsexual are examined.

Common Law

Breach of the Peace

Although cross-dressing in public is not illegal, it is an offense to behave in a manner likely to cause a breach of the peace. The queen's peace is "a normal

447

state of society and any interruption of that peace and good order which ought to prevail in a civilized country is a breach of the peace." A breach may occur when a cross-dressed male enters a ladies' toilet. A cross-dressed male entering a gentlemen's toilet, however, could lead to his being charged with the offense of soliciting or importuning in a public place for immoral purposes (section 21, Sexual Offenses Act, 1986).

Gross Indecency

This has been the charge for male-male sexual contact (even in private) before 1967. Now such contact in private is legal. However, activity involving more than two persons can result in being charged with attempting to procure the commission of an act of gross indecency.

Indecent Assault

Although female-female sex is not an offense per se, a cross-dressed female using a dildo was prosecuted in 1989. Female sexual partners claimed that they did not know their partner was using the artificial phallus and so had not consented to the sex act.

Employment Law

Relevant statutes in employment law are the Employment Protection (consolidation) Act 1978 and the Sex Discrimination Act 1975.

Prior to terminating a worker's employment, employers are required to conduct a fair procedure hearing. This must set out reasons for termination and allow argument by the worker. But these procures are required only if the employee has worked two years on the job (*British Home Stores Limited* v. *Burchell* 1978).

Discrimination is permissible on the basis of sexual orientation or gender identity unless it is sex specific. This means that an opposite sex person would not suffer the same discrimination. If a transvestite or transsexual is dismissed because of his or her status, the legal protection afforded is that against "capricious dismissal." However, unfettered harassment on the basis of gender identity is not permitted. It can be construed as "constructive dismissal" (making it impractical to continue employment).

The cross-dresser who does not cross-dress at work cannot be dismissed because of dressing away from work, providing that the worker has been on the job for two years. However, an employer wanting to dismiss that worker might find a cause of action under the "substantial reason" section of the Employment Act. This is because of the possibility of blackmail to the worker, or the cross-dresser adversely affecting the employer's interest in protecting the business against negative public reaction. The employer need only show, on the balance of probabilities, that the reason for dismissal was "substantial of a kind to justify the dismissal." The criterion is that "any other reasonable employer may have used the same reason for dismissal." The appeals procedure is that a "tribunal at first instance" decides whether the employer was reasonable.

In 1993 a transvestite was dismissed from employment after his Ministry of Defence security clearance was withdrawn because of fear of vulnerability to blackmail. This cross-dresser had been open about his transvestism. The case is on appeal.

In *Calvin v. STC*, 1987, a male job applicant informed a prospective employer of his transsexualism and was denied a job interview. This was found not to be sex discrimination because the employer would not have interviewed a female transsexual either.

Dress Code

It is not sex discrimination to require females to wear a skirt as part of a uniform or to forbid males to wear jewelry. However, a work uniform regulation is discriminatory if applied to one sex only. Under the Sex Discrimination Act of 1975 transvestites and transsexuals are not protected unless they demonstrate that discrimination was motivated by prejudice against the male wearing women's clothes that would not have been effected against the female wearing men's clothes. However, as it plays out, this argument may be difficult to carry.

In January 1995, London newspapers carried a story under the headlines "You Can't Wear a Skirt to Work, Paul," and "Transvestite Loses Fight to Wear Frock." A partially cross-dressing training administrator in a social service department for a London borough had been tolerated by supervisors when he would come to work in tights, blouses, and women's shoes. But when he arrived in a frock he was disciplined. He was accused of bringing the council into disrepute. The cross-dresser took the employer to the industrial tribunal, claiming sex discrimination. He argued, "On an everyday basis I see women wearing individual items of clothing associated with the male such as suits, trousers, shirts and ties."

The tribunal held that the issue was of "appropriateness of dress rather than equality." The employer "had enforced a dress code requiring employees to dress cleanly, neatly and appropriate for their jobs they are doing." The cross-dresser's appeal was dismissed (*Daily Express* 1995, 7; *Daily Mail* 1995, 13).

In a July 30, 1994, article entitled "There's Something Rather Odd about the

School Odd Job Man," *The Sun* reported the dismissal of a newly appointed odd job man at a girls' school after he boasted on television that he dressed up in women's clothes. When the school's headmaster saw a video of the show brought in by a student, the worker was sacked. The headmaster informed him that "his way of life was not something the governor would approve of." He claimed further that the cross-dresser "would get abuse from the girls."

It may not be unfair to fire a worker when co-workers are opposed to their fellow's cross-dressing. But, the industrial tribunal must determine whether the employer acted reasonably in using the worker's cross-dressing as the reason for dismissal or merely as an excuse. A small victory ensued for a cross-dressing defense contractor who was fired as a security risk. When employers learned that he was in contact with a magazine for transvestites, he lost his security clearance and so was unable to continue in his job. However, an industrial tribunal awarded him $5,000 because the employer had not found him alternative work (*The Guardian* 1995, 6)

Some major employers have made provision for transsexuals to continue employment, though not necessarily in the same position, after adopting the new gender role. They include British Rail, British Airways, the Civil Service, British Telecom, British Gas and the National Health Service (McMullan and Whittle, 1994, 66).

Family Law

In divorce law, cross-dressing is regarded by the courts as "unreasonable behavior." Such behaviors are acts that a husband or wife cannot reasonably be expected to tolerate (*Gollins* v. *Gollins*, 1963). A case reported in January 1994, *Re B (a minor) Court of Appeal (Civil Division),* concerned a transvestite husband and father. His wife argued that he had dressed in women's clothing in the child's presence. The judge found that the father was a transvestite or at least engaged in dressing in women's clothing. Women's clothes had been found the in the man's cellar, and plastic breasts and stiletto-heel shoes were found along with underwear, dresses, and a strap-on dildo in the boot (trunk) of his car. The judge accepted as evidence photographs showing the father not only cross-dressing but also with his genitals exposed. The judge, having observed the man throughout the hearing, noted, "I felt instinctively that there was something not quite right about this man."

The court stated that "of course the father's sexual inclination and proclivities, if they are hidden from the children, are of little concern." However, the judge found that the father had a "prurient interest" in the clothes worn by one of his daughters and enjoyed dressing her up. Further, the girl had said, after her contact visit to the father, "daddy was wearing a dress and shoes like mummy," and "daddy wanted to be like mummy."

A consultant child psychiatrist reported,

> it is alleged that the child was exposed to her father's transvestism. As a transvestite cross-dresses for the purpose of sexual excitement, then the child would have been exposed to an adult indulging in a sexual activity. This would have had a consequence over and above the consequence of merely seeing her father in female clothing. The consequence of seeing her father in female clothing might well be minimal. At the most the child is likely to exhibit some confusion about male and female roles. This confusion is likely to engender anxiety . . . a child of this age who witnesses their father in this sort of sexual activity would be likely to be more disturbed. The chances of the child being anxious are greater and it may be that the child will demonstrate some of the consequences of sexual abuse.

The judge recommended no contact between child and father and the father's appeal was dismissed.

Two cases in which I have been an expert witness reached differing conclusions. In one, in Cambridge in 1981, a transsexual father of a pre-school child was denied access (visitation) if he were cross-dressed. In the other, in High Court in London, also in 1981, the trial court held that the transsexual father could have access to his pre-school child only if he were dressed as a man. However, this dressing requirement was overturned on appeal.

Prison Settings

Transvestites or pre-operative male transsexuals convicted of crime will be sent to a male prison. The prison may refuse to provide hormone treatment. Although a post-operative male transsexual will usually be sent to a female prison, there is no rule requiring this. By contrast, both the pre- and post-operative female transsexual will be sent to a female prison (McMullan and Whittle, 1994, 39).

A newspaper article of August 8, 1994, entitled "Jailhouse Frock" (*Daily Star*) reported that a male prisoner, a pre-operative transsexual, was being allowed to wear women's clothing to jail after signing a "transvestite charter." The charter stated, "I, Jane Gantree Pilley, agree to the following rules concerning articles of female clothing being issued in my possession. With the exception of underwear, I will keep the articles in my room at all times (apart from laundry). I will not dress in female clothing except between lock-up at night and unlock in the morning."

The Military

An April 1994 news article entitled "Colonel Kinky is Caught in Frock" (*The Sun*) reported the suspension of an army colonel after he was spotted cross-dressed. He was wearing women's underwear, full-flowing dress, wig, and makeup. A fellow officer said, "He wasn't going to a fancy dress ball. It is highly embarrassing."

Anomalies of Law

Anomalies of sex law relevant to transsexuals in the United Kingdom originate with the decision of *Corbett* v. *Corbett,* dating from 1970. The judge, both a physician and lawyer, held that a transsexual cannot change sex legally, that is via birth certificate change. Although the case was to be limited to the judge's holding regarding the capacity for a post-operative male transsexual to marry as a female, it has been extended to other circumstances involving the legal sex of transsexuals. This stands in contrast to rulings in several other European countries in which some legal recognition of reassigned sex is granted. Because the United Kingdom post-operative male-to-female transsexual is still a male for purposes of the law, the transsexual or a transvestite working as a prostitute (which is per se not illegal) can be charged with soliciting as a man. This is likely to result in a more severe sentence than for a female solicitor (prostitute, not attorney).

The anomaly arises again with regard to section 30, Sexual Offenses Act 1967, prohibiting a man from living off the earnings of a female prostitute or from a man's prostitution (section 5). A post-operative transsexual was convicted of gaining money from a co-prostitute, a female, and their pimp was convicted for living on the proceeds of the transsexual (considered a male) (*R* v. *Tan*).

Another anomaly arises with respect to the charge of rape. Until 1994 males could not be charged with rape of a male. Thus, before the change of law, a male who had forced vaginal intercourse with a post-operative male-to-female transsexual could not be charged with rape. The lesser charge of indecent assault would apply (section 15, Sexual Offenses Act 1956).

Because a transsexual cannot change sex for purposes of marriage, an apparent marriage can be nullified at anytime thereafter. I was a witness in a case where a female partner of a female-to-male transsexual claimed that not until seventeen years after her marriage ceremony did she discover that her husband was female. The marriage was annulled.

European Law

The European Court of Human Rights has emerged as the wild card in several areas of English law, including the sexual. Under the European Convention of Human Rights, article 8 section 1, "everyone has the right to respect for his private and family life, his home and his correspondence." Under section 2, there shall be no "interference by a public authority" except for the protection of health or morals. Under article 10, the European Commission of Human Rights examines whether the interference pursues any legitimate aim under article 8, section 2, and if so whether it is "necessary in a democratic society" for the purpose. Any interference must be proportionate to the legitimate aim pursued.

It has been held that a person's sexual life forms part of his or her "private life" for the purposes of article 8, section 1 (3 ECHR 40, 51). However, the "claim to respect for private life [is] reduced to the extent that the individual [brings] his private life into contact with public life or into close connection with other protected interests" (Application No. 6959/75, 10 DR 100 115).

General Issues

England has a venerable tradition of drag pubs. Here there are stage shows of cross dressed men in drinking houses that may cater to a primarily gay or a primarily straight clientele. England also has the pantomime tradition of Christmas plays. Here the lead male role is played by a woman and the older female role is played by a man.

With respect to transsexual treatment, the United Kingdom has a national health insurance program, the National Health Service (NHS). Since the 1960s the NHS has paid for sex reassignment procedures. The 1969 text I co-edited with John Money, *Transsexualism and Sex Reassignment,* included a chapter reporting the first follow-up results of sex reassignment surgery. It was authored by John Randall, my predecessor in the Gender Identity Clinic at Charing Cross Hospital.

The Gender Identity Clinic at Charing Cross has long made available to patients who request it a card stating, "This card is to indicate that (name) is attending the Gender Identity Clinic at this hospital for assessment of the condition of transsexualism and it is appropriate and necessary as part of this treatment for the patient to wear clothes of the chosen gender. Confirmation may be obtained by contacting the psychiatric department of Charing Cross Hospital." In ten months only one of my patients has requested this card.

Transsexual patients in the United Kingdom change their name formally by statutory declaration or deed poll. The Gender Identity Clinic writes letters to the Home Office for modification of the patient's passport. Driving license changes are straightforward. Support groups exist in the United Kingdom for transsexuals, transvestites, and the partners of both. These include the Beaumont Society, the Beaumont Trust, Women of the Beaumont Society, and the Gender Trust.

Conclusion

The structure of English compared to American law provides the basis of contrasting issues for the cross-dresser. A uniform system of law can help or hurt. Although no local United Kingdom ordinances bar cross-dressing, the refusal to permit birth certificate change is a substantial handicap. The absence of a Bill of Rights in England is a potential hardship to any minority group, but the emergence of the European Court of Human Rights may serve as a check on United Kingdom infringements.

As in the United States, the essential problem confronting cross-dressing is not the law, but medical and general public attitudes. Transsexualism and transvestism are mental disorders within the diagnostic manuals of the American Psychiatric Association and the World Health Organization. While it can be argued that inclusion permits treatment, at least for the transsexual, it also stigmatizes. Cross-dressers remain a poorly understood sexual minority. Conferences such as this may help.

Reference

Corbett v. *Corbett.* (1970) 2 All ER 33.
Daily Express. 1995. You can't wear a skirt to work, Paul. (14 January): 7.
Daily Mail. 1995. Transvestite loses fight to wear frock. (14 January): 13.
Daily Star. 1994. Jailhouse frock. (8 August).
The Guardian. 1995. (16 January): 6.
McMullan, M., and S. Whittle. 1994. *Transvestism, transsexualism and the law.* London: The Beaumont Trust and the Gender Trust.
The Sun. 1994. Colonel Kinky is caught in frock. (April).
———. 1994. There's something rather odd about the school odd job man. (30 July).

For U. S. laws on transsexualism, see Richard Green, *Sexual science and the law* (Cambridge, Mass: Harvard University Press, 1992).

Insurance and the Reimbursement of Transgender Health Care

Lisa Middleton

Transgendered individuals and their health care providers regrettably find too often that public and private health care insurance systems open to others and their needs are closed to the transgendered and our needs. The foundations of discriminatory practices can be found in case law, public policy, and private contracts. While such foundations are not easily undone, such undoing is not impossible. Changing discriminatory practices requires both an understanding of how they came to be and the informed will to effect change.

Standard Exclusionary Language

Both public and private health care programs commonly, but not uniformly, exclude transgender health care. I quote from two policies containing industry-standard and commonly used exclusionary language.

(1) Kaiser Permanente, CalPers, HMO policy, August 1, 1994—Sec. 5-A, Exclusions from Coverage, 13. Services related to sexual reassignment.

(2) Take Care, CalPers, HMO policy, August 1, 1994—General Exclusions and Limitations, A. Plan Exclusions, (33) Sex Change. Any procedure or treatment designed to alter the member's physical characteristics to those of the opposite sex or any other treatment or studies relating to sex transformation.

A reading of the contents of either policy raises questions as to the extent the exclusionary language contradicts other provisions of the policy contract, most specifically, those sections relating to mental health coverages. Should an individual otherwise covered for evaluation or treatment under a policy be *excluded* because the origin of the *condition* requiring such care is related to sexual reassignment?

What is meant by the terms "services related to" and "any procedure or treatment"? Such language is comparatively very broad and sweeping. Is it intended to exclude initial psychiatric care and evaluation as called for by the HBIGDA Standards of Care? Do such exclusions extend to hormone therapy? Or do they relate only to gender reassignment surgery (GRS) operative procedures and hospitalizations? The appellate courts have not been called on to define what is an appropriate standard for specific transgender services that may be excluded by the standard exclusionary language. Absent uniform standards similarly situated transgendered individuals are often treated inconsistently by their individual insurance plans.

Transgender Reimbursement Legal Issues

In the late 1970s and early 1980s there were a number of important cases that addressed the issue of reimbursement for the cost of GRS. In each case the coverage for GRS was sought under a state-operated, federally funded Medicare program.

A. *Doe* v. *State of Minnesota* (257 NW2d, 816. 1977). The Minnesota Supreme Court in Doe found that the Minnesota Medicare plan that provided for a total exclusion of transsexual surgery from eligibility for medical assistance payments was void as arbitrary and unreasonable. The court found that transsexual surgery was singled out for exclusion and therefore violative of federal standards that called for the state *not to reduce benefits solely because of the diagnosis, type of illness or condition.* Additionally the court ruled out a standard that would equate medical necessity with a *guarantee of surgical success.*

B. *Rush* v. *Parham* (440 Fed Sup, 383. 1977) This case is one of two involving Carolyn Rush. Ms. Rush sought reimbursement for GRS under the Medicare plan for the state of Georgia. As in the Doe court, the court found that the expressed language of the state of Georgia barring all transsexual surgery was arbitrary and contrary to federal standards.

This court noted the distinction between permissibly excluded "nontherapeutic elective procedures" and impermissibly excluded "necessary medical treatment" drawn by the U.S. Supreme Court in *Beal* v. *Doe*. The court did not find persuasive the state's argument that GRS was experimental, cosmetic, unsuitable, or unavailable.

On September 15, 1980, the U.S. Court of Appeals Fifth Circuit reversed the court's decision and remanded the case to determine (1) if the state had a policy prohibiting *experimental* services, and (2) if its determination that *transsexual surgery is experimental* was reasonable. The Appeals Court stated "we caution, however, that if defendants simply denied payment for the proposed surgery because it was transsexual surgery, Georgia would now be required to pay for the operation."

C. *Rush* v. *Johnson*, (565 Fed Sup, 856. 1983). This is the single most important precedent case to the exclusion of transgendered people in health care. The issue was whether Georgia had a reasonable foundation for ruling GRS experimental.

The court relied significantly on the *Diagnostic and Statistical Manual* (DSM), referring to it as "an authoritative text which is an expression of the consensus of the psychiatric community as of 1980" that finds "since surgical sex reassignment is a recent development, the long-term course of the disorder with this treatment is unknown." Both plaintiffs and defendants introduced conflicting expert testimony as to the efficacy of GRS as treatment for gender dysphoria. Prominent among those testifying for the state was Dr. John Meyer of the Johns Hopkins Gender Program. He argued for a "psychogenic origin" of transsexuality. He further found that his research (1971–1974) revealed little long-term distinction between those who had undergone surgery and those who had not.

The court quotes Dr. Meyer in finding "substantial evidence presents a picture of growing concern in the medical literature over the long-term effectiveness of sex-reassignment surgery as a generally accepted form of treatment." The court concluded there was *no consensus* in the professional medical community. Perhaps Dr. Meyer's twenty-year-old research and opinions have been invalidated within the scientific community. Within case law, they lack any superseding decision and remain the scientific basis of federal precedent.

Coincidental to the proceedings in the two Carolyn Rush cases, the federal government was active in the research of transgender health care. Based on two studies in 1979 and 1981, the Health Care Financing Administration (HCFA) found that GRS is experimental and issued guidelines barring GRS reimbursement on that basis. The HCFA has not addressed the issue of GRS or transgender-related health care procedures since 1981. The 1979 study was completed by two pharmacologists.

They found "there are no definitive standardized diagnostic tests . . . available for evaluating the transsexual." The effect of psychotherapy on transsexuals was found to be mixed, depending on the researcher. Interestingly, since it is perhaps the only issue two pharmacologists might be considered qualified to address, they found "Hormonal treatment . . . appears to be successful in relieving suffering in the transsexual patient. . . . Complications of hormone therapy in transsexuals have not been reported to any significant extent in the literature."

They found "the surgical component of the treatment of transsexualism remains, within the greater medical community, an experimental procedure . . . at the present level of the state of the art of transsexual surgery, the potential for incapacitating complications of the surgical procedure represents a greater risk of prolonging disability compensation than the primary disorder itself . . . there appears to be a greater incidence of complications for these procedures compared to the average incidence of overall surgical complications."

The 1979 state of the art for GRS remains the basis of federal reimbursement policy.

D. *Pinneke* v. *Preisser* (623 Fed 2d, 546. 1980). This Eighth Circuit U.S. Court of Appeals decision remains one of the most important to transgendered people receiving appropriate health care. The court found that the state "without any formal rule making proceedings or hearings . . . established an irrebuttable presumption that the procedure of sex reassignment surgery can never be medically necessary when the surgery is a treatment for transsexualism and removes healthy, undamaged organs and tissue. *This approach reflects inadequate solicitude for the applicant's diagnosed condition."* The court further quoted from *White* v. *Beal*, supra, 555 Fed 2d, 1152, "that the regulations permit discrimination in benefits based upon the degree of medical necessity but not upon the medical disorder from which the person suffers."

E. *G.B.* v. *Lackner* (145, Cal Rpt, 555. 1978); and *J.D.* v. *Lackner* (145, Cal Rpt, 570. 1978). These two companion cases were decided by the First District Court of Appeal in California. They are significant in that they establish that GRS is *not a cosmetic procedure*. Cosmetic procedures are routinely barred under both private and public health care programs.

Doe, Pinneke, both Rush cases, and the two Lackner cases argue to the point that transsexualism as a *condition* cannot be excluded from coverage. The underpinning of the denial of GRS reimbursement found by the *Rush* v. *Johnson* court was (1) that state was permitted to bar experimental procedures, and (2) that the state had a reasonable foundation for its determination that GRS was experimental.

The exclusion of GRS services has been commonly extended to exclude both GRS and non-GRS transgender health care.

Experimental Medicine Reimbursement Legal Issues

Our procedures have been deemed experimental. Meanwhile in nontransgendered cases, the courts and legislatures are increasingly addressing the question of the obligations of payers for experimental procedures. Private health care plans do permissibly make and interpret their own rules. Nonetheless such practices are subject to judicial review. The legal standard in such cases is the question of "abuse of discretion."

The April 1993 edition of the *Journal of American Medicine* reported in their survey of seventeen cases from 1980–1989 involving unproven and experimental procedures that the plaintiff was successful in fourteen of those cases. The appellate courts have not generally responded however with the degree of sympathy found in juries.

A. *Barnett* v. *Kaiser Foundation Health Plan* (1994 WL 400819 [9th Cir. (Cal.)]). Mr. Barnett required a liver transplant, additionally. he had e-antigen hepatitis. Kaiser denied Mr. Barnett on the basis that (1) liver transplants were experimental, and (2) that Mr. Barnett was medically inappropriate due to his hepatitis.

In evaluating Kaiser's actions, the court used the standard of "arbitrary and capricious": "The touchstone of 'arbitrary and capricious' conduct is unreasonableness." Was Kaiser's action unreasonable? The facts of this case provide a model for judging payer action. Kaiser was able to demonstrate that they had in place a Medical Advisory Committee that reviewed all liver transplant requests, that the committee acted on protocols developed by the UCSF Medical Center, that Mr. Barnett's hepatitis was an absolute contra-indication to transplant under the UCSF protocols, that the committee had authority to make exceptions, and in 120 of 250 requested cases had approved liver transplants, and that the committee was effectively shielded from the financial impacts of their decisions.

One of the more interesting comments in the testimony was that of the head of Kaiser's Medical Advisory Committee that their criteria was under constant review "based on changing literature and views of the profession." (One gathers "constant review," unlike with GRS, indicates a time frame measured in increments of less than decades.)

B. *Boland* v. *King County Medical Blue Shield* (798 Fed Sup, 638. 1992). Mrs. Boland was diagnosed with terminal breast cancer, she sought authorization and reimbursement for high dose chemotherapy with autogolos bone marrow transplant. This is a procedure classified as experimental by Blue Shield. Blue Shield defined experimental in its contract in an industry-standard fashion:

An experimental or investigational service or supply is one that meets at least one of the following:

1. Is under clinical investigation by health professionals and is not generally recognized by the medical profession as tested and accepted medical practice.
2. Requires approval by the Federal Drug Administration or other governmental agency, and such approval has not been granted at the time the service or supply is ordered.
3. Has been classified by the national Blue Cross and Blue Shield Association as experimental or investigational.

In deciding for Blue Shield the court was persuaded that within limits of reasonable discretion, Blue Shield was free to determine medical procedures to be covered. The court relied significantly on finding that the BS/BC association relied upon that which is "generally recognized by the medical profession as tested and accepted medical practice."

C. *Jacob* v. *Blue Cross and Blue Shield of Oregon* (92 Or. App, 259. 1988). This is also a cancer case where plaintiffs sought reimbursement for Gerson therapy received at a clinic in Tijuana, Mexico. The court found for BC/BS. The case is of note for the definition of *medical necessity* as defined by BC/BS—within "accepted medical standards in our service area, it *cannot be omitted without adversely affecting the patient's condition."* Second, while finding for BC/BS the court noted "Blue Cross does not have unlimited discretion to decide what is and is not covered. In determining whether a claim falls within the exclusions, it must apply the objective standards set forth in the exclusions."

D. *Cowan* v. *Myers* (232 Cal. Rptr, 299. 1987). This is a Medicare case. It is significant for its definition of medical necessity and its determination of who properly should determine medical necessity.

Plaintiffs argued that it is the individual physician who should determine in each case what is medically necessary for that patient. The court rejected that argument: "regulations expressly permit the state to limit services on the basis of medical necessity. We are convinced the Act did not intend the physician to be the sole arbiter of medical necessity . . . such a rule [would] result in inconsistent and unfair applications based on variations between physicians."

California regulations had defined *medical necessity* as "that which is medically necessary to protect life or prevent significant disability." The court required California to conform to federal guidelines and include the phrase after "significant disability"—*"or to alleviate severe pain."*

Medical Technology Assessment Practices

How can we judge whether a payer is acting reasonably in making its determinations? Payers, public and private, increasingly rely on what has come to be known as "Medical Technology Assessment Protocols." The practice of developing such protocols is a growing field employing medical, legal, and payer expertise.

In the late 1970s and early 1980s when transgender challenges to reimbursement policies were finding their way into the courts, payers were called on only to answer a two-part question in determining if a procedure is experimental—Is it safe? Is it effective? It was an orientation that was heavily weighted to the experiences of the provider. Providers and payers have come in the past decade to recognize the limits of such an analysis, most particularly the limits it places on the experiences of the patient. Meanwhile payers have certainly noted that new procedures with costs that are unlimited often have benefits that are quite limited. From the *New England Journal of Medicine*, September 1990, with "New Technology Assessment":

> safety and efficacy remains, but . . . [assessments] now encompass the measurement of effectiveness, *considerations of the quality of life, and patients' preferences*, and especially the evaluation of costs and benefits.

The focus of new assessment practices is on the *outcomes* on the procedures applied, the clinical, financial, and the quality of life that results from the application of the medical technology. A modern protocol includes the experiences of the patient:

> The health care system sometimes behaves as if the patient did not matter, the patient *is* the ultimate customer. . . . Two fallacies abound in the health care community concerning information from patients. The first is that patient derived data must be inaccurate or certainly not as accurate as information gleaned from a physician. The second is that the only information one can obtain from patients is their satisfaction with the service they receive. Both of these notions are patently untrue. (Goldfield, Pine, and Pine 1991)

In 1992, the Department of Health and Human Services sponsored a conference on the subject of "New Medical Technology: Experimental or State-of-the-Art." The conference brought together a number of disciplines and sought to provide definition to the process of answering the question, is it experimental? Blue Cross/Blue Shield uses the following five criteria to define experimental:

1. The technology must have final approval from a regulatory body.
2. There must be scientific evidence concerning the effect of the technology on health outcomes— that is, there must be some published evidence about the benefits and risks of using the intervention.
3. The technology must improve net health outcome. Does the person live longer? Is the quality of life better? Does it increase the ability to function?
4. Is the new technology as beneficial as current technologies?
5. Is net approval attainable outside of a research setting? We might stipulate that the technology should only be used in certain settings, but this will not stop the technology from being approved. (Gleeson 1992)

Individual Claim Strategies

My profession is claims administration. I am not an attorney and nothing here should be taken to replace or substitute for the necessary consultation with trained personal legal counsel.

Rule # 1—Don't take no for an answer. No is just the beginning of negotiations.

Rule # 2—Make *all* requests in writing.

Rule # 3—*Insist on answers in writing.*

Rule # 4—*Obtain a receipt and keep your receipts* for anything you pay for out of pocket.

Does your policy contain the standard exclusionary language regarding GRS and related services? Look in the General Exclusions section of the policy contract. If not, congratulations! Your issue is now one of demonstrating the medical necessity of your desired procedure. Key findings that will indicate medical necessity to payer organizations are:

—*Diagnosis, treatment, and procedures conducted in accord with accepted and standard medical practice for this condition. Were HBIGDA Standards followed? If so, that's very important. It is indicative of accepted practice.*

—The absence of this procedure will adversely affect the patient's condition.

—Procedure or service is necessary to protect life, prevent significant disability, or to alleviate severe pain.

—Alternative methods of care were attempted and unsuccessful, e.g., psychotherapy failed to change the underlying condition. The requested care offers a greater opportunity for success than alternative care already delivered or now considered.

If your policy, like most, contains the standard exclusionary language, the issue of medical necessity remains. What is added is the burden of overcoming the contractual exclusion. The strategy I am suggesting in response to the "experimental designation" is to challenge the *process* used by the payer in reaching that designation. Can its designation process for transgender care be shown to be legally deficient in comparison to the practices engaged in by other payers and condoned by the courts in *Barnett* v. *Kaiser, Boland* v. *King County*, and *Jacob* v. *Blue Cross*?

Officials of the health care organizations should be asked the following:

Exactly what is being defined as experimental? Diagnostic examinations and testing? Therapy? Hormones? GRS? (If any procedure related to transgender health care is excluded then that is beginning to sound very similar to a legally suspect exclusion by condition.)

How was the conclusion that it is experimental reached?

On what evidence?

When was the evidence last reviewed?

What literature was reviewed? How timely is that literature?

What are the qualifications of the personnel responsible for making the experimental determination? What experience do they have in the diagnosis and treatment of transgendered people? Was any medical analysis completed prior to the implementation of the exclusion? *Was it an underwriting decision?*

Are they familiar with the procedures requested? with the physicians who have performed or will perform the procedures? with their success/complications rates? Have they attempted to familiarize themselves?

Do they have a medical review committee?

Was this request reviewed by the medical review committee? Why not? On what basis does the medical review committee become involved in an appeal?

Can/Does the medical review committee make exceptions to the bar against reimbursement for experimental services? How often? On what basis? How often do they make exceptions where the patient is transgendered?

By what process does the payer's review procedures attempt to keep up with changes in medical practice? Have they used that process to track developments in transgender health care procedures?

Has a *Technology Assessment Protocol* of the requested procedure been completed? Insist on a copy. When was it done? Does it include patient experience as a criteria? Is there a plan to do an assessment protocol? If so, when and on what basis are procedures denied while the protocol is being developed?

Conclusions

1. Transgendered people *cannot be denied reimbursement based on our condition.*

2. The most controversial or at minimum the most litigated transgender procedure—GRS—has been held to be experimental by Medicare officials and by most private health care plans.

3. Experimental procedures as a class of benefits may be permissibly excluded from coverage. That which is medically necessary may not be excluded.

4. The extension of the coverage exclusion from GRS to non-GRS transgender health care procedures, e.g., hormone therapy, psychological therapy, appears to be founded *not* on medical evidence or case law, but on unchallenged, arbitrary payer actions.

5. The courts have given to the payers the responsibility for determining what is experimental and what is medically necessary. It is a responsibility that is subject to judicial review based on the reasonableness of the decision-making process. Payers may not act in an arbitrary or capricious manner.

6. The courts have held, regardless of express exclusionary language, that to exclude GRS simply because it is GRS would be an unsupportable arbitrary action.

7. Determinations of what is experimental and medically necessary should be based on medical evidence in accord with recognized medical practice.

8. To achieve reimbursement for medical procedures, including transgender procedures, a body of medical evidence must exist that defines accepted, standard, and proven medical practice for a given condition. That is not an argument for any or all of the specific HBIGDA Standards. It is an argument for *recognized standards* in the application of medical services to transgendered people.

9. The *Recommended Guidelines* are to be applauded. Other professionals providing transgender health are needed to come forward and publish within the professional literature evidence that transgender health care treatment procedures—(a) can be reliably diagnosed; (b) are clinically successful; (c) are governed by an accepted consensus of what constitutes normative appropriate care for both diagnosis and treatment; and (d) have medical complications that are, within accepted professional standards, both known and controllable.

Note

This paper was abridged from a version written for the International Conference on Transgender Law and Employment Policy (5707 Firenza St., Houston, Texas 77035), to whom I am deeply indebted.

References

Gleeson, Susan. 1992. Paper presented by the Executive Director, Technology Management Department, Blue Cross and Blue Shield Association at a conference, "New Medical Technology: Experimental or State-of-the-Art," sponsored by the Department of Health and Human Services.

Goldfield, N., M. Pine, and J. Pine. 1991. *Measuring and managing health care quality: Procedures, techniques and protocols.* Gaithersburg, Md.: Aspen Publishers.

Journal of the American Medical Association. 1993.

Kaiser Permanente, CalPers, HMO policy, August 1, 1994—Sec. 5-A, Exclusions from Coverage, 13. Services related to sexual reassignment. Plan Exclusions, (33) Sex Change.

New England Journal of Medicine. 1990. New technology assessment.

Cases

Barnett v. *Kaiser Foundation Health Plan.* (WL 400819 [9th Cir. (Cal.)]). 1994.

Boland v. *King County Medical Blue Shield.* 798 Fed Sup, 638. 1992.

Doe v. *State of Minnesota.* 257 NW2d, 816. 1977.

Cowan v. *Myers.* 232 Cal. Rptr, 299. 1987.

Jacob v. *Blue Cross and Blue Shield of Oregon.* 92 Or. App, 259. 1988.

Kaiser Permanente, Take Care, CalPers, HMO policy, August 1, 1994—General Exclusions and Limitations, *G.B.* v. *Lackner.* 145, Cal Rpt, 555. 1978.

J.D. v. *Lackner.* 145, Cal Rpt, 570. 1978.

Pinneke v. *Preisser.* 623 Fed 2d, 546. 1980. (John Meyer testimony, referring to research done at Johns Hopkins Gender Program [1971–1974].)

Rush v. *Parham.* 440 Fed Sup, 383. 1977.

Rush v. *Johnson.* 565 Fed Sup, 856. 1983.

White v. *Beal,* supra, 555 Fed 2d, 1152.

10

PERSONAL OBSERVATIONS

Introduction

Although social and behavioral scientists can study the transgender phenomenon; and historians and anthropologists can describe its existence in a wide variety of societies; and scholars of literature, music, and art can report on its existence in a wide variety of sources, the personal story still has meaning. The transgendered person has to continually ask, how did I come to be like I am and what am I going to do about it? There is no easy solution. Many men fight it by becoming ever more machismo while others early on decide that they don't want to fight it. Represented in this section are a Catholic priest and a firefighter who underwent sexual reassignment surgery. The priest, Karen Kroll, was no longer recognized as a priest by her church while the firefighter, Michele Kämmerer, went back to her old job, this time as a firewoman instead of a fireman. Rupert Raj represents yet another face of the coin: a female who became a male. As we read their brief autobiographies, we, as editors, can only admire their tenacity and courage in overcoming the obstacles in their search for their true "sexual identity."

Ideally, part of the task of those who have faced what only a few decades ago was the unthinkable—changing one's sex or gender—is to help others face their own demons. This is what Lee Etscovitz is doing, and readers should find her recommendations interesting and applicable to problem areas other than those of gender.

A quite different case is presented by Lynn Edward Harris. Born with

467

ambiguous genitalia and classed and raised as a female, she recounts the efforts she made as an adult to reclaim what she believed was her true sex. Her case emphasizes that some of the biological issues of gender have always faced a small minority of humans of every race and period. It is to be hoped that we will be better able to deal with them in the future than we were in the past.

No series of brief biographies of transgender people would be complete without some reference to Virginia Prince, a person who, after coming to terms with herself, set out to help others and founded a movement. Virginia has always been opinionated, and one of her major efforts has been to try to achieve a precision of language in relation to what individuals in the gendered community call themselves. Virginia has spent the last thirty years of her life living as a woman without benefit of surgery, although early on she did take some hormones. She calls herself a "transgenderist."

This is also the path taken by Kymberleigh Richards, who, like Virginia, started as a transvestite and now calls herself a transgenderist. We hope that by reading these personalized accounts, the scholarly and scientific papers included in this book will come in focus. Transgenderism is a complex topic, and professionals can give no easy answers. Even those who call themselves transgenderists have different solutions to what they see as their own gender problem.

Seventy Years in the Trenches of the Gender Wars

Virginia Prince

I was born in 1912, eighty-two years ago, and I began my interest in cross-dressing when I was about twelve years old. That means that one way or another I have been involved in what has come to be called the "transgender" community for about seventy years. As a matter of fact, I coined the words "transgenderism" and "transgenderist" as nouns describing people like myself who have breasts and live full time as a woman, but who have no intention of having genital surgery. Others soon took to the term and it is now used, erroneously I think, as a collective term for all the various degrees and kinds of cross-dressing. This leaves no simple term for describing those who have changed gender without a change of sex.

In trying to come up with a new term to fill this vacuum, I am proposing "transposeur," meaning one who sets over or rearranges the order of things or takes a position across from or opposite to his original position. This adequately describes what a real transgenderist does—he sets himself up as "herself" and thus rearranges all aspects of his former masculine life. Such a person could be abbreviated as a TP, analogous to a TV, CD, or TS.

Fighting in the trenches of ignorance, intolerance, and bigotry I feel it necessary to get down to basics in language and semantics in order to clarify the many misunderstandings, misconceptions, and mistakes that populate the minds not only of the general public but also in many ways the members of the so-called transgendered community and many a professional too. Thus, in this paper I'd like to discuss some of these areas.

The first is the area of sex versus gender. This ought not to be necessary, but in listening to people talk and reading what they write I find that the proper words for what they mean are often replaced with improper ones that refer to something else.

Simply put, sex is an anatomical/physiological term and its function is reproductive while gender is a psychological/sociological term and its function is to distinguish and identify the social roles and expectations of the two sexes. If two things are related but different, there have to be words for each that do not apply to the other. Were this not so we would not be able to make the distinctions between them, discuss the origins and development of each, study the non-normative or pathological aspects of each, and examine the qualities and characteristics of each.

So what are these words? The sex words both for humans and for animals are male and female, referring to the fact that the former make sperm cells and the latter make egg cells. The gender words are girl and woman, boy and man, referring to the social roles that egg makers and sperm makers generally play. When I hear students, professors, and even some of my own community use the words male and female as adjectives, as in "Why do you wear female clothes" or "She works a male job," I cringe a little. It hurts because such usage perpetuates the misconception that sex and gender are just two words for the same thing and can therefore be used interchangeably.

I might also point out that none of us was born a little boy or a little girl. Just like puppies and kittens, we were born just little males or females, but our indoctrination into a socially prescribed gender role as boy or girl started immediately when the doctor handed us to our mothers. Parents, teachers, peers, coaches, and other adults convert little males into boys who grow into men and little females into girls who grow into women, but the individuals are born, live, and die as males or females.

Another area where things get mixed up and thinking is not clear is in the field of cultural anthropology. It is not uncommon to hear or read anthropologists maintaining that Western ideas of there being only two sexes are wrong in other cultures: that there can be three, five, or whatever, different sexes. But let's face it, nobody would maintain that there were three sexes in dogs or five sexes in monkeys. In addition to the two clear-cut sexes, the sperm makers and the egg makers, there are various types of intersexes both in anatomical presentation and in chromosomal combinations other than the normal XX or XY. It only takes one sperm to fertilize one egg—there is neither a need nor a place for a third gamete, let alone five. Thus there are *not* three, five, or any other number than two, types of gametes made by two specifically different types of individuals called males and females.

The confusion lies in the fact that the anthropologists studying some other cultures find some individuals who live lives a little differently from the standard men or women of that culture. Such persons, like the berdache of the Plains Indians, can make up a third *gender* or lifestyle and be treated differently from either normal men or women. But the anthropologists who term them a third sex just do not understand that anatomical sex and psychosocial gender are not the same things, and they further confuse matters by referring to three or more sexes when what they find and what they mean is three or more gender categories.

The reason for making these points is that thoughts make words and conversely words reflect the thought processes that bring them forth. Thus unclear, incorrect, or imprecise words indicate unclear and imprecise mental concepts. Much damage is done to individuals from failure to realize that sex and gender are *not* synonyms. I tell students in classes I address to think before they speak (or write). If what one is about to say could be said about a dog or other animal, sex is the right word, as are male and female. Animals do not have gender. But if the thought deals with human behavior of some kind, boy/man and girl/woman or the adjectives masculine or feminine are proper.

My next comment is related to the first one. Why is it that some persons are said to be gender dysphoric but that a possible resolution of their condition might be to have sex reassignment surgery (SRS)? How can any sort of surgery, which is a physical invasion or alteration of the body, have any effect on a psychosocial condition, which is what gender is? Of course, it is very likely that if a male is reassigned as a female, "she" will probably attempt to dress, act, and live her life like any other female, and conversely for a female-to-male. But that is behavior and it is a matter of individual choice, and not a condition mandated by the surgery.

I was present at the conference of what subsequently became the Harry Benjamin International Gender Dysphoria Association held at Stanford University fifteen or so years ago when Dr. Norman Fiske first introduced the term "gender dysphoria." Translating "dysphoria" into lay terms, I take it to refer to being uncomfortable, unhappy, or dissatisfied with some condition. Thus I went up to Dr. Fiske afterward and said to him: "Dr. Fiske, if you think that what these people [he had been talking about transsexuals] are suffering from can possibly be helped by sex-altering surgery, why wouldn't it be more appropriate to call the condition sexual dysphoria, since it is their sexual anatomy that they are unhappy about? On the other hand, if what they suffer from is really *gender* dysphoria, how can any kind of surgical intervention possibly help them?"

Of course my point was not seriously heard because I wasn't a physician or a therapist. Instead, I was a "consumer" and as such was not expected to know anything about such a medical/psychological subject as transvestism or transsexuality. I think I knew as much about such topics as he did, but I had learned it from the inside and my own experience, rather than from observing others or reading the literature about other peoples' observations. In spite of my objections the term was accepted and has become part of the lexicon of the so-called transgendered community. I think using it continues to do harm by making people who are really just cross-dressers think they are transsexuals because they like to dress like women. And if people dissatisfied with their gender are really gender dysphoric and if those called gender dysphoric are the ones for whom SRS is intended, then maybe they should arrange to have it. I will say this for SRS—it certainly is a "cure" for cross-dressing! I have never heard of someone who has undergone SRS ever cross-dressing again. How could he? Even natural-born females who adopt various items of mens' clothing are not considered to be cross-dressing.

I am personally a real transgenderist. That is, while still having male genitals I have female-type breasts and I live full-time as a woman. Before I decided on the full-time change I was as *gender* dysphoric as you can get. I was unhappy with having to be a man anymore but I could not see how SRS could help me. I am now very gender *euphoric* with my present lifestyle. I said I was eighty-two, but I don't look, dress, act, feel, or even believe it myself and I attribute my youthful appearance and attitude to the fact that for twenty-six years I have not *had* to be a man. So if you men would like to live to a ripe old age, don't only lower your cholesterol, take vitamin E, etc., but get yourself a dress and heels and join one of the CD clubs. You think I am kidding but I am not. On my birthday last November I discovered I had dyslexia because although I was eighty-two I read it as twenty-eight. It keeps me young.

I think the term "gender dysphoria" and how it was (and is) misapplied is a perfect example of how incorrect language causes misinformation and therefore mistakes in judgments. Fortunately, I have been able to redirect a number of people away from surgery by helping them to understand that sex alteration was not necessary for the solution to their real desires, which were genderal and not sexual. Certainly once a male has had surgery he will also change his gender as a matter of common sense and convenience. But the point is that surgeons cannot change anyone's gender. The person can do it him- or herself without any of the pain, danger, and expense that SRS entails. I fault the physicians, therapists, and psychologists who handle the so-called pre-op transsexuals for not understanding the sex/gender confusion well enough themselves to clarify it to their patients and possibly thereby divert them from surgery.

As a transgenderist (or rather a "transposeur"), I can state from many years of experience that there is nothing that a male person who has had SRS can do that I cannot do without it, except to have sex with a male, which is something in which I have no interest since I am a congenital heterosexual. So unless that is what one is after, why do it? Thus I think "gender dysphoria" is an improper and harmful term for those whose real interest is in losing their male equipment.

It is really ridiculous to say that those claiming to be transsexuals and asking for surgery are suffering from *gender* dysphoria and then seeking to ameliorate that condition with *sexual* surgery. The helping professionals should realize how much damage their adoption of this unfortunate term has done. Disillusion, disappointment, dissatisfaction and even suicide do occur after SRS. None of these sad outcomes need occur if the individuals and their advisors really understood the issues involved before they visited a surgeon. The so-called real life test is a fine idea, but the individual should be encouraged to look upon it as an end in itself and not just a way-point on a different journey.

I am sure there are those among the professionals in this audience who are deeply resent my speaking in this way. It's true I do not have an M.D. degree and neither do I have a degree in psychology, counseling, social service, or any other discipline of that type, so who am I to be saying these things to you? My answer is that I am a highly intelligent person, I have a Ph.D. in a medical science (pharmacology), and was on a medical faculty for a time. I have graduated magna cum laude from the college of bitter experience, majoring in guilt, shame, fear, and isolation like most other cross-dressers. I come from the inside of this gender matter and I share the experience of countless thousands of others both here and abroad. I don't stand outside of it looking in. My medical interests and the need to understand myself led me to study this whole matter rather intensely for many years, so that I think my knowledge of the subject entitles me to speak as pointedly as I have.

The third point I would like to comment on is the continual use by the medical and psychological professions of the term "fetishistic" cross-dressing. While there may be a few isolated individuals who would fit the term, I don't believe it is a valid term when used to identify a large segment of the cross-dressing community. A "fetish" was originally used as a term for some special object in a native medicine man's bag of tricks. It could be a special feather, an animal's claw, a hank of some animal's hair, a horn, or a special colored rock. Whatever it was, it was essential to the medicine man's magic. He couldn't successfully "do his thing" without it. Freud came along and applied the term to any inanimate object to which an individual attached special erotic interest. It was a bit of a stretch because the medicine man's fetish was essential to the success of his magic while sexual fetishes merely *add to* the individual's sexual pleasure and are not generally essential to it. When doctors began treating cross-dressers and found that sexual arousal occurred and often ended up with masturbation and orgasm, the clothing was considered a fetish and the term fetishistic cross-dressing came into use. The implication of the term is that the individual dresses in feminine things in order to get sexually aroused.

This is a misleading since many other things will also lead to arousal, such as seeing a striptease show or an "adult" movie, reading and looking at the pictures in *Playboy, Penthouse,* and several dozen other magazines featuring pictures of nude females. Shouldn't these therefore be considered sexual fetishes too, since they are all arousing in place of an actual female body to play with? But the main difference is that all such activities are indulged in with the expectation of being aroused and possibly enjoying an orgasm. But one doesn't get cross-dressed for the purpose of getting aroused. The dressing itself is a very pleasant experience, and if arousal occurs along with it so much the more enjoyable, in the same way that a piece of pie is enjoyable by itself but a scoop of ice cream on top is even more enjoyable, at least to me.

Almost anything about a woman is appealing and may be erotic to a heterosexual male. Feeling oneself to be a part of her (by dint of wearing the same type of clothes) is a unifying experience deeper than just intercourse alone and therefore is automatically erotic. The point to be made is that the clothes are merely a means to an end, which is that of the feeling of unification, participation, and identity with womanliness. That is the drive behind the dressing and the source of the pleasure and satisfaction in the behavior.

Finally, we come to the big issues of cause and cure. Much effort, thought, and conjecture has gone into these questions, both of which can he dealt with in one simple phrase, namely, "There is *no* cause and there is *no* cure for cross-dressing." Let's take cure first because it is simpler. The word "cure" is largely a medical term and in that field it implies reversing or stopping some undesirable or pathological condition generally thought of as a disease of some sort. Moreover, diseases are generally caused by some outside organism or malfunction within the body or the mind. Cross-dressing is not a disease and no outside agent is involved. Thus it cannot be "cured." If one discontinues some behavior considered harmful, is he "cured"? If so, a cross-dresser could "cure" himself any time he wanted to by simply ceasing to dress up. However, hardly anyone is willing to do that because the behavior is so satisfying to him. If such a person did discontinue the practice, the physical manifestations of it would be gone but the memory and desire would perhaps still be there. The cross-dresser would suffer from a new condition, namely, resentment and frustration at being deprived of the pleasure, regardless of the circumstances that brought about such a decision in the first place. So for all practical purposes cross-dressing is incurable.

All kinds of theories have been put forward as explanations for the cause of this behavior. They run from the ridiculous (astrology and reincarnation) through the unprovable (it was a domineering mother or an absent father or some other flaw in the childhood upbringing, à la Freud) up to the supposedly biological agents like genes and hormones. So when I asserted just now that there was no cause for cross-dressing, I am sure many of you mentally rejected the idea immediately. Isn't cross-dressing an effect and don't all effects have causes? So it would seem, but not in this case. Let me explain. A "cause" is some object, situation, or assertion that acts on some other object or situation to bring about some sort of change in it. But what object or situation was it that was acted on by what other object or situation? Behaviors are results of some interaction and they usually serve to relieve tension or to be a solution to some situation or problem. That being the case one might well ask "What is the problem to which cross-dressing is a solution?" I could tell you but there isn't time to do so here, but think about it a bit. It may give you some new insights into the nature and satisfactions of cross-dressing.

But consider this! All normal babies, regardless of sex, are born with the full complement of human potentials. But the process of growing up is a process of winnowing down the total potentials to select those deemed appropriate by society for young males or females, respectively. These are encouraged, developed, and rewarded. The other potentials—those that would be encouraged in a child of the other sex, are simply left undeveloped and actually discouraged should they appear. But the remaining feminine potentials remain latent in a boy's brain. They constitute what Jung called the anima that exists in all males. And of course the opposite is the animus or masculine potentials in a girl's brain.

Now a potential is simply an unexpressed or inactive ability to do something that the mature organism may ultimately be capable of doing. One of the activities that an older child or adult has the ability to do is to put on different types of clothing. There is nothing complicated about that. So what could motivate a young boy to put on girl's clothing? Certainly two likely answers are curiosity and envy. But regardless of the motivation, when the cross-dresser does it the first time he makes a *discovery*! Just to make it crystal clear, a discovery is the sudden finding of something that has been present all along but not recognized. So when he first puts on something feminine he makes the discovery that it feels good and that the enjoyment is something within himself and therefore a part of himself. It is not due to some event or activity outside of himself. As his cross-dressing develops and more items of apparel are worn, he begins to see his anima in the mirror. She is in three dimensions and real time rather than just being a dry, unreal, psychological postulate. Since this now expressed and realized potential is part of himself and highly pleasurable, there is no reason to give "her" up. Neither is there any motivation to be "cured" by some professional who doesn't understand the inner feeling but feels obligated to try and change the behavior in order to earn his or her fee.

From this explanation I hope you will understand that in my mind there is *no* cause as such for cross-dressing. Rather, it is simply a discovery of those previously buried feminine potentials that were there from birth as a part of our common human inheritance. It should be pointed out that our ideas of what is masculine and what is feminine are arbitrary and culturally determined. Moreover, the division is not the same from one culture to another or from time to time in the same culture.

As a final contribution to this idea I would like to suggest that in today's world there are strong movements away from stereotypes. The bipolarity of the masculine and feminine is so strong that one who is dysphoric about his or her stereotype position has no place to go except in the opposite direction. This adoption of masculine ways, clothes, attitudes, and occupations by women has been the principal manifestation of the Women's Liberation Movement over the past thirty years, and we are used to it. But men's liberation, or the retreat from the former masculine stereotype, is just beginning—with long hair, necklaces, earrings, and more colorful clothing. But I think it will develop much further since I believe cross-dressers are the vanguard of men's liberation. So I suggest that you look at the phenomenon as a kind of personal cultural revolution that will go on in parallel with the changes in women's roles, rather than as some sort of psychological disturbance to be dealt with. Women don't lose their femininity just because they wear pants. And likewise men don't lose their basic masculinity just because they wear a skirt and heels. They have simply added a new dimension to their total personality.

We ain't broke—so stop trying to fix us.

Fighting the Battles

Michele Kämmerer

I would like to tell you a little bit about myself and what my trip as a transsexual has been like, and to give you an idea of how, why, and what I am.

My name is Michele Julia Kämmerer. I am a fifty-year-old woman, fire captain, feminist, father and grandfather, lesbian, political activist, and artist. As a Jodo Shinshu Buddhist I believe that life is a process and that *we are what we do*. I successfully transitioned from male to female within the Los Angeles Fire Department in June 1991, and had sex reassignment surgery in Belgium in 1993.

My father, a German-American Catholic, and my mother, a Swedish Lutheran, were in a very contentious marriage of necessity and habit. And it was hell for me. So the battles I fought were within myself and for survival in a man's world where there was no man there for me. I came through many physical and emotional beatings and learned not to trust and not to talk. I hid my feelings really well and armor-plated myself. I stuffed my feelings deep inside and I survived. Personal adrenalin became my drug of choice via risk-taking adventure. Fun and fear went right along with lipstick and lingerie, fantasy and fucking; it all tied together. My mother died when I was thirteen and I shut down even more, refused to attend her funeral, and went off into fantasy. I was confused about my sex, my gender, and my life, but I kept pushing on. I went through high school immersing myself in the Army Junior ROTC and Boy Scouts. At age seventeen I joined the Navy to get away from problems involving sex with an older woman. In the Navy, I trained as a weather technician, forecaster, upper-air meteorologist, and in photography. I served in Iceland, on two ships. I volunteered for Antarctica and for Navy SEALS. I wanted to go to Vietnam really badly, for more adventure. The captain wouldn't let me off the ship, so I never got to Vietnam. My high school friend married me while I was still in the Navy, and my daughter and son were born after I was discharged.

My goal was to be a Los Angeles firefighter, that sounded like fun . . . it was adventurous and dangerous. I loved running into burning buildings that other people were running from. I loved taking the hose and the nozzle into the hot, dark maw, with smoke so thick you couldn't see your hand in front of your face. We crawled inside of those buildings and we fought fire, our goal was to be first in, to penetrate and get first water on that fire . . . very masculine pursuits. The competition to be first in, to be the best fireman, was immense and it was quite a heady experience. Fighting fire was a wonderful and total mind, body, emotional experience.

Early in my career I divorced and got custody of my two little kids. I was their mother and father for a while. I remarried and my second wife and I raised my children. The urges I had felt all my life were still there, the drive, the motivation, the lust to express my femininity. I went into psychotherapy and discovered Radix, a neo-Reichian method of emotional release work. This is very therapeutic, intense body work that opens you to all your stored feelings of anger and grief. After years of painful work, of opening my armor, my feelings flooded out. Through grief, pain, suffering, and endless tears I discovered myself and I could feel! I accepted and owned my transsexuality, which was a very difficult process. I avoided that word and that concept for a long, long time. But eventually I went through two hundred hours of facial electrolysis. I even dressed as a woman in daylight!

Finally in early 1991, my twenty-second year in the fire department, I told Fire Chief Don Manning that I was a woman, a transsexual woman, and that I would like his help in my transition. He was, of course, shocked, but he ordered the fire department to pay attention to who I was and what I was doing. We have a very highly disciplined organization, and for that I am very thankful. Due to my job performance and the respect I received for my human rights, I was successful in transitioning from male to female in the Los Angeles Fire Department.

So how did I get here? Three things: I stayed in a loving, deeply meaningful process of growth, kept on a career path, and became a Buddhist. I discovered and accepted myself, opened and released my feelings, and included spirituality in my process. I realized that I am a verb, a human be-ing. Whatever I am is what I am doing, right here in the moment; everything else is just a construct, fantasy, or history.

In closing I will read a poem that I heard in a Buddhist service in San Francisco. I thought the priest was reading it directly to me, and all the other people there were just guests. The term used in the poem, "Nembutsu," is a very important concept in Jodo Shinshu Buddhism. It basically means forty-two, the meaning of Life, the Universe, and Everything.

You Are Just Right As You Are

You are just right as you are . . .
    your face,
    your body,
    your name . . .
Your social position,
    wealth, parents, children,
    daughter-in-law and even grandchildren,
    are just right for you.
Your happiness and unhappiness,
    joy and sorrow,
    are just right for you.
Your life has been neither good nor bad . . .
    It has been just right for you.
Whether you go to the Pure Land,
    or fall into hell,
    that place is best suited for you.
Don't think highly of yourself,
    but don't belittle yourself either.
There is neither above or below . . .
    even the time and place of your death,
    is just right for you.
How can it not be just right
    when lived in the world of naturalness,
    the world of Nembutsu . . . ?

—Goromatsu Mayakawa

Metamorphosis: Man in the Making (A Personal and Political Perspective)

Rupert Raj

A self-determinist and individualist by nature, I guess you can call me a "self-made man." Literally. Born a baby girl to my Polish mother and East Indian father, in the maternity ward of the Ottawa General Hospital, on a bleak February morning in 1952, I was a rebel right from the start—screaming my lungs out and kicking up a storm at the ignominy of my entrance onto the stage of life. Hey, what's happening here? Why am I "anatomically incorrect" (not built like my brother)? How could Mother Nature do this to me? I'm supposed to be a boy! I'm not going to take this! Well . . . it was to take me the next twenty years to put things right.

Not your average run-of-the-mill guy, I might seem exotic (or even psychotic) to some people considering that I've led a somewhat unusual life—emerging from the proverbial closet, not once, not twice, but many times. Two of these "rites of passage" have been sexual (both psychologically and physically), the others philosophical (moral and political). In a nutshell, I "came out" initially as a female-to-male transsexual, eventually resolving my gender dysphoria syndrome (I felt like a male "imprisoned" in a woman's body) by means of hormonal and surgical sex reassignment in New York City. In the fall of 1971, I was prescribed biweekly male hormone injections by Dr. Charles Ihlenfeld (former associate of the late Dr. Harry Benjamin), and at the age of nineteen and a half, I went through my second puberty—only this time around, it was a thrill. The following summer, I underwent a radical bilateral mastectomy (my chest "bumps" were a 34C) at the hands of Dr. David Wesser—and a finer set of (man-made) male pecs I have yet to see!

480

Six years later, in July 1978, I again went under the knife—this time for a panhysterectomy (removal of the uterus and the ovaries), which was done at the Sexuality Clinic in Calgary, Alberta. To my disappointment, however, I was not able to follow through with the phalloplasty (construction of an artificial penis) that Dr. Dale Birdsell was then experimenting with on female-to-male transsexuals. One patient had to have as many as nineteen operations to finally create his new male organ, another similarly had to undergo multiple surgeries. Both these "new men" sported scars on their lower torso and thighs, and neither had "balls." Nor could they pee standing up, or get an erection without inserting a stiffening device. Penile sensation and male climax, of course, were too much to hope for at the time. So, I passed on phalloplasty and consoled myself by revaluing my own "micro-prick" (supersensitive and swelled in size by extensive doses of androgen). Though basically your cerebral type, I made good use of my other "head."

Time passed and, once again, I opened the closet door—this time as a bisexual (and androgynous) man. I got "turned on," romantically and sexually, by men *and* women on the basis of their unique individuality, their "humanness," if you will. I wanted—and had—the best of both worlds: the thrilling narcissism of two bronzed and muscled male bodies, gleaming with sweat, grunting and groaning, humping and thumping, as they got hard and "got off" (together or separately), and the exquisite sensation of naked "otherness" between a man and a woman, intimately entangled, skin to skin, honeyed kisses on burning lips and scented hair, each partner pleasuring the most private parts of the other.

In the mid-1970s, during my years out West (Vancouver and Calgary), I had a three-year relationship with a gay-identified, bisexual, female-to-male, preoperative transsexual (he was the dominant, and I the passive, partner). He broke my heart when he "dumped" me in 1979 for a ravishing male-to-female (pre-op). My world was shattered: existential insecurity my constant companion. Then, several years later, in 1982, I had a brief, but intense, love affair with another "new man" (also pre-operative, gay-identified, bisexual, and dominant) whom I visited in Washington, D.C., for two weeks on my summer vacation. This transhomosexual romance was rather short-lived, however, because I was already "attached" at the time and wanted to "stay true" to my fiancee (a soon-to-be-operated-on "new woman"—we never did get married in the end, and eventually split up in 1988). I did manage to remain friends with both of my transgay ex-lovers, though.

So, not only was I androgynous (a man with a masculine gender identity who identified first as a human being, then as a male, with some custom blend of *yin* and *yang*)—and furthermore, a feminist—I was bisexual, too. But wait, that's not all. On top of this, I was also transsexual, of course, and, to some extent, transgenderist (although not, initially, by choice). The androgyny I experienced, therefore, was both social and physical. Talk about your "gender blenders"! Hey, maybe I'm just too complicated for my own good! For instance, I want to be *four* clones at once: a gay man, a lesbian, a straight male, and a bisexual transgenderist androgyne. Well, I'm some combination of the last two and the first, and am presently married (monogamously) to a bisexual "new woman."

And what about the philosophic passageways in my life? What particular philosophical, political and moral milestones helped shape me into the enlightened Renaissance Man of today? Secular humanism, (eco)feminism, "deep" ecology, and Zen Buddhism/Taoism. These four worldviews (as I see it) all share a common precept: the social-democratic principle of inclusiveness, one that embraces all human beings—women and men, black and white, gay and straight, young and old, poor and rich—as well as the "other" animals. The circle of life is an ever-expanding one that circumscribes all.

My own evolution (up the ascending spiral of human consciousness) began on the first turn, with transsexualism and (soon after) gender reassignment. The second turn was my agnostic enlightenment and my encounter with Zen Buddhism and Taoism. Climbing higher, I then experimented with bisexuality, becoming aware of my androgyny, and beginning to form a feminist identity. On the fourth coil, I developed a sense of my "humansexuality," coupled with a reluctant growing acceptance of my physical transgenderism (i.e., my "intersexual" genitals). The fifth coil of the spiral reinforced my commitment to social democracy as *the* universal ethic—the connecting link. The final ascent, so far, has brought me up and around the sixth and seventh links: an affirmation of atheistic humanism and of animal rights (i.e., "ecohumanism"). I continually cycle back to the first turning point in my still-evolving awareness: my transsexualism and what it means to me in terms of my being—and becoming—a fully integrated man-in-the-world.

An interesting aside here concerns the connection among humanism, feminism, androgyny, and bisexuality. I first started calling myself a feminist when I began to read the literature extensively, sometime in the mid-seventies. Then, I guess I got "turned off" by the overly militant, "ball-busting" feminists: the lesbian separatists and other radical purists (like Janice Raymond). Being not only transsexual and androgynous, but bisexual as well (actually, I prefer the term "humansexual"), I changed from identifying as a feminist to thinking of myself as a humanist. In this context, I meant not the secular or even the humanitarian aspect, but rather, the characteristic of being "universally or essentially human," together with the advocacy of gender *and* sexual equality. Out of this initial partial concept of humanism grew my adopted self-label of "humansexual," and later on, my appreciation of the wider meaning of humanism which, ironically, implies an inclusive (substantial) feminism! So, in effect, I've come full circle: from feminist to humanist to ecofeminist-humanist. What a convoluted evolution I continue to pass through to keep on becoming the self-liberated man of today . . .

Turning now from the philosophical, the moral, and the political to the personal. My life, right now, is pretty good, so I can't really complain. I "got my own back" at one of the gender clinicians from Toronto's Clarke Institute of Psychiatry, a rather arrogant psychologist, by announcing my recent betrothal to one of his former patients. Well, ya' shoulda' seen the look of shocked surprise on his face!—who says there's no justice in this world? I have a loving wife (we "tied the knot" in September 1989, and honeymooned in Cleveland, while attending an international gender dysphoria symposium there) and Patches, my cat companion of twelve and a half years, plus close ties with my sister, older brother, sister-in-law, nephew, mother-in-law, and brother-in-law, in addition to several close friends, as well as some twenty folks in nine countries around the world with whom I correspond.

On occasion, I play with the idea of going in for further surgery, such as a "metoidioplasty," performed by Dr. Donald Laub and others. This is a surgical procedure that transforms the existing elongated clitoris into a natural microphallus with full erotic sensibility, capable of orgasm, but not of ejaculation, and that makes use of the labia to form a scrotum (into which artificial testes can be implanted). It is rather tempting given that the overall cosmetic results are quite good, there is virtually no visible scarring, and, if all goes well, one can urinate like a man. The only problem is money—and time—and right now, I don't have either. In other words, this surgery is not a priority for me at the moment. Maybe later on, perhaps . . . we'll see. Until then, I'm used to my body the way it is—and my comfort level is one that I can live with for now.

I have opened a window to my inner self so as to share with you the ongoing evolution of a man in the making: physically, sexually, emotionally, intellectually, politically, and morally. Not, by any means, representative of the larger body of female-to-male transsexuals, I make no apologies. Branded, in the past, by some of these older (pre-1990s) "nouveau male," "moral-majority" mainstreamers as a sexual "outsider" of sorts, I unashamedly exult in my own being—and becoming.

Fluid parameters, ego resilient yet intact, I am what I am. A self-made man, ever-evolving . . .

Note

For those who wish to explore (or re-explore) these valuable worldviews, try reading the following works:

Geller, Thomas. 1990. *Bisexuality: A reader and sourcebook.* Ojai, Calif.: Times Change Press.

Lamont, Corliss. [1949] 1988. *The philosophy of humanism.* New York: Continuum Publishing.

Mellor, Mary. 1992. *Breaking the boundaries: Toward a feminist green socialism.* London: Virago Press.

Ross, Nancy Wilson. 1960. *The world of Zen: An east-west anthology.* New York: Vintage Books.

Singer, June. 1976. *Androgyny: Toward a new theory of sexuality.* Garden City, N.Y.: Anchor Press/Doubleday.

Singer, Peter. [1975] 1990. *Animal liberation.* New York: Avon Books.

Waltham, Clae. 1971. *Chuang Tzu: Genius of the absurd* (Taoism). New York: Ace Books.

The Inner Dimensions of
Gender Transformation

Lee Etscovitz

The following chapter grew out of my own personal struggles with gender dysphoria, as well as out of my observations of other persons struggling with the same basic condition. Underlying these remarks is the fundamental assumption that gender dysphoria is truly a human condition as opposed to being a human choice. In other words, to paraphrase Kim Elizabeth Stuart, it represents an uninvited human situation (1991). Many questions have emerged from what I have personally experienced and professionally observed in terms of this phenomenon. For example, what does the transformation of one's gender entail for the inside of a person, in addition to the all-too-obvious outer changes? What are the inner conflicts and demands, the inner confusions and concerns? Do these various struggles differ among transvestites, transgenderists, and transsexuals? If so, how? Are there certain tasks that a gender dysphoric must face in order to find meaning and fulfillment in life? And what are the processes that can facilitate the resolution of these various inner struggles? What is it, in fact, that a person actually has to do to make sense of it all and to get on with life?

The answers to questions such as these are facilitated by an understanding of what I refer to as "the inner dimensions of gender transformation." I do not mean to imply that the various outer dimensions are of lesser importance. Clothing and hairstyle, for example, are certainly part of the total picture. But to ignore, or at least not to understand, the inner life—the inner substance—of gender transformation is to lessen the chance of a gender dysphoric person's living a meaningful and enjoyable life as a whole person.

In 1991, when I first joined Renaissance Education Association, a support organization for members of the transgendered community, I met JoAnn Roberts, one of the organization's founders. I mentioned to JoAnn that my new membership represented for me a true beginning, a rebirth, in the middle of my chronological life. I also pondered aloud the question of where this beginning would lead and how one goes about making the most of it. JoAnn replied: "You have to name it and claim it." Her remark seemed overly simplistic, which in some ways it was, but it also had some deep implications, deep enough to lead me to a more developed paradigm that I have constructed since in order to help explain the inner tasks of gender transformation. I have now expanded JoAnn's notion of naming it and claiming it to include taming it and framing it. Stated less cryptically, there are at least four major tasks underlying a full personal rebirth, a full sense of inner renewal, as a gender-transformed person. Those tasks are

1. Self-recognition (Naming it)
2. Self-acceptance (Claiming it)
3. Self-integration (Taming it)
4. Self-transcendence (Framing it)

Let me explain what I mean by these four inner tasks. First of all, self-recognition refers to the task of facing oneself in the psychological mirror, facing the fact that one is not only different from other people but also, in this case, somehow transgendered. Self-recognition means an end to any denial of gender wishes and thus an end to any denial of those hard-to-face gender discrepancies in one's life. Nor is self-recognition a one-time effort, for it often takes time to discover just what kind of a transgendered person one really is, whether transvestite, transgenderist, or transsexual. Genuine self-recognition, that is, naming it accurately, is thus very important, in order to give proper shape to one's life, both inner and outer.

A second inner task is that of self-acceptance, going one step beyond self-recognition and accepting the fact that one is a transgendered person, that one is truly different. The task is that of really claiming it, without shame, without guilt, without apology. It means being able at last to say to oneself: "The grass is green, the sky is blue, and I cross-dress." Without self-acceptance—without genuinely feeling that who or what one is, is okay—without such self-affirmation, the individual is embarked on a life of endless pain, frustration, shame, and guilt. Such denial and its negative consequences are usually debilitating, invading one's personal life, relationships, and work efforts. To achieve self-acceptance, on the other hand, is to claim, and therefore to own, that which is everyone's birthright, namely, to be whatever and whoever one is meant to be.

As difficult as self-recognition and self-acceptance are, self-integration is even more difficult, for it represents the means by which the individual begins to achieve a sense of wholeness as a person. Simply as human beings, without any gender issues, we must put our lives together meaningfully and keep them integrated that way. Moreover, there are many aspects of our lives to be integrated, such as the sexual and the spiritual, a point made clear in an article by William R. Stayton (1992). We also have to coordinate our familial and vocational efforts, our vocations and avocations, our goals and abilities, and so on. Integrating our individual lives is a continual challenge.

For the transgendered person, this normal task of self-integration is even more complicated and challenging. How effectively, for example, can a transvestite keep his (or her) cross-dressing a secret as part of a double life? How successfully can a male-to-female transgenderist live and work as a female and still maintain the anatomical and legal status of a male? The same issue pertains to a female-to-male transgenderist. And how smoothly can a transsexual handle the radical personal and social changes that often accompany reassignment surgery? Taming it all and thus gaining meaningful control of one's life as a whole constitute the task of self-integration.

Traditionally, we would end our discussion of the inner tasks of gender transformation at this point, having presented three well-recognized psychological tasks that apply to gender transformation, namely, self-recognition, self-acceptance, and self-integration. But, as I see it, a complete discussion must include yet another inner task, which I refer to as "self-transcendence," a task that is increasingly evident in the growing public and professional interest in spiritual matters and matters of the soul. I have found this fourth task to be the most difficult one to describe and to conceptualize. And yet it has been as much, if not more, a part of my own life as perhaps the other three tasks combined.

To transcend oneself and one's living struggles seems to mean that one has to find, to create, to frame a larger reality within which the struggles can take place and at the same time hold the potential for resolution. A sense of humor about it all also helps to put the daily struggles into a larger framework or perspective. Without this larger framework, without this extraordinary basis for hope and effort, the individual risks hopelessness and failure, for there is no larger perspective, no sense of wider mission, in terms of which to tackle the various pressures of daily life, let alone the pressures of gender dysphoria itself.

Hopefully, the somewhat cryptic notion of naming it, claiming it, taming it, and framing it has now taken on greater meaning, signifying, respectively, self-recognition, self-acceptance, self-integration, and self-transcendence as we have briefly described these four inner tasks. But these four tasks do not in themselves sufficiently explain the inner process that makes possible their fulfillment. Let us now look briefly at such a process to deepen even further our understanding of the inner dimensions of gender transformation.

The process by which each of the four inner tasks is handled can perhaps be best described as a generic, inner process of reaching in, reaching out, and reaching up. The process is generic because the same overall process operates in the case of each inner task. And the process is of an inner nature because it involves the working through of feelings, experiences, and perceptions in terms of one's whole being. For example, to recognize oneself in the deepest sense means one has to "reach in," to be willing to examine one's deepest feelings, hopes, and fears, and to find the courage and strength to go on.

To "reach out," on the other hand, means to relate to other people, to become involved in the world of action and human relations, to make things happen, to be productive, to share oneself with others. Martin Buber, the Jewish philosopher and theologian, sees all real living as meeting, as involving a relationship, whether with God, with people, or with nature (Buber 1958). The point is that, to move in the direction of self-recognition, one must not only reach inward but also reach out to the world. And yet it is in the process of meeting the world, with all its human variety, as well as looking within, that a person begins to discover his or her own uniqueness. A self without boundaries is not really a self, and those boundaries develop more fully in the context of human relationships. In a very real sense, to reach out is also to reach in.

The third aspect of what I have been describing as the generic inner process of gender transformation is that of "reaching up." Reaching out, as we have seen, involves connecting with the immediate world around us and thereby creating more immediate meanings in our daily lives. To "reach up" is to find a wider purpose in life, a wider meaning, to attach oneself to a cause or interest that helps to make one's daily efforts part of something even more significant, more encompassing, more lasting. Out of such an effort we find the strength and courage to live our daily lives. Ernest Becker, basing his ideas on the work of Otto Rank, says, in effect, that we all have to find life projects and allegiances to give our lives meaning and significance (1973). And those same life projects must enhance rather than destroy our lives and the lives of those around us. In other words, we need to create healthy or life-affirming transferences. Attending to one's soul, finding comfort and even empowerment in silence, and staying tuned to one's purpose are some of the ways of reaching up in the direction of greater self-recognition.

What applies to the task of self-recognition also applies to each of the three remaining inner tasks. Without fully illustrating the other three tasks at this time, we can still see the general application of the inner process that I have been describing. For example, self-integration, challenging us to pull our lives together, especially in the face of both inner and outer pressures, can benefit from the process of examining one's feelings, from meeting with other persons, such as in support groups, and from finding ways of making greater sense of it all. Reaching in, reaching out, and reaching up thus comprise the inner process by which each of the four inner tasks of self-recognition, self-acceptance, self-integration, and self-transcendence is fulfilled.

It is my hope that a better understanding of the inner dimensions of gender transformation ultimately contributes to the betterment of life for transvestites, transgenderists, and transsexuals alike, whether through self-help or professional help. In either case, a gender dysphoric must have some means of working through the inner discomfort that at one time or another and to one extent or another invades his or her life. Without an effective approach to the problems demanding resolution, the quality of life, let alone life itself, is threatened. Perhaps the inner tasks and processes outlined here can contribute to the effective approach we are all seeking.

References

Becker, Ernest. 1973. *The denial of death.* New York: Free Press.

Buber, Martin. 1958. *I and thou.* 2d ed. New York: Charles Scribner's Sons.

Etscovitz, Lionel. 1969. Religious education as sacred and profane: An interpretation of Martin Buber. *Religious Education* 64, no. 4.

Stayton, William R. 1992. A theology of sexual pleasure. *SIECUS Report* 20, no. 4.

Stuart, Kim Elizabeth. 1991. *The uninvited dilemma: A question of gender.* Rev. ed. Portland, Ore.: Metamorphous Press.

Transsexuality and Religion:
A Personal Journey

Karen F. Kroll

There is a poem by Robert Frost, entitled "The Road Not Taken," which concludes that the narrator took the road less traveled, "And that has made all the difference." Like the narrator of the poem, I finally had to choose which road to travel on for the rest of my life, and this choice has forever changed the direction of my life.

Making a change is never an easy decision, and at first it may not seem very scary to us, at least as children, but when we grow up and become adults we sometimes get caught up in being afraid of what others will think if we fail in our attempt to change. Many find it easier to hold on to traditional ways and just go with the flow, but this is not the way that a person with gender dysphoria finds peace of self. Inevitably, like countless others before me, I had to make a change that enabled me to know and experience that peace inside myself.

This peace of self was something that I lacked for much of my life. Instead I felt confusion and emotional pain in a major area of my identity. I tried in my early years to understand it, but I was only left with a puzzle that I could not explain. As a teenager I felt like a stranger living in a foreign country and I began to wear a mask to hide my true identity. This mask became an important part of my survival because without it suicide was a real possibility. I began to strike out in anger as an adult, hoping this would relieve the confusion and emotional pain. When this did not work, I tried to kill these feelings by drinking alcohol and by taking drugs to excess. I have been both sober and clean for several years through adoption of a twelve-step program and by facing my feelings of transsexuality, but not without a lot of professional counseling.

490

When a person finally deals with the issue of his or her own gender dysphoria, the potential for causing conflict in regards to individual religious beliefs is very real. In my case, I had to leave an occupation, that of Catholic priest, and begin my work life over again at fifty. Laicization was a very painful process for me because the priesthood had always been a labor of love.

From this experience, I became convinced that religious leaders of various faiths need to find room in their hearts for people in transition. They must remember that God alone is the judge and searcher of a person's heart and they must not forget they are dealing with a person who has come to them for help, not rejection. They need to be willing to journey with transsexuals in order that they may experience the love of God in these encounters, not disillusionment.

A month before I underwent sexual reassignment surgery (SRS) I received a letter from two close friends, both strict Catholics, who believed what I was doing to myself was morally wrong and against the teachings of Jesus. They wondered how I could have survived as a priest in the Catholic Church all those years and do what I was about to do, because the surgery would destroy the body that God had given me to protect and honor. Though their statements cut me right to the bone, in my reply I tried to share my confusion and emotional pain with them and emphasized this was not a spur-of-the-moment decision. I closed my letter by asking them not to write me again if they were only going to condemn me for my decision. I have not heard from them since.

Many transsexuals who come from religious backgrounds may face similar problems, and though many can dismiss or ignore them, I and many others cannot do so. Sexual reassignment surgery raises moral issues, but I think these issues also involve free choice, an issue that goes beyond the two opposite polar schools of thought that dominate religious discourse. One school is generally called "fundamental legalism." It stresses a strict or literal adherence to a set of moral principles within a structured code of conduct. This code defines actions in terms of "black and white." Its adherents refuse to admit there are gray areas or a middle ground in their framework. This rigidity creates two key problems.

The first problem is that adherents of this school of thought take their "black-and-white" concepts and equate them with the divine. By equating them with the divine, they are saying that anyone who cannot accept these concepts cannot be saved by God. Everything must be judged as either right or wrong, and the institution for drawing up these concepts becomes equivalent to God.

The second problem relates to "free will." The fundamental legalism school has difficulty with the existence of the concept since it sees religious concepts only in black and white. If one admits there is a middle ground in morality, then he or she must deal with free will, and this in turn would force acceptance of the fact that individuals are responsible for the free choices that they make in their lives.

Though there are other schools of thought, to my mind the polar opposite of what I have called fundamental legalism is what might be called "situational morality." Its roots can be traced to existential philosophy, which developed after the First World War. The basic premise of this school of thought is that no moral decision can be made by the individual, because the individual is always being governed or determined by various situations in his or her life. In other words, morality is determined by a set of situations that always governs a person's life, and so the individual is not responsible for his or her actions. Ultimately this view denies that the individual is anything more than a robot without any free will. I find this view not much more helpful than the fundamental legalism one.

Helpful to me in dealing with the conflicts and deficiencies in these two approaches was another religious concept, that of the "wholeness of the body." I began by asking a theological question. Is the body by its nature evil? My answer to this question was no, because of my understanding and belief in free will. Yet, like most such questions, it is not one with a simple yes or no answer. To understand these we need to understand two very basic theological and cultural roots from which the Western Christian tradition grew.

The first root is the Jewish religious experience as detailed in the scriptures. In the Book of Genesis, for example, there are two creation accounts. In one of the accounts a human being is created in the image of God, and it is good. In the other account a human being is created from the dust of the earth and God breathes life into that human being. The interesting part of these different accounts is that God did not divide a person into two parts, one part soul and the other part body. A person is a whole being, composed of both body and soul, and created by God.

The second root of Christianity comes from the Hellenistic philosophical and religious experience that has its roots in Platonism. Plato was a dualist. He saw the human being as one part soul and other part body, and the highest part was the soul because it was eternal and above corruption. The body was material and earthly and corruptible and it held the soul a prisoner, and only when a person died could the soul again be free.

These conflicting religious traditions in regard to the soul (or mind) and the body were sources of major conflict in the early Christian Church. One of the first major heresies was Gnosticism, which was based on the premise that only by "pure knowledge" could one be saved, because only then could a person know Jesus Christ. Pure knowledge could only come from the soul since it could not be corrupted like the body. By implication if a person could not learn to control his or her body, there could be no salvation. Though Gnosticism was technically overcome by the more orthodox Christian interpretation, it continued to exist underground, and sprang up over the course of history with a variety of different names.

For example, when the bubonic plague wiped out about a third of the population of Europe during the Middle Ages, one of the theological reasons given for the plague was that people had refused to control their bodies. God had become angry at this and sent a plague to teach them. This viewpoint may sound very barbaric to us today but similar statements have been used to explain the spread of AIDS.

The concept of the corruptibility of the body has played an interesting role in the American experience. The Puritan fathers in New England believed very strongly in the corruptibility of humans, and they established a moral code based on this assumption. Such a moral code would save the world, and this is why in their writings they often saw their settlements as the New Jerusalem.

It is only by studying these moral philosophies and the traditional belief in the corruptibility of the body that transsexuals can begin to understand why this theological concept of body and evil impacts upon our lives. It is a concept that has to be challenged and made the subject of objective reappraisals and of common sense. To some extent this has been going on for a long time. For example, for a time dissecting the body was a serious breach of medical ethics. That concept began to change in the late Middle Ages and resulted in the foundation of modern anatomy. Similarly, the removal of human organs from one body and transplanting them into another body was regarded as totally unacceptable until well into the twentieth century.

In many ways, however, the most sacred part of the body has been the genital areas. They are the inviolate part of the body from a theological and medical point of view, and this belief in inviolability may be at the root of the problems for most people in our society when it comes to SRS. It is a fear of inviolability that must be met head on.

Kim Elizabeth Stuart summed up this problem in her book, *The Uninvited Dilemma.*

> Many opponents of gender congruity bring up the subject of religion, and make statements such as "God made you the way you are, and you have no right to change that." But where are the protests when hopelessly disabled persons are given artificial limbs, joints, or heart valves? According to the logic of those religious protesters, people should not be allowed to take advantage of many of the advances in modern medicine because "God made these people they way they are." Where are the protests when diabetics are injected with insulin derived from animals? Where are the protests when tiny babies . . . are operated on to have birth or genetic defects corrected? Where are the cries . . . when Siamese twins are separated by surgery so that they can live (or one may live) whole, normal lives? Certainly if God made transsexuals, that same God must have made Siamese twins. The implication here, of course, is that transsexuals choose to be the way they are, while others with physical and developmental

birth or genetic defects, and persons who develop medical conditions, do not make choices. That is patent nonsense. No one chooses to be a transsexual any more than one chooses to be a diabetic. . . . The only choice involved for transsexuals is what they are going to do about their condition. The individuals who argue against surgical intervention for transsexuals on religious or moral grounds use spurious arguments, and are hypocritical in the worst sense. They claim to follow the precepts of Jesus who preached the love of God and fellow man, and yet they are perfectly willing to turn their back on their fellow man (or woman), and condemn some to an internal hell based on their interpretations of what is right or wrong. . . . It would behoove those moral adjudicators to keep their own spiritual yard free of weeds instead of constantly spading in other people's gardens. (1983, 96–97)

In a sense I did not have a choice about SRS since my gender dysphoria was always there. But I did have a choice about what to do. I did not choose to have SRS on the spur of the moment, but after a great deal of deep soul searching and professional help. Sexual reassignment surgery was for me a rebirth, because it gave me my life; I was finally in union with my world.

It was for this reason that I made a choice to write this paper. I have seen too many good people over the years hurt by other people, so I could no longer sit on the sidelines. I also wrote it with the hope that it would induce others who feel a need to reflect on issues of transsexuality and religion. It is a moral issue but it is not that simple. Most moral and religious issues never are, but a lot of people would rather make them simple issues for fear of what they might discover about themselves. It is not the asking questions about transsexuality that they fear most in their religious quest, but the answering of our own question about ourselves.

Reference

Stuart, Kim Elizabeth. 1983. *The uninvited dilemma: A question of gender.* Lake Oswegeo, Ore: Metamorphous Press.

A Legal Path of Androgyny

Lynn Edward Harris

I am a clinically diagnosed true hermaphrodite, and although this is a diagnosis with a much longer history than transsexualism, my problems have in many ways been more difficult. Hermaphroditism or androgyny occupies a "gray zone" between the sexes. It is very complex because of the physiological aspect, the human interest factor, and its psychosocial/psychosexual importance. It's been a theme in botany, painting, sculpture, poetry, drama, Greek mythology, and Old Testament scriptures.

I would like to focus upon intersex, the modern term for hermaphroditism (the archaic form), as a social dilemma and how government and bureaucratic agencies address undifferentiated sex within the parameters of only two proscribed sex designations made available: male and female.

I would also like to provide a cursory look at what I personally have experienced in the political arena in the United States, in particular in California. Although there are more personal freedoms in this country than in many others, the bureaucratic process is oftentimes absurd. What I have done, singlehandedly, is break the bureaucratic barrier with a sonic boom by setting what is presumed to be the legal precedent case in California, if not the nation.

I was born in 1950 with a not-so-rare, rather complicated hypothalamic/neuropituitary dysfunction that left me with what Leslie Fiedler termed "intermediate sex" (1978). The syndrome of combined male and female sex characteristics was clinically diagnosed by a team of specialists in 1973. Other than exploratory surgery, and a voluntary, irreversible sterilization for precautionary measures, to this day I remain surgically unaltered and unoperated on, with no cosmetic or reconstructive procedures to better define my internal or external anatomy.

495

Due to the fact my genitalia appeared somewhat ambiguous at birth—and remain to this day at a pre-pubescent stage of arrested development—I was arbitrarily designated by my parents and obstetrician/pediatrician as "female" and reared the same. Inherent in my particular syndrome was a "virilizing factor," so around age five I developed a budding penis; around age eleven to thirteen my voice dropped, and from age fifteen I began shaving almost every day.

Because I knew—even before I could verbalize my thoughts—that I was of indeterminate sex both inside and out, at age twelve I begged my mother to take me to a specialist who could provide me with some answers. The endocrinologist we visited did not examine me, much less ask me to undress, as mother stood by taking full charge of my medical assay. Plaintively, I tried to explain how I was not developing or functioning like any of the other girls in my junior high school. All he said was, "Well, I could put *her* through five hundred dollars' worth of tests, but what would it prove?!"

At that point, inconvenienced by the expense of an apparently wasted office visit and embarrassed by my alleged fabrications, my mother fiercely gripped my arm and, dragging me out of the man's office, shouted with a red face, "You see, you're wrong and I'm right. You're nothing more than a late bloomer. Let nature take its course. So just stop all these wild imaginings. It's all in your head!"

I was not permitted to ever bring up the topic again, and at age nineteen I was asked to leave home for other reasons.

In 1973 at age twenty-three I checked myself into the hospital for three days' worth of laboratory tests, X-rays, and exploratory surgery. Two weeks later the team of specialists (a gynecologist, an internist, and an ophthalmologist) rendered their consensus of opinion: clearly what I had was a congenital anomaly—"an hermaphroditic situation." Since there were no cancers or tumors present anywhere in my body, or even an extra or aberrant chromosome, the exact etiology or causation could not be pinpointed through textbook data available at that time. Although I was deemed sterile from birth and nonreproductive, my chances of pregnancy were 1 in 1,000; and if an accident happened (with my infantile development) it most likely would have been an ectopic hemorrhage, and probably fatal. So I was dismissed and advised by the rather baffled medical doctors, who did state on record that I was "in doubt as to my true sex," "to go home, take your vitamins and good-bye and good luck!"

So from age twenty-three onward my body continued to masculinize rapidly. Still, I had never ovulated, never had a monthly menstrual cycle, never grown breasts or lactated, never gotten pregnant, or developed curvy, child-bearing hips. Even though I had a small, atrophied womb, a nonfunctioning but functional vaginal canal, I was a "non-female." And so nature did, indeed, take its course.

I had a basic male skeletal structure, male musculature, male hair-growth patterns, vocal chords, a slight Adam's apple, an uncircumcised, hypospadiac, boyish penis, empty scrotal lobe halves that never fused, no internal glands to produce seminal fluid or sperm; gonadal mosaicism (fragmented testicular/ovarian tissue); and male genetic patterning and a male-oriented brain.

Twenty-two years later, in 1995, I was invited to participate in a research project at Cedars-Sinai Medical Center (Los Angeles) on intersex and DNA, RNA, and genetic aberrations. My case was reopened, reconfirmed, and expanded upon. With the tremendous advancements made in medical science and research on undifferentiated sex over the past two decades, a specific cause of my own peculiar syndrome may finally be discovered.

I have presented more than sixty lectures at colleges and medical trade seminars, given interviews for nationally syndicated radio and television, and been written up in medical journals and books. In my work on the lecture circuit over the past nine years I have been apprised of 120 other hermaphrodites (U.S. and Europe) and have met in person nine other clinically diagnosed hermaphrodites: four lived as men, four lived as women; and the one who possessed scant bands of gonads lived as a "neuter." With the exception of the last, each had had between one and twenty-five cosmetic or reconstructive surgeries. A few chose to remain with the social gender role in which they were reared. None appeared to live as homosexuals, however, a few, like myself, admitted to being bisexual from childhood. Healthwise, most started out as textbook cases with the customary sterility or mental retardation, or epilepsy; others suffered from pulmonary embolisms, kidney stones, diabetes, edema, etc. By comparison, I have been blessed with excellent health. My chronic hormonal deficiency was treated with supplements to balance my brain chemistry.

Back to my own story. . . . After being mistaken numerous times by people in both social or intimate situations for a mannish lesbian or a male transvestite (lacking breasts) or male transsexual (after testicle removal but prior to penile excision) attired as a woman, my occasional, repressed doubts as to my true gender suddenly became what psychiatrists termed a case of "acute gender dysphoria." I sank into a two-year depression.

Living as a man had never occurred to me until a platonic friend, a metaphysical counselor and avowed homosexual said: "I know you've been so unhappy living as a female, do you think you could do any worse living as a man in society?" He did not coerce, but emotionally bolstered me. I instantly understood how crucial the decision concerning my future well-being was.

Unlike numerous transsexuals I have met, I never felt like one sex "trapped" inside a physical body of the other sex. My penis and vagina always held equal value. Plastic surgery, genital or urological reconstruction, or removal of atrophied, ill-functioning gonads had never been my objective at any time.

The gender role crossover was done "cold turkey." Through the emotional implosion, I finally became in-tune with optimal selfhood after much guilt and recriminations for having been so dense for so long. Gender was just a facade; it was not indelible. Sex had nothing to do with the spirit or force that guided any person. For me to elect to live as a social male in the future seemed a viable solution, and a resolution to the self-delusion and travesty of having lived as a social female. It seemed the safer, more logical, and more comfortable thing to do. I sought relief from an emotional quagmire by divesting myself of everything fake associated with living this counterfeit image on a full-time basis for twenty-nine years.

When I lived as a social female I subconsciously asserted my masculine sensibilities with head ruling heart; now, living as a social male, I subconsciously assert my feminine sensitivities with heart ruling head. Things about my personality that were juxtaposed became equalized.

My physiognomy and my wardrobe changed, but never my sexual preferences. And I grew my facial hair into a full beard.

At a later time my prescient friend quipped, "Why would a so-called heterosexual female want to live as a homosexual?" Far more important to me than actually living as a social male was to fulfill a lifelong inclination to, ostensibly, relate to men as their mental/fraternal equal, not as a tomboy or equal rights-minded feminist—which I never was. Until he informed me of the obvious, only vaguely had I sensed my ultimate destination, but due to self-delusion and ignorance never knew the exact route. I had nothing left to prove to anybody, including myself . . . except become legitimized by the government.

From age twenty-nine to thirty-three I existed in a sexual, legal limbo—living as a man while carrying an old female I.D. I had been carded twice—once by a traffic officer; another time by a sergeant-at-arms in a private club where I'd been a dues-paying member for ten years prior, and barely escaped being turned over to the authorities for allegedly carrying a woman's stolen I.D.—my own. It was time I made my change *legal*.

My internist/endocrinologist—who had treated a few transsexuals but no intersexuals—informed me that, despite my unusual medical history, the courts in California handled any case of transgenderism as a psychiatric issue. Furthermore, the legal prerequisite for a "sex change" was a minimum six months psychological evaluation; also needed was proof that the individual was *not* a "functioning female of child-bearing status." I had already accomplished that via surgical sterilization, exactly ten years before, as proof that I was rendered "non-reproductive"—above and beyond my congenital sterility.

He admonished me to "play the game" with other doctors about needing some sex surgery (penile augmentation, silicone testis implants, hysterectomy, etc.), even though he clearly understood my trepidation. Even in the simplest of elective surgeries, things could go wrong.

I did not consider myself possessing any dramatic genital ailment malformation that would have warranted emergency or even corrective surgical procedures. I was never dissatisfied with my physical or genital construct, and never had had any difficulty either urinating or climaxing.

I collected letters from fourteen friends and relatives who had remained in my life before, during, and after my gender role crossover. After initial interviews with several unsympathetic analysts, I then spent well over a year in therapy with a psychologist. The overseeing psychiatrist gave me an affidavit to present to the court in which he stated he felt I was ready for a legal change of I.D., but probably not surgery at that time.

I followed the Code of Civil Procedure and in February 1983 filed with the Superior Court, County of Los Angeles, State of California, U.S.A., an "Order to Show Cause to Change Name," applying for a change of middle name (from Lynn Elizabeth Harris to Lynn Edward Harris), and a change of sex designation from "F" (female) to "M" (male).

For the following four consecutive weeks I had the customary "fictitious name statement" printed in *Metropolitan News*, a legal journal newspaper.

The court permitted me to both write and plead my own Petition Requesting Court Order for Change of Name and Issuance of New Birth Certificate, case number # C 437625. I researched that the state of California happened to be one of the few states offering not only amended, but brand new Certificates of Live Birth. Some other states in the Union make no provision whatsoever.

The key paragraph in my petition read: "After investigating the pros and cons of radical sex reassignment surgery over the last four years (1979–1983), I have disavowed any desire to risk possible infection, disfigurement, mutilation or rejection of foreign implants." My concluding remark was: "It is with great humility that I entreat the Court in its wisdom to grant a permanent legal remedy to the ambiguity, lack of continuity and presumed fraudulence associated with my present gender status."

My father, an absentee parent most of the time during my childhood and puberty, had originally claimed I was too flat chested and too fat to attract men. Years later, he claimed I looked better as a man than I ever had as a woman. He supported my court action 100 percent and stood up for me in court as my chief character witness. "If Lynn wants to be my son, then I'll call him my son!"

I had purposely not informed my mother of my day in court, sensing she would object or in some way interfere with the proceedings. If she was in denial about my syndrome itself—as if seeing wasn't believing!—she'd likewise be in denial about my using it as a valid, biological excuse for switching to live as a male. Four years earlier when I confronted her with my gender role crossover she declared, "After twenty-nine years living as a female, why bother to change. You're still my daughter, a *she!*"

Armed with my hospital records, surgical reports, the psychiatrist's affidavit, and copies of my old friends' letters, the judge perused only my Petition and Decree Changing Name. He said, "Everything appears to be in order. In that case I see no reason why I shouldn't say '*yes*' and sign this right now." For all the years spent going backwards through hell emotionally, I saw my case favorably adjudicated in about two and a half minutes. That so-called heterosexual (non)-female I lived as for twenty-nine agonizing years did not legally exist any longer. Lynn Elizabeth Harris had become a legal nonentity.

When I informed my mother of my win several months after the fact, she asked if the judge had asked me to drop my pants in court. Her tone was serious and not remotely facetious. I told her if he had asked me to do so, I would have gladly obliged. As far as she was concerned, I was no part of a man, just an impostor who'd perjured myself in court.

After my appointment in Superior Court, I had a thirty-day grace period in which to file the changes with the Department of Social Security (who reissued my original Social Security number with my new name); the Secretary of State (who filed away the changes); and the Department of Vital Statistics (D.V.S.), responsible for all birth records.

The D.V.S. flatly rejected my filing of the matter. As all state and public agencies must by law uphold and enforce all favorable adjudications as they are handed down, it appeared as if the Department of Vital Statistics was attempting to go over the head of the Superior Court and play God!

If you ever want to see a bureaucrat confounded, confront him with something new. The D.V.S. then mailed me a photostatted page from the California Health and Safety Code reading that they, the D.V.S., would issue a new birth certificate only if the filing of my petition were accompanied by a plastic surgeon's affidavit attesting that I'd undergone surgical procedures giving me "characteristics of the opposite sex."

Since I had written medical proof that I was born with "characteristics of *both* sexes," I wrote back the D.V.S. and asked them to explain exactly what *my* "opposite sex" was! Furthermore, there was nothing in their Health and Safety Code that mandated that one must submit to sex reassignment surgery in order to gain characteristics of the opposite sex.

Beyond that, what was heterosexual for me? What was homosexual for me? Two politically militant gay male friends, both attorneys, kidded, "Lynn, you may not have changed your sexual preferences, but you're not gay!"

The D.V.S. would not recant. They mailed me an interim birth certificate reading: "Lynn Edward Harris, Female."

My attorney friends (founders of Legal Foundation for Personal Liberties, a.k.a., National Gay Rights Advocates)—who were never optimistic about my case winning in Superior Court—suggested that since I now had the law on my side, I had three options: be patient and wait for the D.V.S. to come around; sue the state (and win); or hire a lawyer and take my case to an Appellate Court for enforcement. They also recommended I locate a precedent case to use for ammunition.

I researched through the ACLU Transsexual Rights Chapter, the Harry Benjamin International Gender Dysphoria Foundation, and other organizations. Nobody had any information pertinent to my major predicament. My attorney friends then felt safe to say that my own case had become the legal precedent of its kind in California, if not the nation.

I blitzed by-mail the D.V.S. with duplicate copies of my material. I included a letter from another psychiatrist stating that for me a surgical sterilization had been sufficient; that in the best interests of my emotional health I should be recognized as a male, and further unnecessary and dangerous surgical procedures at that time were unwarranted. I also included a letter from another plastic surgeon who gave me a consultation: "In fact, Mr. Harris declines to have surgery for reasons that would be reasonable and logical with any patient irrespective of gender problems . . . and his comportment has been that of a male, for all intents and purposes." He finished by chiding the D.V.S. for its "unconscionable error in not fully processing my case to its fullest degree."

Eventually, the D.V.S. recanted, apologized, and admitted their mishandling of my case from the start. They assured me that my original birth certificate would be frozen and sealed for life, and that they would be sending me not an amended, but a brand-new Certificate of Live Birth reading "Lynn Edward Harris, Male." Their parting words were: "Our computer's already gone into overdrive with the excess paperwork on your file. Just one last thing; promise us you won't ever change back!"

In three weeks my new document arrived. My internist recommended that I apply for a passport (my first ever), "which is government property, and let the state try and take that away from you!"

My passport came up for its tenth-year renewal in 1993.

In 1994 my internist informed me of five transsexual—not intersexual—cases who, apparently on the strength of my presumed legal precedent, obtained amended birth certificates, each without having to "go under the knife."

At present in 1995, sixteen years after living as a social male—the last twelve years as a fully legitimized male citizen—my case has gone uncontested and unchallenged by medical and legal authorities.

I've had the growing up to do for two people and I've benefitted from the unique advantage—beyond bisexuality—afforded me by my gender dichotomy: to live life as a woman *and* as a man in society.

Occasionally on the lecture circuit, I am contacted by befuddled parents of an intersexual infant who have enlisted my advice.

I invited my mother to go with me to see a psychologist with whom I'd collaborated on a two-year research project. During the session, she denied any recollection of our consultation with the specialist back when I was age twelve! To this day, she either will not or cannot bring herself to address me with the male pronoun, but said she'd make an effort.

My internist recently said, "The whole world acknowledges you as a man except your very own mother!"

Justice was done. To win as I did, having both the facts and the law on my side, was an ultimate victory. Although my new birth certificate was only a "piece of paper," it represented everything I'd gone through to obtain it. Avenged were the inequities I'd endured at the hands of two indifferent parents, some inflexible members of the medical orthodoxy, and bureaucrats who had inflated their limited worth.

The court in its wisdom had profoundly empowered and enabled me to actualize my potential and destiny with authenticity as I, a true hermaphrodite, am living life and perceiving it.

Reference

Fiedler, Leslie. 1978. *Freaks: Myths and images of the secret self.* New York: Simon & Schuster.

What Is a Transgenderist?

Kymberleigh Richards

The term "transgenderist" was coined by Virginia Prince to describe someone who lives full time in a gender role opposite to the one that society presumes to attach automatically to one's genetic sex. The gender assigned to me at birth was that of boy and I grew into a man; I now live as a woman, so I am a transgenderist.

Half the time when I tell someone this they say "Oh, well then, you're going to have sex reassignment surgery." However, I have no desire for surgery. The key difference between a transsexual and a transgenderist is that the latter has no burning desire to alter his or her birth genitalia in order to live in society in a role with which he or she feels comfortable. The essence of a transgenderist is that of complete personal identity and comfort with self. If anything, a transgenderist is the absolute best proof that sex does not equal gender, because I'm still sexually, physically a male. Yet, I interact with society, with the world, with my friends in the gender role you see me in twenty-four hours a day, seven days a week.

Unlike a cross-dresser, I don't go back to being Kevin when this conference is over, I will still be Kym. I am always Kym. There are few people in this room whom I have known for years, some of whom knew me before I started living full time as Kym. And they can tell you, "There's no Kevin anymore." Kevin is a social construct that no longer exists. There is no need for me to do it. I can't think for a single reason that I need to put on this societal role of a man.

Granted I am more fortunate than many people because my business is connected to the transgender community. I make my living as editor of *Cross Talk*. That makes it a lot easier because I don't have to shift back and forth in order to protect some image that an employer might want me to fill. I don't have those

503

pressures. I expend a lot of energy in society putting forward the idea that gender role should be a personal decision rather than an assigned role. If someone wants to shift gender roles on a full-time basis there should not be a societal imposed stigma against that. I hope people will eventually understand this, that each of us will be just who we are.

In a recent column in *Cross Talk* Virginia Prince said, "Men are always trying to become, women just are." I became Kym when I transitioned from those roles. Now, almost five years later, I just am Kym. I no longer feel I'm going through the effort of deconstructing one role to construct the other. In that regard, when society says, "People who are transgendered are ill." I say, "Why? I'm perfectly comfortable with who I am. I'm perfectly lucid, and salient, and intelligent. What is it about me that makes you say I'm not well?"

"Well, you're doing this."

"Well, I have a lot fewer issues to deal with, because I'm at peace with myself." Can someone who questions me say the same thing?

The last point I'm going to make deals with a point of semantics. Transgender has come through common usage in our community to mean any type of behavior that challenges dichotomous societal roles. It is an umbrella term that covers the occasional cross-dresser, someone who has the need for sex reassignment surgery, a transgenderist, a post-operative transsexual, or any variation in between. This does not negate the term "transgenderist," and I am still proud to call myself one. Just remember that not everyone who is transgendered is a transgenderist.

Appendix

Standards of Care

The Hormonal and Surgical Sex Reassignment of Gender Dysphoric Persons

1. Introduction

As of the beginning of 1979, an undocumentable estimate of the number of adult Americans hormonally and surgically sex-reassigned ranged from 3,000 to 6,000. Also undocumentable is the estimate that between 30,000 and 60,000 U.S.A. citizens consider themselves to be valid candidates for sex reassignment. World estimates are not available. As of mid-1978, approximately forty centers

Original draft prepared by the founding committee of the Harry Benjamin International Gender Dysphoria Association, Inc.: Paul A. Walker, Ph.D. (Chairperson); Jack C. Berger, M.D.; Richard Green, M.D.; Donald R. Laub, M.D.; Charles L. Reynolds, M.D.; Leo Wollman, M.D.

Original draft approved by the attendees of the Sixth International Gender Dysphoria Symposium, San Diego, California, February 1979. Revised draft (1/80) approved by the majority of the membership of the Harry Benjamin International Gender Dysphoria Association, Inc. Revised draft (3/81) approved by the majority of the membership of the Harry Benjamin International Gender Dysphoria Association, Inc. Revised draft (1/90) approved by the majority of the membership of the Harry Benjamin International Gender Dysphoria Association, Inc. It is this version which is reproduced here. Distributed by the Harry Benjamin International Gender Dysphoria Association, Inc., P.O. Box 1718, Sonoma, CA 95476 (phone 707–938–2871) and the American Educational Gender Information Service, Inc., P. O. Box 33724, Decatur, GA 30033–0724 (phone 404–939–0244).

505

in the Western hemisphere offered surgical sex reassignment to persons having a multiplicity of behavioral diagnoses applied under a multiplicity of criteria.

In recent decades, the demand for sex reassignment has increased as have the number and variety of possible psychologic, hormonal and surgical treatments. The rationale upon which such treatments are offered have become more and more complex. Varied philosophies of appropriate care have been suggested by various professionals identified as experts on the topic of gender identity. However, until the present, no statement of the standard of care to be offered to gender dysphoric patients (sex reassignment applicants) has received official sanction by any identifiable professional group. The present document is designed to fill that void.

2. Statement of Purpose

Harry Benjamin International Gender Dysphoria Association, Inc., presents the following as its explicit statement on the appropriate standards of care to be offered to applicants for hormonal and surgical sex reassignment.

3. Definitions

3.1 Standard of Care

The standards of care, as listed below, are *minimal* requirements and are not to be construed as optimal standards of care. It is recommended that professionals involved in the management of sex reassignment cases use the following as *minimal* criteria for the evaluation of their work. It should be noted that some experts on gender identity recommend that the time parameters listed below should be doubled, or tripled. It is recommended that the reasons for any exceptions to these standards, in the management of any individual case, be very carefully documented. Professional opinions differ regarding the permissibility of, and the circumstances warranting, any such exception.

3.2 Hormonal Sex Reassignment

Hormonal sex reassignment refers to the administration of androgens to genotypic and phenotypic females, and the administration of estrogens and/or progesterones to genotypic and phenotypic males, for the purpose of effecting somatic changes in order for the patient to more closely approximate the physical appearance of the genotypically other sex. Hormonal sex-reassignment does not refer to the administration of hormones for the purpose of medical care and/or research conducted for the treatment or study of non-gender dysphoric medical condition (e.g., aplastic anemia, impotence, cancer, etc.).

3.3 Surgical sex reassignment

Genital surgical sex reassignment refers to surgery of the genitalia and/or breasts performed for the purpose of altering the morphology in order to approximate the physical appearance of the genetically other sex in persons diagnosed as gender dysphoric. Such surgical procedures as mastectomy, reduction mammoplasty, augmentation mammoplasty, castration, orchidectomy, penectomy, vaginoplasty, hysterectomy, salpingectomy, vaginectomy, oophorectomy and phalloplasty in the absence of any diagnosable birth defect or other medically defined pathology, except gender dysphoria, are included in this category labeled surgical sex reassignment.

Non-genital surgical sex reassignment refers to any and all other surgical procedures of non-genital or non-breast sites (nose, throat, chin, cheeks, hips, etc.) conducted for the purpose of effecting a more masculine appearance in a genetic female or for the purpose of effecting a more feminine appearance in a genetic male, in the absence of identifiable pathology which would warrant such surgery regardless of the patient's genetic sex (facial injuries, hermaphroditism, etc.).

3.4 Gender dysphoria

Gender Dysphoria herein refers to that psychological state whereby a person demonstrates dissatisfaction with their sex of birth and the sex role, as socially defined, which applies to that sex, and who requests hormonal and surgical sex reassignment.

3.5 Clinical behavioral scientist*

Possession of an academic degree in a behavioral science does not necessarily attest to the possession of sufficient training or competence to conduct psychotherapy, psychologic counseling, nor diagnosis of gender identity problems. Persons recommending sex reassignment surgery or hormone therapy should have documented training and experience in the diagnosis and treatment of a broad range of psycho-

---

*The drafts of these Standards of Care dated 2/79 and 1/80 require that all recommendations for hormonal and/or surgical sex reassignment be made by licensed psychologists or psychiatrists. That requirement was rescinded, and replaced by the definition in section 3.5, in 3/81.

logic conditions. Licensure or certification as a psychological therapist or counselor does not necessarily attest to competence in sex therapy. Persons recommending sex reassignment surgery or hormone therapy should have the documented training and experience to diagnose and treat a broad range of sexual conditions. Certification in sex therapy or counseling does not necessarily attest to competence in the diagnosis and treatment of gender identity conditions or disorders. Persons recommending sex reassignment surgery or hormone therapy should have proven competence in general psychotherapy, sex therapy, and gender counseling/therapy.

Any and all recommendations for sex reassignment surgery and hormone therapy should be made only by clinical behavioral scientists possessing the following minimal documentable credentials and expertise:

3.5.1

A minimum of a Masters Degree in a clinical behavior science, granted by an institution of education accredited by a national or regional accrediting board.

3.5.2

One recommendation, of the two required for sex reassignment surgery, must be made by a person possessing a doctoral degree (e.g., Ph.D., Ed.D., D.Sc., D.S.W., Psy.D., or M.D.) in a clinical behavioral science, granted by an institution of education accredited by a national or regional accrediting board.

3.5.3

Demonstrated competence in psychotherapy as indicated by a license to practice medicine, psychology, clinical social work, marriage and family counseling, or social psychotherapy, etc., granted by the state of residence. In states where no such appropriate license board exists, persons recommending sex reassignment surgery or hormone therapy should have been certified by a nationally known and reputable association, based on education and experience criteria, and, preferably, some form of testing (and not simply on membership received for dues paid) as an accredited or certified therapist/counselor (e.g., American Board of Psychiatry and Neurology, Diplomate in Psychology from the American Board of Professional Psychologists, Certified Clinical Social Workers, American Association of Marriage and Family Therapists, American Professional Guidance Association, etc.).

3.5.4

Demonstrated specialized competence in sex therapy and theory as indicated by documentable training and supervised clinical experience in sex therapy (in some states professional licensure requires training in human sexuality; also, persons should have approximately the training and experience as required for certification as a Sex Therapist or Sex Counselor by the American Association of Sex Educators, Counselors and Therapists, or as required for membership in the Society for Sex Therapy and Research). Continuing education in human sexuality and sex therapy should also be demonstrable.

3.5.5

Demonstrated and specialized competence in therapy, counseling, and diagnosis of gender identity disorders as documentable by training and supervised clinical experience, along with continuing education.

The behavioral scientists recommending sex reassignment surgery and hormone therapy and the physician and surgeon(s) who accept those recommendations share responsibility for certifying that the recommendations are made based on competency indicators as described above.

4. Principles and Standards

Introduction

4.1.1. PRINCIPLE 1

Hormonal and surgical sex reassignment is extensive in its effects, is invasive to the integrity of the human body, has effects and consequences which are not, or are not readily, reversible, and may be requested by persons experiencing short-termed delusions or beliefs which may later be changed and reversed.

4.1.2. PRINCIPLE 2

Hormonal and surgical sex reassignment are procedures requiring justification and are not of such minor consequence as to be performed on an elective basis.

4.1.3. PRINCIPLE 3

Published and unpublished case histories are known in which the decision to undergo hormonal and surgical sex reassignment was, after the fact, regretted and the final result of such procedures proved to be psychologically dehabilitating to the patients.

4.1.4. STANDARD 1

Hormonal and/or surgical* sex reassignment on demand (i.e., justified simply because the patient has requested such procedures) is contraindicated. It is herein declared to be professionally improper to conduct, offer, administer, or perform hormonal sex reassignment and/or surgical sex reassignment without careful evaluation of the patient's reasons for requesting such services and evaluation of the beliefs and attitudes upon which such reasons are based.

4.2.1. PRINCIPLE 4

The analysis or evaluation of reasons, motives, attitudes, purposes, etc., requires skills not usually associated with the professional training of persons other than clinical behavioral scientists.

4.2.2. PRINCIPLE 5

Hormonal and/or surgical sex reassignment is performed for the purpose of improving the quality of life as subsequently experienced and such experiences are most properly studied and evaluated by the clinical behavioral scientist.

4.2.3. PRINCIPLE 6

Hormonal and surgical sex reassignment are usually offered to persons, in part, because a psychiatric/psychologic diagnosis of transsexualism (see DSM-III, section 302.5X), or some related diagnosis, has been made. Such diagnoses are properly made only by clinical behavioral scientists.

---

*The present standards provide no guidelines for the granting of non-genital/breast cosmetic or reconstructive surgery. The decision to perform such surgery is left to the patient and surgeon. The original draft of this document did recommend the following, however (rescinded 1/80): "Non-genital sex reassignment (facial, hip, limb, etc.) shall be preceded by a period of at least six months during which time the patient lives full-time in the social role of the genetically other sex."

4.2.4. PRINCIPLE 7

Clinical behavioral scientists, in deciding to make the recommendation in favor of hormonal and/or surgical sex reassignment, share the moral responsibility for that decision with the physician and/or surgeon who accepts the recommendation.

4.25. STANDARD 2

Hormonal and surgical (genital and breast) sex reassignment must be preceded by a firm written recommendation for such procedures made by a clinical behavioral scientist who can justify making such a recommendation by appeal to training or professional experience in dealing with sexual disorders, especially the disorders of gender identity and role.

4.3.1. PRINCIPLE 8

The clinical behavioral scientist's recommendation for hormonal and/or surgical sex reassignment should, in part, be based upon an evaluation of how well the patient fits the diagnostic criteria for transsexualism as listed in the DSM-III-R category 302.50, to wit:

> A. Persistent discomfort and sense of inappropriateness about one's assigned sex.
> B. Persistent preoccupation for at least two years with getting rid of one's primary and secondary sex characteristics and acquiring the sex characteristics of the other sex.
> C. The person has reached puberty.[1]

This definition of transsexualism is herein interpreted not to exclude persons who meet the above criteria but who otherwise may, on the basis of their past behavioral histories, be conceptualized and classified as transvestites and/or effeminate male homosexuals or masculine female homosexuals.

4.3.2. PRINCIPLE 9

The intersexed patient (with a documented hormonal or genetic abnormality) should first be treated by procedures commonly accepted as appropriate for such medical conditions.

4.3.3. PRINCIPLE 10

The patient having a psychiatric diagnosis (i.e., schizophrenia) in addition to a diagnosis of transsexualism should first be treated by procedures commonly accepted as appropriate for such nontranssexual psychiatric diagnoses.

4.3.4. STANDARD 3

Hormonal and surgical sex reassignment may be made available to intersexed patients and to patients having nontranssexual psychiatric/psychologic diagnoses if the patient and therapist have fulfilled the requirements of the herein listed standards; if the patient can be reasonably expected to be habilitated or rehabilitated, in part, by such hormonal and surgical sex reassignment procedures; and if all other commonly accepted therapeutic approaches to such intersexed or nontranssexual/psychiatrically/psychologically diagnosed patients have been either attempted, or considered for use prior to the decision not to use such alternative therapies. The diagnosis of schizophrenia, therefore, does not necessarily preclude surgical and hormonal sex reassignment.

Hormonal sex reassignment

4.4.1. PRINCIPLE 11

Hormonal sex reassignment is both therapeutic and diagnostic in that the patient requesting such therapy either reports satisfaction or dissatisfaction regarding the results of such surgery.

4.4.2. PRINCIPLE 12

Hormonal sex reassignment may have some irreversible effects (infertility, hair growth, voice deepening, and clitoral enlargement in the female-to-male patient and infertility and breast growth in the male-to-female patient) and, therefore, such therapy must be offered only under the guidelines proposed in the present standards.

4.4.3. PRINCIPLE 13

Hormonal sex reassignment should precede surgical sex reassignment as its effects (patient satisfaction or dissatisfaction) may indicate or contraindicate later surgical sex reassignment.

4.4.4. STANDARD 4*

The initiation of hormonal sex reassignment shall be preceded by recommendation for such hormonal therapy, made by a clinical behavioral scientist.

4.5.1. PRINCIPLE 14

The administration of androgens to females and of estrogens and/or progesterones to males may lead to mild or serious health-threatening complications.

4.5.2. PRINCIPLE 15

Persons who are in poor health, or who have identifiable abnormalities in blood chemistry, may be at above average risk to develop complications should they receive hormonal medication.

4.5.3. STANDARD 5

The physician prescribing hormonal medication to a person for the purpose of effecting hormonal sex reassignment must warn the patient of possible negative complications which may arise and that physician should also make available to the patient (or refer the patient to a facility offering) monitoring of relevant blood chemistries and routine physical examinations including, but not limited to, the measurement of SGPT in persons receiving testosterone and the measurement of SGPT, bilirubin, triglycerides, and fasting glucose in persons receiving estrogens.

4.6.1. PRINCIPLE 16

The diagnostic evidence for transsexualism (see 4.3.1 above) requires that the clinical behavioral scientist have knowledge, independent of the patient's verbal claim, that the dysphoria, discomfort, sense of inappropriateness and wish to be rid of one's own genitals, have existed for at least two years. This evidence may be obtained by interview of the patient's appointed informant (friend or relative) or it may best be obtained by the fact that the clinical behavioral scientist has professionally known the patient for an extended period of time.

---

*This standard, in the original draft, recommended that the patient must have lived successfully in the social/gender role of the genetically other sex for at least three months prior to the initiation of hormonal sex reassignment. This requirement was rescinded 1/80.

4.6.2. STANDARD 6

The clinical behavioral scientist making the recommendation in favor of hormonal sex reassignment shall have known the patient in a psychotherapeutic relationship for at least three months prior to making said recommendation.

Surgical (genital and/or breast) sex reassignment

4.7.1. PRINCIPLE 17

Peer review is a commonly accepted procedure in most branches of science and is used primarily to ensure maximal efficiency and correctness of scientific decisions and procedures.

4.7.2. PRINCIPLE 18

Clinical behavioral scientists must often rely on possibly unreliable or invalid sources of information (patient's verbal reports or the verbal reports of the patient's families and friends) in making clinical decisions and in judging whether or not a patient has fulfilled the requirements of the herein listed standards.

4.7.3. PRINCIPLE 19

Clinical behavioral scientists given the burden of deciding who to recommend for hormonal and surgical sex reassignment and for whom to refuse such recommendations are subject to extreme social pressure and possible manipulation as to create an atmosphere in which charges of laxity, favoritism, sexism, financial gain, etc., may be made.

4.7.4. PRINCIPLE 20

A plethora of theories exists regarding the etiology of gender dysphoria and the purposes or goals of hormonal and/or surgical sex reassignment such that the clinical behavioral scientist making the decision to recommend such reassignment for a patient does not enjoy the comfort or security of knowing that his or her decision would be supported by the majority of his or her peers.

4.7.5. STANDARD 7

The clinical behavioral scientist recommending that a patient applicant receive surgical (genital and breast) sex reassignment must obtain peer review, in the format of a clinical behavioral scientist peer who will personally examine the patient applicant, on at least one occasion, and who will, in writing, state that he or she concurs with the decision of the original clinical behavioral scientist. Peer review (a second opinion) is not required for hormonal sex reassignment. Nongenital/breast surgical sex reassignment does not require the recommendation of a behavioral scientist. At least one of the two behavioral scientists making the favorable recommendation for surgical (genital and breast) sex reassignment must be a doctoral-level clinical behavioral scientist.*

4.8.1. STANDARD 8

The clinical behavioral scientist making the primary recommendation in favor of genital (surgical) sex reassignment shall have known the patient in a psychotherapeutic relationship for at least six months prior to making said recommendation. That clinical behavioral scientist should have access to the results of psychometric testing (including IQ testing of the patient) when such testing is clinically indicated.

4.9.1. STANDARD 9

Genital sex reassignment shall be preceded by a period of at least twelve months during which time the patient lives full-time in the social role of the genetically other sex.

4.10.1. PRINCIPLE 21

Genital surgical sex reassignment includes the invasion of, and the alteration of, the genitourinary tract. Undiagnosed pre-existing genitourinary disorders may complicate later genital surgical sex reassignment.

4.10.2. STANDARD 10†

Prior to genital surgical sex reassignment a urological examination should be conducted for the purpose of identifying and perhaps treating abnormalities of the genitourinary tract.

---

*In the original and 1/80 version of these standards, one of the clinical behavioral scientists was required to be a psychiatrist. That requirement was rescinded in 3/81.

†This requirement was rescinded 1/90.

4.11.1. Standard 11

The physician administering or performing surgical (genital) sex reassignment is guilty of professional misconduct if he or she does not receive written recommendations in favor of such procedures from at least two clinical behavioral scientists; at least one of which is a doctoral level clinical behavioral scientist and one of whom has known the patient in a professional relationship for at least six months.

Miscellaneous

4.12.1. Principle 22

The care and treatment of sex reassignment applicants or patients often causes special problems for the professionals offering such care and treatment. These special problems include, but are not limited to, the need for the professional to cooperate with education of the public to justify his or her work, the need to document the case history perhaps more completely than is customary in general patient care, the need to respond to multiple, nonpaying, service applicants and the need to be receptive and responsive to the extra demands for services and assistance often made by sex reassignment applicants as compared to other patient groups.

4.12.2. Principle 23

Sex reassignment applicants often have need for post-therapy (psychologic, hormonal, and surgical) follow-up care for which they are unable or unwilling to pay.

4.12.3. Principle 24

Sex reassignment applicants often are in a financial status which does not permit them to pay excessive professional fees.

4.12.4. Standard 12

It is unethical for professionals to charge sex reassignment applicants "whatever the traffic will bear" or excessive fees far beyond the normal fees charged for similar services by the professional. It is permissible to charge sex reassignment applicants for services in advance of the tendering of such services even if such an advance fee arrangement is not typical of the professional's practice. It is permissible to charge patients, in advance, for expected services such as post-therapy follow-up care and/or counseling. It is unethical to charge patients for services which are essentially research and which services do not directly benefit the patient.

4.13.1. PRINCIPLE 25

Sex reassignment applicants often experience social, legal, and financial discrimination not known, at present, to be prohibited by federal or state law.

4.13.2. PRINCIPLE 26

Sex reassignment applicants often must conduct formal or semiformal legal proceedings (i.e., in-court appearances against insurance companies or in pursuit of having legal documents changed to reflect their new sexual and genderal status, etc.).

4.13.3. PRINCIPLE 27

Sex reassignment applicants, in pursuit of what are assumed to be their civil rights as citizens, are often in need of assistance in the form of copies of records, letters of endorsement, court testimony, etc., from the professionals involved in their case.

4.13.4. STANDARD 13

It is permissible for a professional to charge only the normal fee for services needed by a patient in pursuit of his or her civil rights. Fees should not be charged for services for which, for other patient groups, such fees are not normally charged.

4.14.1. PRINCIPLE 28

Hormonal and surgical sex reassignment has been demonstrated to be a rehabilitative, or habilitative, experience for properly selected adult patients.

4.14.2. PRINCIPLE 29

Hormonal and surgical sex reassignment are procedures which must be requested by, and performed only with the agreement of, the patient having informed consent. Sex reannouncement or sex reassignment procedures conducted on infantile or early childhood intersexed patients are common medical practices and are not included in or affected by the present discussion.

4.14.3. PRINCIPLE 30

Sex reassignment applicants often, in their pursuit of sex reassignment, believe that hormonal and surgical sex reassignment have fewer risks than such procedures are known to have.

4.14.4. STANDARD 14

Hormonal and surgical sex reassignment may be conducted or administered only to persons obtaining their legal majority (as defined by state law) or to persons declared by the courts as legal adults (emancipated minors).

4.15.1. STANDARD 15

Hormonal and surgical sex reassignment may be conducted or administered only after the patient applicant has received full and complete explanations, preferably in writing, in words understood by the patient applicant, of all risks inherent in the requested procedures.

4.16.1. PRINCIPLE 31

Gender dysphoric sex reassignment applicants and patients enjoy the same rights to medical privacy as does any other patient group.

4.16.2. STANDARD 16

The privacy of the medical record of the sex reassignment patient shall be safeguarded according to procedures in use to safeguard the privacy of any other patient group.

5. Explication

5.1

Prior to the initiation of hormonal sex reassignment:

5.1.1

The patient must demonstrate that the sense of discomfort with the self and the urge to rid the self of the genitalia and the wish to live in the genetically other sex role have existed for at least two years.

5.1.2

The patient must be known to a clinical behavioral scientist for at least three months and that clinical behavioral scientist must endorse the patient's request for hormone therapy.

5.1.3

Prospective patients should receive a complete physical examination which includes, but is not limited to, the measurement of SGPT in persons to receive testosterone and the measurement of SGPT, bilirubin, triglycerides, and fasting glucose in persons to receive estrogens.

5.2

Prior to the initiation of genital or breast sex reassignment (Penectomy, orchidectomy, castration, vaginoplasty, mastectomy, hysterectomy, oophorectomy, salpingectomy, vaginectomy, phalloplasty, reduction mammoplasty, breast amputation):

5.2.1

See 5.1.1 above.

5.2.2

The patient must be known to a clinical behavioral scientist for at least six months and that clinical behavioral scientist must endorse the patient's request for genital surgical sex reassignment.

5.2.3

The patient must be evaluated at least once by a clinical behavior scientist other than the clinical behavioral scientist specified in 5.2.2 above and that second clinical behavioral scientist must endorse the patient's request for genital sex reassignment. At least one of the clinical behavioral scientists making the recommendation for genital sex reassignment must be a doctoral-level clinical behavioral scientist.

5.2.4

The patient must have been successfully living in the genetically other sex role for at least one year.

5.3

During and after services are provided:

5.3.1

The patient's right to privacy should be honored.

5.3.2

The patient must be charged only appropriate fees and these fees may be levied in advance of services.

Note

1. *DSM-III-R. Diagnostic and Statistical Manual of Mental Disorders.* 3d ed. rev. Washington, D.C.: The American Psychiatric Association, 1987.

Original draft dated February 13, 1979.
Revised draft (1/90) dated January 20, 1980.
Revised draft (3/81) dated March 9, 1981.
Revised draft (11/90) dated January 25, 1990.

About the Editors and Contributors

Mariette Pathy Allen, B.A., M.F.A., is a photographer and the author of *Transformations: Crossdressers and Those Who Love Them.*

Stanley H. Biber, M.D., is a general surgeon practicing in Trinidad, Colorado.

Dr. Walter O. Bockting is affiliated with the Program in Human Sexuality at the University of Minnesota School of Medicine.

Anne Bolin, Ph.D., is an associate professor in the department of sociology at Elon College, in North Carolina.

Winnie Brant, M.S., L.L.D., is president of the Transgenderists Independence Club located in Albany, New York.

Holly Boswell is a transgender educator/activist and founding director of Phoenix Transgender Support.

The late **Bonnie Bullough, R.N., Ph.D.,** was a professor of nursing at the University of Southern California and Emeritus Dean of Nursing at the State University of New York, Buffalo.

Vern L. Bullough, R.N., Ph.D., is a visiting professor of nursing at the University of Southern California and holds the title of Distinguished Professor Emeritus at the State University of New York.

Annette Cardona is a performance artist and professor of theater and dance at the Jersey City State College, New Jersey.

Wang Chuanmin, M.D., works in the Research Center for Plastic Surgery at the Third School of Clinical Medicine in Beijing, China.

Yvonne Cook-Riley is the former executive director of the International Foundation for Gender Education (IFGE), located in Waltham, Massachusetts.

Dallas Denny, M.A., is executive director of the American Educational Gender Information Service (AEGIS) in Decatur, Georgia.

Holly Devor, Ph.D., is a professor in the department of sociology at the University of Victoria, British Columbia, Canada.

Milton Diamond, Ph.D., is a professor in the department of anatomy and reproductive biology at the University of Hawaii in Honolulu.

Mildred Dickemann, Ph.D., is a Professor Emeritus of anthropology at California State University, Hayward.

Keith Dorwick, M.A., A.B.D., teaches in the department of English at the University of Illinois in Chicago.

William B. Dragoin, Ph.D., is a professor in the department of psychology/sociology at Georgia Southwestern College in Americus, Georgia.

James Elias, Ph.D., is the director of the Center for Sex Research at California State University, Northridge.

Lee Etscovitz, Ed.D., is associated with Human Dimensions in Willow Grove, Pennsylvania.

Gretchen Finke, M.S.S.W., works with the Milwaukee Transgender Program at Pathways Counseling Center in Wauwatosa, Wisconsin.

Michael A. Gilbert, Ph.D., is a professor with the department of philosophy at York University in Toronto, Ontario, Canada.

Richard Green, M.D., Ph.D., is a visiting professor at Charing Cross Hospital, Westminster Medical School, and is also a senior research fellow at the Institute of Criminology, Cambridge University. He is an Emeritus Professor of psychiatry at UCLA, Los Angeles.

Lynn Edward Harris resides in Los Angeles, California.

Linda Heidenreich teaches in the department of history at the University of California in San Diego.

Kathryn Helms, A.B., M.Div., a Protestant minister, is a member of the Board of Directors of Tri-Ess and a peer counselor in the transgender community.

William A. Henkin, Ph.D., is in private practice in San Francisco.

Mary Hogan-Finlay, Ph.D., is a professor with the department of psychology at Carlton University in Ottawa, Ontario, Canada.

Bill Jones, Ph.D., teaches in the department of psychology at Carlton University in Ottawa, Ontario, Canada.

Michele Kämmerer is a captain with the Los Angeles Fire Department.

Ariadne Kane, M.Ed., is the Director of the Outreach Institute of Gender Studies and is a founder of Fantasia Fair in Augusta, Maine.

Monica Kendel is a graduate student studying at the University of Victoria in British Columbia, Canada.

Karen F. Kroll, M.Div., lives in Portland, Oregon.

Johnny Madrigal is a writer currently living in Costa Rica.

Lisa Middleton, M.A., is in insurance claims management and reimbursement, specializing in workers' compensation.

Karen J. Nakamura is affiliated with the department of anthropology at Yale University in New Haven, Connecticut.

Lisa Nakamura, Ph.D., teaches in the department of English at Vista College in Berkeley, California.

Nancy Reynolds Nangeroni lives in Cambridge, Massachusetts.

Roger Northway is affiliated with the Milwaukee Transgender Program at Pathways Counseling Center in Wauwatosa, Wisconsin.

Friedemann Pfäfflin, M.D., teaches in the department of psychotherapy at the University of Ulm, Germany

Virginia Prince, Ph.D., is the founder of Tri-Ess, the Society for the Second Self, and is the founding editor of *Transvestia.*

Rupert Raj resides in Toronto, Ontario.

Kymberleigh Richards is publisher and managing editor of *Cross Talk,* which is based in Los Angeles.

Jan Roberts, M.A., works with the American Educational Gender Information Service (AEGIS) in Decatur, Georgia.

Ellen Bayuk Rosenman is an associate professor in the English department at the University of Kentucky in Lexington.

Michael Saffle, Ph.D., is a professor with the department of music and Center for Programs in the Humanities at Virginia Polytechnic Institute.

Jacobo Schifter is the executive editor of *Iconoclasta,* which is based in San Jose, Costa Rica.

David Seil, M.D., is in private practice in Boston, Massachusetts.

The late **Nicholas P. Spanos, Ph.D.,** taught in the department of psychology at Carlton University in Ottawa, Ontario.

Dr. Nancy Strapko. (No information available.)

Louis H. Swartz, Ph.D., L.L.M., R.N., is an associate professor of law and social work at the State University of New York in Buffalo.

Jayne Thomas, Ph.D., is a psychologist who maintains a private practice and is an instructor at various colleges in southern California.

Lynn M. Thompson teaches in the department of English at the University of Miami in Coral Gables, Florida.

Janis Walworth currently resides in Ashby, Massachusetts.

Frederick L. Whitam, Ph.D., is a professor of sociology at Arizona State University in Tempe.

Stephen Whittle, Ph.D., M.A., L.L.B., B.A., is a lecturer in law at Manchester Metropolitan University in Manchester, England. He is also coordinator of the U.K. FTM Network and is vice president of Press for Change.

Xia Zhaoji, M.D., works at the Research Center for Plastic Surgery at the Third School of Clinical Medicine, Beijing Medical University in Beijing, China.